CONVOCAB

ENGLISH-TO-SPANISH
VOCABULARY CONVERSION

CONVOCAB

ENGLISH-TO-SPANISH
VOCABULARY CONVERSION

30,000 WORD HIGH FREQUENCY
SPANISH VOCABULARY
WITH MINIMUM MEMORY EFFORT

ROBERT W. MAYNARD

Published by
CONVOCAB PUBLISHING CO.

Copyright © 1990 by Robert W. Maynard

All rights reserved. No part of this book may be copied or reproduced in any manner whatsoever without written permission from the author. All inquiries should be directed to Robert W. Maynard, 3200 West Calhoun Parkway, Minneapolis, MN 55416.

Library of Congress Catalog Card Number 90-82522

ISBN 0-9626879-0-1

Printed in the United States of America

PREFACE TO CONVOCAB SERIES

With the expanding scope of relationships between people from all parts of the world, the need for multilingual understanding has grown increasingly apparent. Such understanding is essential for the development of full social, cultural, economic and political relationships. The two most important requirements for communication in any language are a familiarity with the grammar and the mastery of a substantial vocabulary. Thanks to a strong common Greek and Latin heritage, the English, French, Italian, Portuguese and Spanish languages are very similar both as to grammar and vocabulary. The CONVOCAB series concentrates on the vocabulary similarities and is designed to provide techniques for converting vocabulary between these languages with a minimum amount of memorization effort. In fact, as much as 80% of the most frequently used 30,000 words in any of these languages can be converted to any of the others without any extensive word to word memorization.

The English to Spanish Vocabulary Conversion version is the first of the CONVOCAB series of 20 separate books or versions of the same book. Each will have English, French, Italian, Portuguese or Spanish as the "base language" and one of the others as the "target language". Each will provide a vocabulary in the target language of 30,000 of the most frequently used words. Although the main focus is placed on those words covered by the conversion techniques, essential nonconverting words are grouped in the appendices in a manner designed to facilitate the learning process. The CONVOCAB series has seven principal objectives:

1. <u>Minimization of "Foreignness" Barrier</u>: Recognition of the similarities between the vocabularies of the five languages will promote a more relaxed and confident approach to handling the written and spoken word in any of these languages. Examination of the series as a whole will indicate how time spent learning any of these languages will be a giant step toward being familiar with them all. The learning task will seem much less formidable once it is realized that more than 80% of an individuals base language vocabulary can be converted to a target language vocabulary with little or no memory effort. Time spent with the lists will develop a familiarity with the word patterns in the target language and facilitate the utilization of existing vocabulary knowledge.

2. <u>Rapid Accumulation of Full Target Language Vocabulary</u>: As contrasted with the traditional practice of aiming for a minimum vocabulary, CONVOCAB's aim is to simplify and accelerate the accumulation of a full working vocabulary in the target language consisting of more than 30,000 of the most frequently used words. Con-

centration on a minimum vocabulary may be helpful during initial efforts to speak and write one of the target languages, but it is a big handicap in developing skills in understanding the language as it is written or spoken in the real world. The conversion approach facilitates the development of a vocabulary practically equivalent to the base language vocabulary reflecting the individual's own level of education and areas of interests. It facilitates ready access to tens of thousands of words in the target language with little more effort than memorizing a few hundred words. There isn't any need for a long period of vocabulary immaturity. The lists build confidence in the use of conversion techniques and open access to the existing wealth of an individual's own base language vocabulary strength.

3. <u>Simplification of Sentence Structure through Better Word Choice:</u> With the availability of a large vocabulary complete with precise and meaningful words, one word may often be used to express an idea that would otherwise require many less meaningful words in a more lengthy and complex sentence structure. For example, the word *proclivity* (Spanish *"proclividad"*) requires less sentence structure than the more verbose "*a natural tendancy in human nature*".

4. <u>Identification of Misleading Vocabulary Similarities</u>: Because there are some words which appear similar in the two languages but have significantly different meanings, caution is often given not to assume a meaning from appearances. A few prize examples of these "misleading cognates" or "false friends" have often been enough to discourage the use of the conversion techniques, but it should be realized that less than 2% of the most frequently used 30,000 words have any such significant deceptive cognate problems. A list of the most important of these problem words appears in the Deceptive Cognate section (p.384) and most are identified by an asterix (*) when they appear in any of the word lists. Familiarity with the 500 or so of these words listed will facilitate confident reliance on convertibility and will take the guesswork and danger out of vocabulary conversion. It should be noted that there are many words which convert as to their primary meaning but not as to secondary or figurative meanings and that there may be some variation in meanings and usage in different countries or regions, but such problems will diminish with exposure to the language.

5. <u>Presentation of Lists Based on Word Endings</u>: Since most of the converting categories are based on word endings, the CONVOCAB lists group words by their endings. For example, verbs which end in *-ize*, are grouped together. This provides lists of words in groupings which identify conversion patterns and which are not readily available in dictionaries or other sources.

6. <u>Arrangement of Non-Conversion Words in Lists to Facilitate the Learning Process</u>: The most frequently used words which don't follow any of CONVOCAB's conversion patterns are presented in the appendix lists according to their function and subject matter. Pronouns, articles, prepositions, conjunctions, special non-converting adjectives, adverbs not derived from adjectives and numbers are listed in separate sections. The listing of words in 40 different subject matter groups at the end of the appendix provides a tool for concentrated study on areas of particular interest.

7. <u>Utilization of Conversion Category Principles to Improve Communication in English with Target Language People</u>. Despite the natural inclination to use simple one-syllable English words when communicating with someone from one of the target language countries not fluent in English, it is far better to use multisyllable words in conversion categories, since more than 85% of the latter and less than 5% of the one-syllable words will be recognizable. For example, a sentence like "John sees the need to work together" is much less likely to be understood by a Spanish-speaking person than the alternative "John comprehends the necessity of cooperation", since the latter is very close to the Spanish "Juan comprende la necesidad de cooperar".

The CONVOCAB approach isn't really contrary to the general view that the newcomer to a language should not be encouraged to translate from his own language. The aim of CONVOCAB is to maximize the use of the vocabulary already known. As familiarity with the target language develops, it will become less and less necessary to go through the base language vocabulary. Thought in the target language will soon replace the need for the conversion step. The CONVOCAB books aren't designed to be used as reference books, but rather as learning tools.

It should be remembered that ideas may be expressed differently in the various languages even though the words in the base language do convert to words in the target language. While the CONVOCAB approach provides the raw material for vocabulary development, idiomatic expressions can be learned best through extended exposure to the target language.

PREFACE TO THE ENGLISH-SPANISH VERSION

The English to Spanish version was chosen as the first in the Series because of the extremely close political, economic, social and literary relationships between the English and Spanish-speaking worlds. English is spoken by as many as a billion people and Spanish by more than 250,000,000 people. Spanish is the official language in more than twenty countries and is fast becoming almost a second language in the United States, particulary in Arizona, California, Florida, New Mexico, New York and Texas. More than 15,000,000 people now speak it in the United States and Canada.

The Series Preface, Contents Outline and Introduction will help clarify the objectives and approach of the CONVOCAB SERIES in general and the English-Spanish version in particular. A preliminary perusal of the following particularly productive categories will provide a feel for the extent of conversion possibilities:

VERBS: *-ine* (p.8); *-ate* (p.12); *-ize* (p.19) and *-ify* (p.33).

NOUNS: *-a* (p.76); *-ence* (p.83); *-tude* (p.87); *-ine* (p.92); *-ive* (p.103); *-ism* (p.113); *-ium* (p.116); *-ion* (p.124); *-o* (p.137); *-ator* (p.146); *-sis* (p.151); *-ist* (p.165) and *-ity* (p.179).

ADJECTIVES: *-ic* (p.258); *-ble* (p.267); *-ile* (p.271); *-ate* (p.274); *-ive* (p.276); *-al* (p.286); *-an* (p.292); *-ar* (p.294); *-ous* (p.296); -ary (p.309) and *-ory* (p.310).

ADVERBS: *-bly* (p.338); -ically (p.339); -ately (p.342); -ally (p.346); -ively (p.344) and -ously (p.349).

CONTENTS OUTLINE

	PAGE
PREFACE TO CONVOCAB SERIES	i
PREFACE TO ENGLISH-SPANISH VERSION	iv
CONTENTS OUTLINE	v
INTRODUCTION	vii

    1. Word Base
    2. Spelling Changes & Accent Marks
    3. List Format

        a) Conversion by Suffix Category

            (1) Conversion Formula
            (2) Conversion Percentage
            (3) Number of Words Listed
            (4) Suffix Meaning
            (5) Cross-Reference
            (6) Deceptive Cognates (Coded *)
            (7) Exception to Conversion Pattern (Coded •)

        b) One-on-One "Pair Word" Conversions
        c) Conversion through Synonyms

WORD CONVERSION LISTS	1
A. VERBS	1
1. Verb Conversion Categories (Category Chart)	2
2. One-on-One "Pair Verb" Conversions	35
3. Verb Conversions through Synonyms	41
B. NOUNS	73
1. Noun Conversion Categories (Category Chart)	74
2. One-on-One "Pair Noun" Conversions	187
Lists of Special One-on-One Conversions	203

                Countries-People   Mountains
                Cities   First Names
                Islands   Months of Year
                Oceans & Rivers   Planets

3. Noun Conversion through Synonyms	211
4. Noun Gender in Spanish	253

		PAGE
C.	ADJECTIVES	255
	1. Adjective Conversion Categories (Category Chart)	256
	2. One-on-One "Pair Adjective" Conversions	311
	3. Adjective Conversion through Synonyms	315
D.	ADVERBS DERIVED FROM ADJECTIVES	337
	1. Adverbs formed from Converting Adjectives (English *-ly* converting to *-mente*)	338
	2. One-on-One "Pair Adverb" Conversions	353
	3. Adverb Conversion through Adjective Synonyms	355

SPELLING CHANGES FROM ENGLISH TO SPANISH — 367

ACCENT MARKS AND ACCENT PLACEMENT — 373

PREFIXES — 375

AUGMENTATIVES — 382

DIMINUTIVES — 383

DECEPTIVE COGNATES — 384

APPENDICES: (AREAS OF NON-CONVERSION) — 395

APPENDIX A - PRONOUN — 396

APPENDIX B - ARTICLES — 398

APPENDIX C - PREPOSITIONS — 398

APPENDIX D - CONJUNCTIONS — 400

APPENDIX E - SPECIAL NONCONVERTING ADJECTIVES — 401

APPENDIX F - SPECIAL NONCONVERTING ADVERBS — 403

APPENDIX G - NUMBERS — 408

APPENDIX H - SPECIAL SUBJECT MATTER LISTS — 411

INTRODUCTION

Since the presentation of vocabulary conversion in this book consists mainly of lists of words in numerous conversion categories and the conclusions drawn from a study of these lists, some background information seems appropriate as to the make up of the lists and the format of the presentation.

1. Word Base

After considerable debate over whether to limit the lists to just a handful of examples for each conversion category or to include most useful words, an arbitrary decision was made to limit the total words listed to approximately 30,000 of the most frequently used English words and their Spanish counterparts. Much shorter lists would fail to reveal the full extent of vocabulary already known, but longer lists would be unwieldy and would seem excessive in view of the fact that the average high school student is believed to use only about 12,000 of the 50,000 or so words he can recognize and the average college graduate uses as few as 15,000 of the 70,000 he can recognize. The total listed actually exceeds 30,000 by a few thousand in order to offset some duplication and the inclusion of some less commonly used words added to help portray a pattern or to complete a subject matter list. The aim is a full vocabulary rather than just a minimum vocabulary.

In preparing the lists and testing the conversion principles, an English word base of over 200,000 words was examined together with the Spanish counterparts of these words. In selecting words to be included in the 30,000 total, extensive use was made of the following studies:-

Henry Kucera and W. Nelson Francis, Frequency Anaylsis of English Usage, Houghton Mifflin Co., Boston 1982.
(Lists approximately 38,000 most frequently used words)

Helen S. Eaton, Semantic Frequency List for English, French, German and Spanish, Univ. of Chicago Press, Chicago 1940.
(Lists approximately 6,000 most frequently used words)

Britannica World Language Dictionary, Funk and Wagnalls, New York, 1964.
(Lists approximately 6,500 most frequently used words)

While erring on the side of including words which follow a conversion pattern, an effort has been made to include most of the important exceptions.

2. Spelling Changes and Accent Marks

The most common spelling changes that occur in converting English words to Spanish words are summarized in the section beginning on page 367. Many of the common spelling changes are used to retain pronunciation characteristics of the root word. Rules for syllable stress and for the use of accent marks are summarized in the section beginning on page 373.

3. Book Format

The presentation deals primarily with verbs, nouns, adjectives, and adverbs derived from adjectives since this is where the conversion benefits are most apparent. Pronouns, articles, prepositions, conjunctions, adverbs not derived from adjectives, numbers and special subject matter lists are covered in the appendices.

The sections dealing with verbs, nouns, adjectives and adverbs are arranged in similar formats and are subdivided into four parts:

a) Conversion Categories:

The conversion categories are arranged in inverse alphabetical order (i.e.: alphabetically from the last letter of the category ending back toward the first letter). For example, conversion categories ending in *-ate* are listed before those ending in *-ity*. This seemingly strange arrangement is necessary since it is often difficult to know which is the first letter of the ending. The Spanish word columns are "justified right" to facilitate the examination of the word endings. Some conversion categories of less value as to number and conversion percentage have been omitted.

In addition to the word list itself, each conversion category contains some or all of the following information:

(1) A title line such as:
"**VERBS:** English -ize = Spanish -izar.   90%   250 Listed".

This title contains the following information:

(a) The conversion formula ("**English** *-ize* = **Spanish** *-izar*.").

(b) The approximate conversion percentage of all words examined in each category ("**90%**"). The total word base examined exceeded 200,000 words, but only 30,000 of the most useful words are listed.

(c) The number of the words listed as being among the 30,000 most frequently used words. ("**250 Listed**").

(2) Cross-reference to other grammatical forms or categories if a helpful conversion relationship exists.

"<u>Cross-Reference:</u> N *-ization*; ADJ *-izable*; V *-ize* "

(3) The meaning of the suffix or other ending where it may be helpful in understanding the meaning of the words.

"The suffix *-cide* denotes a killer or a killing."

(4) A note on the gender of nouns in a conversion category if a significant gender pattern exists.

"<u>Gender</u>: Most are feminine in Spanish."

(5) An asterisk (*) before a listed word to indicate that it may appear alike in the two languages, but that it has significantly different meanings. A list of the most common of these words is set forth in the Deceptive Cognate section (p.384). Familiarity with a few hundred of them will help build confidence in the conversion of tens of thousands of other words.

<u>ENGLISH</u>	<u>SPANISH EQUIVALENT</u>	<u>SPANISH COGNATE</u>	<u>ENGLISH EQUIVALENT</u>
*actual (real)	verdadero	actual	present-day, current
*exit	salida	éxito	success

(6) Spanish verbs, nouns, adjectives and adverbs which don't follow the conversion pattern are identified with a "•" placed after the Spanish word.

<u>ENGLISH</u>	<u>SPANISH</u>	<u>ENGLISH</u>	<u>SPANISH</u>
generalize	generalizar	neutralize	neutralizar
glamorize	embellecer•	oxidize	oxidar•

b) <u>One-on-One Conversions ("Pair-Words")</u>

Words not in a conversion category but which look or sound alike in the two languages are set forth in separate lists. Such words aren't as helpful for vocabulary building as words in a conversion category where words can be learned in bunches, but they are much easier to master than words which have no resemblance in the two languages.

ENGLISH	SPANISH	ENGLISH	SPANISH
attack	ataque, m.	beefsteak	biftec,bistec, m.
cross	cruzar	double	doblar
false	falso	pure	puro

c) Words Convertible through Synonyms

The memorization of English words not in conversion categories nor subject to one-on-one conversion can be minimized by converting a synonym that is in a converting category (i.e.: fast [rapid] = rápido; house [residence] = residencia; get [obtain] = obtener). Since very few one-syllable English words convert to Spanish, they are usually good candidates for conversion through multi-syllable synonyms. The possibilities in synonym conversion are virtually unlimited. Just enough are listed to provide examples for practicing this helpful conversion technique.

ENGLISH	SPANISH NON-CONVERSION	ENGISH SYNONYM	SPANISH CONVERSION
childhood	niñez, f.	infancy	infancia, f.
house	casa, f.	residence	residencia, f.
		domicile	domicilio, m.
		habitation	habitación, f.

4. Key Words Requiring Memorization

Many of the most important words that don't convert from English to Spanish appear as exceptions in the category conversion or pair conversion lists or as entries in the synonym conversion lists. The appendices provide lists of words not covered by any conversion method such as pronouns, articles, prepositions, conjunctions, adverbs not derived from adjectives and numbers. The last appendix in the book beginning on page 411 provides lists of words separated into 40 subject matter groups to facilitate memorization in subject areas of particular interest.

After reading the Prefaces, Contents Outline and Introduction, it will be helpful to skip rapidly through the book, reading the section introductions and category indexes. A glance through the category, "pair-word" and synonym lists should provide convincing evidence that building a Spanish vocabulary up to the level of your English vocabulary isn't as difficult a task as it might have seemed.

WORD CONVERSION LISTS

A. **VERBS**

Verbs warrant special attention because they often serve in both English and Spanish as the base from which corresponding nouns, adjectives and adverbs are formed. For example, the following nouns, adjectives and adverbs are derived from the verb *produce (producir)*:

	ENGLISH	SPANISH
NOUNS:	producer	productor
	production	producción
	productivity	productividad
	product	producto
ADJECTIVES:	productive	productivo
ADVERBS:	productively	productivamente

It is also important to note that verbs in Spanish can often be formed from nouns and adjectives by the addition of certain verbial suffixes such as:

-ear   Added to noun stems to express the use of the noun.

golpe	(a hit)	golpear	(to hit)
teléfono	(a telephone)	telefonear	(to telephone)

-ecer   Added to adjective stems to express the notion of getting or becoming.

húmido	(damp)	humedecer	(to get damp)
obscuro	(dark)	obscurecer	(to get dark)

-izar   Added to noun and adjective stems to express the transfer of the quality involved to an object.

motor	(motor)	motorizar	(to motorize)
tranquilo	(calm)	tranquilizar	(to calm)

The verb lists show only the infinitive form since all the other verb forms are derived from that form and can be dealt with best in the study of grammar. For the same reason, the lists seldom indicate whether a verb is reflexive nor do they identify the preposition that normally follows the verb. The verbs listed are divided into three segments:

(1) Those which are in categories that usually convert from English to Spanish according to the described pattern.

(2) Those which are not in such a category but which do convert on a one-to-one basis.

(3) Those which don't convert directly but which often have one or more synonyms which do convert.

About 3750 Verbs are Listed

1. VERBS IN CONVERTING CATEGORIES

The Verb Category Index lists the English verb ending, the corresponding Spanish verb ending, the percentage of the verbs examined in that category which convert to Spanish according to the pattern (based on examination of a 200,000 word base), the number of verbs (whether convertible or not) included in the list because of the high frequency of use and the category's page location. The conversion category lists contain a total of approximately 1,700 verbs after adjustment for some duplication and synonym listings. Some priority attention might well be given to the categories with the highest conversion percentages and the largest number of verbs listed such as English verbs which end in -duce, -ate, -ine , -ize, -ute, -pose, -form, -mit and -ify, since these categories afford the greatest vocabulary-building benefits. It should be noted that there are very few Spanish conversion counterparts for the English verbs that end in -rd, -ace, -esce, -age, -nge, -ble, -tle, -ase, -ave, -ish, -al, -il, -ll, -ol, -rl, -am, -an, -en, -p, -or, -eer, -er, -ss, -at, -ot, -rt, -ast, -w, -x and -ry nor for one-syllable English verbs. Most of the frequently used of these non-converting verbs are included in the Pair Conversion List (p.35), Synonym Conversion List (p.41) or in the Subject Matter lists of APPENDIX H..

VERB CATEGORY INDEX

ENGLISH	SPANISH	CONV. %	NO LISTED	PG #	ENGLISH	SPANISH	CONV. %	NO LISTED	PG #
-ceed	-ceder	85%	4	4	-serve	-servar	80%	6	19
-end	-ender(ar)	80%	26	4	-i(y)ze	-izar	90%	218	19
-pound	-poner	99%	4	4	-graph	-grafiar	99%	8	21
-scribe	-scribir	99%	8	4	-al	-l(iz)ar	20%	9	22
-ance	-anciar,-ear	65%	8	4	-pel	-peler	65%	6	22
-ence	-enciar,-zar	65%	8	5	-el	-alar,-elar	60%	7	22
-nounce	-nunciar	99%	6	5	-claim	-clamar	75%	8	22
-rce	-rzar,-rciar	90%	6	5	-arm	-armar	99%	4	22
-duce	-ducir	98%	12	5	-firm	-firmar	99%	4	23
-ade	-ar,-dir	80%	12	5	-form	-formar	90%	10	23
-cede	-ceder	85%	8	6	-ign	-n(e)ar	70%	12	23
-ide	-dir	50%	12	6	-tain	-ten(ec)er	80%	13	23
-ude	-uir,-udir,-ar	80%	14	6	-on	-onar	35%	22	24
-e(i)ge	-g(i)ar	95%	4	6	-ern	-ernir,-nar	80%	5	24
-erge	-ergir	85%	6	7	-o	-ar	65%	10	24
-voke	-vocar	99%	6	7	appear	-parecer	99%	4	24
-ale	-alar	99%	5	7	-fer	-ferir	80%	10	24
-ile	-ilar	80%	10	7	-er	-ar,-ir	10%	29	25
-sume	-sumir	95%	4	7	-or	-ecer,-ar	30%	15	25
-ume	-umar	90%	5	8	-cur	-currir	90%	4	25
-vene	-venir	99%	6	8	-ur	-ar	30%	10	26
-ine	-inar	85%	26	8	-press	-primir	90%	10	26
-one	-onar,-poner	90%	10	8	-ss	-sar	35%	10	26
-type	-tipar	85%	4	9	-tract	-traer	90%	10	26
-are	-arar	90%	4	9	-sect	-secar	99%	4	27
-quire	-quirir	99%	3	9	-dict	-decir	65%	5	27
-ire	-irar	80%	14	9	-duct	-ducir	80%	4	27
-ore	-orar	85%	8	9	-struct	-struir	99%	5	27
-ure	-urar	70%	45	10	-ct	-gir,-(ion)ar	15%	38	27
-vise	-visar	90%	6	10	-et	-(e)ar	25%	12	28
-pulse	-pulsar	99%	4	10	-hibit	-hibir	99%	4	28
-ense	-ens(ci)ar	90%	8	10	-mit	-mitir,-eter	95%	14	29
-pose	-poner	95%	20	11	-it	-itar	65%	30	29
-erse	-ersar,-gir	70%	6	11	-lt	-ltar	90%	12	29
-fuse	-fundir	80%	6	11	-ant	-antar	75%	14	30
-use	-usar	80%	10	11	-ent	-entar,-entir	90%	40	30
-ate	-ar	90%	457	12	-ount	-ontar	90%	8	30
-ete	-etar	50%	8	17	-rupt	-mper,-mpir	75%	4	30
-cite	-citar	99%	4	17	-pt	-ptar	85%	12	31
-ite	-ir,-unir	70%	7	17	-part	-partir	99%	4	31
-ote	-otar	70%	10	17	-vert	-vertir	90%	10	31
-bute,-tute &-secute	-uir	99%	14	17	-ert	-ertar	80%	10	31
					-ort	-ortar	55%	20	31
-cute,-fute -mute,-pute	-tar	99%	14	18	-est	-tar,-ir,-sar	65%	22	32
					-ist	-istir	90%	11	32
-ue	-ar	85%	20	18	-ust	-ustar	80%	8	32
-ceive	-cibir	90%	6	18	-ify	-ificar	90%	80	33
-olve	-olver	90%	8	18	-ply	-plicar	85%	6	34
-prove	-probar	65%	6	19	-py	-ar,-iar	99%	6	34

3

VERBS: English -ceed = Spanish -ceder. 85%: 4 Listed

ENGLISH	SPANISH	ENGLISH	SPANISH
exceed	sobrar, exceder	succeed (follow)	suceder
proceed	proseguir, proceder	*succeed (achieve)	tener éxito•

VERBS: English -end = Spanish -ender or -endar. 80%: 26 Listed

ENGLISH	SPANISH	ENGLISH	SPANISH
amend	enmendar	distend	distender
append	añadir•	expend	gastar, expender
apprehend	aprehender	extend	extender
ascend	subir, ascender	*intend	querer hacer, intentar
attend (care)	cuidar, atender	offend	ofender
*attend (be at)	asistir•	portend	pronosticar, augurar•
commend	encomendar, recomender	*pretend (act)	fingir•
comprehend	comprender	pretend (claim)	pretender
condescend	condescender	recommend	recomendar
contend	contender	suspend	suspender
defend	defender	tend	tender
depend	depender	transcend	transcender
descend	bajar, descender	vend	vender

VERBS: English -pound = Spanish -poner. 99%: 4 Listed

ENGLISH	SPANISH	ENGLISH	SPANISH
compound	componer	impound	imponer
expound	exponer	propound	proponer

VERBS: English -scribe = Spanish -scribir. 95%: 8 Listed

ENGLISH	SPANISH	ENGLISH	SPANISH
ascribe	atribuir•	prescribe	prescribir
circumscribe	circunscribir	proscribe	proscribir
describe	describir	subscribe	subscribir
inscribe	inscribir	transcribe	transcribir

VERBS: English -ance = Spanish -anciar or -ancear. 65%: 8 Listed

ENGLISH	SPANISH	ENGLISH	SPANISH
advance	adelantar, avanzar•	entrance	hechizar, fascinar•
balance	balancear	finance	financiar
distance	distanciar	refinance	financiar
enhance	aumentar•	romance	galantear•

VERBS: English *-ence* = Spanish *-enciar* or *-enzar*. 65%: 8 Listed

ENGLISH	SPANISH	ENGLISH	SPANISH
commence	comenzar	inconvenience	incomodar•
evidence	evidenciar	influence	influenciar, influir•
experience (feel)	sentir•	sentence	sentenciar
experience (see)	experimentar	silence	silenciar

VERBS: English *-nounce* = Spanish *-nunciar*. 99%: 6 Listed

ENGLISH	SPANISH	ENGLISH	SPANISH
announce	anunciar	mispronounce	pronunciar mal
denounce	denunciar	pronounce	pronunciar
enounce	enunciar	renounce	renunciar

VERBS: English *-rce* = Spanish *-rzar* or *-rciar*. 90%: 6 Listed

ENGLISH	SPANISH	ENGLISH	SPANISH
coerce	coercer•	enforce	forzar
commerce (make...)	comerciar	force	forzar
divorce	divorciar	reenforce	reforzar

VERBS: English *-duce* = Spanish *-ducir*. 98%: 12 Listed

<u>Cross-Reference:</u>   N -duction, V -duct

ENGLISH	SPANISH	ENGLISH	SPANISH
adduce	aducir	introduce (insert)	introducir
conduce	conducir	produce	producir
deduce	deducir	reduce	reducir
educe	educir	reintroduce	reintroducir
induce	inducir	reproduce	reproducir
*introduce (person)	presentar•	seduce	seducir

VERBS: English *-ade* = Spanish *-ar* or *-dir*. 80%: 12 Listed

ENGLISH	SPANISH	ENGLISH	SPANISH
blockade	bloquear	masquerade	enmascarar
crusade	cruzar	parade	pasear, desfilar•
degrade	degradar	persuade	mover, persuadir
dissuade	disuadir	promenade	pasear•
evade	evadir	retrograde	retrogradar
invade	invadir	serenade	dar serenata•

VERBS: English *-cede* = Spanish *-ceder*.   85%: 8 Listed

Cross-Reference: N *-cession*

ENGLISH	SPANISH	ENGLISH	SPANISH
accede	asentir, acceder	precede	preceder
cede	ceder	recede	retroceder
concede	conceder	retrocede	retroceder
intercede	interceder	secede	separar•

VERBS: English *-ide* = Spanish *-dir*.   50%: 12 Listed

Cross-Reference: N *-ision, -ence*

ENGLISH	SPANISH	ENGLISH	SPANISH
abide	quedar, permanecer•	elide	elidir
coincide	coincidir	preside	presidir
collide	chocar•	provide	suministrar, proveer•
confide	confiar•	reside	residir
decide	decidir	subdivide	subdividir
divide	compartir, dividir	subside	hundir•

VERBS: English *-ude* = Spanish *-udir, -uir* or *-dar*.   80%: 14 Listed

ENGLISH	SPANISH	ENGLISH	SPANISH
allude	aludir	extrude	extrudir
collude	conspirar, coludir	exude	exudar
conclude	concluir	illude	iludir
delude	engañar•	include	incluir
denude	desnudar	occlude	ocluir
elude	eludir	preclude	impedir, excluir•
exclude	excluir	seclude	recluir•

VERBS: English *-ege* and *-ige* = Spanish *-ar* or *-iar*.   95% 4 Listed

ENGLISH	SPANISH	ENGLISH	SPANISH
allege	alegar	privilege	privilegiar
oblige	obligar	renege	renegar

VERBS: English *-erge* = Spanish *-ergir*.   85%:   6 Listed

ENGLISH	SPANISH	ENGLISH	SPANISH
converge	convergir	immerge	sumergir•
diverge	divergir	merge unir,fusionar,	combinar•
emerge	surgir, emerger•	submerge	sumergir

VERBS: English *-voke* = Spanish *-vocar*.   99%   6 Listed

Cross-Reference: N *-vocation*

ENGLISH	SPANISH	ENGLISH	SPANISH
convoke	convocar	provoke	provocar
evoke	evocar	reinvoke	reinvocar
invoke	invocar	revoke	revocar

VERBS: English *-ale* = Spanish *-alar*.   99%:   5 Listed

ENGLISH	SPANISH	ENGLISH	SPANISH
exhale	exhalar	regale	regalar
impale	empalar	scale	escalar
inhale	inhalar		

VERBS: English *-ile* = Spanish *-ilar* or *-iliar*.   80%: 10 Listed

ENGLISH	SPANISH	ENGLISH	SPANISH
beguile	seducir, engañar•	exile	exilar
compile	compilar	profile	perfilar
*defile	contaminar•	reconcile	reconciliar
defile (Mil.)	desfilar	revile	injuriar•
domicile	domiciliar	style	estilar

VERBS: English *-sume* = Spanish *-sumir*.   95%   4 Listed

ENGLISH	SPANISH	ENGLISH	SPANISH
assume	asumir	presume	presumir
consume	consumir	resume	resumir

VERBS: English -*ume* other than -*sume* = Spanish -*umar*.

                                                                                                   90% 5 Listed

ENGLISH	SPANISH	ENGLISH	SPANISH
deplume	desplumar	illume	iluminar
exhume	exhumar	perfume	perfumar
fume	humar		

VERBS: English -*vene* = Spanish -*venir*.　　　　99%: 6 Listed

<u>Cross-Reference</u>:　N -*vention*
　　　　　　　　　　　ADJ -*vening*

ENGLISH	SPANISH	ENGLISH	SPANISH
contravene	contravenir	reconvene	convocar de nuevo•
*convene	convocar, convenir	subvene	subvenir
intervene	intervenir	supervene	supervenir

VERBS: English -*ine* = Spansh -*inar*.　　　　85%: 26 Listed

ENGLISH	SPANISH	ENGLISH	SPANISH
aline (align)	alinear	guillotine	guillotinar
combine	combinar	imagine	figurar, imaginar
confine (imprison)	confinar	incline	inclinar
confine (limit)	limitar•	opine	opinar
decline (worsen)	declinar	outline	esbozar•
*decline (refuse)	rehusar•	predestine	predestinar
define	definir•	predetermine	predeterminar
destine	destinar	quarantine	poner en cuarentena•
determine	determinar	recline	reclinar
discipline	disciplinar	redefine	redefinir
disincline	desinclinar	reexamine	reexaminar
divine (guess)	adivinar	refine	refinar
examine	examinar	undermine	socavar, minar

VERBS: English -*pone* = Spanish -*poner*.　　　　90%: 10 Listed
　　　　　 English -*one* = Spanish -*on(e)ar*.

ENGLISH	SPANISH	ENGLISH	SPANISH
atone	expiar•	intone	entonar
condone	condonar	phone	telefonear
depone	deponer	postpone	posponer
dethrone	destronar	telephone	telefonear
enthrone	entronar	tone	entonar

VERBS: English *-type* = Spanish *-tipar*.   85%: 4 Listed

ENGLISH	SPANISH	ENGLISH	SPANISH
electrotype	electrotipar	stereotype	estereotipar
linotype	linotipar	type	escribir a máquina•

VERBS: English *-are* = Spanish *-arar*.   90%: 4 Listed

ENGLISH	SPANISH	ENGLISH	SPANISH
compare	comparar	ensnare	entrampar•
declare	declarar	prepare	preparar

VERBS: English *-quire* = Spanish *-qui(e)rir*.   99%: 3 Listed

ENGLISH	SPANISH	ENGLISH	SPANISH
acquire	adquirir	require	exigir, requerir
inquire	averiguar, inquirir		

VERBS: Spanish *-ire* other than *-quire* = Spanish *-irar*.
                                                     80%: 14 Listed

Cross-Reference: N *-ation, -irator*
                  ADJ *-iratory, -irable*

ENGLISH	SPANISH	ENGLISH	SPANISH
admire	admirar	perspire	sudar, transpirar•
*aspire	aspirar	respire	respirar
attire	vestir•	retire	retirar
conspire	conspirar	*retire (job)	jubilar•
desire	querer, desear	suspire (sigh)	suspirar
expire	expirar	*transpire	suceder, transpirar
inspire	inspirar	umpire	arbitrar•

VERBS: English *-ore* = Spanish *-orar*.   85%: 8 Listed

ENGLISH	SPANISH	ENGLISH	SPANISH
adore	adorar	*ignore	no hacer caso de•
deplore	deplorar	implore	implorar
explore	explorar	reexplore	reexplorar
*ignore (not know)	ignorar	restore	restaurar

VERBS: English -ure = Spanish -urar.   70%: 45 Listed

ENGLISH	SPANISH	ENGLISH	SPANISH
abjure	abjurar	mature	madurar
adventure	aventurar	measure	medir, mensurar
allure	atraer•	nurture	nutrir•
assure	asegurar•	obscure	obscurecer•
capture	prender, capturar	pasture	pastar•
caricature	caricaturar	perjure	perjurar
censure	censurar	picture	ilustrar•
configure	configurar	pressure	presionar•
conjecture	conjeturar	*procure	lograr, adquirir•
conjure	conjurar	puncture	punzar•
culture	culturar	reassure	aquietar•
cure	curar	rupture	romper•
disfigure	desfigurar	sculpture	esculpir•
endure	soportar, durar	*secure	asegurar•
feature	ofrecer•	*secure	obtener•
figure	figurar	structure	estructurar
fracture	fracturar	suture	suturar
gesture	gesticular	tincture	tinturar
*injure	herir, injuriar	tonsure	tonsurar
insure	asegurar•	torture	torturar
*lecture	disertar•	transfigure	transfigurar
manufacture	manufacturar, fabricar•	treasure	atesorar
		venture (dare)	aventurar

VERBS: English -vise = Spanish -visar.   90% 6 Listed

ENGLISH	SPANISH	ENGLISH	SPANISH
*advise	aconsejar, avisar	revise	revisar
*devise	idear, inventar•	supervise	supervisar
improvise	improvisar	televise	televisar

VERBS: English -pulse = Spanish -pulsar.   99%: 4 Listed

ENGLISH	SPANISH	ENGLISH	SPANISH
expulse (expel)	expulsar	pulse	pulsar
impulse	impulsar	repulse	repulsar

VERBS: English -ense = Spanish -ensar or -enciar.   90%: 8 Listed

ENGLISH	SPANISH	ENGLISH	SPANISH
compense (compensate)	compensar	incense	incensar
condense	condensar	license	licenciar
dispense	dispensar	recompense	recompensar
expense	cargar•	sublicense	sublicenciar

VERBS: English -*pose* = Spanish -*poner*.   **95% 20 Listed**

Cross-Reference: N -*posture*, -*posing*, -*position*, -*poser*
ADJ -*posite*, -*posing*, -*posed*

ENGLISH	SPANISH	ENGLISH	SPANISH
compose	componer	pose	poner
decompose	descomponer	predispose	predisponer
depose	deponer	presuppose	presuponer
dispose	disponer	propose	sugerir, proponer
expose	exponer	*propose (marriage)	declarar•
impose	imponer	reimpose	reimponer
indispose	indisponer	repose	reposar•
interpose	interponer	superimpose	superponer
juxtapose	yuxtaponer	suppose (assume)	suponer
oppose	resistir, oponer	transpose	transponer

VERBS: English -*erse* = Spanish -*ersar* or -*ergir*.   **70%: 6 Listed**

ENGLISH	SPANISH	ENGLISH	SPANISH
converse	conversar	reverse	invertir•
disperse	dispersar	submerse	submergir
immerse	sumergir•	traverse	cruzar, atravesar•

VERBS: English -*fuse* = Spanish -*fundir*.   **80%: 6 Listed**

ENGLISH	SPANISH	ENGLISH	SPANISH
confuse	confundir	infuse	infundir
diffuse	difundir	refuse	rehusar•
effuse	efundir	transfuse	transfundir

VERBS: English -*use* other than -*fuse* = Spanish -*usar*.
          80%: 10 Listed

ENGLISH	SPANISH	ENGLISH	SPANISH
abuse	abusar	enthuse	entusiasmar•
accuse	acusar	excuse	dispensar, excusar
amuse	divertir, entretener•	pause	pausar
cause	causar	recuse	recusar
disabuse	desengañar•	use	usar

VERBS: English *-ate* = Spanish *-ar*.   90% 457 Listed

Suffix meaning: (a) to become (evaporate); (b) to cause to become (invalidate); (c) to form or produce (ulcerate, salivate); (d) to provide or treat with (vacinate, refrigerate); (e) to put in the form of or form by (triangulate); (f) to arrange for (orchestrate); (g) to combine, infuse or treat with (chlorinate, oxygenate).

<u>Cross-Reference</u>:   N: *-ation, -ator, -ate, -ant*
                          ADJ: *-ate, -ated, -atory, -ative, -able*

ENGLISH	SPANISH	ENGLISH	SPANISH
abdicate	abdicar	antiquate	anticuar
abominate	abominar	appreciate (esteem)	apreciar
abrogate	abrogar	*appreciate (increase)	aumentar•
accelerate	acelerar	appropriate	apropiar
accentuate	acentuar	approximate	aproximar
acclimate	aclimatar	arbitrate	arbitrar
accommodate	acomodar	arrogate	arrogar
accumulate	acumular	articulate	articular
activate	activar	asphyxiate	asfixiar
actuate	actuar	assassinate	asesinar
adjudicate	adjudicar	assimilate	asimilar
administrate	administrar	associate	asociar
adulate	adular	attenuate	atenuar
adulterate	adulterar	authenticate	autenticar
advocate	abogar por•	automate,-atize	automatizar
affiliate	afiliar	berate	regañar•
agglomerate	aglomerar	bifurcate	bifurcar
agglutinate	aglutinar	calculate	calcular
aggravate	agravar	calibrate	calibrar
aggregate	agregar	calumniate	calumniar
agitate	agitar	capacitate	capacitar
alienate	enajenar, alienar	capitulate	capitular
alleviate	aliviar	capsulate	capsular
allocate	distribuir•	captivate	cautivar
alternate	alternar	carbonate	carbonatar
amalgamate	amalgamar	castigate	castigar
ameliorate	aliviar, mejorar•	castrate	castrar
amputate	amputar	celebrate	celebrar
animate	animar	chlorinate	clorinar
annihilate	aniquilar	circulate	circular
annotate	anotar	coagulate	coagular
annunciate	anunciar	cogitate	cogitar
antedate	antedatar	collaborate	colaborar
anticipate	anticipar	collate	colar

ENGLISH	SPANISH	ENGLISH	SPANISH
commemorate	conmemorar	degenerate	degenerar
commensurate	conmensurar	dehydrate	deshidratar
commentate	comentar	delate	delatar
commiserate	compadecer•	delegate	delegar
communicate	comunicar	deliberate	deliberar
commutate	conmutar	delineate	delinear
compensate	compensar	demarcate	demarcar
complicate	complicar	demonstrate	demostrar
concentrate	concentrar	denigrate	denigrar
conciliate	conciliar	denominate	denominar
confederate	confederar	denunciate	denunciar
configurate	configurar	depopulate	despoblar
confiscate	confiscar	deprecate	deprecar
conflagrate	conflagrar	*depreciate	depreciar
conglomerate	conglomerar	derogate	derogar
*congratulate	congratular	desecrate	profanar•
	felicitar•	designate	designar
congregate	congregar	desolate	desolar
conjugate	conjugar	deteriorate	deteriorar
connotate	connotar	detonate	detonar
consecrate	consagrar	devaluate	desvalorizar, desvaluar
consolidate	consolidar	devastate	devastar
*constipate	estreñir•	deviate	desviar
consummate	consumar	dictate	dictar
contaminate	contaminar	differentiate	diferenciar
contemplate	contemplar	dilate	dilatar
cooperate	cooperar	disassociate	desasociar
coordinate	coordinar	discriminate	discriminar
copulate	copular	disintegrate	desintegrar
coronate	coronar	dislocate	dislocar
correlate	correlacionar	disorientate	desorientar
corroborate	corroborar	disseminate	diseminar
create	crear	dissimulate	disimular
cremate	cremar	dissipate	disipar
culminate	culminar	dissociate	disociar
cultivate	cultivar	domesticate	domesticar
date	fechar, datar	dominate	dominar
deactivate	desactivar	donate	donar
debate	argüir, debatir•	duplicate	duplicar
debilitate	debilitar	*educate	educar
decaffeinate	descafeinar	effectuate	efectuar
decapitate	decapitar	ejaculate	eyacular
decelerate	disminuir•	*elaborate	elaborar
decimate	diezmar	elate	entusiasmar•
decontaminate	descontaminar	elevate	levantar, elevar
decorate	decorar	eliminate	eliminar
dedicate	dedicar	elongate	alargar•
defalcate	desfalcar	elucidate	elucidar
defecate	defecar	emaciate	demacrar•
deflate	desinflar	emanate	emanar

ENGLISH	SPANISH	ENGLISH	SPANISH
emancipate	emancipar	gesticulate	gesticular
emasculate	castrar, emascular	graduate	graduar
emigrate	emigrar	granulate	granular
emulate	emular	gravitate	gravitar
encapsulate	encapsular	gyrate	girar
enumerate	enumerar	habilitate	habilitar
enunciate	enunciar	habituate	habituar
equate	igualar•	hallucinate	alucinar
equilibrate	equilibrar	hesitate	vacilar•
equivocate	equivocar	hibernate	invernar, hibernar
eradicate	erradicar	humiliate	humillar
*escalate	intensificar•	hydrate	hidratar
*estimate	estimar	hyphenate	unir con guión•
evacuate	evacuar	hypothecate	hipotecar
evaluate	evaluar	illuminate	iluminar
evaporate	evaporar	illustrate	ilustrar
exacerbate	exacerbar	*illustrate	ejemplificar•
exaggerate	exagerar	imitate	imitar
exasperate	exasperar	immigrate	inmigrar
excavate	excavar	immolate	inmolar
excommunicate	excomulgar•	impersonate	imitar•
excoriate	excoriar	implicate	implicar
exculpate	exculpar	imprecate	imprecar
exhilarate	alegrar•	impregnate	impregnar
exonerate	exonerar	inaugurate	inaugurar
expectorate	expectorar	incapacitate	incapacitar
expiate	expiar	incarcerate	encarcelar
expostulate	protestar•	incarnate	encarnar
expropriate	expropiar	incinerate	incinerar
extenuate	extenuar	incorporate	incorporar
exterminate	exterminar	incriminate	incriminar
extirpate	extirpar	incubate	incubar
extrapolate	extrapolar	inculcate	inculcar
extricate	desenredar•	indicate	indicar
fabricate	fabricar	indoctrinate	adoctrinar
facilitate	facilitar	inebriate	emborrachar, embriagar•
fascinate	fascinar	infatuate	infatuar
federate	federar	infiltrate	infiltrar
filtrate	filtrar	inflate	inflar
flagellate	flagelar	infuriate	enfurecer•
fluctuate	fluctuar	ingratiate	congraciar•
foliate	foliar	initiate	iniciar
formulate	formular	innovate	innovar
fornicate	fornicar	inoculate	inocular
frustrate	frustrar	inseminate	inseminar
fulminate	fulminar	insinuate	insinuar
fumigate	fumigar	insolate	insolar
generate	generar	instigate	instigar
germinate	brotar, germinar	insulate	aislar•

ENGLISH	SPANISH	ENGLISH	SPANISH
integrate	integrar	navigate	navegar
intermediate	intermediar	necessitate	necesitar
interpolate	interpolar	negate	negar
interrogate	interrogar	negotiate	negociar
intimate	intimar	nominate	nombrar, nominar
intimidate	intimidar	numerate	numerar
intonate	entonar	obligate	obligar
*intoxicate (poison)	intoxicar	*obliterate	obliterar
(drunk)	emborrachar, embriagar•	obviate	obviar
inundate	inundar	officiate	oficiar
invalidate	anular, invalidar	ondulate	ondular
investigate	investigar	*operate (handle)	manejar•
invigorate	vigorizar•	operate (surgery)	operar
irradiate	irradiar	orchestrate	orquestar
irrigate	irrigar	orientate	orientar
irritate	enfadar, irritar	originate	originar
isolate	aislar•	oscillate	oscilar
iterate	iterar	overestimate	sobreestimar
lacerate	lacerar	ovulate	ovular
laminate	laminar	paginate	paginar
legislate	legislar	palpitate	palpitar
legitimate	legitimar	participate	participar
levitate	elevar•	penetrate	penetrar
liberate	librar, liberar	percolate	filtrar•
liquidate	liquidar	perforate	perforar
litigate	litigar	permeate	infiltrar, penetrar•
locate (situate)	colocar, situar•	perpetrate	perpetrar
*locate (find)	encontrar•	perpetuate	perpetuar
lubricate	lubricar	pirate	piratear
machinate	maquinar	placate	aplacar
mandate	ordenar, mandar	plate	platear
manipulate	manipular	pollinate,-nize	polinizar•
marinate	marinar	pontificate	pontificar
masticate	masticar	populate	poblar•
matriculate	matricular	postulate	postular
mediate	mediar	precipitate	precipitar
medicate	medicar	predestinate	predestinar
meditate	meditar	predicate	predicar
menstruate	menstruar	predominate	predominar
migrate	migrar	prefabricate	prefabricar
militate	militar	premeditate	premeditar
misappropriate	malversar•	preponderate	preponderar
miscalculate	calcular mal	prevaricate	prevaricar
mitigate	mitigar	probate	validar•
moderate	moderar	procrastinate	prosponer, aplazar•
modulate	modular	procreate	procrear
motivate	motivar	prognosticate	pronosticar
mutilate	mutilar	proliferate	proliferar
narrate	narrar	promulgate	promulgar
nauseate	nausear	propagate	propagar

ENGLISH	SPANISH	ENGLISH	SPANISH
propitiate	propiciar	saturate	saturar
prorate	prorratear	scintillate	centellear•
prostrate	postrar	segregate	segregar
pulsate	pulsar	separate	apartar, separar
punctuate	puntuar	sequestrate	secuestrar
quadruplicate	cuadruplicar	simulate	simular
radiate	radiar	situate	situar
reactivate	reactivar	speculate	especular
rebate	reembolsar, rebajar•	stagnate	estancar•
recapitulate	recapitular	stalemate	ahogar, estancar•
reciprocate	reciprocar	stimulate	estimular
reconciliate	reconciliar	stipulate	estipular
recreate	recrear	strangulate	estrangular
recriminate	recriminar	subjugate	subyugar
recuperate	recuperar	sublimate	sublimar
redecorate	redecorar	subordinate	subordinar
reeducate	reeducar	subrogate	subrogar
refrigerate	refrigerar	*substantiate	justificar•
regenerate	regenerar	substantiate	substanciar
regulate	regular	suffocate	sofocar
regurgitate	regurgitar	supplicate	suplicar
rehabilitate	rehabilitar	syncopate	sincopar
reincarnate	reencarnar	syndicate	sindicar
reinstate	restituir, reinstalar•	tabulate	tabular
reintegrate	reintegrar	terminate	terminar
reiterate	reiterar	titillate	titilar
rejuvenate	rejuvenecer•	tolerate	tolerar
*relate	relacionar•	translate	trasladar, traducir•
relate (tell)	contar, relatar	triangulate	triangular
relegate	relegar	triplicate	triplicar
remonstrate	protestar•	truncate	truncar
remunerate	remunerar	ulcerate	ulcerar
renegotiate	negociar de nuevo•	underestimate	desestimar•
renovate	renovar	undulate	ondular
renunciate	renunciar	urinate	orinar
repatriate	repatriar	vacate	vacar
replicate	replicar	vaccinate	vacunar•
reprobate	reprobar	vacillate	vacilar
repudiate	repudiar	validate	validar
resonate	resonar	valuate	avaluar
resuscitate	resucitar	vegetate	vegetar
retaliate	vengar•	venerate	venerar
revaluate	revalorizar•	ventilate	ventilar
reverberate	reverberar	vibrate	vibrar
rotate	girar, rotar	vindicate	vindicar
ruminate	rumiar	violate	violar
salivate	salivar	vitiate	viciar
satiate	saciar	vituberate	vituberar

VERBS: *English -ete = Spanish -etar.*   50%: 8 Listed

ENGLISH	SPANISH	ENGLISH	SPANISH
compete	competir•	deplete	agotar, reducir•
complete	concluir, completar	excrete	excretar
concrete	concretar	secrete (ooze)	secretar
delete	suprimir•	*secrete (hide)	esconder•

VERBS: *English -cite = Spanish -citar.*   99%: 4 Listed

ENGLISH	SPANISH	ENGLISH	SPANISH
cite	citar	incite	incitar
excite	mover, excitar	recite	recitar

VERBS: *English -ite other than -cite = Spanish -ir.*   70%: 7 Listed

ENGLISH	SPANISH	ENGLISH	SPANISH
disunite	desunir	invite	convidar, invitar•
dynamite	dinamitar•	reunite	reunir
expedite	expedir	unite	juntar, unir
ignite	encender•		

VERBS: *English -ote = Spanish -otar.*   70%: 10 Listed

ENGLISH	SPANISH	ENGLISH	SPANISH
connote	connotar	garrote	agarrotar
creosote	creosotar	note	notar
demote	degradar•	promote (push)	promover•
denote	denotar	*promote (rank)	ascender•
devote	dedicar•	vote	votar

VERBS: *English -bute, -cute and -tute = Spanish -uir.*   99%: 14 Listed

Cross-Reference: N *-ution, -utor*

ENGLISH	SPANISH	ENGLISH	SPANISH
attribute	atribuir	prosecute	procesar, proseguir
constitute	constituir	prostitute	prostituir
contribute	contribuir	reconstitute	reconstituir
dilute	diluir	redistribute	redistribuir
distribute	distribuir	restitute	restituir
institute	instituir	retribute	retribuir
persecute	perseguir	substitute	substituir

17

VERBS: English *-cute, -fute, -mute* and *-pute* = Spanish *-utar*.

99%: 14 Listed

ENGLISH	SPANISH	ENGLISH	SPANISH
commute	conmutar	impute	imputar
compute	computar	minute	minutar
confute	confutar	permute	permutar
depute(-ize)	diputar	refute	refutar
dispute	disputar	repute	reputar
electrocute	electrocutar	salute	saludar
execute	ejecutar	transmute	transmutar

VERBS: English *-ue* = Spanish *-ar*.

85%: 20 Listed

ENGLISH	SPANISH	ENGLISH	SPANISH
argue	argumentar	intrigue	intrigar
catalogue	catalogar	issue	emitir•
construe	construir•	league	aliar, ligar
continue	seguir, continuar	plague	plagar
devalue	devaluar	prorogue	prorrogar
dialogue	dialogar	pursue	persequir•
discontinue	descontinuar	rescue	rescatar•
ensue	seguir, suceder•	revalue	revalorizar
fatigue	fatigar	subdue	sojuzgar, subyugar•
harangue	arengar	value	valuar

VERBS: English *-ceive* = Spanish *-cebir* or *-cibir*.

90%: 6 Listed

ENGLISH	SPANISH	ENGLISH	SPANISH
conceive	concebir	perceive	percibir
deceive	engañar•	preconceive	preconcebir
misconceive	concebir mal	receive	recibir

VERBS: English *-olve* = Spanish *-olver*.

90%: 8 Listed

Cross-Reference: N: -olvency, -olution, -ment
                  ADJ: -olvable, -olute

ENGLISH	SPANISH	ENGLISH	SPANISH
absolve	absolver	involve	comprender, incluir•
devolve	devolver	resolve	resolver
dissolve	disolver	revolve	girar, revolver
evolve	desenvolver	solve	resolver

VERBS: English *-prove* = Spanish *-probar*. 65%: 6 Listed

ENGLISH	SPANISH	ENGLISH	SPANISH
approve	aprobar	improve	mejorar•
disapprove	desaprobar	prove	probar
disprove	refutar•	reprove	reprobar

VERBS: English *-serve* = Spanish *-servar*. 80%: 6 Listed

ENGLISH	SPANISH	ENGLISH	SPANISH
conserve	conservar	*preserve	preservar
deserve	merecer•	reserve	reservar
observe	observar	serve	servir•

VERBS: English *-ize* and *-yze* = Spanish *-izar*. 90%: 218 Listed

Suffix meaning: a) to cause to be, become, make conform with or resemble, make (democratize, Americanize, sterilize); b) to become like (crystallize); c) to subject to, treat with, combine with (oxidize, galvanize); d) to engage in, act in a specified way (theorize, soliloquize). Some (marked with a "Z") drop the -iz-.

Cross-References: N -ization, -izer
V -ise

ENGLISH	SPANISH		ENGLISH	SPANISH
acclimatize	aclimatar	Z	capsize	zozobrar•
aggrandize	agrandar	Z	caricaturize	caricaturizar
agonize	agonizar		catechize	catequizar
alkalize	alcalizar		categorize	categorizar
allegorize	alegorizar		catheterize	cateterizar
alphabetize	alfabetizar		cauterize	cauterizar
americanize	americanizar		centralize	centralizar
amortize	amortizar		channelize	canalizar
analyze	analizar		characterize	caracterizar
anesthetize	anestesiar	Z	christianize	cristianizar
antagonize	contrariar, enajenar•		civilize	civilizar
apologize	disculpar•		collectivize	colectivizar
atomize	atomizar		colonize	colonizar
authorize	autorizar		commercialize	comercializar
automatize	automatizar		communize	comunizar
baptize	bautizar		computerize	computerizar
barbarize	barbarizar		criticize	critiquizar
brutalize	brutalizar		crystallize	cristalizar
burglarize	robar•		decentralize	descentralizar
canonize	canonizar		dehumanize	deshumanizar
capitalize	capitalizar		demagnetize	desmagnetizar
				desimantar

ENGLISH	SPANISH	ENGLISH	SPANISH
demilitarize	desmilitarizar	Latinize	latinizar
demobilize	desmovilizar	legalize	legalizar
democratize	democratizar	legitimize	legitimar Z
demoralize	desmoralizar	liberalize	liberalizar
deodorize	desodorizar	lionize	celebrar•
deputize	diputar Z	localize	localizar
despotize	despotizar	macadamize	macadamizar
destabilize	desestablizar	magnetize	magnetizar
devitalize	desvitalizar	martyrize	martirizar
dialyze	dializar	maximize	aumentar, maximizar
digitalize	digitalizar	mechanize	mecanizar
disorganize	desorganizar	memorialize	conmemorar•
divinize	divinizar	memorize	memorizar
dogmatize	dogmatizar	mercerize	mercerizar
dramatize	dramatizar	mesmerize	encantar, hipnotizar•
economize	economizar	metabolize	metabolizar
electrolyze	electrolizar	metallize	metalizar
emphasize	acentuar, enfatizar•	metaphorize	metaforizar
energize	energizar	methodize	metodizar
equalize	egualar Z	militarize	militarizar
eulogize	elogiar Z	mineralize	mineralizar
exorcize	exorcizar	minimize	minimizar
extemporize	improvisar•	mobilize	movilizar
exteriorize	exteriorizar	modernize	modernizar
familiarize	familiarizar	monetize	monetizar
federalize	federalizar	monopolize	monopolizar
fertilize	fertilizar	moralize	moralizar
finalize	finalizar	motorize	motorizar
formalize	formalizar	narcotize	narcotizar
fossilize	fosilizar	nasalize	nasalizar
fraternize	fraternizar	nationalize	nacionalizar
galvanize	galvanizar	naturalize	naturalizar
generalize	generalizar	neutralize	neutralizar
Germanize	germanizar	normalize	normalizar
glamorize	embellecer•	notarize	certificar•
gormandize	glotonear•	novelize	novelizar
gutturalize	guturalizar	optimize	optimar Z
harmonize	armonizar	organize	organizar
homogenize	homogeneizar	ostracize	excluir•
hospitalize	hospitalizar	oxidize	oxidar Z
humanize	humanizar	paganize	paganizar
hypnotize	hipnotizar	paralyze	paralizar
hypothesize	formar una hipótesis•	particularize	particularizar
idealize	idealizar	pasteurize	pasteurizar
idolize	idolatrar•	patronize	patrocinar Z
immobilize	inmovilizar	penalize	penalizar
immortalize	inmortalizar	personalize	personalizar
immunize	inmunizar	philosophize	filosofar Z
individualize	individualizar	plagiarize	plagiar Z
industrialize	industrializar	pluralize	pluralizar
ionize	ionizar	poetize	poetizar
italicize	enfatizar, subrayar•	polarize	polarizar
itemize	detallar•	pollinize	polinizar
jeopardize	arriesgar•	polymerize	polimerizar

ENGLISH	SPANISH	ENGLISH	SPANISH
popularize	popularizar	standardize	estandardizar
pressurize	presurizar	sterilize	esterilizar
prologuize	prologar Z	stigmatize	estigmatizar
prophetize	profetizar	stylize	estilizar
psychoanalyze	psicoanalizar	subsidize	dar subsidio•
publicize	publicar Z	summarize	resumir•
pulverize	pulverizar	syllabize	silabizar
rationalize	racionalizar	syllogize	silogizar
*realize	realizar	symbolize	simbolizar
recapitalize	recapitalizar	*sympathize	simpatizar
recognize	reconocer•	synchronize	sincronizar
regularize	regularizar	syndicalize	sindicalizar
remilitarize	remilitarizar	synthesize	sintetizar
reorganize	reorganizar	systematize	sistematizar
republicanize	republicanizar	tantalize	tentar•
revitalize	revitalizar	temporize	contemporizar, temporizar
revolutionize	revolucionar Z	terrorize	aterrorizar
romanticize	romantizar	theologize	teologizar
sanitize	sanear•	theorize	teorizar
satirize	satirizar	totalize	totalizar
scandalize	escandalizar	tranquilize	tranquilizar
schematize	esquematizar	traumatize	traumatizar
scrupulize	escrupulizar	tyrannize	tiranizar
scrutinize	escrutar•	unionize	sindicar•
secularize	secularizar	universalize	universalizar
sensitize	sensibilizar•	urbanize	urbanizar
singularize	singularizar	utilize	utilizar
socialize	socializar	vaporize	vaporizar
solemnize	solemnizar	victimize	victimar Z
soliloquize	soliloquiar Z	visualize	imaginar•
sovietize	sovietizar	vitalize	vitalizar
specialize	especializar	vocalize	vocalizar
spiritualize	espiritualizar	vulcanize	vulcanizar
stabilize	estabilizar	vulgarize	vulgarizar

VERBS: English *-graph* = Spanish *-grafiar.* **99%: 8 Listed**

Cross-Reference: N *-graph, -grapher, -graphy*
ADJ *-graphic*

ENGLISH	SPANISH	ENGLISH	SPANISH
autograph	autografiar	mimeograph	mimeografiar
calligraph	caligrafiar	photograph	fotografiar
graph	grafiar	radiograph	radiografiar
lithograph	litografiar	telegraph	telegrafiar

VERBS: English *-al* often = Spanish *-lar* or *-izar*.   20%: 9 Listed

ENGLISH	SPANISH	ENGLISH	SPANISH
appeal	apelar	reveal	divulgar, revelar
congeal	helar, congelar	rival	rivalizar
corral	acorralar	seal	sellar
equal	igualar	total	totalizar
pedal	pedalear		

VERBS: English *-pel* = Spanish *-peler*.   65%: 6 Listed

ENGLISH	SPANISH	ENGLISH	SPANISH
compel	obligar, compeler	impel	impeler
dispel	dispersar•	propel	propulsar, impeler•
expel	expulsar, expeler	repel	repeler

VERBS: English *-el* other than *-pel* often = Spanish *-alar* or *-elar*.   60%: 7 Listed

ENGLISH	SPANISH	ENGLISH	SPANISH
cancel	cancelar	parcel	parcelar
channel	acanalar	rebel	rebelar
model	modelar	remodel	remodelar
nickel	niquelar		

VERBS: English *-claim* = Spanish *-clamar*.   75%: 8 Listed

ENGLISH	SPANISH	ENGLISH	SPANISH
acclaim	aclamar	disclaim	repudiar•
claim	reclamar	exclaim	exclamar
counterclaim	contrademandar•	proclaim	proclamar
declaim	declamar	reclaim	reclamar

VERBS: English *-arm* = Spanish *-armar*.   99%: 4 Listed

ENGLISH	SPANISH	ENGLISH	SPANISH
alarm	alarmar	disarm	desarmar
arm	armar	rearm	rearmar

VERBS: English *-firm* = Spanish *-firmar*. 99%: 4 Listed

Cross-Reference: N -firmation; ADJ -firmative

ENGLISH	SPANISH	ENGLISH	SPANISH
affirm	afirmar	reaffirm	reafirmar
confirm	confirmar	reconfirm	reconfirmar

VERBS: English *-form* = Spanish *-formar*. 90%: 10 Listed

ENGLISH	SPANISH	ENGLISH	SPANISH
chloroform	cloroformizar•	perform	ejectutar•
conform	conformar	preform	preformar
deform	deformar	reform	reformar
form	formar	transform	transformar
inform	avisar, advertir, informar	uniform	uniformar

VERBS: English *-ign* = Spanish *-nar* or *-near*. 70%: 12 Listed

ENGLISH	SPANISH	ENGLISH	SPANISH
align	alinear	malign	difamar•
assign	asignar	realign	realinear
campaign	hacer campaña•	reign	reinar
consign	consignar	resign (quit)	renunciar•
deign	dignar	resign (give in)	resignar
design	dibujar, diseñar	sign	firmar, signar

VERBS: English *-tain* = Spanish *-tener* or *-tenecer*. 80%: 13 Listed

ENGLISH	SPANISH	ENGLISH	SPANISH
abstain	abstener	*entertain	divertir, entretener
appertain	pertenecer	maintain	mantener
ascertain	averiguar•	obtain	conseguir, obtener
attain	alcanzar•	pertain	pertenecer
contain	contener	retain	retener
detain	detener	sustain	sostener
entertain	entretener		

VERBS: English -on sometimes = Spanish -onar.   35%:   22 Listed

ENGLISH	SPANISH	ENGLISH	SPANISH
abandon	abandonar	pension	pensionar
blazon	blasonar	proportion	proporcionar
button	abotonar	provision	aprovisionar
caption	encabezar•	question	cuestionar
caution	caucionar	ration	racionar
commission	comisionar	reason	razonar
condition	condicionar	recondition	renovar, restaurar•
function	funcionar	sanction	sancionar
mention	mencionar	season	sazonar
occasion	ocasionar	section	seccionar
pardon	perdonar	station	estacionar

VERBS: English -ern = Spanish -ernar or -ernir.   80%:   5 Listed

ENGLISH	SPANISH	ENGLISH	SPANISH
concern	concernir	intern	internar
discern	discernir	pattern	imitar, modelar•
govern	gobernar		

VERBS: English -o = Spanish -ar.   65%:   10 Listed

ENGLISH	SPANISH	ENGLISH	SPANISH
echo	repetir, resonar•	shampoo	lavar•
embargo	embargar	stucco	estucar
folio	foliar	tango	bailar tango•
lasso	lazar	torpedo	torpedear
radio	radiar	veto	vetar

VERBS: English -appear = Spanish -parecer.   99%:   4 Listed

ENGLISH	SPANISH	ENGLISH	SPANISH
appear (sight)	asomar, aparecer	disappear	desaparecer
*appear (seem)	parecer	reappear	reaparecer

VERBS: English -fer = Spanish -ferir.   80%:   10 Listed

Cross-Reference: N: -ference

ENGLISH	SPANISH	ENGLISH	SPANISH
*confer	conferir	pilfer	ratear, robar•
defer	deferir	prefer	preferir
differ	diferenciar, diferir	refer	aludir, referir
infer	inferir	suffer	padecer, sufrir
offer	ofrecer•	transfer	transferir

VERBS: English *-er* sometimes = Spanish *-ar.*   10%: 25 Listed

ENGLISH	SPANISH	ENGLISH	SPANISH
administer	administrar	filter	filtrar
alter	cambiar, alterar	inter	enterrar
carpenter	carpintear	minister	administrar
center	centrar	number	numerar
cipher	cifrar	order	pedir, ordenar
consider	considerar	ponder	ponderar
decipher	descifrar	prosper	prosperar
disinter	desenterrar	reconsider	reconsiderar
dismember	desmembrar	recover	recobrar
encipher	cifrar	reenter	volver a entrar
encounter	encontrar	register	registrar
engender	engendrar	temper (steel)	templar
*enter	entrar		

VERBS: English *-er* sometimes = Spanish *-ir.*   10%: 4 Listed

ENGLISH	SPANISH	ENGLISH	SPANISH
discover	descubrir	rediscover	redescubrir
re-cover	recubrir	render	rendir

VERBS: English *-or* sometimes = Spanish *-ar.*   30%: 12 Listed

ENGLISH	SPANISH	ENGLISH	SPANISH
anchor	anclar	enamor	enamorar
censor	censurar	honor	honrar
clamar	clamar	labor	laborar
color	colorear	savor	saborear
discolor	descolorar	succor	socorrar
dishonor	deshonrar	vapor	vaporar

VERBS: English *-or* sometimes = Spanish *-ecer.*   10%: 3 Listed

ENGLISH	SPANISH	ENGLISH	SPANISH
abhor	aborrecer	favor	favorecer
disfavor	desfavorecer		

VERBS: English *-cur* = Spanish *-currir.*   90%: 4 Listed

ENGLISH	SPANISH	ENGLISH	SPANISH
concur	concurrir	occur	ocurrir
incur	incurrir	*recur	repetir•

25

VERBS: English *-ur* other than *-cur* often = Spanish *-ar*.
30%: 10 Listed

ENGLISH	SPANISH	ENGLISH	SPANISH
augur	augurar	dishonour	deshonrar
colour	colorar	enamour	enamorar
contour	contornear	murmur	murmurar
devour	devorar	savour	saborear
discolour	descolorar	sulphur	sulfurar

VERBS: English *-press* = Spanish *-primir*.   90%: 10 Listed

Cross-Reference: N *-sion, -sor, -sibility*; ADJ *-sible, -sive*

ENGLISH	SPANISH	ENGLISH	SPANISH
compress	comprimir	impress	impresionar•
decompress	descomprimir	oppress	oprimir
depress	deprimir	reimpress	reimprimir
express	expresar•	repress	reprimir
impress (stamp)	imprimir	suppress	suprimir

VERBS: English *-ss* other than *-press* often = Spanish *-sar* or *-zar*.
10 Listed

ENGLISH	SPANISH	ENGLISH	SPANISH
amass	amasar	profess	profesar
confess	confesar	progress	progresar
*embarrass	turbar, embarazar	regress	regresar
pass	pasar	surpass	sobrepasar
process	procesar	trespass	trespasar

VERBS: English *-tract* = Spanish *-traer*.   90%: 10 Listed

Cross-Reference: N *-tion, -actor*; ADJ *-active*

ENGLISH	SPANISH	ENGLISH	SPANISH
abstract	abstraer	extract	extraer
attract	atraer	protract	prolongar•
contract	contraer	retract	retraer
detract	detraer	subcontract	sustraer
distract	distraer	subtract	deducir, subtraer

VERBS: English *-sect* = Spanish *-secar.*   99%: 4 Listed

ENGLISH	SPANISH	ENGLISH	SPANISH
bisect	bisecar	intersect	intersectar
dissect	disecar	trisect	trisecar

VERBS: English *-dict* = Spanish *-decir.*   65%: 5 Listed

ENGLISH	SPANISH	ENGLISH	SPANISH
addict	enviciar•	interdict	interdecir
contradict	contradecir	predict	predecir
indict	acusar•		

VERBS: English *-duct* = Spanish *-ducir.*   80%: 4 Listed

Cross-Reference: N *-ductance, -ductility, -duction, -ducto*
ADJ *-ductive,* V *-duce*

ENGLISH	SPANISH	ENGLISH	SPANISH
abduct	secuestrar•	*deduct	deducir
conduct	conducir	*induct	inducir

VERBS: English *-struct* = Spanish *-struir.*   99%: 5 Listed

ENGLISH	SPANISH	ENGLISH	SPANISH
construct	construir	obstruct	obstruir
destruct	destruir	reconstruct	reconstruir
instruct	enseñar, instruir		

VERBS: English *-ct* sometimes = Spanish *-ar.*   15%: 20 Listed

ENGLISH	SPANISH	ENGLISH	SPANISH
act	actuar	infect	infectar
affect (pretend)	afectar	inject	inyectar
collect	colectar	interconnect	conectar
connect	juntar, conectar	object	oponer, objetar
disinfect	desinfectar	project	proyectar
detect	percibir, detectar	prospect	explorar, prospectar
disconnect	separar, desconectar	reflect	reflejar
effect	efectuar	refract	refractar
eruct	eructar	respect	respetar
expect	aguardar, esperar	subject	someter, sujetar

VERBS: English *-ect* sometimes = Spanish *-ionar*.

                                                             10%: 8 Listed

ENGLISH	SPANISH	ENGLISH	SPANISH
collect	cobrar, coleccionar	perfect	perfeccionar
confect	confeccionar	react	reaccionar
inflect	inflexionar	reflect	reflexionar
inspect	inspeccionar	select	escoger, seleccionar

VERBS: English *-ct* sometimes = Spanish *-gir* or *-ger*.

                                                            15%: 10 Listed

ENGLISH	SPANISH	ENGLISH	SPANISH
afflict	afligir	erect	erigir
astrict	astringir	exact	exigir
correct	corregir	inflict	infligir
direct	dirigir	protect	proteger
elect	elegir	restrict	restringir

VERBS: English *-et* sometimes = Spanish *-ar* or *-ear*.

                                                        25%: 12 Listed

ENGLISH	SPANISH	ENGLISH	SPANISH
banquet	banquetear	fillet	filetear
bayonet	bayonetear	interpret	interpretar
buffet	abofetear	misinterpret	interpretar mal
coquet	coquetear	quiet	aquietar
diet	adietar	reinterpret	reinterpretar
disquiet	inquietar	trumpet	trompetear

VERBS: English *-hibit* = Spanish *-hibir*.   **99%: 4 Listed**

        Cross-Reference: N *-tion*, *-itor*; ADJ *-tive*

ENGLISH	SPANISH	ENGLISH	SPANISH
cohibit	cohibir	inhibit	inhibir
exhibit	exhibir	prohibit	prohibir

VERBS: English *-mit* = Spanish *-mitir, -mitar* or *-meter.*

95%: 14 Listed

Cross-Reference: N *-tance, -mission, -mitment, -mittal, -missibility*
ADJ *-missible, -missive*

ENGLISH	SPANISH	ENGLISH	SPANISH
*admit (enter)	admitir	omit	omitir
admit (concede)	conceder•	permit	dejar, permitir
commit	cometer	remit	remitir
delimit	delimitar	retransmit	retransmitir
demit	dimitir	submit	someter
emit	emitir	transmit	transmitir
limit	limitar	vomit	vomitar

VERBS: English *-it* other than *-mit* and *-exhibit* = Spanish *-ar.*

65%: 30 Listed

ENGLISH	SPANISH	ENGLISH	SPANISH
accredit	acreditar	exploit	explotar
acquit	exculpar•	forefeit	confiscar•
audit	revisar•	inhabit	habitar
benefit	beneficiar	inherit	heredar
cohabit	cohabitar	merit	merecer•
counterfeit	falsificar•	orbit	dar vueltas•
credit	acreditar	profit	aprovechar, ganar•
debit	adeudar•	quit	quitar
delimit	delimitar	recruit	reclutar
deposit	depositar	reedit	reeditar
discredit	desacreditar	revisit	visitar
disinherit	desheredar	solicit	solicitar
*edit	editar, redactar•	spirit	animar•
elicit	obtener, provocar•	transit	transitar
exit	salir•	visit	visitar

VERBS: English *-lt* = Spanish *-ltar.*   **90%: 12 Listed**

ENGLISH	SPANISH	ENGLISH	SPANISH
asphalt	asfaltar	exult	exultar
assault	asaltar	fault	faltar
catapult	catapultar	insult	insultar
consult	consultar	occult	ocultar
default	faltar	result	resultar
exalt	exaltar	revolt	rebelar, revolucionar•

VERBS: English *-ant* = Spanish *-antar*.   75%: 14 Listed

ENGLISH	SPANISH	ENGLISH	SPANISH
chant	cantar	plant	plantar
covenant	convenir•	recant	retractar•
decant	decantar	replant	replantar
disenchant	desencantar	supplant	suplantar
enchant	encantar	transplant	trasplantar
gallant	galantear	warrant (guarantee)	asegurar•
implant	implantar	warrant (justify)	justificar•

VERBS: English *-ent* = Spanish *-entar* or *-entir*.   90%: 40 Listed

ENGLISH	SPANISH	ENGLISH	SPANISH
absent	ausentar	implement	cumplir•
accent	acentuar•	indent	dentar, endentar
assent	asentir	instrument	instrumentar
augment	aumentar	invent	inventar
cement	cimentar	lament	lamentar
circumvent	circunvenir•	misrepresent	representar mal
comment	comentar	orient	orientar
complement	complementar	ornament	ornamentar
compliment	complimentar	patent	patentar
consent	consentir	present (introduce)	presentar
content	contentar	prevent	prevenir•
dement	dementar	regiment	regimentar
disorient	desorientar	reinvent	reinventar
dissent	disentir	relent	aplacar•
document	documentar	repent	arrepentir
experiment	experimentar	represent	representar
ferment	fermentar	resent	resentir
foment	fomentar	segment	segmentar
fragment	fragmentar	supplement	suplementar
frequent	frecuentar	torment	atormentar

VERBS: English *-ount* = Spanish *-ontar*.   90%: 8 Listed

ENGLISH	SPANISH	ENGLISH	SPANISH
account	contar	dismount	desmontar
*amount to	montar	mount	montar
count	contar	recount	relatar, recontar
discount	descontar	surmount	superar•

VERBS: English *-rupt* = Spanish *-romper* or *-rumpir*.   75%: 4 Listed

ENGLISH	SPANISH	ENGLISH	SPANISH
corrupt	corromper	interrupt	interrumpir
disrupt	perturbar, trastornar•	irrupt	irrumpir

VERBS: English *-pt* other than *-rupt* = Spanish *-ptar* or *-ntar*.
                                                                85%: 12 Listed

ENGLISH	SPANISH	ENGLISH	SPANISH
accept	aceptar	exempt	eximir de, exentar
adapt	adaptar	intercept	interceptar
adopt	adoptar	opt	optar
attempt	atentar	preempt	supeditar, apropiar•
co-opt	co-optar	receipt	extender recibo•
except	exceptuar•	tempt	tentar

VERBS: English *-part* = Spanish *-partir*.   99%: 4 Listed

ENGLISH	SPANISH	ENGLISH	SPANISH
compart	compartir	impart	impartir
depart	partir	part	separar, partir

VERBS: English *-vert* = Spanish *-vertir*.   90%: 10 Listed

<u>Cross-Reference</u>: N *-sion*

ENGLISH	SPANISH	ENGLISH	SPANISH
advert	advertir	invert	invertir
avert	apartar, desviar•	pervert	pervertir
controvert	controvertir	reconvert	reconvertir
convert	convertir	revert	revertir
*divert	divertir	subvert	subvertir

VERBS: English *-cert (-sert)* = Spanish *-certar (-sertar)*.
                                                                80%: 10 Listed

ENGLISH	SPANISH	ENGLISH	SPANISH
assert	afirmar, asertar	dissert	disertar
concert	concertar	insert	insertar
desert	desertar	reassert	reafirmar•
disconcert	desconcertar	reinsert	reinsertar

(Similarily: alert = alertar, but exert = ejercer)

VERBS: English *-ort* = Spanish *-ortar*.   55%: 20 Listed

ENGLISH	SPANISH	ENGLISH	SPANISH
abort	abortar	export	exportar
comfort	confortar	extort	extorsionar•
comport	comportar	import	importar
consort	asociar•	purport	implicar•
contort	contornear•	reimport	reimportar
deport	deportar	*report	informar, relatar•
discomfort	incomodar•	resort	apelar•
distort	distorcionar, torcer•	retort	acudir, retorcer•
escort	escoltar•	*support	sostener, soportar
exhort	exhortar	transport	transportar

31

VERBS: English *-est* = Spanish *-tar, -ir , -rir* or *-sar*.

                                                              65%:   22 Listed

ENGLISH	SPANISH	ENGLISH	SPANISH
*arrest (halt)	detener•	ingest	ingerir
arrest (jail)	arrestar	interest	interesar
attest	atestiguar•	*invest (finance)	invertir•
congest	congestionar•	invest (install)	investir
*contest	disputar•	manifest	manifestar
crest	encrestar	molest	molestar
detest	detestar	protest	protestar
digest	digerir	reforest	reforestar
divest	desposeer•	request	solicitar, pedir•
harvest	recoger•	suggest	sugerir
infest	infestar	vest	vestir

VERBS: English *-ist* = Spanish *-istir*.   **90%:   11 Listed**

                   Cross-Reference: N *-ence*; ADJ *-ent*

ENGLISH	SPANISH	ENGLISH	SPANISH
*assist	ayudar, asistir	insist	insistir
coexist	coexistir	persist	persistir
consist	consistir	preexist	preexistir
desist	desistir	resist	resistir
enlist	alistar•	subsist	subsistir
exist	existir		

VERBS: English *-ust* = Spanish *-ustar*.   **80%:   8 Listed**

ENGLISH	SPANISH	ENGLISH	SPANISH
adjust	ajustar	exhaust	agotar•
*disgust	disgustar	incrust	incrustar
encrust	incrustar	joust	justar
entrust	confiar•	readjust	reajustar

VERBS: English *-ify* = Spanish *-ificar*.   **90%: 80 Listed**

Suffix used to form verbs meaning (a) to make, cause, become (deify); (b) to cause to have, imbue with (dignify, glorify); (c) become (emulsify).

Cross-Reference: N *-ification, -ifier, -ifying*
ADJ *-ficative, -ficatory, -ifying*

ENGLISH	SPANISH	ENGLISH	SPANISH
acidify	acidificar	mortify	mortificar
amplify	ampliar, amplificar	mummify	momificar
beatify	beatificar	mystify	mistificar
beautify	embellecer•	nitrify	nitrificar
calcify	calcificar	notify	notificar
certify	certificar	nullify	nulificar
clarify	clarificar	ossify	osificar
classify	clasificar	pacify	pacificar
codify	codificar	personify	personificar
crucify	crucificar	petrify	petrificar
damnify	damnificar	purify	purificar
decertify	descertificar	qualify	calificar
declassify	volver a clasificar	quantify	cuantificar
dehumidify	deshumedecer•	ramify	ramificar
deify	deificar	ratify	ratificar
densify	densificar	reclassify	reclasificar
dignify	dignificar	rectify	rectificar
disqualify	descalificar	reunify	reunificar
diversify	diversificar	reverify	reverificar
dulcify	dulcificar	revivify	revivificar
edify	edificar	sanctify	santificar
electrify	electrificar	saponify	saponificar
emulsify	emulsionar•	satisfy	contentar, satisfacer•
exemplify	ejemplificar	scarify	escarificar
falsify	falsificar	scorify	escorificar
fortify	fortificar	signify	significar
fructify	fructificar	simplify	simplificar
gasify	gasificar	solidify	solidificar
glorify	glorificar	specify	especificar
*gratify	gratificar	stratify	estratificar
horrify	horrorizar•	stultify	invalidar, frustrar•
humidify	humedecer•	•terrify	aterrorizar•
identify	identificar	testify	testificar
indemnify	indemnizar•	typify	tipificar
intensify	intensificar	unify	unificar
justify	justificar	verify	averiguar, verificar
magnify	magnificar	versify	versificar
metrify	metrificar	vilify	difamar, envilecer•
modify	modificar	vitrify	vitrificar
mollify	molificar	vivify	vivificar

VERBS: English -*ply* = Spanish -*plicar* or -*plir*.   85%:   6 Listed

ENGLISH	SPANISH	ENGLISH	SPANISH
apply	aplicar	multiply	multiplicar
comply	cumplir	reply	responder, replicar
imply	implicar	supply	abastecer

VERBS: English -*py* = Spanish -*piar* or -*par*.   99%:   6 Listed

ENGLISH	SPANISH	ENGLISH	SPANISH
copy	copiar	photocopy	fotocopiar
microcopy	microcopiar	preoccupy	preocupar
occupy	ocupar	spy	espiar

2. VERBS CONVERTING ON A ONE-TO-ONE BASIS WITHOUT ANY CATEGORY PATTERN

The verbs in this list are easily learned because of the similarities in spelling or pronunciation in the two languages. While most of the frequently used "pairs" appear in this list, they are just a fraction of the English verbs that can be converted to Spanish on a word-to-word basis without a category pattern.

554 Listed

ENGLISH	SPANISH	ENGLISH	SPANISH
abate	abatir	bandage	vendar
abhor	aborrecer	banquet	banquetear
abolish	abolir	base	basar
abound	abundar	baste (sew)	bastear
abscond	esconder	bat	batear
absorb	absorber	bayonet	bayonetear
accompany	acompañar	beat (pound)	golpear, batir
accomplish	cumplir	becalm	calmar
*accord	convenir, acordar	blaspheme	blasfemar
accustom	acostumbrar	block	bloquear
act (do)	actuar	bombard	bombardear
add (include)	añadir	bore (tire)	fastidiar, aburrir
adhere	adherir	bowl	bolear
adjudge	adjudicar	box (fight)	boxear
admonish	amonestar	boycott	boicotear
adorn	adornar	buoy	boyar
advance	avanzar	cable (-graph)	cablegrafiar
advantage (have..)	aventajar	calm	calmar
advocate	abogar	camouflage	camuflar
affix	fijar	camp (encamp)	acampar
affront	afrentar	campaign	hacer campaña
aid (help)	ayudar	careen	carenar
air	airear	caress	acariciar
alert	alertar	cause (make)	causar
ally	aliar	cease (stop)	cesar
amble	amblar	cede	ceder
annex	anexar	chant	cantar
annoy	irritar, enojar	charge (ELEC)	cargar
annul	anular	charge (debit)	cargar
appear	aparecer	charge (commission)	encargar
applaud	aplaudir	chirp	chirriar
approve	aprobar	chloroform	cloroformizar
argue	argüir	cinch	cinchar
arrive	llegar, arribar	circle	circular, circundar
arm	armar	circumvent	circunvenir
atrophy	atrofiar	cite (quote)	citar
attack	atacar	claim	reclamar
attest	atestiguar	class (-ify)	clasificar
avenge	vengar	clear up	aclarar
avoid	evitar	cluck	cloquear
ballot	votar, balotar	coast	costear

ENGLISH	SPANISH	ENGLISH	SPANISH
coerce	coercer	deprive	privar de
collect	colegir, colectar	derive	derivar
color	colorar	desire	desear
combat	combatir	despair	desesperar
command	comandar	destroy	destrozar, destruir
commerce	comerciar	detail	detallar
compact	comprimir	diagnose	diagnosticar
compete	competir	diminish	disminuir
comply	cumplir	disappear	desaparecer
comprise	comprender	disband	desbandar
compromise	comprometer	discard	descartar
condemn	condenar	discharge (gun)	descargar
condole	condoler	discover	descubrir
confide	confiar	discuss	discutir
confound	confundir	disdain	desdeñar
confront	confrontar	disembark	desembarcar
conquer	conquistar	disfavor	desfavorecer
console	consolar	disinherit	desheredar
constrain	constreñir	dismay	desmayar
construe	construir	disobey	desobedecer
contact	poner en contacto	disorder (put in)	desordenar
contrast	contrastar	dispair (drive to..)	desesperar
control	regular, controlar	dispatch	despachar
convalesce	convalecer	displace	desplazar
convince	convencer	displease	desagradar, desplacer
convoy	convoyar	distil	destilar
convulse	convulsionar	distort	torcer, distorcionar
correspond	corresponder	*distinguish	distinguir
corrode	corroer	disturb	perturbar, turbar
cost	costar	divulge	divulgar
counsel	aconsejar	dose	dosificar
couple	acoplar	double	doblar
court (woo)	cortejar	doubt	dudar
cover	tapar, cubrir	drain	desaguar, drenar
cross	cruzar	drug	narcotizar, drogar
cruise	viajar, cruzar	dynamite	dinamitar
cube	cubicar	eclipse	eclipsar
curve (bend)	encorvar, curvar	effect	efectuar
cut	cortar	effloresce	eflorecer, florecer
damage	dañar	embalm	embalsamar
dance	bailar, danzar	embark	embarcar
debark	desembarcar	embellish	embellecer
debate	debatir	embrace	abrazar
debut	debutar	embroider	bordar
decipher	descifrar	embroil	embrollar
decree	decretar	emerge	emerger
defame	difamar	emphasize	enfatizar
define	definir	employ	emplear
defraud	defraudar	emulsify	emulsionar
defy	desafiar	encamp	acampar
dehumidify	deshumedecer	encipher	cifrar
delight	deleitar	encircle	circundar
demand	demandar	encounter	encontrar
demolish	demoler	endorse	endosar
deprave	depravar	engrave	grabar

ENGLISH	SPANISH	ENGLISH	SPANISH
enlist	alistar	grease	engrasar
enoble	ennoblecer	group	agrupar
enrich	enriquecer	grunt	gruñir
ensconce	esconder	guarantee	garantizar
enslave	esclavizar	guard	guardar
enthuse	entusiasmar	guide	guiar
entitle	entitular, titular	have	tener, haber
envelop	envolver	hiss	sisear
envenom	envenenar	horrify	horrorizar
*envy	envidiar	howl (growl)	aullar
equip	equipar	humidify	humedecer
erode	roer, erosionar	idolize	idolatrar
err	errar	*ignorant (be..of)	ignorar
escape	escapar	imbibe (drink)	beber
escort	acompañar, escoltar	imbue	imbuir
establish	establecer	impede	impedir
*esteem	estimar	implode	implosionar
estrange	extrañar	important (be..)	importar
excommunicate	excumulgar	importune	importunar
exercise	ejercer, ejercitar	impoverish	empobrecer
exert	ejercer	impress	impresionar
expand	extender, expandir	imprint	imprimir
expect	soponer, esperar	imprison	aprisionar
experience	experimentar	impugn	impugnar
explain	explicar	incommode	incomodar
express	expresar	increase	crecer
expunge	expungar	indemnify	indemnizar
extinguish	extinguir	influence	influir
extort	extorsionar	infringe	infringir
fail	fallar	infuriate	enfurecer
favor	favorecer	ingratiate	congraciar
feign	disimular, fingir	inhabit	habitar
fillet	filetear	inherit	heredar
film	filmar	install	instalar
filter (strain,sift)	filtrar	instill	instilar
fix (make fast)	fijar	intend	intentar
flame	flamear	interfere	interferir
flank	flanquear	interlace	entrelazar
flirt	flirtear	interrupt	interrumpir
float	flotar	interview	entrevistar
flourish	florecer	*invest	invertir
flow	correr, fluir	invigorate	vigorizar
flower	florecer	invite	invitar
focus	enfocar	irrupt	irrumpir
forage	forrajear	isolate	aislar
forge (metal)	forjar	judge	juzgar
found (base)	fundar	know (acquainted)	conocer
frown	fruncir	lace	enlazar
fry	freír	lance	lancear
gain (win)	ganar	languish	languidecer
garnish	guarnecer	launch	lanzar
gas	gasear	level	nivelar
gloss	glosar	line up (align)	alinear
grace	agraciar	liquefy	licuar, licuefacer
grade (level)	graduar	list	alistar

ENGLISH	SPANISH
live (be alive)	vivir
locate (put)	colocar
lynch	linchar
malfunction	funcionar mal
maltreat	maltratar
manage	manejar
maneuver	maniobrar
march	marchar
margin	marginar
mark	marcar, mercadear
martyr	martirizar
marvel	maravillar
mask	enmascarar
mass	amasar
menace	amenazar
measure	mensurar, medir
mend	remendar, enmendar
merit	merecer
mine	minar
misconstrue	construir mal
misguide	guiar mal
misjudge	juzgar mal
mold	moldear
moo	mugir
move (shift)	mover
move (emotion)	conmover
murmer	murmurar
mutiny	amotinar
name	nombrar
nourish (nurture)	nutrir
number	numerar
obey	obedecer
obscure	obscurecer
obsess	obsesionar
offer	ofrecer
ordain	mandar, ordenar
order	pedir, ordenar
pace	pasear
pack	empacar
paint	pintar
pair	parear
pale	palidecer
palm	palmear
paraphrase	parafrasear
park	estacionar, aparcar
parry	parar
paste	empastar
pasture	pastar
patrol	patrullar
pause	pausar
pave	pavimentar
pay	pagar
peck	picar

ENGLISH	SPANISH
pedal	pedalear
peel (husk)	descortezar, pelar
perch	emperchar
perish	morir, perecer
persevere	perseverar
perturb	perturbar
phone	telefonear
phosphoresce	fosforescer
phrase	frasear
pile	apilar
pillage	pillar
pilot	pilotar, pilotear
pine	penar
plan	planear
plant	plantar
plate	platear
please	placer
plumb	aplomar
point out	apuntar
polish (shine)	bruñir, pulir
ponder	ponderar
populate	poblar
possess	posesionar, poseer
post (station)	apostar
practice	practicar
prefix	prefijar
prejudge	prejuzgar
prejudice	perjudicar
preordain	preordenar
presage	presagiar
pressure	presionar
prevail	prevalecer
prevent	impedir, prevenir
price	preciar
prick	picar
print	imprimir
profane	profanar
program	programar
prolong	prolongar
promise	prometer
promote	promover
propose	proponer
protect	proteger
prove	demostrar, probar
provide	proveer
publish	publicar
punch (pierce)	picar, punchar
purge	purgar
pursue	perseguir
question	cuestionar
quiet	aquietar
quit (leave)	quitar
quote	cotizar

ENGLISH	SPANISH	ENGLISH	SPANISH
return	retornar	revive	revivir
rarefy	rarificar, enrarecer	revoke	revocar
raze	rasar	rhyme	rimar
react	reacionar	ridicule	ridiculizar
rebate	rebajar	risk (take chance)	arriesgar
recess	estar de receso	rival	rivalizar
recognize	reconocer	rob (steal)	robar
recoil	recular	roll	rodar
recover	recobrar	route	derrotar
redeem	redimir	ruin (wreck)	deshacer, arruinar
redefine	redefinir	ruminate	rumiar
rediscover	descubrir de nuevo	sabotage	sabotear
redouble	redoblar	sacrifice	sacrificar
redound	redundar	salt	salar
reelect	reelegir	salute	saludar
reestablish	restablecer	salvage	salvar
refrain	refrenar	sanitize	sanear
refresh	refrescar	satisfy	satisfacer
refuge (take..)	refugiar	save (rescue)	salvar
refuse	rehusar	savour	saborear
*register	registrar	scald	escaldar
reimburse	reembolsar	scale	escalar
reinstall	reinstalar	scalp	escalpar
rejoice	alegrar, regocijar	scrutinize	escrutar
rejuvenate	rejuvenecer	sculpture	esculpir
relate	relacionar	seal	sellar
relax	relajar	season	sazonar
relieve (duty)	relevar	second	secundar
remedy	remediar	secure	asegurar
remember	remembrar	sense	sentir
remodal	remodelar	sensitize	sensibilizar
remove	remover	serenade	dar serenata
render	rendir	serve (attend)	servir
renew	renovar	shock (jolt)	chocar
*rent (hire)	arrendar	signal	señalar
repair	reparar	ski	esquiar
repeat	repetir	slave (enslave)	esclavizar
replace	reponer, reemplazar	solder	soldar
reply	replicar	solve	resolver
repose	reposar	sound	sonar
reprimand	reprender	space	espaciar
reproach	reprochar	spice	condimentar, especiar
requisition	requisar	spy	espiar
rescue	rescatar	stamp (mark)	estampar
resemble	semejar	strangle	estrangular
resound	resonar	study	estudiar
respond	contestar, responder	style	estilar
restrain	restringir	submerge	sumergir
retain	retener	suborn	sobornar
retard	retardar	succor	socorrar
retort	retorcer	succumb	sucumbir
revaluate	revalorizar	surge (spurt)	surgir
revere	reverenciar	surprise	sorprender

ENGLISH	SPANISH	ENGLISH	SPANISH
survive	sobrevivir	turn (lathe, go around)	tornear
suspect	sospechar	unbutton	desabotonar
telescope	telescopar	uncork	descorchar
temper (steel)	templar	uncouple	desacoplar
tempt	tentar	uncover	descubrir
terrify	aterrorizar	underestimate	desestimar
title	titular	unlace	desenlazar
toast	tostar	unroll	desenrollar
touch	tocar	usurp	usurpar
tow (pull)	atoar	vaccinate	vacunar
trace	trazar	vagabond	vagar, vagabundear
train (coach)	entrenar	vanish	desvanecer
trap	entrapar, atrapar	varnish	barnizar
travail	trabajar	vary	variar
traverse	atravesar	*veil	velar
treat (handle)	tratar	vest	vestir
tremble	temblar	villify	envilecer
triumph	triunfar	vote	votar
trot	trotar	wade	vadear
trumpet	trompetear	zone	zonificar

3. FREQUENTLY-USED ENGLISH VERBS NOT CONVERTIBLE INTO SPANISH EXCEPT INDIRECTLY THROUGH ENGLISH SYNONYMS

Most of the nonconverting verbs listed in the second column of the list are essential for a full Spanish vocabulary, but almost all of the Spanish synonym conversions in the fourth column are given in the English-Spanish dictionary as equivalents for one or more meanings of the English verbs in the first column.

1500 Listed

ENGLISH VERB	SPANISH NON-CONVERSION	ENGLISH SYNONYMS	SPANISH CONVERSION
abduct	raptar	sequester	secuestrar
abet	apoyar, instigar	induce, incite	inducir, incitar
abhor (hate)	odiar	detest	detestar
abide (stay)	quedar, permanecer	continue, tolerate	continuar, tolerar
able (be..)	poder		
abridge	acortar	abbreviate, condense	abreviar, condensar
account for	dar cuenta de	explain	explicar
accrue	proceder	accumulate, result	acumular, resultar
ache	doler, ansiar	suffer	sufrir
achieve	lograr, tener éxito	execute, realize	ejecutar, realizar
acknowledge	reconocer	admit, confess	admitir, confesar
acquaint	enterar	inform, familiarize	informar, familiarizar
acquainted(be.)	conocer	perceive	percibir
acquiesce	acceder	assent, consent	asentir, consentir
acquit	relevar	exonerate, exculpate	exonerar, exculpar
act (behave)	portar(se)	conduct (self)	conducir(se)
act (take action)	actuar	procede	proceder
add (sum up)	añadir	sum, aggregate	sumar, agregar
address	poner las señas	direct, consign	dirigir, consignar
adjourn	aplazar	suspend	suspender
*admit (concede)	aceptar	concede, confess	conceder, confesar
advantage(take)	aprovechar(se) de	benefit from	beneficiar
*advertize	poner anuncios	announce	anunciar
advise	aconsejar, advertir	recommend, suggest	recomendar, sugerir
affect (feign)	fingir	simulate	simular
affect	afectar	influence	influir
afford (allow)		permit, provide	permitir, proveer
age (grow old)	envejecer	mature	madurar
agree (accord)	acordar, convenir	concur, coincide	concurrir, coincidir
agree (consent)	asentir	consent, accede	consentir, acceder
agree with	estar de acuerdo	concur	concurrir
aim (gun)	asestar	point, direct	apuntar, dirigir
aim (try)	proponer(se)	aspire	aspirar
allocate, allot	repartir	distribute, assign	distribuir, asignar
allow (let)	dejar	permit, concede	permitir, conceder
allure	tentar	fascinate, attract	fascinar, atraer

ENGLISH VERB	SPANISH NON-CONVERSION	ENGLISH SYNONYMS	SPANISH CONVERSION
amaze	asombrar	surprise	sorprender
amount to	montar a, ascender	sum to	sumar
amuse	*divertir	entertain, recreate	entretener, recrear
anger	enfadar, enojar	infuriate, irritate	enfurecer, irritar
annoint	untar, ungir		
annoy (irk)	fastidiar	molest, irritate	molestar, irritar
answer	*contestar	respond, reply	responder, replicar
antagonize	enajenar	provoke	provocar
ape	remedar	imitate	imitar
apologize	disculpar(se)	excuse	excusar(se)
appeal (beg)	exhortar	supplicate, implore	suplicar, implorar
appease	calmar, apaciguar	placate, mitigate	aplacar, mitigar
apply (for job)	pedir	solicite	solicitar
appoint		name, designate	nombrar, designar
apportion	repartir	distribute, prorate	distribuir, prorratear
appraise	tasar	evaluate	evaluar
appreciate(val)	subir de valor	augment	aumentar
apprise	dar parte a	inform, notify	informar, notificar
approach	acercar(se)	approximate	aproximar(se)
arise	levantar(se)	surge, ascend	surgir, ascender
arouse	despertar	excite, stimulate	excitar, estimular
arrange (place)	fijar	locate, adjust	colocar, ajustar
arrange (plan)	ordenar, ajustar	regulate, organize	arreglar, organizar
arrest (halt)	parar	detain, arrest	detener, arestar
ascertain	averiguar, comprobar	determine	determinar
ask (question)	preguntar	inquire	inquerir
ask for	pedir, rogar	solicite, supplicate	solicitar, suplicar
assail	acometer	assault, attack	asaltar, atacar
assemble(gather)	recoger, reunir	amass, congregate	amasar, congregar
assemble(mount)	ensamblar	mount	montar
assess	gravar, multar	evaluate, judge	evaluar, juzgar
assist (help)	auxiliar	aid	ayudar
assuage	aplacar, calmar	mitigate, alleviate	mitigar, aliviar
assume		suppose, presume	suponer, presumir
assure	asegurar	convince, affirm	convencer, afirmar
astound(aston.)	maravillar, asombrar	surprise	sorprender
atone	dar reparación	expiate	expiar
attach (fasten)	añadir, juntar, ligar	add, unite	añadir, unir
attain	lograr, conseguir	realize, obtain	realizar, obtener
attempt (try)	tratar, probar	intend	intentar
attend(presence)	asistir	frequent	frecuentar
attend(wait on)	cuidar	serve, assist	servir, asistir
attest	atestiguar	certify, testify	certificar, testificar
attire	ataviar, vestir	cover, invest	cubrir, *investir
auction	rematar, subastar	vend	vender
avail oneself	aprovechar(se)	benefit from	beneficiar
avert (turn)	desviar, apartar	avoid	evitar
avert (prevent)	impedir	prevent	prevenir
avoid (shun)	evitar	elude	eludir
avow	reconocer	declare, admit	declarar, admitir
await	aguardar	expect	esperar
aware (be..)	tener conocimiento	be informed	ser informado
awaken (arouse)	despertar	excite	excitar
award	otogar, adjudicar	confer, assign	conferir, asignar

ENGLISH VERB	SPANISH NON-CONVERSION	ENGLISH SYNONYMS	SPANISH CONVERSION
babble	parlotear		
bait (tease)		provocate, torment	provocar, atormentar
bait (trap)	atraer, tentar	trap	atrapar
bake	asar, cocer en horno		
balloon (blow up)		inflate, augment	inflar(se), aumentar
bandage	vendar, fajar		
bang (door)	golpear		
banish	desterrar, expulsar	deport, exile	deportar, exiliar
bank	tener cuenta	deposit	depositar
bankrupt	hacer quebrar	ruin	arruinar
bar (keep out)	impedir	exclude, prohibit	excluir, prohibir
bare		reveal, denude	revelar, desnudar
bargain	pactar	negotiate	negociar
bark (bay)	ladrar		
bathe	bañar, lavar	inundate	inundar
be	estar, ser		
beam (radio)		direct, emit	dirigir, emitir
bear (child)	parir, dar a luz	produce	producir
bear (carry)	llevar, cargar	transport	transportar
bear (endure)	soportar, sostener	suffer, tolerate	sufrir, tolerar
beat (defeat)	derrotar, vencer	conquer	conquistar
beat (pound)	batir, golpear		
beat (pulsate)	latir	palpitate, pulsate	palpitar, pulsar
beautify	hermosear	adorn, embellish	adornar, embellecer
become	hacer(se), llegar a acostar(se)		
bed (go to..)			
beg (beseech)	rogar, mendigar, pedir	implore, supplicate	implorar, suplicar
beget	causar, suscitar	engender, procreate	engendrar, procrear
begin	empezar, principiar	commence, initiate	comenzar, iniciar
beguile	engañar	seduce	seducir
behave (act)	portar(se)	conduct self	conducir(se)
behead	degollar	decapitate	decapitar
behold	mirar	observe, contemplate	observar, contemplar
belie	desmentir	falsify, contradict	falsear, contradecir
believe	creer	opine, have faith	opinar, tener fe
belittle	menospreciar	reduce, minimize	reducir, minimizar
bellow (roar)	bramar, rugir, gritar		
belong	ser de, corresponder	pertain to	pertenecer
bend (curve)	doblar	curve, incline	curvar, inclinar
bequeath (leave)	legar	transmit	transmitir
beseech	instar	implore, supplicate	implorar, suplicar
bestow (grant)	otorgar	confer, concede	conferir, conceder
bet (wager)	jugar, apostar		
betray	traicionar	violate, denounce	violar, denunciar
beware	tener cuidado	guard (be on..)	guardar(se)
bewilder	aturdir	disconcert	desconcertar
bill (charge)	facturar	charge	cargar
bind (book)	encuadernar		
bind (tie)	atar, liar, amarrar	unite	unir
bind (oblige)	comprometer	obligate	obligar
bite	morder, picar (bug)		
blame (censure)	culpar	censure, reproach	censurar, reprochar
blast	volar	bombard	bombardear
blaze	arder, llamear	flame	flamear

43

ENGLISH VERB	SPANISH NON-CONVERSION	ENGLISH SYNONYMS	SPANISH CONVERSION
bleach (whiten)	blanquear	uncolor, pale	descolorar, palidecer
bleat	balar		
bleed	sangrar		
blend (mix)	mezclar	harmonize, combine	armonizar, combinar
bless	alabar, bendecir	consecrate	consagrar
blind	cegar	obscure	obscurecer
block	bloquear, estorbar	obstruct	obstruir
bloom (blossom)		prosper, flower	prosperar, florecer
blot (stain)	manchar, tachar	supress	suprimir
blow (nose)	sonar		
blow (air)	soplar		
blow (sound)	tocar		
blow up (air)		amplify, inflate	ampliar, inflar
blow up (bang)	estallar	detonate	detonar
blunder	tropezar	err	errar
blunt	embotar, desafilar	mitigate	mitigar
blush	ruborizar(se)		
board	abordar	embark	embarcar
boast (brag)	ostentar, jactar(se)	lard up	alardear
boil	bullir, hervir		
bomb		bombard	bombardear
bond (stick)	ligar, pegar	unite	unir
bond (guarantee)	hipotecar	guarantee	garantizar
book (reserve)		reserve	reservar
bore (drill)	taladrar, barrenar	perforate	perforar
born (be..)	nacer		
borrow	tomar prestado	appropriate	apropiar(se)
boss	mandar	direct, supervise	dirigir, supervisar
bother (vex)	fastidiar(se)	molest, perturb	molestar, perturbar
bounce	brincar, rebotar		
bounce back		recuperate	recuperar(se)
bow (greet)	inclinar(se)	salute	saludar
brace	apuntalar	fortify, reinforce	fortificar, reforzar
braid	hacer trenzas	interlace	entrelazar
brake	frenar		
brave	arrostrar, afrontar		
break	quebrar, romper	fracture	fracturar
breakfast	desayunar(se)		
breathe		respire	respirar
breed	criar	engender, procreate	engendrar, procrear
brew	elaborar	fabricate	fabricar
bribe		suborn	sobornar
brief	resumir	instruct, inform	instruir, informar
brighten	abrillantar	illuminate, clarify	iluminar, aclarar
bring together	juntar	unite, reconcile	unir, reconciliar
bring	traer	conduct	conducir
bring up	criar	*educate	educar
broadcast	difundir, radiar	transmit, emit	transmitir, emitir
broaden	ensanchar(se)	amplify	ampliar
broil	asar	toast	tostar
brood (hatch)	empollar	incubate	incubar
brood (meditate)	cavilar	meditate	meditar
bruise	magullar, golpear	contusion (cause..)	contusionar
brush	cepillar		

ENGLISH VERB	SPANISH NON-CONVERSION	ENGLISH SYNONYMS	SPANISH CONVERSION
bubble	burbujear		
buckle	abrochar		
bud	brotar	germinate, flower	germinar, florecer
budget	presupuestar	economize	economizar
build	edificar	construct, erect	construir, erigir
bump (run into)		shock	chocar
burden	agobiar, cargar		
burglarize		rob	robar
burn	quemar, arder	consume	consumir
burst	estallar, romper	*explode	explotar
bury	sepultar	inter	enterrar
buy	comprar	acquire	adquirir
buzz	zumbar		
bypass	desviar	avoid	evitar
cable		cablegraph	cablegrafiar
call forth	llamar	evoke	evocar
call(be called)	llamar(se)		
call out	gritar	exclaim	exclamar
call together	reunir	convoke	convocar
call upon		invoke, visit	invocar, visitar
can (be able)	poder	be able, be capable	ser hábil, ser capaz
canvass	escudriñar	examine, solicit	examinar, solicitar
care (concern)	ocupar(se)	interest (be...)	interesar(se)
care for	cuidar	attend to	atenter
caress	acariciar		
carry	llevar, cargar	transport	transportar
carry out	cumplir	execute, complete	ejecutar, completar
carve	tallar, trinchar	sculpture	esculpir
cash	cambiar	convert	convertir
cast (throw)	echar, lanzar, tirar		
catch	*coger	trap, capture	atrapar, capturar
catch up	alcanzar		
caution	advertir, prevenir	admonish	amonestar
chafe (rub)	frotar	irritate, exacerbate	irritar, exacerbar
chain	encadenar		
chair (lead)		preside	presidir
challenge	desafiar	dispute, cuestion	disputar, cuestionar
*chance(take a)	aventurar	risk	arriesgar
change	mudar, cambiar	alter, modify	alterar, modificar
chaperon		accompany	acompañar
charge (price)	cobrar, pedir		
charge(accuse)		acuse	acusar
charm	atraer	enchant, fascinate	encantar, fascinar
charter (boat)	fletar		
chase (out)	echar	expel	expeler
chase (pursue)		pursue	perseguir
chasten,-tize		castigate	castigar
chat	charlar		
chatter (talk)	parlotear		
chatter (teeth)	castañetear		
cheat	engañar, estafar	defraud	defraudar
check(restrain)	reprimir	contain, impede	contener, impedir
check (test)	comprobar	verify, examine inspect	verificar, examinar inspeccionar

ENGLISH VERB	SPANISH NON-CONVERSION	ENGLISH SYNONYMS	SPANISH CONVERSION
cheer (clap)	vitorear	applaud	aplaudir
cheer up	alentar, alegrar	animate	animar
cherish	querer, amar	*esteem, appreciate	estimar, apreciar
chew	rumiar	masticate	mascar, masticar
chill	enfriar	refrigerate	refrigerar
chip	cortar, picar		
chirp	gorjear		
choke (stifle)	ahogar	strangle, suffocate	estrangular, sofocar
choke (by neck)	ahogar	strangulate	estrangular
choose	escoger	select, elect	seleccionar, elegir
chop (cut up)	picar, cortar		
christen		baptize	bautizar
claim	reclamar	affirm	afirmar
clang		resonate	resonar
clap (applaud)	vitorear	applaud, acclaim	aplaudir, aclamar
clasp	estrechar, apretar		
clean	limpiar, fregar	purify	purificar
clear up		clarify	aclarar, clarificar
clear table	quitar la mesa		
clear (of guilt)		absolve	absolver
climax		culminate	culminar
climb (rise)	subir, trepar	ascend, escalate	ascender, escalar
cling	agarrar, apegar(se)	adhere	adherir(se)
clip (cut)	cortar		
close (finish)	acabar	conclude, terminate	concluir, terminar
close (shut)	cerrar, encerrar		
clot	aburujar, cuajar	coagulate	coagular
clothe (dress)	vestir, arropar		
cluster	amontonar	group	agrupar
coach		train	entrenar
coax	instar	persuade	persuadir
code (encode)		encipher	cifrar
collapse	derrumbar, caer(se)		
collect (gather)	cobrar, recoger	amass, aggregate	amasar, agregar
collide		shock (crash)	chocar
comb	peinar		
come (arrive)	venir, llegar	arrive	arribar
come back	volver, regresar	return	retornar
come forward	adelantar	advance	avanzar
come out	salir		
command	regir	ordain, mandate	ordenar, mandar
commandeer	requisar	confiscate	confiscar
complain	quejar(se)	lament	lamentar
complete	acabar, completar	terminate	terminar
comprise	comprender	include	incluir
conceal (hide)	ocultar, esconder		
concoct		fabricate, prepare	fabricar, preparar
conflict	luchar, pugnar	contend, oppose	contender, oponer(se)
connive	disimular	conspire, intrigue	conspirar, intrigar
conquer	vencer, conquistar	triumph	triunfar
conscript	alistar	recruit	reclutar
consort	juntar	associate	asociar
*contest	luchar, discutir	dispute, contend	disputar, contender
		question	cuestionar
contrive	idear	invent	inventar

ENGLISH VERB	SPANISH NON-CONVERSION	ENGLISH SYNONYMS	SPANISH CONVERSION
convey (ideas)		communicate, impart	comunicar, impartir
convey (things)	llevar	transport	transportar
convict		condemn	condenar
cook	guisar, cocinar, cocer		
cool (chill)	enfriar	refresh	refrescar
correct	corregir	rectify, remedy	rectificar, remediar
corrupt	corromper	pervert, suborn	pervertir, sobornar
cough	toser		
counsel	aconsejar	consult	consultar
countenance	sancionar	tolerate, approve	tolerar, aprobar
counterfeit	contrahacer	falsify, imitate	falsificar, imitar
couple	acoplar	connect	conectar
court	galantear	enamor	enamorar
cover	cubrir, tapar		
covet	codiciar	desire	desear
crack (split)	hender, romper		
crackle (creak)	crujir, crepitar		
crash	estrellar(se)	shock	chocar
crave (yearn)	anhelar, ansiar	desire	desear
crawl (creep)	arrastrar(se)		
cripple (lame)	lisiar, estropear	mutilate	mutilar
croak (frog)	graznar		
cross out	tachar, borrar		
cross over	cruzar	traverse	atravesar
crouch	agachar(se)		
crown		coronate	coronar
crumble	desmoronar(se)		
crush	abrumar, apretar exprimir, aplastar		
cry (weep)	llorar	lament	lamentar
*cry (scream)	gritar, chillar		
curb	refrenar, reprimir	restrain	restringir
curl	rizar		
curse (swear)	maldecir	blaspheme	blasfemar
curve (bend)	encorvar	double	doblar
cut (mow, shear)	segar, cortar, entrojar		
cut (wound)	herir, cortar		
cut off	mermar, rebajar	isolate	aislar
damage	dañar, lastimar	prejudice	perjudicar
damn	maldecir	condemn	condenar
dampen (wet)	mojar	humidify	humedecer
dangle (hang)	pender, colgar	suspend	suspender
dare	atrever(se), osar	provoke, risk	provocar, arriesgar
darken (get..)	anochecer	obscure	obscurecer
darn	zurcir	mend	remendar
dart (dash)	lanzar(se), correr		
daunt	desanimar	intimidate	intimidar
dawn	amanecer, alborear		
day dream	ilusionar(se)	fantasize	fantasear
daze (dazzle)	aturdir, deslumbrar		
deal (..in)	tratar, comerciar	traffic	traficar
debase	rebajar	degrade	degradar
decay (rot)	decaer	putrefy, decompose	pudrir, descomponer
deceive (trick)	engañar, burlar	defraud	defraudar
decelerate		diminish, retard	disminuir, retardar

ENGLISH VERB	SPANISH NON-CONVERSION	ENGLISH SYNONYMS	SPANISH CONVERSION
*decline(say no)	rechazar	refuse, negate	rehusar, negar
decode	decodificar	decipher	descifrar
decrease	aminorar	diminish, reduce	disminuir, reducir
deem	opinar	consider, judge	considerar, juzgar
deepen	profundizar		
deface	estropiar	disfigure, mutilate	desfigurar, mutilar
defeat	derrotar, superar	vanquish, frustrate	vencer, frustrar
defect		desert	desertar
defile	corromper, ensuciar	contaminate	contaminar
defy	desafiar, enfrentar	resist	resistir
deign	dignar(se)	permit, concede	permitir, conceder
delay	dilatar, demorar tardar, atrasar	defer, postpone	diferir, posponer
delete	tachar	supress	suprimir
deliver	entregar, repartir	consign	consignar
deliver (free)		liberate	liberar
demand	exigir	require, demand	requerir, demandar
demote		degrade	degradar
deny	rechazar	negate, repudiate	negar, repudiar
depict	pintar	describe, represent	describir, representar
deplete	agotar	reduce, diminish	reducir, disminuir
deride	burlar(se)	ridicule	ridiculizar
desecrate		profane	profanar
deserve		merit	merecer
despise	despreciar	disdain	desdeñar
detach	destacar	separate	separar
detect	detectar	discover, perceive	descubrir, percibir
deter	impedir	dissuade, refrain	disuadir, refrenar
detour	deviar(se)		
develop	desarrollar	foment, form	fomentar, formar
devise	idear	invent, conceive	inventar, concebir
devote	consagrar	dedicate	dedicar
die	morir, fallecer		
dig (scoop)	cavar	excavate	excavar
dine	comer, cenar		
dip (plunge)	hundir, bañar	submerge	sumergir
disable	lisear	incapacitate	incapacitar
disagree	diferir	dissent	disentir
disallow	rechazar	prohibit, annul	prohibir, anular
disappoint	desengañar	frustrate disillusion	frustrar desilusionar
disassemble		dismount, disarm	desmontar, desarmar
disbar (debar)		exclude, expel	excluir, expulsar
disburse	desembolsar	pay	pagar
discard	descartar	abandon, renounce	abandonar, renunciar
discharge(gun)	disparar, descargar		
discharge(job)	despedir		
disclaim	negar, rechazar	repudiate, renounce	repudiar, renunciar
disclose		divulge, reveal	divulgar, revelar
discomfort	incomodar	preoccupy, molest	preocupar, molestar
discourage	desanimar, desesperar	dissuade	disuadir
disgrace	desgradar	dishonor discredit	deshonorar desacreditar
disguise	disfrazar	mask	enmascarar
dislike	tener aversión		

ENGLISH VERB	SPANISH NON-CONVERSION	ENGLISH SYNONYMS	SPANISH CONVERSION
dismantle		dismount	desmontar
dismay	espantar, desanimar	consternate	consternar
dismiss	despedir, echar	remove	remover
disown	renegar, desconocer	repudiate	repudiar
dispel	desvanecer	dissipate, disperse	disipar, dispersar
display	desplegar, mostrar	exhibit	exhibir
displease	desagradar	disgust	disgustar
disprove	confutar	refute	refutar
disrupt	trastornar	perturb, obstruct	perturbar, obstruir
distort	distorcionar, torcer	deform, falsify	deformar, falsear
distress	afliger, angustiar		
distrust	desconfiar	suspect	sospechar
disturb	inquietar	molest, perturb	molestar, perturbar
dive	bucear, zambullir	submerge	sumergir(se)
divest	quitar, deprivar	dispossess, deprive	desposeer, deprivar
dizzy (make..)	aturdir, marear		
do	hacer, cumplir	act	actuar
do again	rehacer	repeat	repetir
do without	prescindir	omit	omitir
doom		condemn, destine	condenar, destinar
double	doblar	duplicate	duplicar
draft (draw up)	bosquejar, redactar		
draft (conscript)		recruit	reclutar
drag (pull)	sacar, tirar, arrastrar		
drain	desaguar, agotar		
draw (sketch)	dibujar		
draw back	retroceder	retire	retirar
draw near	acercar(se)	approximate	aproximar
draw up	redactar	formulate	formular
dream	soñar	imagine, fantasize	imaginar, fantasear
dress (clothe)	vestir		
dress (cure)		cure	curar
dress (trim)		decorate, adorn	decorar, adornar
drift	derivar, vagar	float	flotar
drill (bore)	taladrar	perforate	perforar
drill (discip.)	ejercitar	practice	practicar
drink	beber, tomar, tragar		
drip	gotear		
drive (car)	ir, manejar	conduct, guide	conducir, guiar
drive (propel)	echar	impel	impeler
drive away	alejar, apartar		
drive back	rechazar	repel	repeler
drive out (chase)	echar		
drizzle	lloviznar, rociar		
droop	inclinar(se)	languish	languidecer
drop (let fall)	dejar caer		
drop	caer		
drown	ahogar		
drunk (get..)	embriagar		
dry (parch)	secar	dehydrate	deshidratar
dull (blunt)	embotar, desafilar		
dull (numb)	adormecer	paralyse	paralisar
dull (tarnish)	empañar, deslustrar		
dwell (live)	alojar, morar	reside, inhabit	residir, habitar

49

ENGLISH VERB	SPANISH NON-CONVERSION	ENGLISH SYNONYMS	SPANISH CONVERSION
dye	teñir	color	colorar
earn (deserve)		merit	merecer
earn	ganar, conseguir	obtain	obtener
ease		aleviate, mitigate	aliviar, mitigar
eat	comer	devour	devorar
echo	repercutir	resonate, reverberate	resonar, reverberar
*edit	redactar		
eject	expulsar, despedir	expel	expelar
elate	engorgullecer	enthuse, exalt	entusiasmar, exaltar
*embarass	turbar, avergonzar	embarass, confound disconcert	embarasar, confundir desconcertar
embezzle	malversar	defalcate	desfalcar
embody	encarnar	personify, include	personificar, incluir
emphasize	enfatizar	accent	acentuar
employ (use)	emplear	utilize, use	utilizar, usar
empower	habilitar	authorize	autorizar
empty (a river)	desembocar		
empty	descargar	vacate	vaciar
enable	posibilitar	capacitate, permit	capacitar, permitir
enact	decretar	promulgate	promulgar
enclose	encerrar, rodear	include	incluir
encourage	alentar, fomentar	animate, stimulate	animar, estimular
encroach	meter(se) en	usurp, invade	usurpar, invadir
end (finish)	acabar, cesar	terminate, conclude	terminar, concluir
endeavor (try)	intentar, tratar de	force self	esforzar(se)
endow	dotar	donate	donar
endure	soportar, sufrir	tolerate, sustain	tolerar, sostener
enforce	ejercitar	impose, obligate	imponer, obligar
engage (be..in)	tomar parte en	occupy(one's self)	ocupar(se) en
engage (hire)	alquilar	contract, employ	contratar, emplear
enhance	acrecentar	augment	aumentar
enjoin	ordenar, mandar	prescribe, prohibit	prescribir, prohibir
enjoy	gozar de, disfrutar		
enjoy self	divertir(se)		
enlarge	agrandar	amplify, augment	ampliar, aumentar
enlighten		illuminate, clarify	iluminar, aclarar
enliven	alegrar	animate	animar
enough (be..)	bastar	suffice	ser suficiente
enrage (anger)	enfadar, encolerizar	infuriate	enfurecer
enroll	enscribir	enlist, register	alistar, registrar
ensnare	entrampar	trap	atrapar
ensue	seguir(se)	result	resultar
entail	acarrear	occasion, implicate	ocasionar, implicar
entangle(snare)	enredar	embroil	embrollar
enter(register)		inscribe, register	inscribir, registrar
entertain(guest)	hospedar, agasajar		
entice	atraer	tempt, seduce	tentar, seducir
entomb	sepultar	inter	enterrar
entrance	hechizar	fascinate	fascinar
entrust	entregar, encargar	confide	confiar
envisage(-sion)	prever	imagine, conceive	imaginar, concebir
equate		equal, compare	igualar, comparar
erase (rub out)	borrar	eradicate, extirpate	erradicar, extirpar
erect	edificar	construct, erect	construir, erigir
erode	roer, gastar	corrode	corroer

ENGLISH VERB	SPANISH NON-CONVERSION	ENGLISH SYNONYMS	SPANISH CONVERSION
escalate		augment, intensify	aumentar, intensificar
eschew	esquivar, rehuir	avoid	evitar
escort	escoltar	accompany	acompañar
estrange	extrañar, apartar		
even	emparear	level, equal(-ize)	nivelar, igualar
evict	desalojar	expel, dispossess	expulsar, desposeer
excel	superar, aventajar, sobresalir	distinguish (self)	distinguir(se)
exchange	cambiar, permutar	alter, vary	alterar, variar
excise	cortar	extirpate	extirpar
exercise	ejercer	practice, train	practicar, entrenar
exhaust	agotar, cansar	dissipate	disipar
*exit	salir	depart	partir
expand(increase)		amplify, augment	ampliar, aumentar
expand	expandir(se)	extend	extender
expect	aguardar, esperar		
expense		charge	cargar
experience	sentir	sense, experiment	sentir, experimentar
		observe	observar
explain	explicar	clarify	aclarar
*explode	estallar, explotar	detonate	detonar
extemporize	repentizar	improvise	improvisar
extol (praise)	alabar	exalt	exaltar
face	arrostrar, enfrentar	confront	confrontar, afrontar
fade (color)	palidecer	discolor, obscure	decolorar, obscurecer
fade (wilt)	marchitar	debilitate	debilitar
fail	fracasar, faltar, fallar		
faint	desmayar(se)		
fall (tumble)	caer		
fall asleep	dormir(se)		
fancy	figurar	imagine	imaginar
farm	labrar	cultivate	cultivar
fashion (make)	idear, moldear, hacer	form, invent	formar, inventar
fast	ayunar		
fasten (join)	trabar, fijar, juntar	secure, fix, attach	asegurar, fijar, atar
fathom (depth)	sondear, sondar	test profundity	profundizar
fathom (grasp)	profundizar	comprehend	comprender
fatten	engordar, cebar	enrich	enriquecer
fear (dread)	temer, tener miedo		
feature	mostrar	offer, characterize	ofrecer, caracterizar
feed	dar de comer, alimentar, nutrir	nourish	nutrir
feel (sense)	sentir	experience, perceive	experimentar, percibir
feel (touch)	tocar, tentar		
feel sorry	sentir		
fein	fingir	pretend	pretender
fetch (get)	traer, buscar		
fight	luchar, pelear	combat, battle	combatir, batallar
file (scrape)	limar		
file (store)	archivar, ordenar	register, classify	registrar, clasificar
fill	llenar	occupy, satisfy	ocupar, satisfacer
find	hallar	encounter, discover	encontrar, descubrir
find out	averiguar	inform oneself	informar(se) sobre
fine	multar, castigar	penalize	penar, penalizar

ENGLISH VERB	SPANISH NON-CONVERSION	ENGLISH SYNONYMS	SPANISH CONVERSION
finish	acabar	finalize, terminate	finalizar, terminar
fish	pescar		
fit (adapt)	convenir, colocar	adapt, adjust accomodate	adapatar, ajustar acomodar
fix (determine)		determine, define	determinar, definir
fix (repair)	arreglar, fijar	repair, adjust	reparar, ajustar
fix up	arreglar, acomodar		
flatter	lisonjear, halagar	adulate	adular
flee (run away)	huir, fugar	escape	escapar
flood	anegar	inundate	inundar
fly	volar	float	flotar
foam	espumar		
foil	contrarrestar	frustrate, annul	frustrar, anular
fold	plegar	double over	doblar
follow (obey)	seguir	observe	observar
follow (result)		result	resultar
follow (series)	seguir	*succeed	suceder
forbid	prevenir, vedar	prohibit	prohibir
ford	vadear	traverse	atravesar
forebear		abstain, desist	abstener, desistir
forecast	predecir	prognosticate	prognosticar
foreclose	impedir	exclude	excluir
foresake		abandon	abandonar
foresee	prever	anticipate	anticipar
forestall	prevenir	impede, exclude	impedir, excluir
foretell	predecir	prognosticate	prognosticar
forfeit	perder	confiscate	confiscar
forge (falsify)	falsear	falsify	falsificar
forget	olvidar(se)		
forgive	remitir (debt)	pardon, condone	perdonar, condonar
forgo	privar(se) de	renounce, cede	renunciar, ceder
forsake	dejar	abandon, renounce	abandonar, renunciar
forward	enviar, reexpedir	remit	remitir
foster (further)	adelantar	foment, promote	fomentar, promover
found	fundar	establish	establecer
founder	fracasar, hundir		
frame (picture)	encuadrar, enmarcar		
frame (draft)	planchar, construir	form, formulate	formar, formular
free (rid)	desembarazar	liberate, emancipate	libertar, emancipar
freeze (ice)	helar	congeal	congelar
freshen		refresh	refrescar
fret (worry)	quejar, irritar(se)	preoccupy oneself	preocupar(se)
frighten (scare)	espantar, asustar	terrorize, alarm	aterrorizar, alarmar
frown	fruncir		
fulfill	cumplir, llenar	realize, satisfy	realizar, satisfacer
fun (have ..)	divertir(se)		
fun (make..of)	burlar(se), reír(se)	ridicule	ridiculisar
furnish (house)	amueblar		
furnish (supply)	suministrar	provide	proveer
gamble	jugar, apostar	risk	arriesgar
garden		cultivate	cultivar
garner	almacenar	accumulate	acumular
gasp (pant)	boquear, jadear		
gather (group)	reunir, juntar	congregate	congregar
gather	amasar, recoger, coger	accumulate	acumular

ENGLISH VERB	SPANISH NON-CONVERSION	ENGLISH SYNONYMS	SPANISH CONVERSION
gaze	mirar	contemplate	contemplar
get (acquire)	lograr, conseguir	acquire, obtain	adquirir, obtener
	admitir, cobrar	receive, procure	recibir, procurar
get away		escape	escapar(se)
get back		recover	recobrar
get dressed	vestir(se)		
get ready		prepare	preparar
get married	casar(se)		
get out	salir, bajar de	descend	descender
get together		reunion (reunite)	reunir(se)
get up (arise)	levantar(se)		
gild	dorar	eluminate	eluminar
give back	devolver, volver		
give	dar, entregar	donate	donar
give (present)	regalar	donate	donar
give up	rendir	renounce, abandon	renunciar, abandonar
gladden (be glad)	alegrar(se) de		
glance	vislumbrar		
gleam (glare)	brillar, destellar		
glide	resbalar, deslizar		
glow (glare)	lucir, brillar		
glue	pegar, encolar		
gnaw	roer		
go	andar, ir	march	marchar
go around	rodear	circle	circular
go away (leave)	ir(se), marchar(se)	depart	partir
go back	retroceder, volver		
go before		precede	preceder
go down	bajar	descend	decender
go forward	adelantar	advance	avanzar
go in		enter	entrar
go out	salir	depart	partir
go to bed	acostar(se)		
go through	pasar por	traverse, penetrate	atravesar, penetrar
go up (mount)	subir	ascend	ascender
go with		accompany	acompañar
good-by (say..)	despedir(se)		
good time (have.)	divertir(se)		
gossip	murmurar, chismear		
grab	arrebatar, coger	seize	asir
grade (level)	graduar	level	nevelar
grade (evaluate)	calificar	classify	clasificar
grant (bestow)	otorgar	concede, dispense	conceder, dispensar
grasp (grab)	prender, coger	seize	asir
grate (squeek)	crujir, rechinar		
graze (flock)	pacer	pasture	pastar
grease	engrasar	lubricate	lubricar
greet	dar la bienvenida	salute	saludar
grieve	apenar(se)	lament, afflict	lamentar, afligir(se)
grin	sonreír		
grind	moler, triturar	pulverize	pulverizar
grip (seize)	prender, agarrar	seize	asir
groan (moan)	gemir		
grope	tentar		
grow	crecer, brotar	mature	madurar

53

ENGLISH VERB	SPANISH NON-CONVERSION	ENGLISH SYNONYMS	SPANISH CONVERSION
grow old	envejecer	mature	madurar
growl (howl)	gruñir		
grumble	quejar(se), gruñir		
guess	adivinar, acertar	conjecture, suppose	conjeturar, suponer
guide	guiar	direct, conduct	dirigir, conducir
hail	granizar		
halt (stop)	parar(se)	detain, desist	detener, desistir
hand over	entregar		
handle (manage)		manage, direct, guide	manejar, dirigir, guiar
handle (touch)	tocar	manipulate	manipular
hang (dangle)	colgar, pender	suspend	suspender
hang (execute)	ahorcar	execute	ejecutar
happen	*suceder, acontecer	pass, occur	pasar, ocurrir
harass	agobiar, acosar	molest	molestar
harden	endurecer		
harm	dañar, herir	prejudice	perjudicar
harvest	recoger, cosechar		
hasten (hurry)	apresurar, apurar	accelerate	acelerar
hatch	empollar	incubate	incubar
hate (loath)	odiar	abhor, detest	aborrecer, detestar
haul (pull)	tirar, arrastrar		
haunt (frequent)	rondar	frequent	frequentar
have	haber, tener	possess	poseer
have to (must)	deber		
hazard	poner en peligro	risk	arriesgar
head	encabezar	direct, preside	dirigir, presidir
heal (cure)	sanar	cure, remedy	curar, remediar
hear (heed)	oír, escuchar		
heat (warm)	acalorar, calentar		
help	auxiliar, socorrer	aid	ayudar
hesitate	titubear	vacillate	vacilar
hide	esconder, ocultar		
hike	caminar	march	marchar
hinder	estorbar, retardar	obstruct, impede	obstruir, impedir
hint	intimar	insinuate, allude	insinuar, aludir
hire (employ)	alquilar	contract, employ	contratar, emplear
hit (strike, tap)	golpear, tapir		
hoard (save)	ahorar	accumulate, treasure	acumular, atesorar
hoe	cavar, azadonar		
hold	tener	contain	contener
hold back (stop)	reprimir	detain, contain	detener, contener
hollow	ahuecar	excavate	excavar
hope	esperar		
howl	latir, aullar		
hug (clasp)	estrechar	embrace	abrazar
hum	zumbar		
humble		humiliate	humillar
hunger (be..)	tener hambre		
hunt	buscar, casar		
hurry (hasten)	apresurar, apurar	accelerate	acelerar
hurt (harm)	herir, dañar	prejudice	perjudicar
hurt (suffer)	doler	suffer	sufrir
hush (quiet)	acallar	quiet, calm	aquietar, calmar
ill (become..)	enfermar(se)		

ENGLISH VERB	SPANISH NON-CONVERSION	ENGLISH SYNONYMS	SPANISH CONVERSION
immerse	hundir	submerge	sumergir
impair	dañar	deteriorate	deteriorar
impersonate	fingir	imitate	imitar
impinge	violar	invade, usurp	invadir, usurpar
imprison	aprisionar	incarcerate	encarcelar
improve	mejorar	reform, perfect	reformar, perfeccionar
inconvenience		incommode, molest	incomodar, molestar
increase	crecer, subir	amplify, augment	ampliar, aumentar
indict	procesar	accuse	acusar
indulge	consentir, mimar	satisfy	satisfacer
*injure	lastimar, herir	damage	dañar
insulate	apartar	isolate, separate	aislar, separar
insure	asegurar	protect	proteger
*introduce(pers)		present	presentar
intrude	meter por fuerza	molest, impose	molestar, imponer
*invest	invertir		
invoice	facturar		
involve	enredar	include, implicate	incluir, implicar
issue	echar, brotar	emit, distribute	imitir, distribuir
italicize	subrayar	emphasize	enfatizar
itch	picar		
itemize		detail, enumerate	detallar, enumerar
jeopardize		risk	arriesgar
jerk	sacudir, tirar		
join (fasten)	añadir, juntar	enlace, unite	enlazar, unir
join (group)	ensamblar	associate, ally	asociar, aliar
joke (jest)	bromear		
journey	viajar		
judge	juzgar	determine, evaluate	determinar, evaluar
jump(leap,skip)	saltar, brincar		
keep (save)	guardar	conserve, guard	conservar, guardar
keep back		retain	retener
keep from(avoid)		abstain, avoid	abstener, evitar
keep from(stop)		impede, exclude	impedir, excluir
keep quiet	callar(se)	guard silence	guardar silencio
keep up (cont)	seguir	maintain, continue	mantener, continuar
kick	patear		
kill (slay)	matar	assassinate	asesinar
kindle	encender	inflame, provoke	inflamar, provocar
kiss	besar		
knead (mould)	amasar	mold, form	moldear, formar
kneel	arrodillar(se)		
knit	tejer		
knock (hit)	golpear		
knock (door)	llamar, tocar		
knot	anudar		
know (acquainted)	conocer		
know (info)	saber		
know (not to..)	desconocer	ignorant of (be..)	ignorar
label	rotular	mark	marcar
lack(be lacking)	faltar, carecer	need	necesitar
lag (linger)	retrasar(se)	retard	retardar(se)
lampoon	pasquinar	satirize	satirizar
land (plane)	aterrizar		
land(go ashore)		disembark	desembarcar
lapse	caducar	pass, prescribe	pasar, prescribir

ENGLISH VERB	SPANISH NON-CONVERSION	ENGLISH SYNONYMS	SPANISH CONVERSION
lash (whip)	azotar		
last (continue)	durar, sobrevivir	subsist, endure continue	subsistir, durar continuar
late (be..)		tardy (be..)	tardar
laud (praise)	loar, alabar	eulogize	elogiar
laugh (chuckle)	reír		
launch (start)	lanzar	initiate	iniciar
lavish	prodigar, derrochar		
lay (put)	echar, poner	locate, deposit	colocar, depositar
lay down	acostar(se), deponer		
lay waste	asolar, arrasar	devastate	devastar
lead (be ahead)	ser el primero		
lead	llevar, mandar	conduct, direct guide, induce	conducir, dirigir guiar, inducir
lean	apoyar(se)	incline	inclinar(se)
learn	aprender	study	estudiar
lease (rent, let)	arrendar, alquilar		
leave behind	dejar atrás		
leave (bequeath)	legar		
leave (foresake)	desamparar	abandon	abandonar
leave (go away)	ir(se), marchar(se) dejar, salir	depart	partir
leave (take..)	salir, despedir(se)		
leave out		omit, exclude	omitir, excluir
lend (loan)	prestar		
lengthen		enlarge, prolong	alargar, prolongar
lessen		reduce, diminish	reducir, disminuir
let (allow)	dejar	permit	permitir
libel	calumniar	defame	difamar
lick	lamer		
lie (falsify)	mentir	falsify	falsificar
lie down	descansar, acostar		
lift	levantar, alzar	elevate	elevar
light (kindle)	encender		
light (up)	alumbrar	illuminate	iluminar
lighten (weight)	aligerar	alleviate	aliviar
like (care for)	gustar, querer		
liken	asemejar	compare	comparar
limp	cojear		
line (draw)	rayar, bordear	delineate, align	delinear, alinear
linger (tarry)	morar, retrasar(se)		
link	eslabonar, ligar	connect	conectar
lisp	balbucir, cecear		
listen	escuchar, oír		
live (be alive)	vivir	exist	existir
live (dwell)	morar, alojar	inhabit, reside	habitar, residir
load	llenar, cargar		
loaf	halaganear holgazanear		
loathe (hate)	odiar	detest, abhor	detestar, aborrecer
locate	colocar	situate	situar
lock	cerrar		
long for (crave)	anhelar, ansiar	desire	desear
look at (scan)	mirar	contemplate	contemplar
look for (search)	buscar		
look like	parecer	resemble	semejar
look over	repasar, recorrer	examine	examinar
loom	surgir	appear	aparecer

ENGLISH VERB	SPANISH NON-CONVERSION	ENGLISH SYNONYMS	SPANISH CONVERSION
loose (loosen)	desatar, desliar	liberate, disunite	libertar, desunir
lose	perder		
love	amar, querer		
lower	bajar	diminish	diminuir
lull (quiet)	sosegar	placate, calm	aplacer, calmar
lunch	comer, almorzar		
lure		seduce, tempt	seducir, tentar
madden (craze)	enloquecer	infuriate	enfurecer
mail (post)	echar al correo		
maim	lisear, estropear	mutilate	mutilar
make believe		pretend	pretender
make	hacer, elaborar	create, fabricate	crear, fabricar
		construct, form	construir, formar
make fun of	burlar(se) de	ridicule	ridiculizar
make out	divisar	distinguish	distinguir
make up		constitute	constituir
make up for		compensate	compensar
malign	calumniar	defame	difamar
manage	manejar	direct, administer	dirigir, administrar
mar (deform)	dañar, menoscabar	disfigure, mutilate	disfigurar, mutilar
market	marcadear	vend, distribute	vender, distribuir
marry (wed)	casar		
massacre	matar	assassinate	asesinar
master	vencer	dominate	dominar
mate	casar	pair	aparear
matter		be important	importar
may, might	poder	be permitted	ser permitido
mean (intend)		intend	tener intención
mean (..to say)	querer decir	signify	significar
measure	mensurar, medir		
meddle	meter(se)	intervene	intervenir
meet (assemble)		reunion	reunir
meet (introd.)	ser presentado a		
meet (run into)		encounter	encontrar
mellow (ripen)	suavizar	mature	madurar
melt (thaw)	derretir, fundir	dissolve, dilute	disolver, diluir
memorialize		commemorate	conmemorar
mend	componer, remendar	repair	reparar
merge		combine, fuse	combinar, fusionar
mesmerize	encantar	hypnotize	hipnotizar
milk (exploit)		exploit	explotar
milk (extract)		extract	extraer
mill	moler		
mind (care for)	cuidar	attend	atender
mind (obey)		obey	obedecer
mind (object)		disapprove, oppose	desaprobar, oponer
mislay	perder, extraviar		
misplace	perder, colocar mal		
miss	faltar, dejar de	err	errar
mistaken (be...)	equivocar(se)	err	errar
mistrust	desconfiar	doubt	dudar
misunderstand	comprender mal		
	entender mal		
mix (blend)	mezclar	combine	combinar
moan (groan)	gemir		
mock	mofar, burlar	disdain	desdeñar
	despreciar	ridicule	ridiculizar

57

ENGLISH VERB	SPANISH NON-CONVERSION	ENGLISH SYNONYMS	SPANISH CONVERSION
moisten (wet)	mojar	humidify	humedecer
mortgage	hipotecar		
mould (knead)	amasar		
mount (go up)	montar, subir	ascend	ascender
mourn (wail)	doler, llorar	lament	lamentar
move (residence)	mudar(se)		
move toward	acercar(se)	approximate	aproximar
mow (cut)	segar, cortar		
mumble	barbotar		
murder (kill)	matar	assassinate	asesinar
muse		meditate	meditar
must (have to)	deber	be necessary	necesitar
mutter	refunfuñar	murmur	murmurar
nail	clavar		
name (appoint)	nombrar	designate	designar
name (entitle)	nombrar, llamar	entitle, denominate	titular, denominar
narrow	estrechar	reduce, limit	reducir, limitar
need (require)	necesitar	require	requerir
neglect	descuidar	abandon	abandonar
neigh	relinchar		
night (spend..)	pasar la noche		
nod	cabecear	incline head	inclinar(se)
*note (-tice)	notar	observe	observar
notice (notify)	anunciar, advertir	notify	notificar
notarize		certify, authorize	certificar, autorizar
numb (deaden)	adormecer	paralyse	paralizar
nurse	cuidar	attend	atender
oil	aceitar	lubricate	lubricar
open	abrir		
operate (handle)	actuar, marchar	manage, function	manejar, funcionar
open (event)	principiar	inaugurate, initiate	inaugurar, iniciar
order (buy)	pedir	acquire	adquirir
order (direct)	ordenar	mandate	mandar
ostracize		exclude	excluir
ought	deber		
oust	echar	expel	expulsar
outfit		equip	equipar
outlaw		prohibit	prohibir
outline	esbozar, bosquejar	profile	perfilar
outnumber	superar en número	exceed	exceder
overcome (conq)	vencer, derrotar, rendir	conquer, subjugate dominate	conquistar, subyugar domar
overflow	desbordar, rebozar	inundate	inundar
overhaul	desmontar	repair, revise	reparar, revisar
overlap	superponer(se)	coincide	coincidar
override	imponer(se)	abrogate, annul	abrogar, anular
overtake	adelantar, alcanzar		
overthrow	vencer, volcar	dethrone	destronar
overturn (upset)	volcar, tumbar		
overwhelm	arrollar, aplastar	submerge	sumergir
owe (debt)	deber, adeudar		
own	ser dueño de	possess	poseer
pack	hacer el baúl		
paddle	remar		
pant (gasp)	jadear	suspire, palpitate	suspirar, palpitar

ENGLISH VERB	SPANISH NON-CONVERSION	ENGLISH SYNONYMS	SPANISH CONVERSION
park	parquear	station	estacionar
part (partake)	tomar parte	participate	participar
partition	repartir	divide, section	dividir, seccionar
paste (stick)	pegar		
pat	golpear		
patch		mend, repair	remendar, reparar
pattern		imitate, model, copy	imitar, modelar, copiar
pawn	empeñar, pignorar		
pay off		liquidate	liquidar
pay	pagar	compensate, remunerate	recompensar, remunerar
peak	encumbrar	culminate	culminar
peal (ring)	sonar, tocar		
pension	pensionar, jubilar		
people		populate	poblar
perch	posar(se)		
percolate	colar	filter	filtrar
perform	desempeñar, hacer	execute	ejecutar
perish	morir, perecer	succumb	sucumbir
permeate		penetrate, infiltrate	penetrar, infiltrar
perplex	embrollar, aturdir	confound	confundir
perspire	transpirar, sudar		
peruse	escudriñar	examine	examinar
pervade	extender(se)	penetrate, saturate	penetrar, saturar
pester	fastidiar	molest	molestar
pet (stroke)	frotar, mimar	caress	acariciar
petition	rogar, pedir	implore, suplicate	implorar, suplicar
pick (choose)	escoger	select, elect	seleccionar, elegir
pick (gather)	*coger		
pick up	recoger, levantar		
pickle	escabechar, encurtir		
picture		illustrate, imagine	ilustrar, imaginar
pierce	traspasar	perforate	perforar
pilfer	ratear, hurtar	rob	robar
pinch	pellizcar, apretar		
pioneer		explore, initiate	explorar, iniciar
pitch	lanzar, echar, tirar		
pity	compadecer		
*place (put)	poner, meter, colocar	situate, deposit	situar, depositar
place (take..)	*suceder	occur	ocurrir
plan	planear, idear	project	proyectar
play (game)	jugar		
play (MUS)	tocar		
play (role)	hacer el papel		
plead (beg)		implore, suplicar	implorar, suplicar
please	placer, agradar, gustar, complacer	satisfy	satisfacer
pledge (warrant)	prender, empeñar	promise	prometer
plot (draw)		trace, delineate	trazar, delinear
plot (scheme)	conjurar, tramar	conspire	conspirar
plow (plough)	arar, labrar	cultivate	cultivar
plow (waves)	surcar		
plunder	despojar, pillar	sack, rob	saquear, robar
plunge (dip)	hundir, arrojar	submerge	sumergir

ENGLISH VERB	SPANISH NON-CONVERSION	ENGLISH SYNONYMS	SPANISH CONVERSION
point out	apuntar, señalar, mostrar	indicate	indicar
poison		envenom	envenenar
		contaminate	contaminar
pollute	corromper	contaminate	contaminar
pool (combine)	juntar, reunir	combine	combinar
portend	presagear	augur, prognosticate	augurar, pronosticar
portray (paint)	retratar	represent, paint	representar, pintar
position	colocar, poner	situate	situar
post (station)	apostar	situate	situar
pound	golpear, martillear	pulverize	pulverizar
pour	derramar, verter, vaciar, echar		
power (take..)	apoderar(se)		
praise (extol)	alabar, exaltar	eulogize, adulate	elogiar, adular
pray	orar, regar, rezar	supplicate, implore	suplicar, implorar
preach	predicar	sermonize, exhortar	sermonear, exhortar
preclude	impedir	exclude, avoid	excluir, evitar
predict	predecir, profetizar	augur, prognosticate	augurar, pronosticar
preface	empezar	prologuize, introduce	prologar, introducir
press (iron)	planchar		
press (squeeze)	exprimir, apretar		
pretend	aparentar	feign, simulate	fingir, simular
prevent		impede, avoid	impedir, evitar
print	imprimir	stamp, publish	estampar, publicar
probate		validate, legalize	validar, legalizar
probe	sondar, sondear	inquire	inquirir
procrastinate	aplazar, dilatar	be tardy	tardar
*procure	lograr, conseguir	acquire, obtain	adquirir, obtener
profit (benefit)	aprovechar	gain, benefit	ganar, beneficiar
prompt	impulsar, mover	incite, inspire	incitar, inspirar
propose (marriage)	declarar(se)		
protract	alargar, levantar	prolong	prolongar
protrude (project)	resaltar, sobresalir		
prove (establish)	probar, comprobar	establish	establecer
pull down	derribar	demolish	demoler
pull (drag, tug)	tirar, sacar		
pull up (uproot)	arrancar		
pump	bombear		
punish	penar	castigate	castigar
purchase (buy)	comprar	acquire	adquirir
purport	aparentar	imply, signify	implicar, significar
pursue	perseguir, buscar		
push (shove)	empujar	impel	impeler
put (place)	colocar, poner	situate	situar
put down (quell)		repress	reprimir
put in (install)		install	instalar
put in charge	encargar		
put off	aplazar	defer, postpone	diferir, posponer
put on	poner(se)	apply	aplicar
put out	apagar	extinguish	extinguir
put up (lodge)	hospedar		

ENGLISH VERB	SPANISH NON-CONVERSION	ENGLISH SYNONYMS	SPANISH CONVERSION
put up (build)	levantar, alojar	construct	construir
put (place)	meter, poner, colocar	situate	situar
puzzle	desconcertar	confound	confundir
quack (duck)	graznar		
quake	temblar		
quarrel	reñirse, pelear	altercate, discuss	altercar, discutir
quell	domar	repress, calm	reprimir, clamar
quench	apagar	extinguish	extinguir
question (ask)	preguntar	interrogate	interrogar
question (doubt)		doubt	dudar
quicken	apresurar, apurar	accelerate	acelerar
		stimulate	estimular
quiet (lull)	callar	calm, placate	calmar, aplacar
		tranquilize	tranquilizar
*quit (leave)	dejar, salir de	desist, abandon	desistir, abandonar
quote	cotizar	cite	citar
race	correr contra	compete with	competir con
rain	llover		
raise (lift)	alzar, levantar	elevate	elevar
raise (children)	criar	*educate	educar
rally	rehacer, recobrar	reanimate	reanimar
range	ordinar	fluctuate, vary	fluctuar, variar
ransom	rescatar	liberate	liberar
rape	estuprar	violate	violar
rate	calcular, calificar	estimate, value	estimar, valorar
rate (deserve)		merit	merecer
ravage	asolar, violar	devastate, destroy	devastar, destruir
rave	desvariar, delirar		
reach (arrive)	llegar	arrive	arribar
reach (attain)	alcanzar		
read	leer		
ready	apercibir	prepare	preparar
*realize (be aware)	dar cuenta de		
reap	cosechar		
rebuke (reproach)	reprender, regañar	censure, reproach	censurar, reprochar
rebut	contradecir	refute	refutar
recall (remind)	recordar	remember	rememorar
recall (revoke)	llamar, retirar	revoke, annul	revocar, anular
recant		retract, revoke	retractar, revocar
recess	entrar en receso	suspend	suspender
reckon	contar	calculate, compute	calcular, computar
recondition			
*record	protocolizar	inscribe, consign	inscribir, consignar
recount (tell)	contar	relate, enumerate	relatar, enumerar
recover (get well)	sanar	recuperate	recuperar
recover	recobrar		
redress	enmender	remedy, repair	remediar, reparar
		rectify	rectificar
refer to		allude, attribute	aludir, atribuir
refer (direct to)	enviar	remit, refer	remitir, referir
refund	restituir, devolver	reimburse	reembolsar
regain		recover, recuperate	recobrar, recuperar
regard (watch)	mirar	observe	observar

61

ENGLISH VERB	SPANISH NON-CONVERSION	ENGLISH SYNONYMS	SPANISH CONVERSION
regard (consider)		consider	considerar
regard (esteem)		respect, appreciate	respetar, apreciar
register (letter)		certify	certificar
regret	sentir	deplore, lament	deplorar, lamentar
rehearse	ensayar	repeat, recite	repetir, recitar
reinstate	reponer	reinstall	reinstalar
reject	rechazar, rehusar	repel	repeler
rejoice	alegrar, regocijar		
relay	difundir	transmit	transmitir
release (let go)	soltar	discharge	descargar
relieve (ease)	desahogar, librar	alleviate, mitigate	aliviar, mitigar
relinquish		abandon, renounce	abandonar, renunciar
relish	encantar, gozar de	savour	saborear
rely on	atener(se)	depend on	depender
remain	quedar, sequir, permanecer, restar	continue	continuar
*remark	advertir	comment, observe	comentar, observar
remind	recordar, acordar		
remonstrate	sermonear	protest, object	protestar, objetar
remove	quitar	eliminate, extirpate	eliminar, extirpar
*rent (hire)	arrendar, alquilar		
repay	pagar, devolver	reimburse	reembolsar
repeal	derogar	revoke, annul	revocar, anular
		abolish, rescind	abolir, rescindir
		abrogate	abrogar
replenish	llenar de nuevo	restore	restaurar
reply	contestar	respond	responder
*report	contar, narrar	relate, inform	relatar, informar
request	pedir, rogar	demand, solicit	demandar, solicitar
rescue	rescatar	save, recover	salvar, recobrar
resemble	parecer a, semejar		
resign (quit)	resignar, dimitir	renounce, abdicate	renunciar, abdicar
*rest (repose)	descansar	repose	reposar
resurrect	revivir	resuscitate	resucitar
retail	vender a menor		
*retire (job)	jubilar		
*retreat		retire	retirar(se)
return (give back)	devolver		
return (go back)	volver, regresar	revert	revertir
reverse	trastornar, cambiar	invert, transpose	invertir, transponer
review	repasar	examine, analyze	examinar, analizar
revive	revivir	resuscitate, restore	resucitar, restaurar
revolt	revolucionar	rebel	rebelar(se)
reward	premiar	recompense	recompensar
rid	desembarazar	liberate from	librar(se) de
ride	pasear, ir		
ride (horse)	montar, cabalgar		
ridicule	burlar(se)		
rig	arreglar, ataviar	equip, adorn	equipar, adornar
right (be...)	tener razón		
ring (sound)	tocar, sonar	resound	resonar
rip	arrancar, rasgar		
ripen		mature	madurar

ENGLISH VERB	SPANISH NON-CONVERSION	ENGLISH SYNONYMS	SPANISH CONVERSION
ripple	murmurar, rizarse	undulate	ondular
rise (increase)	alzar	extend, augment	extender, aumentar
rise (stand)	levantar(se), ponerse de pie		
rise	levantar, subir	ascend, elevate	ascender, elevar
roam (wander)	errar, vagar		
roar (bellow)	rugir, bramar		
roast	asar	toast	tostar
rock (roll)	balancear, mecer, cunear	oscillate	oscilar
roll	rodar, arrollar	revolve	revolver
romance	galantear	fantasize	fantasear
rot	pudrir	decompose	descomponer
row	remar		
rub (chafe)	friccionar, frotar		
rue (regret)	sentir	lament, repent	lamentar, arrepentir
rule (draw lines)	rayar		
rule (govern)	regir, imperar	govern, direct	gobernar, dirigir
run (on foot)	correr		
run (machine)	marchar		
run away (flee)	huir, fugar(se)	escape	escapar
run into	chocar, topar		
run through	recorrer	traverse	atravesar
rush	apresurar(se)		
rust	enmohecer(se)	oxidize	oxidar
safeguard	salvaguardar	protect, defend	proteger, defender
sail (navigate)		navigate	navegar
sail (set...)		embark	embarcar
save (keep)	guardar, ahorrar	conserve, economize	conservar, economizar
save up (hoard)	ahorrar, economizar		
saw	serrar		
say (again)		repeat, reiterate	repetir, reiterar
say	decir	express, recite	expresar, recitar
		indicate, pronounce	indicar, pronunciar
say good-by	despedir(se)		
scan	mirar	examine, inspect	examinar, inspeccionar
scare (frighten)	espantar, asustar	alarm, intimidate	alarmar, intimidar
scatter	esparcir	disperse	dispersar
scent (perfume)		perfume	perfumar
school	enseñar	educate, instruct	educar, instruir
scold	reprender, regañar, reñir	admonish	amonestar
scorn (despise)	despreciar, mofar	disdain	desdeñar
scourge (punish)	azotar	castigate	castigar
scout	reconocer	explore	explorar
scrape	raspar, arañar		
scrape (clean)	limpiar		
scratch	rascar, rayar		
scream	gritar, chillar		
screen (shelter)	abrigar, ocultar	protect	proteger
screw	atornillar		
scrub (scour)	limpiar, fregar		
search (look for)	buscar	examine	examinar
seat	sentar	install	instalar

ENGLISH VERB	SPANISH NON-CONVERSION	ENGLISH SYNONYMS	SPANISH CONVERSION
secede		separate from	separar(se)
*secure (obtain)	conseguir	obtain	obtener
see	ver	observe, perceive	observar, percibir
seed (sow)	sembrar		
seek (search)	buscar, pedir	aspire, solicite	aspirar, solicitar
seem		appear	parecer
seize	agarrar, *coger, prender, asir		
select (choose)	escoger	elect	elegir
sell		vend	vender
send (ship)	mandar, enviar	dispatch, remit	despachar, remitir
send forth	alejar	emit	emitir
service		maintain, repair	mantener, reparar
set (place)	poner, ubicar, meter	locate, situate	colocar, situar
set (sun)	poner(se)		
set (table)	poner la mesa		
settle (agree)	convenir	decide, clarify	decidir, clarificar
settle (arrange)	arreglar	fix	fijar
settle (establish)	colocar	establish	establecer
settle (resolve)	componer, arreglar	satisfy, resolve	satisfacer, resolver
sever	romper	disunite, divide separate, cut	desunir, dividir separar, cortar
sew (stitch)	coser		
shade	sombrear		
shake hands	estrechar		
shake	sacudir, estremecer	agitate	agitar
shame	avergonzar	humiliate, dishonor	humillar, deshonrar
shape	ahormar, labrar	form, mould model, plan	formar, moldear modelar, planear
share	compartir, repartir	divide, prorate	dividir, prorratear
sharpen	aguzar, afilar		
shatter	estrellar, romper		
shave	afeitar		
shed (leaves)	deshojar(se)		
shelter	abrigar, refugiar	protect, defend	proteger, defender
shield	escudir	protect, defend	proteger, defender
shift (move)	cambiar	move	mover
shine	lucir, brillar		
ship	mandar, enviar	dispatch, remit	despachar, remitir
shiver	estremecer, tiritar	tremble	temblar
shock (emotions)	conmover	offend scandalize	ofender, escandalizar
shoot	disparar, tirar		
shop	ir de compras		
shorten	acortar	abbreviate, reduce	abreviar, reducir
should	deber		
shout (shriek)	chillar, gritar	clamor	clamar
shove	empujar	impel	empeler, empellar
show	mostrar	demonstrate manifest	demostrar manifestar
show up		appear	aparecer
shriek	chillar, gritar		
shrink	encoger	contract, diminish	contraer, disminuir
shut	cerrar, encerrar		
shut out (bar)		exclude, prohibit	excluir, prohibir
sift (strain)	tamizar, cerner, colar	filter	filtrar

ENGLISH VERB	SPANISH NON-CONVERSION	ENGLISH SYNONYMS	SPANISH CONVERSION
sigh	suspirar, gemir		
sign	firmar	subscribe	subscribir
signal	señalar	communicate, advise	comunicar, avisar
silence	callar	repress	reprimir
silent (be..)	callar(se)		
sin	pecar		
sing	cantar		
sink (founder)	hundir(se)	submerge	sumergir
sip	sorber		
sit (seat)	sentar(se)		
skate	patinar		
sketch	esbozar, bosquejar		
skid	resbalar, patinar		
skin	descarnar	peel	pelar
skip	pasar por alto	omit	omitir
skip (jump)	saltar, brincar		
slander	calumniar	defame	difamar
slant (slope)	oblicuar	incline	inclinar
slap	abofetear	insult	insultar
slay (kill)	matar	assassinate	asesinar
sleep (go to.)	dormir(se), adormecer		
sleep (nap)	dormitar, dormir		
slice (split)	rebanar, cortar	divide	dividir
slide (slip)	resbalar, deslizar		
slow	retrasar	retard, reduce	retardar, reducir
smash	aplastar, romper	destroy	destrozar, destruir
smell	oler, olfatear		
smile	sonreír		
smoke	humear, fumar		
smooth	alisar	plane	aplanar
smuggle		contraband	contrabandear
sneeze	estornudar		
sniff	husmear, aspirar		
snore	roncar		
snow	nevar		
soak	empapar, mojar		
soar	remontar	elevate	elevar(se)
sob	sollozar		
soften	suavizar, ablandar	mollify	molificar
soil (dirty)	ensuciar, manchar		
sojourn	morar, permanecer	reside	residir
solve	solucionar	resolve	resolver
soothe		calm, alleviate, tranquilize	calmar, aliviar, tranquilizar
sorry (be..)	sentir	lament	lamentar
sort	ordenar	classify	clasificar
sound (ring)	sonar, tocar		
sow (seed)	sembrar		
spank	zurrar		
spare (let go)		pardon	perdonar
spare (avoid)		avoid	evitar
spare (save)	ahorrar	economize	economizar
sparkle	chispear, brillar		
speak (utter)	hablar	express	expresar(se)
spell	escribir, deletrar		

ENGLISH VERB	SPANISH NON-CONVERSION	ENGLISH SYNONYMS	SPANISH CONVERSION
spend (money)	gastar		
spend (time)	pasar		
spice	condimentar	season	sazonar
spill (tip)	volcar, derramar, tumbar		
spin (revolve)	girar	turn	tornear
spin (thread)	hilar		
spit	escupir	expectorate	expectorar
splash	salpicar		
splice	juntar	unite	unir
split	hender, agrietar	divide, part	dividir, partir
spoil (child)	mimar		
spoil (decay)	podrir, corromper	decompose	descomponer
sponsor	fiar, patrocinar	guarantee	garantizar
spot (stain)	manchar		
sprain	torcer		
spray (sprinkle)	esparcir, rociar		
spread (expand)	tender	extend	extender
spread	esparcir, untar	disseminate	diseminar
spirit	alentar	animate	animar
sprout	brotar		
spurn	rechazar, despreciar	disdain	desdeñar
spurt	echar	surge	surgir
square	cuadrar		
squeak	chirriar, rechinar		
squeeze (press)	exprimir, apretar	compress	comprimir
stab	apuñalar		
stagger	titubear	vacilate	vacilar
stain (spot)	manchar		
stain (wood)	teñir		
stammer	balbucear, tartamudear		
stamp (foot)	patear		
stamp (stamp)	timbrar		
stampede	espantar	precipitate	precipitar
stand	estar de pie		
stand out	resaltar		
stand (bear)	soportar, aguantar	suffer, sustain, tolerate	sufrir, sostener tolerar
stare (peer)	mirar		
start (begin)	empezar	commence, initiate	comenzar, iniciar
start out (leave)		depart	partir
starve	hambrear		
state (say)	decir, precisar	declare, express	declarar, expresar
stay (remain)	permanecer, quedar		
steady		stabilize, calm	estabilizar, calmar
steal (rob)	hurtar	rob	robar
steer	guiar, manejar	conduct, govern navigate, direct	conducir, gobernar navegar, dirigir
step (tread)	dar un paso, pisar		
stick	pegar	adhere	adherir
stifle (choke)	ahogar	suffocate	sofocar
sting (insect)	picar		
stink	heder, apestar, oler		
stir	batir, mezclar	agitate, excite revolve, animate	agitar, excitar revolver, animar
stitch (sew)	coser		

ENGLISH VERB	SPANISH NON-CONVERSION	ENGLISH SYNONYMS	SPANISH CONVERSION
stoop (bend)	encorvar(se)	double up	doblar(se)
stoop (debase)	bajar	condescend	condescender
stop (halt)	parar, atajar, dejar de, acabar	cease, detain, desist, suspend, terminate	cesar, detener, desistir, suspender, terminar
stop up	tapar, tupir	obstruct	obstruir
store	almacenar	accumulate	acumular
strain (pour)	colar, tamizar		
stray	vagar, extraviar, errar		
stream	correr	flow	fluir
strengthen	fortalecer, reforzar	intensify, fortify	intensificar, fortificar
stress	subrayar	accentuate	acentuar
*stretch(extend)	alargar, estirar	extend	extender
strike (hit)	chocar, batir, pegar, golpear		
strike (picket)	declarar(se) en huelga		
strip	quitar, despojar	denude	desnudar
strive	esforzar(se), luchar	dispute	disputar
stroke (rub)	acariciar, frotar		
stroll	pasear(se)		
struggle	luchar, forcejar	combat	combatir
stuff	cebar, rellener, llenar		
stumble (trip)	tropezar		
stutter	tartamudear		
subdue (quell)	vencer, someter	subjugate, subject	subyugar, sujetar
sublease	subarrendar		
subside	hundir, apaciguar	calm	calmar
*succeed	tener éxito	triumph	triunfar
suck	aspirar, mamar, chupar		
sue	procesar	demand, supplicate	demandar, suplicar
suffice	bastar	be sufficient	ser suficiente
suit (fit)	convenir	conform, satisfy	conformar, satisfacer
sum up	resumir	recapitulate	recapitular
summon	llamar	convoke, evoke	convocar, evocar
sup	cenar, comer		
supply	abastecer, surtir	provide	proveer
support (weight)	aguantar, apoyar	sustain	sostener
support (doubt)		confirm, corroborate	confirmar, corroborar
sure (make..)	asegurar	verify	verificar
surmise		conjecture, suppose	conjeturar, suponer
surpass	sobresalir, sobrar, superar, sobrepasar	exceder	exceder
surrender	rendir(se), entregar	cede, abandon	ceder, abandonar
surround	rodear, ceñir	encircle	cercar
survey	reconocer	examine, inspect	examinar, inspeccionar
suspect	sospechar	imagine, conjecture	imaginar, conjeturar
swallow	tragar, tomar	ingest	ingerir
sway (swing)	mecer, balancear(se)	oscilate, vacilate	oscilar, vacilar
swear (cuss)	maldecir	blaspheme	blasfemar
swear (vow)	jurar		
sweat	sudar		

ENGLISH VERB	SPANISH NON-CONVERSION	ENGLISH SYNONYMS	SPANISH CONVERSION
sweep	barrer		
sweeten	azucarar	dulcify	dulcificar, endulzar
swell	hinchar, engrosar	inflate	inflar(se)
swerve	desviar(se)		
swim	nadar		
sympathize	compadecer		
taint	manchar	contaminate	contaminar
take a walk	pasear(se)	march	marchar
take advantage	aprovechar(se)		
take away	restar, llevar, quitar	separate	separar
take back	sacar, retirar, devolver		
take care of	cuidar	attend	atender
take leave	despedir(se)		
take off	desnudar, quitar(se)	amputate	amputar
take	tomar, *coger, agarrar	capture	capturar
take out	sacar	extract	extraer
take part		participate	participar
take power	apoderar(se)		
talk (converse)	hablar, charlar	converse	conversar
tame	domar	domesticate	domesticar
tap (pat)	golpear		
tape (measure)	medir		
tape (sound)	grabar		
tarnish (dull)	deslucir, empañar	discolor	descolorar
tarry (linger)	retrasar(se), demorar		
taste	gustar, probar	savour	saborear
tax	tasar, imponer, cargar		
teach	enseñar	instruct	instruir
team	formar un equipo	associate	asociar
tear (rip, rend)	rasgar, desgarrar	divide	dividir
tease	embromar, fastidiar	molest, torment	molestar, tormentar
tell (relate)	contar, decir	relate, narrate	relatar, narrar
tempt	tentar	seduce, solicit	seducir, solicitar
tend (incline)	tender	incline	inclinar
tend (watch)	vigilar, cuidar	attend	atender
tender		offer, propose	ofrecer, proponer
		present	presentar
test	ensayar, probar	examine, analyze	examinar, analizar
thank	agradecer, dar gracias		
thaw	derretir, deshelar		
thicken	espesar	condense	condensar
think (reflect)	pensar	reflect	reflexionar
		consider	considerar
think (believe)	creer, pensar	suppose	suponer
thirst	tener sed		
thrash (grain)	trillar		
threaten	amagar	menace	amenazar
thrill	estremecer	excite, delight	excitar, deleitar
thrive	crecer, medrar	prosper	prosperar
throb	pulsar	palpitate, vibrate	palpitar, vibrar
throw (pitch, cast, hurl)	lanzar, echar, arrojar, tirar		
thumb through	hojear		
thunder	tronar		

ENGLISH VERB	SPANISH NON-CONVERSION	ENGLISH SYNONYMS	SPANISH CONVERSION
thwart	contrariar	frustrate, impede	frustrar, impedir
tie (bind)	atar, liar, amarrar	restrain	restringer
tie (score)	empatar	equal	igualar
tighten	tensar, apretar, estrechar		
till	labrar	cultivate	cultivar
tilt (slant)	ladear	incline	inclinar
tint	teñir, matrizar	color	colorar, colorear
tip (gratuity)	dar propina		
tip	ladear	incline	inclinar
tip over	volcar, tumbar		
tire (weary)	cansar	fatigue, bore	fatigar, aburrir
toast (honor)	brindar	salute	saludar
toil (work)	trabajar	labor	laborar, labrar
touch	tocar, probar, manosear		
touch (emotion)		move	conmover
tour (travel)	viajar, recorrer, andar	navigate	navigar
tow (pull)	sacar, tirar, remolcar		
trade	tratar, comerciar	negotiate, traffic	negociar, traficar
train	enseñar, entrenar	instruct, prepare educar, discipline	instruir, preparar *educar, disciplinar
translate	traducir	convert, explain	convertir, explicar
travel	caminar, viajar		
traverse	atravesar	cross	cruzar
tread (step)	pisar, andar, caminar		
treat (handle)	tratar	attend, cure	atender, curar
treble		triple	triplicar
trick (deceive)	engañar, trampear, burlar		
trim	ornar, ordenar	decorate, adorn	decorar, adornar
trip	tropezar		
trouble	inquietar, afligir	perturb, molest	perturbar, molestar
trust	fiar, tener confianza	confide, depend	confiar, depender
try (endeavor)	tratar, intentar	attempt	tentar
try on	ensayar	prove	probar(se)
tug	sacar, tirar, arrastrar		
tumble (fall)	caer, rodar, derrumbar		
tune	entonar	harmonize, adjust	armonizar, ajustar
turn (convert)	cambiar	convert	convertir
turn around	volver, girar	revolve	revolver
twist (wring)	torcer, retorcer	deform	deformar
type	escribir a máquina		
umpire		arbitrate, judge	arbitrar, juzgar
unbutton	desabontonar		
uncover	destapar	discover	descubrir
undergo	pasar, padecer	suffer, sustain	sufrir, sostener
underline	subrayar	accentuate	acentuar
understand	entender	comprehend	comprender
undertake	emprender	commit to	acometer
undo	deshacer, desatar, abrir	annul, repair	anular, reparar
undress	desvestir	denude	desnudar
unearth	desenterrar	exhume, excavate	exhumar, excavar
unfasten	desatar, desabrochar		
unfold	desplegar, desarrollar desenvolver, desdoblar	discover, reveal extend	descubrir, revelar extender

ENGLISH VERB	SPANISH NON-CONVERSION	ENGLISH SYNONYMS	SPANISH CONVERSION
unionize		syndicate	sindicalizar
unload	descargar	unpack	desempacar
uphold	apoyar	sustain, defend	sostener, defender
upset	tumbar, volcar		
upset (disturb)	incomodar	perturb, molest disconcert, agitate	perturbar, molestar desconcertar, agitar
*urge	alentar, instar, exigir	exhort, incite	exhortar, incitar
use	usar	employ	emplear
use up	gastar, agotar	consume	consumir
utter	decir, hablar	pronounce, express articulate, emit	pronunciar, expresar articular, emitir
value	preciar, valorar, tasar valorizar	esteem, estimate appreciate	estimar apreciar
vamp		seduce	seducir
vanish	desvanecer	disappear	desaparecer
vex (anger)	enfadar	irritate	irritar
vex (bother)	fastidiar	molest, annoy, irritate, afflict	molestar, enojar irritar, afligir
vie	cortejar, contender	compete, rival	competir, rivalizar
view (see)	ver, mirar	examine, consider inspect	examinar, considerar inspeccionar
vizualize	concebir	imagine	imaginar
voice		express, proclaim	expresar, proclamar
void (annul)		annul, invalidate	anular, invalidar
void (empty)	vaciar	evacuate	evacuar
vouch	comprobar	verify, attest	verificar, atestiguar
vow	jurar	promise	prometer
voyage	viajar		
wade	vadear		
wag (tail)	sacudir, colear	agitate, move	agitar, mover(se)
wail	gemir, aullar	lament	lamentar
wait (for)	esperar, aguardar		
wait on		serve, attend	servir, atender
waive	descartar	renounce, suspend abandon, repudiate	renunciar, suspender abandonar, repudiar
wake	despertar(se)	alert	alertar
walk (stroll)	andar, caminar, pasear	march	marchar
wander (roam)	errar, vagar, desviarse		
want (wish)	querer	desire	desear
warm (heat)	calentar, recalentar		
warn	advertir, prevenir	alert, advise admonish	alertar, avisar amonestar
warp	torcer	pervert, deform	pervertir, deformar
warrant (back)	abonar	guarantee	garantizar
warrant (merit)		justify	justificar
wash	lavar, fregar, limpiar	purify	purificar
waste	malgastar, agotar, perder	dissipate, consume	disipar, consumir
watch (guard)	vigilar	guard	guardar
watch (observe)	velar, mirar	observe	observar
water	regar	irrigate, dilute	irrigar, diluir
wave	ondear	float, agitate	fotar, agitar
waver	oscilar	vacilate, doubt	vacilar, dudar
weaken	enflaquecer	debilitate	debilitar
wear (clothes)	llevar, poner, traer		
wear out	desgastar, gastar	consume	consumir

ENGLISH VERB	SPANISH NON-CONVERSION	ENGLISH SYNONYMS	SPANISH CONVERSION
weave	tejer	interlace	entrelazar
wed (marry)	casar(se)	unite	unir
weed	desherbar, arrancar	extirpate, eliminate	extirpar, eliminar
weep (cry)	llorar	lament	lamentar
weigh	pesar, medir		
welcome	dar la bienvenida	accept	aceptar
weld	soldar, juntar	unite	unir
westernize		occidentalize	occidentalizar
wet (drench)	empapar, mojar	humidify	humedecer
whet	afilar, despertar	stimulate	estimular
whip (lash)	azotar, golpear	flagellate	flagelar
whisper	cuchichear, susurrar		
whistle	silbar, pitar		
whiten	blanquear		
widen	ensanchar	amplify	ampliar
win (gain)	vencer, ganar	triumph, prevail	triunfar, prevalecer
wind (watch)	dar cuerdo a		
wink	pestañear, parpadear		
wipe	frotar, enjugar, secar, limpiar		
wish	querer, pedir	desire	desear
withdraw	quitar, apartar	retire, retract	retirar, retractar
wither (fade)	marchitar, secar(se)		
withhold	contener	retain	retener
withstand		resist	resistir
witness (see)	ver	be present	presenciar
witness (bear.)	testimoniar	attest, testify	atestar, testificar
wonder (marvel)	admirar(se), pasmar	marvel	maravillar(se)
wonder (ques.)	pensar, preguntar(se)	doubt	dudar
woo (court)	enamorar, galantear	court	cortejar
work (operate)		operate, function	operar, funcionar
work (toil)	trabajar	labor	laborar
work together		colaborate	colaborar
worry (fret)	inquietar, apurar(se)	torment, preoccupy	atormentar, preocupar
worsen	empeorar	aggravate	agravar
worship	reverenciar	adore, honor	adorar, honrar
worth (be..)	valer		
wound	herir	damage	dañar
wrap	envolver	roll up	enrollar
wreck	aniquilar, destrozar	destroy, ruin	destruir, arruinar
wrestle	luchar		
wring (twist)	retorcer		
wring out	escurrir, exprimir		
wrinkle	arrugar		
write	escribir		
wrong (to be.)	equivocar(se)	err	errar
yawn	bostezar		
yearn (crave)	ansiar, anhelar	desire	desear
yell (shout)	gritar, chillar	exclaim	exclamar
yield (give up)	rendir	capitulate, cede	capitular, ceder

B. NOUNS

For the purposes of the listings, nouns are divided into three segments:

1. Those which are in categories that usually convert from English to Spanish according to a uniform pattern. (Approximately 8,000 Listed)

2. Those which are not in such a category but which do convert on a one-on-one basis. (Approximately 2,500 Listed)

3. Frequently-used English nouns not convertible into Spanish but which often have one or more synonyms which do convert. (Approximately 2,000 Listed)

Approximately 4,500 additional frequently-used nouns are included in the 40 subject matter lists of Appendix H..

If the noun can be either masculine or feminine, depending on the gender of the person, only the masculine is given. The notes on page 252 may help in determining the gender of nouns and in identifying changes in the meaning of some nouns depending on their gender. Because of space limitation, only the singular form of nouns is given in the lists, but Spanish nouns ending in a vowel can usually be made plural by adding -s [*la casa (house)* =*las casas* (houses)] and those ending in a consonant are usually made plural by adding -es [*el mes (month)* = *los meses (months)*]

Total of Approximately 17,000 Nouns Listed

1. NOUNS IN CONVERTING CATEGORIES

The Noun Category Index lists the English noun ending, the corresponding Spanish noun ending, the percentage of the verbs examined in that category which convert to Spanish according to the stated pattern (based on examination of a 200,000 word base), the number of nouns (whether convertible or not) included in the list because of the high frequency of use and the category's page location. The conversion category lists contain a total of approximately 8,000 nouns after adjustment for duplication and synonym listings. Special attention should be given to the categories with the highest conversion percentages and the largest numbers of nouns in the category (i.e.: *-a, -ence, -tude, -ine, -ate, -ive, -al, -ism, -ium, -ion, -o, -ator, -sis, -itis, -us, -ent, -ist, -ency* and *-ity*) since these afford the greatest vocabulary-building benefit.

NOUN CATEGORY INDEX

ENGLISH	SPANISH	CONV. %	NO. LISTED	PAGE NO	ENGLISH	SPANISH	CONV. %	NO. LISTED	PAGE NO
-a,-ah	-a	95%	366	76	-ise	-iso(a),-icio	35%	12	97
-maniac	-ómano,-íaco	99%	6	79	-ulse	-ulso(a)	95%	3	97
-ac	-íaco, -aque	70%	14	79	-nse	-nso(a),-ión	70%	12	98
-ic	-ico(a)	85%	72	80	-ose	-osa	99%	12	98
-ad	-ada	95%	10	80	-pse	-pse(o), -psis	65%	8	98
-oid	-oide(s)	98%	24	81	-rse	-rso(a)	80%	11	98
-id	-ido(a), -ide	90%	14	81	-sse	-sa,-se,-za(o)	80%	8	99
-phobe	-ófobo	99%	6	81	-use	-uso(a)	85%	16	99
-ice	-icio(a)	40%	38	82	-ate	-ado(a), -ato	75%	81	99
-ance	-a(e)ncia,-anza	30%	60	82	-ate	CHEM -ado(to)	98%	22	100
-ence	-encia	90%	182	83	-ete	-eta, -ete	85%	5	100
-ade	-ada(o), -ata	80%	37	85	-ite	CHEM -ito(a)	99%	16	101
-cide	-cida, -cidio	99%	32	86	-ite	NAT -ita	98%	8	101
-ide	CHEM -ido, -uro	98%	21	86	-ite	-ito(a), -ite	70%	21	101
-ode	-odo(a)	90%	13	87	-ote	-oto(a), -ote	95%	8	101
-lude	-ludio	99%	3	87	-tte	-eta	70%	19	102
-tude	-tud	90%	34	87	-ute	-uto(a), -udo	80%	19	102
-age	-aje	25%	42	88	-ogue	-ogo	95%	18	102
-ege	-egio	65%	6	88	-gue	-g(u)a,-gue	95%	16	103
-ige	-igio	99%	2	88	-que	-co(a)	70%	16	103
-fuge	-uga(o),-ugio	95%	4	88	-ive	-ivo(a)	85%	85	103
-cycle	-ciclo,-icleta	99%	8	89	-é	-e,-é	55%	52	104
-cle	-culo(a)	85%	35	89	-arch	-arca(o)	95%	8	105
-angle	-ángulo	99%	4	89	-graph	-grafo,-grafía	99%	18	105
-phile	-ófilo	99%	10	90	-ish	-és(esa)	50%	10	106
-ile	-il,-il(i)o(a)	70%	22	90	-path	-pata	99%	6	106
-ole	-olo(a), -ole	80%	13	90	-i	-i,-í,-e	85%	48	106
-ule	-ulo(a)	85%	19	91	-al	-al,-alo(a)	70%	172	107
-me	-mo(a),me,-men	90%	37	91	-el	-lla,-el,elo(a)	50%	86	109
-ane	-ano(a), -án	95%	16	91	-ol	CHEM -ol	95%	12	110
-ene	-eno(a)	85%	16	92	-ol	-ol,-olo(a)	75%	18	110
-ine	-ino(a),-ín	90%	104	92	-ul	-ul	95%	8	110
-one	-ono(a),-ón	95%	22	93	-ful		-	14	111
-une	-una(o)	85%	8	94	-yl	-ilo	95%	8	111
-scope	-scopio	99%	14	94	-gram	-gramo(a)	99%	14	111
-ope	-ope,-opo(a)	90%	10	94	-em	-ema,-em, -ima	85%	20	112
-type	-tipo	95%	6	95	-gm	-gma	99%	4	112
-sphere	-sfera	95%	8	95	-ithm	-itmo	99%	4	112
-ire	-rio	85%	16	95	-lm	-lmo(a), -lm	90%	9	112
-ore	-oro(a)	95%	12	95	-form	-forma(o),-forme	95%	6	113
-ure	-ura	65%	112	96	-rm	-rma(o)		8	113
-ese	-és, -esa	95%	14	97	-asm	-asma(o)	90%	8	113

ENGLISH	SPANISH	CONV. %	NO. LISTED	PAGE NO	ENGLISH	SPANISH	CONV. %	NO. LISTED	PAGE NO
-ism	-ismo	95%	252	113	-it	-ito(a)-ido,-it	65%	44	157
-ium	-io	99%	84	116	-alt	-alto, -alt	99%	5	158
-um	-o, -um	85%	58	117	-ult	-lto(a),-tima	80%	15	158
-onym	-ónimo	99%	10	118	-ant	-a(e)nte	75%	96	158
-ician	-ico,-ista	80%	22	118	-ment	-m(i)ento	30%	98	159
-arian	-ario	85%	24	118	-ent	-ente, -to	85%	110	160
-an	-ano(a),-án,-io	80%	74	119	-ot	-ot(e),-oto(a)	60%	32	162
-gen	-geno(a)	95%	10	120	-pt	-pto(a),-ito	55%	14	162
-en	-en, -no(a)	50%	44	121	-rt	-rto, -rte	35%	22	162
-in	CHEM -ina	95%	42	121	-ast	-asto(a)-aste	90%	12	163
-in	-án,-én,-én	-	26	122	-est	-esto(a),-és	60%	24	163
-gon	GEOM -agono	99%	6	123	-icist	-ísico, -ico	90%	10	163
-gon	-gón	75%	8	123	-ologist	-ólogo	98%	58	164
-lion	-llón	75%	12	123	-apist	-peuta	99%	4	164
-ion	-ión	95%	1221	124	-i(y)st	-ista	90%	240	165
-oon	-ón	60%	20	135	-ut	-uta, -ut	95%	8	167
-tron	-trón	99%	6	135	-xt	-xto	99%	3	167
-on	-ón, -no(a)	80%	160	136	-u	-ú,-u	95%	10	167
-o	-o	85%	190	137	-x	-x,-ice,-z	90%	47	168
-oo	-ú	80%	12	139	-cracy	-cracía	99%	10	169
-ar	-ar, -ar(i)o	75%	50	140	-acy	-acía, -ión	60%	34	169
-eer	-ero(a)	70%	20	140	-ancy	-a(e)ncia,-ión	75%	34	170
-grapher	-ógrafo	99%	16	141	-ency	-encia	85%	64	170
-ifier	-ificador	90%	24	141	-dy	-día,dia(o)	70%	22	171
-meter	-metro	99%	28	142	-ology	-ología	95%	54	172
-(iz)er	-izador	85%	28	142	-gy	-gía,-gia(o)	90%	16	172
-er(doer)	-dor	-	100	143	-archy	-arquía,-cado	99%	8	173
-er(doer)	-tor	-	18	144	-graphy	-grafía	99%	22	173
-er(doer)	-sor	-	12	144	-pathy	-patía	99%	8	173
-er(doer)	-nte	-	12	144	-ly	-lio(a),-lea	85%	19	174
-i(y)r	-ir, -iro	95%	9	145	-nomy	-nomía	99%	6	174
-dor	-dor	90%	18	145	-tomy	-tomía	99%	12	174
-sor	-sor	75%	27	145	-my	-ía, -ia	60%	14	174
-ator	-ador	95%	130	146	-ny	-nia(o),-nía	85%	50	175
-ctor	-ctor	75%	50	147	-py	-pia,-pía	95%	18	175
-or	-or	70%	136	148	-ary	-ario(a),-ar	80%	72	176
-ur	-ur,-ur(i)o(a)	-	18	149	-ery	-ería,-erio	20%	24	176
-as	-as	70%	14	149	-ory	-orio(a),-ario	80%	40	177
-ics	-ica,-ia,-ismo	95%	60	150	-metry	-metría	99%	12	177
-sis	-sis	95%	50	151	-try	-tría,-terio(a)	50%	30	178
-itis	-itis	99%	24	151	-ury	-uria(o)	65%	12	178
-is	-is	70%	28	152	-sy	-sía, -sia	70%	26	178
-os	-os	85%	10	152	-ety	-edad	70%	16	179
-ess	FEM -esa,-ra	80%	25	152	-acity	-acidad	90%	14	179
-ess	-eso(a)	-	19	153	-icity	-icidad	99%	22	180
-us	-o(a), -us	90%	96	153	-idity	-idez	90%	24	180
-ocrat	-ócrata	99%	8	154	-ality	-alidad	90%	87	180
-at	-ato(a),-at(e)	70%	20	155	-bility	-bilidad	95%	135	181
-act	-acto, -ato	90%	14	155	-arity	-aridad	90%	26	183
-nct	-nto	99%	4	155	-osity	-osidad	99%	14	183
-uct	-ucto(a)	99%	8	155	-ivity	-ividad	90%	26	184
-ct	-cto, -eto	65%	30	156	-ity	-i(e)dad,-ez(a)	90%	192	184
-et	-eto(a),-ete	99%	14	156	-ty	-idad,-tad,-ía	55%	40	186
-et	-eto(a),-et(e)	30%	58	156	-xy	-xia, -jía	90%	6	186

NOUNS: English -a and -ah = Spanish -a.   95%: 366 Listed

English names of countries and diseases ending in *-a* usually follow this conversion rule. Country names ending in *-a* are included in the list of countries beginning on page 203.

<u>Gender</u>: Most are feminine in Spanish. The few that change the *-a* to *-o* are masculine

ENGLISH	SPANISH		ENGLISH	SPANISH	
ablepsia	ablepsia,	f.	bazooka	bazuka,	f.
abscissa	abscisa,	f.	begonia	begonia,	f.
adenoma	adenoma,	m.	belladonna	belladona,	f.
agenda	agenda,	f.	beta	beta,	f.
alfalfa	alfalfa,	f.	boa	boa,	f.
Allah	Alá,	m.	bonanza	bonanza,	f.
algebra	álgebra,	f.	bravura	bravura,	f.
alleluia(h)	aleluya,	f.	Buddha	Buda,	m.
alpaca	alpaca,	f.	cabana	cabaña,	f.
alpha	alfa,	f.	cadenza	cadencia,	f.
*alumna	ex-alumna,	f.•	cafeteria	cafetería,	f.
ambrosia	ambrosía,	f.	camellia	camelia,	f.
ammonia	amoníaco,	m.•	*camera	cámera,	f.
amnesia	amnesia,	f.	canasta	canasta,	f.
amoeba	ameba,	f.	candelabra	candelabro,	m.
anaconda	anaconda,	f.	cantata	cantata,	f.
anaesthesia	anestesia,	f.	capita	capita,	f.
analgesia	analgesia,	f.	carcinoma	carcinoma,	m.
anathema	anatema,	f.	carioca	carioca,	f.
anemia	anemia,	f.	casbah	casba,	f.
angina	angina,	f.	catalpa	catalpa,	f.
anglophilia	anglofilia,	f.	cathedra	cátedra,	f.
anglophobia	anglofobia,	f.	cedilla	cedilla,	f.
angora	angora,	m.	charisma	carisma,	m.
anorexia	anorexia,	f.	chimera	quimera,	f.
antenna	antena,	f.	china	china,	f.
aorta	aorta,	f.	chinchilla	chinchilla,	f.
area	área,	f.	*cholera	cólera,	m.
*arena	arena,	f.	cinema	cine,	m.•
aria	aria,	f.	cinerama	cinerama,	m.
armada	armada,	f.	citronella	cidronela,	f.
aroma	aroma,	m.	cleptomania	cleptomanía,	f.
arrhythmia	arritmia,	f.	cobra	cobra,	f.
asphyxia	asfixia,	f.	cochlea	cóclea,	f.
asthma	asma,	f.	cocoa	cacao,	m.•
aura	aura,	f.	cola	cola,	f.
aurora	aurora,	f.	*coma	coma,	m.
azalea	azalea,	f.	*comma	coma,	f.
bacteria	bacteria,	f.	concertina	concertina,	f.
ballerina	ballerina,	f.	conga	conga,	f.
balsa	balsa,	f.	copra	copra,	f.
*banana	plátano, banano,	m.	copula	cópula,	f.
barracuda	barracuda,	f.	cordillera	cordillera,	f.
basilica	basílica,	f.	cornea	córnea,	f.

ENGLISH	SPANISH	ENGLISH	SPANISH
cornucopia	cornucopia, f.	gladiola	gladiolo, m.
corolla	corola, f.	glaucoma	glaucoma, m.
corona	corona, f.	gondola	góndola, f.
criteria	criterio, m.	gonorrhea	gonorrea, f.
cupola	cúpula, f.	gorgonzola	gorgonzola, f.
cyclorama	ciclorama, m	gorilla	gorila, m.
czarina	czarina, f	guava	guayaba, f.
dahlia	dalia, f.	guerrilla	guerrilla, f.
data	datos, m. •	hacienda	hacienda, f.
delta	delta, f.	harmonica	armónica, f.
dementia	demencia, f.	hematoma	hematoma, m.
diarrhea	diarrea, f.	hemophilia	hemofilia, f.
dilemma	dilema, m.	hernia	hernia, f.
diorama	diorama, f.	hosanna	hosanna, m.
diphtheria	difteria, f.	hula	hula, f.
diploma	diploma, m.	hydra	hidra, f.
dipsomania	dipsomanía, f.	hydrangea	hidrangea, f.
dogma	dogma, m.	hydrophobia	hidrofobia, f.
drachma	dracma, f.	hyena	hiena, f.
drama	drama, m.	hyperbola	hipérbola, f.
duenna	dueña, f.	hypochondria	hipocondría, f.
duma	duma, f.	hypothermia	hipotermia, f.
dyslexia	dislexia, f.	hysteria	histeria, f.
dyspepsia	dispepsia, f.	idea	idea, f.
dysplasia	displasia, f.	iguana	iguana, f.
eczema	eczema, m.	impalla	impala, f.
edema	edema, m.	indicia	indicio, m.
egomania	egomanía, f.	inertia	inercia, f.
emphysema	enfisema, m.	influenza	influenza, f.
enchilada	enchilada, f.	insignia	insignia, f.
encyclopedia	enciclopedia, f.	insomnia	insomnio, m.
enema	enema, f.	iota	iota, f.
enigma	enigma, m.	junta	junta, f.
era	era, f.	kappa	kappa, f.
errata	errata, f.	kleptomania	cleptomanía, f.
et cetera	etcétera	larva	larva, f.
euphoria	euforia, f.	lasagna	lasaña, f.
euthanasia	eutanasia, f.	lava	lava, f.
extra (tip)	extra, m.	lemma	lema, m.
extravaganza	extravaganza, f.	leucoma	leucoma, f.
fantasia	fantasía, f.	leukemia	leucemia, f.
farina	harina, f.	lira	lira, f.
fauna	fauna, f.	llama	llama, f.
fibula	fíbula, f.	loggia	logia, f.
fiesta	fiesta, f.	lymphoma	linfoma, m.
flora	flora, f.	Madonna	Madona, f.
flotilla	flotilla, f.	Mafia	mafia, f.
formica	formica, f.	magenta	magenta, f.
formula	fórmula, f.	magnesia	magnesia, f.
forsythia	forsitia, f.	magnolia	magnolia, f.
fuchsia	fucsia, f.	maharaja	maharajá, m.
*gala	gala, f.	mahatma	mahatma, m.
gamma	gamma, f.	malaria	malaria, f.
gardenia	gardenia, f.	mamma	mamá, f.
geisha	geisha, f.	mania	manía, f.

ENGLISH	SPANISH	ENGLISH	SPANISH
manila	manila, f.	pasta	pasta, f.
manna	maná, m.	patina	pátina, f.
manta	manta, f.	peninsula	península, f.
maraca	maraca, m.	penumbra	penumbra, f.
margarita	margarita, f.	persona	persona, f.
marijuana	marihuana, f.	peseta	peseta, f.
marimba	marimba, f.	petunia	petunia, f.
marina	marina, f.	phenomena	fenómena, f.
*mascara	máscara, f.	phobia	fobia, f.
Mecca	Meca, f.	piranha	piraña, f.
medusa	medusa, f.	pizza	piza, f.
megalomania	megalomanía, f.	pizzeria	picería, f.
melancholia	melancolía, f.	placenta	placenta, f.
melanoma	melanoma, f.	plasma	plasma, f.
melodrama	melodrama, m.	plaza	plaza, f.
melomania	melomanía, f.	plethora	plétora, f.
mesa	mesa, f.	pleura	pleura, f.
Messiah	Mesías, m.	pneumonia	pulmomía, neumonía, f.
mica	mica, f.	poinciana	poinciana, f.
miasma	miasma, f.	polka	polca, f.
militia	milicia, f.	prima-donna	prima-donna, f.
Minerva	Minerva	propaganda	propaganda, f.
minutia	minucia, f.	puma	puma, m.
miscellanea	miscelánea, f.	pupa	pupa, f.
mocha	moca, f.	pyorrhea	piorrea, f.
myopia	miopía, f.	pyromania	piromanía, f.
naphtha	nafta, f.	quota	cuota, f.
nausea	náusea, f.	raja(h)	rajá, m.
nebula	nebulosa, f.•	regalia	regalía, f.
neuralgia	neuralgia, f.	regatta	regata, f.
nirvana	nirvana, m.	replica	réplica, f.
nostalgia	nostalgia, f.	retina	retina, f.
novella	novela, f.	rotunda	rotunda, f.
novena	novena, f.	rumba	rumba, f.
nymphomania	ninfomanía, f.	russophobia	rusofobia, f.
onomatopoeia	onomatopeya, f.	rutabaga	rutabaga, f.
omega	omega, f.	*saga	saga, f.
opera	ópera, f.	saliva	saliva, f.
operetta	opereta, f.	salmonella	salmonela, f.
ophthalmia	oftalmía, f.	samba	samba, f.
orchestra	orquesta, f.	sarcoma	sarcoma, f.
pagoda	pagoda, f.	sarsaparilla	zarzaparrilla, f.
pajama	pijama, m.	sauna	sauna, f.
palaestra	palestra, f.	savanna	sabana, f.
pampa	pampa, f.	schizophrenia	esquizofrenia, f.
panacea	panacea, f.	sciatica	ciática, f.
panama (hat)	panamá, m.	scintilla	centella, f.
panatela	panatela, f.	sepia	sepia, f.
panda	panda, m.	sequoia	secoya, f.
panorama	panorama, f.	Shah	sha, m.
papa	papá, m.	sienna	siena, f.
papaya	papaya, f.	*sierra	sierra, f.
paprika	paprika, f.	siesta	siesta, f.
*parabola	parábola, f.	silica	sílice, f.•
paranoia	paranoia, f.	sinfonia	sinfonía, f.
paraplegia	paraplejía, f.	soda	soda, f.
pariah	paria, f.	sofa	sofá, m.

ENGLISH	SPANISH	ENGLISH	SPANISH
sonata	sonata, f.	tuba	tuba, f.
spatula	espátula, f.	*tuna	atún, m.•
stamina	vigor, m.•	tundra	tundra, f.
stanza	estancia, f.	umbrella	paraguas, m.•
stigma	estigma, m.	urethra	uretra, f.
subpoena	citación, f.•	utopia	utopía, f.
sulfa	sulfa, f.	uvula	úvula, f.
sultana	sultana, f.	vagina	vagina, f.
swastika	svástica, f.	vanilla	vainilla, f.
taffeta	tafetán, m.•	vendetta	vendetta, f.
tapioca	tapioca, f.	veranda	veranda, f.
tarantula	tarántula, f.	vertebra	vértebra, f.
tempera	tempera, f.	via	vía, f
tequila	tequila, f.	vice-versa	viceversa, m.
terra	tierra, f.	vicuña	vicuña, f.
terracotta	terracota, f.	villa	villa, f.
theta	theta, f.	viola	viola, f.
tiara	tiara, f.	virtuosa	virtuosa, f.
tibia	tibia, f.	visa	visa, f.
toga	toga, f.	viscera	vísceras, f.
Torah	tora, f.	vista	vista, f.
tortilla	tortilla, f.	vodka	vodka, m.
toxemia	toxemia, f.	xenophobia	xenofobia, f.
trachea	tráquea, f.	Yoga	Yoga, m.
trauma	trauma, m.	yucca	yuca, f.
trivia	trivialidades, f.•	zebra	cebra, zebra, f.
troika	troica, f.	zinnia	cinnia, zinia, f.

NOUNS: English -*maniac* = Spanish -*ómano* (80%) or -*íaco* (20%).
                                                               99%: 6 Listed
    Gender: Most are masculine in Spanish unless referring to a feminine person.

ENGLISH	SPANISH	ENGLISH	SPANISH
dipsomaniac	dipsómano, m.	megalomaniac	megalómano, m.
kleptomaniac	cleptómano, m.	nymphomaniac	ninfómana, f.
maniac	maníaco, m.	pyromaniac	piromaníaco, m.

NOUNS: English -*ac* other than -*maniac* = Spanish -*íaco* or -*aque*.
                                                               70%: 14 Listed
    Gender: Most are masculine in Spanish unless referring to a feminine person.

ENGLISH	SPANISH	ENGLISH	SPANISH
almanac	almanaque, m.	hemophiliac	hemofílico, m.•
aphrodisiac	afrodisíaco, m.	hypochondriac	hipocondríaco, m.
bivouac	vivac, vivaque, m.	insomniac	insomníaco, m.
cardiac	cardíaco, m.	sacroiliac	sacroilíaco, m.
cognac	coñac, m.•	shellac	laca, f.•
demoniac	demoníaco, m.	sumac	zumaque, m.
elegiac	elegíaco, m.	zodiac	zodíaco, m.

NOUNS: English -ic = Spanish -ico or -ica. 85%: 72 Listed

Gender: Most are masculine in Spanish unless referring to a feminine person.

ENGLISH	SPANISH	ENGLISH	SPANISH
agnostic	agnóstico, m.	garlic	ajo, m.•
alcoholic	alcohólico, m.	heretic	hereje, m.•
analgesic	analgésico, m.	logic	lógica, f.
anesthetic	anestésico,-tético, m.	hieroglyphic	jeroglífico, m.
antibiotic	antibiótico, m.	lunatic	loco, lunático, m.
antiseptic	antiséptico, m.	lyric (poet)	lírico, m.
Arabic	árabe, m.•	lyric (poem)	lírica, f.
Arctic	ártico, m.	magic	magia, f.•
arithmetic	aritmética, f.	mechanic	mecánico, m.
arsenic	arsénico, m.	medic	médico, m.
ascetic	asceta, m.•	mimic	mimo, m.•
Asiatic	asiático, m.	mosaic	mosaico, m.
Atlantic	Atlántico, m.	music	música, f.
attic	desván, ático, m.	Pacific	Pacífico, m.
Catholic	católico, m.	panic	pánico, m.
ceramic(s)	cerámica, f.	picnic	picnic, m.•
characteristic	característica, f.	plastic	plástico, m.
classic	clásico, m.	polemic	polémica, f.
cleric	clérigo, m.•	public	público, m.
clinic	clínica, f.	relic	reliquia, f.•
colic	cólico, m.	republic	república, f.
comic	cómico, m.	rhetoric	retórica, f.
cosmetic(s)	cosmético, m.	romantic	romántico, m.
critic	crítico, m.	rubric	rúbrica, f.
cynic	cínico, m.	skeptic	escéptico, m.
diabetic	diabético, m.	spastic	espástico, m.
domestic	doméstico, m.	static	estática, f.
eccentric	excéntrico, m.	statistic(s)	estadística, f.
ecclesiastic	eclesiástico, m.	syndic	síndico, m.
elastic	elástico, m.	synthetic	sintético, m.
epic	epopeya, épica, f.	tactic(s)	táctica, f.
epidemic	epidemia, f.•	tonic	tónico, m.
epileptic	epiléptico, m.	topic	tema,f.;sujeto,tópico, m.
ethic	ética, f.	traffic	circulación,tráfico, m.
*fabric	tela, f.;tejido, m.•	tropic	trópico, m.
fanatic	fanático, m.	tunic	túnica, f.

NOUNS: English -ad = Spanish -ada. 95%: 10 Listed

Gender: Most are feminine in Spanish.

ENGLISH	SPANISH	ENGLISH	SPANISH
ballad	balada, f.	nomad	nómada, f.
dryad	dríada, f.	Olympiad	olimpiada, f.
gonad	gónada, f.	salad	ensalada, f.
Iliad	Ilíada, f.	tetrad	tetrada, f.
myriad	miríada, f.	triad	triada, f.

NOUNS: English *-oid* = Spanish *-oide* (90%) or *-oides* (8%).
                                                            98%: 24 Listed
<u>Gender</u>: Most are masculine in Spanish.

ENGLISH	SPANISH	ENGLISH	SPANISH
adenoid	adenoides, m.	paranoid	paranoide, m.
alkaloid	alcaloide, m.	planetoid	planetoide, m.
anthropoid	antropoide, m.	polaroid	polaroide, m.
asteroid	asteroide, m.	rhomboid	romboide, m.
celluloid	celuloide, m.	schizoid	esquizoide, m.
colloid	coloide, m.	solenoid	solenoide, m.
ellipsoid	elipsoide, m.	spheroid	esferoide, m.
fibroid	fibroide, m.	steroid	esteroide, m.
hemorrhoid	hemorroide, f.	tabloid	tabloide, m.
metalloid	metaloide, m.	thyroid	tiroides, m.
meteoroid	meteorito, m.•	trapezoid	trapezoide, m.
paraboloid	paraboloide, m.	typhoid	tifoides, m.

NOUNS: English *-id* other than *-oid* = Spanish *-ido* (a) (70%)
   or *-ide* (20%).   **90%: 14 Listed**

<u>Gender</u>: Most are masculine in Spanish.

ENGLISH	SPANISH	ENGLISH	SPANISH
acid	ácido, m.	hybrid	híbrido, m.
antacid	antiácido, m.	invalid	inválido, m.
aphid	áfido, m.	liquid	líquido, m.
bicuspid	bicúspide, m.	orchid	orquídea, f.•
cupid	cupido, m.	pyramid	pirámide, f.
druid	druida, f.	rapid (stream)	rápido, m.
fluid	flúido, m.	solid	sólido, m.

English nouns ending in *-hood* have no pattern of conversion to Spanish.

NOUNS: English *-phobe* = Spanish *-ófobo*.   **99%: 6 Listed**
The combining form *-phobe* denotes fearing or hating.

<u>Gender</u>: All are masculine in Spanish.

ENGLISH	SPANISH	ENGLISH	SPANISH
anglophobe	anglófobo, m.	hydrophobe	hidrófobo, m
Francophobe	francófobo, m.	Russophobe	rusófobo, m
Hispanophobe	hispanófobo, m.	xenophobe	xenófobo, m

NOUNS: Many English nouns ending in -ice = Spanish -icio(a).
                                                40%: 38 Listed

Gender: There is no reliable pattern of gender in Spanish.

ENGLISH	SPANISH	ENGLISH	SPANISH
accomplice	cómplice, m.•	justice	justicia, f.
*advice	consejo, aviso, m.•	licorice	regalíz, m.•
apprentice	aprendiz, m.•	malice	malicia, f.
armistice	armisticio, m.	*notice	anuncio, aviso, m.•
artifice	artificio, m.	*notice	notificación, f.•
auspice	auspicio, m.	novice	novicio, m.
avarice	avaricia, f.	*office (place)	oficina, f.•
benefice	beneficio, m.		despacho, escritorio, m.•
caprice (whim)	capricho, m.•	*office (position)	oficio, m.
cowardice	cobardía, f.•		cargo, puesto, m.•
crevice	hendedura, f.•	orifice	orificio, m.
dentifrice	dentífrico, m.	*police	policía, f.
device	aparato, m.•	practice	ejercicio, m; práctica, f.
device (mark)	lema, divisa, f.•	precipice	precipicio, m.
disservice	deservicio, m.	prejudice	prejuicio, m.
edifice	edificio, m.	price	precio, m.
hospice	hospicio, m.	sacrifice	sacrificio, m.
injustice	injusticia, f.	service	servicio, m.
interstice	intersticio, m.	solstice	solsticio, m.
invoice	factura, f.•	vice	vicio, m.

NOUNS: Many English nouns ending in -ance = Spanish -ancia, -encia or -anza.
                                                30%: 60 Listed

The suffix -ance used in forming nouns from verbs or from adjectives ending in -ant denotes action, quality, state or result. Frequently-used nouns ending in -ance not following these conversion patterns are listed with the one-on-one conversion nouns or with the synonym conversion nouns.

Gender: All are feminine in Spanish.

ENGLISH	SPANISH	ENGLISH	SPANISH
abundance	abundancia, f.	assonance	asonancia, f.
acceptance	aceptación, f.•	balance (phys)	balanza, f.
advance	avance, m.•	capacitance	capacitancia, f.
alliance	alianza, f.	circumstance	circunstancia, f.
ambulance	ambulancia, f.	clairvoyance	clarividencia, f.•
*appearance (looks)	apariencia, f.	concomitance	concomitancia, f.
appurtenance	pertenancia, f.	concordance	concordancia, f.
arrogance	arrogancia, f.	connivance	connivencia, f.
assistance	asistencia, f.	consonance	consonancia, f.

ENGLISH	SPANISH	ENGLISH	SPANISH
dance	danza, f.	lance	lanza, f.
dissonance	disonancia, f.	luminance	luminancia, f.
distance	distancia, f.	nonresistance	no resistencia, f.
elegance	elegancia, f.	observance	observancia, f.
entrance	entrada, f.•	ordinance	ordenanza, f.
exorbitance	exorbitancia, f.	perseverance	perseverancia, f.
extravagance	extravagancia, f.	pittance	pitanza, f.
exuberance	exuberancia, f.	predominance	predominancia, f.
finance	finanza, f.	preponderance	preponderancia, f.
flagrance	flagrancia, f.	protuberance	protuberancia, f.
fragrance	fragancia, f.	redundance	redundancia, f.
France	Francia, f.	reflectance	reflectancia, f.
ignorance	ignorancia, f.	remembrance	remembranza, f.
impedance	impedancia, f.	repugnance	repugnancia, f.
importance	importancia, f.	resistance	resistencia, f.
inheritance	herencia, f.	resonance	resonancia, f.
insignificance	insignificancia, f.	substance	substancia, f.
*instance	instancia, f.	temperance	temperancia, f.
intemperance	intemperancia, f.	tolerance	tolerancia, f.
intolerance	intolerancia, f.	vengeance	venganza, f.
jubilance	júbilo, m.•	vigilance	vigilancia, f.

NOUNS: English -ence = Spanish -encia.   90%: 182 Listed

The suffix -ence forming abstract nouns corresponding to adjectives ending in -ent signifies *action, state* or *quality*.

Cross-Reference: N -ency; ADJ -ent

Gender: Almost all are feminine gender in Spanish.

ENGLISH	SPANISH	ENGLISH	SPANISH
abhorrence	aborrecimiento, m.•	complacence	complacencia, f.
absence	ausencia, f.	concupiscence	concupiscencia, f.
abstinence	abstinencia, f.	*concurrence	concurrencia, f.
acquiescence	aquiescencia, f.	condescendence	condescendencia, f.
adherence	adherencia, f.	condolence	condolencia, f.
adolescence	adolescencia, f.	*conference	conferencia, f.
affluence	afluencia, f.	*confidence	confianza, f.•
ambience	ambiente, m.•	confidence	confidencia, f.
ambivalence	ambivalencia, f.	confluence	confluencia, f.
antecedence	antecedencia, f.	congruence	congruencia, f.
*audience(session)	audiencia, f.	conscience	consciencia, f.
*audience(group)	auditorio, m.•	consequence	consecuencia, f.
belligerence	beligerancia, f.•	consistence	consistencia, f.
beneficence	beneficencia, f.	contingence	contingencia, f.
benevolence	benevolencia, f.	continence	continencia, f.
cadence	cadencia, f.	convalescence	convalecencia, f.
circumference	circunferencia, f.	*convenience	conveniencia, f.
coalescence	coalescencia, f.	convergence	convergencia, f.
coexistence	coexistencia, f.	corpulence	corpulencia, f.
coherence	coherencia, f.	correspondence	correspondencia, f.
coincidence	coincidencia, f.	credence	creencia, f.
*competence	competencia, f.	decadence	decadencia, f.

ENGLISH	SPANISH	ENGLISH	SPANISH
deference	deferencia, f.	infrequence	infrecuencia, f.
dependence	dependencia, f.	inherence	inherencia, f.
deterrence	disuasión, f.•	innocence	inocencia, f.
difference	diferencia, f.	insipience	insipiencia, f.
diffidence	timidez, f.•	insistence	insistencia, f.
diligence	diligencia, f.	insolence	insolencia, f.
disobedience	desobediencia, f.	insurgence	insurrección, f.•
dissidence	disidencia, f.	intelligence	inteligencia, f.
divergence	divergencia, f.	interference	interferencia, f.
ebullience	ebullición, f.•	intermittence	intermitencia, f.
effervescence	efervescencia, f.	intransigence	intransigencia, f.
efflorescence	eflorescencia, f.	intumescence	intumescencia, f.
eloquence	elocuencia, f.	iridescence	iridiscencia, f.
emergence	emergencia, f.	irreverence	irreverencia, f.
eminence	eminencia, f.	jurisprudence	jurisprudencia, f.
equivalence	equivalencia, f.	lenience	lenidad, f.•
essence	esencia, f.	license	licencia, f.
*evidence	evidencia, f.	luminescence	luminiscencia, f.
excellence	excelencia, f.	magnificence	magnificencia, f.
exigence	exigencia, f.	maleficence	maleficencia, f.
existence	existencia, f.	malevolence	malevolencia, f.
experience	experiencia, f.	munificence	munificencia, f.
flatulence	flatulencia, f.	negligence	negligencia, f.
fluorescence	fluorescencia, f.	obedience	obediencia, f.
fraudulence	fraudulencia, f.	obsolesence	desuso, m.•
frequence	frequencia, f.	*occurrence	suceso, m; ocurrencia, f.
grandiloquence	grandilocuencia, f.	omnipotence	omnipotencia, f.
immanence	inmanencia, f.	omnipresence	omnipresencia, f.
imminence	inminencia, f.	omniscience	omnisciencia, f.
impatience	impaciencia, f.	opalescence	opalescencia, f.
impertinence	impertinencia, f.	opulence	opulencia, f.
impotence	impotencia, f.	patience	paciencia, f.
improvidence	improvidencia, f.	penitence	penitencia, f.
imprudence	imprudencia, f.	permanence	permanencia, f.
impudence	impudencia, f.	persistence	persistencia, f.
inadvertence	inadvertencia, f.	pertinence	pertinencia, f.
incandescence	incandescencia, f.	pestilence	pestilencia, f.
incidence	incidencia, f.	phosphorescence	fosforescencia, f.
incoherence	incoherencia, f.	preadolescence	preadolescencia, f.
incompetence	incompetencia, f.	precedence	precedencia, f.
incongruence	incongruencia, f.	preeminence	preeminencia, f.
inconsequence	inconsecuencia, f.	preexistence	preexistencia, f.
inconsistence	inconsistencia, f.	preference	preferencia, f.
incontinence	incontinencia, f.	prescience	presciencia, f.
*inconvenience	inconveniencia, f.	presence	presencia, f.
independence	independencia, f.	prevalence	frecuencia, f.•
indifference	indiferencia, f.	prominence	prominencia, f.
indigence	indigencia, f.	providence	providencia, f.
indolence	indolencia, f.	prudence	prudencia, f.
indulgence	indulgencia, f.	quiescence	quiecencia, f.
inexistence	inexistencia, f.	quintessence	quintaesencia, f.
inexperience	inexperiencia, f.	recurrence	repetición, f.•
inference	inferencia, f.	reference	referencia, f.
influence	influencia, f.	reminiscence	reminiscencia, f.

ENGLISH	SPANISH	ENGLISH	SPANISH
remittence (MED)	remitencia, f.	subsistence	subsistencia, f.
residence	residencia, f.	succulence	suculencia, f.
resilience	resiliencia, f.	teleconference	teleconferencia, f.
resurgence	resurgimiento, m.•	transcendence	transcendencia, f.
reticence	reticencia, f.	transference	transferencia, f.
reverence	reverencia, f.	transience	transitoriedad, f.•
science	ciencia, f.	translucence	translucidez, f.•
*sentence	frase, f.•	transparence	transparencia, f.
sentence (court)	sentencia, f.	truculence	truculencia, f.
sequence	secuencia, f.	turbulence	turbulencia, f.
silence	silencio, m.•	urgence	urgencia, f.
stridence	estridencia, f.	valence	valencia, f.
submergence	sumergimiento, m.•	vehemence	vehemencia, f.
subservience	subordinación, f.•	violence	violencia, f.
subsidence	subsidencia, f.	virulence	virulencia, f.

NOUNS: English -*ade* = Spanish -*ada(o)* or -*ata*.

80%: 37 Listed

The suffix -*ade* denotes (a) the act of (blockade); (b) result or product of (pomade); (c) participant in an action (brigade); (d) a drink made from (lemonade).

Gender: Most are feminine in Spanish.

ENGLISH	SPANISH	ENGLISH	SPANISH
accolade	acolada, f.	fusillade	fusilamiento, m.•
alidade	alidada, f.	grade	grado, m.
ambuscade	emboscada, f.	grenade	granada, f.
arcade	arcada, f.	jade	jade, m.•
balustrade	balaustrada, f.	lemonade	limonada, f.
barricade	barricada, f.	limeade	limonada, f.
blockade	bloqueo, m.•	marmalade	mermelada, f.
brigade	brigada, f.	masquerade	mascarada, f.
brocade	brocado, m.	orangeade	naranjada, f.•
cascade	cascada, f.	palisade	palizada, f.
cavalcade	cabalgata, f.•	*parade	paseo, m.; parada, f.
charade	charada, f.		cortejo, m.
colonnade	columnata, f.	pomade	pomada, f.
comrade	camarada, m.	promenade	paseo, m.•
crusade	cruzada, f.	renegade	renegado, m.
decade	década, f.	serenade	serenata, f.
escapade	escapada, f.	spade (cards)	espada, f.
esplanade	explanada, f.	stockade	estacada, f.
facade	fachada, f.	tirade	diatriba, f.•

NOUNS: English- *cide* = Spanish *-cida* and *-cidio*.
99%:   32 Listed
The suffix *-cide* denotes killer or a killing.

Gender: Most are masculine unless the killer is clearly a feminine person.

ENGLISH		SPANISH	
		THE KILLER OF--	THE KILLING OF--
algaecide	(algae)	algacida, m.	algacidio, m.
fratricide	(brother)	fratricida, m.	fratricidio, m.
fungicide	(fungus)	fungicida, m.	fungicidio, m.
genocide	(people)	genocida, m.	genocidio, m.
germicide	(germs)	germicida, m.	germicidio, m.
herbicide	(plants)	herbicida, m.	herbicidio, m.
homicide	(man)	homicida, m.	homicidio, m.
infanticide	(infants)	infanticida, m	infanticidio, m.
insecticide	(insects)	insecticida, m.	insecticidio, m.
matricide	(mother)	matricida, m.	matricidio, m.
patricide	(country)	patricida, m.	patricidio, m.
pesticide	(pests)	insecticida, m.•	insecitcidio, m.•
regicide	(king)	regicida, m.	regicidio, m.
sororicide	(sister)	sororicida, m.	sororicidio, m.
suicide	(self)	suicida, m.	suicidio, m.
vermicide	(worms)	vermicida, m.	vermicidio, m.

NOUNS: English chemical nouns ending in *-ide* or *-yde* = Spanish *-ido* or *-uro*.   98%: 21 Listed
(There are hundreds of such chemical words.)

Gender: Most are masculine in Spanish.

ENGLISH	SPANISH	
arsenide	arsénido, m.	
bromide		bromuro, m.
carbide		carburo, m.
chloride		cloruro, m.
cyanide		cianuro, m.
dioxide	dióxido, m.	
fluoride		fluoruro, m.
formaldehyde	formaldehído, m.	
glycoside	glicósido, m.	
hydride		hidruro, m.
hydrochloride	hidroclorato, m.•	
hydrosulfide		hidrosulfuro, m.
hydroxide	hidróxido, m.	
monoxide	monóxido, m.	
nitride		nitruro, m.
nucleotide	nucleótido, m.	
oxide	óxido, m.	
peroxide	peróxido, m.	
sulfide		sulfuro, m.
telluride		telururo, m.
tetrachloride		tetracloruro, m.

NOUNS: English -ode = Spanish -odo or -oda.   90%: 13 Listed

Gender: Most are masculine in Spanish.

ENGLISH	SPANISH	ENGLISH	SPANISH
abode	domicilio, m.•	electrode	electrodo, m.
anode	ánodo, m.	episode	episodio, m.•
cathode	cátodo, m	mode	moda, f.
code	código, m.•	node	nudo, m.
commode	cómoda, f.	ode	oda, f.
diode	diodo, m.	photocathode	fotocátodo, m.
dynode	dinodo, m.		

NOUNS: English -lude = Spanish -ludio.   99%: 3 Listed

Gender: All are masculine in Spanish

ENGLISH	SPANISH	ENGLISH	SPANISH
interlude	interludio, m.	prelude	preludio, m.
postlude	postludio, m.		

NOUNS: English -tude = Spanish -itud(e).   90%: 34 Listed

The suffix -tude often forms nouns corresponding to English -ness.

Gender: All are feminine in Spanish.

ENGLISH	SPANISH	ENGLISH	SPANISH
altitude	altura, altitud, f.	latitude	latitud, f.
amplitude	amplitud, f.	longitude	longitud, f.
aptitude	aptitud, f.	magnitude	magnitud, f.
attitude	actitud, f.	multitude	multitud, f.
beatitude	beatitud, f.	platitude	trivialidad, f.•
certitude	certitud, f.	plenitude	plenitud, f.
disquietude	inquietud, f.	promptitude	prontitud, f.
exactitude	exactitud, f.	*pulchritude	pulcritud, f.
fortitude	fortaleza, f.•	quietude	quietud, f.
gratitude	gratitud, f.	rectitude	rectitud, f.
inaptitude	ineptitud, f.	servitude	servitud, f.
incertitude	incertidumbre, f.•	similitude	similitud, f.
ineptitude	ineptitud, f.	solicitude	solicitud, f.
infinitude	infinitud, f.	solitude	soledad, f.•
ingratitude	ingratitud, f.	turpitude	turpitud, f.
inquietude	inquietud, f.	verisimilitude	verisimilitud, f.
lassitude	lasitud, f.	vicissitude	vicisitud, f.

87

NOUNS: Many English-*age* nouns = Spanish -*aje*.

25%: 42 Listed

Gender: Most are masculine in Spanish.

ENGLISH	SPANISH	ENGLISH	SPANISH
advantage	provecho,m;vantaja, f.•	homage	homenaje, m.
amperage	amperaje, m.	language	idioma,f.; lenguaje, m.
anchorage	anclaje, m.	lineage	linaje, m.
arbitrage	arbitraje, m.	massage	masaje, m.
*baggage (MIL)	bagaje, m.	message	mensaje, m.
bandage	venda,f.;vendaje, m.	montage	montaje, m.
camouflage	camuflaje, m.	ohmage	ohmiaje, m.
carriage (horse)	carruaje, m.	passage	pasaje, m.
cartage	carretaje, m.	percentage	percentaje, m.
cleavage	clivaje, m.	personage	personaje, m.
cordage	cordaje, m.	photomontage	fotomontaje, m.
*courage	valor, m.;coraje, f.	pillage	pillaje, m.
disadvantage	desventaje, m.	plumage	plumaje, m.
drainage	drenaje, m.	potage (soup)	potaje, m.
equipage	equipaje, m.	reportage	reportaje, m.
espionage	espionaje, m.	sabotage	sabotaje, m.
foliage	ramaje, follaje, m.	savage	salvaje, m.
forage	forraje, m.	tonnage	tonelaje, f.
fuselage	fuselaje, m.	vassalage	vasallaje, m.
garage	cochera,f.;garaje, m.	voltage	voltaje, m.
hemorrhage	hemorragia, f.•	wattage	vatiaje, m.

NOUNS: English -*ege* = Spanish -*egio*.

65%: 6 Listed

Gender: Most are masculine in Spanish.

ENGLISH	SPANISH	ENGLISH	SPANISH
*college	colegio, m.	protégé	protegido, m.•
cortege	cortejo, m.•	sacrilege	sacrilegio, m.
privilege	privilegio, m.	sortilege	sortilegio, m.

NOUNS: English -*ige* = Spanish -*igio*.

99%: 2 Listed

Gender: Most are masculine in Spanish.

ENGLISH	SPANISH	ENGLISH	SPANISH
prestige	prestigio, m.	vestige	vestigio, m.

NOUNS: English -*fuge* = Spanish -*fuga (o)* or -*fugio*.

95%: 4 Listed

Gender: Most are masculine in Spanish.

ENGLISH	SPANISH	ENGLISH	SPANISH
centrifuge	centrífuga, f.	subterfuge	subterfugio, m.
refuge	asilo, refugio, m.	vermifuge	vermífugo, m.

NOUNS: Nouns ending in *-ble* seldom convert uniformly to Spanish. Some are included in the one-on-one and synonym conversion lists.

NOUNS: English *-cycle* = Spanish *-ciclo* or *-cicleta*.
                                              99%: 8 Listed

    Gender: Most are feminine in Spanish.

ENGLISH	SPANISH	ENGLISH	SPANISH
bicycle	bicicleta, f.	monocycle	monociclo, m.
cycle	ciclo, m.	motorcycle	motocicleta, f.
kilocycle	kilociclo, m.	tricycle	triciclo, m.
megacycle	megaciclo, m.	unicycle	monociclo, m•

NOUNS: English *-cle* other than *-cycle* = Spanish *-culo(a)*.
                                              85%: 35 Listed

    Gender: Most are masculine in Spanish.

ENGLISH	SPANISH	ENGLISH	SPANISH
article	artículo, m.	obstacle	obstáculo, m.
auricle	aurícula, f.	oracle	oráculo, m.
barnacle	percebe, m.•	particle	partícula, f.
carbuncle	carbúncula, f.	pinnacle	pináculo, m.
chicle	chicle, m.	radicle	radícula, f.
chronicle	crónica, f.•	receptacle	receptáculo, m.
circle	círculo, m.	reticle	retículo, m.
clavicle	clavícula, f.	semicircle	semicírculo, m.
corpuscle	corpúsculo, m.	spectacle	espectáculo, m.
cubicle	cubículo, m.	tabernacle	tabernáculo, m.
cuticle	cutícula, f.	tentacle	tentáculo, m.
debacle	debacle, m.•	testicle	testículo, m.
follicle	folículo, m.	tubercle	tubérculo, m.
icicle	carámbano, m.•	uncle	tío, m.•
manacle	manilla, f.•	vehicle	vehículo, m.
miracle	milagro, m.•	ventricle	ventrículo, m.
monocle	monóculo, m.	vesicle	vesícula, f.
muscle	músculo, m.		

NOUNS: English *-angle* = Spanish *-ángulo*.   **99%: 4 Listed**

    Gender: All are masculine in Spanish.

ENGLISH	SPANISH	ENGLISH	SPANISH
angle	ángulo, m.	rectangle	rectángulo, m.
quadrangle	cuadrángulo, m.	triangle	triángulo, m.

NOUNS: English *-phile* = Spanish *-ófilo*.   99%:   10 Listed

The combining form *-phile* denotes loving, liking or favorably disposed to.

    Gender: All are masculine in Spanish.

ENGLISH	SPANISH	ENGLISH	SPANISH
Anglophile (UK)	anglófilo, m.	Hispanophile (Sp.)	hispanófilo, m.
audiophile (Hi-Fi)	audiófilo, m.	oenophile (wine)	enófilo, m.
bibliophile (books)	bibliófilo, m.	Russophile (Russia)	rusófilo, m.
discophile (records)	discófilo, m.	Sinophile (China)	sinófilo, m.
Francophile (Fr.)	francófilo, m.	theophile (God)	teófilo, m.

NOUNS: English *-ile* other than *-phile* = Spanish *-il*, *-ilo(a)* or *-ilio*.   70%:   22 Listed

    Gender: Almost all are masculine in Spanish.

ENGLISH	SPANISH	ENGLISH	SPANISH
automobile	automóvil, m.	missile	proyectil, cohete, m.•
campanile	campanil, m.	mobile	móvil, m.
crocodile	cocodrilo, m.	percentile	percentil, m
domicile	domicilio, m.	profile	perfil, m.
exile (status)	exilio, m.	projectile	proyectil, m.
exile (person)	exiliado, m.•	quartile	cuartil, m.
facsimile	facsímile, m.•	reptile	reptil, m.
file (line)	fila, f.	simile	símil, m.
Gentile	cristiano, gentil, m.	style	estilo, m.
imbecile	imbécil, m.	textile	tejido, textil, m.
juvenile	menor, joven, m.•	thermopile	termopila, f.

NOUNS: English *-ole* = Spanish *-olo(a)* or *-ole*.   80%:   13 Listed

This category does not include compounds of *hole* and *pole* which don't follow any helpful conversion pattern.

    Gender: Most are feminine in Spanish.

ENGLISH	SPANISH	ENGLISH	SPANISH
arteriole	arteriola, f.	console	consola, f.
aureole	aureola, f.	creole	criollo, m.
barcarole	barcarola, f.	hyperbole	hipérbole, f.
bronchiole	bronquíolo, m.	oriole	oriol, m.•
cabriole	cabriola, f.	parole	liberación, f.•
camisole	camisola, f.	stole (wrap)	estola, f.
casserole	cacerola, f.		

NOUNS: English -*ule* = Spanish -*ula(o)*.   **85%: 19 Listed**

The suffix -*ule* is often added to nouns to form diminutives.
Gender: Evenly masculine and feminine in Spanish.

ENGLISH	SPANISH	ENGLISH	SPANISH
ampule	ampolleta, f.•	mule	mula, f.
capsule	cápsula, f.	nodule	nódulo, m.
crepuscule	crepúsculo, m.	ovule	óvulo, m.
ferule	férula, f.	ridicule	ridículo, m.
globule	glóbulo, m.	schedule	horario, m.; cédula, f.
granule	gránulo, m.	spherule	esférula, f.
lobule	lobulillo, m.•	spicule	espícula, f.
locule	lóculo, m.	tubule	túbulo, m.
module	módulo, m.	vestibule	vestíbulo, m.
molecule	molécula, f.		

NOUNS: English -*me* = Spanish -*mo* , -*ma* , -*me* or -*men*.
90%: 37 Listed
Gender: Evenly masculine and feminine.in Spanish

ENGLISH	SPANISH	ENGLISH	SPANISH
aerodrome	aeródromo, m	monochrome	monocromo, m.
centime	céntimo, m.	morpheme	morfema, f.
chrome	cromo, m.	pantomime	pantomimo, m.
chromosome	cromosoma, m.	passtime	pasatiempo, m.•
costume	traje, m.•	perfume	perfume, m.
crime	crimen, m.	phoneme	fonema, f.
dome	domo, m.	plume	pluma, f.
enzyme	enzima, f.	regime	régimen, m.
epitome	epítome, m.	rhizome	rizoma, f.
extreme	extremo, m.	rhyme	rima, f.
fame	fama, f.	Rome	Roma, f.
gendarme	gendarme, m.	scheme	plan, m; esquema, f.
gnome	gnomo, m.	syndrome	síndrome, m.
gram	gramo, m.	theme	tema, f.
hippodrome	hipódromo, m.	tome	tomo, m.
income	ingresos, renta, f.•	volume	volúmen, m.
mercurochrome	mercurocromo, m.	welcome	bienvenida, f.•
metronome	metrónomo, m.		

NOUNS: English -*ane* = Spanish -*ano(a)* or -*án*.
95%: 16 Listed
Gender: Almost all are masculine in Spanish.

ENGLISH	SPANISH	ENGLISH	SPANISH
aeroplane	aeroplano, m.	membrane	membrana, f.
airplane	aeroplano, m.	methane	metano, m.
aquaplane	acuaplano, m.	monoplane	monoplano, m.
biplane	biplano, m.	octane	octano, m.
butane	butano, m.	plane	plano, m.
cellophane	celofán, m.	polyurethane	poliuretano, m.
hurricane	huracán, m.	propane	propano, m.
hydroplane	hidroplano, m.	urethane	uretano, m.

NOUNS: English -ene = Spanish -eno(a).   85%:   16 Listed
Most of these are nouns related to chemistry,

<u>Gender</u>:   Most are masculine in Spanish.

ENGLISH	SPANISH	ENGLISH	SPANISH
acetylene	acetileno, m.	naphthalene	naftaleno, m.
benzene	benceno, m.	neoprene	neopreno, m.
carotene	caroteno, m.	phosgene	fosgeno, m.
damascene	damasceno, m.	polyethylene	polietileno, m.
ethylene	etileno, m.	polypropylene	polipropileno, m.
gangrene	gangrena, f.	polystyrene	poliestireno, m.
hygiene	higiene, f. •	scene	escena, f.
kerosene	queroseno, m.	styrene	estireno, m.

NOUNS: English -ine = Spanish -ina(o) or -in.
                                    90%: 104 Listed
Hundreds of nouns in the fields of chemistry, biochemistry, botany, pharmacy, biology and mineralogy follow this pattern.

<u>Gender</u>:   Most of these nouns are feminine in Spanish.
Those that are masculine usually end in -o.

ENGLISH	SPANISH	ENGLISH	SPANISH
aborigine	aborígene, m. •	concubine	concubina, f.
adrenaline	adrenalina, f.	confine	confín, m.
amine	amina, f.	cosine	coseno, m.
amphetamine	anfetamina, f.	cosmoline	cosmolina, f.
aniline	anilina, f.	crinoline	crinolina, f.
anodyne	anodino, m.	cuisine	cocina, f.
aquamarine	aguamarina, f.	dauphine	delfina, f.
Argentine	argentino, m.	decline	ruina, declinación, f. •
argentine	argentina, f.	dentine	dentina, f.
arsine	arsina, f.	discipline	disciplina, f.
beguine	beguina, f.	divine	divino, m.
benzedrine	bencedrina, f.	doctrine	doctrina, f.
benzine	bencina, f.	dramamine	dramamina, f.
benzocaine	benzocaína, f.	endocrine	endocrina, f.
bovine	bovino, m.	engine	motor, m., máquina, f. •
brigantine	brigantina, f.	ermine	armiño, m.
Byzantine	bizantino, m.	famine	hambre, f. •
caffeine	cafeína, f.	feline	felino, m.
calamine	calamina, f.	figurine	figurina, f.
canine	canino, m.	fluorine	fluorina, f.
carbine	carabina, f.	gabardine	gabardina, f.
carmine	carmín, m.	gasoline	gasolina, f.
chlorine	cloro, m. •	gelatine	gelatina, f.
cocaine	cocaína, f.	glycerine	glicerina, f.
codeine	codeína, f.	grenadine	granadina, f.
columbine	aguileña, f. •	guillotine	guillotina, f.
combine	segadora, f. •	heroine	heroína, f.

ENGLISH	SPANISH	ENGLISH	SPANISH
histamine	histamina, f.	porcupine	puerco espín, m.
incline	declive, m.•	ptomaine	ptomaína, f.
intestine	intestino, m.	quarantine	cuarentina, f.
iodine	yodo, m.•	quinine	quinina, f.
jasmine	jazmín, m.	ravine	barranca, f.•
latrine	letrina, f.	routine	rutina, f.
libertine	libertino, m.	saccharine	sacarina, f.
limousine	limosina, f.	saline	salina, f.
line	línea, f.•	sardine	sardina, f.
machine	máquina, f.	sine	seno, m.
magazine (store,gun)	almacén, m.•	spine	espina, f.
magazine (booklet)	revista, f.•	strychnine	estricnina, f.
mandoline	mandolina, f.	submarine	submarino, m.
marine	marino, m.	supine	supino, m.
medicine	medicina, f.	tambourine	tamborino, m.
mezzanine	entresuelo, m.•	tangerine	tangerino, m.
migraine	migraña, f.	trampoline	trampolín, m.
mine	mina, f.	tuberculine	tuberculina, f.
morphine	morfina, f.	turbine	turbina, f.
nectarine	nectarino, m.	turpentine	trementina, f.•
nicotine	nicotina, f.	urine	orina, f.
novocaine	novocaína, f.	ultramarine	ultramarino, m.
oleomargarine	oleomargarina, f.	vaccine	vacuna, f.•
Philippine	filipino, m.	Vaseline	vaselina, f.
pine	pino, m.	wine	vino, m.

NOUNS: English -one = **Spanish** -ono(a) or -ón.

95%: 22 Listed

Gender: Slightly more than half are masculine in Spanish.

ENGLISH	SPANISH	
	-ona,-ono	-ón
	75%	20%
baritone	barítono, m.	
cone	cono, m.	
cortisone	cortisona, f.	
cyclone		ciclón, m.
dictaphone	dictáfono, m.	
earphone	audífono, m.	
gramophone	gramófono, m.	
hormone	hormona, f.	hormón, m.
megaphone	megáfono, m.	
methadone	metadona, f.	
microphone	micrófono, m.	
minestrone		minestrón, m.
monotone	monotonía, f.•	
ozone	ozono, m.	
saxophone	saxófono, m.	
silicone		silicón, m.
telephone	teléfono, m.	
throne	trono, m.	
tone	tono, m.	
trombone		trombón, m.
xylophone	xilófono, m.	
zone	zona, f.	

NOUNS: English *-une* = Spanish *-una(o)*.   85%:   8 Listed

    Gender: Most are feminine in Spanish.

ENGLISH	SPANISH	ENGLISH	SPANISH
commune	comuna, f.	Neptune	Neptuno, m
dune	duna, f.	prune	ciruela, pruna, f.
fortune	suerte, fortuna, f.	tribune	tribuno, m.
misfortune	infortuna, f.	tune	tonada, f. •

NOUNS: English *-scope* = Spanish *-scopio*.   99%: 14 Listed

    Cross-Reference: N *-scopy*; A *-scopic*
    Gender: All are masculine in Spanish.

ENGLISH	SPANISH	ENGLISH	SPANISH
electroscope	electroscopio, m.	periscope	periscopio, m.
fluoroscope	fluoroscopio, m.	radarscope	radariscopio, m.
gyroscope	giroscopio, m.	seismoscope	sismoscopio, m.
horoscope	horóscopo, m. •	spectroscope	espectroscopio, m.
kaleidoscope	caleidoscopio, m.	stereoscope	estereoscopio, m.
kinescope	cinescopio, m.	stethoscope	estetoscopio, m.
microscope	microscopio, m.	telescope	telescopio, m.

NOUNS: English *-ope* other than *-scope* = Spanish *-ope* or *-opo(a)*.   90%: 10 Listed

    Cross-Reference: N *-thropy, -thropist, -thropism*; ADJ *-thropic*
    Gender: Most are masculine in Spanish

ENGLISH	SPANISH -ope	SPANISH -opo, -opa	Exceptions
antelope	antílope, m.		
envelope			sobre, m. •
Europe		Europa, f.	
heliotrope		heliotropo, m.	
isotope		isótopo, m.	
misanthrope		misántropo, m.	
myope	miope, m.		
philanthrope		filántropo, m.	
radioisotope		radioisótopo, m.	
syncope	síncope, m.		

NOUNS: English -*type* = Spanish -*tipo*.   95%:   6 Listed

    Gender: Almost all feminine in Spanish.

ENGLISH	SPANISH	ENGLISH	SPANISH
linotype	linotipo, m.	teletype	teletipo, m.
prototype	prototipo, m.	tintype	ferrotipo, m. •
stereotype	estereotipo, m.	type	tipo, m.

NOUNS: English -*sphere* = Spanish -*sfera*.   95%:   8 Listed

    Gender: Almost all are feminine in Spanish.

ENGLISH	SPANISH	ENGLISH	SPANISH
atmosphere	atmósfera, f.	ionosphere	ionosfera, f.
bathysphere	batiesfera, f.	sphere	esfera, f.
hemisphere	hemisferio, m. •	stratosphere	estratósfera, f.
hydrosphere	hidrosfera, f.	troposphere	troposfera, f.

NOUNS: English -*ire* = Spanish -*rio* or -*iro*.   85%: 16 Listed

    Gender: Almost all feminine in Spanish.

ENGLISH	SPANISH	ENGLISH	SPANISH
armoire	armario, m.	millionaire	millonario, m.
attire	atavio, m. •	questionnaire	cuestionario, m.
billionaire	billonario, m.	repertoire	repertorio, m.
concessionaire	concesionario, m.	sapphire	zafiro, m.
desire	deseo, m. •	satire	sátira, f. •
doctrinaire	doctrinario, m.	solitaire	solitario, m.
empire	empirio, m.	umpire	árbitro, m. •
legionnaire	legionario, m.	vampire	vampiro, m.

NOUNS: English   -*phore* = Spanish -*fora*   95%: 12 Listed
              -*pore* = Spanish -*pora*
              -*vore* = Spanish -*voro*

    Gender: Most are masculine in Spanish.

ENGLISH	SPANISH	ENGLISH	SPANISH
blastopore	blastóporo, m.	insectivore	insectivoro, m.
carnivore	carnívoro, m.	metaphore	metáfora, f.
commodore	comodoro, m.	omnivore	omnivoro, m.
endospore	endóspora, f.	semaphore	semáforo, m.
gymnospore	gimnosporo, m.	spore	espora, f.
herbivore	herbívoro, m.	sycamore	sicomoro, m.

NOUNS: English -ure = Spanish -ura.   65%:   112 Listed

The suffix -ure denotes the act or result of an action, agent or instrument of an action or state of being.

<u>Gender</u>: Almost all are feminine in Spanish.

ENGLISH	SPANISH	ENGLISH	SPANISH
acupuncture	acupuntura, f.	foreclosure	exclusión, f.•
adventure	aventura, f.	forfeiture	confiscación, f.•
agriculture	agricultura, f.	fracture	fractura, f.
allure	atracción, f.•	furniture	mueble, m.•
aperture	abertura, f.	future	porvenir, futuro, m.
architecture	arquitectura, f.	gesture	gesto, m.•
armature	armadura, f.	gesture	ademán, m.
brochure	folleto, m.•	horticulture	horticultura, f.
candidature	candidatura, f.	indenture	escritura, f.•
capture	presa, captura, f.	infrastructure	infraestructura, f.
caricature	caricatura, f.	investiture	investidura, f.
censure	censura, f.	juncture	juntura, f.
closure	clausura, f.	*lecture	disertación, f.•
cloture	clausura, f.	*lecture	conferencia, f.•
composure	compostura, f.	legislature	legislatura, f.
conjecture	conjetura, f.	leisure	ocio, m.•
conjuncture	coyuntura, f.	literature	literatura, f.
countermeasure	represalia, f.•	manicure	manicura, f.
countersignature	contrafirma, f.•	manufacture	fabricación, f.•
creature	criatura, f.		manufactura, f.
culture	cultura, f.	manure	estiércol, abono, m.•
*cure	curación, cura, f.	*measure	medida, f.•
curvature	curvatura, f.	miniature	miniatura, f.
debenture	obligación, f.•	misadventure	desventura, f.
denture	dentatura, f.	mixture	mescla, mixtura, f.
departure	desviación, f.•	moisture	humedad, f.•
departure	partida, salida, f.•	nature	naturaleza, natura, f.
disclosure	revelación, f.•	nomenclature	nomenclatura, f.
displeasure	desagrado, m.•	overture (MUS	obertura, f.
disvestiture	despojo, m.•	overture	proposición, f.•
enclosure	anexo, m.•	pasture	pasto, m.; pastura, f.
enclosure	cercamiento, m.•	pedicure	pedicuro, m.
epicure	epicúreo, m.•	picture	cuadro, m.; pintura, f.•
erasure	borradura, f.•	pleasure	gusto, placer, m.•
expenditure	gasto, m.•	posture	postura, f.
exposure	exposición, f.•	prefecture	prefectura, f.
facture	factura, f.	pressure	presión, f.•
failure (bkpcy)	quiebra, f.•	primogeniture	primogenitura, f.
failure	falta, fracaso, m.•	procedure	procedimiento, m.•
feature (attrib.)	rasgo, m.•	projecture	proyectura, f.
feature (face)	facciones, f.•	puncture	puntura, f.
figure (form)	figura, f.	rapture	delirio, rapto, m.•
figure (number)	cifra, f.•	recapture	recobro, m.•
fissure	fisura, f.	rotogravure	rotograbado, m.•
fixture	cosa fija, f.•	rupture	ruptura, f.

ENGLISH	SPANISH		ENGLISH	SPANISH	
scripture	escritura,	f.	suture	sutura,	f.
sculpture	escultura,	f.	temperature	temperatura,	f.
seizure	secuestro,	m.•	tenure	tenencia,	f.•
sepulture	sepultura,	f.	texture	textura,	f.
*signature (MUS)	signatura,	f.	tincture	tintura,	f.
signature	firma,	f.•	torture	tortura,	f.
sinecure	sinecura,	f.	treasure	tesoro,	m.•
stature	talla, estatura,	f.	venture	riesgo, m.; ventura,	f.
stricture	estrictura,	f.	venture	empresa, operación,	f.•
structure(parts)	estructura,	f.	verdure	verdor, m.; verdura,	f.
structure(thing)	construcción,	f.•	vulture	buitre,	m.•

NOUNS: English -*ese* denoting nationality or language = Spanish -*és* or -*esa*.

95%: 14 Listed

Cross-Reference: Separate List of Countries and People p.203

Gender: The -*és* denoting a male person or the language is masculine and the -*esa* denoting a female person is feminine.

ENGLISH	SPANISH		ENGLISH	SPANISH	
Burmese	birmanés, m. -esa,	f.	Maltese	maltés, m. -esa,	f.
Cantonese	cantonés, m. -esa,	f.	Pekingese	pekinés, m. -esa,	f.
Chinese	chino, m. -esa,	f.•	Portuguese	portugués, m. -esa,	f.
Congolese	congolés, m. -esa,	f.	Sengalese	sengalés, m. -esa,	f.
Japanese	japonés, m. -esa,	f.	Siamese	siamés, m. -esa,	f.
Javanese	javanés, m. -esa,	f.	Viennese	vienés, m. -esa,	f.
Lebanese	libanés, m. -esa,	f.	Vietnamese	vietnamés, m. -esa,	f.

NOUNS: English -*ise* sometimes = -*iso(a)*, -*eso(a)* or -*icio(a)*.

35%: 12 Listed

Gender: Most are feminine in Spanish

ENGLISH	SPANISH		ENGLISH	SPANISH	
camise (chemise)	camisa,	f.	mayonnaise	mayonesa,	f.
*compromise	compromiso,	m.	paradise	paraíso,	m.
exercise	ejercicio,	m.	premise	premisa,	f.
franchise	franquicia,	f.	promise	promesa,	f.
marquise	marquesa,	f.	surprise	sorpresa,	f.
Marseillaise	Marsellesa,	f.	turquoise	turquesa,	f.

NOUNS: English -*ulse* = Spanish -*ulso(-a)*. 95%: 3 Listed

ENGLISH	SPANISH		ENGLISH	SPANISH	
impulse	impulso,	m.	repulse	repulsa,	f.
pulse	pulso,	m.			

NOUNS: English *-nse* = Spanish *-nso(a)* or *-ión*.

70%: 12 Listed

ENGLISH	SPANISH	ENGLISH	SPANISH
defense	defensa, f.	nonsense	disparate, m.•
expanse	extensión, f.•	offense	ofensa, f.
expense	gasto, costo, m.•	pretense	pretensión, f.
frankincense	incienso, m.	recompense	recompensa, f.
incense	incienso, m.	response	respuesta, f.•
license	permiso,m;licencia, f.•	suspense	suspensión, f.

NOUNS: English *-ose* denoting chemical substances = Spanish *-osa*.

99%: 12 Listed

<u>Gender</u>: All are feminine in Spanish.

ENGLISH	SPANISH	ENGLISH	SPANISH
cellulose	celulosa, f.	lactose	lactosa, f.
dextroglucose	dextroglucosa, f.	maltose	maltosa, f.
dextrose	dextrosa, f.	nitrocellulose	nitrocelulosa, f.
fructose	fructosa, f.	sucrose	sucrosa, f.
glucose	glucosa, f.	triose	triosa, f.
heptose	heptosa, f.	viscose	viscosa, f.

Also following a similar conversion pattern:

prose	prosa, f.	rose	rosa, f.
repose	reposo, m.		

NOUNS: English *-pse* = Spanish *-pse, -pso* or *-psis*.

65%: 8 Listed

<u>Gender</u>: Most are masculine in Spanish.

ENGLISH	SPANISH	ENGLISH	SPANISH
Apocalypse	Apocalipsis, m.	ellipse	elipse, m.
collapse	derrume, m.•	lapse	lapso, m.
*collapse (MED)	colapso, m.	relapse	recaída, f.•
eclipse	eclipse, m.	synapse (PHYS)	sinapsis, m.

NOUNS: English *-rse* = Spanish *-rso(a)*.

80%: 11 Listed

<u>Gender</u>: Most are masculine in Spanish.

ENGLISH	SPANISH	ENGLISH	SPANISH
concourse	concurso, m.	remorse	remordimiento, m.•
converse	conversa, f.	reverse	revés, reverso, m.
course	curso, m.	traverse	traversaño, m.•
discourse (speech)	discurso, m.	universe	universo, m.
inverse	inverso, m.	verse	verso, m.
recourse	recurso, m.		

NOUNS: English -sse = Spanish -sa, -se or -zo(a).

80%: 8 Listed

ENGLISH	SPANISH	ENGLISH	SPANISH
bagasse	bagazo, m.	impasse	impase, m.
bouillabaisse	bullabesa, f.	largesse	largueza, f.
crevasse	hendura, grieta, f.•	noblesse	nobleza, f.
finesse	finura, sutileza, f.•	posse	posse, m.

NOUNS: English -use = Spanish -usa or -uso.

85%: 16 Listed

ENGLISH	SPANISH	ENGLISH	SPANISH
abuse	abuso, m.	menopause	menopausia, f.•
applause	aplauso, m.	misuse	mal uso, m.
blouse	blusa, f.	Muse	musa, f.
cause	causa, f.	pause	pausa, f.
clause	cláusula, f.•	recluse	solitario, m.•
disuse	desuso, m.	refuse	basura, f.•
excuse	disculpa, excusa, f.	spouse	esposo, m.
hypotenuse	hipotenusa, f.	use	uso, m.

NOUNS: English -ate other than chemical terms = Spanish -ado(a), -ato or -ate.

75%: 81 Listed

The suffix -ate often denotes an office, function, official, group of officials or agents (*episcopate, potentate, directorate*); or a person or thing that is the object of an action (*legate*).

ENGLISH	SPANISH	ENGLISH	SPANISH
advocate	abogado, m.	degenerate	degenerado, m.
affiliate	afiliada, f.	delegate	delegado, m.
aggregate	agregado, m.	dictate	dictado, m.
alternate	substituto, m.•	doctorate	doctorado, m.
associate	socio, m.•	duplicate	duplicado, m.
baccalaureate	bachillerato, m.	effeminate	efeminado, m.
caliphate	califato, m.	electorate	electorado, m.
candidate	candidato, m.	emirate	emirato, m.
celibate	célibe, m.•	estate	finca, f.; estado, m.
certificate	certificado, m.	*estimate	estimación, f.•
chocolate	chocolate, m.	expatriate	expatriado, m.
climate	clima, m.•	graduate	graduado, m.
cognate	cognado, m.		licenciado, m.•
confederate	confederado, m.	illiterate	ignorante, m.•
conglomerate	conglomerado, m.	ingrate	ingrato, m.
consulate	consulado, m.	initiate	iniciado, m.
coordinate	coordinada, f.	inmate	residente, m.•
debate	debate, m.	intestate	intestado, m.

ENGLISH	SPANISH	ENGLISH	SPANISH
intimate	íntimo, m.•	private (MIL)	soldado raso, m.•
karate	karate, m.	probate	validación, f.•
laminate	lámina, f.•	profligate	libertino, m.•
laureate	laureado, m.	protectorate	protectorado, m.
lectorate	lectorado, m.	quadruplicate	cuadruplicado, m.
legate	legado, m.	*rebate	rebaja, f.•
magistrate	magistrado, m.	reprobate (REL)	réprobo, m.•
magnate	magnate, m.	senate	senado, m.
mandate	mandato, m.	sophisticate	mundano, m.•
moderate	moderado, m.	stalemate	empate, m.•
novitiate	noviciado, m.	state	estado, m.
opiate	opiato, m.	subordinate	subordinado, m.
ordinate	ordenada, f.	substrate	substrato, m.
palate	paladar, m.•	sultanate	sultanato, m.
patriarchate	patriarcado, m.	surrogate	substituto, m.•
pirate	pirata, m.	syndicate	sindicato, m.
plate	plato, m.	template	modelo, m.•
postgraduate	postgraduado, m.		plantilla, f.•
postulate	postulado, m.	triplicate	triplicado, m.
potentate	potentado, m.	triumvirate	triunvirato, m.
predicate	predicado, m.	ultimate	último, m.•
prelate	prelado, m.	unfortunate	infortunado, m.
primate (REL)	primado, m.	vertebrate	vertebrado, m.
primate (ZOOL)	primate, m.	vulgate	vulgata, f.

NOUNS: English chemical and mineral nouns ending in -ate = Spanish -ado or -ato.   98%: 22 Listed
(There are hundreds of these nouns.)

Gender: Almost all are masculine in Spanish.

ENGLISH	SPANISH	ENGLISH	SPANISH
acetate	acetado, m.	ferrate	ferrato, m.
barbiturate	barbiturato, m.	filtrate	filtrado, m.
bicarbonate	bicarbonato, m.	fulminate	fulminato, m.
carbohydrate	carbohidrato, m.	glycerate	glicerato, m.
carbonate	carbonato, m.	hydrate	hidrato, m.
chelate	quelado, m.	nitrate	nitrato, m.
chlorate	clorato, m.	phosphate	fosfato, m.
citrate	citrato, m.	silicate	silicato, m.
concentrate	concentrado, m.	solvate	solvato, m.
condensate	condensado, m.	sublimate	sublimado, m.
cyclamate	ciclamato, m.	sulfate (sulphate)	sulfato, m.

NOUNS: English -ete = Spanish -eta or -ete.   85%: 5 Listed

ENGLISH	SPANISH	ENGLISH	SPANISH
aesthete	esteta, f.	machete	machete, m.
athlete	atleta, m.	spirochete	espiroqueta, f.
*concrete	hormigón, m.•		

NOUNS: English *-ite* denoting minerals or chemicals = Spanish *-ita* or *-ito*. **99%: 16 Listed**
(There are hundreds of such nouns.)

ENGLISH	SPANISH	ENGLISH	SPANISH
anthracite	antracita, f.	leucite	leucita, f.
bauxite	bauxita, f.	lignite	lignito, m.
cordite	cordita, f.	lucite	lucita, f.
dolomite	dolomita, f.	manganite	manganita, f.
dynamite	dinamita, f.	meteorite	meteorito, m.
ferrite	ferrita, f.	stalactite	estalactita, f.
granite	granito, m.	stalagmite	estalagmita, f.
graphite	grafito, m.	vulcanite	vulcanita, f.

NOUNS: English *-ite* denoting a member of a group of people = Spanish *-ita*. **98%: 8 Listed**

Cross-Reference: Separate List of Countries and People p.203
Gender: Usually masculine unless reference is to a female.

ENGLISH	SPANISH	ENGLISH	SPANISH
Canaanite	cananeo, m.•	Jacobite	jacobita, m.
Hittite	hitita, m.	Levite	levita, m.
Ishmaelite	ismaelita, m.	Mennonite	menonita, m.
Israelite	israelita, m.	Semite	semita, m.

NOUNS: English *-ite* other than minerals, chemicals and human groups often = Spanish *-ito(a)* or *-ite*. **70%: 21 Listed**

Gender: Almost all are masculine in Spanish.

ENGLISH	SPANISH	ENGLISH	SPANISH
appetite	apetito, m.	plebiscite	plebiscito, m.
composite	compuesto, m.•	prerequisite	requisito previo, m.•
elite	élite, m.	preterite	pretérito, m.
erudite	erudito, m.	proselyte	prosélito, m.
favorite	favorito, m.	requisite	requisito, m.
finite	finito, m.	respite	pausa, f.; respiro, m.•
hypocrite	hipócrita, m.	rite	ceremonia, f.; rito, m.
mesquite	mezquita, f.	satellite	satélite, m.
neophyte	neófito, m.	suburbanite	suburbano, m.•
opposite	contrario, opuesto, m.•	termite	termite, m.
parasite	parásito, m.		

NOUNS: English *-ote* = Spanish *-oto(a)* or *-ote*. **95%: 8 Listed**

ENGLISH	SPANISH	ENGLISH	SPANISH
anecdote	anécdota, f.	creosote	creosota, f.
antidote	antídota, f.	garrote	garrote, m.
compote	compota, f.	*note	nota, f.
coyote	coyote, m.	vote	votación, f.; voto, m.

NOUNS: English -tte = Spanish -eta.   70%: 19 Listed

Gender: Most are feminine in Spanish.

ENGLISH	SPANISH	ENGLISH	SPANISH
briquette	briqueta, f.	marionette	marioneta, f.
brochette	asador, m.•	pirouette	pirueta, f.
brunette	moreno, m.•	rosette	roseta, f.
cassette	cajita, f.•	roulette	ruleta, f.
cigarette	cigarrillo, m.•	serviette	servilleta, f.
corvette	corbeta, f.	silhouette	silueta, f.
croquette	croqueta, f.	statuette	estatuilla, f.•
etiquette	etiqueta, f.	vignette	viñeta, f.
gazette	gaceta, f.	vinaigrette	vinagreta, f.
lunette	luneta, f		

NOUNS: English -ute = Spanish -uto, -uta or -udo.
80%: 19 Listed

ENGLISH	SPANISH	ENGLISH	SPANISH
absolute	absoluto, m.	mute	mudo, m.
attribute	atributo, m.	parachute	paracaídas, f.•
brute	bruto, m.	prostitute	prostituta, f.
compute	cómputo, m.	repute	reputación, f.•
dispute	disputa, f.	route	ruta, f.
disrepute	descrédito, m.•	salute	saludo, m.
evolute (GEOM)	evoluta, f.	statute	ley, f.; estatuto, m.
hirsute	hirsuto, m.	substitute	substituto, m.
institute	instituto, m.	tribute	tributo, m.
minute	minuto, m.		

NOUNS: English -gogue and -logue = Spanish -gogo and -logo.
95%: 18 Listed

Gender: All are masculine in Spanish.

ENGLISH	SPANISH	ENGLISH	SPANISH
analogue	análogo, m.	ideologue	ideólogo, m.
apologue	apólogo, m.	monologue	monólogo, m.
catalogue	catálogo, m.	mystagogue	mistagogo, m.
chronologue	cronólogo, m.	pedagogue	pedagogo, m.
decalogue	decálogo, m.	prologue	prólogo, m.
demagogue	demagogo, m.	sialagogue	sialagogo, m.
dialogue	diálogo, m.	sinologue	sinólogo, m.
epilogue	epílogo, m.	synagogue	sinagogo, m.
homologue	homólogo, m.	theologue	teólogo, m.

NOUNS: English -gue other than -gogue and -logue = -ga, -gua or -gue.   95%: 16 Listed

ENGLISH	SPANISH	ENGLISH	SPANISH
colleague	colega, m.	merengue (dance)	merengue, m.
dengue (MED)	dengue, m.	morgue	morgue, m.
fatigue	fatiga, f.	pirogue	piragua, f.
harangue	arenga, f.	plague	plaga, f.
intrigue	intriga, f.	Prague	Praga, f.
league (MEAS)	legua, f.	rogue	bribón, m.•
league (group)	liga, legua, f.	tongue (ANAT)	lengua, f.•
meringue	merengue, m.	vogue	moda, boga, f.•

NOUNS: English -que = Spanish -co or -ca.   70%: 16 Listed

ENGLISH	SPANISH	ENGLISH	SPANISH
antique	antigüedad, f.•	discotheque	discoteca, f.
arabesque	arabesco, m.	Martinique	Martinica, f.
baroque	barroco, m.	mystique	mística, f.
boutique	tienda, f.•	physique	figura, f.; físico, m.
burlesque	parodia, farsa, f.•	plaque	placa, f.
catafalque	catafalco, m.	relique	reliquia, f.•
communiqué	comunicación, f.•	technique	técnica, f.
critique	crítica, f.	torque	torsión, f.•

NOUNS: English -ive = Spanish -ivo(a).   85%: 85 Listed

Gender: Most are masculine in Spanish.

ENGLISH	SPANISH	ENGLISH	SPANISH
ablative	ablativo, m.	corrosive	corrosivo, m.
abrasive	abrasivo, m.	curative	curativo, m.
accusative	acusativo, m.	dative	dativo, m.
additive	aditivo, m.	defensive	defensiva, f.
adhesive	adhesivo, m.	demonstrative	demonstrativo, m.
adjective	adjetivo, m.	derivative	derivativo, m.
affirmative	afirmativa, f.	detective	detective, m.•
alternative	alternativa, f.	determinative	determinativo, m.
aperitive	aperitivo, m.	digestive	digestivo, m.
archive	archivo, m.	diminutive	diminutivo, m.
attributive	atributo, m.•	directive	mandato, m.•
captive	cautivo, m.	elective	curso electivo, m.
collective	colectividad, f.•	exclusive	exclusiva, f.
comparative	comparativo, m.	executive	ejecutivo, m.
conjunctive	conjunción, f.•	expletive	expletiva, f.
connective	conectivo, m.	explosive	explosivo, m.
*conservative	conservador, m.•	fixative	fijativo, m.
contraceptive	contraceptivo, m.	fugitive	fugitivo, m.
cooperative	cooperativa, f.	genitive	genitivo, m.
corrective	correctivo, m.	imperative	imperativo, m.
correlative	correlativo, m.	incentive	incentivo, m.

ENGLISH	SPANISH	ENGLISH	SPANISH
indicative	indicativo, m.	positive	positivo, m.
infinitive	infinitivo, m.	possessive	posesivo, m.
initiative	iniciativa, f.	preparative	preparativo, m.
interrogative	interrogatorio, m.•	prerogative	prerrogativa, f.
intransitive	intransitivo, m.	preservative	preservativo, m.
invective	invectiva, f.	preventive	prevención, f.•
laxative	laxativo, m.	primitive	primitivo, m.
locomotive	locomotora, f.•	progressive	progresista, f.•
missive	misiva, f.	prospective	prospectiva, f.
motive	motivo, m.	purgative	purgante, m.•
narrative	narrativa, f.	reflexive	reflexivo, m.
*native	natural, aborigen, m.•	*relative	pariente, m.•
negative	negativa, f.	relative (GRAM)	relativo, m.
negative (photo)	negativo, m.	representative	representante, m.•
nominative	nominativo, m.	restorative	restaurativo, m.
objective	propósito, objetivo, m.	sedative	sedativo, m.
offensive	ofensiva, f.	subjunctive	subjuntivo, m.
olive	oliva, f.	substantive	substantivo, m.
operative	operario, m.•	subversive	subversivo, m.
palliative	paliativo, m.	superlative	superlativo, m.
partitive	partitiva, f.	vocative	vocativo, m.
perspective	perspectiva, f.		

NOUNS: English nouns ending in sounded -e = Spanish -e or -é. 55%: 52 Listed

Gender: Most are masculine in Spanish.

ENGLISH	SPANISH	ENGLISH	SPANISH
acme	cima, f.; colmo, m.•	jubilee	jubileo, m.•
acne	acné, f.	Kamikaze	Kamikaze, m.
adobe	adobe, m.	karate	karate, m.
Apache	apache, m.	machete	machete, m.
apostrophe	apóstrofe, m.	matinee	matiné, f.
cabriole	cabriolé, m.	naiveté	candidez, f.•
café	café, m.	negligee	negligé, m.
canapé	canapé, m.	pedigree	pedigee, m.
carafe	garrafe, m.	posse	posse, m.
catastrophe	catástrofe, m.	protégé	protegido, m.•
Chile	Chile, m.	psyche	psique, m.
cliché	cliché, m.	purée	puré, m.
coffee	café, m.	recipe	receta, f.•
committee	comité, m.	résumé	resumen, m.•
consommé	consomé, m.	sake (drink)	sake, m.
coyote	coyote, m.	simile	símil, m.•
devotee	devoto, m.•	soufflé	souffle, m.
dilettante	diletante, m.	sundae	helado, m.•
divorcé	hombre divorciado, m.•	tee (golf)	tee, m.
exposé	exposición, f.•	teepee	tepee, m.
facsimile	facsímile, m.	tilde (accent)	tilde, m.
fiancé	novio, prometido, m.•	toupee	tupé, m.
finale	final, m.•	troche	pastilla, f.•
forte	fuerte, m.	tsetse	tsetsé, m.
guarantee	guarantía, f.•	ukulele	ukelele, m.
habitué	frequentador, m.•	vigilante	vigilante, m.

NOUNS: English -*ing* (gerund) = Spanish infinitive.

The infinitive of a verb in Spanish can be used as the subject or object of a sentence where English normally uses the -*ing* form.

El leer no es difícil en español.
Reading isn't difficult in Spanish.

NOUNS: English -*arch* = Spanish -*arca(o)*.   95%:   8 Listed

<u>Gender</u>:   Most are masculine in Spanish.

ENGLISH	SPANISH	ENGLISH	SPANISH
arch	arco, m.	monarch	monarca, m.
ecclesiarch	eclesiarca, m.	oligarch	oligarca, m.
hierarch	jerarca, m.	patriarch	patriarca, m.
matriarch	matriarca, f.	Plutarch	Plutarco, m.

NOUNS: English -*graph* = Spanish -*grafo* or -*grafía*.

99%: 18 Listed

<u>Cross-Reference</u>: N -*grapher*, -*graphy*; ADJ -*graphic*

ENGLISH	SPANISH	ENGLISH	SPANISH
autograph	autógrafo, m.	lithograph	litografía, f.
cardiograph	cardiógrafo, m.	mimeograph	mimeógrafo, m.
choreograph	coreógrafo, m.	monograph	monografía, f.
cinematograph	cinematógrafo, m.	paragraph	párrafo, parágrafo, m.
diagraph	diágrafo, m.	phonograph	fonógrafo, m.
epigraph	epígrafo, m.	photograph	fotografía, f.
graph	grafía, f.	seismograph	sismógrafo, m.
holograph	hológrafo, m.	subparagraph	subparágrafo, m.
homograph	homógrafo, m.	telegraph	telégrafo, m.

Following a similar conversion pattern are several other nouns ending in -*ph* such as the following:

ENGLISH	SPANISH	ENGLISH	SPANISH
caliph	califa, m.	nymph	ninfa, f.
epitaph	epitafio, m.	triumph	triunfo, m.

NOUNS: English *-ish* in nouns of nationality or language = Spanish- *és*. 50%: 10 Listed

Cross-Reference: Separate List of Countries and People (p.203)

Gender: When used to describe a person's nationality, these nouns take the gender of the person to which they refer.

ENGLISH	SPANISH	ENGLISH	SPANISH
British	bretón, m.•	Polish	polaco, m.•
Danish	danés, m.	Scotish	escocés, m.
English	inglés, m.	Spanish	español, m.•
Finnish	finlandés, m.	Swedish	sueco, m.•
Irish	irlandés, m.	Turkish	turco, m.•

NOUNS: English *-path* = Spanish *-pata*. 99%: 6 Listed

Cross-Reference: N *-pathy*, *-pathist*; ADJ *-pathic*

Gender: All are masculine in Spanish.

ENGLISH	SPANISH	ENGLISH	SPANISH
allopath	alópata, m.	neuropath	neurópata, m.
cardiopath	cardiópata, m.	osteopath	osteópata, m.
naturopath	naturópata, m.	psychopath	psicópata, m.

NOUNS: English *-i* = Spanish *-i*, *-í* or *-e*. 85%: 48 Listed

Gender: Most are masculine in Spanish.

ENGLISH	SPANISH	ENGLISH	SPANISH
Afghani	afgano, m.•	Helsinki	Helsinki, m.
alibi	pretexto, alibí, m.	hi-fi	hi-fi, m.
alkali	álcali, m.	Hindi	hindi, m.
beriberi	beriberi, m.	Hindustani	indostani, m.
bikini	bikini, m.	Israeli	Israelí, m.
broccoli	brócoli, m.	Karachi	Karachi, m.
cadi (judge)	cadí, m.	khaki	caqui, m.
chianti	quianti, m.	kiwi	kiwí, m.
chili	chile, m.	macaroni	macarrones, m.•
confetti	confeti, m.	Malawi	Malawi, m.
coolie	peón, culí, m.	Mali	Malí, m.
daiquiri	daiquirí, m.	martini	martini, m.
effendi	efendi, m.	Miami	Miami, m.
Haiti	Haití, m.	mufti	mufti, m.
hara-kari	harakiri, m.	Nairobi	Nairobi, m.
Hawaii	Hawaii, m.	Nazi	Nazi, m.

ENGLISH	SPANISH	ENGLISH	SPANISH
Pakistani	Pakistani, m.	ski	esquí, m.
potpourri	popurrí, m.	Tahiti	Tahití, m.
rabbi	rabino, rabí, m.	taxi	taxi, m.
ravioli	ravioles, m.•	Thai	Tai, m.
safari	safari, m.	Tripoli	Trípoli, m.
salami	salame, m.	yanqui	yanqui, m.
sari	sari, m.	yogi	yogi, m.
Saudi	Saudi, m.	zucchini	calabacín, m.•

NOUNS: English -al = -al or -alo(a).　　　　70%: 172 Listed

<u>Gender</u>: Most converting to -al are masculine in Spanish.

ENGLISH	SPANISH	ENGLISH	SPANISH
accrual	incremento, m.•	*crystal	cristal, m.
acquittal	absolución, f.•	cymbal (music)	címbalo, m.
admiral	almirante, m.•	decimal	decimal, m.
aerial	antena, f.•	denial	negación, f.•
animal	animal, m.	diagonal	diagonal, f.
appeal	apelación, f.•	dial	esfera, f.; dial, m.
appeal	súplica, f.•	differential	diferencial, f.
appraisal	evaluación, f.•	disapproval	desaprobación, f.•
approval	aprobación, f.•	dismissal	despedida, f.•
arousal	excitación, f.•	dispersal	dispersión, f.•
arrival	venida, llegada, f.•	disposal	disposición, f.•
arsenal	arsenal, m.	disproval	refutación, f.•
Baal	Baal, m.	editorial	editorial, m.
bacchanal	bacanal, m.	equal	igual, m.
betrayal	traición, f.•	espousal	esponsales, m.•
betrothal	compromiso, m.•	essential	esencial, m.
burial	entierro, m.	festival	fiesta, festival, m.
cabal	cábala, f.	final	final, m.
canal	canal, m.	fundamental	fundamento, m.•
cannibal	caníbal, m.	funeral	funeral, m.
capital (city)	capital, f.	general	general, m.
capital (wealth)	capital, m.	heterosexual	heterosexual, m.
cardinal (MATH)	cardinal, m.	homosexual	homosexual, m.
cardinal (REL)	cardenal, m.	horizontal	horizontal, f.
carnival	carnaval, m.	hospital	hospital, m.
cathedral	catedral, f.	humeral	humeral, m.
centennial	centenario, m.•	hymnal	hímnico, m.•
central	central, m.	ideal	ideal, m.
cereal	cereal, m.	immortal	inmortal, m.
chaparral	chaparral, m.	*individual	individuo, m.•
chemical	producto químico, m.•	initial	inicial, f.
choral	coral, m.	integral (math)	integral, m.
collateral	colateral, m.	intellectual	intelectual, m.
coral	coral, m.	interval	intervalo, m.
cordial	cordial, m.	jackal	chacal, m.
*corporal	cabo, caporal, m.	*journal	diario, periódico, m.•
corral	corral, m.	lateral	lateral, m.
credential	credencial, f.	liberal	liberal, m.
criminal	criminal, m.	local	local, m.

ENGLISH	SPANISH	ENGLISH	SPANISH
madrigal	madrigal, m.	rebuttal	refutación, f.•
mammal	mamífero, m.•	reciprocal	recíproco, m.•
manual	manual, m.	recital	recital, m.
marshal	mariscal, m.	referral	referencia, f.•
marsupial	marsupial, m.	refusal	negativa, repulsa, f.•
material	tela, f; material, m.	rehearsal	ensayo, m.; prueba, f.•
medal	medalla, f.	removal	remoción, f.•
*memorial	monumento, memorial, m.	renewal	renovación, f.•
metal	metal, m.	rental	renta, arrendamiento, m.•
mineral	mineral, m.	reprisal	represalia, f.•
moral(s)	moral, f.	residual	residuo, m.•
mortal	mortal, m.	retrieval	recobro, m.•
mural	mural, m.	reversal	inversión, f.•
musical	comedia musical, f.	revival	restauración, f.•
national	nativo, nacional, m.	ritual	ritual, m.
Nepal	Nepal, m.	rival	rival, m.
neutral	neutral, m.	sandal	sandalia, f.•
numeral	cifra, f.; número, m.•	scandal	escándalo, m.
occidental	occidental, m.	semifinal	semifinal, m.
official	funcionario, m.•	Senegal	Senegal, m.
opal	ópalo, m.	sepal	sépalo, m.
ordeal	ordalía, f.•	serial	serial, m.
ordinal	número ordinal, m.	signal	señal, f.
oriental	oriental, m.	sisal	sisal, m.
original	original, m.	special	especial, m.
oval	óvalo, m.	spiral	espiral, f.
pedal	pedal, m.	spiritual (music)	espiritual, m.
pedestal	pedestal, m.	subtotal	subtotal, m.
pentothal	pentotal, m.	supernatural	sobrenatural, m.
periodical	periódico, m.•	survival	supervivencia, f.•
perusal	lectura cuidadosa, f.•	terminal	términal, m.
petal	pétalo, m.	territorial	territorial, m.
phenobarbital	fenobarbital, m.	testimonial	testimonial, m.
plural	plural, m.	total	suma, f.; total, m.
portal	portal, m.	transferral	transferencia, f.•
portrayal	representación, f.•	transmittal	transmisión, f.•
Portugal	Portugal, m.	tribunal	tribunal, m.
postal (card)	postal, f.	triennial	trienio, m.•
potential	potencial, m.	universal	universal, m.
principal	principal, m.	urinal	urinal, m.
prodigal	pródigo, m.•	vandal	vándalo, m.
professional	profesional, m.	vassal	vasallo, m.
proposal	propuesta, oferta, f.•	vertical	vertical, m.
quetzal	quetzal, m.	vestal	vestal, f.
radical	radical, m.	vial	ampolleta, f.•
rascal	pícaro, bribón, m.•	vocal	vocal, f.
reappraisal	revaluación, f.•	zeal	celo, m.•

NOUNS: English -el = Spanish -el, -elo(a) or -llo(a).
50%: 86 Listed

Gender: Most are masculine in Spanish

ENGLISH	SPANISH	ENGLISH	SPANISH
angel	ángel, m.	*label	rótulo, m.; etiqueta, f.•
apparel	aparejo, m.•	lapel	solapa, f.•
archangel	arcángel, m.	laurel	laurel, m.
babel	babel, m.	level	nivel, m.
barrel	barril, m.•	libel	difamación, f.; libelo, m.
betel (nut)	betel, m.	mackerel	caballa, f.•
bevel	bisel, m.•	mandrel	mandril, m.•
bowel	intestino, m.•	mantel	manto, m.•
brothel	burdel, m.•	marvel	maravilla, f.•
bushel	fanega, f.•	minstrel	juglar, trovador, m.•
camel	camello, m.	model	modelo, m.
caramel	caramelo, m.	morsel	bocado, m.•
carpel	carpelo, m.	motel	motel, m.
carrousel	carrusel, m.	muscatel	vino muscatel, m.
*cartel	sindicato, cartel, m.	mussel	mejillón, m.•
channel	canalizo, canal, m.•	navel	ombligo, m.•
chapel	capilla, f.	nickel	níquel, m.
chattel	bienes muebles, m.•	novel	novela, f.
chisel	cincel, m.	panel	panel, m.
cidadel	ciudadela, f.	parallel	paralela, f.
colonel	coronel, m.	parcel	paquete, m.•
counsel	abogado, consejo, m.•	*pastel	pastel, m.
damsel	damisela, f.	personnel	personal, m.
decibel	decibel, m.	pretzel	bizcocho, m.•
diesel	diesel, m.	quarrel	riña, querella, f.
*duel	duelo, m.	rebel	rebelde, m.•
duffel	muletón, m.•	scalpel	escalpelo, m.
easel	atril, m.•	scoundrel	pícaro, bribón, m.•
enamel	esmalte, m.•	sentinel	centinela, m.
flannel	franela, f.	sequel	secuela, f.
fuel	combustible, m.•	shovel	pala, f.•
funnel	embudo, m.•	shrapnel	shrapnel, m.
gavel	mallete, m.•	snorkel	esnórquel, m.
gospel	evangelio, credo, m.•	squirrel	ardilla, f.•
gravel	cascajo, m.; grava, f.•	tassel	borla, f.•
hostel	hostería, posada, f.•	towel	toalla, f.
hotel	hotel, m.	travel	viaje, m.•
infidel	infiel, m.	trowel	llana, trulla, f.•
Israel	Israel, m.	tunnel	túnel, m.
jewel	joya, f.•	vessel(jar)	vasija, f.; vaso, m.•
keel	quilla, f.	vessel(boat)	barco, buque, m.•
kennel	perrera, f.•	vowel	vocal, f.
kernel	grano, m.; semilla, f.•	weasel	comadreja, f.•

NOUNS: English *-ol* in nouns dealing with chemistry = Spanish *-ol*.   95%: **12 Listed**
(Only a few of the many such nouns are listed)

<u>Gender</u>: All are masculine in Spanish.

ENGLISH	SPANISH	ENGLISH	SPANISH
aerosol	aerosol, m.	glycol	glicol, m.
alcohol	alcohol, m.	hydrosol	hidrosol, m.
cholesterol	colesterol, m.	menthol	mentol, m.
creosol	creosol, m.	thiokol	tiocol, m.
ethanol	etanol, m.	thiophenol	tiofenol, m.
glycerol	glicerol, m.	viosterol	viosterol, m.

NOUNS: English *-ol* in nouns not dealing with chemistry = Spanish *-ol* or *-olo(a)*.   75%: **18 Listed**

<u>Gender</u>: All are masculine in Spanish.

ENGLISH	SPANISH	ENGLISH	SPANISH
bristol	bristol, m.	parasol	parasol, m.
cacerol	cacerola, f.	patrol	patrulla, f.
capitol	capitolio, m.•	pistol	pistola, f.
carol	canción, f.•	protocol	protocolo, m.
control	control, m.	saracol	saracola, f.
entresol	entresuelo, m.	school	escuela, f.
frijol	frijol, m.	symbol	símbolo, m.
idol	ídolo, m.	Tyrol	Tirol, m.
Mongol	mongol, m.	vitriol	vitriolo, m.

NOUNS: English *-ul* other than *-ful* = Spanish *-ul*.   95%: **8 Listed**

<u>Gender</u>: All are masculine in Spanish.

ENGLISH	SPANISH	ENGLISH	SPANISH
caracul	caracul, m.	karakul	caracul, m.
consul	cónsul, m.	mogul	mogol, m.•
Istanbul	Estambul, m.	proconsul	procónsul, m.
Kabul	Kabul, m.	vice-consul	vicecónsul, m.

NOUNS: English nouns ending in *-ful* have no helpful pattern for conversion to Spanish except that the concept of quanity measure is often expressed in Spanish by the Spanish measure word alone or by adding *-ada(o)* or *-illo(a)*.

14 Listed

ENGLISH	SPANISH	ENGLISH	SPANISH
armful	brazado, m.	mouthful	bocada, f.
eyeful	ojeada, f.	nestful	nidada, f.
barrelful	barrilada, f.	pocketful	bosillo, m.
basketful	cestada, f.	spadeful	palada, f.
cupful	tasa, f.	spoonful	cucharada, f.
glassful	vaso, m.	teaspoonful	cucharilla, f.
handful	puñada, f.	wagonful	carretada, f.

NOUNS: English *-yl* = Spanish *-ilo*.   **95%: 8 Listed**

(Most are chemical or mineral nouns. Only a few of the many such commonly used nouns are listed.)

Gender: All are masculine in Spanish.

ENGLISH	SPANISH	ENGLISH	SPANISH
butyl	bútilo, m.	methyl	metilo, m.
carbonyl	carbonilo, m.	polyvinyl	polivinilo, m.
dactyl	dáctilo, m.	thionyl	tionilo, m.
ethyl	etilo, m.	vinyl	vinilo, m.

NOUNS: English *-gram* = Spanish *-grama(o)*.   **99%: 14 Listed**

Gender: All are masculine in Spanish including those which end in *-a*.

ENGLISH	SPANISH	ENGLISH	SPANISH
anagram	anagrama, m.	kilogram	kilogramo, m.
cablegram	cablegrama, m.	milligram	miligramo, m
cryptogram	criptograma, m.	monogram	monograma, m.
decigram	decigramo, m.	parallelogram	paralelogramo, m
diagram	diagrama, m.	program	programa, m.
epigram	epigrama, m.	radiogram	radiograma, m.
gram	gramo, m.	telegram	telegrama, m.

The following nouns also convert with a similar *-am* = *-ama(o)* pattern: **4 Listed**

ENGLISH	SPANISH	ENGLISH	SPANISH
amalgam	amalgama, f.	cream	nata, crema, f.
balsam	balsamo, m.	madam	madama, f.

NOUNS: English *-em* = Spanish *-ema*, *-em* or *-ima*.
                                                85%: 20 Listed
   Gender: Most are masculine in Spanish.

ENGLISH	SPANISH	ENGLISH	SPANISH
anthem	himno, m.•	Moslem	musulmán, m.•
diadem	diadema, f.	poem	poema, m.
disesteem	desestima, f.	postmortem	postmórtem, m.
emblem	emblema, f.	problem	problema, m.
esteem	estima, f.	requiem	réquiem, m.
gem	joya, gema, f.	stratagem	estratagema, f.
harem	herén, harem, m.	system	sistema, m.
item	detalle, ítem, m.	tandem	tándem, m.
mayhem	pandemónium, m.•	theorem	teorema, m.
modem	modem, m.	totem	tótem, m.

NOUNS: English *-gm* = Spanish *-gma*.   99%: 4 Listed

   Gender: All are masculine in Spanish.

ENGLISH	SPANISH	ENGLISH	SPANISH
apothegm	apotegma, m.	epiphragm	epifragma, m.
diaphragm	diafragma, m.	paradigm	paradigma, m.

NOUNS: English *-ithm* = Spanish *-itmo*.   99%: 4 Listed

   Gender: All are masculine in Spanish.

ENGLISH	SPANISH	ENGLISH	SPANISH
algorithm	algoritmo, m.	logarithm	logaritmo, m.
antilogarithm	antilogaritmo, m.	rhythm	ritmo, m.

NOUNS: English *-lm* = Spanish *-lmo(a)* or *-lm*.   90%: 9 Listed

   Gender: Most are masculine in Spanish.

ENGLISH	SPANISH	ENGLISH	SPANISH
calm	calma, f.	microfilm	microfilm, m.
elm	olmo, m.	napalm	napalm, m.
film	pelicula, f.; film, m.	realm	reino, m•
palm	palma, f.	Stockholm	Estocolmo, m.
psalm	salmo, m.		

NOUNS: English -form = Spanish -forma(o) or -forme.
95%: 6 Listed

ENGLISH	SPANISH	ENGLISH	SPANISH
chloroform	cloroformo, m.	platform (RR)	andén, m. •
form	forma, f.	reform	reforma, f.
platform	plataforma, f.	uniform	uniforme, m.

The following nouns also convert with a similar -rmo(a) pattern.
8 Listed

ENGLISH	SPANISH	ENGLISH	SPANISH
alarm	alarma, f.	isotherm	isotgerma, f.
endoderm	endodermo, m.	norm	norma, f.
endosperm	endosperma, f.	pachyderm	pacquidermo, m.
*firm	casa, firma, f.	sperm	sperma, f.

NOUNS: English -asm = Spanish -asma or -asmo.
90%: 8 Listed

Gender: Most are masculine in Spanish.

ENGLISH	SPANISH	ENGLISH	SPANISH
endoplasm	endoplasma, f.	phantasm	fantasma, m.
enthusiasm	entusiasmo, m.	protoplasm	protoplasma, m.
neoplasm	neoplasma, m.	sarcasm	sarcasmo, m.
orgasm	orgasmo, m.	spasm	espasmo, m.

NOUNS: English -ism = Spanish -ismo.   95%: 252 Listed

The noun-forming suffix -ism denotes the act, practice or result of (terrorism); the condition of being (barbarism); the doctrine, theory or principle of (socialism); the devotion to (nationalism); an instance, example or peculiarity of (Gallicism) or an abnormal condition caused by (alcoholism).

Most of the exceptions are nouns formed from nonconverting roots (bossism, hoboism, leftism). The -ic- and -an- found in the English endings -icism and -ianism are often not retained in the conversion to Spanish.

Cross-Reference: N -ist; ADJ -istic
Gender: Almost all are masculine in Spanish.

ENGLISH	SPANISH	ENGLISH	SPANISH
anarchism	anarquismo, m.	activism	activismo, m.
absenteeism	ausentismo, m.	adventurism	aventurismo, m.
absolutism	absolutismo, m.	aestheticism	esteticismo, m.

113

ENGLISH	SPANISH	ENGLISH	SPANISH
agnosticism	agnosticismo, m.	cubism	cubismo, m.
agrarianism	agrarismo, m.	cynicism	cinismo, m.
albinism	albinismo, m.	Dadaism	dadaísmo, m.
alcoholism	alcoholismo, m.	Darwinism	darvinismo, m.
alpinism	alpinismo, m.	defeatism	derrotismo, m.
altruism	altruismo, m.	deism	deísmo, m.
amateurism	amateurismo, m.	despotism	despotismo, m.
Americanism	americanismo, m.	determinism	determinismo, m.
amorphism	amorfismo, m.	dogmatism	dogmatismo, m.
anachronism	anacronismo, m.	dualism	dualismo, m.
analogism	analogismo, m.	egalitarianism	igualitarismo, m.
anarchism	anarquismo, m.	egocentrism	egocentrismo, m.
aneurism	aneurisma, f.	egoism	egoísmo, m.
Anglicism	anglicismo, m.	egotism	egotismo, m.
animalism	animalismo, m.	embolism	embolismo, m.
animism	animismo, m.	emotionalism	emocionalismo, m.
antagonism	antagonismo, m.	empiricism	empirismo, m.
anticommunism	anticomunismo, m.	eroticism	erotismo, m.
antisemitism	antisemitismo, m.	escapism	escapismo, m.
aphorism	aforismo, m.	estheticism	esteticismo, m.
asceticism	ascetismo, m.	euphemism	eufemismo, m.
astigmatism	astigmatismo, m.	evangelism	evangelismo, m.
atavism	atavismo, m.	evolutionism	evolucionismo, m.
atheism	ateísmo, m.	exhibitionism	exhibicionismo, m.
athleticism	atletismo, m.	existentialism	existencialismo, m.
authoritarianism	autoritarismo, m.	exorcism	exorcismo, m.
autism	autismo, m.	exoticism	exotismo, m.
baptism	bautismo, baptismo, m	expansionism	expansionismo, m.
bimetallism	bimetalismo, m.	expressionism	expresionismo, m.
Bolshevism	bolchevismo, m.	extremism	extremismo, m.
botulism	botulismo, m.	Fabianism	fabianismo, m.
Buddhism	budismo, m.	fanaticism	fanatismo, m.
Calvinism	calvinismo, m.	Fascism	fascismo, m.
cannibalism	canibalismo, m.	fatalism	fatalismo, m.
capitalism	capitalismo, m.	favoritism	favoritismo, m.
carnalism	carnalismo, m.	federalism	federalismo, m.
Castroism	castrismo, m.	feminism	feminismo, m.
cataclysm	cataclismo, m.	feudalism	feudalismo, m.
catechism	catequismo, m.	formalism	formalismo, m.
Catholicism	catolicismo, m.	fraternalism	fraternalismo, m.
centralism	centralismo, m.	functionalism	funcionalismo, m.
chauvinism	chauvinismo, m.	fundamentalism	fundamentalismo, m.
classicism	clasicismo, m.	futurism	futurismo, m.
clericalism	clericalismo, m.	galvanism	galvanismo, m.
collectivism	colectivismo, m.	gradualism	gradualismo, m.
colonialism	colonialismo, m.	hedonism	hedonismo, m.
commercialism	comercialismo, m.	heroism	heroísmo, m.
communism	comunismo, m.	Hinduism	hinduismo, m.
conceptualism	conceptualismo, m.	historicism	historicismo, m.
Confucianism	confucianismo, m.	humanism	humanismo, m.
conservatism	conservatismo, m.	humanitarianism	humanitarismo, m.
creationism	creacionismo, m.	hypnotism	hipnotismo, m.
criticism	crítica, f.	idealism	idealismo, m.

ENGLISH	SPANISH	ENGLISH	SPANISH
imperialism	imperialismo, m.	organism	organismo, m.
impressionism	impresionismo, m.	ostracism	ostracismo, m.
individualism	individualismo, m.	pacifism	pacifismo, m.
industrialism	industrialismo, m.	paganism	paganismo, m.
intellectualism	intelectualismo, m.	Pan-Arabism	panarabismo, m.
irrationalism	irracionalismo, m.	pantheism	panteísmo, m.
isolationism	aislacionismo, m.	parallelism	paralelismo, m.
jingoism	jingoísmo, m.	paternalism	paternalismo, m.
journalism	periodismo, m. •	patriotism	patriotismo, m.
Judaism	judaísmo, m.	pauperism	pauperismo, m.
lesbianism	lesbianismo, m.	peculiarism	peculiarismo, m.
liberalism	liberalismo, m.	perfectionism	perfeccionismo, m.
literalism	literalismo, m.	pessimism	pesimismo, m.
localism	localismo, m.	Pietism	pietismo, m.
Lutheranism	luteranismo, m.	plagiarism	plagio, m. •
lyricism	lirismo, m.	pluralism	pluralismo, m.
magnetism	magnetismo, m.	polytheism	politeísmo, m.
mannerism	manerismo, m.	popularism	popularismo, m.
Marxism	marxismo, m.	positivism	positivismo, m.
masochism	masoquismo, m.	pragmatism	pragmatismo, m.
materialism	materialismo, m.	primitivism	primitivismo, m.
mechanism	mecanismo, m.	prism	prisma, f. •
mercantilism	mercantilismo, m.	professionalism	profesionalismo, m.
mesmerism	mesmerismo, m.	protagonism	protagonismo, m.
metabolism	metabolismo, m.	protectionism	proteccionismo, m.
Methodism	metodismo, m.	Protestantism	protestantismo, m.
microorganism	microorganismo, m.	provincialism	provincialismo, m.
militarism	militarismo, m.	pugilism	pugilismo, m.
millenarianism	milenarismo, m.	purism	purismo, m.
modernism	modernismo, m.	Puritanism	puritanismo, m.
Mohammedanism	mahometismo, m. •	racism	racismo, m.
monarchism	monarquismo, m.	radicalism	radicalismo, m.
monasticism	monaquismo, m. •	rationalism	racionalismo, m.
monism	monismo, m.	realism	realismo, m.
monotheism	monoteísmo, m.	recidivism	recidivismo, m.
muhammadanism	mahomatismo, m. •	reformism	reformismo, m.
mysticism	misticismo, m.	regionalism	regionalismo, m.
narcissism	narcismo, m.	relativism	relativismo, m.
nationalism	nacionalismo, m.	Republicanism	republicanismo, m.
naturalism	naturalismo, m.	revisionism	revisionismo, m.
Nazism	nazismo, m.	rheumatism	reumatismo, m.
negativism	negativismo, m.	ritualism	ritualismo, m.
neo-classicism	neoclasicismo, m.	romanticism	romanticismo, m.
nepotism	nepotismo, m.	sadism	sadismo, m.
neutralism	neutralismo, m.	scepticism	escepticismo, m.
nihilism	nihilismo, m.	schism	cisma, f.
nomadism	nomadismo, m.	secularism	secularismo, m.
nonism	nonismo, m.	segregationism	segregacionismo, m.
nudism	nudismo, m.	self-criticism	autocrítica, f. •
objectivism	objetivismo, m.	sensationalism	sensacionalismo, m.
obstructionism	obstruccionismo, m.	sensualism	sensualismo, m.
opportunism	oportunismo, m.	sentimentalism	sentimentalismo, m.
optimism	optimismo, m.	separatism	separatismo, m.

ENGLISH	SPANISH	ENGLISH	SPANISH
sexism	sexismo, m.	terrorism	terrorismo, m.
shintoism	sintoísmo, m.	totalitarianism	totalitarismo, m.
skepticism	escepticismo, m.	tourism	turismo, m.
socialism	socialismo, m.	transvestism	transvestismo, m.
solecism	solecismo, m.	truism	truismo, m.
somnambulism	somnambulismo, m.	unionism	unionismo, m.
spiritualism	espiritualismo, m.	universalism	universalismo, m.
statism	estatismo, m.	urbanism	urbanismo, m.
stigmatism	estigmatismo, m.	utilitarianism	utilitarismo, m.
stoicism	estoicismo, m.	vandalism	vandalismo, m.
subjectivism	subjetivismo, m.	vegetarianism	vegetarianismo, m.
surrealism	surrealismo, m.	ventriloquism	ventriloquia, f. •
syllogism	silogismo, m.	vocalism	vocalismo, m.
symbolism	simbolismo, m.	voluntarism	voluntarismo, m.
synchronism	sincronismo, m.	vulgarism	vulgarismo, m.
syndicalism	sindicalismo, m.	witticism	chiste, m. •
synergism	sinergismo, m.	Zionism	sionismo, m.

The following nouns also convert with a similar -sm conversion pattern: 99%: 2 Listed

ENGLISH	SPANISH	ENGLISH	SPANISH
macrocosm	macrocosmo, m.	microcosm	microcosmo, m.

NOUNS: English -ium = Spanish -io(a).

99%: 84 Listed

The suffix -ium often indicates the name of a chemical element.

Gender: Almost all are masculine in Spanish.

ENGLISH	SPANISH	ENGLISH	SPANISH
actinium	actinio, m.	compendium	compendio, m.
aluminium	aluminio, m.	condominium	condominio, m.
ammonium	amonio, m.	consortium	consorcio, m.
aquarium	acuario, m.	cranium	cráneo, m.
atrium	atrio, m.	crematorium	crematorio, m.
*auditorium	auditorio, m.	decennium	decenio, m.
bacterium	bacteria, f.	delirium	delirio, m.
barium	bario, m.	delphinium	delfinio, m.
beryllium	berilio, m.	effluvium	efluvio, m.
biennium	bienio, m.	eluvium	eluvio, m.
butyl-lithium	butilo-litio, m.	Elysium	Elísio, m.
cadmium	cadmio, m.	emporium	emporio, m.
calcium	calcio, m.	encomium	encomio, m.
cambium	cambio, m.	equilibrium	equilibrio, m.
cerium	cerio, m.	europium	europio, m.
chromium	cromo, m. •	gallium	galio, m.
cilium	cilio, m.	geranium	geranio, m.
collegium	colegio, m.	germanium	germanio, m.
colloquium	coloquio, m.	gymnasium	gimnasio, m.
columbium	columbio, m.	helium	helio, m.
honorarium	honorario, m.	iridium	iridio, m.
indium	indio, m.	lithium	litio, m.

ENGLISH	SPANISH	ENGLISH	SPANISH
magnesium	magnesio, m.	proscenium	proscenio, m.
medium	medio, m.	radium	radio, m.
medium (spirit)	medium, m. •	rhenium	renio, m.
millennium	milenio, m.	ruthenium	rutenio, m.
moratorium	moratoria, f.	sanatorium	sanatorio, m.
myocardium	miocardio, m.	sanitarium	sanitario, m.
neptunium	neptunio, m.	selenium	selenio, m.
odium	odio, m.	sodium	sodio, m.
opium	opio, m.	solarium	solana, f. •
opprobrium	oprobio, m.	stadium	estadio, m.
palladium	paladio, m.	stibonium	estibonio, m.
pandemonium	pandemonio, m.	symposium	simposio, m.
planetarium	planetario, m.	tedium	tedio, m.
plutonium	plutonio, m.	tellurium	telurio, m.
podium	podio, m.	thorium	torio, m.
polonium	polonio, m.	titanium	titanio, m.
potassium	potasio, m.	uranium	uranio, m.
premium	premio, m.	vanadium	vanadio, m.
presidium	presidio, m.	zirconium	zirconio, m.

NOUNS: English *-um* other than *-ium* = Spanish *-o(a)* or *-um*.

85%: 58 Listed

Gender: Most are masculine in Spanish.

ENGLISH	SPANISH	ENGLISH	SPANISH
album	álbum, m.	modicum	pequeña cantidad, f. •
alum	alumbre, m. •	momentum	momento, m.
aluminum	aluminio, m.	museum	museo, m.
annum	año, m.	nostrum	panacea, f. •
asylum	asilo, m.	opossum	oposum, m.
athenaeum	ateneo, m.	optimum	óptimo, m.
carborundum	carborundo, m	pabulum	pábulo, m.
cerebellum	cerebelo, m.	pendulum	péndulo, m.
cerebrum	cerebro, m.	petroleum	petróleo, m.
chrysanthemum	crisantemo, m.	platinum	platino, m.
coliseum	coliseo, m.	possum	oposum, m.
continuum	continuo, m.	quantum	quantum, m.
curriculum	currículum, m.	quorum	quórum, m.
datum	dato, m.	rectum	recto, m.
decorum	decoro, m.	referendum	referéndum, m.
factotum	factótum, m.	residuum	residuo, m.
forum	foro, m.	rostrum	rostro, m.
fulcrum	fulcro, m.	septum	septo, m.
gum	goma, f.	serum	suero, m.
gypsum	yeso, m. •	sorghum	sorgo, m.
hilum	hilo, m.	spectrum	espectro, m.
infinitum	infinito, m.	sputum	esputo, m.
linoleum	linóleo, m.	sternum	esternón, m. •
lyceum	liceo, m.	substratum	substrato, m.
magnum	magnum, m.	sum	suma, f.
mausoleum	mausoleo, m.	talcum	talco, m.
maximum	máximum, máximo, m.	tantrum	berrinche, m. •
memorandum	memorándum, m.	ultimatum	ultimátum, m.
minimum	mínimum, mínimo, m.	vacuum	vacío, m.

NOUNS: English -*onym* = Spanish -*ónimo*.   99%: 10 Listed

> Gender: All are masculine in Spanish.

ENGLISH	SPANISH	ENGLISH	SPANISH
acronym	acrónimo, m.	metonym	metónimo, m.
anonym	anónimo, m.	paronym	parónimo, m.
antonym	antónimo, m.	pseudonym	seudónimo, m.
eponym	epónimo, m.	synonym	sinónimo, m.
homonym	homónino, m.	tautonym	tautónimo, m.

NOUNS: English -*ician* = Spanish -*ico* or -*ista*.   80%: 22 Listed

> The suffix -*ician* is used in forming nouns meaning a person engaged in, practicing or specializing in a specified field.

> Gender: Almost always masculine unless a female person is clearly indicated.

ENGLISH	SPANISH	ENGLISH	SPANISH
academician	académico, m.	musician	músico, m.
beautician	cosmetólogo, m.•	obstetrician	obstétrico, m.
clinician	clínico, m.	optician	óptico, m.
diagnostician	diagnóstico, m.	patrician	patricio, m.•
dietitian	diético, m.	pediatrician	pediatra, m.•
electrician	electricista, m.	physician	médico, m.•
geopolitician	geopolítico, m.	politician	político, m.
logician	lógico, m.	statistician	estadístico, m.
magician	mágico, m.	tactician	táctico, m.
mathematician	matemático, m.	technician	técnico, m.
mortician	funerario, m.•	theoretician	teórico, m.

NOUNS: English -*arian* = Spanish -*ario*.   85%: 24 Listed

> The suffix -*arian* is used in forming nouns denoting age, sect, social belief or occupation.

> Gender: All are masculine in Spanish unless clearly referring to a female person.

ENGLISH	SPANISH	ENGLISH	SPANISH
antiquarian	anticuario, m.	doctrinarian	doctrinario, m.
authoritarian	autoritario, m.	egalitarian	igualitario, m.
barbarian	bárbaro, m.•	equalitarian	igualitario, m.
centenarian	centenario, m.	grammarian	gramático, m.•
disciplinarian	disciplinario, m.	humanitarian	humanitario, m.

ENGLISH	SPANISH	ENGLISH	SPANISH
libertarian	libertario, m.	sexagenerian	sexagenario, m.
*librarian	bibliotecario, m.•	totalitarian	totalitario, m.
octogenarian	octogenario, m.	Trinitarian	trinitario, m.
parliamentarian	parlementario, m.	Unitarian	unitario, m.
proletarian	proletario, m.	utilitarian	utilitario, m.
sectarian	sectario, m.	vegetarian	vegetariano, m.•
seminarian,-ist	seminarista, m.•	veterinarian	veterinario, m.

NOUNS: English -*an* other than -*ician*, -*arian*, and -*man* (equi- (valent to English -*man*) = Spanish -*ano* (45%), -*án* (30%) or -*io* (5%).

Sub-Groups combined = 80%: 74 Listed

ENGLISH	SPANISH			
	-ano(a) (45%)	-án (30%)	-io (5%)	Others
American	americano, m.			
amphibian			anfibio, m.	
artisan	artesano, m.			
bipartisan			bipartidario, m.	
Brahman		brahmán, m.		
cancan		cancán, m.		
caravan	caravana, f.			
catamaran		catamarán, m.		
charlatan		charlatán, m.		
Christian	cristiano, m.			
civilian				civilista, m.
comedian				cómico, m.
cordovan		cordobán, m.		
courtesan	cortesana, f.			
custodian			custodio, m.	
dean		deán, m.		
diocesan	diocesano, m.			
divan		diván, m.		
equestrian				jinete, m.•
Estonian			estonio, m.	
fustian		fustán, m.		
gentian	genciana, f.			
guardian		guardián, m.		tutor, m.•
historian				historiador, m.
human	humano, m.			
Italian	italiano, m.			
Indian	indiano, m.			
Jordan		Jordán, m.		
khan		kan, m.		
Koran		Corán, m.		
lesbian	lesbiana, f.			
Leviathan		leviatán, m.		
Lutheran	luterano, m.			
Malaysian			malasio, m.	
Martian	marciano, m.			
median			medio, m.	

ENGLISH	SPANISH -ano(a) (45%)	-án (30%)	-io (5%)	Others
meridian	meridiano, m.			
Muhammadan	mahometano, m.			
ocean	océano, m.			
orangutan		orangután, m.		
organ(body)	órgano, m.			
organ(MUS)	órgano, m.			
orphan	huérfano, m.			
paean		peón, m.•		
pagan	pagano, m.			
partisan	partisano, m.			
pecan	pacana, f.			
pedestrian		peatón, m.•		
pelican	pelícano, m.			
plan	plano, m.			
plebeian			plebeyo, m.	
publican	publicano, m.			
Puritan	puritano, m.			
Republican	republicano, m.			
Roman	romano, m.			
ruffian		rufián, m.		
sampan		sampán, m.		
Satan		Satán, m.		
sedan		sedán, m.		
slogan				lema, f.•
sultan		sultán, m.		
talisman		talismán, m.		
tartan		tartán, m.		
theologian				teólogo, m.•
thespian				actor, m.•
Titan		Titán, m.		
toboggan		tobogán, m.		
turban				turbante, m.
utopian				utopista, m.
vegetarian	vegetariano, m.			
veteran	veterano, m.			
Victorian	victoriano, m.			
*villan				bribón, m.•
woman				mujer, f.•

Nouns ending in -*an* denoting nationality are listed in the special list beginning on page 203.

NOUNS: English -*gen* = Spanish -*geno(a)*.   95%: 10 Listed
(Only a few of the most common are listed to show the pattern.)

Gender: Almost all are masculine in Spanish.

ENGLISH	SPANISH	ENGLISH	SPANISH
androgen	andrógeno, m.	hallucinogen	alucinógeno, m.
antigen	antígeno, m.	halogen	halógeno, m.
carcinogen	carcinógeno, m.	hydrogen	hidrógeno, m.
collagen	colágena, f.	nitrogen	nitrógeno, m.
estrogen	estrógeno, m.	oxygen	oxígeno, m.

NOUNS: English *-en* other than *-gen* often = *-en* or *-no(a)*.
                                                    50%: 44 Listed
  Gender: Most are masculine in Spanish.

ENGLISH	SPANISH	ENGLISH	SPANISH
abdomen	abdomen, m.	lichen	liquen, m.
acumen	engenio, cacumen, m.	linen	lino, m.
albumen	albúmina, f.	lumen	lumen, m.
alien	forastero, extranjero, m.•	maiden	soltera, muchacha, f.•
amen	amén, m.	mitten	mitón, m.•
aspen	álamo, m.•	omen	augurio, presagio, m.•
bitumen	bitumen, m.	oven	horno, m.
burden	carga, obligacion, f.•	oxen	buey, m.•
canteen	cantina, f.	platen	platina, f.
chicken	pollo, m.•	pollen	polen, m.
citizen	ciudadano, m.•	raven	cuervo, m.•
dozen	docena, f.	regimen	régimen, m.
Eden	Edén, m.	sateen	satén, m.
garden	jardín, m.•	semen	semen, m.
gluten	gluten, m.	siren	sirena, f.
haven	asilo, puerto, abrigo, m.•	specimen	espécimen, m.
heathen	pagano, m.•	stamen	estambre, m.•
heaven	cielo, paraíso, m.•	token	señal, f.; símbolo, m.•
hyphen	guión, f.•	tungsten	tungsteno, m.
kindergarten	kindergarten, m.	vixen	zorra, f.•
kitchen	cocina, f.•	warden	vigilante, carcelero, m.•
kitten	gatito, m.•	yen (currency)	yen, m.

NOUNS: English science words ending in *-in* = Spanish
  -ina(o).   **95%: 42 Listed**
  There are hundreds of nouns in this category

  Cross-Reference: N *-ine*

  Gender: Almost all are feminine in Spanish.

ENGLISH	SPANISH	ENGLISH	SPANISH
adrenalin	adrenalina, f.	globin	globina, f.
agglutinin	aglutinina, f.	glycerin	glicerina, f
albumin	albúmina, f.	hemoglobin	hemoglobina, f.
antitoxin	antitoxina, f.	heparin	heparina, f.
aspirin	asperina, f.	heroin	heroína, f.
aureomycin	aureomicina, f.	insulin	insulina, f.
benzoin	benzoína, f.	lanolin	lanolina, f.
botulin	botulina, f.	niacin	niacina, f.
casein	caseína, f.	nitroglycerin	nitroglicerina, f.
cocain	cocaína, f.	mycin	micina, f.
dentin	dentina, f.	novocain	novocaína, f.
dextrin	dextrina, f.	paraffin	parafina, f.
fibrin	fibrina, f.	pectin	pectina, f.
gelatin	gelatina, f.	penicillin	penicilina, f.

ENGLISH	SPANISH	ENGLISH	SPANISH
pepsin	pepsina, f.	stearin	estearina, f.
protein	proteína, f.	streptomycin	estreptomicina, f.
prothrombin	protrombina, f.	tannin	tanino, m.
resin	resina, f.	terramycin	terramicina, f.
riboflavin	riboflavina, f.	thyrotrophin	tirotropina, f.
rosin	resina, f.	toxin	toxina, f.
saccharin	sacarina, f.	vitamin	vitamina, f.

Some other English nouns ending in -*in* follow a similar conversion pattern although not in a reliable conversion category.

22 Listed

Gender: No reliable pattern for gender in Spanish.

ENGLISH	SPANISH	ENGLISH	SPANISH
assassin	asesino, m.	penguin	pinqúino, m.
Bedouin	beduíno, m.	poplin	popelina, f.
bobbin	bobina, f.	porcelain	porcelana, f.
curtain	cortina, f.	resin	resina, f.
domain	dominio, m.	ruin	ruina, f.
grain	grano, m.	Spain	España, f.
javelin	jabalina, f.	terrain	terreno, m.
Latin	latino, m.	train	treno, m
mandarin (BOT)	mandarino, m.	tuberculin	tuberculina, f.
mandolin	mandolina, f.	vein	vena, f.
muslin	muselina, f.	*villain	villano, m.

NOUNS: Some English nouns ending in -*in* = Spanish -*án*, -*én*,-*en*, or -*ín*.

26 Listed

Gender: Almost all are masculine in Spanish.

ENGLISH	SPANISH	ENGLISH	SPANISH
Benjamin	Benjamín, m.	Mandarin	mandarin, m.
Berlin	Berlín, m.	margin	margen, m.
Brahmin	brahmán, m.	moccasin	mocasín, m.
captain	capitán, m.	origin	origen, m.
chamberlain	chambelán, m.	paladin	paladín, m.
dauphin	delfín, m.	poplin	polelín, m.
dolphin	delfín, m.	refrain	refrán, m.
Dublin	Dublín, m.	Sanhedrin	sanedrín, m.
disdain	desdén, m.	satin	satén, m.
florin	florín, m.	train	tren, m.
harlequin	arlequín, m.	violin	violín, m.
Kremlin	Kremlin, m.	virgin	virgen, f.
Latin	Latín, m.	zeppelin	zepelín, m.

NOUNS: English geometry nouns ending in -gon = Spanish -ágono.

                                                               99%: 6 Listed

The Suffix -gon denotes a figure having a specified number of angles.

                      Cross-Reference: ADJ -onal

Gender: All are masculine in Spanish.

ENGLISH	SPANISH	ENGLISH	SPANISH
decagon	decágono, m.	octagon	octágono, m.
heptagon	heptágono, m.	pentagon	pentágono, m.
hexagon	hexágono, m.	polygon	polígono, m.

NOUNS: English -gon other than geometry terms = Spanish -gón.

                                    75%: 8 Listed

Gender: Most are masculine in Spanish.

ENGLISH	SPANISH	ENGLISH	SPANISH
argon	argón, m.	Oregon	Oregón, m
dragon	dragón, m.	paragon	modelo, m.•
flagon	jarro, m.•	Saigon	Saigón, m.
jargon	jerga, f.•	*wagon	carro, vagón, m.

NOUNS: English -lion = Spanish -llón.

                                    75%: 12 Listed

Gender: Most are masculine in Spanish.

ENGLISH	SPANISH	ENGLISH	SPANISH
battalion	batallón, m.	million	millón, m.
billion	mil millones, billón, m.	pavilion	pabellón, m.
bullion	oro en barras, m.•	rebellion	rebelión, f.
cotillion	cotillón, m.	stallion	semental, m.•
lion	león, m.•	trillion	trillón, m.
medallion	medallón, m.	vermilion	bermellón, m.

NOUNS: English *-ion* except *-lion* = Spanish *-ión*. The *-t-* in nouns ending in *-gestion* doesn't change to *-c-*.

                                                                  95%: 1221 Listed

Gender: Almost all are feminine in Spanish.
Many of the exceptions to the pattern are masculine.

ENGLISH	SPANISH	ENGLISH	SPANISH
abbreviation	abreviación, f.	affection	cariño, afección, f.
abdication	abdicación, f.	affiliation	afiliación, f.
abduction	abducción, f.	affirmation	afirmación, f.
aberration	aberración, f.	affliction	aflicción, f.
abjection	abyección, f.	agglomeration	aglomeración, f.
ablation	ablación, f.	agglutination	aglutinación, f.
ablution	ablución, f.	aggravation	agravación, f.
abnegation	abnegación, f.	aggregation	agregación, f.
abolition	abolición, f.	aggression	agresión, f.
abomination	abominación, f.	agitation	agitación, f.
abortion	aborto, m.•	alienation	alienación, f.
abrasion	abrasión, f.	alimentation	alimentación, f.
abrogation	abrogación, f.	allegation	alegación, f.
absolution	absolución, f.	alleviation	alivio, m.•
absorption	absorción, f.	alliteration	aliteración, f.
abstention	abstención, f.	allocation	distribución, f.•
abstraction	abstracción, f.	allusion	alusión, f.
acceleration	aceleración, f.	alteration	alteración, f.
accentuation	acentuación, f.	altercation	altercación, f.
accession	accesión, f.	alternation	alternación, f.
acclamation	aclamación, f.	amalgamation	amalgamación, f.
accommodation	acomodación, f.	ambition	ambición, f.
accordion	acordeón, m.•	amelioration	amelioración, f.
accreditation	acreditación, f.	ammunition	(plur.) munición, f.
accretion	acreción, f.	amortization	amortización, f.
accumulation	acumulación, f.	amplification	amplificación, f.
accusation	acusación, f.	amputation	amputación, f.
acquisition	adquisición, f.	animation	animación, f.
action	acción, f.	annexation	anexión, f.•
activation	activación, f.	annihilation	aniquilación, f.
actuation	actuación, f.	annotation	anotación, f.
adaptation	adaptación, f.	annunciation	anunciación, f.
addiction	enviciamiento, m.•	anticipation	anticipación, f.
addition	adición, f.	apparition	aparición, f.
adhesion	adhesión, f.	appellation	apelación, f.
adjudication	adjudicación, f.	application	aplicación, f.
administration	administración, f.	*application	solicitud, f.•
admiration	admiración, f.	appreciation	apreciación, f.
admission (entry)	entrada, f.•	apprehension	aprehensión, f.
admission	admisión, f.	approbation	aprobación, f.
admonition	admonición, f.	appropriation	apropiación, f.
adoption	adopción, f.	approximation	aproximación, f.
adoration	adoración, f.	arbitration	arbitraje, m.•
adulation	adulación, f.	argumentation	argumentación, f.
adulteration	adulteración, f.	articulation	articulación, f.
aeration	aeración, f.	ascension	ascensión, f.
affectation	afectación, f.	aspersion	aspersión, f.

ENGLISH	SPANISH		ENGLISH	SPANISH	
asphyxiation	asfixia,	f.•	coalition	coalición,	f.
aspiration	aspiración,	f.	codification	codificación,	f.
assassination	asesinato,	m.•	coeducation	coeducación,	f.
assertion	aserción,	f.	coercion	coerción,	f.
assimilation	asimilación,	f.	cohabitation	cohabitación,	f.
association	asociación,	f.	cohesion	cohesión,	f.
*assumption	asunción,	f.	collaboration	colaboración,	f.
attention	atención,	f.	collation	colación,	f.
attestation	atestación,	f.	collection	colección,	f.
attraction	atracción,	f.	collision	colisión,	f.
attrition	atrición,	f.	collusion	colusión,	f.
auction	subasta,	f.•	colonization	colonización,	f.
audition	audición,	f.	coloration	coloración,	f.
augmentation	aumentación,	f.	combination	combinación,	f.
authentication	autenticación,	f.	combustion	combustión,	f.
authorization	autorización,	f.	commemoration	conmemoración,	f.
automation	automación,	f.	commendation	recomendación,	f.
aversion	aversión,	f.	commiseration	conmiseración,	f.
aviation	aviación,	f.	commission (fee)	comisión,	f.
avocation	avocación,	f.	commission (group)	comisión,	f.
bastion	bastión,	m.	commotion	conmoción,	f.
beatification	beatificación,	f.	communication	comunicación,	f.
benediction	bendición,	f.•	communion	comunión,	f.
bifurcation	bifurcación,	f.	communization	comunización,	f.
bunion	bunio,	m.•	commutation	conmutación,	f.
calcification	calcificación,	f.	companion	compañero,	m.•
calculation	cálculo,	m.•	compassion	compasión,	f.
calibration	calibración,	f.	compensation	compensación,	f.
cancellation	cancelación,	f.	*compensation	remuneración,	f.•
canonization	canonización,	f.	*competition	competencia,	f.
capitalization	capitalización,	f.		concurso,	m.•
capitulation	capitulación,	f.	compilation	compilación,	f.
caption	título,	m.•	*completion	cumplimiento,	m.•
carnation	clavel doble,	m.•		terminación,	f.•
carrion	carroña,	f.•	*complexion	tez, complexión,	f.
castigation	castigación,	f.	complication	complicación,	f.
castration	castración,	f.	composition	composición,	f.
causation	causalidad,	f.•	comprehension	comprensión,	f.
cauterization	cauterización,	f.	compression	compresión,	f.
caution	precaución,	f.•	compulsion	compulsión,	f.
celebration	celebración,	f.	compunction	compunción,	f.
centralization	centralización,	f.	computation	computación,	f.
centurion	centurión,	m.	concentration	concentración,	f.
certification	certificación,	f.	conception (PHYS)	concepción,	f.
cessation	cesación,	f.	*conception (idea)	concepto,	m.•
cession	cesión,	f.	concession	concesión,	f.
champion	campeón,	m.•	conciliation	conciliación,	f.
chlorination	cloración,	f.•	conclusion	conclusión,	f.
circulation	circulación,	f.	concoction	fabricación,	f.•
circumlocution	circunlocución,	f.	concussion	concusión,	f.
citation	citación,	f.	condemnation	condenación,	f.
civilization	civilización,	f.	condensation	condensación,	f.
clarification	clarificación,	f.	condescension	condescendencia,	f.•
classification	clasificación,	f.	*condition	condición,	f.
coagulation	coagulación,	f.	condonation	condonación,	f.

ENGLISH	SPANISH	ENGLISH	SPANISH
conduction	conducción, f.	conversion	conversión, f.
*confection	dulce, confección, f.	*conviction (crime)	condena, f.
confederation	confederación, f.	conviction (feeling)	convicción, f.
confession	confesión, f.	convocation	convocación, f.
configuration	configuración, f.	convulsion	convulsión, f.
confirmation	confirmación, f.	cooperation	cooperación, f.
confiscation	confiscación, f.	coordination	coordinación, f.
conflagration	conflagración, f.	coronation	coronación, f.
conformation	conformación, f.	corporation	corporación, f.
confrontation	confrontación, f.	corporation	sociedad anónima, f.•
confusion	confusión, f.	correction	corrección, f.
congestion	congestión, f.	correlation	correlación, f.
conglomeration	conglomeración, f.	corroboration	corroboración, f.
congratulation	congratulación, f.	corrosion	corrosión, f.
	felicitación, f.•	corrugation	corrugación, f.
*congregation	congregación, f.	corruption	corrupción, f.
congregation (REL)	feligreses, m.•	creation	creación, f.
conjugation	conjugación, f.	cremation	cremación, f.
conjunction	conjunción, f.	criterion	criterio, m.•
connection (MECH)	conexión, f.	crucifixion	crucifixión, f.
connotation	connotación, f.	culmination	culminación, f.
conscription	conscripción, f.	cultivation	cultivación, f.
consecration	consagración, f.	cushion	cojín, m.; almohada, f.•
conservation	conservación, f.	damnation	damnación, m.
consideration	consideración, f.	dandelion	diente de león, m.•
*consolation	consuelo, m.•	deactivation	desactivación, f.
consolation	consolación, f.	debarkation	desembarco, m.•
consolidation	consolidación, f.	decapitation	decapitación, f.
constellation	constelación, f.	*deception	engaño, m.; decepción, f.
consternation	consternación, f.	decimation	pérdida, f.•
*constipation	estreñimiento, m.•	decision	decisión, f.
constitution	constitución, f.	declaration	declaración, f.
constriction	constricción, f.	declination	declinación, f.
construction	construcción, f.	decomposition	descomposición, f.
consultation	consultación, f.	decompression	descompresión, f.
consummation	consumación, f.	decoration	decoración, f.
consumption (MED)	consunción, f.	dedication	dedicación, f.
*consumption (use)	consumo, m.•	deduction	deducción, f.
contagion	contagio, m.•	defamation	difamación, f.
contamination	contaminación, f.	defecation	defecación, f.
contemplation	contemplación, f.	defection	defección, f.
contention	contención, f.	definition	definición, f.
continuation	continuación, f.	deflation	deflación, f.
contortion	contorsión, f.	deflection	deflección, f.
contraception	contracepción, f.	deformation	deformación, f.
contraction	contracción, f.	degeneration	degeneración, f.
contradiction	contradicción, f.	degradation	degradación, f.
contravention	contravención, f.	dehydration	deshidratación, f.
contribution	contribución, f.	deification	deificación, f.
contrition	contrición, f.	dejection	melancolía, f.•
contusion	contusión, f.	delegation	delegación, f.
convection	convección, f.	deletion	borradura, f.•
convention	convención, f.	deliberation	deliberación, f.
convention	pacto, m.; alianza, f.•	delineation	delineación, f.
conversation	conversación, f.	delusion	engaño, m.; ilusión, f.•

ENGLISH	SPANISH	ENGLISH	SPANISH
demarcation	demarcación, f.	digression	digresión, f.
demolition	demolición, f.	dilation	dilatación, f.
demonstration	demostración, f.	dilution	dilución, f.
demonstration	manifestación, f.•	dimension	dimensión, f.
demoralization	desmoralización, f.	diminution	disminución, f.
demotion	desgradación, f.•	*direction	dirección, f.
denomination	denominación, f.	disaffection	desafección, f.
denotation	denotación, f.	disaffiliation	desafiliación, f.
denunciation	denunciación, f.	disconsolation	desconsolación, f.
deodorization	desodorización, f.	discretion	discreción, f.
depletion (MED)	depleción, f.	discrimination	discriminación, f.
*depletion (COM)	disminución, f.•	discussion	discusión, f.
*deportation	deportación, f.	disembarkation	desembarco, m.•
deposition	deposición, f.	disfiguration	desfiguración, f.
depravation	depravación, f.	disillusion	disilusión, f.
deprecation	deprecación, f.	disinclination	desinclinación, f.
*depreciation	depreciación, f.	disinfection	desinfección. f.
depredation	depredación, f.	disintegration	desintegración, f.
depression (hole)	depresión, f.	dislocation	dislocación, f.
*depression (mind)	abatimiento, m.•	disorientation	desorientación, f.
deprivation	deprivación, f.	dispensation	dispensación, f.
depuration	depuración, f.	dispersion	dispersión, f.
deputation	diputación, f.	disposition	disposición, f.
dereliction	abandono, m.•	disposition (temper)	genio, m.•
derision	irrisión, f.•	dispossession	deposeimiento, m.•
derivation	derivación, f.	disruption	perturbación, f.•
derogation	derogación, f.	dissatisfaction	descontento, m.•
descension	descensión, f.	dissection	disección, f.
description	descripción, f.	dissemination	diseminación, f.
desecration	profanación, f.•	dissension	disensión, f.
desegregation	desegregación, f.	dissertation	disertación, f.
desertion	deserción, f.	dissimulation	disimulación, f.
designation	designación, f.	dissipation	disipación, f.
desolation	desolación, f.	dissociation	disociación, f.
desperation	desesperación, f.	dissolution	disolución, f.
destination	destino, m.•	dissuasion	disuasión, f.
*destination	destinación, f.	distillation	destilación, f.
destitution	destitución, f.	distinction	distinción, f.
destruction	destrucción, f.	distortion	distorsión, f.
detection	detección, f.	distraction	distracción, f.
detention	detención, f.	distribution	distribución, f.
deterioration	deterioración, f.	diversification	diversificación, f.
determination	determinación, f.	diversion	diversión, f.
detestation	detestación, f.	divination	divinación, f.
detonation	detonación, f.	division	división, f.
detraction	detracción, f.	documentation	documentación, f.
devaluation	devaluación, f.	domestication	domesticación, f.
devastation	devastación, f.	domination	dominación, f.
deviation	desviación, f.	dominion	dominio, m.•
devotion	devoción, f.	donation	donación, f.
dictation	dictado, m.•	dramatization	dramatización, f.
diction	dicción, f.	duplication	duplicación, f.
differentiation	diferenciación, f.	duration	duración, f.
diffusion	difusión, f.	ebullition	ebulición, f.
digestion	digestión, f.	economization	economización, f.

127

ENGLISH	SPANISH	ENGLISH	SPANISH
edification	edificación, f.	examination (test)	examen, m. •
edition	edición, f.	exasperation	exasperación, f.
*education	educación, f.	excavation	excavación, f.
effusion	efusión, f.	exception	excepción, f.
ejaculation	eyaculación, f.	excitation	excitación, f.
ejection	eyección, f.	exclamation	exclamación, f.
*elaboration	elaboración, f.	exclusion	exclusión, f.
elation	elación, f.	excommunication	excomunión, f. •
election	elección, f.	excretion	excreción, f.
electrocution	electrocución, f.	excursion	excursión, f.
elevation	elevación, f.	execution	ejecución, f.
elimination	eliminación, f.	exemption	exención, f.
elision	elisión, f.	exertion	ejercicio, m. •
elocution	elocución, f.	exhalation	exhalación, f.
elongation (MED)	elongación, f.	exhaustion	agotamiento, m. •
elongation	extensión, f. •	exhibition	exhibición, f.
elucidation	elucidación, f.	exhilaration	alegría, f. •
emancipation	emancipación, f.	exhortation	exhortación, f.
emasculation	emasculación, f.	exhumation	exhumación, f.
embarkation (cargo)	embarque, m. •	exoneration	exoneración, f.
embarkation (people)	embarco, m. •	expansion	expansión, f.
emersion	emersión, f.	*expectation	expectación, f.
emigration	emigración, f.	expedition	expedición, f.
emission	emisión, f.	experimentation	experimentación, f.
emotion	emoción, f.	expiation	expiación, f.
emulation	emulación, f.	expiration	expiración, f.
emulsion	emulsión, f.	explanation	explicación, f. •
enervation	enervación, f.	explication	explicación, f.
enumeration	enumeración, f	exploitation	explotación, f.
enunciation	enunciación, f.	exploration	exploración, f.
equalization	igualación, f. •	explosion	explosión, f.
equation	ecuación, f.	exportation	exportación, f.
equivocation	equivocación, f.	exposition	exposición, f.
eradication	erradicación, f.	expression	expresión, f.
erection	erección, f.	expropriation	expropiación, f.
erosion	erosión, f.	expulsion	expulsión, f.
erudition	erudición, f.	expurgation	expurgación, f.
eruption	erupción, f.	extension	extensión, f.
escalation	escalada, f. •	extenuation	extenuación, f.
*estimation	estimación, f.	extermination	exterminio, m. •
estimation	valoración, f.	extinction	extinción, f.
evacuation	evacuación, f.	extirpation	extirpación, f.
evaluation	evaluación, f.	extortion	extorsión, f.
evangelization	evangelización, f.	extraction	extracción, f.
evaporation	evaporación, f.	extradition	extradición, f.
evasion	evasión, f.	extrapolation	extrapolación, f.
eviction	evicción, f.	extrusion	extrusión, f.
evocation	evocación, f.	exultation	exultación, f.
evolution	evolución, f.	fabrication	fabricación, f.
evulsion	evulsión, f.	facilitation	facilitación, f.
exacerbation	exacerbación, f.	faction	facción, f.
exaggeration	exageración, f.	falsification	falsificación, f.
exaltation	exaltación, f.	familiarization	familiarización, f.

ENGLISH	SPANISH	ENGLISH	SPANISH
fascination	fascinación, f.	hypertension	hipertensión, f.
fashion (style)	moda, f.•	hypnotization	hipnotización, f.
federalization	federalización, f.	idealization	idealización, f.
federation	federación, f.	identification	identificación, f.
felicitation	felicitación, f.	ignition	ignición, f.
fermentation	fermentación, f.	illumination	iluminación, f.
fertilization	fertilización, f.	illusion	ilusión, f.
fiction	novela, ficción, f.	illustration (example)	ejemplo, m.•
filtration	filtración, f.	illustration (sketch)	estampa, f.•
fission	fisión, f.	illustration	ilustración, f.
fixation	fijación, f.	imagination	imaginación, f.
flection,flexion	flexión, f.	imitation	imitación, f.
flirtation	flirteo, m.•	immersion	inmersión, f.
flotation	flotación, f.	immigration	inmigración, f.
fluctuation	fluctuación, f.	immolation	inmolación, f.
fluoridation	fluorización, f.	immunization	inmunización, f.
formalization	formalización, f.	impaction	impacción, f.
formation	formación, f.	impartation	impartación, f.
formulation	formulación, f.	imperfection	imperfección, f.
fornication	fornicación, f.	impersonation	imitación, f.•
fortification	fortificación, f.	implantation	implantación, f.
*foundation	fundación, f.	implementation	ejecución, f.•
foundation (bldg)	fundamento, m.•	implication	implicación, f.
fraction	fracción, f.	importation	importación, f.
fragmentation	frangmentación, f.	imposition	imposición, f.
fraternization	fraternización, f.	imprecation	imprecación, f.
*friction	fricción, f.	imprecision	imprecisión, f.
fruition	fruición, f.	impregnation	impregnación, f.
frustration	frustración, f.	impression	impresión, f.
fumigation	fumigación, f.	improvisation	improvisación, f.
function	función, f.	impulsion	impulsión, f.
fusion	fusión, f.	imputation	imputación, f.
generalization	generalización, f.	inaction	inacción, f.
generation	generación, f.	inactivation	inactivación, f.
genuflection	genuflexión, f.	inauguration	inauguración, f.
germination	germinación, f.	incantation	encantamiento, m.•
gestation	gestación, f.	incapacitation	incapacitación, f.
gesticulation	gesticulación, f.	incarceration	encarcelación, f.
glorification	glorificación, f.	incarnation	encarnación, f.
gradation	gradación, f.	inception	principio, m.•
graduation	graduación, f.	incision	incisión, f.
granulation	granulación, f.	inclination	inclinación, f.
*gratification	gratificación, f.	inclusion	inclusión, f.
gravitation	gravitación, f.	incorporation	incorporación, f.
gyration	giro, m.•	incrimination	incriminación, f.•
habitation	habitación, f.	incrustation	incrustación, f.
hallucination	alucinación, f.	incubation	incubación, f.
harmonization	harmonización, f.	inculcation	inculcación, f.
hesitation	hesitación, f.	incursion	incursión, f.
hibernation	hibernación, f.	indecision	indecisión, f.
homogenization	homogeneización, f.	indemnification	indemnización, f.•
hospitalization	hospitalización, f.	indentation	sangría, f.•
humiliation	humillación, f.	indication	indicación, f.

129

ENGLISH	SPANISH		ENGLISH	SPANISH	
indigestion	indigestión,	f.	interrelation	correlación,	f.•
indignation	indignación,	f.	interrogation	interrogación,	f.
indirection	tortuosidad,	f.•	interruption	interrupción,	f.
indiscretion	indiscreción,	f.	intersection	intersección,	f.
indisposition	indisposición,	f.	intervention	intervención,	f.
induction	inducción,	f.	*intimation	intimación,	f.
inebriation	ebriedad,	f.•	intimidation	intimidación,	f.
infatuation	infatuación,	f.	intonation	entonación,	f.
infection	infección,	f.	intoxication(MED)	intoxicación,	f.
infestation	infestación,	f.	*intoxication(drunk)	embriaguez,	f.•
infiltration	infiltración,	f.	introduction	introducción,	f.
inflammation	inflamación,	f.	*introduction	presentación,	f.•
inflation	inflación,	f.	introspection	introspección,	f.
inflection	inflexión,	f.	intrusion	intrusión,	f.
information(know)	información,	f.	intuition	intuición,	f.
*information (news)	noticias,	f.•	inundation	inundación,	f.
infraction	infracción,	f.	invalidation	invalidación,	f.
infuriation	enfurecimiento,	m.•	invasion	invasión,	f.
infusion	infusión,	f.	invention	invención,	f.
ingestion	ingestión,	f.	*inversion	inversión,	f.
inhalation	inhalación,	f.	investigation	investigación,	f.
inhibition	inhibición,	f.	invigoration	vigorización,	f.
initiation	iniciación,	f.	invitation	invitación,	f.
injection	inyección,	f.	invocation	invocación,	f.
injunction	mandato,	m.•	involution	involución,	f.
innovation	innovación,	f.	ionization	ionización,	f.
inoculation	inoculación,	f.	irradiation	irradiación,	f.
inquisition	inquisición,	f.	irresolution	irresolución,	f.
inscription	inscripción,	f.	irrigation (MED)	irrigación,	f.
insemination	inseminación,	f.	irrigation	riego,	m.•
insertion	inserción,	f.	irritation	irritación,	f.
insinuation	insinuación,	f.	irruption	irrupción,	f.
inspection	inspección,	f.	isolation	aislamiento,	m.•
inspiration	inspiración,	f.	itemization	especificación,	f.•
installation	instalación,	f.	*jubilation	júbilo,	m.•
instigation	instigación,	f.	junction	unión,	f.•
instillation	instilación,	f.	jurisdiction	jurisdicción,	f.
institution	institución,	f.	justification	justificación,	f.
instruction	instrucción,	f.	juxtaposition	yuxtaposición,	f.•
insulation	aislamiento,	m.•	laceration	laceración,	f.
insurrection	insurrección,	f.	lamentation	lamentación,	f.
integration	integración,	f.	lamination	laminación,	f.
intention	intención,	f.	legation	legación,	f.
interaction	interacción,	f.	legion	legión,	f.
interception	interceptación,	f.	legislation	legislación,	f.
intercession	intercesión,	f.	lesion	lesión,	f.
interjection	interjección,	f.	levitation	levitación,	f.
interlineation	interlineación,	f.	libation	libación,	f.
intermission	intermisión,	f.	liberalization	liberalización,	f.
intermutation	intermutación,	f.	liberation	liberación,	f.
interpellation	interpelación,	f.	limitation	limitación,	f.
interpolation	interpolación,	f.	liquidation	liquidación,	f.
interpretation	interpretación,	f.	litigation	litigación,	f.

ENGLISH	SPANISH	ENGLISH	SPANISH
localization	localización, f.	nomination	nominación, f.
*location	colocation, f.•	*nomination	nombramiento, m.•
locomotion	locomoción, f.	normalization	normalización, f.
lotion	loción, f.	notation	anotación, f.
lubrication	lubricación, f.	notification	notificación, f.
magnification	magnificación, f.	notion	noción, f.
malediction	maldición, f.	novation	novación, f.
malformation	malformación, f.	nullification	anulación, f.•
malnutrition	desnutrición, f.	nutrition	nutrición, f.
manifestation	manifestación, f.	obfuscation	ofuscación, f.
manipulation	manipulación, f.	objection	objeción, f.
mansion	mansión, f.	obligation	obligación, f.
mastication	masticación, f.	*obliteration(MED)	obliteración, f.
masturbation	masturbación, f.	obliteration	borradura, f.•
matriculation	matriculación, f.	oblivion	olvido, m.•
maturation	maduración, f.	observation	observación, f.
mechanization	mecanización, f.	obsession	obsesión, f.
mediation	mediación, f.	obstruction	obstrucción, f.
medication	medicación, f.	*occasion	ocasión, f.
meditation	meditación, f.	occlusion	oclusión, f.
memorization	memorización, f.	occupation	ocupación, f.
menstruation	menstruación, f.	omission	omisión, f.
mention	mención, f.	ondulation	ondulación, f.
migration	migración, f.	onion	cebolla, f.•
militarization	militarización, f.	operation	operación, f.
mission	misión, f.	*operation	funcionamiento, m.•
mitigation	mitigación, f.	opinion	opinión, f.
mobilization	movilización, f.	opposition	oposición, f.
moderation	moderación, f.	oppression	opresión, f.
modernization	modernización, f.	option	opción, f.
modification	modificación, f.	*oration	oración, f.
modulation	modulación, f.	orchestration	orquestación, f.
molestation	molestia, f.•	ordination	ordenación, f.
mollification	molificación, f.	organization	organización, f.
monopolization	monopolización, f.	orientation	orientación, f.
moralization	moralización, f.	origination	origen, m.•
mortification	mortificación, f.	ornamentation	ornamentación, f.
motion (movement)	movimiento, m.•	oscillation	oscilación, f.
motion (proposal)	moción, f.	ossification	osificación, f.
motivation	motivación, f.	ostentation	ostentación, f.
multiplication	multiplicación, f.	ovation	ovación, f.
mummification	momificación, f.	oxidation	oxidación, f.
munition	munición, f.	pacification	pacificación, f.
mutation	mutación, f.	pagination	paginación, f.
mutilation	mutilación, f.	palpitation	palpitación, f.
mystification	mistificación, f.	paralyzation	paralización, f.
narration	narración, f.	participation	participación, f.
nation	nación, f.	partition	partición, f.
naturalization	naturalización, f.	passion	pasión, f.
navigation	navegación, f.	pasteurization	pasteurización, f.
negation	negación, f.	penalization	penalización, f.
negotiation	negociación, f.	penetration	penetración, f.
neutralization	neutralización, f.	pension	pensión, f.

ENGLISH	SPANISH	ENGLISH	SPANISH
perception	percepción, f.	prescription	prescripción, f.
percussion	percusión, f.	*prescription	receta, f.•
perdition	perdición, f.	presentation	presentación, f.
perfection	perfección, f.	preservation	preservación, f.
perforation	perforación, f.	pression	presión, f.
perfusion (MED)	perfusión, f.	presumption	presunción, f.
*perfusion	aspersión, f.•	presupposition	presuposición, f.
permission	permiso, m.•	*pretension	pretensión, f.
peroration	peroración, f.	prevarication	prevaricación, f.
perpetration	perpetración, f.	prevention	prevención, f.
perpetuation	perpetuación, f.	prevision	previsión, f.
*persecution	persecución, f.	privation	privación, f.
personalization	personalización, f.	probation	probación, f.
personification	personificación, f.	procession	procesión, f.
perspiration	sudor, m.•	proclamation	proclamación, f.
persuasion	persuasión, f.	procrastination	dilación, f.•
perturbation	perturbación, f.	procreation	procreación, f.
perversion	perversión, f.	production	producción, f.
petition	petición, f.	profession	profesión, f.
petrification	petrificación, f.	profusion	profusión, f.
pigmentation	pigmentación, f.	prognostication	pronosticación, f.
pinion	piñón, m.•	progression	progresión, f.
plantation	plantación, f.	prohibition	prohibición, f.
polarization	polarización, f.	projection	proyección, f.
*pollution	contaminación, f.•	proliferation	proliferación, f.
pollution (MED)	polución, f.	prolongation	prolongación, f.
polymerization	polimerización, f.	*promotion	promoción, f.
pontification	pontificación, f.	*promotion (job)	ascenso, m.•
popularization	popularización, f.	promulgation	promulgación, f.
population	población, f.	pronunciation	pronunciación, f.
portion	porción, f.	propagation	propagación, f.
position	posición, f.	propitiation	propiciación, f.
possession	posesión, f.	proportion	proporción, f.
potion	poción, f.	proposition	proposición, f.
precaution	precaución, f.	propulsion	propulsión, f.
precipitation	precipitación, f.	proscription	proscripción, f.
*precision	precisión, f.	prosecution	prosecución, f.
preclusion	prevención, f.•	prostitution	prostitución, f.
preconception	preconcepción, f.	prostration	postración, f.
precondition	precondición, f.	protection	protección, f.
predestination	predestinación, f.	protestation	protestación, f.
predication	predicación, f.	protrusion	protrusión, f.
prediction	predicción, f.	provision	provisión, f.
predilection	predilección, f.	provocation	provocación, f.
predisposition	predisposición, f.	publication	publicación, f.
predomination	predominación, f.	pulsation	pulsación, f.
preemption	prioridad, f.•	pulverization	pulverización, f.
prefabrication	prefabricación, f.	punctuation	puntuación, f.
premeditation	premeditación, f.	purgation	purgación, f.
premonition	premonición, f.	purification	purificación, f.
preoccupation	preocupación, f.	putrefaction	putrefacción, f.
*preparation	preparación, f.	qualification	calificación, f.
preposition	preposición, f.	*question	pregunta, cuestión, f.

ENGLISH	SPANISH	ENGLISH	SPANISH
*quotation (price)	cotización, f.•	rejection	repudio, rechazo, m.•
quotation (citation)	citación, f.•	rejuvenation	rejuvenecimiento, m.•
radiation	radiación, f.	relation	relación, f.
ramification	ramificación, f.	*relation (relative)	pariente, m.•
ratification	ratificación, f.	relaxation	relajación, f.
ration	ración, f.	relegation	relegación, f.
reaction	reacción, f.	religion	religión, f.
reactivation	reactivación, f.	remission	remisión, f.
reaffirmation	reafirmación, f.	remonstration	protesta, f.•
realization	realización, f.	remuneration	remuneración, f.
rebellion	rebelión, f.	rendition	rendición, f.
recalculation	recalculación, f.	renegotiation	renegociación, f.
recapitulation	recapitulación, f.	renovation	renovación, f.
reception	recepción, f.	renumeration	renumeración, f.
recession	recesión, f.	renunciation	renunciación, f.
reciprocation	reciprocación, f.	reorganization	reorganización, f.
recision	rescisión, f.	reorientation	reorientación, f.
recitation	recitación, f.	reparation	reparación, f.
reclamation	reclamación, f.	repercussion	repercusión, f.
recognition	reconocimiento, m.•	repetition	repetición, f.
*recollection	recuerdo, m.•	repletion	repleción, f.
recommendation	recomendación, f.	replication	réplica, f.•
reconciliation	reconciliación, f.	representation	representación, f.
reconstruction	reconstrucción, f.	repression	represión, f.
reconversion	reconversión, f.	reprobation	reprobación, f.
recreation	recreación, f.	reproduction	reproducción, f.
recreation (play)	recreo, m.•	repudiation	repudiación, f.
recrimination	recriminación, f.	repulsion	repulsión, f.
rectification	rectificación, f.	reputation	reputación, f.
recuperation	recuperación, f.	requisition	requisición, f.
redaction	redacción, f.	rescission	rescisión, f.
redemption	redención, f.	reservation	reservación, f.
reduction	reducción, f.	*resignation (job)	renuncia, f.•
reelection	reelección, f.	resignation	resignación, f.
reevaluation	reevaluación, f.	resolution	resolución, f.
reexamination	reexaminación, f.	respiration	respiración, f.
*reflection (thought)	reflexión, f.	restitution	restitución, f.
*reflection (image)	reflejo, m.•	restoration	restauración, f.
reformation	reformación, f.	restriction	restricción, f.
reformulation	reformulación, f.	resumption	reasunción, f.
refraction	refracción, f.	resurrection	resurrección, f.
refrigeration	refrigeración, f.	resuscitation	resuscitación, f.
refutation	refutación, f.	retaliation	represalia, f.•
regeneration	regeneración, f.	retardation	retardación, f.
regimentation	regimentación, f.	retention	retención, f.
region	región, f.	retraction	retracción, f.
registration	registro, m.•	retribution	retribución, f.
regression	regresión, f.	retrovision	retrovisión, f.
regularization	regularización, f.	reunification	reunificación, f.
regulation	regla, regulación, f.	reunion	reunión, f.
regurgitation	regurgitación, f.	revaluation	revaluación, f.
rehabilitation	rehabilitación, f.	revelation	revelación, f.
reincarnation	reencarnación, f.	reverberation	reverberación, f.
reiteration	reiteración, f.	reversion	reversión, f.

133

ENGLISH	SPANISH	ENGLISH	SPANISH
revision	revisión, f.	stupefaction	estupefacción, f.
revitalization	revitalización, f.	stylization	estilización, f.
revivification	revivificación, f.	subdivision	subdivisión, f.
revocation	revocación, f.	subjection	sujeción, f.
revolution	revolución, f.	subjugation	subyugación, f.
revulsion	repugnancia, f.•	sublimation	sublimación, f.
*revulsion (MED)	revulsión, f.	submersion	sumersión, f.
rotation	rotación, f.	submission	submisión, f.
ruination	ruina, f.•	subordination	subordinación, f.
salutation	salutación, f.	subrogation	subrogación, f.
salvation	salvación, f.	subscription	subscripción, f.
sanctification	santificación, f.	*substantiation	justificación, f.•
sanction	sanción, f.	substitution	substitución, f.
sanitation	saneamiento, m.•	subtraction	substracción, f.
satisfaction	satisfacción, f.	subvention	subvención, f.
saturation	saturación, f.	subversion	subversión, f.
scorpion	escorpión, m.	succession	sucesión, f.
secession	secesión, f.	suction	succión, f.
secretion	secreción, f.	suffocation	sofocación, f.
section	sección, f.	suggestion(PSYCH)	sugestión, f.
sedation	sedación, f.	*suggestion	sugerencia, f.•
sedimentation	sedimentación, f.	summarization	sumario, m.•
sedition	sedición, f.	summation	suma, f.•
seduction	seducción, f.	superstition	superstición, f.
segmentation	segmentación, f.	supervention	supervención, f.
segregation	segregación, f.	supervision	supervisión, f.
selection	selección, f.	supplantation	suplantación, f.
sensation	sensación, f.	supplementation	suplementación, f.
sensitization	sensitización, f.	supplication	suplicación, f.
separation	separación, f.	supposition	suposición, f.
sequestration	secuestración, f.	suppression	supresión, f.
session	sesión, f.	suspension	suspensión, f.
signification	significación, f.	suspicion	sospecha, f.•
simplification	simplificación, f.	sterilization	esterilización, f.
simulation	simulación, f.	synchronization	sincronización, f.
situation	situación, f.	syndication	sindicación, f.
socialization	socialización, f.	tabulation	tabulación, f.
solicitation	solicitación, f.	taxation	impuestos, m.•
solidification	solidificación, f.	television	televisión, f.
solution	solución, f.	temptation	tentación, f.
sophistication	sofisticación, f.	tension (physical)	tensión, f.
specialization	especialización, f.	tension (emotion)	ansiedad, f.•
specification	especificación, f.	termination	terminación, f.
speculation	especulación, f.	toleration	tolerancia, f.•
stabilization	estabilización, f.	torsion	torsión, f.
stagnation	estancación, f.•	traction	tracción, f.
standardization	uniformación, f.•	tradition	tradición, f.
starvation	hambre, f.•	transaction	transacción, f.
station	estación, f.	transcription	transcripción, f.
sterilization	esterilización, f.	transformation	transformación, f.
stimulation	estimulación, f.	transfusion	transfusión, f.
stipulation	estipulación, f.	transgression	transgresión, f.
strangulation	estrangulación, f.	transition	transición, f.
stratification	estratificación, f.	translation	traslación, f.
			traducción, f.

ENGLISH	SPANISH	ENGLISH	SPANISH
transmission	transmisión, f.	vegetation	vegetación, f.
transmutation	transmutación, f.	veneration	veneración, f.
transpiration	transpiración, f.	ventilation	ventilación, f.
transplantation	trasplante, m.•	verbalization	verbalización, f.
transportation	transportación, f.	verification	verificación, f.
transposition	transposición, f.	version	versión, f.
trepidation	trepidación, f.	vesication (MED)	vesicación, f.
triangulation	triangulación, f.	vexation	enfado, m.;vejación, f.
tribulation	tribulación, f.	vibration	vibración, f.
ulceration	ulceración, f.	victimization	victimación, f.•
unction	unción, f.	vilification	difamación, f.•
undulation	ondulación, f.	vindication	vindicación, f.
unification	unificación, f.	violation	violación, f.
union	unión, f.	vision	vista, visión, f.
union (labor)	sindicato, m.•	vision (foresight)	previsión, f.
unionization	sindicalización, f.•	visitation	visitación, f.
urbanization	urbanización, f.	visualization	visualización, f.•
urination	urinación, f.	vitalization	vitalización, f.
usurpation	usurpación, f.	vitiation	corrupción, f.•
utilization	utilización, f.	vituperation	vituperación, f.
vacation	(plur) vacación, f.	vivisection	vivisección, f.
vaccination	vacunación, f.•	vocalization	vocalización, f.
vacillation	vacilación, f.	vocation	vocación, f.
validation	validación, f.	volition	volición, f.
valuation	valuación, f.	vulcanization	volcanización. f.
vaporization	vaporización, f.	vulgarization	vulgarización, f.
variation	variación, f.	Zion	Sión, f.

NOUNS: **English -oon = Spanish -ón.**   **60%: 20 Listed**

<u>Gender</u>: Most are masculine in Spanish.

ENGLISH	SPANISH	ENGLISH	SPANISH
baboon	babuino, m.•	macaroon	macarrón, m.
balloon	globo, balón, m.	maroon	rojo obscuro, m.•
bassoon	bajón, m.	monsoon	monzón, m.
buffoon	bufón, m.	octoroon	ochavón, m.
*cartoon	caricatura, f.•	platoon	pelotón, m.
cocoon	capullo, m.•	pontoon	pontón, m.
doubloon	doblón, m.	raccoon	mapache, m.•
dragoon	dragón, m.	saloon	salón, m.
harpoon	arpón, m.	tycoon	taicún, m.•
lagoon	laguna, f.•	typhoon	tifón, m.

NOUNS: **English -tron = Spanish -trón.**   **99%: 6 Listed**

<u>Gender</u>: All are masculine in Spanish.

ENGLISH	SPANISH	ENGLISH	SPANISH
cyclotron	ciclotrón, m.	neutron	neutrón, m.
dynatron	dinatrón, m.	photoelectron	fotoelectrón, m.
electron	electrón, m.	positron	positrón, m.

NOUNS: English *-on* other than *-gon, -ion, -oon* and *-tron*
= Spanish *-ón, -no(a)* or *-onte*.   80%: 160 Listed

<u>Gender</u>: Most are masculine in Spanish.

ENGLISH	SPANISH	ENGLISH	SPANISH
abandon	abandono, m.	dacron	dacrón, m.
aileron	alerón, m.	deacon	diácono, m.
Amazon	amazona, f.	decathlon	decatlón, m.
Anglo-Saxon	anglosajón, m.	demon	demonio, m.•
apron	delantal, m.•	don	don, m.
argon (CHEM)	argón, m.	dragon	dragón, m.
Armageddon	Armagedón, m.	dungeon	calaboza, f.•
arson	incendio, m.•	echelon	escalón, m.
bacon	tocino, m.•	eon	eón, m.
badminton	badminton, m.	epsilon	épsilon, m.
baron	barón, m.	falcon	halcón, m.
baton	bastón, m.	*felon	felón, m.
beacon	faro, m.•	galleon	galeón, m.
bison	bisonte, m.	gallon	galón, m.
blazon	blasón, m.	garrison	guarnición, f.•
bludgeon	cachipora, f.•	gibbon (ZOOL)	gibón, m.
bonbon	bombón, m.	gibson	gibson, m.
Boston	Boston, m.	glutton	glotón, m.
bouillon	caldo, m.•	guidon	guión, m.
bourbon	borbón, m.	halcyon	alción, m.
Briton	britano, m.	heron	garza, f.•
button	botón, m.	horizon	horizonte, m.
caisson	cajón, m.	hydrocarbon	hidrocarburo, m.•
caldron	calderón, m.	icon	icono, m.
*cannon	cañón, m.	ion	ion, m.
*canon (LAW)	canon, m.	iron (metal)	hierro, m.•
canton	cantón, m.	iron (flat)	plancha, f.•
canyon	cañón, m.	jargon	jerga, f.•
capon	capón, m.	kiloton	kilotón, m.
*carbon	carbono, carbón, m.	lemon	limón, m.
carillon	carillón, m.	lesson	lección, f.
carton	caja, f., cartón, m.	lexicon	lexicón, m.
chameleon	camaleón, m.	liaison	vinculación, f.•
*chaperon	chaperona, f.	luncheon	almuerzo, m.•
chevron	galón, cheurón, m.	mammon	mammón, m.
chiffon	chifón, m.	marathon	maratón, m.
cinnamon	canelo, m.•	*mason	albañil, m.•
citron	cidro, m.•	mason (freemason)	masón, m.
colon (ANAT)	colon, m.	mastodon	mastodonte, m.
*colon (GRAM)	dos puntos, m.•	matron	matrona, f.
comparison	comparación, f.	megaton	megatón, m.
cordon	cordón, m.	melodeon (MUS)	melodión, m.
cotillon	cotillón, m.	melon	melón, m.
cotton	algodón, m.•	methadon	metadona, f.
cotyledon	cotiledón, m.	micron	micrón, m.
coupon	taló, cupón, m.	Mormon	mormón, m.
crayon	lápiz, creyón, m.	moron	morón, m.
crimson	carmesí, m.•	mutton	carne de carnero, f.•

ENGLISH	SPANISH	ENGLISH	SPANISH
Napoleon	Napoleón, m.	salmon	salmón, m.
neon	neón, m.	salon	salón, m.
neuron	neurona, f.	Samson	Samsón, m.
nylon	nilón, m.	Saxon	sajón, m.
orlon	orlón, m.	season (spice)	sazón, m.
orthicon	orticón, m.	*season (year)	estación, f.•
oxymoron	oxímoron, m.	semicolon	punto y coma, m.•
pantheon	panteón, m.	sermon	sermón, m.
pardon	perdón, m.•	sexton	sacristán, m.•
parson	clérgico, pastor, m.•	silicon	silicio, m.•
Parthenon	Partenón, m.	simpleton	simplón, m.
*patron	patrón, m.	si(y)phon	sifón, m.
pentagon	pentágono, m.	skeleton	esqueleto, m.•
peon	peón, m.	squadron	escuadrón, m.
person	tipo, m., persona, f.	sturgeon	esturión, m.
phenomenon	fenómeno, m.	surgeon	cirujano, m.•
photon	fotón, m.	*talon (claw)	talón, m.
pigeon(dove)	paloma,f,pichón, m.	tampon	tampón, m.
piston	pistón, m.	tarpon (fish)	tarpón, m.
piton (tool)	pitón, m.	teflon	teflón, m.
plankton	plancton, m.	tendon	tendón, m.
poison	veneno, m.•	Teuton	teutón, m.
pompon	pompón, m.	thoron	torón, m.
prison	carcel,m; prisión, f.	treason	traición, f.
proton	protón, m.	triton	tritón, m.
pylon	pilón, m.	unison	unisón, m.
python	pitón, m.	venison	carne de venado, f.•
radon	radón, m.	wagon	carro,m; carreta, f.•
rayon	rayón, m.	weapon	arma, f.•
reason	causa, razón, f.	Yukon	Yukón, m.
rhododendron	rododendro, m.•	Zion	Sión, m.
ribbon	listón,m.; cinta, f.•	zircon	zircón, m.

NOUNS: English *-o* other than *-oo* = Spanish *-o*.

85%: 190 Listed

Gender: Almost all are masculine in Spanish.

ENGLISH	SPANISH	ENGLISH	SPANISH
adagio	adagio, m.	*auto	auto, m.
aficionado	aficionado, m.	autogyro	autogiro, m.
agio	agio, m.	avocado	aguacate, m.•
Alamo	Alamo, m.	banjo	banjo, m.
albino	albino, m.	basso	bajo, m.•
allegro	alegro, m.	bingo	bingo, m.
alter-ego	alter ego, m.	bolero	bolero, m.
*alto	contralto, m.	bolo	bolo, m.
antipasto	entremés, m.•	bongo	bongó, m.
Apollo	Apolo, m.	*bozo	tipo, m.•
archipelago	archipiélago, m.	braggadocio	fanfarrón, m.•
armadillo	armadillo, m.	bravado	bravata, f.•
audio	audio, m.	buffalo	bisonte, búfalo, m.

137

ENGLISH	SPANISH	ENGLISH	SPANISH
burro	burro, m.	hobo	vagabundo, m.•
cacao	cacao, m.	homo	homo, m.
Cairo	Cairo, m.	imbroglio	embrollo, m.
calico	calicó, m.	impetigo	impétigo, m.
calypso	calipso, m.	impresario	empresario, m.
cameo	camafeo, m.•	indigo	índigo, m.
canto	canto, m.	inferno	infierno, m.
carabao	carabao, m.	innuendo	insinuación, f.•
*cargo	cargamento, carga, f.•	intermezzo	intermezzo, m.
casino	casino, m.	ipso	ipso, m.
cello	violoncelo, m.•	judo	judo, m.
centavo	centavo, m.	kilo	kilo, m.
cigarillo	cigarrillo, m.	kimono	kimono, m.
coco	coco, m.	lasso	lazo, m.
Colorado	Colorado, m.	libido	libido, m.
commando	comando, m.	libretto	libreto, m.
concerto	concierto, m.	limbo	limbo, m.
Congo	Congo, m.	lobo	lobo, m.
contralto	contralto, m.	logo	logo, m.
credo	credo, m.	lumbago	lumbago, m.
crescendo	crescendo, m.	maestro	maestro, m.
cruzeiro	cruzeiro, m.	magneto	magneto, f.
desperado	malhechor, m.•	majordomo	mayordomo, m.
ditto	ídem, m.•	mambo	mambo, m.
dodo	dodo, m.	mango	mango, m.
domino	dominó, m.	manifesto	manifiesto, m.
duo	dúo, m.	memento	memento, m.
dynamo	dínamo, m.	*memo	nota, f.;memorándum, m.•
echo	eco, m.	metro	metro, m.
ego	ego, m.	Mexico	Méjico, México, m.
*embargo	embargo, m.	micro	micro, m.
embryo	embrión, f.•	Mikado	micado, m.
scudo (coin)	escudo, m.	Monaco	Mónaco, m.
Eskimo	esquimal, m.•	mosquito	mosquito, m.
Esperanto	esperanto, m.	*motto	mote, m.; lema, f.•
espresso	expreso, m.	mulatto	mulato, m.
falsetto	falsete, m.•	negro	negro, m.
fandango	fandango, m.	nuncio	nuncio, m.
fiasco	fiasco, m.	officio	oficio, m.
Filipino	filipino, m.	Ontario	Ontario, m.
flamingo	flamenco, m.•	oratorio	oratorio, m.
folio	folio, m.	oregano	orégano, m.
fresco	fresco, m.	Oslo	Oslo, m.
gaucho	gaucho, m.	patio	patio, m.
generalissimo	generalísimo, m.	peccadillo	pecadillo, m.
Gestapo	gestapo, m.	*peso	peso, m.
ghetto	ghetto, m.	photo	foto, m.
gigolo	gigolo, m.	piano	piano, m.
grotto	gruta, f.•	piccolo	flautín, m.•
guano	guano, m.	pimiento	pimiento, m.
gusto	gusto, m.	pistachio	pistacho, m.
gyro	giro, m.	pizzicato	pizzicato, m.
halo	halo, m.	placebo	placebo, m.
hero	héroe, m.•	polio	polio(mielitis), m.

ENGLISH	SPANISH	ENGLISH	SPANISH
Politburo	politburó, m.	staccato	staccato, m.
politico	político, m.	stereo	estereo, m.
polo	polo, m.	stiletto	estilete, m.•
pompano (fish)	pómpano, m.	stucco	estuco, m.
poncho	poncho, m.	studio	estudio, m.
portfolio	cartera, f.•	Tabasco	Tabasco, m.
portico	pórtico, m.	tango	tango, m.
potato	papa, patata, f.•	telephoto	telefoto, m.
presidio	presidio, m.	tempo	tempo, m.
presto	presto, m.	terrazzo	terrazo, m.
proviso	condición, f.•	tobacco	tobaco, m.
pueblo	pueblo, m.	Tokyo	Tokio, m.
Puerto Rico	Puerto Rico, m.	tomato	tomate, m.•
quebracho (BOT)	quebracho, m.	tornado	tornado, m.
Quito	Quito, m.	Toronto	Toronto, m.
*radio	radio, m.	torpedo	torpedo, m.
ratio	relación, proporción, f.•	torso	torso, m.
rococo	rococó, m.	trio	trío, m.
*rodeo	rodeo, m.	tuxedo	esmoquin, m.•
salvo	salva, f.•	ultimo	último, m.
Santiago	Santiago, m.	vertigo	vértigo, m.
Santo Domingo	Santo Domingo, m.	veto	veto, m.
scenario	escenario, m.	video	video, m.
silo	silo, m.	violoncello	violoncelo, m.
sirocco (wind)	siroco, m.	virtuoso	virtuoso, m.
solo	solo, m.	volcano	volcán, m.•
sombrero	sombrero, m.	yo-yo	yoyó, m.
soprano	soprano, m.	*zero	cero, m.

NOUNS: English *-oo* = Spanish *-ú* or *-o*.   80%: 12 Listed

Gender: All are masculine in Spanish.

ENGLISH	SPANISH	ENGLISH	SPANISH
bamboo	bambú, m.	moo	mu, m.
cashoo	cachú, m.	shampoo	champú, m.
cuckoo	cuco, cucú, m.	taboo	tabú, m.
Hindoo	hindú, m.	tattoo	tataje, m.•
igloo	iglú, m.	voodoo	vodú, m.
kangeroo	cangro, m.•	zoo	zoo, m.•

NOUNS: English -ar = Spanish -ar or -ar(i)o.
　　　　　　　　　　　　　　　　　　　　75%: 50 Listed
　　Gender: Most are masculine in Spanish.

ENGLISH	SPANISH	ENGLISH	SPANISH
altar	altar, m.	isobar	isobaro, m.
bazaar	bazar, m.	jaguar	jaguar, m.
beggar	mendigo, m.•	mandibular	mandibular, m.
binocular	binóculo, m.•	molar	molar, m.
Bolivar	Bolivar	mortar (gun, bowl)	mortero, m.•
burglar	ladrón, m.•	mortar (plaster)	argamasa, f.•
bursar	tesorero, m.•	nectar	néctar, m.
Caesar	César	*particular	detalle, particular, m.
calendar	calendario, m.	perpendicular	perpendicular, m.
caterpillar	oruga, f.•	*pillar	pilar, m.
caviar	caviar, m.	poplar	álamo, m.•
cedar	cedro, m.•	radar	radar, m.
cellar	sótano, m.; cueva, f.•	registrar	registrador, m.•
cheddar	cheddar, m.	regular	regular, m.
*cigar	puro, cigarro, m.	*scholar	sabio, escolar, m.
circular	círculo, circular, m.	seminar	seminario, m.
*collar	cuello, m.•	singular	singular, m.
commissar	comisario, m.	sonar	sonar, m.
cougar	cuguar, m.	sugar	azúcar, m.
czar	czar, m.	tartar	tártaro, m.
dollar	dólar, m.	Tsar	czar, m.
funicular	funicular, m.	vernacular	vernácular, f.
grammar	gramática, f.•	vicar	vicario, m.
guitar	guitarra, f.•	vinegar	vinagre, m.•
hangar	hangar, m.	Zanzibar	Zanzíbar, m.

NOUNS: English ending in -eer = Spanish -ero(a).
　　　　　　　　　　　　　　　　　　　　70%: 20 Listed
The suffix -eer usually denotes a person that does a specified thing.

　　Gender: Almost all are masculine in Spanish.

ENGLISH	SPANISH	ENGLISH	SPANISH
auctioneer	subastador, m.•	musketeer	mosquetero, m.
bandoleer	bandolera, f.	mutineer	amotinado, m.•
buccaneer	bucanero, m.	pioneer	explorador, pionero, m.
cannoneer	cañonero, m.	pistoleer	pistolero, m.
carabineer	carabinero, m.	profiteer	logrero, m.•
career	carrera, f.	racketeer	extorsionista, m.•
*engineer	ingeniero, m.	reindeer	reno, m.•
engineer (RR)	maquinista, m.•	trumpeteer	trompetero, m.
financeer	financiero, m.	veneer	chapa, f.•
fusileer	fusilero, m.	volunteer	voluntario, m.•
mountaineer	montañero, m.		

NOUNS: English *-grapher* = Spanish *-grafo*.   98% 16 Listed

Cross-References: N *-graph, -graphy*; A *-graphic*

Gender: All are masculine in Spanish.

ENGLISH	SPANISH	ENGLISH	SPANISH
autobiographer	autobiógrafo, m.	geographer	geógrafo, m.
autographer	autógrafo, m.	lithographer	litógrafo, m.
biographer	biógrafo, m.	oceanographer	oceanógrafo, m.
calligrapher	calígrafo, m.	photographer	fotógrafo, m.
cartographer	cartógrafo, m.	stenographer	estenógrafo, m.
choreographer	coreógrafo, m.	telegrapher	telegrafista, m.•
cryptographer	criptógrafo, m.	topographer	topógrafo, m.
demographer	demógrafo, m.	typographer	tipógrafo, m.

NOUNS: English *-ifier* = Spanish *-ificador*.   90%: 24 Listed

The suffix *-ifier* denotes the doer of the action of *-ify* verbs.

Cross-Reference: V *-ify*; N *-ification*; ADJ *-ed*

Gender: All are masculine in Spanish.

ENGLISH	SPANISH	ENGLISH	SPANISH
amplifier	amplificador, m.	nullifier	anulador, m.•
certifier	certificador, m.	pacifier	pacificador, m.
classifier	clasificador, m.	purifier	purificador, m.
codifier	codificador, m.	qualifier	calificador, m.
dehumidifier	deshumedecador, m.•	reclassifier	reclasificador, m.
falsifier	falsificador, m.	rectifier	rectificador, m.
fortifier	fortificador, m.	simplifier	simplificador, m.
glorifier	glorificador, m.	specifier	especificador, m.
humidifier	humedecador, m.•	unifier	unificador, m.
justifier	justificador, m.	verifier	verificador, m.
magnifier	amplificador, m.•	villifier	difamador, m.•
modifier	modificador, m.	vivifier	vivificador, m.

NOUNS: English *-meter* = Spanish *-metro*. 99%: 28 Listed

The suffix *-meter* denotes:
a) a device for measuring a specified thing (thermometer)
b) a specified number of meters (kilometer)
c) a specified fraction of a meter (centimeter)
d) having a specified number of metrical feet (pentameter)

Cross-Reference: N *-metry*; ADJ *-metrical*
Gender: All are masculine in Spanish.

ENGLISH	SPANISH	ENGLISH	SPANISH
accelerometer	acelerómetro, m.	*meter	metro, m.
actinometer	actinómetro, m.	micrometer	micrómetro, m.
altimeter	altímetro, m.	millimeter	milímetro, m.
amperemeter	amperímetro, m.	odometer	odómetro, m.
anemometer	anemómetro, m.	parameter	parámetro, m.
barometer	barómetro, m.	pedometer	pedómetro, m.
calorimeter	calorímetro, m.	pentameter	pentámetro, m.
centimeter	centímetro, m.	perimeter	perímetro, m.
decimeter	decímetro, m.	pyrometer	pirómetro, m.
densimeter	densímetro, m.	spectrometer	espectrómetro, m.
diameter	diámetro, m.	speedometer	velocímetro, m. •
hexameter	hexámetro, m.	tachometer	tacómetro, m.
hydrometer	hidrómetro, m.	thermometer	termómetro, m.
kilometer	kilómetro, m.	voltmeter	voltímetro, m.

NOUNS: English *-izer* or *-yzer* = Spanish *-izador*.
  85%: 28 Listed

The suffix *-izer* denotes the doer of the action of *-ize* verbs.

Cross-Reference: V *-ize* ; N *-ization*

Gender: All are masculine in Spanish unless referring specifically to a female doer in which case an *-a* is added to the *-izador*.

ENGLISH	SPANISH	ENGLISH	SPANISH
analyzer	analizador, m.	moralizer	moralizador, m.
appetizer	aperitivo, m. •	neutralizer	neutralizador, m.
atomizer	atomizador, m.	organizer	organizador, m.
centralizer	centralizador, m.	paralyzer	paralizador, m.
colonizer	colonizador, m.	plagiarizer	plagiario, m. •
criticizer	criticador, m. •	pulverizer	pulverizador, m.
economizer	economizador, m.	reorganizer	reorganizador, m.
equalizer	igualador, m. •	socializer	socializador, m.
evangelizer	evangelizador, m.	stabilizer	estabilizador, m.
generalizer	generalizador, m.	sterilizer	esterilizador, m.
gormandizer	glotón, m. •	synchronizer	sincronizador, m.
hypnotizer	hipnotizador, m.	tranquilizer	tranquilizador, m.
mobilizer	movilizador, m.	vaporizer	vaporizador, m.
modernizer	modernizador, m.	vocalizer	vocalizador, m.

NOUNS: Many other *-er* doer nouns also convert to Spanish *-dor*, but there is no general pattern to assure this conversion.
100 Listed

<u>Gender</u>: All are masculine in Spanish unless referring specifically to a female doer in which case an *-a* is added to the *-dor*.

ENGLISH	SPANISH	ENGLISH	SPANISH
abuser	abusador, m.	gainer	ganador, m.
accuser	acusador, m.	importer	importador, m.
adapter	adaptador, m.	importuner	importunador, m.
adjuster	adjustador, m.	improviser	improvisador, m.
admirer	admirador, m.	inciter	incitador, m.
announcer	anunciador, m.	informer	informante, informador, m.
appraiser	apreciador, m.	inhaler	inhalador, m.
arbiter	árbitro, arbitrador, m.	injurer	injuriador, m.
blasphemer	blasfemador, m.	inquirer	inquiridor, m.
boxer	boxeador, m.	inspirer	inspirador, m.
censurer	censurador, m.	installer	instalador, m.
civilizer	civilizador, m.	laborer	labrador, m.
commuter	conmutador, m.	marauder	merodeador, m.
computer	computador, m.	marker	marcador, m.
condenser	condensador, m.	microcomputer	microcomputador, m.
conditioner	acondicionador, m.	minicomputer	minicomputador, m.
conjurer	conjurador, m.	molester	molestador, m.
conspirer	conspirador, m.	moulder	moldeador, m.
consumer	consumidor, m.	multiplier	multiplicador, m.
contender	contendor, m.	observer	observador, m.
converter	convertidor, m.	originator	originador, m.
copier	copiador, m.	planter	plantador, m.
counter	contador, m.	preserver	preservador, m.
declarer	declarador, m.	programmer	programador, m.
defrauder	defraudador, m.	provider	visor, proveedor, m.
designer	diseñador, m.	reasoner	razonador, m.
dispatcher	despachador, m.	receiver	recibidor, m.
dispenser	dispensador, m.	reconciler	reconciliador, m.
disputer	disputador, m.	recruiter	reclutador, m.
distiller	destilador, m.	refiner	refinador, m.
distributer	distribuidor, m.	reformer	reformador, m.
enchanter	encantador, m.	refuter	refutador, m.
establisher	establecedor, m.	repairer	reparador, m.
examiner	examinador, m.	repeater	repetidor, m.
exhibiter	exhibidor, m.	responder	respondedor, m.
expander	expandidor, m.	restorer	restaurador, m.
expediter	expedidor, m.	server	servidor, m.
experimenter	experimentador, m.	silencer	silenciador, m.
exploiter	explotador, m.	skier	esquiador, m.
explorer	explorador, m.	strangler	estrangulador, m.
exporter	exportador, m.	suspender	suspendedor, m.
floater	flotador, m.	sustainer	sustentador, m.
fomenter	fomentador, m.	tempter	tentador, m.
forger	forjador, m.	tormenter	atormentador, m.
founder	fundador, m.	torturer	torturador, m.

ENGLISH	SPANISH	ENGLISH	SPANISH
transferer	transferidor, m.	transposer	transponedor, m.
transformer	transformador, m.	treater	tratador, m.
transmuter	transmutador, m.	trotter	trotador, m.
transplanter	trasplantador, m.	usurper	usurpador, m.
transporter	transportador, m.	vender	vendedor, m.

NOUNS: Some English doer nouns ending in *-er* = Spanish *-tor*.

18 Listed

Gender: All are masculine in Spanish.

ENGLISH	SPANISH	ENGLISH	SPANISH
composer	compositor, m.	inscriber	inscriptor, m.
describer	descriptor, m.	introducer	introductor, m.
deserter	desertor, m.	producer	productor, m.
erecter	erector, m.	proscriber	proscriptor, m.
exacter	exactor, m.	prospecter	prospector, m.
executer	ejecutor, m.	receiver	receptor, m.
expounder	expositor, m.	resister	resistor, m.
extinguisher	extintor, m.	sculpter	escultor, m.
inducer	inductor, m.	seducer	seductor, m.

NOUNS: Some English doer nouns ending in *-er* = Spanish *-sor*.

12 Listed

Gender: All are masculine in Spanish.

ENGLISH	SPANISH	ENGLISH	SPANISH
apprehender	aprehensor, m.	inverter	inversor, m.
defender	defensor, m.	offender	ofensor, m.
deluder	delusor, m.	persuader	persuasor, m.
diffuser	difusor, m.	propeller	propulsor, m.
emitter	esmisor, m.	represser	represor, m.
invader	invasor, m.	transmitter	transmisor, m.

NOUNS: Some English doer nouns ending in *-er* = Spanish *-nte*.

12 Listed

Gender: All are masculine in Spanish.

ENGLISH	SPANISH	ENGLISH	SPANISH
commander	comandante, m.	pretender	pretendiente, m.
dissenter	disidente, m.	remitter	remitente, m.
dissolver	disolvente, m.	resolver	resolvente, m.
fertilizer	fertilizante, m.	sympathizer	simpatizante, m.
informer	informante, m.	theorizer	teorizante, m.
oxidizer	oxidante, m.	voter	votante, m.

NOUNS: English *-ir* or *-yr* preceded by a consonant = Spanish *-ir* or *-iro*.   95%:   9 Listed

<u>Gender</u>: Almost all are masculine in Spanish.

ENGLISH	SPANISH	ENGLISH	SPANISH
elixir	elixir, m.	nadir	nadir, m.
emir	emir, m.	satyr	sátiro, m.
fakir	faquir, m.	souvenir	recuerdo, m. •
martyr	mártir, m.	zephyr	céfiro, m.
mohair	mohair, m.		

NOUNS: English *-dor* = Spanish *-dor*.   90%:   18 Listed

<u>Gender</u>: Most are masculine in Spanish.

ENGLISH	SPANISH	ENGLISH	SPANISH
ambassador	embajador, m.	matador	matador, m.
ardor	ardor, m.	odor	olor, m.
candor	candor, m.	picador	picador, m.
condor	cóndor, m.	splendor	esplendor, m.
conquistador	conquistador, m.	sudor (sweat)	sudor, m.
corridor	corredor, m.	toreador	toreador, m.
cuspidor	escupidera, f. •	troubadour	trovador, m.
Ecuador	Ecuador, m.	Tudor	Tudor, m.
humidor	humidificador, m.	vendor	vendedor, m.

NOUNS: English *-sor* = Spanish *-sor*.   75%:   27 Listed

<u>Cross-Reference</u>: V *-ess*, *-ise*, *-or*, *-cede* ; N *-nse*

<u>Gender</u>: Almost all are masculine in Spanish.

ENGLISH	SPANISH	ENGLISH	SPANISH
advisor	consejero, m. •	predecessor	predecesor, m.
aggressor	agresor, m.	processor	procesor, m.
assessor	asesor, m.	professor	profesor, m.
censor	censor, m.	promisor	prometidor, m. •
compressor	compresor, m.	revisor	revisor, m.
condensor	condensador, m. •	sensor	sensor, m.
confessor	confesor, m.	sponsor	fiador, garante, m. •
divisor	divisor, m.	successor	sucesor, m.
extensor	extensor, m.	supervisor	supervisor, m.
lessor	arrendador, locador, m. •	suppressor	supresor, m.
licensor	concedente, m. •	suspensor	suspensor, m.
oppressor	opresor, m.	transgressor	transgresor, m.
possessor	poseedor, posesor, m. •	visor	visera, f. •
precursor	precursor, m.		

NOUNS: English -ator = Spanish -ador or -ante. 95%: 130 Listed

The suffix -ator denotes the doer of the action of -ate verbs.

Cross-Reference: V -ate; N -ion; ADJ -ative, -able, -ed

Gender: Almost all are masculine in Spanish.

ENGLISH	SPANISH	ENGLISH	SPANISH
abbreviator	abreviador, m.	donator	donador, m.
accelerator	acelerador, m.	duplicator	duplicador, m.
accommodator	acomodador, m.	educator	educador, m.
accumulator	acumulador, m.	*elevator(storage)	elevador, m.
activator	activador, m.	elevator (lift)	ascensor, m.•
actuator	actuador, m.	emancipator	emancipador, m.
administrator	administrador, m.	equator	ecuador, m.
adulator	adulador, m.	eradicator	extirpador, m.•
adulterator	adulterador, m.	escalator	escalera, f.•
agitator	agitador, m.	evaporator	evaporador, m.
alligator	caimán, m.•	exaggerator	exagerador, m.
alternator	alternador, m.	excavator	excavador, m.
animator	animador, m.	exterminator	exterminador, m.
amalgamator	amalgamador, m.	fabricator	fabricador, m.
annotator	anotador, m.	generator	generador, m.
applicator	aplicador, m.	gladiator	gladiador, m.
arbitrator	arbitrador, m.	illuminator	iluminador, m.
aspirator	aspirador, m.	illustrator	ilustrador, m.
aviator	aviador, m.	imitator	imitador, m.
calculator	calculador, m.	impersonator	imitador, m.•
calibrator	calibrador, m.	incinerator	incinerador, m.
castigator	castigador, m.	incorporator	incorporador, m.
collaborator	colaborador, m.	incubator	incubador, m.
collator	colador, m.	indicator	indicador, m.
commentator	comentador, m.	inhalator	inhalador, m.
conciliator	conciliador, m.	initiator	iniciador, m.
conservator	conservador, m.	innovator	innovador, m.
consolidator	consolidor, m.•	instigator	instigador, m.
conspirator	conspirador, m.	insulator	aislador, m.•
contaminator	contaminador, m.	integrator	integrador, m.
coordinator	coordinador, m.	interrogator	interrogador, m.
corroborator	corroborante, m.	investigator	investigador, m.
creator	creador, m.	legislator	legislador, m.
cultivator	cultivador, m.	liberator	liberador, m.
curator	conservador, m.•	liquidator	liquidador, m.
decorator	decorador, m.	litigator	litigante, m.
delegator	delegador, m.	lubricator	lubricador, m.
demonstrator	demostrador, m.	manipulator	manipulador, m.
denigrator	denigrador, m.	mediator	mediador, m.
denominator	denominador, m.	meditator	meditador, m.
detonator	detonador, m.	moderator	moderador, m.
dictator	dictador, m.	modulator	modulador, m.
discriminator	discriminador, m.	mutilator	mutilador, m.
disseminator	diseminador, m.	narrator	narrador, m.

ENGLISH	SPANISH	ENGLISH	SPANISH
navigator	-gante, navegador, m.	refrigerator	refrigerador, m.
negotiator	negociador, m.	regulator	regulador, m.
nominator	nombrador, nominador, m.	relator	relator, relatador, m.
numerator	numerador, m.	renovator	renovador, m.
operator	operador, m.	respirator	respirador, m.
orator	orador, m.	resuscitator	resucitador, m.
originator	originador, m.	senator	senador, m.
oscillator	oscilador, m.	separator	separador, m.
participator	participante, m.	simulator	simulador, m.
penetrator	penetrador, m.	spectator	espectador, m.
percolator	percolador, m.	speculator	especulador, m.
perpetrator	perpetrador, m.	stimulator	estimulador, m.
prevaricator	prevaricador, m.	tabulator	tabulador, m.
procrastinator	dilatador, m.•	terminator	terminador, m.
procreator	procreador, m.	testator	testador, m.
procurator	procurador, m.	translator	traductor, m.•
prognosticator	pronosticador, m.	valuator	avaluador, m.
promulgator	promulgador, m.	ventilator	ventilador, m.
propagator	propagador, m.	vibrator	vibrador, m.
pulsator	pulsador, m.	vindicator	vindicador, m.
radiator	radiador, m.	violator	violador, m.

NOUNS: English *-ctor* = Spanish *-ctor*.   75%: 50 Listed

Cross-Reference: V *-ct*; N *-ction*; ADJ *-ctive*

Gender: All are masculine in Spanish.

ENGLISH	SPANISH	ENGLISH	SPANISH
*abductor	raptor, abductor, m.	injector	inyector, m.
actor	actor, m.	inspector	inspector, m.
benefactor	benefactor, m.	instructor	instructor, m.
chiropractor	quiropractor, m.	lector	lector, m.
collector	colector, m.	objector	objetor, m.
conductor (ELEC)	conductor, m.	obstructor	obstructor, m.
*conductor (MUS)	director, m.•	predictor	predictor, m.
*conductor (RR)	revisor, m.•	proctor	censor, vigilante, m.•
connector	conector, m.	projector	proyector, m.
constrictor	constrictor, m.	prospector	prospector, m.
constructor	constructor, m.	protector	protector, m.
contractor	contratante, m.•	protractor	prolongador, m.•
corrector	corrector, m.	reactor	reactor, m.
deflector	deflector, m.	rector	rector, m.
destructor	destructor, m.	redactor	redactor, m.
detector	detector, m.	reflector	reflector, m.
detractor	detractor, m.	refractor	refractor, m.
director	director, m.	retractor	retractor, m.
*doctor (MED)	médico, m.•	sector	sector, m.
doctor (ACAD)	doctor, m.	selector	selector, m.
ejector	eyector, m.	semiconductor	semiconductor, m.
elector	elector, m.	subcontractor	subcontratista, m.•
extractor	extractor, m.	tractor	tractor, m.
factor	factor, m.	vector	vector, m.
inductor	inductor, m.	victor	vencedor, m.•

**NOUNS: English *-or* other than *-dor, -sor, -ator* and *-ctor* =
Spanish *-or*.   70%: 136 Listed**

<u>Gender</u>:   Most are masculine in Spanish.

ENGLISH	SPANISH	ENGLISH	SPANISH
ancestor	antecesor, ascendiente, m.•	governor	gobernador, m.
anchor	ancla, f.•	grantor	otorgador, donador, m.•
arbor	glorieta, f.; árbol, m.•	guarantor	fiador, m.•
ardor	ardor, m.	harbor	puerto, m.•
armor	armadura, f.•	honor	honra, f.; honor, m.
auditor	interventor, auditor, m.	horror	horror, m.
author	escritor, autor, m.	humor	humor, m.
*bachelor	soltero, m.•	impostor	impostor, m.
behavior	conducta, f.•	inferior	inferior, m.
camphor	alcanfor, m.	inheritor	heredero, m.•
cantor	chantre, m.•	inhibitor	inhibidor, m.
capacitor	condensador, m.•	inquisitor	inquisidor, m.
captor	capturador, m.	interceptor	interceptor, m.
carburetor	carburador, m.	interior	interior, m.
chancellor	canciller, m.•	interlocutor	interlocutor, m.
clamor	clamor, m.	inventor	inventor, m.
clangor	clangor, m.	investor	inversionista, m.•
coauthor	coautor, m.	janitor	portero, m.•
color	color, m.	juror	jurado, m.•
competitor	competidor, f.	labor	labor, f.
conqueror	conquistador, m.•	liquor	licor, m.
consignor	consignador, m.	major	comandante, mayor, m.
contributor	contribuidor, m.	manor	solar, m.; finca, f.•
conveyor	transportador, m.•	*mayor	alcalde, m.•
councillor	consejero, m.•	mentor	mentor, m.
counselor	consejero, m.•	metaphor	metáfora, f.•
creditor	acreedor, m.	meteor	meteoro, m.•
debtor	deudor, m.	minor	menor, m.
demeanor	comportamiento, m.•	mirror	espejo, m.•
depositor	depositador, m.	misbehavior	mala conducta, m.•
disfavor	disfavor, m.	misdemeanor	delito menor, m.•
dishonor	deshonra, f; deshonor, m.	monitor	monitor, m.
distributor	distribuidor, m.	monsignor	monseñor, m.
dolor	dolor, m.	mortgagor	deudor, m.•
donor	donador, m.	motor	motor, m.
*editor	redactor, m.•	neighbor	vecino, m.•
emperor	emperador, m.	odor	olor, m.•
endeavor	empeño, m.•	pallor	palor, m.
error	equivocación, f; error, m.	parlor	sala, f.•
executor	ejecutor, m.	pastor	pastor, m.
exhibitor	exhibidor, m.	persecutor	perseguidor, m.
exterior	exterior, m.	posterior	trasero, m.•
favor	favor, m.	preceptor	preceptor, m.
fervor	fervor, m.	primogenitor	primogenitor, m.
flavor	sabor, m.•	progenitor	progenitor, m.
furor	furor, m.	proprietor	propietario, m.•

148

ENGLISH	SPANISH		ENGLISH	SPANISH	
prosecutor	acusador,	m.•	surveyor	agrimensor,	m.•
purveyor	proveedor,	m.•	tambour	tambor,	m.
rancor	rencor,	m.	tenor	tenor,	m.
razor	navaja de afeitar,	f.•	terror	espanto, miedo, terror,	m.
razor (blade)	hoja de afeitar,	m.•	tormentor	atormentador,	m.
receptor	receptor,	m.	torpor (MED)	torpor,	m.
resistor	resistor,	m.	traitor	traidor,	m.
rigor	rigor,	m.	transferor	transferidor,	m.
rotor	rotor,	m.	transistor	transistor,	m.
rumor	rumor,	m.	tremor	temblor, tremor,	m.
sailor	marinero,	m.•	tricolor	tricolor,	m.
savior	salvador,	m.•	tumor	tumor,	m.
savor	sabor,	m.	tutor	preceptor, tutor,	m.
sculptor	escultor,	m.	valor	valor,	m.
*senior	persona mayor,	m.•	vapor	vapor,	m.
solicitor	solicitador,	m.	vigor	vigor,	m.
squalor	escualidez,	f.•	visitor	visitante, visitador,	m.
stupor	estupor,	m.	visor	visera,	f.•
superior	superior,	m.	warrior	guerrero,	m.•

NOUNS: Some English nouns ending in *-ur* = Spanish *-ur*, *-urio* or *-uro(a)*.   **18 Listed**

ENGLISH	SPANISH		ENGLISH	SPANISH	
amateur	amateur,	m.	hour	hora,	f.
augur	augur,	m.	imprimatur	imprimátur,	m.
centaur	centauro,	m.	minotaur	minotauro,	m.
connoisseur	perito, conocedor,	m.•	monseigneur	monseñor,	m.
contour	contorno,	m.•	murmur	murmullo,	m.•
dinosaur	dinosaurio,	m.	seigneur	señor,	m.
femur (ANAT)	fémur,	m.	succour	socorro,	m.
furfur (dandruff)	fúrfura,	f.	sulphur	azufre,	m.•
glamour	glamour,	m.	tambour	tambor,	m.

NOUNS: English *-as* = Spanish *-as*.   **70%: 14 Listed**

ENGLISH	SPANISH		ENGLISH	SPANISH	
alias	alias,	m.	gas	gasolina, f.; gas,	m.
atlas	atlas,	m.	Honduras	Honduras,	f.
bias	prejuicio,	m.•	pancreas	páncreas,	m.
canvas	lona,	f.•	plexiglas	plexiglás,	m.
Christmas	Navidad,	f.•	pyjamas	pijamas,	f.
Dallas	Dallas,	m.	sassafras	sasafrás,	m.
fracas	tumulto,	m.•	Texas	Texas,	m.

NOUNS: English *-ics* = Spanish *-ica* (70%), *-ia* (20%) or *-ismo* (5%).
95%: 60 Listed

The suffix *-ics* is used to form plural nouns meaning (a specified) art, science, practice or systems. Not included in this conversion category are many English nouns ending in *-ics* which are really just the plural form of nouns ending in *-ic* (i.e.: classics, basics, characteristics, comics, diagnostics, heroics, hieroglyphics, lyrics, mosaics, narcotics, Olympics, specifics, tropics, etc.).

Gender: Almost all are feminine in Spanish. They are usually construed as singular nouns. The exceptions which convert to *-ismo* are masculine in Spanish.

ENGLISH	SPANISH	ENGLISH	SPANISH
acrobatics	acrobacia, f.	hydrodynamics	hidrodinámica, f.
acoustics	acústica, f.	hydromechanics	hidromecánica, f.
aeronautics	aeronáutica, f.	linguistics	lingüística, f.
astrophysics	astrofísica, f.	logistics	logística, f.
athletics	atletismo, m.	macroeconomics	macroeconomía, f.
ballistics	balística, f.	mathematics	matemática, f.
biometrics	biométrica, f.	mechanics	mecánica, f.
calisthenics	calistenia, f.	melodramatics	melodramática, f.
ceramics	cerámica, f.	metaphysics	metafísica, f.
chromatics	cromática, f.	obstetrics	obstetricia, f.
civics	cívica, f.	optics	óptica, f.
cosmetics	cosmético, m.	orthodontics	ortodoncia, f.
diagnostics	diagnóstica, f.	orthopedics	ortopedia, f.
dialectics	dialéctica, f.	pedagogics	pedagogía, f.
didactics	didáctica, f.	pediatrics	pediatría, f.
dietetics	dietética, f.	periodontics	periodoncia, f.
dramatics	dramática, f.	phonemics	fonémica, f.
dynamics	dinámica, f.	phonetics	fonética, f.
economics	economía, f.	physics	física, f.
electronics	electrónica, f.	plastics	plástica, f.
esthetics	estética, f.	polemics	polémica, f.
ethics	ética, f.	politics	política, f.
genetics	genética, f.	pragmatics	pragmática, f.
geodetics	geodesia, f.	pyrotechnics	pirotecnia, f.
geopolitics	geopolítica, f.	semantics	semántica, f.
geriatrics	geriatría, f.	statistics	estadística, f.
graphics	gráfica, f.	tactics	táctica, f.
gymnastics	gimnástica, f.	therapeutics	terapéutica, f.
hermeneutics	hermenéutica, f.	thermodynamics	termodinámica, f.
hydraulics	hidráulica, f.	ultrasonics	ultrasónica, f.

NOUNS: English *-sis* = Spanish *-sis*.   95% 50 Listed
(There are hundreds of these *-sis* nouns.)

Gender: Most are feminine in Spanish.

ENGLISH	SPANISH	ENGLISH	SPANISH
analysis	análisis, m.	narcosis	narcosis, f.
antithesis	antítesis, f.	necrosis	necrosis, f.
basis	base, f. •	nemesis	vengador, m. •
catalysis	catálisis, f.	neurosis	neurosis, f.
catharsis	catarsis, f.	oasis	oasis, m.
chassis	chasis, m.	osmosis	ósmosis, f.
cirrhosis	cirrosis, f.	paralysis	parálisis, f.
crisis	crisis, f.	parenthesis	paréntesis, m.
diaeresis	diéresis, f.	pathogenesis	patogénesis, f.
diagnosis	diagnosis, f.	periphrasis	perífrasis, f.
dialysis	diálisis, f.	peristalsis	peristalsis, f.
diathesis	diátesis, f.	photosynthesis	fotosíntesis, f.
electrolysis	electrólisis, f.	prognosis	prognosis, f.
ellipsis	elipsis, f.	psoriasis	psoríasis, f.
emphasis	énfasis, f.	psychoanalysis	psicoanálisis, f.
fibrosis	fibrosis, f.	psychosis	psicosis, f.
genesis	génesis, f.	sclerosis	esclerosis, f.
Genesis	génesis, m.	stenosis	estenosis, f.
halitosis	halitosis, f.	synopsis	sinopsis, f.
hydrolysis	hidrólisis, f.	synthesis	síntesis, f.
hypnosis	hipnosis, f.	thesis	tesis, f.
hypothesis	hipótesis, f.	thrombosis	trombosis, f.
metamorphosis	metamorfosis, f.	trichinosis	triquinosis, f.
metastasis	metástasis, f.	tuberculosis	tuberculosis, f.
mononucleosis	mononucleosis, f.	urinalysis	urinálisis, f.

NOUNS: English *-itis* = Spanish *-itis*.   99%: 24 Listed
(There are over a hundred of these *-itis* nouns.)

The suffix *-itis* signifies an inflamatory disease or inflamation of a specified part or organ of the body.

Gender: All are feminine in Spanish.

ENGLISH	SPANISH	ENGLISH	SPANISH
appendicitis	apendicitis, f.	hepatitis	hepatitis, f.
arthritis	artritis, f.	ileitis	ileítis, f.
bronchitis	bronquitis, f.	laryngitis	laringitis, f.
bursitis	bursitis, f.	meningitis	meningitis, f.
colitis	colitis, f.	neuritis	neuritis, f.
conjunctivitis	conjuntivitis, f.	pancreatitis	pancreatitis, f.
dermatitis	dermatitis, f.	peritonitis	peritonitis, f.
diverticulitis	diverticulitis, f.	phlebitis	flebitis, f.
encephalitis	encefalitis, f.	pleuritis	pleuritis, f.
enteritis	enteritis, f.	retinitis	retinitis, f.
gastritis	gastritis, f.	ten(d)onitis	tenonitis, f.
gingivitis	gingivitis, f.	tonsillitis	tonsilitis, f.

NOUNS: English -is other than -sis and -itis = Spanish -is.
70%: 28 Listed

ENGLISH	SPANISH	ENGLISH	SPANISH
acropolis	acrópolis, f.	glottis	glotis, f.
Adonis	Adonis, m.	iris (eye)	iris, m.
aegis	égida, f.•	*iris (BOT)	lirio, m.•
axis (ANAT)	axis, m.	mantis	mantis, f.
*axis	eje, m.•	marquis	marqués, m.•
basis	base, f.•	Memphis	Menfis, f.
bourgeois	burguesía, f.•	metropolis	metrópoli, f.•
chablis	chablis, f.	Paris	París, m.
challis	chalí, m.•	pelvis	pelvis, f.
croquis	croquis, m.	précis	resumen, m.•
cutis	cutis, m.	prophylaxis	profilaxis, f.
debris	restos, m.•	syphilis	sífilis, f.
digitalis	digital, -ina, f.•	tennis	tenis, m.
epidermis	piel, epidermis, f.	trellis	enrejado, m.•

NOUNS: English -os other than plurals = Spanish -os.
85%: 10 Listed

Gender: Almost all are masculine in Spanish.

ENGLISH	SPANISH	ENGLISH	SPANISH
albatros	albatros, m.	Laos	Laos, m.
asbestos	asbesto, m.•	pathos	pathos, m.
chaos	caos, m.	pharos	faros, m.
cosmos	cosmos, m.	rhinoceros	rinoceronte, m.•
ethos	genio, m.•	thermos	termos, m.

NOUNS: English -ess added to nouns to designate a feminine person = Spanish -esa, -ra or -iz.
80%: 25 Listed

ENGLISH	-ess = -esa 25%	-ess = -ra 55%	-iz & Other Patterns
actress			actriz, f.
adulteress		adúltera, f.	
adventuress		aventurera, f.	
baroness	baronesa, f.		
countess	condesa, f.		
deaconess	diaconisa, f.		
duchess	duquesa, f.		
empress			emperatriz, f.
governess		gobernadora, f.	
heiress		heredera, f.	
hostess			anfitriona, f.•
instructress		instructora, f.	institutriz, f.
laundress		lavandera, f.	
lioness			leona, f.
marquess	marquesa, f.		
mistress		señora, f.•	
mistress			concubina, f.•
negress			negra, f.

ENGLISH	SPANISH		
	-ess = -esa 25%	-ess = -ra 55%	-iz & Other Patterns
poetess			poeta, f.
princess	princesa, f.		
sculptress		escultora, f.	
seamstress		costurera, f.•	
stewardess		camarera, f.•	asistenta, f.•
tigress	tigresa, f.		
waitress		camarera, f.•	

Some other English nouns ending in -ss follow similar conversion patterns.   **19 Listed**

ENGLISH	SPANISH	ENGLISH	SPANISH
abscess	absceso, m.	mass	masa, f.
abyss	abismo, m.•	mass (REL)	misa, f.
access	acceso, m.	pass	paso, m.
albatross	albatros, m.•	press	prensa, f.
compress	compresa, f.	process	proceso, m.
congress	congreso, m.	progress	progreso, m.
cypress	ciprés, m.	prowess	proeza, f.
excess	exceso, m.	regress	regreso, m.
express	expreso, m.	Swiss	suizo, m.
ingress	ingreso, m.		

NOUNS: English nouns ending in *-ness* don't convert directly to Spanish, but the *-ity* alternative form of these nouns usually converts to *-idad* in Spanish.

Cross-Reference: N -ity

NOUNS: English *-us* = Spanish *-o* or *-us*.   90%:   96 Listed

Gender: Almost all are masculine in Spanish.

ENGLISH	SPANISH	ENGLISH	SPANISH
abacus	ábaco, m.	bonus	prima, f.•
*alumnus	ex-alumno, m.•	cactus	cacto, m.
amicus	amico, m.	calculus	cálculo, m.
animus	animo, m.	callus	callo, m.
anus	ano, m.	campus	ciudad universitaria, f.•
apparatus	aparato, m.	caucus	comité político, m.•
asparagus	espárrago, m.	Celsius	Celsio, m.
autobus	autobus, m.	census	censo, m.
bacillus	bacilo, m.	chorus	coro, m.

ENGLISH	SPANISH	ENGLISH	SPANISH
circus	circo, m.	narcissus	narciso, m.
cirrus	cirro, m.	nautilus	nautilo, m.
coitus	coito, m.	nexus	nexo, m.
colossus	coloso, m.	nucleolus	nucléolo, m.
Confusius	Confucio, m.	nucleus	núcleo, m.
consensus	consenso, m.	octopus	pulpo, óctopo, m.
corpus	cuerpo, m.	Olympus	Olimpo, m.
crocus	croco, m.	omnibus	ómnibus, m.
cumulus	cumulo, m.	onus	carga, f. •
Damascus	Damasco, m.	opus	opus, m.
discus	disco, m.	Orpheus	Orfeo, m.
esophagus	esófago, m.	papyrus	papiro, m.
eucalyptus	eucalipto, m.	phallus	falo, m.
exodus	éxodo, m.	phosphorus	fósforo, m.
fetus (foetus)	feto, m.	Pius	Pío, m.
focus	foco, m.	Prometheus	Prometeo, m.
fungus (MED)	fungo, m.	prospectus	prospecto, m.
fungus (BOT)	hongo, m.	pus	pus, m.
genius	genio, m.	radius	radio, m.
genus	género, m. •	rhombus	rombo, m.
gladiolus	gladiolo, m.	sarcophagus	sarcófago, m.
hiatus	hiato, m.	sinus	seno, m.
hibiscus	hibisco, m.	situs	lugar, m., localidad, f. •
hippopotamus	hipopótamo, m.	status	estato, m.
humerus	húmero, m.	stimulus	estímulo, m.
humus	humus, m.	Stradivarius	Estradivario, m.
iambus	yambo, m.	streptococcus	estreptococo, m.
ignoramus	ignorante, m. •	stylus	estilo, m.
impetus	ímpetu, m. •	surplus	sobrante, excedente, m. •
incubus	íncubo, m.	syllabus	sílabo, m.
isthmus	istmo, m.	terminus	término, m.
Jesus	Jesús, m.	tetanus	tétanos, m. •
Leviticus	Levítico, m.	thesaurus	tesauro, m.
litmus	tornasol, m. •	thrombus	trombo, m.
locus	sitio, lugar, m. •	typhus	tifus, m.
lotus	loto, m.	uterus	útero, m.
mandamus	mandamiento, m. •	Venus	Venus, f.
minus	menos, m. •	virus	virus, m.
mucus	mucus, muco, m.	walrus	morsa, f. •

NOUNS: English *-crat* = Spanish *-ócrata*.   99%: 8 Listed

Gender: All are masculine in Spanish.

ENGLISH	SPANISH	ENGLISH	SPANISH
aristocrat	aristócrata, m.	physiocrat	fisiócrata, m.
autocrat	autócrata, m.	plutocrat	plutócrata, m.
bureaucrat	burócrata, m.	technocrat	tecnócrata, m.
democrat	demócrata, m.	theocrat	teócrata, m.

NOUNS: English -at other than -crat = Spanish -ata(o), -ate, -ado or -at.   70%: 20 Listed

<u>Gender</u>: Most are masculine in Spanish.

ENGLISH	SPANISH	ENGLISH	SPANISH
acrobat	acróbata, m.	format	formato, m.
automat	autómata, m.	habitat	hábitat, m.
caveat	advertencia, f.•	kumquat (BOT)	kuncuat, m.
combat	combate, m.	lariat	lazo, m.•
commissariat	comisariato, m.	proletariat	proletariado, m.
concordat	concordato, m.	rat	rata, f.
cravat	corbata, f.	repeat	repetición, f.•
defeat	derrota, f.•	retreat	retiro, m.•
diplomat	diplomático, m.•	secretariat	secretariado, m.
fiat	fiat, m.	thermostat	termostato, m.

NOUNS: English -act = Spanish -acto or -ato(a).   90%: 14 Listed

<u>Gender</u>: Most are masculine in Spanish.

ENGLISH	SPANISH	ENGLISH	SPANISH
abstract	extracto, m.•	extract	extracto, m.
act	acto, m.	fact	hecho, m.; realidad, f.•
artifact	artefacto, m.	impact	impacto, m.
cataract	catarata, f.	pact	pacto, m.
*compact	convenio, m; pacta, f.	subcontract	subcontrato, m.
contact	contacto, m.	tact	tacto, m.
contract	contrato, m.	tract	tracto, m.

NOUNS: English -nct = Spanish -nto.   99%: 4 Listed

<u>Gender</u>: Most are masculine in Spanish.

ENGLISH	SPANISH	ENGLISH	SPANISH
adjunct	adjunto, m.	instinct	instinto, m.
defunct	difunto, m.	precinct	recinto, m.

NOUNS: English -uct = Spanish -ucto(a).   99%: 8 Listed

<u>Gender</u>: Most are masculine in Spanish.

ENGLISH	SPANISH	ENGLISH	SPANISH
aqueduct	acueducto, m.	misconduct	mala conducta, f.
byproduct	subproducto, m.	product	producto, m.
conduct	conducta, f.	usufruct	usufructo, m.
duct	conducto, m.	viaduct	viaducto, m.

NOUNS: English -ct other than -act, -nct and -uct = Spanish -cto(a) or -eto.   65%: 30 Listed

Gender: Most are masculine in Spanish.

ENGLISH	SPANISH	ENGLISH	SPANISH
addict	adicto, m.	intellect	intelecto, m.
affect	sentimiento, m.•	neglect	descuido, abandono, m.•
architect	arquitecto, m.	*object (thing)	cosa, f; objeto, m.
aspect	aspecto, m.	object (aim)	propósito, m.•
conflict	conflicto, m.	pact	pacto, m.
convict	convicto, m.	prefect	prefecto, m.
defect	defecto, m.	project	proyecto, m.
derelict	derelicto, m.	prospect	expectación, f.•
dialect	dialecto, m.	respect	respeto, m.
disrespect	falta de respeto, f.	retrospect	retrospección, f.•
district	distrito, m.	sect	secta, f.
edict	edicto, m.	subject	tema, f.; sujeto, m.
effect	efecto, m.	*subject	súbdito, vasallo, m.•
imperfect	imperfecto, m.	suspect	sospechoso, m.•
insect	insecto, m.	verdict	sentencia, f; veredicto, m.

NOUNS: English music words ending in -et = Spanish -eto(a), -ete or -et.   99%: 14 Listed

Gender: Most are masculine in Spanish.

ENGLISH	SPANISH	ENGLISH	SPANISH
ballet	ballet, m.	quintet	quinteto, m.
castanet	castañeta, f.	sestet	sexteto, m.
clarinet	clarinete, m.	sextet	sexteto, m.
duet	dueto, m.	sonnet	soneto, m.
minuet	minuete, m.	spinet	espineta, f.
octet	octeto, m.	triplet	tripleto, m.
quartet	cuarteto, m.	trumpet	trompeta, f.

NOUNS: About 30% of the other English nouns ending in -et follow the same conversion pattern and = Spanish -eto(a), -ete or -et.   58 Listed

Gender: Almost all those converting to -ete or -eto are masculine in Spanish while those converting to -eta are feminine.

ENGLISH	SPANISH	ENGLISH	SPANISH
alphabet	alfabeto, m.	basset	basset, m.
amulet	amuleto, m.	bayonet	bayoneta, f.
banquet	banquete, m.	billet	billete, m.

ENGLISH	SPANISH	ENGLISH	SPANISH
bonnet	gorro, m.; boneta, f.	magnet	imán, magneto, m.
bracelet	pulsera, f; brazalete, m.	mallet	mallete, m.
buffet	bufet, m.	minaret	minarete, m.
cabaret	cabaret, m.	musket	mosquete, m.
*cabinet (GOVT)	gabinete, m.	packet	paquete, m.
cadet	cadete, m.	pallet	paleta, f.
chalet	chalet, m.	pamphlet	folleto, panfleto, m.
chrochet	crochet, m.	parakeet	periquito, m.
civet (ZOOL)	civeto, m.	parapet	parapeto, m.
claret	clarete, m	parquet	parqué, parquet, m.
comet	cometa, f.	picket	piquete, m.
coquet	coqueta, f.	planet	planeta, f.
cricket (game)	criquet, m.	poet	poeta, m.
croquet	croquet, m.	prophet	profeta, m.
cutlet	chuleta, f.	racket (tennis)	raqueta, f.
diet	dieta, f.	sachet	sachet, m.
epithet	epíteto, m.	scarlet	escarlata, f.
facet	faceta, f.	secret	secreto, m.
filet	filete, m.	sherbet	sorbete, m.
gauntlet	guantelete, m.	Soviet	soviet, m.
gourmet	gourmet, m.	stylet	estilete, m.
hatchet	hacheta, f.	tablet (paper)	tableta, f.
islet	isleta, f.	tablet (MED)	pastilla, tableta, f.
jacket	saco, chaqueta, f.	Tibet	Tíbet, m.
jennet	jinete, f.	tourniquet	torniquete, m.
lancet	lanceta, f.	violet (BOT)	violeta, f.

NOUNS: English pronounced -it = Spanish -ito(a), -ido or -it.
65%: 44 Listed

ENGLISH	SPANISH	ENGLISH	SPANISH
affidavit	afidávit, m.	*habit (custom)	costumbre, f.
ambit	ámbito, m.	hypocrit	hipócrita, m.
audit	examen de cuentas, m.•	hermit	ermitaño, m.•
bandit	bandido, m.	Jesuit	jesuita, m.
benefit	ventaja, f; benefico, m.•	limit	confín, límite, m.
biscuit	bizcocho, m.•	merit	mérito, m.
circuit	circuito, m.	orbit	órbita, f.
conduit	conducto, m.•	permit	permiso, m.•
credit	crédito, m.	preterit	pretérito, m.
culprit	culpado, m.•	profit	ganancia, f.•
debit	débito, m.		beneficio, provecho, m.•
deficit	déficit, m.	pulpit	púlpito, m.
demerit	demérito, m.	pundit	erudito, m.•
deposit	depósito, m.	rabbit	conejo, m.•
digit (number)	dígito, m.	sanskrit	sánscrito, m.
digit (finger)	dedo, m.•	spirit	ánimo, espíritu, m.•
discredit	descrédito, m.	summit	cumbre, cima, f.•
esprit	espíritu, m.•	thermit (CHEM)	termita, f
exhibit	exhibición, f.•	transit	tránsito, m.
*exit	salida, f.•	unit	unidad, f.•
gambit	gambito, m.	visit	estancia, visita, f.
*habit (dress)	hábito, m.	vomit	vómito, m.

157

NOUNS: English -alt = Spanish -alto or -alt.

99%: 5 Listed

ENGLISH	SPANISH	ENGLISH	SPANISH
asphalt	asfalto, m.	gestalt	gestalt, m.•
basalt	basalto, m.	malt	malta, f.
cobalt	cobalto, m.		

NOUNS: English -ult = Spanish -lto(a) or -última.

80% 15 Listed

ENGLISH	SPANISH	ENGLISH	SPANISH
adult	adulto, m.	indult	indulto, m.
antepenult	antepenúltima, f.	insult	insulto, m.
assault	ataque, asalto, m.	penult	penúltima, f.
catapult	catapulta, f.	result	resultado, resulta, f.
cult	culto, m.	somersault	salto mortal, m.•
default	falta, f.	tumult	tumulto, m.
fault (blame)	culpa, f.•	vault (jump)	salto, m.•
fault	defecto, m; falta, f.		

NOUNS: English -ant = Spanish -ante or -ente.

75%: 96 Listed

The suffix -ant meaning a person or thing that performs (the specified act) is often used to form nouns from verbs.

Gender: Most are masculine in Spanish unless clearly a female person.

ENGLISH	SPANISH	ENGLISH	SPANISH
accountant	contador, m.•	confidant	confidente, m.
adjutant	ayudante, m.	consonant	consonante, f.
adulterant	adulterante, f.	constant	constante, f.
anticoagulant	anticoagulante, m.	consultant	consejero, m.•
appellant	apelante, m.	contaminant	contaminante, m.
applicant	solicitante, m.•	contestant	contendiente, m.•
aspirant	aspirante, m.	coolant	enfriador, m.•
assailant	asaltante, m.	covenant	contrato, convenio, m.•
assistant	ayudante, asistente, m.	croissant	panecillo, m.•
*attendant	ayudante, asistente, m.•	currant (BOT)	grosella, f.•
celebrant	celebrante, m.	debutant	debutante, f.
claimant	reclamante, m.•	defendant	acusado, demandado, m.•
clairvoyant	clarividente, m.•	deodorant	desodorante, m.
coagulant	coagulante, m.	dependant	dependiente, m.
combatant	combatiente, m.	descendant	descendiente, m.
commandant	comandante, m.	determinant	determinante, m.
communicant	comunicante, m.	dilettant	diletante, m.

ENGLISH	SPANISH	ENGLISH	SPANISH
disinfectant	desinfectante, m.	peasant	campesino, m.•
elegant	elegante, m.	pedant	pedante, m.
elephant	elefante, m.	penchant	inclinación, f.•
emigrant	emigrante, m.	pendant	pendiente, m.
entrant	entrante, m.	pennant	insignia, f.; pendón, m.•
gallant	galán, m.•	pheasant	faisán, m.•
giant	gigante, m.	*plant	planta, f.•
habitant	habitante, m.	propellant	propulsor, m.•
hydrant	boca de agua, f.•	Protestant	protestante, m.
immigrant	inmigrante, m.	quadrant	cuadrante, m.
independant	independiente, m.	radiant	radiante, m.
*infant	criatura, f.; infante, m.	refrigerant	refrigerante, m.
informant	informante, m.	registrant	registrador, m.•
inhabitant	habitante, m.	remnant	remanente, m.
instant	instante, m.	restaurant	restaurante, m.
invariant (MATH)	invariante, f.	resultant (MATH)	resultante, m.
irritant	irritante, m.	ruminant (ZOOL)	rumiante, m.
itinerant	viadante, m.•	secant (MATH)	secante, f.
lieutenant	lugarteniente, m.•	sergeant	sargento, m.•
litigant	litigante, m.	servant	servidor, sirviente, m.
lubricant	lubricante, m.	sextant	sextante, m.
mendicant	mendicante, m.	stimulant	estimulante, m.
merchant	comerciante, mercador, m.•	supplicant	suplicante, m.
migrant	migrante, m.	sycophant	sicofante, m.
militant	militante, m.	tenant	arrendatario, m.•
mitigant	mitigante, m.	transplant	trasplante, m.
mutant	mutante, m.	truant	haragán, tunante, m.•
negotiant	negociante, m.	tyrant	déspota, tirano, m.•
occupant	ocupante, m.	vagrant	vago, vagabundo, m.•
pageant	exhibición teatral, f.•	variant	variante, f.
participant	participante, m.	warrant	decreto, orden, m.•

NOUNS: About 30% of the English nouns ending in -*ment* = Spanish -*mento* or -*miento*. **98 Listed**

Gender: Almost all are masculine in Spanish.

ENGLISH	SPANISH	ENGLISH	SPANISH
abandonment	abandonamiento, m.	condiment	condimento, m.
accompaniment	acompañamiento, m.	confinement	confinamiento, m.
alignment	alineamiento, m.	contentment	contentamiento, m.
aliment	alimento, m.	department	departamento, m.
apartment	apartamento, m.	deportment	comportamiento, m.
*argument	disputa, f; argumento, m.	detachment	destacamento, m.
armament	armamento, m.	detriment	detrimento, m.
*cement	cemento, m.	discernment	discernimiento, m.
commandment	orden, mandamiento, m.	disenchantment	desencantamiento, m.
comment	comento, m.	disfigurement	desfiguramiento, m.
compartment	compartimiento, m.	dismemberment	desmembramiento, m.
complement	complemento, m.	displacement	desplazamiento, m.
compliment	elogio, m.•	document	documento, m.
comportment	comportamiento, m.	element	elemento, m.

ENGLISH	SPANISH	ENGLISH	SPANISH
embellishment	embellecimiento, m.	liniment	linimento, m.
emblazonment	blasonamiento, m.	lodgment	alojamiento, m.•
emolument	emolumento, m.	medicament	medicamento, m.
emplacement	emplazamiento, m.	misalignment	desalineamiento, m.
encampment	campamento, m.	mistreatment	maltratamiento, m.
enchantment	encantamiento, m.	moment	momento, m.
encirclement	encerramiento, m.	monument	monumento, m.
enlacement	enlazamiento, m.	movement	movimiento, m.
enlistment	alistamiento, m.	nutriment	alimento, nutrimento, m.
enrichment	enriquecimiento, m.	ornament	ornamento, m.
entertainment	entretenimiento, m.	parliament	parlamento, m.
entrenchment	atrincheramiento, m.	pavement	acera, f, pavimento, m.
envelopment	envolvimiento, m.	payment	pago, pagamiento, m.
establishment	establecimiento, m.	permanent (wave)	permanente, m.
estrangement	extrañamiento, m.	pigment	pigmento, m.
evolvement	desenvolvimiento, m.	predicament	predicamento, m.
excrement	excremento, m.	presentiment	presentimiento, m.
experiment	experimento, m.	recruitment	reclutamiento, m.
ferment	fermento, m.	refinement	refinamiento, m.
filament	filamento, m.	regiment	regimiento, m.
firmament	firmamento, m.	renouncement	renunciamiento, m.
fragment	fragmento, m.	requirement	requerimiento, m.
fundament	fundamento, m.	resentment	resentimiento, m.
impediment	impedimento, m.	*retirement	retiramiento, m.
implement	implemento, m.	rudiment	rudimento, m.
impoverishment	empobrecimiento, m.•	sacrament	sacramento, m.
increment	aumento, incremento, m.	sediment	poso, sedimento, m.
inducement	inducimiento, m.	segment	sección, f.; segmento, m.
instrument	instrumento, m.	sentiment	sentimiento, m.
interment	enterramiento, m.	supplement	suplemento, m.
internment	internamiento, m.	temperament	temperamento, m.
involvement	envolvimiento, m.	testament	testamento, m.
lament	lamento, m.	*torment	tormento, m.
ligament	ligamento, m.	treatment (MED)	tratamiento, m.
lineament	lineamento, m.	vestment	vestimenta, f.

NOUNS: English -ent other than -ment = Spanish -ente or -ante with a few converting instead to -ento.   85%: 110 Listed

Gender: Almost all are masculine in Spanish.

ENGLISH	SPANISH	ENGLISH	SPANISH
accent	acento, m.	antecedent	antecedente, m.
accident(chance)	casualidad, f.•	ascent	ascenso, m.•
accident(mishap)	accidente, m.	assent	asentimiento, m.•
adherent	adherente, m.	astringent	astringente, m.
adolescent	adolescente, m.	belligerent	beligerante, m.
Advent	Adviento, m.	cement	cemento, m.
affluent	afluente, m.	cent	centavo, m.•
agent	agente, m.	client	cliente, m.

ENGLISH	SPANISH	ENGLISH	SPANISH
coefficient	coeficiente, m.	intent	tención, f; intento, m.
component	componente, m.	intransigent	intransigente, m.
concurrent	concurrente, m.	liquefacient	licuefaciente, m.
confident	confidente, m.	malcontent	malcontento, m.
confluent	confluente, m.	microcurrent	microcorriente, m.
consent	consentimiento, m.•	moment	momento, m.
consequent (MATH)	consecuente, m.	nonresident	no residente, m.
constituent	constituyente, m.	nutrient	alimento nutritivo, m.•
content	contenido, m.•	occident	occidente, m.
continent	continente, m.	opponent	contrario, antagonista, m.•
contingent	contingente, m.	orient	oriente, m.
convalescent	convaleciente, m.	*parent	padres, m.•
convent	convento, m.	patent	patente, m.
*correspondent	correspondiente, m.	patient	paciente, m.
cotangent	cotangente, m.	pendent	pendiente, m.
crescent	creciente, m.	penitent	penitente, m.
crosscurrent	contracorriente, m.	percent	por ciento, m.
current	corriente, m.	permanent	permanente, m.
decedent	difunto, m.•	photocurrent	fotocorriente, m.
deficient	deficiente, m.	portent	presagio, portento, m.
delinquent	delincuente, m.	preadolescent	preadolescente, m.
dependent	dependiente, m.	precedent	precedente, m.
deponent	deponente, m.	present (time)	presente, m.
descendent	descendiente, m.	*present (gift)	regalo, presente, m.
descent	descenso, m.•	president	presidente, m.
detergent	detergente, m.	proponent	proponente, m.
deterrent	factor disuasivo, m.•	quotient (MATH)	cuociente, m.
diluent	diluente, m.	recipient	recipiente, m.
discontent	descontento, m.	regent	regente, m.
dissolvent	disolvente, m.	*rent	renta, f.
dissent	disenso, m.•	resident	residente, m.
dissident	disidente, m.	respondent	respondedor, m.•
docent	docente, m.	rodent	roedor, m.•
effluent	efluente, m.	salient	saliente, m.
emollient	emoliente, m.	serpent	serpiente, f.
equivalent	equivalente, m.	solvent	solvente, m.
event	suceso, evento, m.	student	estudiante, m.
expedient	expediente, m.	stupefacient	estupefaciente, m.
exponent	exponente, m.	subagent	subagente, m.
extent	grado, m.; extensión, f.•	subcontinent	subcontinente, m.
gradient	gradiente, m.	superintendent	superintendente, m.
grandparent	abuelo, m.•	*talent	engenio, talento, m.
incident	incidente, m.	tangent	tangente, m.
incumbent	ocupante, m.•	torrent	torrente, m.
independent	independiente, m.	transient	transiente, m.
ingredient	ingrediente, m.	trident	tridente, m.
insolvent	insolvente, m.	unguent (ointment)	ungüento, m.
insurgent	insurgente, m.	vice-president	vicepresidente, m.

NOUNS: English *-ot* = Spanish *-ot, -oto(a)* or *-ote*.
60%: 32 Listed

ENGLISH	SPANISH	ENGLISH	SPANISH
abbot	abate, m. •	idiot	idiota, m.
aliquot	alícuota, f.	ingot	lingote, m.
apricot	albaricoque, m. •	maggot	gusano, m.; cresa, f. •
ballot	paleleta, balota, f.	marmot	marmota, f.
bigot	intolerante, fanático, m. •	mascot	mascota, f.
carrot	zanahoria, f. •	ocelot	ocelote, m.
chariot	carro, m. •	parrot	loro, papagayo, m. •
cheviot	cheviot, m.	patriot	patriota, m.
compatriot	compatriota, m.	pilot	piloto, m.
copilot	copiloto, m.	pivot	pivote, m.
Cypriot	cipriota, m.	polyglot	políglota, f.
depot	estación, f.; depósito, m. •	riot	tumulto, motín, m. •
despot	déspota, m.	robot	robot, m.
divot	tepe, m. •	spigot	espita, f. •
harlot	zorra, prostituta, f. •	turbot	turbot, m.
Huguenot	hugonot, m.	zealot	fanático, partidario, m. •

NOUNS: English *-pt* = Spanish *-pto (a)* or *-ito*.
55%: 14 Listed

ENGLISH	SPANISH	ENGLISH	SPANISH
attempt	tentativa, f; intento, m. •	manuscript	manuscrito, m.
concept	concepto, m.	postscript	posdata, f. •
conscript	recluta, conscripto, m.	precept	precepto, m.
contempt	desprecio, desdén, m. •	receipt	receta, f.; recibo, m. •
crypt	cripta, f.	subscript	subíndice, m. •
Egypt	Egipto, m.	transcript	copia, f. •
excerpt	excerpta, f.	transept	transepto, m.

NOUNS: Some English *-rt* nouns = Spanish *-rto* or *-rte*.
35%: 22 Listed

Many nouns ending in *-rt* not following this pattern are included in the noun pair or synonym conversion lists.

ENGLISH	SPANISH	ENGLISH	SPANISH
airport	aeropuerto, m.	fort	fortaleza, fuerte, f.
art	arte, m.	heliport	helipuerto, m.
cohort	cohorte, f.	introvert	introvertido, m. •
concert	concierto, m.	part	parte, f.
consort	consorte, m.	passport	pasaporte, m.
convert	converso, m. •	port	puerto, m.
counterpart	contraparte, f.	report	reporte, m.
court (royal)	corte, f.	sport	deporte, m.
desert	yermo, desierto, m. •	subpart	subparte, f.
expert	experto, m.	support	soporte, m.
extrovert	extrovertido, m. •	transport	transporte, m.

NOUNS: English *-ast* = Spanish *-asto(a)* or *-ste*.

                                                                                    90%: 12 Listed

Most scientific words ending in *-blast* and *-plast* convert to *-blasto* and *-plasto* respectively.

ENGLISH	SPANISH	ENGLISH	SPANISH
ballast	balasto, m.	enthusiast	entusiasta, m.
coast	litoral, m.; costa, f.	gymnast	gimnasta, m.
contrast	contraste, m.	iconoclast	iconoclasta, f.
dynast	dinasta, f.	northeast	nordeste, m.
east	este, m.	past	pasado, m.•
endoblast	endoblasto, m.	southeast	sudoeste, m.

NOUNS: English *-est* other than superlatives = Spanish *-esto(a)* or *-és*.
                                    60%: 24 Listed

Gender: Those converting to *-és* are masculine in Spanish. The others are mixed in gender.

ENGLISH	SPANISH	ENGLISH	SPANISH
arrest	arresto, m.	interest(attention)	atención, f.•
behest	orden, mandato, m.•	interest (rate)	interés, m.
bequest	legado, m.; donación, f.•	interest (concern)	interés, m.
conquest	conquista, f.•	interest(share)	participación, f.•
contest	concurso, conflicto, m.•	manifest	manifiesto, m
crest	cresta, f.	palimpsest	palimpsesto, m.
digest	digesto, m.	pest	peste, f.•
disinterest	desinterés, m.	protest	protesta, f.
forest	bosque, m.; selva, f.•	request	súplica, demanda, f.•
harvest	cosecha, f.•	rest (remainder)	resto, m.
incest	incesto, m.	tempest	tormenta, tempestad, f.•
inquest	encuesta, f.	west	oeste, m.•

NOUNS: English *-icist* = Spanish *-ísico* or *-ico*.   **90%: 10 Listed**

Gender: All are masculine in Spanish.

ENGLISH	SPANISH	ENGLISH	SPANISH
astrophysicist	astrofísico, m.	geophysicist	geofísico, m.
biophysicist	biofísico, m.	lyricist	lírico, m.
classicist	clasicista, m.•	physicist	físico, m.
empiricist	empírico, m.	pharmacist	farmacéutico, m.
ethicist	ético, m.	romanticist	romántico, m.

The following nouns ending in *-chemist* follow the same coversion pattern:

chemist	químico, m.	biochemist	bioquímico, m.

NOUNS: English *-ologist* = Spanish *-ólogo* or occasionally
-ista. 98%: 58 Listed

The suffix *-ologist* means a specialist in the particular branch of learning or science.

Cross-Reference: N *-ist, -ology, -ism*; ADJ *-ist, -logical*

Gender: All are masculine in Spanish.

ENGLISH	SPANISH	ENGLISH	SPANISH
anthologist	antólogo, m.	morphologist	morfólogo, m.
anthropologist	antropólogo, m.	musicologist	musicólogo, m.
apologist	apologista, m.	mythologist	mitólogo, m.
archaeologist	arqueólogo, m.	neurologist	neurólogo, m.
astrologist	astrólogo, m.	ophthalmologist	oftalmólogo, m.
bacteriologist	bacteriólogo, m.	orchidologist	orquidólogo, m.
biologist	biólogo, m.	ornithologist	ornitólogo, m.
carcinologist	carcinólogo, m.	osteologist	osteólogo, m.
cardiologist	cardiólogo, m.	paleontologist	paleontólogo, m.
chronologist	cronólogo, m.	pathologist	patólogo, m.
climatologist	climatólogo, m.	penologist	penalista, m.
cosmologist	cosmólogo, m.	pharmacologist	farmacólogo, m.
criminologist	criminólogo, m.	phenologist	fenólogo, m.
dermatologist	dermatólogo, m.	philologist	filólogo, m.
ecologist	ecólogo, m.	phonologist	fonólogo, m.
embryologist	embriólogo, m.	physiologist	fisiólogo, m.
entomologist	entomólogo, m.	proctologist	proctólogo, m.
epidemiologist	epidemiólogo, m.	psychologist	psicólogo, m.
ethnologist	etnólogo, m.	radiologist	radiólogo, m.
etymologist	etimólogo, m.	rhinologist	rinólogo, m.
gastrologist	gastrólogo, m.	seismologist	sismólogo, m.
genealogist	genealogista, m.	serologist	serólogo, m.
geologist	geólogo, m.	sociologist	sociólogo, m.
gerontologist	gerontólogo, m.	technologist	tecnólogo, m.
gynecologist	ginecólogo, m.	theologist	teólogo, m.
immunologist	inmunólogo, m.	toxicologist	toxicólogo, m.
lexicologist	lexicólogo, m.	urologist	urólogo, m.
meteorologist	meteorólogo, m.	virologist	virólogo, m.
mineralogist	mineralogista, m.	zoologist	zoólogo, m.

NOUNS: English *-therapist* and *-therapeutist* = Spanish
-peuta. 99%: 4 Listed

Cross-Reference: N *-ist, -therapy*; ADJ *-peutic*

Gender: All are masculine in Spanish.

ENGLISH	SPANISH	ENGLISH	SPANISH
physiotherapist	fisioterapeuta, m.	radiotherapist	radioterapeuta, m.
psychotherapist	psicoterapeuta, m.	therapist	terapeuta, m.

NOUNS: English *-ist* other than *-ologist, -icist, -urgist, -pathist* and *-therapist* = Spanish *-ista*. English *-urgist* = *úrgico* (*metalúrgico*) and *-pathist* = *-pata* (*neurópata*).

90%: 240 Listed

ENGLISH	SPANISH	ENGLISH	SPANISH
abolitionist	abolicionista, m.	chauvinist	chauvinista, m.
abortionist	abortista, m.•	chemist	químico, m.•
abstractionist	abstracionista, f.	chiropodist	quiropodista, m.
accompanist	acompañante, m.•	Christ	Cristo, m.•
accordionist	acordionista, m.	clarinetist	clarinetista, m.
activist	activista, m.	classicist	clasicista, m.
Adventist	adventista, m.	colonialist	colonialista, m.
agriculturist	agricultor, m.•	colonist	colono, m.•
agronomist	agrónomo, m.•	columnist	columnista, m.
alarmist	alarmista, m.	communist	comunista, m.
alchemist	alquimista, m.	conformist	conformista, m.
allegorist	alegorista, m.	contortionist	contorsionista, m.
allergist	alergista, m.	cubist	cubista, m.
alpinist	alpinista, m.	cultist	cultor, m.•
altruist	altruista, m.	cyclist	ciclista, m.
amethyst	amatista, m.	defeatist	derrotista, m.•
amorist	amante, m.•	deist	deísta, m.
analyst	analista, m.	dentist	dentista, m.
anarchist	anarquista, m.	dogmatist	dogmatista, m.
anatomist	anatomista, m.	dramatist	dramaturgo, m.•
anesthetist	anestesista, m.	*druggist (chemist)	droguista, m.
animist	animista, m.		farmacéutico, m.•
annalist	analista, m.	duelist	duelista, m.
antagonist	antagonista, m.	economist	economista, m.
anti-communist	anticomunista, m.	editorialist	editorialista, m.
archivist	archivista, m.	egoist	egoísta, m.
arsonist	incendiario, m.•	egotist	egotista, m.
artist	artista, m.	escapist	escapista, m.
atheist	ateo, ateísta, m.	essayist	ensayista, m.
automobilist	automovilista, m.	evangelist	evangelista, m.
Baptist	bautista, baptista, m.	evolutionist	evolucionista, m.
bicyclist	biciclista, m.	exhibitionist	exhibicionista, m.
bigamist	bígamo, m.•	existentialist	existencialista, m.
Bolshevist	bolchevique, m.•	exorcist	exorcista, m.
botanist	botanista, m.	expansionist	expansionista, m.
Buddhist	budista, m.	expressionist	expresionista, m.
cacophonist	cacofonista, m.	extortionist	extorsionista, m.
calligraphist	calígrafo, m.•	extremist	extremista, m.
Calvinist	calvinista, m.	Fascist	fascista, m.
canonist	canonista, m.	fatalist	fatalista, m.
capitalist	capitalista, m.	federalist	federalista, m.
caricaturist	caricaturista, m.	feminist	feminista, m.
cartoonist	caricaturista, m.•	feudalist	feudalista, m.
casuist	casuista, m.	finalist	finalista, m.
catalyst	catalizador, m.•	florist	florista, m.
cellist (MUS)	violoncelista, m.	flutist	flautista, m.
centrist	centrista, m.	folklorist	folklorista, m.

ENGLISH	SPANISH	ENGLISH	SPANISH
fundamentalist	fundamentalista, m.	novelist	novelista, m.
futurist	futurista, m.	nudist	nudista, m.
generalist	generalista, m.	oboist	oboísta, m.
guitarist	guitarrista, m.	obstructionist	obstruccionista, m.
harpist	arpista, m.	oculist	oculista, m.
Hebraist	hebraísta, m.	opportunist	oportunista, m.
hedonist	hedonista, m.	optimist	optimista, m.
horticulturist	horticultor, m.•	optometrist	optometrista, m.
humanist	humanista, m.	organist	organista, m.
humorist	humorista, m.	orthodontist	ortodontista, m.
hygienist	higienista, m.	orthopedist	ortopedista, m.
hymnist	himnista, m.	osteopathist	osteópata, m.•
hypnotist	hipnotista, m.	pacifist	pacifista, m.
idealist	idealista, m.	palmist	palmista, m.
imperialist	imperialista, m.	pantheist	panteísta, m.
impressionist	impresionista, m.	Papist	papista, m.
individualist	individualista, m.	parachutist	paracaidista, m.•
industrialist	industrialista, m.	perfectionist	perfeccionista, m.
internist	internista, m.	pessimist	pesimista, m.
isolationist	aislacionista, m.	philanthropist	filántropo, m.•
jingoist	jingoísta, m.	philatelist	filatelista, m.
*journalist	periodista, m.•	pianist	pianista, m.
jurist	jurista, m.	podiatrist	podiátra, m.
leftist	izquierdista, m.•	polygamist	polígamo, m.•
legalist	legalista, m.	populist	populista, m.
linguist	linguista, m.	positivist	positivista, m.
list	lista, f.	pragmatist	pragmatista, m.
literalist	literalista, m.	pro-communist	procomunista, m.
liturgist	liturgista, m.	prohibitionist	prohibicionista, m.
lobbyist	cabildero, m.•	projectionist	proyeccionista, m.
machinist	maquinista, m.	propagandist	propagandista, m.
manicurist	manicurista, m.	protagonist	protagonista, m.
Marxist	marxista, m.	protectionist	proteccionista, m.
masochist	masoquista, m.	psalmist	salmista, m.
materialist	materialista, m.	psychiatrist	psiquiatra, m.•
medalist	medallista, m.	psychoanalyst	psicoanalista, m.
medievalist	medievalista, m.	psychopathist	psicópta, f.•
metallurgist	metalúrgico, m.•	publicist	publicista, m.
Methodist	metodista, m.	pugilist	pugilista, m.
militarist	militarista, m.	purist	purista, m.
miniaturist	miniaturista, m.	racist	racista, m.
modernist	modernista, m.	rapist	raptor, m.•
monarchist	monárquico, m.•	rationalist	racionalista, m.
monogamist	monogamista, m.	*realist	realista, m.
monopolist	monopolista, m.	receptionist	recepcionista, m.
moralist	moralista, m.	reformist	reformista, m.
motorcyclist	motorciclista, m.	regionalist	regionalista, m.
motorist	motorista, m.	reservist	reservista, m.
muralist	muralista, m.	revolutionist	revolucionario, m.•
nationalist	nacionalista, m.	*royalist	realista, m.•
naturalist	naturalista, m.	sadist	sadista, m.
neo-classicist	neoclasicista, m.	satirist	satírico, m.•
neutralist	neutralista, m.	saxophonist	saxofonista, m.
nihilist	nihilista, m.	scientist	científico, m.•

ENGLISH	SPANISH	ENGLISH	SPANISH
secessionist	secesionista, m.	taxidermist	taxidermista, m.
secularist	secularista, m.	telegraphist	telegrafista, m.
segregationist	segregacionista, m.	terrorist	terrorista, m.
semifinalist	semifinalista, m.	theorist	teórico, m.*
sensationalist	sensacionalista, m.	tobacconist	tabaquero, m.*
sentimentalist	sentimentalista, m.	tourist	turista, m.
separatist	separatista, m.	traditionalist	tradicionalista, m.
socialist	socialista, m.	trapezist	trapecista, m.
soloist	solista, m.	trombonist	trombón, m.*
specialist	especialista, m.	typist	mecanógrafo, m.*
spiritualist	espiritualista, m.	unionist	sindicalista, m.*
strategist	estratega, m.*	universalist	universalista, m.
stylist	estilista, m.	urbanist	urbanista, m.
subjectivist	subjectivista, m.	ventriloquist	ventrílocuo, m.*
suffragist	sufragista, m.	violinist	violinista, m.
surrealist	surrealista, m.	violist	violista, m.
symbolist	simbolista, m.	vocalist	vocalista, m.
Taoist	taoísta, m.	Zionist	sionista, m.

NOUNS: English -ut = Spanish -uta or -ut. 95%: 8 Listed

Gender: Almost all are masculine in Spanish.

ENGLISH	SPANISH	ENGLISH	SPANISH
aeronaut	aeronauta, m.	Beirut	Beirut, m.
aquanaut	acuanauta, m.	cosmonaut	cosmonauta, m.
Argonaut	argonauta, m.	debut	debut, m.
astronaut	astronauta, m.	gamut	gama, f.*

NOUNS: English -xt = Spanish -xto. 99%: 3 Listed

Gender: All are masculine in Spanish.

ENGLISH	SPANISH	ENGLISH	SPANISH
context	contexto, m.	text	texto, m.
pretext	pretexto, m.		

NOUNS: English -u preceded by a consonant or not more than one vowel (i.e.: not *chateau*) = Spanish -ú or -u. 95% 10 Listed

Gender: Almost all are masculine in Spanish.

ENGLISH	SPANISH	ENGLISH	SPANISH
Bantu	bantú, m.	Manchu	manchú, m.
caribou	caribú, m.	menu	menú, m.
guru	maestro, m.*	Peru	Perú, m.
Hindu	hindú, m.	Urdu	urdu, m.
jiu-jitsu	jiu-jitsu, m.	Zulu	zulú, m.

NOUNS: English nouns ending in *-x* = Spanish *-x, -z, -ice , -jo* or *-ora*.   90%: 47 Listed

ENGLISH	SPANISH			
	-x	-z	-ice	-jo(a), -ora & Miscel.
administratrix				administradora, f.
annex				anexo, m.
anthrax	ántrax, m.			
anticlimax	anticlímax, m.			
apex			ápice, m.	
appendix	apéndix, m.		apéndice, m.	
arbitratrix				arbitradora, f.
aviatrix		aviatriz, f.		aviadora, f.
borax	bórax, m.			
calyx		cáliz, m.		
cervix		cerviz, m.		
cicatrix		cicatriz, f.		
cirmcumflex				circunflejo, m.
climax	clímax, m.			
coccyx	cóccix, m.			
complex				complejo, m.
cortex				corteza, f.
crucifix				crucifijo, m.
crux				punto crítico, m.
directrix		directriz, f.		directora, f.
duplex	dúplex, m.			
equinox				equinoccio, m.
executrix				testamentaria, f.
flux				flujo, m.
helix	hélix, m.		hélice, m.	
index			índice, m.	
larynx				laringe, f.
latex	látex, m.			
lynx			lince, m.	
matrix		matriz, f.		
onyx	ónix, m.		ónice, m.	
paradox				paradoja, f.
phalanx				falange, f.
phoenix	fénix, m.			
prefix				prefijo, m.
reflex				reflejo, m.
sex				sexo, m.
silex	sílex, m.			
sphynx				esfinge, f.
suffix				sufijo, m.
syntax				sintaxis, f.
telex	télex, m.			
testatrix				testadora, f.
thorax	tórax, m.			
vertex			vértice, m.	
vortex			vórtice, m.	
Zerox	Zerox, m.			

NOUNS: English *-cracy* = Spanish *-cracia*.   99%: 10 Listed

The ending *-cracy* denotes a specified type of government.

Gender: All are feminine in Spanish.

ENGLISH	SPANISH	ENGLISH	SPANISH
aristocracy	aristocracia, f.	hierocracy	hierocracia, f.
autocracy	autocracia, f.	plutocracy	plutocracia, f.
bureaucracy	burocracia, f.	polycracy	policracia, f.
democracy	democracia, f.	technocracy	tecnocracia, f.
gerontocracy	gerontocracia, f.	theocracy	teocracia, f.

NOUNS: English *-acy* other than *-cracy* sometimes = *-acia*, *-ción*, *-ado* or *-idad*.   60%: 34 Listed

Gender: Most are feminine in Spanish.

ENGLISH	SPANISH	ENGLISH	SPANISH
accuracy	exactitud, f.•	inaccuracy	inexactitud, f.•
adequacy	adecuación, f.	inadequacy	inadecuación, f.
advocacy	apoyo, m.•	indelicacy	indelicadeza, f.•
candidacy	candidatura, f.•	inefficacy	ineficacia, f.
celibacy	celibato, m.•	intimacy	intimidad, f.•
confederacy	confederación, f.	intricacy	intrincación, f.•
conspiracy	conspiración, f.	legacy	herencia, f; legado, m.
contumacy	contumacia, f.	legitimacy	legitimidad, f.
degeneracy	degeneración, f.	literacy	alfabetismo, m.•
delicacy	delicadeza, f.•	lunacy	locura, demencia, f.•
diplomacy	diplomacia, f.	obstinacy	obstinación, f.
effeminacy	afeminación, f.	papacy	papado, m.
efficacy	eficacia, f.	pharmacy	farmacia, f.
fallacy	falacia, f.	piracy	piratería, f.•
illegitimacy	ilegitimidad, f.	primacy	primacía, f.
illiteracy	analfabetismo, m.•	privacy	retiro, m.•
immediacy	inmediación, f.	supremacy	supremacía, f.

Following a similar *-cía* conversion pattern:

ENGLISH	SPANISH
prophecy	profecía, f.

NOUNS: English -ancy = Spanish -ancia, -encia, -ión or -idad.
75%: 34 Listed

The suffix *-ancy* is used in forming nouns from verbs or from adjectives ending in *-ant* and denoting action, quality, state or result.

Cross-Reference: N *-ance, -ence, -ency*

Gender: Most all are feminine in Spanish.

ENGLISH	SPANISH	ENGLISH	SPANISH
accountancy	contabilidad, f.	infancy	infancia, f.
ascendancy	ascendiente, m.•	instancy	instancia, f.
blatancy	estridencía, f.•	irrelevancy	irrelevancia, f.
buoyancy	flotación, f.•	malignancy	malignidad, f.
constancy	constancia, f.	militancy	militancia, f.
discrepancy	discrepancia, f.	occupancy	ocupación, f.
dissonancy	disonancia, f.	pregnancy	preñeza, f; embarazo, m.•
dormancy	inactividad, f.•	preponderancy	preponderancia, f.
elegancy	elegancia, f.	redundancy	redundancia, f.
expectancy	expectativa, f.•	relevancy	relevancia, f.
fancy (fantasy)	fantasía, f.•	reluctancy	reluctancia, f.
fancy (notion)	capricho, m.•	repugnancy	repugnancia, f.
flagrancy	flagrancia, f.	tenancy	tenencia, f.
flippancy	ligereza, f.•	truancy	haraganeria, f.•
fragrancy	fragrancia, f.	vacancy	vacancia, f.
hesitancy	hesitación, f.	vagrancy	vagancia, f.
inconstancy	inconstancia, f.	vibrancy	vibración, f.

NOUNS: English -ency = Spanish -encia.   85%: 64 Listed

The suffix *-ency* (equivalent to *-ence*) is used to form abstract nouns corresponding to adjectives ending in *-ent* meaning act, fact, quality, state, result or degree.

Cross-Reference: N *-ence*, ADJ *-ent*

Gender: Almost all are feminine in Spanish.

ENGLISH	SPANISH	ENGLISH	SPANISH
absorbency	absorbencia, f.	*competency	competencia, f.
abstinency	abstinencia, f.	*complacency	complacencia, f.
agency (firm)	agencia, f.	congruency	congruencia, f.
agency (instrum.)	medio, m.•	consistency	consistencia, f.
apparency	apariencia, f.	continency	continencia, f.
ascendency	ascendencia, f.	contingency	contingencia, f.
astringency	astringencia, f.	currency	moneda corriente, f.•
belligerency	beligerancia, f.•	decency	decencia, f.
clemency	clemencia, f.	deficiency	deficiencia, f.
cogency	fuerza lógica, f.•	delinquency	delincuencia, f.

ENGLISH	SPANISH	ENGLISH	SPANISH
dependency	dependencia, f.	insolvency	insolvencia, f.
despondency	desaliento, m.•	insufficiency	insuficiencia, f.
efficiency	eficiencia, f.	latency	latencia, f.
emergency	emergencia, f.	leniency	lenidad, f.•
equivalency	equivalencia, f.	malevolency	malevolencia, f.
excellency	excelencia, f.	permanency	permanencia, f.
exigency	exigencia, f.	potency	potencia, f.
expediency	comodidad, f.•	presidency	presidencia, f.
fluency	afluencia, f.	proficiency	habilidad, f.•
frequency	frecuencia, f.	regency	regencia, f.
impotency	impotencia, f.	residency	residencia, f.
inadvertency	inadvertencia, f.	resiliency	resiliencia, f.
incipiency	principio, m.•	solvency	solvencia, f.
inclemency	inclemencia, f.	stringency	severidad, f.•
incoherency	incoherencia, f.	sufficiency	suficiencia, f.
incompetency	incompetencia, f.	tangency	tangencia, f.
inconsistency	inconsistencia, f.	tendency	tendencia, f.
incumbency	incumbencia, f.	translucency	translucidez, f.•
indecency	indecencia, f.	transparency	transparencia, f.
inefficiency	ineficiencia, f.	truculency	truculencia, f.
infrequency	infrecuencia, f.	urgency	urgencia, f.
inherency	inherencia, f.	virulency	virulencia, f.

NOUNS: English -dy = Spanish -día or -dia(o).

70%: 22 Listed

ENGLISH	SPANISH	ENGLISH	SPANISH
antibody	anticuerpo, m.•	melody	melodía, f.
bastardy	bastardía, f.	Normandy	Normandía, f.
body	cuerpo, m.•	parody	parodia, f.
brandy	aguardiente, coñac, m.•	perfidy	perfidia, f.
candy	dulce, confite, m.•	prosody	prosodia, f.
comedy	comedia, f.	psalmody	salmodia, f.
custody	custodia, f.	remedy	remedio, m.
eddy	remolino, m.•	rhapsody	rapsodia, f.
jeopardy	riesgo, peligro, m.•	study	estudio, m.
lady	dama, señora, f.•	subsidy	subsidio, m.
malady	enfermedad, f.•	tragedy	tragedia, f.

NOUNS: English *-logy* = Spanish *-logía*.   95%: 54 Listed

The ending *-logy* usually denotes a science, doctrine or theory.

Cross-References: N *-logist*

Gender: Almost all are feminine in Spanish.

ENGLISH	SPANISH	ENGLISH	SPANISH
analogy	analogía, f.	mineralogy	mineralogía, f.
anthology	antología, f.	morphology	morfología, f.
anthropology	antropología, f.	musicology	musicología, f.
*apology	apología, f.	mythology	mitología, f.
archaeology	arqueología, f.	neurology	neurología, f.
astrology	astrología, f.	numerology	numerología, f.
bacteriology	bacteriología, f.	ophthalmology	oftalmología, f.
biology	biología, f.	ornithology	ornitología, f.
cardiology	cardiología, f.	pathology	patología, f.
chronology	cronología, f.	penology	penología, f.
cosmology	cosmología, f.	pharmacology	farmacología, f.
criminology	criminología, f.	philology	filología, f.
dermatology	dermatología, f.	phonology	fonología, f.
doxology	doxología, f.	phraseology	fraseología, f.
ecology	ecología, f.	physiology	fisiología, f.
embryology	embriología, f.	psychology	psicología, f.
epidemiology	epidemiología, f.	radiology	radiología, f.
ethnology	etnología, f.	sociology	sociología, f.
etymology	etimología, f.	tautology	tautología, f.
eulogy	elogio, m.•	technology	tecnología, f.
genealogy	genealogía, f.	terminology	terminología, f.
geology	geología, f.	theology	teología, f.
gynecology	ginecología, f.	toxicology	toxicólogía, f.
ideology	ideología, f.	trichology	tricología, f.
immunology	inmunología, f.	trilogy	trilogía, f.
meteorology	meteorología, f.	virology	virología, f.
methodology	metodología, f.	zoology	zoología, f.

NOUNS: English *-gy* other than *-ology* = Spanish *-gia(o)* or *-gía*.   90%: 16 Listed

Gender: Most are feminine in Spanish.

ENGLISH	SPANISH	ENGLISH	SPANISH
allergy	alergia, f.	lethargy	letargo, m.•
clergy	clero, clérigo, m.•	liturgy	liturgia, f.
crystallurgy	cristalurgia, f.	metallurgy	metalurgia, f.
demagogy	demagogia, f.	orgy	orgía, f.
effigy	efigie, f.•	pedagogy	pedagogía, f.
elegy	elegía, f.	prodigy	prodigio, m.
energy	energía, f.	strategy	estrategia, f.
geophagy	geofagia, f.	synergy	sinergia, f.

NOUNS: English -archy = Spanish -arquía or -arcado.
                                                     99%: 8 Listed

The suffix *-archy* denotes ruling or that which is ruled.

Cross-Reference: N *-arch*

Gender: Most are feminine in Spanish.

ENGLISH	SPANISH	ENGLISH	SPANISH
anarchy	anarquía, f.	monarchy	monarquía, f.
autarchy	autarquía, f.	oligarchy	oligarquía, f.
hierarchy	jerarquía, f.	patriarchy	patriarcado, m.
matriarchy	matriarcado, m.	tetrarchy	tetrarquía, f.

NOUNS: English -graphy = Spanish -grafía.   **99%: 22 Listed**

The suffix *-graphy* denotes a writing, drawing, description, discourse, science, etc..

Cross-Reference: N *-graph, -grapher*; ADJ *-graphical*

Gender: All are feminine in Spanish.

ENGLISH	SPANISH	ENGLISH	SPANISH
autobiography	autobiografía, f.	geography	geografía, f.
bibliography	bibliografía, f.	lithography	litografía, f.
biogeography	biogeografía, f.	oceanography	oceanografía, f.
biography	biografía, f.	orthography	ortografía, f.
calligraphy	caligrafía, f.	photography	fotografía, f.
cartography	cartografía, f.	pornography	pornografía, f.
choreography	coreografía, f.	radiography	radiografía, f.
cinematography	cinematografía, f.	stenography	estenografía, f.
cryptography	criptografía, f.	telegraphy	telegrafía, f.
crystography	cristografía, f.	topography	topografía, f.
demography	demografía, f.	typography	tipografía, f.

NOUNS: English -pathy = Spanish -patía.   **99%: 8 Listed**

The ending *-pathy* usually denotes feeling, suffering, disease or treatment of disease.

Cross-Reference: N *-pathia*; ADJ *-pathic*

Gender: All are feminine in Spanish.

ENGLISH	SPANISH	ENGLISH	SPANISH
antipathy	antipatía, f.	osteopathy	osteopatía, f.
apathy	apatía, f.	psychopathy	psicopatía, f.
empathy	empatía, f.	*sympathy	simpatía, f.
neuropathy	neuropatía, f.	telepathy	telepatía, f.

NOUNS: English -ly = Spanish -lio(a), -lía or -lea. 85%: 19 Listed

ENGLISH	SPANISH	ENGLISH	SPANISH
anomaly	anomalía, f.	lily	lirio, m.
antimonopoly	antimonopolio, m.	melancholy	melancolía, f.
assembly	reunión, asamblea, f.	microcephaly	microcefalia, f.
duopoly	duopolio, m.	monopoly	monopolio, m.
emboly (MED)	embolia, f.	oligopoly	oligopolio, m.
family	familia, f.	panoply	panoplia, f.
homily	homilía, f.	reply	respuesta, f.•
Italy	Italia, f.	Sicily	Sicilia, f.
jelly	jalea, f.	supply	oferta, provisión, f.•
July	julio, m.		abastecimiento, m.•

NOUNS: English -nomy = Spanish -nomía.   99%: 6 Listed

The ending -nomy denotes the systematized knowledge of....

<u>Gender:</u> All are feminine in Spanish.

ENGLISH	SPANISH	ENGLISH	SPANISH
agronomy	agronomía, f.	economy	economía, f.
astronomy	astronomía, f.	gastronomy	gastronomía, f.
autonomy	autonomía, f.	physiognomy	fisionomía, f.

NOUNS: English -tomy = Spanish -tomía.   99%: 12 Listed

The ending -tomy denotes a cutting, dividing or operation.

<u>Gender:</u> All are feminine in Spanish.

ENGLISH	SPANISH	ENGLISH	SPANISH
anatomy	anatomía, f.	hysterectomy	histerectomía, f.
appendectomy	apendectomía, f.	lobotomy	lobotomía, f.
colostomy	colostomía, f.	mastectomy	mastectomía, f.
dichotomy	dicotomía, f.	phlebotomy	flebotomía, f.
embolectomy	embolectomía, f.	tonsillectomy	tonsilectomía, f.
gastrectomy	gastrectomía, f.	vasectomy	vasectomía, f.

NOUNS: English -my other than -nomy and -tomy = Spanish -ia or -ía.   60%: 14 Listed

ENGLISH	SPANISH	ENGLISH	SPANISH
academy	academia, f.	infamy	infamia, f.
alchemy	alquimia, f.	monogamy	monogamia, f.
army	ejército, m.•	mummy	momia, f.
bigamy	bigamia, f.	poligamy	poligamia, f.
blasphemy	blasfemia, f.	pygmy	pigmeo, m.•
enemy	enemigo, m.•	sodomy	sodomía, f.
hypothermy	hipotermia, f.	taxidermy	taxidermia, f.

NOUNS: English -ny = Spanish -nia(o) or -nía.   85%: 50 Listed

Gender: Most are feminine in Spanish.

ENGLISH	SPANISH	ENGLISH	SPANISH
acrimony	acrimonia, f.	larceny	hurto, m.•
*agony	agonía, f.	litany	letanía, f.
alimony	pensión, f.•	mahogany	caoba, f.•
balcony	balcón, m.•	matrimony	matrimonio, m.
barony	baronía, f.	miscellany	miscelánea, f.•
botany	botánica, f.•	misogyny	misoginia, f.
cacophony	cacofonía, f.	monotony	monotonía, f.
calumny	calumnia, f.	mutiny	motín, m.•
ceremony	ceremonia, f.	neoteny	neotenia, f.
colony	colonia, f.	parsimony	parsimonia, f.
company	compañía, f.	patrimony	patrimonio, m.
destiny	destino, m.•	peony	peonía, f.
disharmony	inarmonía, f.	progeny	progenie, f.•
ebony	ébano, m.•	pyrotechny	pirotecnia, f.
Epiphany	epifanía, f.	scrutiny	escrutinio, m.
euphony	eufonía, f.	simony	simonía, f.
felony	felonía, f.	symphony	sinfonía, f.
gluttony	glotonería, f.•	synchrony	sincronía, f.
harmony	armonía, f.	synchrony	sincronía, f.
hegemony	hegemonía, f.	syntony	sintonía, f.
hominy	maíz, m.•	telephony	telefonía, f.
homogeny	homogenia, f.	testimony	testimonio, m.
homogony	homogonía, f.	theophany	teofanía, f.
ignominy	ignominia, f.	tyranny	tiranía, f.
irony	ironía, f.	villainy	villanía, f.

NOUNS: English -py = Spanish -pia or -pía.   95%: 18 Listed

Gender: Most are feminine in Spanish.

ENGLISH	SPANISH	ENGLISH	SPANISH
canopy	pabellón, m.•	misanthropy	misantropía, f.
chemotherapy	quimioterapia, f.	philanthropy	filantropía, f.
copy	copia, f.	photocopy	fotocopia, f.
electrotherapy	electroterapia, f.	physiotherapy	fisioterapia, f.
fluoroscopy	fluoroscopia, f.	psychotherapy	psicoterapia, f.
horoscopy	horoscopia, f.	radiotherapy	radioterapia, f.
hydrotherapy	hidroterapia, f.	satrapy	satrapía, f.
mechanotherapy	mecanoterapia, f.	therapy	terapia, f.
microscopy	microscopia, f.	telescopy	telescopia, f.

NOUNS: English -ary = Spanish -ario(a) or -ar.   80%: 72 Listed

The suffix -ary denotes (a) relating to, connected with (dictionary); (b) relating to (military).

Gender: Most are masculine in Spanish.

ENGLISH	SPANISH	ENGLISH	SPANISH
actuary	actuario, m.	intermediary	intermediario, m.
adversary	adversario, m.	itinerary	itinerario, m.
anniversary	aniversario, m.	judiciary	judicatura, f.*
apiary	apiario, m.	legionary	legionario, m.
apothecary	boticario, m.*	*library	biblioteca, f.*
auxiliary	auxiliar, m.	luminary	luminar, m.
aviary	aviario, m.	mercenary	mercenario, m.
beneficiary	beneficiario, m.	military	militares, m.*
boundary	límite, termino, m.*	missionary	misionero, m.*
burglary	robo, m.*	mortuary	morgue, m.*
Calvary	Calvario, m.	notary	notario, m.
canary	canario, m.	obituary	necrología, obituario, m.
capillary	vaso capilar, m.*	ordinary	ordinario, m.
centenary	centenario, m.	ovary	ovario, m.
commentary	comentario, m.	penitentiary	penitenciario, m.
commissary	comisario, m.	preliminary	preliminar, m.
contemporary	contemporáneo, m.*	primary	elección preliminar, f.*
contrary	contrario, m.	proprietary	proprietario, m.
corollary	corolario, m.	quandary	dilema, f.*
depositary	depositario, m.	reactionary	reaccionario, m.
diary	diario, m.	revolutionary	revolucionario, m.
dictionary	diccionario, m.	rosary	rosario, m.
dignitary	dignatario, m.	salary	sueldo, salario, m.
dispensary	dispensario, m.	*sanctuary	santuario, m.
documentary	documental, m.*	secretary	secretario, m.
dromedary	dromedario, m.	seminary	seminario, m.
emissary	emisario, m.	statuary	estatuario, m.
epistolary	epistolario, m.	subsidiary	subsidiaria, f.
estuary	estuario, m.	summary	resumen, sumario, m.
February	febrero, m.*	supernumerary	supernumerario, m.
fiduciary	fiduciario, m.	tertiary	terciario, m.
functionary	funcionario, m.	tributary	tributario, m.
glossary	glosario, m.	vagary	capricho, m.*
granary	granero, m.*	veterinary	veterinario, m.
incendiary	incendiario, m.	visionary	visionario, m.
infirmary	enfermería, f.*	vocabulary	vocabulario, m.

NOUNS: English -ery sometimes = -ería(o) or -erio(a).
20%: 24 Listed
Gender: Most are feminine in Spanish.

ENGLISH	SPANISH	ENGLISH	SPANISH
adultery	adulterio, m.	battery (MIL)	batería, f.
artery	arteria, f.	bravery	bravura, f.*
artillery	artillería, f.	cemetery	cementerio, m.

ENGLISH	SPANISH	ENGLISH	SPANISH
chancery	cancillería, f.•	monastery	monasterio, m.
comradery	camaradaría, f.	mummery	mumería, f.
distillery	destilería, f.	mystery	misterio, m.
dysentery	disentería, f.	perfumery	perfumería, f.
gallery	galería, f.	periphery	periferia, f.
lottery	lotería, f.	presbytery	presbiterio, m.
machinery	maquinaria, f.	refinery	refinería, f.
mastery	maestría, m.	surgery	cirugía, f.
*misery	miseria, f.	tannery	tenería, f.

NOUNS: English -ory = Spanish -orio(a), -ario or -ría.
80%: 40 Listed

The suffix -ory often denotes a place or a thing for.

Gender: Most are masculine in Spanish.

ENGLISH	SPANISH	ENGLISH	SPANISH
accessory	accesorio, m.	lavatory	lavatorio, m.
allegory	alegoría, f.	memory	recuerdo, m.; memoria, f.
armory	armería, f.	observatory	observatorio, m.
category	categoría, f.	oratory	oratorio, m.
chicory	achicoria, f.	promontory	promontorio, m.
conservatory	conservatorio, m.	purgatory	purgatorio, m.
consistory	consistorio, m.	rectory	rectoría, f.
contributory	contribuidor, m.•	reformatory	reformatorio, m.
cosignatory	cosignatario, m.	repertory	repertorio, m.
crematory	crematorio, m.	responsory	responsorio, m.
depository	depositario, m.	signatory	signatario, m.
directory	directorio, m.	story	cuento, historia, f.•
*dormitory	dormitorio, m.	story (floor)	piso, m.•
*factory	fabrica, factoría, m.	suppository	supositorio, m.
glory	gloria, f.	territory	territorio, m.
history	cuenta, historia, f.	theory	teoría, f.
interrogatory	interrogatorio, m.	tory	conservador, m.•
inventory	inventario, m.	trajectory	trayectoria, f.
ivory	marfil, m.•	vainglory	vanagloria, f.
laboratory	laboratorio, m.	victory	victoria, f.

NOUNS: English -metry = Spanish -metría.
99%: 12 Listed

The suffix -metry denotes the process, art or science of measuring.

Cross-References: N -meter; ADJ -metrical

Gender: All are feminine in Spanish.

ENGLISH	SPANISH	ENGLISH	SPANISH
asymmetry	asimetría, f.	pluviometry	pluviometría, f.
barometry	barometría, f.	seismometry	sismometría, f.
crystallometry	cristalometría, f.	symmetry	simetría, f.
geometry	geometría, f.	telemetry	telemetría, f.
isometry	isometría, f.	thermometry	termometría, f.
optometry	optometría, f.	trigonometry	trigonometría, f.

NOUNS: English *-try* other than *-metry* = Spanish *-tría*, *-tería* or *-terio*. 50%: 30 Listed

<u>Gender</u>: Most are feminine in Spanish.

ENGLISH	SPANISH	ENGLISH	SPANISH
ancestry	linaje, m.•	infantry	infantería, f.
artistry	arte, f.•	ministry	ministerio, m.
bigotry	intolerancia, f.•	musketry	mosquetería, f.
biochemistry	bioquímica, f.•	pageantry	espectáculo, m.•
carpentry	carpentería, f.	pantry	despensa, f.•
chemistry	química, f.	pastry	pastelería, f.•
country	campo, m.•	pleasantry	broma, f.•
country	país, m.; nación, f.•	poetry	poesía, f.•
coquetry	coquetería, f.	poultry	aves de corral, m.•
entry	entrada, f.•	psychiatry	psiquiatría, f.
forestry	silvicultura, f.•	registry	registro, m.•
gallantry	galantería, f.	sentry	centinela, f.•
gentry	nobleza, f.•	sophistry	sofistería, f.
idolatry	idolatría, f.	tapestry	tapicería, f.•
industry	industria, f.	vestry	vestuario, m.•

NOUNS: English *-ury* = Spanish *-urio(a)* or *-uría*. 65%: 12 Listed

ENGLISH	SPANISH	ENGLISH	SPANISH
augury	augurio, m.	*luxury	lujo, m.•
century	siglo, centuria, f.	mercury	mercurio, m.
fury	furor, furia, f.	penury	penuria, f.
injury (harm)	daño, injuria, f.	perjury	perjurio, m.
*injury (wound)	lesión, herida, f.•	treasury	tesorería, f.
jury	jurado, m.•	usury	usura, f.•

NOUNS: English *-sy* = Spanish *-sía* or *-sia*. 70%: 26 Listed

<u>Gender</u>: Most are feminine in Spanish.

ENGLISH	SPANISH	ENGLISH	SPANISH
apostasy	apostasía, f.	fantasy	fantasía, f.
autopsy	autopsia, f.	gypsy	gitano, m.•
biopsy	biopsia, f.	heresy	herejía, f.•
catalepsy	catalepsia, f.	hypocrisy	hipocresía, f.
controversy	controversia, f.	idiosyncrasy	idiosincrasia, f.
courtesy	cortesía, f.	jealousy	celo, m.•
curtsy	hecha, f.•	leprosy	lepra, f.•
daisy	margarita, f.•	palsy	parálisis, f.•
discourtesy	descortesía, f.	pansy	pensamiento, m.•
dropsy	hidropesía, f.•	phantasy	fantasía, f.
ecstasy	éxtasis, m.•	pleurisy	pleuresía, f.
embassy	embajada, f.•	poesy	poesía, f.
epistasy	epistasia, f.	pussy	gatito, m.•

NOUNS: English *-ety* = Spanish *-edad*.   70%: 16 Listed

Gender: All are feminine in Spanish.

ENGLISH	SPANISH	ENGLISH	SPANISH
anxiety	ansia, ansiedad, f.	piety	piedad, f.
entirety	totalidad, entereza, f.•	propriety	propiedad, f.
gaiety	jovialidad, alegría, f.•	safety	seguridad, f.•
impiety	impiedad, f.	sobriety	sobriedad, f.
impropriety	impropiedad, f.	society	sociedad, f.
inebriety	inebriedad, f.	subtlety	sutileza, f.•
naivety	candidez, ingenuidad, f.•	surety	fianza, seguridad, f.
notoriety	notoriedad, f.	variety	variedad, f.

NOUNS: English *-ity* usually = *-idad*.

Since English nouns ending in *-ity* are usually derived from adjectives and retain the conversion patterns of those adjectives, these nouns are subdivided into separate lists for nouns derived from each of the main adjective conversion categories plus a miscellaneous *-ity* list. Approximately 95% of all the *-ity* nouns other than those which have an *-idity* ending convert to *-idad* in Spanish. The suffix *-ity* usually denotes state, character or condition. The English usually has a *-ness* form as well.

Gender: Almost all are feminine in gender.

**1. English *-acity* (from *-acious* adjectives) = Spanish *-acidad*.
                                                              90%:   14 Listed**

The exceptions usually convert to *-acia* in Spanish

Cross-Reference: ADJ *-acious*

ENGLISH	SPANISH	ENGLISH	SPANISH
audacity	audacia, f.•	pugnacity	pugnacidad, f.
capacity	capacidad, f.	rapacity	rapacidad, f.
incapacity	incapacidad, f.	sagacity	sagacidad, f.
loquacity	locuacidad, f.	tenacity	tenacidad, f.
mendacity	mendacidad, f.	veracity	veracidad, f.
perspicacity	perspicacidad, f.	vivacity	vivacidad, f.
pertinacity	pertinacia, f.•	voracity	voracidad, f.

2. English -icity (mainly from -ic adjectives) = Spanish -icidad.
99%: 22 Listed

Cross-Reference: ADJ -ic

ENGLISH	SPANISH	ENGLISH	SPANISH
authenticity	autenticidad, f.	felicity	felicidad, f.
catholicity	catolicidad, f.	historicity	historicidad, f.
complicity	complicidad, f.	imbecility	imbecilidad, f.
concentricity	concentricidad, f.	multiplicity	multiplicidad, f.
domesticity	domesticidad, f.	periodicity	periodicidad, f.
duplicity	duplicidad, f.	plasticity	plasticidad, f.
eccentricity	excentricidad, f.	publicity	publicidad, f.
egocentricity	egocentricidad, f.	rusticity	rusticidad, f.
elasticity	elasticidad, f.	simplicity	simplicidad, f.
electricity	electricidad, f.	specificity	especificidad, f.
excentricity	excentricidad, f.	toxicity	toxicidad, f.

3. English -idity (from -id Adjs) = Spanish -idez.
90%: 24 Listed

Cross-Reference: ADJ -id

ENGLISH	SPANISH	ENGLISH	SPANISH
acidity	acidez, f.	morbidity	morbidez, f.
aridity	aridez, f.	nudity	desnudez, f.
avidity	avidez, f.	placidity	placidez, f.
fluidity	fluidez, f.	putridity	putridez, f.
frigidity	frigidez, f.	rancidity	rancidez, f.
humidity	humedad, f.•	rapidity	rapidez, f.
hyperacidity	hiperacidez, f.	rigidity	rigidez, f.
insipidity	insipidez, f.	solidity	solidez, f.
intrepidity	intrepidez, f.	stolidity	estolidez, f.
invalidity	invalidez, f.	stupidity	estupidez, f.
liquidity	liquidez, f.	timidity	timidez, f.
lucidity	lucidez, f.	validity	validez, f.

4. English -ality (from -al adjectives) = Spanish -alidad.
90%: 87 Listed

Cross-Reference: ADJ -al

ENGLISH	SPANISH	ENGLISH	SPANISH
abnormality	anormalidad, f.	carnality	carnalidad, f.
*actuality	realidad, f.•	causality	causalidad, f.
amorality	amoralidad, f.	commerciality	comercialidad, f.
artificiality	artificialidad, f.	confidentiality	confiden-cialidad, f.
banality	banalidad, f.		
bestiality	bestialidad, f.	congeniality	congenialidad, f.
brutality	brutalidad, f.	constitutionality	constitu-cionalidad, f.

ENGLISH	SPANISH	ENGLISH	SPANISH
cordiality	cordialidad, f.	morality	moralidad, f.
criticality	criticalidad, f.	mortality	mortalidad, f.
criminality	criminalidad, f.	municipality	municipalidad, f.
duality	dualidad, f.	musicality	musicalidad, f.
equality	igualdad, f.	mutuality	mutualidad, f.
essentiality	esencialidad, f.	nationality	nacionalidad, f.
eventuality	eventualidad, f.	neutrality	neutralidad, f.
fatality	fatalidad, f.	normality	normalidad, f.
finality	finalidad, f.	originality	originalidad, f.
formality	formalidad, f.	partiality	parcialidad, f.
frugality	frugalidad, f.	personality	personalidad, f.
functionality	funcionalidad, f.	plurality	pluralidad, f.
generality	generalidad, f.	potentiality	potencialidad, f.
geniality	afabilidad, f.•	practicality	viabilidad, f•
homosexuality	homosexualidad, f.	principality	principalidad, f.
hospitality	hospitalidad, f.	provinciality	provincialidad, f.
illegality	ilegalidad, f.	punctuality	puntualidad, f.
illiberality	iliberalidad, f.	quality	c(u)alidad, f.
immateriality	inmaterialidad, f.	rationality	racionalidad, f.
immorality	inmoralidad, f.	reality	realidad, f.
immortality	inmortalidad, f.	sensuality	sensualidad, f.
impartiality	imparcialidad, f.	sentimentality	sentimentalismo, m•
impracticality	impracticabilidad, f.•	sexuality	sexualidad, f.
		speciality	especialidad, f.
individuality	individualidad, f.	spirituality	espiritualidad, f.
informality	informalidad, f.	superficiality	superficialidad, f.
instrumentality	agencia, f.•	technicality	tecnicidad, f•
intellectuality	intelectualidad, f.	temporality	temporalidad, f.
irrationality	irracionalidad, f.	territoriality	territorialidad, f.
joviality	jovialidad, f.	tonality	tonalidad, f.
legality	legalidad, f.	totality	totalidad, f.
lethality	letalidad, f.	triviality	trivialidad, f.
liberality	liberalidad, f.	unilaterality	unilateralidad, f.
locality	localidad, f.	universality	universalidad, f.
marginality	marginalidad, f.	venality	venalidad, f.
materiality	materialidad, f.	verticality	verticalidad, f.
mentality	mentalidad, f.	virtuality	virtualidad, f.
modality	modalidad, f.	vitality	vitalidad, f.

5. English *-bility* (from *-ble* adjectives) = Spanish *-bilidad*.
95%: 135 Listed

Cross-Reference: ADJ *-ble*

ENGLISH	SPANISH	ENGLISH	SPANISH
ability	habilidad, f.	advisability	conveniencia, f.•
acceptability	aceptabilidad, f.	affability	afabilidad, f.
accessibility	accesibilidad, f.	amiability	amabilidad, f.
accountability	contabilidad, f.	applicability	aplicabilidad, f.
adaptability	adaptabilidad, f.	audibility	audibilidad, f.
adjustability	ajustabilidad, f.	availability	disponibilidad, f.•
admissibility	admisibilidad, f.	avoidability	evitabilidad, f.•

ENGLISH	SPANISH	ENGLISH	SPANISH
capability	capacidad, f.•	inexcusability	inexcusabilidad, f.
comparability	comparabilidad, f.	inexorability	inexorabilidad, f.
compatibility	compatibilidad, f.	inexplicability	inexplicabilidad, f.
compressibility	compresibilidad, f.	infallibility	infalibilidad, f.
contestability	contestabilidad, f.	inflexibility	inflexibilidad, f.
convertibility	convertibilidad, f.	inscrutability	inescrutabilidad, f.
credibility	credibilidad, f.	insensibility	insenibilidad, f.
culpability	culpabilidad, f.	inseparability	inseparabilidad, f.
curability	curabilidad, f.	insolubility	insolubilidad, f.
debility	debilidad, f.	instability	inestabilidad, f.
deductibility	deducibilidad, f.	intelligibility	inteligibilidad, f.
desirability	convenencia, f.•	invincibility	invencibilidad, f.
destructibility	destructibilidad, f.	inviolability	inviolabilidad, f.
determinability	determinabilidad, f.	invisibility	invisibilidad, f.
digestibility	digestibilidad, f.	invulnerability	invulnerabilidad, f.
disability	inhabilidad, f.•	irascibility	irascibilidad, f.
divisibility	divisibilidad, f.	irrefutability	irrefutabilidad, f.
durability	durabilidad, f.	irresistibility	irrestistibilidad, f.
eligibility	elegibilidad, f.	irresponsibility	irresponsabilidad, f.
enforceability	exigibilidad, f.•	irrevocability	irrevocabilidad, f.
excitability	excitabilidad, f.	irritability	irritabilidad, f.
fallibility	falibilidad, f.	legibility	legibilidad, f.
feasibility	viabilidad, f.•	liability	responsabilidad, f.•
flexibility	flexibilidad, f.	maneuverability	maniobrabilidad, f.•
gullibility	credulidad, f.•	mobility	movilidad, f.
illegibility	ilegibilidad, f.	navigability	navegabilidad, f.
immobility	inmovilidad, f.	negotiability	negociabilidad, f.
immutability	inmutabilidad, f.	nobility	nobleza, f.•
impeccability	impecabilidad, f.	notability	notabilidad, f.
impossibility	imposibilidad, f.	operability	operabilidad, f.
impracticability	impracticalidad, f.•	palatability	aceptabilidad, f.•
improbability	improbabilidad, f.	patentability	patentabilidad, f.
inability	inabilidad, f.	penetrability	penetrabilidad, f.
inaccessibility	inaccesibilidad, f.	perfectibility	perfectibilidad, f.
inadmissibility	inadmisibilidad, f.	permeability	permeabilidad, f.
inalterability	inalterabilidad, f.	permissibility	permisibilidad, f.
inapplicability	inaplicabilidad, f.	plausibility	credibilidad, f.•
incalculability	incalculabilidad, f.	possibility	posibilidad, f.
incapability	incapacidad, f.•	practicability	viabilidad, f.•
incomparability	incomparabilidad, f.	preferability	preferibilidad, f.
incompatibility	incompatibilidad, f.	presentability	presentabilidad, f.
inconceivability	inconcebibilidad, f.	probability	probabilidad, f.
inconvertibility	inconvertibilidad, f.	questionability	cuestionabilidad, f.
incredibility	incredibilidad, f.	reasonability	racionalidad, f.•
incurability	incurabilidad, f.	reliability	fiabilidad, f.•
indefensibility	indefendibilidad, f.	respectability	respetabilidad, f.
indefinability	indefinibilidad, f.	responsibility	responsibilidad, f.
indigestibility	indigestibilidad, f.	reversibility	reversibilidad, f.
indispensability	indispensabilidad, f.	revocability	revocabilidad, f.
		sensibility	sensibilidad, f.
indisputability	indisputabilidad, f.	sociability	sociabilidad, f.
indivisibility	indivisibilidad, f.	solubility	solubilidad, f.
ineligibility	inelegibilidad, f.	stability	estabilidad, f.
inevitability	inevitabilidad, f.	suggestibility	sugestibilidad, f.

ENGLISH	SPANISH	ENGLISH	SPANISH
suitability	conveniencia, f.•	variability	variabilidad, f.
susceptibility	susceptibilidad, f.	venerability	venerabilidad, f.
tangibility	tangibilidad, f.	viability	viabilidad, f.
tranferability	transferibilidad, f.	vincibility	vencibilidad, f.
transmissibility	transmisibilidad, f.	visibility	visibilidad, f.
unacceptability	inaceptabilidad, f.	volubility	volubilidad, f.
unsociability	insociabilidad, f.	vulnerability	vulnerabilidad, f.

6. English -arity (from -ar adjectives) = Spanish -aridad.
90%: 26 Listed

Cross-Reference: ADJ -ar

ENGLISH	SPANISH	ENGLISH	SPANISH
angularity	angularidad, f.	particularity	particularidad, f.
barbarity	barbaridad, f.	peculiarity	peculiaridad, f.
charity	caridad, f.	polarity	polaridad, f.
circularity	circularidad, f.	popularity	popularidad, f.
clarity	claridad, f.	rarity	raridad, f.
disparity	disparidad, f.	rectangularity	rectangularidad, f.
familiarity	familiaridad, f.	regularity	regularidad, f.
hilarity	hilaridad, f.	similarity	semejanza, f.•
insularity	insularidad, f.	solidarity	solidaridad, f.
irregularity	irregularidad, f.	triangularity	triangularidad, f.
jocularity	jocosidad, f.•	unfamiliarity	desconocimiento, m.•
muscularity	muscularidad, f.	unpopularity	impopularidad, f.
parity	paridad, f.	vulgarity	vulgaridad, f.

7. English -osity (from -ous or -ose adjectives) = Spanish -osidad.
99%: 14 Listed

Cross-Reference: ADJ -ous, -ose

ENGLISH	SPANISH	ENGLISH	SPANISH
animosity	animosidad, f.	pomposity	pomposidad, f.
curiosity	curiosidad, f.	porosity	porosidad, f.
ferocity	ferocidad, f.	religiosity	religiosidad, f.
generosity	generosidad, f.	scrupulosity	escrupulosidad, f.
impetuosity	impetuosidad, f.	verbosity	verbosidad, f.
luminosity	luminosidad, f.	virtuosity	virtuosidad, f.
monstrosity	monstruosidad, f.	viscosity	viscosidad, f.

8. English -ivity (from -ive adjectives) = Spanish -ividad.

90 %: 26 Listed

Cross-Reference: ADJ -ive

ENGLISH	SPANISH	ENGLISH	SPANISH
activity	actividad, f.	negativity	negatividad, f.
captivity	cautividad, f.	objectivity	objetividad, f.
collectivity	colectividad, f.	passivity	pasividad, f.
conductivity	conductividad, f.	perceptivity	perceptividad, f.
creativity	creatividad, f.	productivity	productividad, f.
destructivity	destructividad, f.	radioactivity	radioactividad, f.
exclusivity	exclusividad, f.	reactivity	reactividad, f.
expressivity	expresividad, f.	receptivity	receptividad, f.
festivity	festividad, f.	relativity	relatividad, f.
impassivity	impasibilidad, f.•	retroactivity	retroactividad, f.
inactivity	inactividad, f.	selectivity	selectividad, f.
insensitivity	insensibilidad, f.•	sensitivity	sensibilidad, f.•
nativity	natividad, f.	subjectivity	subjetividad, f.

9. English -ity nouns not having an adjectival counterpart in the eight categories listed above usually also = Spanish -idad, -edad, -dad or -ez(a).

90%: 192 Listed

ENGLISH	SPANISH	ENGLISH	SPANISH
absurdity	disparate, absurdo, m.•	chastity	castidad, f.
adversity	adversidad, f.	Christianity	cristiandad, f.
affinity	afinidad, f.	city	ciudad, f.
agility	agilidad, f.	civility	civilidad, f.
alacrity	alacridad, f.	clarity	claridad, f.
alkalinity	alcalinidad, f.	*commodity	mercancía, f.•
ambiguity	ambigüidad, f.	commodity	comodidad, f.
amenity	amenidad, f.	community	comunidad, f.
amity	amisdad, f.•	complexity	complexidad, f.
annuity	anualidad, f.•	conformity	conformidad, f.
anonymity	carácter anónimo, m.•	congruity	congruidad, f.
antiquity	antigüedad, f.	consanguinity	consanguinidad, f.
anxiety	ansiedad, f.	continuity	continuidad, f.
asperity	aspereza, f.	convexity	convexidad, f.
assiduity	asiduidad, f.	credulity	credulidad, f.
atrocity	atrocidad, f.	crudity	crudeza, f.
austerity	austeridad, f.	deformity	deformidad, f.
authority	autoridad, f.	deity	deidad, f.
benignity	benignidad, f.	density	densidad, f.
brevity	brevedad, f.	depravity	depravación, f.•
calamity	calamidad, f.	dexterity	*destreza, f.
cavity	cavidad, f.	dignity	dignidad, f.
celebrity	celebridad, f.	disunity	disunion, f.•
celerity	celeridad, f.	diversity	diversidad, f.
charity	caridad, f.	divinity	divinidad, f.

ENGLISH	SPANISH	ENGLISH	SPANISH
docility	docilidad, f.	laity	laicos, m.•
ductility	ductilidad, f.	laxity	laxidad, f.
enmity	enemistad, f.•	levity	frivolidad, f.•
enormity	enormidad, f.	longevity	longevidad, f.
entity	entidad, f.	magnanimity	magnanimidad, f.
equanimity	ecuanimidad, f.	majority	mayoría, f.•
equity	equidad, f.	malignity	malignidad, f.
eternity	eternidad, f.	masculinity	masculinidad, f.
extremity	extremidad, f.	maternity	maternidad, f.
facility	facilidad, f.	maturity	maturez, f.•
falsity	falsedad, f.	maturity (bond)	vencimiento, m.•
fecundity	fecundidad, f.	mediocrity	mediocridad, f.
felicity	felicidad, f.	minority	minoría, minoridad, f.
femininity	femineidad, f.	mobility	movilidad, f.
ferocity	ferocidad, f.	modernity	modernidad, f.
fertility	fertilidad, f.	mundanity	mundanidad, f.
fidelity	fidelidad, f.	necessity	necesidad, f.
fragility	fragilidad, f.	nonconformity	disconformidad, f.
fraternity	fraternidad, f.	nudity	desnudez, f.•
frivolity	frivolidad, f.	nullity	nulidad, f.
futility	futilidad, f.	obesity	obesidad, f.
gentility	gentileza, f.	obscenity	obscenidad, f.
*gratuity	donación, f.•	obscurity	obscuridad, f.
gravity	gravedad, f.	oddity	singularidad, f.•
heredity	herencia, f.•	opportunity	oportunidad, f.
homogeneity	homogeneidad, f.	paternity	paternidad, f.
hostility	hostilidad, f.	paucity	escasez, f.•
humanity	humanidad, f.	perpetuity	perpetuidad, f.
humility	humildad, f.	perplexity	perplejidad, f.
identity	identidad, f.	perversity	perversidad, f.
immaturity	inmadurez, f.•	pity	piedad, f.
immensity	inmensidad, f.	posterity	posteridad, f.
immunity	inmunidad, f.	precocity	precocidad, f.
importunity	importunidad, f.	priority	prioridad, f.
impunity	impunidad, f.	privity	conocimiento, m.•
impurity	impureza, f.	probity	probidad, f.
incongruity	incongruencia, f.•	proclivity	proclividad, f.
incredulity	incredulidad, f.	profanity	profanidad, f.
indemnity	indemnidad, f.	profundity	profundidad, f.
indignity	indignidad, f.	prolixity	prolijidad, f.
inequity	inequidad, f.	promiscuity	promiscuidad, f.
inferiority	inferioridad, f.	propensity	propensión, f.•
infertility	infertilidad, f.	prosperity	prosperidad, f.
infidelity	infidelidad, f.	proximity	proximidad, f.
infinity	infinidad, f.	puerility	puerilidad, f.
infirmity	enfermedad, f.	purity	pureza, puridad, f.
*ingenuity	ingeniosidad, f.•	quantity	cantidad, f.
inhumanity	inhumanidad, f.	reciprocity	reciprocidad, f.
iniquity	iniquidad, f.	rotundity	rotundidad, f.
insanity	insania, locura, f.•	salinity	salinidad, f.
insecurity	inseguridad, f.	sanctity	santidad, f.
insincerity	insinceridad, f.	*sanity	sensatez, f.•
integrity	integridad, f.	scarcity	escasez, f.
intensity	intensidad, f.	security	seguridad, f.

185

ENGLISH	SPANISH	ENGLISH	SPANISH
*security	valores, m.•	tranquillity	tranquilidad, f.
senility	senilidad, f.	Trinity	Trinidad, f.
seniority	prioridad, f.•	ubiquity	ubicuidad, f.
serenity	serenidad, f.	unanimity	unanimidad, f.
severity	severidad, f.	uniformity	uniformidad, f.
sincerity	sinceridad, f.	unity	unidad, f.
solemnity	solemnidad, f.	university	universidad, f.
sonority	sonoridad, f.	urbanity	urbanidad, f.
sorority	sororidad, f.	utility	utilidad, f.
spontaneity	espontaneidad, f.	vanity	vanidad, f.
sterility	esterilidad, f.	varsity	universidad, f.•
suavity	suavidad, f.	velocity	velocidad, f.
subtility	sutilidad, f.	*versatility	versatilidad, f.
superiority	superioridad, f.	vicinity	vecindad, f.
taciturnity	taciturnidad, f.	virginity	virginidad, f.
temerity	temeridad, f.	virility	virilidad, f.
tenuity	tenuidad, f.	volatility	volatilidad, f.

NOUNS: English *-ty* other than *-ety*, *-ity* and *-asty* often = *-dad*, *-tad* or *-ía*.   55%: 40 Listed

ENGLISH	SPANISH	ENGLISH	SPANISH
admiralty	almirantazgo, m.•	loyalty	fidelidad, lealtad, f.
amnesty	amnestía, f.	majesty	majestad, f.
beauty	belleza, f.•	modesty	modestia, f.
booty	botín, despojo, m.•	novelty	novedad, f.
bounty	liberalidad, f.•	osteoplasty	osteoplastia, f.
*casualty	casualidad, f.	party (pol.)	grupo, partido, m.•
certainty	certeza, certidumbre, f.•	party (social)	fiesta, reunión, f.•
cruelty	crueldad, f.	party (accomplice)	cómplice, m.•
deity	deidad, f.	penalty	castigo, m; penalidad, f.
deputy	diputado, m.•	plenty	abundancia, plenitud, f.•
difficulty	dificultad, f.	poverty	pobreza, f.
*dishonesty	deshonestidad, f.	property	bienes, m.; propiedad, f.
disloyalty	deslealtad, f.	puberty	pubertad, f.
duty	deber, m.•	realty	bienes raíces, m.•
dynasty	dinastía, f.	royalty	realeza, f.•
*faculty	facultad, f.	sovereignty	soberanía, f.
frailty	flaqueza, debilidad, f.•	specialty,-ity	especialidad, f.
guaranty	guarantía, f.	travesty	parodia, farsa, f.•
*honesty	honradez, honestidad, f.	treaty	convenio, tratado, m.•
liberty	libertad, f.	warranty	guarantía, seguridad, f.•

NOUNS: English *-xy* = Spanish *-xia* or *-jía*.   90%: 6 Listed

<u>Gender:</u>   Almost all are feminine in Spanish.

ENGLISH	SPANISH	ENGLISH	SPANISH
apoplexy	apoplejía, f.	heterodoxy	heterodoxia, f.
epoxy	epoxia, f.	orthodoxy	ortodoxia, f.
galaxy	galaxia, f.	proxy	poder, m.•

2. NOUNS CONVERTING TO SPANISH ON A ONE-ON-ONE BASIS - "PAIR CONVERSIONS"

There are many English nouns not falling within any of the conversion categories but which are so similar in spelling and/or sound in English and Spanish that very little memorization effort is needed. About 1,700 of the most common such nouns are set forth in this list. Approximately 800 more are included in the special noun pair lists beginning on page 203.

ENGLISH	SPANISH	ENGLISH	SPANISH
abbey	abadía, f.	air	aire, m.
abbott	abate, m.	airforce	fuerza aérea, f.
aborigines	aborígenes, m.	airline	aerolínea, f.
abortion	aborto, m.	airplane	aeroplano, m.
abscess	absceso, m.	airport	aeropuerto, m.
absence	ausencia, f.	alabaster	alabastro, m.
absentee	ausente, m.	alleviation	alivio, m.
absurdity	absurdo, m.	alliance	alianza, f.
abyss	abismo, m.	ally	aliado, m.
acceptance	aceptación, f.	altitude	altura, f.
acclaim	aclamación, f.	amber	ámbar, m.
accomodation	acomodamiento, m.	ambience	ambiente, m.
accompanist	acompañante, m.	amen	amén, m.
accomplice	cómplice, m.	ammonia	amoníaco, m.
accord	acuerdo, m.	ammunition	municiones, f.
accordion	acordeón, m.	amount	monto, m.
account	cuenta, f.	ampere	amperio, m.
accountant	contador, m.	amphitheater	anfiteatro, m.
accused	acusado, m.	ancester	antecesor, m.
ace	*as, m.	anchor	ancla, f.
acre	hectárea, f.; acre, m.	anchorage	anclaje, m.
adage	adagio, m.	anchovy	anchova, f.
adequacy	adecuación, f.	anglophobe	anglófobo, m.
adjustment	ajusto, m.	anguish (distress)	angustia, f.
admiral	admirante, m.	anise	anís, m.
admonishment	admonición, f.	annals	anales, m.
adobe	adobe, m.	annex	anexo, m.
adornment	adorno, m.	annexation	anexión, f.
adulterer	adúltero, m.	announcement	anuncio, m.
advantage	ventaja, f.	annulment	anulación, f.
adventurer	aventurero, m.	antichrist	anticristo, m.
adverb	adverbo, m.	antique	antigüedad, f.
advice	aviso, m.	anxiety	ansia, f.
aerodrome	aeródromo, m.	apertif	apertivo, m.
affront	afrenta, f.	apostle	apóstol, m.
agate (Min)	ágata, f.	apparel	aparejo, m.
aggrandizement	agrandamiento, m.	•appeal	apelación, f.
aggressiveness	agresividad, f.	appendage	apéndice, m.
agronomist	agrónomo, m.	appendics	apéndice, m.
aid (help)	ayuda, f.	applause	aplauso, m.
aide	ayudante, m.	apprentice	aprendiz, m.

187

ENGLISH	SPANISH	ENGLISH	SPANISH
apprenticeship	aprendizaje, m.	ball (bullet)	bala, f.
appropriateness	propiedad, f.	ball (dance)	baile, m.
approval	aprobación, f.	ballet	baile, ballet, m.
aptness	aptitud, f	band (gang)	banda, f.
Arab	árabe, m.	band (MUS)	banda, f.
Arabic	árabe, m.	band (ribbon)	faja, banda, f.
arbiter	árbitro, m.	bandage	venda, f.
arbitrariness	arbitrariedad, f.	bank (FIN)	banco, m.
arbitration	arbitraje, m.	banker	banquero, m.
arc	arco, m.	banking	banca, f.
arch	arco, m.	bankrupcy	quiebra, bancarrota, f.
archbishop	arzobisbo, m.	banner (flag)	bandera, f.
archdiocese	archidiócesis, f.	bar (rod)	barra, f.
ark	arca, f.	bar (tavern)	bar, m.
*arm(s)	armamento, m.; arma, f.	barbarian	bárbaro, m.
arrival	llegada, f.; arribo, m.	barbecue	barbacoa, f.
art	arte, f.	barber	barbero, m.
artilleryman	artillero, m.	bard (poet)	poeta, bardo, m.
asbestos	asbesto, m.	barracks	cuarteles, barracas, f.
ascent	ascenso, m.	barrel	barril, m.
asp	áspid, m.	barrier	barrera, f.
asparagus	espárrago, m.	bark (boat)	barca, f.; barco, m.
asphyxiation	asfixia, f.	base	fundamento, m.; base, f.
ass	burro, asno, m.	baseball	béisbal, m.
assasination	asesinato, m.	basin	bacía, vasija, f.
assemblyman	asambleísta, m.	basis	base, f.
associate	socio, m.	bastard	bastardo, m.
assurance	aseguración, f.	bastille	bastilla, f.
asterisk(s)	asterisco, m.	bat	bate, m.
astronomer	astrónomo, m.	batiste	batista, f.
astuteness	astucia, f.	batsman	bateador, m.
athletics	atletismo, m.	batter (mix)	batido, m.
atom	átomo, m.	batter (hitter)	bateador, m.
atomic bomb	bomba atómica, f.	battle	batalla, f.
atrophy	atrofía, f.	bay	bahía, f.
attack	ataque, m.	beast	fiera, res, bestia, f.
audacity	audacia, f.	bee	abeja, f.
*audience	auditorio, m.	beefsteak	biftec, bistec, m.
augmentation	aumento, m.	benediction	bendición, f.
auspices	auspicios, m.	benefit	beneficio, m.
autumn	otoño, m.	Bible	Biblia, f.
avenue	avenida, f.	biceps	bíceps, m.
avocado	aguacate, m.	bigamist	bígamo, m.
avoidance	evitación, f.	bigamy	bigamia, f.
axiom	axioma, f.	bile	bilis, f.
azimuth	azimut, m.	bill (currency)	billete, m.
baby (babe)	niño, bebé, m.	billiard	billar, m.
bagatelle	bagatela, f.	binoculars	binóculo, m.
balance sheet	balance, m.	biped	bípedo, m.
balcony	balcón, m.	bishop	obisbo, m.
bale	bala, f.	bismuth	bismuto, m.
*ball (sphere)	pelota, bola, f.	bison	bisonte, m.

ENGLISH	SPANISH	ENGLISH	SPANISH
bivouac	vivac, m.	calculation	cálculo, m.
*blank	blanco, m.	calibre	calibre, m.
block	bloque, m.	calm	calma, f.
blockade	bloqueo, m.	calorie	caloría, f.
blockage	bloqueo, m.	camaraderie	camaradería, f.
blouse	blusa, f.	*camp	campamento, campo, m.
boat(row)	bote, m.	campaign	campaña, f.
Bolshevik	bolchevique, m.	cancer	cancer, m.
bomb	bomba, f.	candidacy	candidatura, f.
bomb (atomic)	bomba atómica, f.	candidness	candidez, f.
bombardier	bombardero, m.	cane	caña, f.
bombardment	bombardeo, m.	canker	cancro, m.
bomber	bombardero, m.	cannonball	bala de cañón, m.
bond (COM)	bono, m.	canoe	canoa, f.
boomerang	bumerang, m.	cape (coat)	capa, f.
boot	bota, f.	cape (GEOG)	cabo, m.
booty	botín, m.	capitol	capitolio, m.
border (edge)	borde, m.	Capricorn	Capricornio, m.
boredom	aburrimiento, m.	captain	capitán, m.
bottle	botella, f.	captancy	capitanía, f.
bouillabaisse	bullabesa, f.	*car	coche, carro, m.
boulevard	bulevar, m.	carafe	garrafa, f.
bourgeoisie	burguesía, f.	caravelle	caravela, f.
bowl	bol, m.	*card (playing)	naipe, m.; carta, f.
boxer	boxeador, m.	caress	caricia, f.
boxing	boxeo, m.	caries	caries, f.
boycott	boicoteo, boicot, m.	carnage	carnicería, f.
bravery	bravura, f.	carp (fish)	carpa, f.
breach (gap)	brecha, f.	carpenter	carpintero, m.
breeze	brisa, f.	*cart	carreta, f.; carro, m.
bridge (cards)	bridge, m.	carter	carretero, m.
bridle	brida, f.	cartilage	cartílago, m.
brilliance	brillantez, f.	cartridge	cartucho, m.
brioche	brioche, m.	case (event)	caso, m.
bronze	bronce, m.	casern	caserna, f.
brooch (broach)	broche, m.	cashmere	cachemira, f.
brush	cepillo, m.; brocha, f.	caste	casta, f.
bruskness	brusquedad, f.	castle	castillo, m.
bulb (BOT)	bulbo, m.	cat	gato, m.
bulwark	baluarte, m.	catacomb	catacumba, f.
bunion	bunio, m.	catalyst	catalizador, m.
buoy	boya, f.	catarrh	catarro, m.
burgess	burgés, m.	catheter	catéter, m.
bus	ómnibus, autobús, m.	cauliflower	coliflor, m.
bust	busto, m.	cause	causa, f.; motivo, m.
buzzard	busardo, m.	caution	precaución, f.
cabin	cabaña, f.	cavalier	caballero, m.
cabaret (club)	cabaret, f.	cavalry	caballería, f.
cabinet (GOV)	gabinete, m.	cave	cueva, f.
cable	cable, m.	cavern	caverna, f.
cadaver	cadáver, m.	cedar	cedro, m.
*cafe	café, m.	celibate (bachelor)	célibe, m.

189

ENGLISH	SPANISH	ENGLISH	SPANISH
cell (organic)	célula, f.	clime (climate)	clima, f.
censorship	censoria, censura, f.	cloister	claustro, m.
cent	céntimo, centavo, m.	clone	clon, m.
centennial	centenario, m.	clove	clavo, m.
center	medio, centro, m.	club (assoc.)	club, m.
centipede	centípedo, m.	coach (car)	vagón, coche, m.
certainty	certeza, f.	coachman	cochero, m.
chalice	cáliz, m.	coast (shore)	litoral, m.; costa, f.
champagne	champaña, f.	cocktail	coctel, m.
champion	campeón, m.	cocoa	cacao, m.
championship	campeonata, f.	coconut	coco, m.
chancellor	canciller, m.	code	código, m.
chancre	chancro, m.	codicil	codicilio, m.
channel	canal, m.	coffee	café, m.
chant	canto, m.	cognac	coñac, m.
chaplain	capellán, m.	cointreau	cointreau, m.
chapter	capítulo, m.	coke	coque, m.
*character (nature)	carácter, m.	coldcream	colcrén, m.
chauffeur	chófer, m.	collar	cuelo, m.
check (bank)	cheque, m.	collie	collie, m.
checkmate	jaque mate, m.	colloquy	coloquio, m.
cheese	queso, m.	colonist	colono, m.
chemist	químico, m.	coloring	colorante, m.
chemistry	química, f.	column	columna, f.
cherry	cereza, f.	combustible	combustible, m.
cherub(-im)	querubín, m.	comestible	comestible, m.
chestnut	castaño, m.	Comintern	comintern, m.
chief (head)	jefe, m.	commencement	comienzo, m.
chimney	chimenea, f.	commerce	comercio, m.
chimpanzee	chimpancé, m.	commissioner	comisionado, m.
Chinese	chino, m.	committee	comité, m.
chisel	cincel, m.	communiqué	comunicación, f.
chlorine	cloro, m.	companion	compañero, m.
chocolate	chocolate, m.	companionship	compañerismo, m.
choir	coro, m.	comparison	comparación, f.
chorale	coral, m.	compass (drawing)	compás, m.
chord	cuerda, f.	competition	competencia, f.
Christ	Cristo, m.	composer	compositor, m.
Christendom	cristiandad, f.	composit	compuesto, m.
chrome	cromo, m.	compost	abono, compuesto, m.
chromosome	cromosoma, f.	comradeship	camaradaría, f.
chronicle	crónica, f.	concave	cóncavo, m.
cider	sidra, f.	*conception (idea)	concepto, m.
cigarette	cigarrillo, m.	conche	concha, f.
cinema	cine, m.	concierge	conserje, m.
cipher	cifro, m.	conciseness	concisión, f.
cistern	cisterna, f.	condescension	condescendencia, f.
claim	reclamación, f.	condom	condón, m.
class	clase, f.	condonement	condonación, f.
clause	cláusula, f.	conferee	conferido, m.
clavichord	clavicordio, m.	confessional	confesionario, m.
clergyman (cleric)	clérigo, m.	confidence	confianza, f.
clerkship	clérigo, m.	conformance	conformidad, f.
clientele	clientela, f.	Congressman	congresista, f.

ENGLISH	SPANISH	ENGLISH	SPANISH
conifer	conífero, m.	courtier	cortesano, m.
connoisseur	conocedor, m.	courtiousness	cortesía, f.
conquerer	conquistador, m.	courtship	corte, f.
conquest	conquista, f.	covenant	convenio, m.
consciousness	conciencia, f.	coward	cobarde, m.
consent	consentimiento, m.	cowardice	cobardía, f.
conservative	conservador, m.	crater	cráter, m.
conserve	conserva, f.	cravat	corbata, f.
consignee	consignatario, m.	creditor	acreedor, m.
consignment	consignación, f.	creed	credo, m.
*consolation	solaz, f.; consuelo, m.	crime	delito, crimen, m.
constraint	constreñimiento, m.	criterion	criterio, m.
*consumption	consumo, m.	cross	cruz, f.
contagion	contagio, m.	croupier	crupié, m
content(s)	contenido, m.	crown	corona, f.
contentedness	contento, m.	crudity	crudeza, f.
continuance	continuación, f.	cruise	crucero, m.
contour	contorno, m.	cruiser	crucero, m.
contraband	contrabando, m.	crusader	cruzado, m.
contrabass (MUS)	contrabajo, m.	crust	costra, f.
contractor	contratante, m.	cube	cubo, m.
contratemps	contratiempo, m.	*cup (trophy)	copa, f.
controller	controlador, m.	curio	curiosidad, f.
convention	convenio, m.	curry	cari, m.
convert	converso, m.	curtain	cortina, f.
convoy	convoy, m.	curve	curva, f.
coolie	culí, m.	custodianship	costodia, f.
copper	cobre, m.	custom	costumbre, f.
*copy	copia, f.	cycling	ciclismo, m.
coquette	coquetón, m.	cylinder	cilindro, m.
cord	cuerda, f.; cordón, m.	cypress	ciprés, m.
cork	corcho, m.	cyst	vesicula, f.; quiste, m.
cornice	cornisa, f.	dachshund	dachshund, m.
corp	cuerpo, m.	dagger	puñal, m.; daga, f.
corps	cuerpo, corps, m.	dame	doña, dama, f.
correspondent	corresponsal, m.	dance	baile, danza, f.
corsair	corsario, m.	dart	dardo, m.
corset	corsé, m.	data	datos, m
cortege	cortejo, m.	*date (fruit)	dátil, m.
cosine	coseno, m.	day	día, m.
cossack	cosaco, m.	dean	deán, m.
*cost	precio, costo, m.	debacle	debacle, m.
cot	catre, m.	debarkation	desembarco, m.
council	consejo, concilio, m.	debt	deuda, f.
counsel	consejo, m.	decease	fallecimiento, deceso, m.
count (title)	conde, m.	decline	declinación, f.
count	cuenta, f.	decree	decreto, m.
counterattack	contraataque, m.	defalcation	defalco, m.
counterbalance	contrabalanza, f.	defender	defensor, m.
counterpart	contraparte, f.	defiance	desafío, m.
couple	copla, f.	delicateness	delicadez, f.
couplet	copla, f.	deliciousness	delicia, f.
course (drift)	curso, m.	*delight, -fulness	deleite, f.
*court (royal)	corte, f.	demagoguery	demagogia, f.
		demand (ECON)	demanda, f.

ENGLISH	SPANISH	ENGLISH	SPANISH
demon	demonio, m.	disunity	disunión, f.
denouncement	denuncia, f.	dividend	dividendo, m.
denture	dentatura, f.	divorce	divorcio, m.
departure	salida, partida, f.	divorcee	divorciada, f.
depot	deposito, m.	dock	dique, m.
depravity	depravación, f.	documentary	documental, m.
dervish	derviche, m.	dolphin	delfín, m.
descent	descendencia,f;descenso, m.	domain	dominio, m.
design (drawing)	diseño, m.	dominance	predominio, m.
desire	gana, f.; deseo, m.	dominion	dominio, m.
despair	desesperación, f.	donee	donatario, m.
despatch	despacho, m.	donor	dador, donante, m.
destiny	destino, m.	dosage	dosificación, f.
destroyer	destructor,destróyer, m.	dose	dosis, f.
detail	detalle, m.	double	doble, m.
detective	detective, m.	doubt	duda, f.
devotee	devoto, m.	douche	ducha, f.
diabetes	diabetes, f.	dredge	draga, f.
diamond	diamante, m.	drug	medicina, droga, f.
diatribe	diatriba, f.	drugstore	droguería, f.
dictation	dictado, m.	duchy	ducado, m.
dictatorship	dictadura, f.	duke	duque, m.
dictum	dictamen, m.	dukedom	ducado, m.
dike	dique, m.	eagle	águila, f.
dinghy	dinga, f.	east	este, m.
diocese	diócesis, f.	ebony	ébano, m.
diphthong	diptongo, m.	ecstacy	éxtasis, écstasi, m.
directness	derechura, f.	effigy	efigie, f.
directorship	directorado, m.	elf	duende, enano, elfo, m.
dirigible	dirigible, m.	elm	olmo, m.
disappearance	desaparición, f.	*embarkation	embarco, m.
disarmament	desarme, m.	embarrassment	embarazo, m.
disaster	desastre, m.	embassy	embajada, f.
disc	disco, m.	embrace	abrazo, m.
discharge	disparo,m; descarga, f.	embryo	embrión, f.
disciple	discípulo, m.	emerald	esmeralda, f.
discontentment	descontento, m.	employ	empleo, m.
discontinuance	descontinuación, f.	employee	empleado, m.
discord	discordia, f.	employment	empleo, m.
discount	rebaja,f.; descuento, m.	enchantment	encanto, m.
discoverer	descubridor, m.	enclave	enclave, m.
discovery	descubrimiento, m.	encounter	encuentro, m.
disdain	desdén, m.	endorsee	endosado, m.
*disgrace	desgracia, f.	endorsement	endoso, m.
*disgust	disgusto, m.	enemy	enemigo, m.
disillusionment	desilusión, f.	engineering	ingeniería, f.
disinheritance	desheredación, f.	English	inglés, m.
disk	disco, m.	enmity	enemistad, f.
*dismay	desmayo, m.	ensign (flag)	enseña, f.
disorder	desorden, m.	enslavement	esclavitud, f.
*dispach	despacho, m.	entirety	entereza, f.
dispersement(-sal)	dispersión, f.	entrance (entry)	entrada, f.
disposal	disposición, f.	envoy	enviado, m.
distributorship	distribuidor, m.	envy	*envidia, f.
disturbance	disturbio, m.	epidemic	epidemia, f.

ENGLISH	SPANISH	ENGLISH	SPANISH
episode	episodio, m.	finances	finanzas, m.
epistle	epístola, f.	financing	financiamiento, m.
epoch	época, f.	finesse	finura, f.
epsom	epsomita, f.	fineness	fineza, f.
equalization	igualación, f.	finish	fin, m.
equipment	*equipo, equipaje, m.	firmness	firmeza, f.
escalation	escalada, f.	fjord	fiordo, m.
escalator	escalera, f.	flame	llama, f.
escape	escape, m.	flamingo	flamenco, m.
escort	escolta, f.	flank (side)	llado, m.; flanco, m.
Eskimo	esquimal, m.	flask	frasco, m.
esprit	espíritu, m.	fleet	flota, f.
essay	ensayo, m.	flirtation	flirteo, m.
esteem	estimación, f.	*float	flotador, m.
*estimate	estimación, f.	flourish	floreo, m.
ether	éter, m.	flow (tide)	flujo, m.
eunuch	eunuco, m.	flower	flor, f.
exactness	exactitud, f.	flu	influenza, f.
exam	examen, m.	flute	flauta, f.
examination	examen, m.	flux	flujo, m.
*example	ejemplar, ejemplo, m.	folklore	folklore, m.
excitement	excitación, f.	football (soccer)	*fútbal, m.
expectancy	expectativa, f.	force	vigor, m.; fuerza, f.
explanation	explicación, f.	forceps	forceps, m.
export	exportación, f.	fort	fuerte, f.
exposé	exposición, f.	fortress	fortaleza, f.
exposure	exposición, f.	fossil	fósil, m.
extacy	éxtasis, m.	foundry	fundición, m.
extent	extensión, f.	fountain	fuente, f.
extermination	exterminio, m.	foyer	foyer, m.
extrovert	extrovertido, m.	franc	franco, m.
fable	fábula, f.	franchise	franquicia, f.
face (surface)	faz, f.	frankness	franqueza, f.
fair	feria, f.	fraud (deceit)	engaño, fraude, m.
faith (trust)	fe, f.	freemasonry	masonería, f.
falconer	halconero, m.	freight	flete, m.
falsehood	falsedad, f.	French	francés, m.
fanfare	fanfarria, f.	frenzy	frenesí, m.
farce	farsa, f.	freshness	frescura, f.
*fault(defect)	defecto, m; falta, f.	friar	fraile, m.
*feast	fiesta, f.	fritter	fritilla, f.
felt	fieltro, m.	front (fore)	faz, frente, f.
fervency	fervor, m.	frontier	frontera, f.
fetish	fetiche, m.	fruit	fruto, m.; fruta, f.
feud	feudo, m.	functioning	funcionamiento, m.
fever	fiebre, m.	fund(s)	fondo, m.
fez	fez, m.	fundimental	fundamento, m.
fiber	fibra, f.	funding	fundación, f.
fierceness	fiereza, f.	fuse	fusible, m.
fife	flautín, pífano, m.	gable	gablete, m.
fig	higo, m.	*gain	ganancia, f.
filibuster	filibustero, m.	galley	galera, f.
film	película, f.; film, m.	gallop	galope, m.
filter	filtro, m.	galosh	galocha, f.
finale	final, m.	gamut	gama, f.

193

ENGLISH	SPANISH	ENGLISH	SPANISH
garden	jardín, m.	gyration	giro, m.
gardner	jardinero, m.	Hades	hades, m.
gargle	gárgara, f.	ham	jamón, m.
gargoyle	gárgola, f.	hammock	hamaca, f.
garnish	guarnición, f.	hamster	hámster, m.
garrison	guarnición, f.	handicap	handicap, m.
gas station	gasolinera, f.	harness	arneses, m.
gauze	gasa, f.	harp	arpa, f.
gazelle	gacela, f.	hashish	hachich, m.
gendarmerie	gendarmería, f.	hatchet	hacha, f.
gender	sexo, género, m.	hay	paje, heno, m.
gene	gen, m.	Hebrew	judío, hebreo, m.
genie	genio, m.	hectare	hectária, f.
gentility	gentileza, f.	heir	heredero, m
germ	microbio, germen, m.	helicopter	helicoptero, m.
gerund	gerundio, m.	helmet	casco, yelmo, m.
gesture	gesto, m.	hemisphere	hemisferio, m.
geyser	géiser, m.	hemophiliac	hemofílico, m.
*gin	ginebra, f.	henry (ELEC)	henrio, m.
ginger	jengibre, m.	herald	heraldo, m.
glacier	glaciar, m.	heraldry	heráldica, f.
gland	glandula, f.	herb	yerba, hierba, f.
globe	orbe, globo, m.	heretic	hereje, m.
gloss	glosa, f.	heritage	herencia, f.
golf	golf, m.	hermitage	ermita, f.
golfer	golfista, m.	hero	héroe, m.
gondolier	gondolero, m.	herring	arenque, m.
gong	gong, m.	hertz (PHYS)	hertzio, m.
goulash	gulash, m.	hestitance	hesitación, f.
gout	gota, f.	hex	hechizo, m.
governance	gobernación, f.	historian	historiador, m.
government	gobierno, m.	hockey	hockey, m.
grace	genileza, gracia, f.	holocaust	holocausto, m.
graciousness	gracia, f.	homerun	jonrón, m.
graffiti	grafitos, m.	horizon	horizonte, m.
grain	grano, m.	hour	hora, f.
grammar	gramática, f.	howl	aullido, m.
grandeur	grandeza, f.	humidity	humedad, f.
grange	granja, f.	hygiene	higiene, f.
gratefulness	gratitud, f.	hymn	himno, m.
gravel	grava, f.	idiocy	idiotez, f.
grease (fat)	manteca, grasa, f.	idyll	idilio, m.
grippe	gripe, f.	image	imagen, f.
gross (measure)	gruesa, f.	immaturity	inmadurez, f.
group	grupo, m.	import(s)	importaciones, f.
guarantee	guarantía, f.	*import	sentido, m.; importancia, f.
guard	guardia, f.; guarda, f.	impurity	impureza, f.
guardianship	guardianía, f.	inappropriateness	impropiedad, f.
guidance	guía, f.	incitement	incitación, f.
guide	guía, f.	incongruity	incongruencia, f.
guitar	guitarra, f.	indecisiveness	indecisión, f.
*gulf (bay)	golfo, m.	indemnification	indemnización, f.
gum (chewing)	chicle, m.; goma, f.	index finger	índice, m.
gutter	arroyo, m.; gotera, f.	indication	indicio, m.
gym	gimnasio, m.	individual	individuo, m.

ENGLISH	SPANISH	ENGLISH	SPANISH
indoctrination	adoctrinamiento, m.	labour	labor, f.
inebriation	ebriedad, f.	labyrinth	laberinto, m.
ineptness	ineptitud, f.	lackey	lacayo, m.
inertness	inercia, f.	lacquer	barniz, m.; laca, f.
influence	influjo, m.	lagoon	laguna, f.
infuriation	enfurecimiento, m.	lake	lago, m.
ingenuity	ingeniosidad, f.	lamp	lámpara, f.
inhabitant	habitante, m.	language	lengua, f.
inheritance	herencia, f.	lantern	linterna, f.
insert	inserción, f.	lasciviousness	lascivia, f.
insurrectionist	insurrecto, m.	launch	lancha, f.
interest (rate)	interés, m.	leader	líder, m.
interim	ínterin, m.	legatee	legatario, m.
intermission	intermedio, m.	legend	leyenda, f.
intern	interno, m.	legume	legumbre, f.
internee	internado, m.	leniency (-ience)	lenidad, f.
interpreter	intérprete, m.	lens	lente, f.
introvert	introvertido, m.	lentil (BOT)	lenteja, f.
intruder	instruso, m.	leopard	leopardo, m.
invitee	invitado, m.	leper	leproso, m.
iodine	yodo, m.	leprosy	lepra, f.
ire	ira, f.	lethargy	letargo, m.
isle (island)	isla, f.	lettace	lechuga, f.
isolation	aislamiento, m.	letter (ABCs)	letra, f.
jacquard	jacquard, m.	licensee	licenciado, m.
jade	jade, m.	lieutenant	teniente, m.
jalousie	celosía, f.	lilac	lila, f.
jar (urn,vase)	jarra, f.	*lily	lirio, m.
jazz	jazz, m.	lime	limón, m.
jeep	jeep, m.	line	línea, f.
jelly	jalea, f.	lingerie	lencería, f.
jersey	jersey, m.	liqueur	licor, m.
jig (MUS)	jiga, f.	liter	litro, m.
jockey	jinete, jokey, m.	literary person	literato, m.
jonquil (BOT)	junquillo, m.	litter (bed)	camilla, litera, f.
jot	jota, f.	livery	uniforme, m.; librea, f.
journey	viaje, m.; jornada, f.	lobe	lóbulo, m.
joust	justa, f.	locale	localidad, f.
*jubilance(-lation)	júbilo, m.	locomotive	locomotora, f.
jubilee	jubileo, m.	lodge	posada, logia, f.
judiciary	judicatura, f.	lot (batch)	lote, m.
juice	jugo, m.	lucre	lucro, m.
juniper	junípero, m.	luster	lustre, m.
jury	jurado, m.	*luxury	lujo, m.
just	justo, m.	lycee	liceo, m.
justness	justicia, f.	lymph	linfa, f.
juvenile	joven, m.	lynx	lince, m.
Kamikase	Kamikase, m.	lyre	lira, f.
kangeroo	canguro, m.	macaroni	macarrones, m.
kayak	kayak, m.	magic	magia, f.
keel	quilla, f.	magician	mago, m.
kilowatt	kilovatio, m.	maintenance	mantenimiento, m.
kindergarten	kindergarten, m.	maize	maíz, m.
kiosk	quiosco, m.	majority	mayoría, f.
knot	nudo, m.	malignance	malignidad, f.

ENGLISH	SPANISH	ENGLISH	SPANISH
mandible	mandíbula, f.	miner	minero, m.
mandril	mandril, m.	minister (GOVT)	ministro, m.
manganese	manganese, m.	mint (BOT)	menta, f.
mangoose	mangosta, f.	minuend	minuendo, m.
manikin	maniquí, m.	minutes	actas, minutas, f.
manner	modo, m.; manera, f.	miscellany	miscelánea, f.
maneuverability	maniobrabilidad, f.	missionary	misionero, m.
manoeuvre	maniobra, f.	misuse	mal uso, m.
mansard	mansarda, f.	mitre	mitra, f.
*mantle	manto, m.	mitten	mitón, m.
map	carta, f.; mapa, m.	mix	mixtura, f.
marble (MIN)	mármol, m.	mizzen	mesana, f.
march	marcha, f.	modiste	modista, f.
mariner	marinero, marino, m.	mogul	mogol, m.
*mark (sign)	símbolo, m.; marca, f.	molasses	melaza, f.
mark	marca, f.	mold (form)	matriz, f.; molde, m.
market	marcado, m.	molestation	molestia, f.
marquis	marqués, m.	mollusk	molusco, m.
marquise	marquesa, f.	monarchist	monárquico, m.
martyrdom	martirio, m.	money	dinero,m.;plata,moneda, f.
marvel	maravilla, f.	monk	monje, m.
mask	máscara, f.	monkey	mono, m.
mass (pile)	montón, m.; masa, f.	monolith	monolito, m.
mass (religious)	misa, f.	monosyllable	monosílabo, m.
masseur	masajista, m.	monseigneur	monseñor, m.
mast	mástil, m.	monster	monstro, m.
master	maestro, m.	moon	luna, f.
math	matemática, f.	morale	moral, f.
matter	materia, f.	morals	moral, moralidad, f.
maturity	madurez, f.	Moses	Moisés, m.
maxim	máxima, f.	mosque	mezquita, f.
mayonnaise	mayonesa, f.	moss	musgo, m.
meeting	reunión, f.; mitin, m.	mother	madre, f.
megawatt	megavatio, m.	motif	motivo, m.
member	miembro, m.	motorbike	motocicleta, f.
memoir	memoria, f.	motorboat	bote a motor, m.
menace	amenaza, f.	moulding	moldura, f.
merchandise	mercancía, f.	mountain (mount)	montaña, f.
merchant	mercador, m.	mounting (jewels)	montadura, f.
message	mensaje, m.	move	movimiento, m.
messenger	mensajero, m.	multiple	múltiplo, m.
Messiah	Mesías, m.	multiplicand	multiplicando, m.
metallurgist	metalúrgico, m.	murmur	murmullo, m.
method	método, m.	muscilage	muscilago, m.
metropolis	metrópoli, f.	muslin	gasa, musalina, f.
microbe	microbio, m.	mustache	bigote, mostacho, m.
microfilm	microfilm, m.	mustang	mustango, m.
microsecond	microsegundo, m.	mustard	mostaza, f.
mil	mil, m.	mute	mudo, m.
mildew	mildiú, mildeu, m.	mutiny	motín, m.
mile	milla, f.	myrrh	mirra, f.
military man	militar, m.	myrtle	mirto, m.
militiaman	miliciano, m.	myth	mito, m.
mimic	mimo, m.	name	nombre, m.
mimicry	mímica, f.	nanosecond	nanosegundo, m.

ENGLISH	SPANISH	ENGLISH	SPANISH
naturalness	naturalidad, f.	palace	palacio, m.
nerve	nervio, m.	paleness	palidez, f.
niche	nicho, m.	palm tree	palmera, palma, f.
nobility	nobleza, f.	panache	penacho, m.
nobleman	noble, m.	panther	pantera, f.
nocturne	nocturno, m.	pantofle	pantufla, f.
node	nudo, m.	paper	papel, m.
nominee	nómino, m.	papistry	papismo, m.
noncompliance	incomplimiento, m.	par	paridad, f.
normalcy	normalidad, f.	*parable	parábola, f.
north	norte, m.	parachute	paracaídas, m.
North Pole	Polo Norte, m.	paradise	paraíso, m.
northeast	nordeste, m.	paraphrase	paráfrasis, f.
northwest	noroeste, m.	park	parque, m.
nude	desnudo, m.	part	parte, f.
novelty	novedad, f.	participle	participio, m.
number	número, m.	parting	partida, f.
nymph	ninfa, f.	party (politics)	partido, m.
obelisk	obelisco, m.	pass (permit)	*permiso, pase, m.
oboe	oboe, m.	passage	pasillo, paso, m.
obstinacy (-ness)	obstinación, f.	passenger	pasajero, m.
octahedron	octaedro, m.	past	pasado, m.
octave	octava, f.	paste	pasta, f.
odyssey	odisea, f.	pastille	pastilla, f.
offer	ofrecimiento, m.; oferta, f.	pastime	pasatiempo, m.
offering	oferta, f.	pastorale	pastoral, f.
*office	oficina, f.	pasturage	pastura, f.
officer	oficial, m.	patrician	patricio, m.
officialdom	oficialidad, f.	patronage	patrocinio, m.
ogre	ogro, m.	pay	pagamento, m.; paga, f.
oil	aceite, óleo, m.	payment	pago, pagamento, m.
opaqueness	opacidad, f.	peace (pax)	paz, f.
operand	operando, m.	peak	cima, f.; pico, m.
operative	operario, m.	*pear	pera, f.
opposite	opuesto, m.	pear tree	peral, m.
orb	orbe, m.	pearl	perla, f.
orchid	orquídea, f.	pediatrician	pediatra, m.
ordeal	ordalía, f.	peer	par, m.
order (arrangement)	orden, m.	penance	penitencia, f.
ordinand	ordenando, m.	pennant	pendón, m.
orphanage	orfanato, m.	penny	penique, m.
other	otro, m.	Pentecost	Pentecostés, m.
ottoman	otomana, f.	people	pueblo, m.
ounce	onza, f.	percale	percal, m.
overpayment	pago excesivo, m.	perch	percha, f.
oyster	ostra, f.	period (time)	plazo, período, m.
pace (gait)	marcha, f.; paso, m.	permafrost	permafrost, m.
pack (package)	paquete, m.	permalloy	permalloy, m.
*page (book)	página, f.	permission (permit)	permiso, m.
page (messenger)	paje, m.	personnel	personal, m.
pain	dolor, m.; pena, f.	pertinacity	pertinacia, f.
paint	pintura, f.	pervert	pervertido, m.
painter	pintor, m.	pest	pestilencia, peste, f.
painting	pintura, f.	petard	petardo, m.
pair (couple)	pareja, f.; par, m.	phantom	fantasma, f.

ENGLISH	SPANISH	ENGLISH	SPANISH
pharisee	fariseo, m.	polyhedron	poliedro, m.
Pharoh	faraón, m.	polymer	polímero, m.
phase	fase, f.	polysyllable	polisílabo, m.
pheasant	faisán, m.	pomp	pompa, f.
philanthropist	filántropo, m.	pontiff	pontífice, m.
philanthropy	filantropía, f.	poop (stern)	popa, f.
philodendron	filodendro, m.	poor	pobre, m.
philosopher	filósofo, m.	populace	populacho, m.
philosophy	filosofía, f.	porch	porche, m.
phone	teléfono, m.	pore	poro, m.
*phrase	frase, f.	pork (pig)	cerdo, puerco, m.
pick	pico, m.	port	puerto, m.
picnic	picnic, m.	portage	porteo, m.
piece	pieza, f.	porter (bldg)	portero, m.
pigeon	paloma, f.; pichón, m.	porter (carrier)	portador, m.
pigmy	pigmeo, m.	porthole	porta, f.
pike	pica, f.	pose	postura, f.
pile (mass,mound)	masa, pila, f.	post (pole)	palo, poste, m.
pill	píldora, f.	post (position)	puesto, m.
pineapple	piña, f.	pot	pote, m.
ping-pong	ping-pong, m.	potash	potasa, f.
pipe (smoking)	pipa, f.	potato	papa, patata, f.
pique	rencor, pique, m.	power	poder, m.
piracy	piratería, f.	practitioner	practicante, m.
pistil (BOT)	pistilo, m.	preamble	preámbulo, m.
pity	lastima, piedad, f.	predominance	predominio, m.
place (square)	plaza, f.	preface	prólogo, prefacio, m.
plagiarism	plagio, m.	preliminary	preliminar, m.
plagiarist	plagiario, m.	presage	presagio, m.
plaid	tartán, plaid, m.	press (news)	prensa, f.
plan	proyecto, plano, m.	pressure	presión, f.
planning	planificación, f.	pretentiousness	pretensión, f.
plaque	placa, f.	preventive	prevención, f.
plaster	yeso, emplasto, m.	prey	presa, f.
platoon	pelotón, m.	price (cost)	precio, m.
playing cards	cartas, f.	price list	lista de precios, f.
pleasure	agrado, placer, m.	primate (ZOOL)	primate, m.
plexiglass	plexiglás, m.	prince	príncipe, m.
plot	complot, m.	principle	principio, m.
plumb	plomo, m.	prisoner (MIL)	prisionero, m.
plummer	plomero, m.	procedure	procedimiento, m.
poetry	poesía, f.	proceeding	proceder, m.
pogrom	pogrom, m.	prodigal	pródigo, m.
point (item)	pico, m.; punta, f.	produce	producto, m.
point (dot)	punto, m.	progeny	progenie, f.
point (sharp end)	punta, f.	proletariat	proletariado, m.
poker (cards)	póquer, póker, m.	promise	promesa, f.
pole (post)	palo, m.	promptness	prontitud, f.
pole (GEOG)	polo, m.	pronoun	pronombre, m.
Pole, Polish	polaco, m.	proof	prueba, f.
policeman	policía, f.	propensity	propensión, f.
*policy (contract)	póliza, f.	prophecy	profecía, f.
*policy (plan)	política, f.	proposal	propuesta, f.
polyester	poliester, m.	proprietor	propietario, m.
polygamist	polígamo, m.	prosecution	proceso, m.

ENGLISH	SPANISH	ENGLISH	SPANISH
proverb	proverbio, m.	recruit	recluta, f.
provider	proveedor, m.	referral	referencia, f.
province	provincia, f.	*reflection (image)	reflejo, m.
provost	alcalde, preboste, m.	refreshment	refresco, m.
prow	proa, f.	refugee	refugiado, m.
prowess	proeza, f.	register (registry)	registro, m.
protégée	protegido, m.	registering (-tration)	registro, m.
psalm	salmo, m.	registrar	registrador, m.
psalter	salterio, m.	*reign (rule period)	reinado, m.
psychiatrist	psiquiatra, m.	reimbursement	reembolso, m.
pudding	budín, m.	*rein (bridle)	freno, m.; rienda, f.
pulley	garrucha, polea, f.	reindeer	reno, m.
pullover	pulóver, m.	reinforcement	refuerzo, m.
pumice	pómez, f.	rejuvenation	rejuvenecimiento, m.
*punch (blow)	puñada, f.	relationship	relación, f.
punch (drink)	ponche, m.	relic	reliquia, f.
pupil (eye)	pupila, f.	*relief (ART)	relieve, m.
*pupil (school)	alumno, pupilo, m.	remembrance	remembranza, f.
purgative	purgante, m.	remorse	remordimiento, m.
purge	purgación, f.	renaissance	renacimiento, m.
purple	púrpura, f.	rent (rental)	alquiler, m.; renta, f.
pygmy	pigmeo, m.	repair	reparación, f.; reparo, m.
Quaker	cuáquero, m.	repairman	reparador, m.
quart	cuarto de galón, m.	repentence	arrepentimiento, m.
quarter	cuarto, m.	replacement	reemplazo, m.
quiet	silencio, m.; quietud, f.	replication	réplica, f.
*quotation (price)	cotización, f.	reply	réplica, f.
rabies	hidrofobia, rabia, f.	reporter	reportero, repórter, m.
race (human)	raza, f.	repose (rest)	reposo, m.
rail (train)	riel, rail, m.	representative	representante, m.
ramp	rampa, f.	reprisal	represalia, f.
ranch	hacienda, f.; rancho, m.	reproach	reproche, m.
rancher	ganadero, ranchero, m.	reprobate	réprobo, m.
rank (level)	rango, m.	repute	reputación, f.
rapist	raptor, m.	rescue	rescate, m.
rapture	rapto, m.	reserve	reserva, f.
*rat	rata, f.; ratón, m.	residue (residual)	residuo, m.
rationale	razón, f.	resource	medio, recurso, m.
ravioli	ravioles, m.	respite	respiro, m.
ray (beam)	rayo, m.	response	respuesta, f.
readjustment	reajuste, m.	rest (remainder)	resto, m.
realignment	realinación, f.	result	resultado, m.
reappearance	reaparición, f.	résumé	resumen, m.
rearmament	rearme, m.	resurgence	resurgimiento, m.
reasoning	razonamiento, m.	retardation	retardo, m.
rebate	rebaja, f.	retreat	retirada, f.
rebel	rebelde, m.	retrospect	retrospección, f.
*receipt	recibo, m.	return	regreso, retorno, m.
receiver	receptor, m.	revenge (vengiance)	venganza, f.
recipe	receta, f.	revolt	rebelión, revuelta, f.
reciprocal	recíproco, m.	*revolver	revólver, m.
reconnaissance	reconocimiento, m.	rhinoceros	rinoceronte, m.
record (sports)	récord, m.	rhododendron	rododendro, m.
recovery	recobro, m.	rhubarb	ruibarbo, m.
recreation	recreo, m.	ribaldry	ribaldería, f.

199

ENGLISH	SPANISH	ENGLISH	SPANISH
riches (wealth)	riqueza, f.	seigneur	señor, m.
ridiculousness	ridiculez, f.	semester	semestre, m.
rifle	fusil, rifle, m.	sense (feel)	sentido, m.
risk (danger)	peligro, riesgo, m.	sensitiveness	sensibilidad, f.
rivalry	rivalidad, f.	sentry	cintinela, f.
roastbeef	rosbif, m.	sepulcher	sepulcro, m.
robbery	robo, m.	Septuagint	Septuaginta, f.
robustness	robustez, f.	seraphim	serafín, m.
rock	piedra, roca, f.	series	sucesión, serie, f.
rodent	roedor, m.	seriousness	seriedad, f.
role (part)	papel, rol, m.	serve	servicio, m.
*roll (paper)	rollo, m.	setter (dog)	sétter, m.
roller	rodillo, m.	sex	sexo, m.
rose bush	rosal, m.	shawl	chal, m.
rosette	roseta, f.	shellac	laca, f.
rotisserie	rotisería, f.	sherbet	sorbete, m.
round (shot)	rondo, m.	sheriff	jerife, m.
route (road)	camino, m.; ruta, f.	sherry	jerez, m.
royalist	realista, m.	shock	susto, choque, m.
ruble	rublo, m.	sign (mark)	señal, seña, f.
ruby	rubí, m.	sign (indication)	signo, m.
rudeness	rudeza, f.	signal	señal, f.
rugby	rugby, m.	significance	significación, f.
rum	ron, m.	silicon	silicio, m.
rupee	rupia, f.	similarity	similitud, f.
sabateur	saboteador, m.	sine	seno, m.
sabbath	sabat, m.	site	sitio, m.
*sable	cebellina, f.	skeleton	esqueleto, m.
sack (bag, pouch)	saco, m.	slalom	slalom, m.
sahib	sahib, m.	slave	esclavo, m.
saint	santo, m.	slavery	esclavitud, f.
sainthood (-liness)	santidad, f.	sluice	esclusa, f.
*salad	ensalada, f.	snob	esnob, m.
salamander	salamandra, f.	snobbery	esnobismo, m.
*salt	sal, f.	snorkle	esnórquel, m.
salt shaker	saltero, m.	soil (earth)	tierra, f.; suelo, m.
salvage	salvamento, m.	solace	solaz, m.
sandal	sandalia, f.	solar system	sistema solar, f.
sandwich	emparedado, sandwich, m.	solarium	solana, f.
sapphire	zafiro, m.	solder	soldadura, f.
sarong	sarong, m.	soldier	militar, soldado, m.
Saturn	Saturno, m.	sole (shoe)	suela, f.
sauce (gravy)	salsa, f.	soliloquy	soliloquio, m.
savior	salvador, m.	sound	sonido, son, m.
scale	escala, f.	*soup	sopa, f.
scepter	cetro, m.	South Pole	Polo Sur, m.
school	escuela, f.	southeast	sudeste, m.
scientist	científico, m.	southwest	suroeste, m.
scruple	escrúpulo, m.	soverign	soberano, m.
sculpter	escultor, m.	space (room)	espacio, m.
seacoast	costa, f.	Spanish	español, m.
seal (stamp)	timbre, sello, m.	species	género, m.; especie, f.
second	segundo, m.	*spice	especia, f.
secrecy	secreto, m.	spinach	espinaca, f.
security	aseguración, f.	spirit	espíritu, m.

ENGLISH	SPANISH	ENGLISH	SPANISH
sponge	esponja, f.	tamale	tamal, m.
sport(s)	*deporte, m.	tamborin	tamboril, m.
spouse	esposa, f.; esposo, m.	tank	cisterna, f.; tanque, m.
spume	espuma, f.	tapestry	tapicería, f.
sputnik	sputnik, m.	tardiness	tardanza, f.
spy	espía, f.	*tariff	tarifa, f.
squad (-dron)	escuadra, f.	tart	torta, f.
squalor	escualidez, f.	tavern	taberna, f.
stable	establo, m.	taxicab	taxi, m.
stake (post)	estaca, f.	tea	té, m.
stamp	estampa, f.	teak	teca, f.
stampede	estampida, f.	teat	teta, f.
stamping	estampa, f.	technicality	tecnicidad, f.
standard	bandera, estandarte, f.	tee (golf)	tee, m.
statesman	estadista, m.	tempest	tempestad, f.
statue	estatua, f.	*temple (bldg)	templo, m.
steak	biftec, m.	tender (R.R.)	ténder, m.
stencil	esténcil, m.	tenderness	ternura, f.
stevedore	estibador, m.	tenure	tenencia, f.
stiletto	estilete, m.	term	término, m.
stipend	estipendio, m.	terrace	terraza, f.
stomach	estómago, m.	terrain	terreno, m.
story	historia, f.	terrier	terrier, m.
stove	estufa, f.	tetanus	tétanos, m.
strait	estrecho, m.	theater	teatro, m.
strategist	estratega, m.	theologian	teólogo, m.
study	estudio, m.	theorist	teórico, m.
style	estilo, m.	tiger	tigre, m.
suaveness	suavidad, f.	time	tiempo, m.
subaltern	subalterno, m.	tint	tinte, m.
subcommittee	subcomité, f.	tissue	gasa, f.; tisú, m.
subornation	soborno, m.	title	título, m.
subtitle	subtítulo, m.	toast	tostada, f.
subtlety	sutileza, f.	toaster	tostadora, f.
subtrahend	substraendo, m.	toleration(-rance)	tolerancia, f.
suburb	arrabal, suburbio, m.	tomato	tomate, m.
suburbanite	suburbano, m.	tomb	sepulcro, m.; tumba, f.
succour	socorro, m.	ton	tonelada, f.
suffering	sufrimiento, m.	tonsil	tonsila, f.
suffrage	sufragio, m.	torch	antorcha, f.
sugar cane	caña, f.	torque	torsión, f.
sulky	sulky, m.	torte	torta, f.
sulpher	azufre, m.	tortoise	tortuga, f.
supermarket	supermarcado, m.	toupee	tupé, m.
surgery	cirugía, f.	tournament	torneo, m.
surprise	sorpresa, f.	tourney	torneo, m.
suspicion	sospecha, f.	towel	toalla, f.
sustenance	sustento, m.	tower	torre, f.
sweater	suéter, m.	trace	vestigo, m.; traza, f.
syllable	sílaba, f.	train	treno, m.
symptom	síntoma, f.	trainer	entrenador, m.
synod	sínodo, m.	training	entrenamiento, m.
syntax	sintaxis, m.	trance	trance, m.
syringe	jeringa, f.	transfer(-feral)	transferencia, f.
table (chart)	tabla, f.	trapeze	trapecio, m.
taffeta	tafetán, m.	treason	traición, f.

ENGLISH	SPANISH	ENGLISH	SPANISH
treasure	tesoro, m.	value	valor, m.
treasurer	tesorero, m.	valve	válvula, f.
treasury	tesorería, f.	vanguard	vanguardia, f.
treaty	tratado, m.	variable	variable, f.
tremor (trembling)	tremblor, m.	variance	variación, f.
trench	trinchera, f.	varnish	barniz, m.
tribe	tribu, f.	vase	vaso, m.
triceps	tríceps, m.	vegetable	legumbre, vegetal, f.
triple	triple, m.	*veil	velo, m.
tripod	trípode, m.	venom	veneno, m.
triumph	triunfo, m.	ventriloquist	ventrílocuo, m.
trivia	trivialidades, f.	verb	verbo, m.
trolley	trole, m.	verbiage	verbosidad, f.
troop	grupo, m.; tropa, f.	vermouth	vermut, m.
trophy	trofeo, m.	vernier	vernier, m.
trot	trote, m.	vespers	vísperas, f.
trout	trucha, f.	victim	víctima, f.
trumpeteer	trompetero, m.	vigil	vigilia, f.
trunk (tree)	tronco, m.	vinegar	vinagre, m.
trust	consorcio, trust, m.	vineyard	viña, f.
tube	tubo, m.	viper	víbora, f.
tubing	tube, m.	virtue	virtud, f.
tulip	tulipán, m.	viscount	vizconde, m.
tuna	atún, m.	visor	visera, f.
tune	tonada, f.	vogue	moda, boga, f.
Turk, Turkish	turco, m.	vogurt	yogurt, m.
turn	turno, m.	voice	voz, f.
turpentine	trementina, f.	volcano	volcán, m.
turtle	tortuga, f.	volleyball	vóleibol, m.
tutelage	tutela, f.	volt	voltio, m.
tycoon	taicún, m.	voter	votante, m.
type	tipo, m.	waffle	wafle, m.
tyrant	tirano, m.	waltz	vals, m.
ulcer	úlcera, f.	watt	vatio, m.
ultimate	último, m.	west	oeste, m.
unemployment	desempleo, m.	whisky	whiski, m.
unicorn	unicornio, m.	*wine	vino, m.
unit	unidad, f.	X-ray	rayo, m.
urn	urna, f.	yacht	yate, m.
usher	ujier, m.	yankee	yanqui, m.
usury	usura, f.	yard	yarda, f.
utensil	utensilio, m.	yoke (tool)	yugo, m.
vaccine	vacuna, f.	zeal	ardor, fervor, celo, m.
vaccination	vacunación, f.	Zenith	zenit, m.
vagabond	vagabundo, m.	zigzag	zigzag, m.
vagueness	vaguedad, f.	zinc	cinc, zinc, m.
valise	valija, f.	zither	cítara, f.
valley (glen, vale)	valle, m.	zoo	zoo, m.

SPECIAL SUBJECT MATTER LISTS OF NOUN PAIRS

COUNTRIES, REGIONS AND THEIR PEOPLE
Almost all are pair converters.

310 Listed

COUNTRY OR REGION		ITS PEOPLE	
ENGLISH	SPANISH	ENGLISH	SPANISH
Abyssinia	Abisinia	Abyssinian	abisinio
Afghanistan	Afganistán	Afghan	afgano
Africa	Africa	African	africano
Albania	Albania	Albanian	albanés
Algeria	Argelia	Algerian	argelino
Alsace	Alsacia	Alsatian	alsaciano
America	América	American	americano
Anarctic	Anártico		
Arabia	Arabia	Arab(-ian)	árabe
Arctic	Artico		
Argentina	Argentina	Argentinian	argentino
Armenia	Armenia	Armenian	armenio
Asia	Asia	Asian	asiático
Australia	Australia	Australian	australiano
Austria	Austria	Austrian	austríaco
Bavaria	Baviera	Bavarian	bávaro
Belgium	Bélgica	Belgian	belga
Bengal	Bengala	Bengalese	bengalí
Bermuda	Bermudas	Bermudian	bermudiano
Bolivia	Bolivia	Bolivian	boliviano
Brazil	(el) Brasil	Brazilian	brasileño
Britain	Bretaña	British,-ton	bretón
Bulgaria	Bulgaria	Bulgarian	búlgaro
Burgundy	Borgoña	Burgundian	borgoñon
Burma	Birmania	Burmese	birmano
California	California	Californian	californiano
Canada	(el) Canadá	Canadian	canadiense
Catalonia	Cataluña	Catalan	catalán
Central America	América Central	Cent.American	centroamericano
Chile	Chile	Chilean	chileno
China	(la) China	Chinese	chino
Colombia	Colombia	Colombian	colombiano
Congo	Congo	Congolese	congoleño
Costa Rica	Costa Rica	Costa Rican	-queño,costarricense
Crete	Creta	Cretan	cretense
Croatia	Croacia	Croat(-ian)	croata
Cuba	Cuba	Cuban	cubano
Czechoslovakia	Checoslovakia	Czech	checoslovaco
Denmark	Dinamarca	Dane	danés
Dom. Rep.	República Dominicana	Dominican	dominicano
Ecuador	(el) Ecuador	Ecuadorian	ecuatoriano
Egypt	Egipto	Egyptian	egipcio
England	Inglaterra	English(-man)	inglés
Estonia	Estonia	Estonian	estonio
Ethiopia	Etiopía	Ethiopian	etíope

203

COUNTRY OR REGION		ITS PEOPLE	
ENGLISH	**SPANISH**	**ENGLISH**	**SPANISH**
Finland	Finlandia	Finn	finlandés
Florida	Florida	Floridian	floridano
France	Francia	Frenchman	francés
Germany	Alemania	German	alemán, germano
Gibraltar	Gibraltar	Gibralter native	gibraltareño
Great Britain	(la) Gran Bretaña	Britain	británico
Greece	Grecia	Greek	griego
Greenland	Groenlandia	Greenlander	groenlandés
Guatemala	Guatemala	Guatemalan	guatemalteco
Guiana	Guayana	Guianese	guayanés
Haiti	Haití	Haitian	haitiano
Hisp.-América	Hispano-América	So.American	hispano-americano
Holland	Holanda	Dutchman	holandés
Honduras	Honduras	Honduran	hondureño
Hungary	Hungría	Hungarian	húngaro
Iceland	Islandia	Icelander	islandés
India	India	Indian	indio
Iran	Irán	Iranian	iranio, iraní
Iraq	Irak, Iraq	Iraqui	iraqués
Ireland	Irlanda	Irishman	irlandés
Islam	Islam	Islamite	musulmán, islamita
Israel	Israel	Israeli	israelita
Italy	Italia	Italian	italiano
Jamaica	Jamaica	Jamaican	jamaicano
Japan	(el) Japón	Japanese	japonés
Java	Java	Javanese	javanés
Jordan	Jordania	Jordanian	jordano
Kashmir	Cachemira	Kashmiri	cachemiro
Kenya	Kenya	Kenyan	keniano
Kuwait	Kuwait	Kuwaiti	kuwaiti
Korea	Corea	Korean	coreano
Laos	Laos	Laotian	laosiano
Lapland	Laponia	Laplander (Lapp)	lapón
Latin America	América Latina	Latin American	latinoamericano
Latvia	Latvia	Latvian	latvio
Lebanon	Líbano	Lebanese	libanés
Liberia	Libería	Liberian	liberiano
Libya	Libia	Libyan	libio
Lithuania	Lituania	Lithuanian	lituano
Low Countries	Países Bajos	Netherlander	holandés
Luxembourg	Luxemburgo	Luxembourgian	luxemburgés
Majorca	Mallorca	Majorcan	mallorquín
Malaysia	Malasia	Malasian	malasio
Manchuria	Manchuria	Manchurian	manchú
Mexico	Méjico, México	Mexican	mejicano
Minorca	Menorca	Minorcan	menorquín
Morocco	Marruecos	Moroccan	marroquí
Nepal	Nepal	Napalese	nepalés
Netherlands	Países Bajos, Holanda	Netherlander	holandés
New Zealand	Nueva Zelandia	New Zealander	neocelandés
Newfoundland	Terranova		
Nicaragua	Nicaragua	Nicaraguan	nicaragüense, -güeño
Nigeria	Nigeria	Nigerian	nigeriano
Normandy	Normandía	Norman	normando
No.America	América del Norte	North American	norteamericano

COUNTRY OR REGION		ITS PEOPLE	
ENGLISH	SPANISH	ENGLISH	SPANISH
Norway	Noruega	Norwegian	noruego
Nova Scotia	Nueva Escocia	Nova Scotian	nuevoescocés
Pakistan	Pakistán	Pakistani	paquistaní
Palistine	Palestina	Palestinian	palestino
Panama	Panamá	Panamanian	panameño
Paraguay	(el) Paraguay	Paraguayan	paraguayo
Persia	Persia	Persian	persa
Peru	(el) Perú	Peruvian	peruano
Philippines	(las) Filipinas	Philippine	filipino
Poland	Polonia	Pole	polaco
Polynesia	Polinesia	Polynesian	polinesio
Portugal	Portugal	Portuguese	portugués
Prussia	Prusia	Prussian	prusiano
Puerto Rico	Puerto Rico	Puerto Rican	puertorriqueño
Rumania	Rumania	Rumanian	rumano
Russia	Rusia	Russian	ruso
Salvador (El-)	(el) Salvador	Salvadorian	salvadoreño
Sardinia	Cerdeña	Sardinian	sardo
Saudi Arabia	Arabia Saudita	Saudi Arabian	árabe saudita
Saxony	Sajonia	Saxon	sajón
Scandinavia	Escandinavia	Scandinavian	escandinavo
Scotland	Escocia	Scots	escocés
Sengal	Sengal	Sengalese	sengalés
Serbia	Servia	Serbian	servio
Siam	Siam	Siamese	siamés
Sicily	Sicilia	Sicilian	siciliano
Singapore	Singapur		
So. America	América del Sur	South American	sudamericano
South Africa	Sudáfrica	South African	sudafricano
Soviet Union	Unión Soviético	Soviet	soviético
Spain	España	Spaniard	español
Sudan	Sudán	Sudanese	sudanés
Sweden	Suecia	Swede	sueco
Switzerland	Suiza	Swiss	suizo
Syria	Siria	Syrian	sirio
Tahiti	Tahití	Tahitian	tahitiano
Tanzania	Tanzania	Tanzanian	tanzaniano
Tasmania	Tasmania	Tasmanian	tasmaniano
Texas	Tejas	Texan	tejano
Thailand	Tailandia	Thai, Tai	tailandés, tai
Tibet	Tíbet	Tibetan	tibetano
Tunisia	Túnez	Tunisian	tunecino
Turkey	Turquía	Turk	turco
Tyrol	Tirol	Tyrolean	tirolés
Ukrain	Ucrania	Ukranian	ucranio, ucraniano
United Kingdom	Reino Unido		
United States	(los) Estados Unidos	American	yanqui, estadounidense gringo, norteamericano
Uruguay	(el) Uruguay	Uruguayan	uruguayo
Venezuela	(el) Venezuela	Venezuelan	venezolano
Vietnam	Vietnam	Vietnamese	vietnamés, vietcong
Wales	Gales	Welsh	galés
West Indies	Indias Occidentales	West Indian	antillano
Yemen	Yemen	Yemeni	yemenita
Yugoslavia	Yugoslavia	Yugoslav,-vian	yugoeslavo

OTHER NOUNS OF NATIONALITY, ORIGEN OR BELIEF
Almost all are pair converters.

8 Listed

ENGLISH	SPANISH	ENGLISH	SPANISH
Christian	cristiano	Jew	judío
Hebrew	hebreo	Muslim	musulmán
Hindustani	indostani	Viking	vikingo
Indian	indio	Yankee	yanqui

CITIES
Almost all are pair converters. **126 Listed**

ENGLISH	SPANISH	ENGLISH	SPANISH
Algiers	Argel	Geneva	Ginebra
Amsterdam	Amsterdam	Genoa	Génova
Asuncion	Asunción	Ghent	Gante
Athens	Atenas	Hague	La Haya
Avignon	Aviñón	Hamburg	Hamburgo
Babylon	Babilonia	Hanoi	Hanoi
Baghdad	Bagdad	Havana	La Habana
Baltimore	Baltimore	Helsinki	Helsinki
Bangkok	Bangkok	Hong Kong	Hong Kong
Barcelona	Barcelona	Istanbul	Estambul
Beirut	Beirut	Jerusalem	Jerusalén
Belgrade	Belgrado	Kabul	Kabul
Berlin	Berlín	La Paz	La Paz
Berne	Berna	Lausanne	Lausana
Bethlehem	Belén	Leningrad	Leningrado
Bogota	Bogotá	Lima	Lima
Bologna	Bolonia	Lisbon	Lisboa
Bordeaux	Bordeos	Liverpool	Liverpool
Boston	Boston	London	Londres
Bremen	Bremen	Los Angeles	Los Angeles
Brussels	Bruselas	Lucerne	Lucerna
Bucharest	Bucarest	Lyons	Lión
Budapest	Budapest	Madrid	Madrid
Buenos Aires	Buenos Aires	Managua	Managua
Cadiz	Cádiz	Manila	Manila
Cairo	Cairo	Marseille	Marsella
Calcutta	Calcuta	Mecca	Meca
Caracas	Caracas	Melbourne	Melbourne
Ceylon	Ceilán	Memphis	Menfis
Chicago	Chicago	Miami	Miami
Cologne	Colonia	Milan	Mílan
Constantinople	Constantinopla	Montevideo	Montevideo
Copenhagen	Copenhague	Montreal	Montreal
Cordoba	Córdoba	Moscow	Moscú
Damascus	Damasco	Nairobi	Nairobi
Detroit	Detroit	Naples	Nápoles
Dover	Dóver	Nazareth	Nazaret
Dresden	Dresde	New Delhi	Nueva Delhi
Edinburgh	Edimburgo	New Orleans	Nueva Orleáns
Florence	Florencia	New York	Nueva York

ENGLISH	SPANISH	ENGLISH	SPANISH
Nice	Niza	Santo Domingo	Santo Domingo
Oporto	Oporto	Sao Paulo	San Pablo
Oslo	Oslo	Sebastopol	Sebastopol
Ottawa	Ottawa	Seville	Sevilla
Paris	París	Seoul	Seúl
Peiping, Peking	Peiping, Pekín	Sidney	Sidney
Philadelphia	Filadelfia	Singapore	Singapur
Pittsburgh	Pittsburgo	Stalingrad	Stalingrado
Port-au-Prince	Puerto Príncipe	Stockholm	Estocolmo
Prague	Praga	Tangier	Tánger
Pretoria	Pretoria	Taipei	Taipeh
Quebec	Quebec	Tel Aviv	Tel Aviv
Quito	Quito	Tokyo	Tokio
Rangoon	Rangún	Toronto	Toronto
Rio de Janeiro	Río de Janeiro	Tripoli	Trípoli
Rome	Roma	Tunis	Túnez
Saigon	Saigón	Turin	Turín
Salzburg	Salzburgo	Venice	Venecia
San Francisco	San Francisco	Veracruz	Veracruz
San José	San José	Versailles	Versalles
San Juan	San Juan	Vienna	Viena
San Salvador	San Salvador	Warsaw	Varsovia
Santiago	Santiago	Washington	Washington

ISLANDS
Most are pair converters.   **38 Listed**

ENGLISH	SPANISH	ENGLISH	SPANISH
Aleutians	Islas Aleutas	Guam	Guam, Guaján
Antilles	Antillas	Hawaiian Islands	Islas Hawái
Balearic Islands	Islas Baleares	Hebrides	Hébridas
Barbados	Barbados	Hispaniola	La Española
Bermuda	Islas Bermudas	Indies	Las Indias
British Islands	Islas Británicas	Jamaica	Jamaica
Cameroons	Camerún	Madagascar	Madagascar
Canary Islands	Islas Canarias	Majorca	Mallorca
Cape Verde	Islas del Cabo Verde	Martinique	Martinica
Caroline Islands	Islas Carolinas	Minorca	Menorca
Corsica	Córcega	Philippines	Filipinos
Crete	Creta	Puerto Rico	Puerto Rico
Cuba	Cuba	Sardinia	Cerdeña
Curaçao	Curazao	Sicily	Sicilia
Cyprus	Chipre	Tobago	Tobago
East Indies	Indias Orientales	Virgen Islands	Islas Vírgenes
Easter Islands	Islas de Pascua	West Indies	Antillas
Falkland Islands	Islas Malvinas	Windward Isles	Islas de Barlovento
Granada	Granada	Zanzibar	Zanzibar

OCEANS, RIVERS AND OTHER BODIES OF WATER
Most are pair converters. **38 Listed**

ENGLISH	SPANISH	ENGLISH	SPANISH
Adriatic Sea	Mar Adriático	Lake Geneva	Lago de Ginebra
Aegean Sea	Mar Egeo	Loire	Loira
Amazon	Amazonas	Mediterranean	Mar Mediterráneo
Atlantic Ocean	Océano Atlántico	Mississippi	Misisipí
Baltic Sea	Mar Báltico	Niger	Níger
Black Sea	Mar Negro	Nile	Nilo
Bosporus	Bósforo	North Sea	Mar del Norte
Caribbean	Mar Caribe	Pacific Ocean	Océano Pacífico
Caspian Sea	Mar Caspio	Persian Gulf	Golfo Pérsico
China Sea	Mar de la China	Red Sea	Mar Rojo
Danube	Danubio	Rhine	Rin, Rhin
Dardanelles	Dardanelos	Rhone	Ródano
Dead Sea	Mar Muerto	Rio Grande	Río Grande
Dnieper	Dniéper	River Plate	Río de la Plata
Elbe	Elba	Salt Lake	Lago Salado
English Channel	Paso de Calais	Sein	Sena
	la Mancha	Strait of Gibralter	Estrecho de
Ganges	Ganges		Gibralter
Indian Ocean	Océano índico	Thames	Támesis
Lake Constance	Lago de Constanza	Yellow River	Río Amarillo

MOUNTAINS
Most are pair converters. **10 Listed**

ENGLISH	SPANISH	ENGLISH	SPANISH
Alps	Alpes	Caucasus	Cáucaso
Andes	Andes	Dolomites	Dolomites
Appalachians	Apalaches	Pyrenees	Pireneos
Apennines	Apeninas	Rockies	Montes Rocosos
Carpathians	Montes Cárpatos	Urals	Montes Urales

FIRST NAMES
Most are pair converters. **240 Listed**

ENGLISH	SPANISH	ENGLISH	SPANISH	ENGLISH	SPANISH
Abraham	Abrahán	Alphonse,-so	Alfonso	Basil	Basilio
Adam	Adán	Amy	Amata	Beatrice	Beatriz
Adelaide	Adelaida	Andrew	Andrés	Benedict	Benito
Adele	Adela	Anna, Ann(e)	Ana	Benjamin	Benjamin
Adolph(us)	Adolfo	Anthony	Antonio	Bernard	Bernardo
Adrian	Adrián	Antoinette	Antonia	Bertha	Berta
Agatha	Agata	Archibald	Archibaldo	Bertram	Bertrán
Agnes	Inés	Arnold	Arnaldo	Bridget	Brígida
Alan, Allen	Alano	Arthur	Arturo	Calvin	Calvino
Albert	Alberto	Augustus	Augusto	Camille	Camila
Alexander	Alejandro	Barbara	Bárbara	Caroline	Carolina
Alfred	Alfredo	Barnaby	Barnabé	Casimir	Casimiro
Alice	Alicia	Bartholomew	Bartolomé	Casper	Gaspar

ENGLISH	SPANISH	ENGLISH	SPANISH	ENGLISH	SPANISH
Catharine	Catalina	Godfrey	Godofredo	Lucius	Lucio
Cecil	Cecilio	Grace	Engracia	Lucy	Lucía
Charles	Carlos	Gregory	Gregorio	Luke	Lucas
Charlotte	Carlota	Gustav	Gustavo	Luther	Lutero
Christian	Cristiano	Gustavus	Gustavo	Marcel	Marcelo
Christina	Cristina	Guy	Guido	Marcellus	Marcelo
Christine	Cristina	Hannah	Ana	Margaret	Margarita
Christopher	Cristóbal	Harold	Haraldo	Marian	Mariana
Cicely	Cecilia	Harry	Enrique	Marie, Maria	María
Claire	Clara	Helen	Elena	Marius	Mario
Clara	Clara	Henrietta	Enriqueta	Marjorie	Margarita
Claude	Claudio	Henry	Enrique	Mark	Marcos, Marco
Claudia	Claudia	Herbert	Heriberto	Martha	Marta
Conrad	Conrado	Herman	Germán	Martin	Martín
Constance	Constanza	Hillary	Hilario	Mary	María
Cornelius	Cornelio	Homer	Homero	Matilda	Matilde
Cyrus	Ciro	Horace	Horacio	Matthew	Mateo
Daisy	Margarita	Hortense	Hortensia	Maurice	Mauricio
Daniel	Daniel	Hubert	Huberto	Maximilian	Maximiliano
David	David	Hugo, Hugh	Hugo	Michael	Miguel
Dennis	Dionisio	Humphrey	Hunfredo	Nathan	Natán
Dominic	Domingo	Ignatius	Ignacio	Nathaniel	Nataniel
Dorothy	Dorotea	Immanuel	Manuel	Nicholas	Nicolás
Edmund	Edmundo	Irene	Irene	Noah	Noé
Edward	Eduardo	Isaac	Isaac	Olga	Olga
Eleanor	Leonor	Isabel	Isabel	Oliver	Oliverio
Elizabeth	Isabel	Isidor	Isidoro	Otto	Otón
Ellen	Elena	Jacob	Jacobo	Patrick	Patricio
Elsa	Alicia	James	Jaime, Diego	Paul	Pablo
Emanuel	Manuel	Jaspar	Gaspar	Paula, Pauline	Paula
Emily	Emilia	Jean, Jane	Juana	Peter	Pedro
Emma	Ema	Jennie, Joan	Juana	Philip	Filipe
Erasmus	Erasmo	Jeremy	Jeremías	Philippa	Filipa
Ernest	Ernesto	Jerome	Jerónimo	Phineas	Fineas
Esther	Ester	Jesus	Jesús	Prudence	Prudencia
Eugene	Eugenio	John	Juan	Quentin	Quintín
Eustace	Eustaquio	Jonah	Jonás	Rachel	Raquel
Eva	Eva	Jonathan	Jonatán	Ralph	Rafael
Felicia	Felicia	Joseph	José	Randolph	Randolfo
Felix	Félix	Josephine	Josefina	Raymond	Ramón, Raimundo
Ferdinand	Fernando	Joshua	Josué	Rebecca	Rebeca
Florence	Florencia	Judith	Judit	Reginald	Reginaldo
Frances	Francisca	Julia	Julia	René	Renato
Francis	Francisco	Julian	Julián	Richard	Ricardo
Frank	Francisco	Julius	Julio	Robert	Roberto
Fred(-erick)	Federico	Justin	Justino	Roderic	Rodrigo
Gabrielle	Gabriela	Katherine	Catalina	Roger	Roger
Genevieve	Genoveva	Kathleen	Catalina	Roland	Rolando
Geoffrey	Geofredo	Laura	Laura	Ronald	Renaldo
George	Jorge	Lawrence	Lorenzo	Rosalie	Rosalía
Geraldine	Gerarda	Leon, Leo	León	Rosamond	Rosamunda
Gerard	Gerardo	Leonard	Leonardo	Rose	Rosa
Gertrude	Gertrudis	Leopold	Leopoldo	Rosemarie	Rosa María
Gilbert	Gilberto	Louis	Luis	Rudolph	Rodolfo
Giles	Gil	Louise	Luisa	Rueben	Rueben

209

ENGLISH	SPANISH	ENGLISH	SPANISH	ENGLISH	SPANISH
Rufus	Rufo	Susan, -ana	Susana	Victor	Víctor
Rupert	Ruperto	Sylvia	Silvia	Vincent	Vicente
Ruth	Rut	Terence	Terencio	Virgil	Virgilio
Sampson	Sansón	Thadeus	Tadeo	Virginia	Virginia
Samuel	Samuel	Theodore	Teodoro	Vivian	Bibiana
Sarah	Sara	Theresa	Teresa	Walter	Gualterio
Saul	Saúl	Thomas	Tomás	Wilhelmina	Guillermina
Silvester	Silvestre	Timothy	Timoteo	William	Guillermo
Solomon	Salomón	Titus	Tito	Winifred	Genoveva
Sophia	Sofía	Tobias, Toby	Tobías	Xavier	Javier
Stephen	Esteban	Valentine	Valentín	Zachary, -riah	Zacarías

MONTHS
All are convertering pairs.   12 Listed

ENGLISH	SPANISH	ENGLISH	SPANISH
January	enero, m.	July	julio, m.
February	febrero, m.	August	agosto, m.
March	marzo, m.	September	septiembre, m.
April	abril, m.	October	octubre, m.
May	mayo, m.	November	noviembre, m.
June	junio, m.	December	diciembre, m.

NAMES OF PLANETS
All are converting pairs except Earth.   9 Listed

ENGLISH	SPANISH	ENGLISH	SPANISH
Earth	Tierra, f.	Pluto	Plutón, m.
Jupiter	Júpiter, m.	Saturn	Saturno, m.
Mars	Marte, m.	Uranus	Urano, m.
Mercury	Mercurio, m.	Venus	Venus, m.
Neptune	Neptuno, m.		

3. FREQUENTLY-USED ENGLISH NOUNS NOT CONVERTIBLE INTO SPANISH EXCEPT INDIRECTLY THROUGH ENGLISH SYNONYMS

The nouns in this list are predominantly one-syllable nouns, compound nouns, exceptions to converting categories and nouns in non-converting categories such as *-ness, -ful, -ing, -hood* and *-ship*. In most cases where the English noun has no Spanish counterpart listed in the second column, the Spanish noun in the last column is given by the English-Spanish dictionary as the usual counterpart of the English noun. This list represents only a small fraction of the nouns that can be converted through synonyms.

2055 Listed

ENGLISH	SPANISH NON-CONVERSION	ENGLISH SYNONYM	SPANISH CONVERSION
abatement	descuento, m.	diminution	disminución, f.
abeyance	espera, f.	suspension	suspensión, f.
ability	habilidad, f.	capacity	capacidad, f.
abode	morada, f.	domicile	domicilio, m.
		residence	residencia, f.
abridgement	resumen, m.	abbreviation	abreviación, f.
accomplishment	logro, m.	consummation	consumación, f.
		realization	realización, f.
accord	acuerdo, m.	harmony	armonía, f.
accordance	acuerdo, m.	comformity	conformidad, f.
account (report)	cuenta, relación, f.	narration	narración, f.
accuracy	esmero, m.	exactitude	exactitud, f.
		precision	precisión, f.
achievement	ejecución, f.	realization	realización, f.
acknowledgement	reconocimiento, m.	admission	admisión, f.
acquaintance	conocimiento, m.	familiarity	familiaridad, f.
acquital	descargo, m.	absolution	absolución, f.
acreage		area	área, f.
act (deed)	escritura, f.	instrument	instrumento, m.
		protocol	protocolo, m.
*addition (MATH)	adición, f.	sum	suma, f.
address (post)	señas, f.	direction	dirección, f.
address (speech)	alocución, f.	discourse	discurso, m.
addressee	consignatario, m.	destination	destinatario, m.
adjournment	aplazamiento, m.	suspension	suspensión, f.
admission (entry)	aceso, m.	entrance (-try)	entrada. f.
advance (-ement)	adelanto, m.	progress	progreso, m.
advertisement	aviso, m.	announcement	anuncio, m.
advertising		publicity	publicidad, f.
		propaganda	propaganda, f.
advice	consejo, m.	opinion	opinión, f.
		consultation	consultación, f.
adviser	consejero, m.	consultor	consultor, m.
aerial		antenna	antena, f.
affair (matter)	asunto, m.; cosa, f.	*question	cuestión, f.
		subject	sujeto, m.
agreeableness	amenidad, f.	affability	afabilidad, f.
age (oldness)	edad, vejez, f.	antiquity	antigüedad, f.
age (epoch)	generación, f.	epoch, era	época, era, f.

ENGLISH	SPANISH NON-CONVERSION	ENGLISH SYNONYM	SPANISH CONVERSION
agreement	convenio, m.	contract, accord	contrato, acuerdo, m.
ailment	dolencia, f.	infirmity	enfermedad, f.
aim (objective)	fin, m.	objective	objetivo, m.
aim (gun)	tiro, m.	pointing	puntería, f.
air (tune)	aire, m.; tonada, f.	melody	melodía, f.
aisle	pasadizo, crujía, f.	passage	pasillo, m.
alcove	gabinete, m.	niche	nicho, m.
alert	aviso, m.	alarm	alarma, f.
alertness	cuidado, m; agudeza, f.	vigilance	vigilancia, f.
alibi	coartada, f.	pretext, excuse	pretexto, m; excusa, f.
all	todo	totality	totalidad, f.
allegiance	fidelidad, f.	loyalty	lealtad, f.
alligator		cayman	caimán, m.
		crocodile	crocodrilo, m.
allocation	repartición, f.	distribution	distribución, f.
allotment	lote, m.	distribution	distribución, f.
	asignación, f.	quota, portion	cuota, porción, f.
allowance		permission	permiso, m.
		authorization	autorización, f.
		concession	concesión, f.
		indulgence	indulgencia, f.
allure (-ment)	encanto, m.	attraction	atracción, f.
		fascination	fascinación, f.
alms	limosna, f.	charity	caridad, f.
aloofness	retraimiento, m.	indifference	indiferencia, f.
alternate	suplente, m.	substitute	substituto, m.
amazement	asombro, m.	surprise	sorpresa, f.
amendment	enmienda, f.	correction	corrección, f.
amount	monto, importe, m.	quantity, sum	cantidad, suma, f.
amusement	pasatiempo, m.	diversion	diversión, f.
	distracción, f.	recreation	recreo, m.
ancestry	abolengo, m.	lineage	linaje, m.
anger	cólera, ira, f.	indignation	indignación, f.
	enfado, enojo, m.	fury	furia, f.
anointment	ungimiento, m.	consecration	consagración, f.
annoyance	disgusto, fastidio, m.	molestation	molestia, f.
anthem	cántico, m.	hymn	himno, m.
apartheid		segregation	segregación, f.
appliance (tool)	artefacto, m.	apparatus	aparato, m.
		instrument	instrumento, m.
appointee		elected one	electo, m.
appointment	nombramiento, m.	designation	designación, f.
appointment	compromiso, m; cita, f.	obligation	obligación, f.
apportionment	prorrateo, reparto, m.	distribution	distribución, f.
appraisal	valoración, f.	evaluation	evaluación, f.
appraiser	tasador, m.	evaluater	evaluador, m.
approach	acercamiento, m.	approximation	aproximación, f.
approval	consentimiento, m.	approbation	aprobación, f.
area	terreno, m.; área, f.	zone, region	zona, región, f.
	superficie, f.	space	espacio, m
arousal	despertar, m.	excitement	excitación, f.
arrangement	arreglo, m.	disposition	disposición, f.
array	serie, f.; orden, m.	formation	formación, f.
article	cosa, f.	object	objeto, m.
ascertainment	averiguación, f.	determination	determinación, f.

ENGLISH	SPANISH NON-CONVERSION	ENGLISH SYNONYM	SPANISH CONVERSION
assertiveness	dogmatismo, m.	aggressivity	agresividad, f.
assessment	tasación, f.	valuation	avaluación, f.
assignment	deber, m.	charge (resp)	encargo, m.
assignment (LAW)	asignación, f.	cession	cesión, f.
*assistance	apoyo, auxilio, m.	aid, assistance	ayuda,*asistencia, f.
assortment	surtido, m.	collection	colección, f.
assurance	aseguración, f.	promise	promesa, f.
astonishment	pasmo, asombro, m.	surprise	sopresa, f.
atonement	reparación, f.	expiation	expiación, f.
		compensation	compensación, f.
		redemption	redención, f.
attachment	fijación, f.	union, adhesion	unión, adhesión f.
attachment (LAW)		embargo	embargo, m.
attainment	logro, m.	realization	realización, f.
attempt	intento, ensayo, m.		
*attendance	*asistencia, f.	presence	presencia, f.
attorney (LAW)	abogado, m.	procurator	procurador, m.
attorney (agent)	apoderado, m.	legal agent	agente legal, m.
average (fair)	promedio, m.	mediocrity	mediocridad, f.
average (medium)	término medio, m.		
award	premio, m.	honor	honor, m.
awareness	conocimiento, m.	conscience	conciencia, f.
awe	pavor, espanto, m.	reverence	reverencia, f.
awkwardness	torpeza, f.	ineptitude	ineptitud, f.
axe	segur, f.	hachet	hacha, f.
back (..side)	dorso, m.	reverse	revés, m.
backbone	espina dorsal, f.	spine	espinazo, m.
backer	partidario, m.	financer	financiador, m.
background	fondo, m.	ambiance, past	ambiente, pasado, m.
badge	divisa, placa, f.	symbol	símbolo, m.
		insignia	insignia, f.
badness	maldad, f.	maliciousness	malicia, f.
bag (suitcase)	maleta, f.	sack, valise	saco, m.; valija, f.
baggage	maletas, f.	equipment	equipaje, m.
bailment	entrega, f.	deposit	depósito, m.
balance	contrapeso, m.	equilibrium	equilibrio, m.
ban	proscripción, f.	prohibition	prohibición, f.
band leader		conductor	conductor, m.
banishment	destierro, m.	exile	exilio, m.
		deportation	deportación, f.
bankruptcy	quiebra,bancarrota,f.	insolvency	insolvencia, f.
bar (block)	barrera, f.	obstacle	obstáculo, m.
		impediment	impedimento, m.
bar (cafe)	bar, m.	cantine,tavern	cantina, taberna, f.
bargain (pact)	trato, m.	pact,convention	pacto, convenio, m.
bargain (deal)	ganga, f.	opportunity	oportunidad, f.
bargaining	regateo, trato, m.	pact	pacto, m.
barn	granero, m.	stable	establo, m.
barnyard	patio de granja, m.	corral	corral, m.
barrenness	yermo, m.	sterility	esterilidad, f.
bashfulness	vergüenza,f;pudor, m.	timidity	timidez, f.
bat (animal)	murciélago, m.	vampire	vampiro, m.
batch	cúmulo,m.;cochura, f.	lot	lote, m.
beads	gotas, f.	rosary	rosario, m.
beam (light)	haz, m.	ray	rayo, m.

213

ENGLISH	SPANISH NON-CONVERSION	ENGLISH SYNONYM	SPANISH CONVERSION
bearer		porter	portador, m.
bearing (body)	aire, porte, m.	manner, presence	maneras, presencia, f.
bearings	rumbo, m.	orientation	orientación, f.
beat	tiempo, golpe, m.	rhythm	ritmo, m.
beating (heart)	latido, m.	pulsation	pulsación, f.
beautician		cosmetologist	cosmetólogo, m.
beauty	hermosura, belleza, f.		
bedroom	alcoba, f.	dormitory	dormitorio, m.
beginner	iniciador, m.	novice	novicio, m.
		apprentice	aprendiz, m.
beginning	principio, m.	commencement	comienzo, m.
		origen	origen, m.
behalf	en nombre de	benefit, favor	beneficio, favor, m.
		interest	interés, m.
behavior	comportamiento, m.	conduct	conducta, f.
being (human)	ser, m.	creature	criatura, f.
being	vida, f.	existence	existencia, f.
belief	creencia, f.	creed, opinion	credo, m.; opinión, f.
believability		credibility	creibilidad, f.
bellboy	botones, m.	page	paje, m.
belly	vientre, m; barriga, f.	stomach	estómago, m.
belongings	pertenencias, f.	property	propiedad, f.
bend	vuelta, f.	curve	curva, f.
bent (penchant)	afición, propensión, f.	tendancy	tendencia, f.
	disposición, f.	inclination	inclinación, f.
bequest	legado, m.	donation	donación, f.
bereavement	duelo, desconsuelo, m.	affliction	aflicción, f.
best	mejor, m.	optimum	óptimo, m.
bestowing	don, m.	donation	donación, f.
betrayer	delator, m.	traitor	traidor, m.
bewilderment	aturdimiento, m.	perplexity	perplejidad, f.
bias	propensión, f.	prejudice	prejuicio, m.
bid	propuesta, postura, f.	offer	oferta, f.
bigotry	fanatismo, m.	intolerance	intolerancia, f.
bike		bicycle	bicicleta, f.
bill (exch.)	giro, m.	letter	letra, f.
bill (invoice)	factura, cuenta, f.	note	nota, f.
birth	parto, nacimiento, m.	origin	origen, f.
bit (fragment)	pedacito, poquito, m.	fragment	fragmento, m.
bitterness	amargura, f.	acridity, rancor	acritud, f.; rencor, m.
blame	culpa, f.	censure	censura, f.
blast	ráfaga, f.	explosion	explosión, f.
		discharge	descarga, f.
blemish	tacha, mancha, f.	imperfection	imperfección, f.
blend	mezcla, f.	mixture	mixtura, f.
		combination	combinación, f.
blessing	gracia, f.	benediction	bendición, f.
blind (window)	persiana, f.	jalousie	celosía, f.
bliss (rapture)	felicidad, f.	ecstacy	éxtasis, m.
blossom (bloom)	brote, m; floración, f.	flower (-ing)	flor, m.
blow (hit)	porrazo, golpe, m.	disaster	desastre, m.
bluff	engaño, farallón, m.	deception	decepción, f.
blunder	disparate, m.	error	error, m.
bluntness	aspereza, f.	bruskness	brusquedad, f.
boat	bote, m.; chalupa, f.	launch, bark	lancha, f.; barco, m.

ENGLISH	SPANISH NON-CONVERSION	ENGLISH SYNONYM	SPANISH CONVERSION
body (corpse)	cuerpo, m.	cadaver	cadáver, m.
boldness	intrepidez, f.	audacity	audacia, f.
bond (tie)	enlace, lazo, m.	union	unión, f.
bondage	cautividad, f.	slavery	esclavitud, f.
book	libro, m.	volume, tome	volumen, tomo, m.
boom (ECON)		prosperity	prosperidad, f.
boor	grosero, campesino, m.	rustic	rústico, m.
boost	empuje, m.	impulse, aid	impulso, f; ayuda, f.
booth (stall)	puesto, m.; barraca, f.	kiosk	quiosco, m.
border	limite, confín, m.	frontier	frontera, f.
boredom	aburrimiento, m.	tedium	tedio, m.
boss	amo, m.; patrón, m.	chief	jefe, m.
bother	incomodidad, f.	molestation disturbance	molestia, f. disturbio, m.
bottom	fondo, m.	base	base, f.
bound(s), -dry	término, m.	limit, confine frontier	límite, confín, m. frontera, f.
bow (ship)		prow	proa, f.
bow (curve)		curve, arc	curvo, arco, m.
bow (nod)	saludo, m.	reverence	reverencia, f.
bowel(s)	entrañas, tripas, f.	intestines	intestinos, m.
box	caja, f.	compartment	compartimiento, m.
boy (lad)	muchacho, mozo, m.	adolescent	adolescente, m.
brace	abarazadera, grapa, f.	support	soporte, m.
bracket	puntal, m.; reprisa, f.	support	soporte, m.
braid	cinta, trenza, f.		
brake	freno, m.	control	control, m.
branch (limb)	rama, f.	tributary	tributario, m.
brand (mark)	tizón, m.	mark	marca, f.
brandy	aguardiente, m.	cognac	coñac, m.
brass	latón, m.	copper, bronze	cobre, bronce, m.
breach (LAW)	contravención, f.	rupture infraction	ruptura, f. infracción, f.
breadth (width)	espacio, m; anchura, f.	latitude extension	latitud, f. extensión, f.
break	rotura, f.	rupture	ruptura, f.
break (pause)	descanso, m.	pause, interval	pausa, intervalo, m.
breakage	rompimiento, m.	fracture	fractura, f.
breath	aliento, m.	respiration	respiración, f.
breeches	calzón, m.	pantaloons	pantalones, m.
breed (stock)		race, species caste, class	raza, especie, f. casta, clase, f.
bribery		subornation	soborno, m.
briefcase	maletín, m; cartera, f.	portfolio	portafolio, m.
briefness		brevity conciseness	brevedad, f. concisión, f.
brightness	fulgor, m.	luminosity brilliance splendor	luminosidad, f. brillantez, f. esplendor, m.
brightness	viveza, f.	intelligence sagacity	inteligencia, f. sagacidad, f.
brim (edge)	orilla, f.	border, margen	borde, margen, m.
brim (hat)	ala, f.	margin	margen, m.
bringing up	cría, f.	*education	educación, f.

ENGLISH	SPANISH NON-CONVERSION	ENGLISH SYNONYM	SPANISH CONVERSION
broker	corredor, m.	agent	agente, m.
		commission man	comisionista, m.
brood	nidado, m.; cría, f.	progeny	progenie, f.
brotherhood	hermanidad, f.	fraternity	fraternidad, f.
bruise	magulladora, f.	contusion	contusión, f.
bubble	burbuja, f.	ampule	ampolla, f.
bug	bicho, m.	insect	insecto, m.
bugle	clarín, m.	trumpet, cornet	trumpeta, corneta, f.
builder		constructor	constructor, m.
building (act of)		construction	construcción, f.
building	casa, f.	edifice	edificio, m.
bulk (size)	tamaño, m.	magnitude	magnitud, f.
		volume	volumen, m.
bullet		ball	bala, f.
bully	fanfarrón, m.	abuser	abusador, m.
bum	holgazán, m.	vagabond	vago, vagabundo, m.
bunch	conjunto, racimo, m.	group	grupo, m.
bundle	haz, bulto, fardo, m.	package	paquete, m.
buoyancy	flotabilidad, f.	flotation	flotación, f.
bureau (chest)	tocador, m.	commode	cómoda, f.
bureau (office)	despacho, m.	office	oficina, f.
burglary	ratería, f.	robbery	robo, m.
burial	sepultura, f.	interment	entierro, m.
burlesque		farce, parody	farsa, parodia f.
burning	quema, quemadora, f.	combustion	combustión, f.
bus		autobus	autobús, m.
		omnibus	ómnibus, m.
business	negocios, m.	occupation	ocupación, f.
		profession	profesión, f.
bursting	estallido, m.	explosion	explosión, f.
butt	mango, cabo, m.	extremity	extremo, m.
by-product	subproducto, m.	derivative	derivado, m.
		residue	residuo, m.
bystander(s)	circunstante, m.	spectator	espectador, m.
cab (hack)	coche, m.	taxi	taxi, m.
cake	bizcocho, pastel, m.	torte	torta, f.
call (cry)	grito, m; llamada, f.	exclamation	exclamación, f.
caller	llamador, m.	visiter	visita, visitante, m.
candy (sweet)	confite, dulce, m.	bonbon	bonbón, m.
caption	encabezamiento, m.	title	titular, título, m.
car (carriage)	coche, m.	wagon (RR)	vagón, m.
*car (auto)	coche, carro, m.	automobile	automóvil, m.
carbon (copy)		copy	copia, f.
carcass		cadaver	cadáver, m.
cardboard	cartulina, f.	carton	cartón, m.
*care (concern)	cuidado, m.	preoccupation	preocupación, f.
		solicitude	solicitud, f.
care (attention)	cautela, f.	attention	atención, f.
care (custody)		custody	custodia, f.
carefulness	cautela, f; cuidado, m.	attention	atención, f.
carelessness	descuido, m.	negligence	negligencia, f.
		indifference	indiferencia, f.
carriage (stance)	porte, m.	presence	presencia, f.
carriage	carruaje, m.	coach, car	coche, carro, m.

ENGLISH	SPANISH NON-CONVERSION	ENGLISH SYNONYM	SPANISH CONVERSION
carrier	cargador, m.	porter	portador, m.
	mandadero, m.	transporter	transportador, m.
carrying out		execution	ejecución, f.
		realization	realización, f.
cart	coche, m.	carriage	carro, m; carreta, f.
cartoon	dibujo animado, m.	caricature	caricatura, f.
cartoonist		caricaturist	caricaturista, f.
cask	tonel, m.; cuba, f.	barrel	barril, m.
cast		mold, mould	moldura, f.; molde, m.
catch (hitch)		difficulty	dificultad, f.
		impediment	impedimiento, m.
caterer	abastecedor, m.	provider	proveedor, m.
cesspool	pozo negro, m.	latrine	letrina, f.
*chagrin	*disgusto, m.	mortification	mortificación, f.
chairman		president	presidente, m.
chairmanship		presidency	presidencia, f.
challenge	reto, desafío, m.	objection	objeción, f.
chance (fate)	casualidad, suerte, f.	fortune	fortuna, f.
chance	ocasión, f.	opportunity	oportunidad, f.
chance(s)		probability	probabilidad, f.
*chance		possibility	posibilidad, f.
change	cambio, m; mudanza, f.	transformation	transformación, f.
		modification	modificación, f.
chap (fellow)	mozo, chico, m.	subject	sujeto, m.
character (stage)	personaje, m.	part	parte, f.
charge (price)	gasto, m.	price, cost	precio, costo, m.
charge (accus.)	alegato, m.	accusation	acusación, f.
charge (duty))	cargo, m.; tarea, f.	responsibility	responsabilidad, f.
charm	encanto, m; gracia, f.	attractiveness	atractivo, m.
charmer	mago, m.	enchanter	encantador, m.
chart	cuadro, m.	table, map	tabla, mapa, f.
		diagram	diagrama, f.
chat	charla, f.	conversation	conversación, f.
chateau		castle	castillo, m.
check (control)	freno, m.	control	control, m.
		repression	represión, f.
check (exam)	chequeo, m.	inspection	inspección, f.
		verification	verificación, f.
cheer (joy)	alegría, f.	humor	humor, m.
cheer (clap)	vítor, grito, m.	applause	aplauso, m.
cheeriness	alegría, f.	joviality	jovialidad, f.
		animation	animación, f.
childhood	niñez, f.	infancy	infancia, f.
childishness	niñeria, f.	puerility	puerilidad, f.
chime	campanas, f.	carillon	carillón, m.
chip (piece)	pedazo, trozo, m.	fragment	fragmento, m.
choice		election, option	elección, opción, f.
		selection	selección, f.
		preference	preferencia, f.
chum	compinche, m.	companion	compañero, m.
		comrade	camarada, m.
church	iglesia, f.	temple	templo, m.
citizen	ciudadano, m.	compatriat	compatriota, m.
claim	derecho, reclamo, m.	pretension	pretensión, f.
	reclamación, f.	petition, demand	petición, demanda, f.

ENGLISH	SPANISH NON-CONVERSION	ENGLISH SYNONYM	SPANISH CONVERSION
claimant	reclamante, m.	demander	demandante, m.
clash	choque, m.	collision	colisión, f.
clash (fight)	contienda, lucha, f.	discord	discordia, f.
clearance	despejo, m.	liquidation	liquidación, f.
		evacuation	evacuación, f.
clearance	aprobación, f.	permission	permiso, m.
		authorization	autorización, f.
clearness	perspicacia, f.	clarity	claridad, f.
cliff (bluff)	risco, m.	precipice	precipicio, m.
climb	subidero, m.	ascent	ascenso, m.
cloak		cape, mantle	capa, f.; manto, m.
cloister	claustro, m.	convent	convento, m.
		monastery	monasterio, m.
close	fin, m.	termination	terminación, f.
		conclusion	conclusión, f.
closeness	cercanía, f.	proximity	proximidad, f.
		contiguousness	contigüidad, f.
closet	armario, ropero, m.	*cabinet	gabinete, m.
clot	grumo, m.	coagulation	coágulo, m.
cloth	paño, m.; tela, f.	material	material, m.
cloudiness	nebulosidad, f.	obscurity	obscuridad, f.
clown	payaso, m.	buffoon, mime	bufón, mimo, m.
clue	pista, f.	indication	indicio, m.
coach (leader)	maestro, m.	trainer	entrenador, m.
coal	carbón, m.	anthracite	antracita, f.
coals (hot)	brasa, f.		
coarseness	aspereza, grosería, f.	vulgarity	vulgaridad, f.
coat	abrigo, m.; saco, m.	cape	capa, f.
	americana, f.	jacket	chaqueta, f.
cockiness	descaro, m.	impertinence	impertinencia, f.
coffin	cajón, ataúd, m.		
cognizance	conocimiento, m.	comprehension	comprensión, f.
		perception	percepción, f.
coil	rollo, carrete, m.	spiral	espiral, f.
coin	dinero, m.	money	moneda, f.
coldness	frio, m.; frialdad, f.	frigidity	frigidez, f.
collarbone		clavicle	clavícula, f.
comb (bird)		crest	cresta, f.
comedian	comediante, m.	comic	cómico, m.
comfort	alivio, comodidad, f.	solace	solaz, m.
comfort (care)		consolation	consuelo, m.
comity	urbanidad, f.	courtesy	cortesía, f.
command (order)	mando, orden, m.	mandate	mandato, m.
comment (remark)	comento, m.	observation	observación, f.
		commentary	comentario, m.
commitment	compromiso, m.	obligation	obligación, f.
commonwealth	comunidad, f.	state	estado, m.
company (guest)	visita, f; huésped, m.	invitee	invitado, m.
compass (area)	círculo, m.	space, ambit	espacio, ámbito, m.
		circumference	circunferencia, f.
compensation		remuneration	remuneración, f.
compensation	desagravio, m.	indemnification	indemnización, f.
		reparation	reparación, f.
		recompense	recompensa, f.

ENGLISH	SPANISH NON-CONVERSION	ENGLISH SYNONYM	SPANISH CONVERSION
*competence	competencia, f.	capacity	capacidad, f.
		aptitude	aptitud, f.
complaint	queja, f.	lament	lamento, m.
*completion	cumplimiento, m.	termination	terminación, f.
compliance		submission	sumisión, f.
concealment	escondimiento, m.		
conceit	orgullo, m.	vanity	vanidad, f.
		presumption	presunción, f.
concern (BUS)	negocio, m.; casa, f.	establishment	establecimiento, m.
concern (worry)	inquietud, f.	anxiety	ansiedad, f.
concoction	mezcla, f.	fabrication	fabricación, f.
		mixture	mixtura, f.
concurrence	concurrencia, f.	accord	acuerdo, m.
*conference	conferencia, f.	consultation	consulta(ción), f.
	entrevista, f.	deliberation	deliberación, f.
confrere	compañero, socio, m.	colleague	colega, f.
contempt	desprecio, m.	disdain	desdén, m.
contrivance	invención, f.	artifice	artificio, m.
conveyance	traspaso, m; cesión, f.	transmission	transmisión, f.
conveyor (load)	portador, m.	transporter	transportador, m.
conveyor (title)	cedente, m.		
*conviction (LAW)		condemnation	condena, f.
conviction	convencimiento, m.	persuasion	persuasión, f.
	creencia firme, f.		
conviviality	buen humor, m.	joviality	jovialdad, f.
copy	copia, f.	imitation	imitación, f.
copycat	remedador, m.	imitator	imitador, m.
core	corazón, m.	center, nucleus	centro, núcleo, m.
corn	grano, m.	cereal, maize	cereal, maíz, m.
corpse	difunto, m.	cadaver	cadáver, m.
cost (price)	costo, m.; costa, f.	price	precio, m.
couch (sofa)	lecho, m.	sofa, divan	sofá, f.; diván, m.
council	concilio, consejo, m.	junta	junta, f.
counterpart	contraparte, f.	equivalent	equivalente, m.
		double, pair	doble, m.; pareja, f.
		duplicate	duplicado, m.
country	país, m.; patria, f.	nation	nación, f.
countryman	paisano, m.	compatriot	compatriota, m.
couple	copla, f.	pair	par, m.; pareja, f.
courageousness	ánimo, m.	valor	valor, m.
		intrepidity	intrepidez, f.
court (yard)	atrio, m.	patio, corral	patio, corral, m.
court (LAW)	corte, f.	forum, tribunal	foro, tribunal, m.
covenant	convenio, m.	contract, pact	contrato, pacto, m.
		accord	acuerdo, m.
coverage	reportaje, m.	treatment	tratamiento, m.
covetousness	avidez, codicia, f.	avarice	avaricia, f.
crack	quiebra, grieta, f.	rupture	ruptura, f.
	hendedura, f.		
craft (trade)	oficio, m.	occupation, art	ocupación, f; arte, m.
craft (skill)	astucia, f.	artifice	artificio, m.
craft (boat)	embarcación, f.	bark	barco, m.
crash	choque, m.	collision	colisión, f.
craze	demencia, locura, f.	mania	manía, f.

ENGLISH	SPANISH NON-CONVERSION	ENGLISH SYNONYM	SPANISH CONVERSION
crossing (act)	travésia, f.	passage, transit	pasaje, tránsito, m.
crossing (place)	cruce, m.	intersection	intersección, f.
crowd (throng)	gente, muchedumbre, f.	multitude	multitud, f.
crown	guirnalda, f.	corona	corona, f.
cruise	crucero, m.	excursion	excursión, f.
cry	grito, m.	exclamation	exclamación, f.
		clamor	clamor, m.
cue	apunte, m.	signal	señal, f.
cunning	astucia, f.	subtlety	sutileza, f.
cunning (craft)	habilidad, f.	artifice	artificio, m.
	distreza, f.	astuteness	astucia, f.
curb (restraint)	freno, m.	restriction	restricción, f.
curse	imprecación, f.	malediction	maldición, f.
	reniego, m.	blasphemy	blasfemia, f.
curtailment	acortamiento, m.	restriction	restricción, f.
		reduction	reducción, f.
custard	natilla, f.	flan	flan, m.
customer	marchante, m.	client	cliente, m.
cut	herida, f.; corte, m.	incision	incisión, f.
cutlass	alfanje, m.	machete	machete, m.
dad	padre, m.	papa	papá, m.
damage	daño, perjuicio, m.	deterioration	deterioro, m.
dampness		humidity	humedad, f.
dancer	bailador, m.	ballerina	bailarina, f.
danger (peril)	peligro, m.	risk	riesgo, m.
dare	desafío, m.	provocation	provocación, f.
daring	atrevimiento, m.	audacity	audacia, f.
	arrojo, m.; bravura, f.		
dark (-ness)	noche, m; tinieblas, f.	obscurity	obscuridad, f.
darling	amado, querido, m.	favorite	favorito, m.
*date (calendar)	fecha, f.	day	día, m.
date (apptmt)	cita, f.	compromise	compromiso, m.
daydream	ensueño, m.	illusion	ilusión, f.
daze	aturdimiento, m.	trance	trance, m.
deadlock	estancamiento, m.	impasse	empate, m.
deal (contract)	negocio, trato, m.	pact	pacto, m.
dealer	negociante, m.	vendor	vendedor, m.
dealing	trato, m.	negotiation	negociación, f.
dealings	tratos, m.	relations	relaciones, f.
		conduct	conducta, f.
debarment		exclusion	exclusión, f.
debasement	rebajamiento, m.	degradation	degradación, f.
debauchery	sensualidad, f.	libertinism	libertinaje, f.
		corruption	corrupción, f.
debt	deuda, f.	obligation	obligación, f.
decanter		jar, carafe	jarra, garrafa, f.
decay	podredura, f.	decadence	decadencia, f.
		decomposition	descomposición, f.
		putrefaction	putrefacción, f.
deceitfulness	engaño, m.	fraudulence	fraudulencia, f.
		falseness	falsedad, f.
deck (ship)	cubierta, f.	platform	plataforma, f.
decrease	mengua, f.	diminution	disminución, f.
deed (act)	hecho, m.	act	acción, f.; acto, m.

ENGLISH	SPANISH NON-CONVERSION	ENGLISH SYNONYM	SPANISH CONVERSION
deed (instrument)	escritura, f.	instrument title	instrumento, m. título, m.
deepness	hondura, f.	profundity intensity	profundidad, f. intensidad, f.
defacement	estrapeo, m.	mutilation disfiguration deformation	mutilación, f. disfiguración, f. deformación, f.
defector		deserter	desertor, m.
defendant	(Civil) demandado, m.	accused (Crim.)	acusado, m.
defilement	profanación, f.	contamination corruption	contaminación, f. corrupción, f.
degree		grade, range	grado, rango, m.
dejection	abatimiento, m.	melancholy depression	melancolía, f. depresión, f.
delay	dilacción, demora, f. retraso, plazo, m.	tardiness	tardanza, f.
delight	gozo, m.; alegría, f. delicia, f.	enchantment	encanto, m.
deliverance	rescate, m.	liberation salvation redemption	liberación, f. salvación, f. redención, f.
delivery	entrega, f.	transfer	transferencia, f.
demand (reqmt)		exigency necessity	exigencia, f. necesidad, f.
demeanor	semblante, porte, m.	comportment conduct	comportamiento, m. conducta, f.
den (lair)	guarida, f.; cubil, m.	cavern	caverna, f.
denial	rechazo, m. desmentida, f.	negation repudiation	negación, f. repudiación, f.
*depletion	agotamiento, m.	diminution reduction	disminución, f. reducción, f.
depth	hondura, f.	profundity	profundidad, f.
desert (merit)		merit	merecimiento, m.
desecration		profanation	profanación, f.
detachment	despego, m.	indifference disinterest	indiferencia, f. desinterés, m.
detachment	despegadura, f.	separation	separación, f.
deterrence	refrenamiento, m.	dissuasion	disuasión, f.
development	desarrollo, m.	exploitation	explotación, f.
development	suceso, m.	occurrence	ocurrencia, f.
device	artefacto, m.	apparatus	aparato, m.
devil	diablo, m.	demon, Satan	demonio, satán, m.
die	matriz, m.	mould, stamp	molde, m; estampa, f.
diehard	reacio, m.	intransigent	intransigente, m.
diet	dieta, f,; régimen, m.	alimentation	alimentación, f.
diffidence	apocamiento, m.	timidity	timidez, f.
din (clamor)	ruido, estrépito, m.	clamor	clamoreo, m.
dinner	comida, cena, f.	banquet	banquete, f.
dirt (filth)	suciedad, mugre, f.	contamination	contaminación, f.
disagreement	desacuerdo, m.	dissension dispute	disención, f. disputa, f.
disappointment	desengaño, m.	disillusion	desilusión, f.
disarrangement	desarreglo, m.	disorder	desorden, m.

ENGLISH	SPANISH NON-CONVERSION	ENGLISH SYNONYM	SPANISH CONVERSION
disarray	desarreglo, m.	disorder	desorden, m.
		confusion	confusión, f.
disavowment (-al)		repudiation	repudiación, f.
disbelief		incredulity	incredulidad, f.
		skepticism	escepticismo, m.
discharge (job)	despedida, f.	separation	separación, f.
disclosure	divulgación, f.	revelation	revelación, f.
discouragement	desaliento, m.; desánimo, m.	dismay	desmayo, m.
disease	dolencia, f.; mal, m.	infirmity	enfermedad, f.
*disgrace	vergüenza, f.	dishonor	deshonra, f.
		stigma, ignominy	estigma, ignominia, f.
disguise	disfraz, m.	mask	máscara, f.
*disgust	hastío, m.	repugnance	repugnancia, f.
		aversion	aversión, f.
dish (container)	vajilla, f.	plate	plato, m.
dislike		aversion	aversión, f.
		repugnance	repugnancia, f.
		antipathy	antipatía, f.
*dismay	desaliento, m.; desánimo, m.	consternation	consternación, f.
display	muestra, f.	exposition	exposición, f.
		demonstration	demostración, f.
		exhibition	exhibición, f.
displeasure	desagrado, m.	disgust	*disgusto, m.
disregard	descuida, f.	no attention	desatención, f.
		negligence	negligencia, f.
dissatisfaction	desagrado, m.	discontent	descontento, m.
*distress	dolor, m.; pena, f.	misery	miseria, f.
		anguish	angustia, f.
		affliction	aflicción, f.
distrust	desconfianza, f.	suspicion	sospecha, f.
		doubt	duda, f.
ditch (water)	zanja, acequia, f.	canal	canal, m.
dive	zambullido, salto, m.		
dizziness	desvanecimiento, m.	vertigo	vértigo, m.
docket	cédula, f.	register	registro, m.
doctor (MD)	médico, f.	doctor (degree)	doctor, m.
dodge	regate, m.	evasion	evasiva, f.
		artifice	artificio, m.
doggedness	contumacia, f.	tenacity	tenacidad, f.
		obstinacy	obstinación, f.
doing(s)	hechos, m.	actions	accións, f.
		activities	actividades, f.
dole	repartimiento, m.; limosna, f.	distribution	distribución, f.; don, m.
donkey	asno, m.	burro	burro, m.
doom	muerte, f.	perdition, ruin	perdición, ruina, f.
		fatality	fatalidad, f.
door	puerta, f.	entrance	entrada, f.
dormancy	quietud, f.; sueño, m.	inactivity	inactividad, f.
		lethargy	letargo, m.
dot	puntillo, dote, m.	point	punto, m.

ENGLISH	SPANISH NON-CONVERSION	ENGLISH SYNONYM	SPANISH CONVERSION
dough	masa, f.	pasta	pasta, f.
dove (pigeon)	paloma, f.	pigeon	pichón, m.
downfall	caída, f.	ruin	ruina, f.
downtown		center	centro, m.
draft (report)		project	proyecto, m.
draft (MIL)	cuota, leva, f.	conscription	conscripción, f.
draftee	quinto, m.	conscript	conscripto, m.
		recruit	recluta, m.
drape	colgadura, f.	curtain	cortina, f.
drawers (chest)	cajón, m.	*commode	cómoda, f.
dread (fear)	espanto, miedo, m.	terror	temor, terror, m.
dream	sueño, m.	illusion	ilusión, f.
dreamer	soñador, m.	visionary	visionario, m.
dressing	relleno, aderezo, m.	sauce	salsa, f.
dressmaker	costurera, f.	modiste	modista, f.
drive	paseo, m.	excursion	excursión, f.
driver	cochero, m.	chauffeur	conductor, chofer, m.
drop (fall)	caída, f.	descent	descenso, m.
drop (droplet)	poco, m.; gota, f.		
drug (narcotic)		narcotic	narcótico, m.
drug (medicine)	droga, f.	medicine	medicina, f.
drugstore	droguería, botica, f.	pharmacy	farmacia, f.
drunk	ebrio, borracho, m.		
drunkenness	embriaguez, f.		
dryness	sequedad, f.	aridity	aridez, f.
duct	conducto, tubo, m.	canal	canal, m.
duress	coacción, prisión, f.	compulsion	compulsión, f.
dust	polvo, m.		
duty (task)	tarea, f.; deber, m.	obligation	obligación, f.
dwarf	enano, m.	pygmy	pigmeo, m.
dwelling	morada, vivienda, f.	habitation	habitación, f.
	casa, f.	residence	residencia, f.
		domicile	domicilio, m.
dye	tintura, f.	tint	tinte, m.
eagerness (zeal)	afán, m.; avidez, f.	anxiety	ansiedad, f.
earring	arete, m.	pendant	pendiente, m.
earth (planet)	mundo, m.; tierra, f.	globe	globo, m.
ease (comfort)	comodidad, f.	tranquility	tranquilidad, f.
		serenity	serenidad, f.
		repose	reposo, m.
ease (facility)	soltura, f.	facility	facilidad, f.
edge (brim, rim)	orilla, f.	border, margen	borde, margen, m.
edible		comestible	comestible, m.
effectiveness	(LAW) vigencia, f.	efficacy	eficacia, f.
effort	esfuerzo, m.		
*embarrassment	vergüenza, f.	disconcerting	desconcierto, m.
		perplexity	perplejidad, f.
		confusion	confusión, f.
embodiment	encarnación, f.	personification	personificación, f.
employer	empleador, m.	patron	patrón, patrono, m.
emptiness		vacuum	vacio, vacuidad, f.
enactment		promulgation	promulgación, f.
enamel	esmalte, m.		

ENGLISH	SPANISH NON-CONVERSION	ENGLISH SYNONYM	SPANISH CONVERSION
encore		repetition	repetición, f.
encouragement	aliento, m.	stimulus	estímulo, m.
encroachment		intrusion	intrusión, f.
		usurpation	usurpación, f.
		invasion, abuse	abuso, m; invasión, f.
encumbrance	embarazo, m.; carga, f.	impediment	impedimento, m.
end (-ing)	termino, fin, cabo, m.	conclusion	conclusión, f.
		termination	terminación, f.
end		extremity	extremidad, f.
end (purpose)	propósito, m.	object	objeto, m.
endeavor	esfuerzo, empeño, m.	intention (aim)	intento, m.
endowment	dote, m.; dotación, f.	funding	fundación, f.
endurance	aguante, m.	resistance	resistencia, f.
		patience	paciencia, f.
enforcement	coacción, f.	imposition	imposición, f.
		application	aplicación, f.
engagement (date)	compromiso, m.	obligation	obligación, f.
	cita, f.	promise	promesa, f.
engine	motor, m.	machine	máquina, f.
engine (RR)		locomotive	locomotora, f.
enhancement	mejoría, f.	augmentation	aumento, m.
enjoyment	placer, goce, m.	delight	deleite, m.
	disfrute, m.		
enlargement	ampliación, f.	aggrandizemnt	agrandamiento, m.
		augmentation	aumento, m.
		extension	extensión, f.
		expansion	expansión, f.
enlightenment	esclarecimiento, m.	instruction	instrucción, f.
enrollment	alistamiento, m.	registration	registro, m.
		matriculation	matriculo, m.
ensign (Navy)	alférez, m.	sublieutenant	subteniente, m.
enticement	incitación, f.	temptation	tentación, f.
		seduction	seducción, f.
entirety	entereza, f.	totality	totalidad, f.
entrails	entrañas, f.	tripe	tripa, f.
		intestines	intestinos, m.
entrepreneur	contratista, m.	impresario	empresario, m.
environment	cercanía, f.	ambience	ambiente, m.
environs	alrededores, m.	suburbs	suburbios, m.
eradicator	quitamanchas, f.	extirpater	extirpador, m.
errand	recado, m.	mandate	mandato, m.
escapee	prófugo, m.	fugitive	fugitivo, m.
escort	escolta, f.	accompanist	acompañante, m.
escrow	plica, f.	deposit	depósito, m.
eve	noche, f.	vesper	víspera, f.
	anochecer, m.		
event	acontecimiento, m.	incident	incidente, m.
	evento, suceso, m.	consequence	consecuencia, f.
evil (wicked)	mal, m.; maldad, f.	perversity	perversidad, f.
excitement	excitación, f.	animation,	animación, f.
		emotion	emoción, f.
exertion	esfuerzo, m.	exercise	ejercicio, m.
exit	éxit, m.; salida, f.	departure	partida, f.

ENGLISH	SPANISH NON-CONVERSION	ENGLISH SYNONYM	SPANISH CONVERSION
expanse	espacio, m.	extension	extensión, f.
expense	gasto, m.	cost	costo, m.
expert	perito, m.	expert	experto, m.
exploit	hazaña, proeza, f.		
fact	hecho, m.	reality	realidad, f.
failure	fracaso, m.	fault, fiasco	falta, f.; fiasco, m.
fairness	rectitud, equidad, f.	justice impartiality	justicia, f. imparcialidad, f.
fairy (sprite)	duende, m.; hada, f.		
faith (creed)	fe, f.	religion, creed	religión, credo, m.
faith (trust)	fe, f.	confidence	confianza, f.
faithfulness	lealtad, f.	fidelity	fidelidad, f.
fake	impostura, f.	falsification imitation	falsificación, f. imitación, f.
fall (season)		autumn	otoño, m.
fall (tumble)	caída, f.		
falls	catarata, f.	cascade	cascada, f.
fan (coolant)	abanico, m.	ventilator	ventilador, m.
fancy (notion)	capricho, m.	imagination idea, impression	imaginación, f. idea, impresión, f.
fare (rate)		tariff, passage	tarifa, f.; pasaje, m.
farewell	salida, despedida, f.	adios	adiós, m.
farmer	granjero, labrador, m.	agriculturist	agricultor, m.
farming	labranza, f.	agriculture cultivation	agricultura, f. cultivo, m.
farsightedness	perspicación, f. previsión, f.	prudence	prudencia, f.
fashion	figura, hechura, f.	mode, style vogue	moda, f.; estilo, m. boga, f.
fast	ayuno, m.	abstinence	abstinencia, f.
fat (lard)	sebo, m.; manteca, f.	grease	grasa, f.
fate (doom)	sino, m.; suerte, f.	destiny	destino, m.
fatherhood		paternity	paternidad, f.
fatness	gordura, f.	obeisity	obesidad, f.
*fault	falta, f.	defect, error imperfection	defecto, error, m. imperfección, f.
fault (blame)	culpa, f.	responsibility imperfection	responsibilidad, f. imperfección, f.
fear (fright)	miedo, temor, m.	terror	terror, m.
feasibility		viability	viabilidad, f.
feast (banquet)	festín, m.; fiesta, f.	banquet	banquete, m.
feat	hazaña, f.	prowess	proeza, f.
feather		plume	pluma, f.
features	rostro, m.; figura, f.	physiognomy	fisonomía, f.
fee	derechos, m.	honorarium remuneration stipend	honorario, m. remuneración, f. estipendio, m.
feed	comida, f.	forage alimentation	foraje, m. alimentación, f.
feeding	alimento, m.	nutrition	nutrición, f.
feel, -ing	tacto, m.	sensation	sensación, f.
feeling	sentimiento, m.	emotion sensitivity	emoción, f. sensibilidad, f.
fellow (chap)	sujeto, m.	individual	individuo, m.

ENGLISH	SPANISH NON-CONVERSION	ENGLISH SYNONYM	SPANISH CONVERSION
fellow (assoc)	compañero, m.	associate	asociado, m.
fellow worker		colleague	colega, f.
fellowship	confraternidad, f.	camaraderie	camaradería, f.
		community	comunidad, f.
fervency	fervor, m.	ardor devotion	ardor, m; devoción, f
fetter (chain)	grillo, m.; cadena, f.	impediment	impedimento, m.
fiddle		violin	violín, m.
fiddler		violinist	violinista, m.
field (sphere)	campo, m.	sphere	esfera, f.
fiend	loco, adicto, m.	fanatic	fanático, m.
fierceness	fiereza, f.	ferocity	ferocidad, f.
fight (struggle)	lucha, pelea, f.	conflict	conflicto, m.
fighter	luchador, guerrero, m.	boxer	boxeador, m.
	peleador, m.	combantant	combatiente, m.
figment		fiction	ficción, f.
		invention	invención, f.
figure (number)		cipher, number	cifra, f.; numero, m
file (papers)	actas, f.	archive	archivo, m.
		registry	registro, m.
find, -ing	hallazgo, m.	discovery	descubrimiento, m.
		invention	invención, f.
fine	multa, f.	penalty	pena, penalidad, f.
finesse	finura, sutileza, f.	refinement	refinamiento, m.
fir	abeto, m.	pine	pino, m.
fire	fuego, incendio, m.		
fireplace	hogar, m.	chimney	chimenea, f.
firmness	firmeza, fijeza, f.	stability	estabilidad, f.
first	primero, m.	original	original, m.
fit (in size)	talle, f.; ajuste, m.	cut	corte, m
fitness	propiedad, f.	aptitude	aptitud, f.
flag (standard)	bandera, f; pabellón, m.	standard	estandarte, m.
flair	instinto, m.	style	estilo, m.
		aptitude	aptitud, f
flake	pedacito, m; escama, f.		
flamboyance	resplandor, m.	ostentation	ostentación, f.
flame	fuego, m.; llama, f.		
flat (apartment)	piso, m.	apartment	apartamento, m.
flattery	lisonaje, f.	adulation	adulación, f.
flavor	gusto, m.	savor, season	sabor, sazón, m.
flaw	grieta, f.	defect	defecto, m.
		imperfection	imperfección, f.
fleet	flota, f.	armada, squadron	armada, escuadra, f.
flier	volador, m.	aviator	aviador, m.
flight	vuelo, m.		
flight (retreat)	fuga, huida, f.	escape, evasion	escape, m; evasión, f.
flirt	galanteador, m.	coquette	coqueta, f.
flood	crecida, f.; diluvio, m.	inundation	inundación, f.
flour		farina	harina, f.
flu		grippe	gripe, f.
		influenza	influenza, f.
foam	espuma, f.		
foe		enemy	enemigo, m.
		adversary	adversario, m.
		antagonist	antagonista, m.

ENGLISH	SPANISH NON-CONVERSION	ENGLISH SYNONYM	SPANISH CONVERSION
folk	gente, f.; pueblo, m.	nation, race	nación, raza, f.
follower	partidario, m.	disciple	discípulo, m.
following	acompañamiento, m.	cortege	cortejo, m.
	partidarios, m.	party (group)	partido, m.
folly	locura, tontaría, f.	stupidity	estupidez, f.
		temerity	temeridad, f.
fondness	cariño, m.; afición, f.	inclination	inclinación, f.
food (feeding)	comida, f.	alimentation	alimento, m.
fool (dunce)	necio, tonto, m.	imbecile	imbécil, m.
foolishness	disparate, tontería, f.	ridiculousness	ridiculez, f.
footsoldier	soldado de pie, m.	infantryman	infante, m.
foray	correría, f; saqueo, m.	pillage	pillaje, m.
		incursion	incursión, f.
forbearance	refrenamiento, m.	patience	paciencia, f.
		abstention	abstención, f.
forecast	pronóstico, m.	prophecy	profesía, f.
		prediction	predicción, f.
forecaster		pronosticator	pronosticador, m.
foreclosure	privación, f.	exclusion	exclusión, f.
foreigner	forastero, m.	stranger	extranjero, m.
			extraño, m.
foreknowledge		prescience	presciencia, f.
forerunner	heraldo, m.	precursor	precursor, m.
foreward	advertencia, f.	preface	prefacio, m.
		prologue	prólogo, m.
		preamble	preámbulo, m.
		introduction	introducción, f.
forfeiture	comiso, m.; pérdida, f.	confiscation	confiscación, f.
forgery		falsification	falsificación, f.
		adulteration	adulteración, f.
forgetfulness	descuido, olvido, m.	amnesia	amnesia, f.
forgiveness		pardon	perdón, m.
		indulgence	indulgencia, f.
fracas	alboroto, m.	tumult	tumulto, m.
framework	armazón, f.	skeleton	esqueleto, m.
freedom		liberty	libertad, f.
freeing		emancipation	emancipación, f.
freight	flete, m.	cargo	carga, f.
friar (monk)	fraile, m.	monk	monje, m.
friend	amigo, m.	ally, companion	aliado, compañero, m.
friendship	amigabilidad, f.	amity	amistad, f.
fright (fear)	susto, miedo, temor, m.	terror	terror, m.
	espanto, m.		
fringe	fleco, m.	border, margen	borde, margen, m.
front, fore	frente, faz, f.	facade	fachada, f.
frontage	frente, f.	facade	fachada, f.
fuel		combustible	combustible, m.
fulfillment	cumplimiento, m.	realization	realización, f.
fullness	plenitud, llenura, f.	abundance	abundancia, f.
fun	burla, diversión, f.	recreation	recreo, m.
		entertainment	entretenimiento, m.
funnel (ship)		chimney	chimenea, f.
furlough	licencia, f.	permission	permiso, m.
gait	marcha, f.	pace	paso, m.

ENGLISH	SPANISH NON-CONVERSION	ENGLISH SYNONYM	SPANISH CONVERSION
gaiety	alegría, f.	joviality	jovialidad, f.
gale (storm)	ventarrón, m.	tempest	tempestad, f.
gall (BIOCHEM)	hiel, f.	bile	bilis, f.
gall (nerve)	aspereza, f.	rancor	rencor, m.
game (play)	juego, m.	sport	deporte, m.
gang (band)	pandilla, cuadrilla, f.	band	banda, f.
gangster	pisolero, pandillero, m.	bandit	bandido, m.
gap	hueco, m.	breach	brecha, f.
garnishment (LAW)		embargo	embargo, m.
		retention	retención, f.
garnishment		adornment	adorno, m.
		ornament	ornamento, m.
gate (city--)	puerta, f.; portón, m.	entrance	entrada, f.
gateway	portal, m.	entrance	entrada, f.
gathering	agrupación, f.	reunion	reunión, f.
gauge	medida, f.	norm	norma, f.
gavel		mallet	mallete, m.
gear (things)		equipment	equipo, m.
geniality		affability	afabilidad, f.
		cordiality	cordialidad, f.
gentile	gentil, m.	Christian	cristiano, m.
gentleman	hidalgo, caballero, m.		
gentleness	benignidad, bondad, f.	suaveness	suavidad, f.
		docility	docilidad, f.
gentry	alta burguesía, f.	nobility	nobleza, f.
germ	germen, m.	microbe	microbio, m.
ghost (phantom)	fantasma, f.	specter	espectro, m.
		apparition	aparición, f.
gift (present)	regalo, don, m.	donation	donación, f.
	obsequio, m.	present	presente, m.
girdle	faja, cintura, f.	corset	corsé, m.
glade	raso, claro, m.		
gladness (glee)	alegría, f.; gozo, m.	*jubilation	júbilo, m.
glance (glimpse)	mirada, ojeada, f.		
glass (material)	vidrio, m.	crystal	cristal, m.
gleam	destello, m.	ray	rayo, m.
gleeclub	orfeón, m.	chorus	coro, m.
glen (dale)	hoya, f.	valley	valle, m.
gloom (sorrow)	tristeza, f.; dolor, m.	melanchnoly	melancolía, f.
gloom (darkness)	tenebrosidad, f.	obscurity	obscuridad, f.
glow	brillo, m.	splendor	resplandor, m.
glue	goma, cola, f.	adhesive	adjesivo, m.
goal (aim)	fin, propósito, m.	objective	objetivo, m.
goblet	tazón, m.	cup	copa, f.
God	Dios, m.	deity	deidad, f.
good	provecho, bien, m.	advantage	ventaja, f.
		benefit	beneficio, m.
goodness	bondad, f.	virtue	virtud, f.
goods (wares)	géneros, bienes, m.	merchandise	mercancía, f.
goodwill	buena voluntad, f.	benevolence	benevolencia, f.
gorge	garganta, f.	canyon, pass	cañón, paso, m.
gormandizer	tragón, m.	glutton	glotón, m.
gourmet	gastrónomo, m.	epicure	epicúreo, m.
gospel	evangelio, m.	creed	credo, m.

ENGLISH	SPANISH NON-CONVERSION	ENGLISH SYNONYM	SPANISH CONVERSION
gossiper	chismoso, m.	murmurer	murmurador, m.
governess	gobernante, aya, f.	instructress	institutriz, f.
grade (class)	grado, rango, año, m.	class	clase, f.
grant	otorgamiento, m.	concession	cesión, f.
		permission	permiso, m.
		donation	donación, f.
grantee	cesionario, m.	donee	donatario, m.
grantor	cedente, otorgante, m.	donor	donador, m.
grasp (hold)	presa, f.; abrazo, m.	control	control, m.
*gratuity	propina, f.	donation	donación, f.
grave (tomb)	sepulcro, f.	tomb	tumba, f.
		sepulcher	sepultura, f.
graveyard		cemetery	cementerio, m.
gravy	jugo, caldo, m.	sauce	salsa, f.
greatness	grandeza, f.	magnitude	magnitud, f.
greed (-iness)	codicia, f.	avarice	avaricia, f.
green (-ness)	verde, m.	verdure	verdura, f.
greeting(s)	saludo, m.	salutations	salutaciones, f.
grief (sorrow)	dolor, pesar, m.	affliction	aflicción, f.
	pesadumbre, f.	pain	pena, f.
grievance	agravio, m.	injustice	injusticia, f.
grip (grasp)	apretón, m.	press	presa, f.
groan (moan)	gemido, quejido, m.		
*grocery	abacería, bodega, f.	spicery	especiería, f.
groove	ranura, f.	channel	acanaladura, f.
ground	tierra, f.	soil, terrain	suelo, terreno, m.
		territory	territorio, m.
ground (basis)	causa, f.	base, reason	base, razón, f.
group (class)		class	clase, f.
		category	categoría, f.
grower	agricultor, criador, m.	cultivator	cultivador, m.
growth	crecimiento, m.	expansion	expansión, f.
growth (develop)	desarrollo, m.	augmentation	aumento, m.
grub	gusano, m.	larva	larva, f.
grudge	rencor, m.	animosity	animosidad, f.
guess	barrunto, m.	supposition	soposición, f.
		conjecture	conjetura, f.
guest	huésped, m.	invited one	invitado, m.
guidance	consejo, m.; guía, f.	direction	dirección, f.
guild	gremio, m.	association	asociación, f.
		society	sociedad, f.
guilt	delito, m.; culpa, f.	culpability	culpabilidad, f.
guise	cara, f.	appearance	apariencia, f.
		form	forma, f.
gullet	gola, f.	esophagus	esófago, m.
gun (rifle)	fusil, m; escopeta, f.	cannon, rifle	cañon, rifle, m.
gunner		artilleryman	artillero, m.
guru	líder, guía, m.	master	maestro, m.
gush	chorro, m.	effusion	efusión, f.
guy (fellow)	tio, tipo, muchacho, m.	subject	sujeto, m.
gypsy	gitano, m.		
habitué	parroquiano, m.	frequenter	frequentador, m.
half	medio, m.; mitad, f.		
hall (entry)	pasillo, m.	vestibule	vestíbulo, m.

229

ENGLISH	SPANISH NON-CONVERSION	ENGLISH SYNONYM	SPANISH CONVERSION
handbook		manual, guide	manual, m.; guía, f.
handling	manejo, m.	manipulation	manipulación, f.
happiness	alegría, dicha, f.	felicity	felicidad, f.
harassment	acosamiento, m.	molestation	molestia, f.
harbour	anclaje, m.	port	puerto, m.
hardness	dureza, f.	firmness	firmeza, f.
hardship	penuria, f.	privation	privación, f.
		solidity	solidez, f.
harlot	zorra, puta, f.	prostitute	prostituta, f.
harm	mal, perjuicio, m.	damage	daño, m.
harmlessness		innocuousness	innocuidad, f.
		innocence	inocencia, f.
harshness	aspereza, f.	severity	severidad, f.
		cruelty	crueldad, f.
haste	prisa, f.	celerity	celeridad, f.
		precipitation	precipitación, f.
hatchery	criadero, m.	incubator	incubadero, m.
hate (hatred)	odio, m.	aversion	aversión, f.
		abhorrence	aborrecimiento, m.
haughtiness	altivez, f.	arrogance	arrogancia, f.
haven	abrigo, m.	asylum, refuge	asilo, refugio, m.
havoc	estrango, m.	devastation	devastación, f.
hawk		falcon	halcón, m.
hazard	peligro, m.	risk	riesgo, m.
head (chief)		chief	jefe, m.
heading, -line	encabezamiento, m.	title	título, m.
headquarters	jefatura, sede, f.	central office	oficina central, f.
health	salubridad, salud, f.	sanity	sanidad, f.
heap (pile)	montón, m.	pile	pila, f.
hearing	oído, m.	audience	audiencia, f.
heartache	tristeza, f.;pesar, m.	anguish	angustia, f.
heat (warmth)	calor, m.	temperature	temperatura, f.
heathen		barbarian, pagan	bárbaro, pagano, m.
heating	calentamiento, m.	calefaction	calefacción, f.
heaven	cielo, m.	paradise	paraíso, m.
heed	cuidado, m.	attention	atención, f.
height (top)	colmo, m.	eminence	eminencia, f.
height (alt.)		altitude	altitud, altura, f.
hell		inferno	infierno, m.
help	auxilio, m.; ayuda, f.	*assistance	asistencia, f.
		succor	socorro, m.
helper	ayudante, auxilar, m.	assistant	asistente, m.
hem	bastilla, f.;borde, m.	margin	margen, m.
highness	alteza, f.	altitude	altura, f.
hindrance	embarazo, estorbo, m.	impediment	impedimento, m.
		obstacle	obstáculo, m.
hint	indirecta, f.	insinuation	insinuación, f.
		indication	indicio, m.
		suggestion	sugestión, f.
hinterland		interior	interior, m.
hoax	engaño, m.; broma, f.	fraud	fraude, m.
hobo	vago, m.	vagabond	vagabundo, m.
hog	cochino, cerdo, m.	pork(-er)	puerco, m.
holder	tenedor, m.	possessor	poseedor, posesor, m.

ENGLISH	SPANISH NON-CONVERSION	ENGLISH SYNONYM	SPANISH CONVERSION
holdings	pertenencia, f.	property	propiedades, f.
hole	agujero, hueco, hoyo, m.	cavity, cave	cavidad, cueva, f.
		aperture	abertura, f.
		orifice	orificio, m.
holiday	día de fiesta, m.	vacation	vacación, f.
holiness	beatitud, f.	saintliness	santidad, f.
hollow	hueco, m.	cavity	cavidad, f.
		depression	depresión, f.
home	hogar, m.; casa, f.	residence	residencia, f.
		domicile	domicilio, m.
homesickness	añoranza, f.	nostalgia	nostalgia, f.
hope	esperanza, f.	desire, faith	deseo, m.; fé, f.
hopelessness		desperation	desesperación, f.
horn (bugle)	trompa, corneta, f.	trumpet	trompeta, f.
horsemanship	manejo, m.	equitation	equitación, f.
host	anfitrión, huesped, m.	host	hospedero, m.
house	casa, f.; hogar, m.	residence	residencia, f.
		domicile	domicilio, m.
house (boarding)	casa de huéspedes, f.	pension	pensión, f.
household	casa, f.	family	familia, f.
hub	cubo, m.	center	centro, m.
hue (shade)	matiz, tinte, f.	color	color, m.
hug		embrace	abrazo, m.
hum	zumbido, susurro, m.	murmur	murmullo, m.
hunger	hambre, f.	desire	deseo, m.
hurry (rush)	prisa, f.	urgency	urgencia, f.
hurt	herida, f.; daño, m.	lesion	lesión, f.
husband	marido, m.	spouse	esposo, m.
husbandry	manejo, m.	agriculture	agricultura, f.
hut (shed)	choza, f.	cabin	cabaña, f.
hyphen	guión, m.		
ice	hielo, m.		
ice cream	helado, m.	sherbet	sorbete, m.
*idiom	yerga, f.; modismo, m.	dialect	dialecto, m.
idleness	pereza, ociosidad, f.	indolence	indolencia, f.
illness	mal, m.; dolencia, f.	infirmity	enfermedad, f.
*illustration		example	ejemplo, m.
impairment	daño, menoscabo, m.	deterioration	deterioro, m.
impersonator	intérprete, m.	imitator	imitador, m.
implementation	cumplimiento, m.	execution	ejecución, f.
import(-ance)	importancia, f.	significance	significación, m.
imprint		impression	impresión, f.
		mark	marca, f.
improvement	mejoramiento, m.	progress	progreso, m.
inaccuracy	incorrección, f.	inexactitude	inexactitud, f.
		error	error, m.
		equivocation	equivocación, f.
inadequacy		insufficiency	insuficiencia, f.
income	ingresos, m.	rent	renta, f.
	utilidades, f.		
increase	crecimiento, m.	augmentation	aumento, m.
indictment	denuncia, f.	accusation	acusación, f.
	proceso, m.		
inductee		recruit	recluta, f.

231

ENGLISH	SPANISH NON-CONVERSION	ENGLISH SYNONYM	SPANISH CONVERSION
infringement		infraction	infracción, f.
		transgression	transgresión, f.
		violation	violación, f.
injunction	orden, precepto, m.	mandate	mandato, m.
injury (wound)	daño, m.; herida, f.	lesion	lesión, f.
inn	posada, fonda, f.	hostel	hostería, f.
innuendo	indirecta, f.	insinuation	insinuación, f.
inquiry (ques)	pregunta, f.	question	cuestión, m.
inquiry (search)		investigation	investigación, f.
		inquest	encuesta, f.
insanity	locura, f.	dementia	demencia, f.
inset		insertion	inserción, f.
inside(s)		interior	interior, m.
		contents	contenido, m.
insight	agudeza de ingenio, f.	perspicacity	perspicacia, f.
		discernment	discernimiento, m.
installment	entrega, f.	installation	instalación, f.
installment(pay)	plazo, m.; cuota, f.	partial payment	pago parcial, m.
instrumentality	medio, m.	agency	agencia, f.
insurgence		insurrection	insurrección, f.
		rebellion	rebelión, f.
intercourse(sex)	cópula, f.	coitus	coito, m.
intercourse(soc)	intercambio, m.	communication	comunicación, f.
interest (share)		participation	participación, f.
*introduction		presentation	presentación, f.
issue (descent)	prole, f.	progeny	progenie, f.
issue,-ance		emission	emisión, f.
itemization		specification	especificación, f.
ivory	marfil, m.		
jackass	burro, m.	ass	asno, m.
jail	cárcel, m.	prison	prisión, f.
jam	confitura, f.	marmalade	mermelada, f.
jellyfish		medusa	medusa, f.
jeopardy	peligro, m.	risk	riesgo, m.
Jew	judío, m.	Israelite	israelita, m.
job	trabajo, m.; obra, f.	employment	empleo, m.
job (task)	tarea, f.	labor	labor, m.
joint	juntura, junta, f.	union	unión, f.
jolt	golpe, m.	impact	impacto, m.
journal	diario, m.	periodical	periódico, m.
journey	viaje, m.	passage	pasaje, m.
joy	alegría, f.; gozo, m.	jubilation	júbilo, m.
judge	juez, m.	arbitrator	árbitro, m.
judgment	criterio, m.	reason	razón, f.
judgment		decision	decisión, f.
		opinion	opinión, f.
judgment (LAW)	dictamen, juicio, m.	sentence	sentencia, f.
jug (pitcher)	botija, f.	jar	jarra, f.; jarro, m.
keeper	guarda, m.	custodian	custodio, m.
		guardian	guardián, f.
keeping up		maintaining	mantenimiento, m.
kernel	semilla, f.	grain	grano, m.
kettle	olla, marmita, f.	caldron	caldera, f.
kidnapper	raptor, m.	sequestrator	secuestrador, m.

ENGLISH	SPANISH NON-CONVERSION	ENGLISH SYNONYM	SPANISH CONVERSION
killer	homicida, matador, m.	assassin	asesino, m.
kind (sort)	especie,f.;género, m.	class, tenor variety	clase,f.; tenor, m. variedad, f.
kindness	bondad,amabilidad, f.	benevolence	benevolencia, f.
king	rey, m.	monarch	monarca, m.
kingdom		reign	reino, m.
kiss	beso, m.		
knave (wretch)	pícaro, m.	villain	villano, m.
knob	tirador, m.	button	botón, m.
knot	nudo, m.		
knowledge	entendimiento, m. conocimiento, m.	information	información, f.
lab		laboratory	laboratorio, m.
label (tag)	etiqueta,f.;letrero, m. rótulo, m.	mark	marca, f.
laborer	obrero, m.	operator	operario, m.
lace	encaje, m.	cord	cordón, m.
lack	falta, f.	deficiency	deficiencia, f.
lampoonist		satirist	satirista, f.
land (area)	país, suelo, m.	territory	territorio, m.
landlord	arrendador, m.	proprietor	propietario, m.
lard(fat)	manteca, f.	grease	grasa, f.
largeness	amplitud, f.	magnitude	magnitud, f.
last		ultimate	último, m.
laugh,laughter	risa, f.		
law (statute)	ley, f.	code,statute legislation	código, estatuto, m. legislación, f.
law	derecho, m.	jurisprudence	jurisprudencia, f.
lawsuit	pleito, proceso, m. juicio, m.	litigation	litigio, m.
lawyer	licenciado, m.	jurist advocate	jurista, m. abogado, m.
layer	capa, f.	stratum	estrato, m.
laziness	pereza, f.	indolence	indolencia, f.
lead (ahead)	delantera, f.	initiative	iniciativa, f.
leader (MIL)	jefe, m.	commander	comandante, m.
leader (MUS)		conductor	conductor, m.
leadership	jefatura, f.	direction	dirección, f.
leaf (BOT)	hoja, f.	foliage	follaje, m.
leak	agujero, gotero, m.	escape	escape, m.
leaning		tendency propensity proclivity inclination	tendencia, f. propensión, f. proclividad, f. inclinación, f.
learning	sabiduría,f.; saber, m.	erudition	erudición, f.
least	menor, m.	minimum	mínimo, m.
leather	piel, cuero, m.		
leave (abs.)	licencia, f.	permission authorization	permiso, m. autorización, f.
*lecture		dissertation	disertación, f.
*lecture		conference	conferencia, f.
leeway		margin	margen, m.
left	izquierda, f.		
length	largo, m.	longitude	longitud, f.

ENGLISH	SPANISH NON-CONVERSION	ENGLISH SYNONYM	SPANISH CONVERSION
lengthening	alargamiento, m.	prolongation	prolongación, f.
		extension	extensión, f.
lens	lente, m.	crystal	cristal, m.
letter (mail)	carta, f.	epistle	epístola, f.
levee		dike	dique, m.
levity	ligereza, f.	frivolity	frivolidad, f.
levy (tax)	recaudación, f.	imposition	imposición, f.
liability	riesgo, m.	responsibility	responsabilidad, f.
		obligation	obligación, f.
liar	mentiroso, m.	falsifier	falsificador, m.
lie	mentira,f.;embuste, m.	falsehood	falsedad, f.
life	viveza, f.	animation	animación, f.
life	vida, f.; vivir,ser, m.	existence	existencia, f.
light	luz, f.	illumination	iluminación, f.
		clarity	claridad, f.
lighting	alumbrado, m.	illumination	iluminación, f.
	encendido, m.	ignition	ignición, f.
lightness	ligereza, f.	frivolity	frivolidad, f.
lightness		luminosity	luminosidad, f.
likelihood		probability	probabilidad, f.
likeness	semejanza, f.	similarity	similitud, f.
liking	agrado, m.; afición, f.	preference	preferencia, f.
limb (body)		member	miembro, m.
		extremity	extremidad, f.
line (row)		file	fila, f.
line (rope)	cuerda, f.	cord	cordón, cordel, m.
lining	forro, m.	interior	interior, m.
linkage	enlace, m.	union	unión, f.
livelihood	mantenimiento, m.	subsistence	subsistencia, f.
liveliness	viveza, f.	vivacity	vivacidad, f.
		animation	animación, f.
living	vida, f.	subsistence	subsistencia, f.
load	cargamento, m.	cargo	carga, f.
lobby (hall)	pasillo, m.	vestibule	vestíbulo, m.
		foyer	foyer, m.
lock (sluice)		sluice	esclusa, f.
locket	relicario, m.	medallion	medallón, m.
lockjaw	tristmo, m.	tetanus	tétano, m.
lodging	hospedaje, m.	habitation	habitación, f.
log	leño, m.	trunk	tronco, m.
loneliness	tristeza, f.	solitude	soledad, f.
longing	gana, f.; anhelo, m.	desire	deseo, m.
look(s)(mien)	cara, f.;gesto,aire, m.	appearance	apariencia, f.
look(glimpse)	mirada, ojeada, f.		
loop	vuelta, f.	lasso	lazo, m.
loophole		escape	escapatorio, m.
		excuse	excusa, f.
looseness	aflojamiento, m.	licence	licencia, f.
loot	saqueo, m.	pillage	pillaje, m.
lord	señor, dueño, m.	patron	patrón, m.
loss	pérdida, f.	privation	privación, f.
lot (fate)	sorteo, m.; suerte, f.	opportunity	oportunidad, f.
lot (share)	lote, m.	part, portion	parte, porción, f.
lounge		salon	salón, m.

ENGLISH	SPANISH NON-CONVERSION	ENGLISH SYNONYM	SPANISH CONVERSION
love	amor, cariño, m.	devotion	devoción, f.
luck	suerte, f.	fortune	fortuna, f.
lull		calm	calma, f.
lump	terrón, m.	protuberance	protuberancia, f.
lunacy	locura, f.	dementia	demencia, f.
lust	codicia, lujuria, f. anhelo, m.	lasciviousness	lascivia, f.
luxury	lujo, m.	pomp	pompa, f.
madness	locura, f.; extravío, m.	mania, fury	manía, furia, f.
maid (servant)	criada, moza, f.	servant	sirvienta, f.
mail	correo, m.	correspondence	correspondencia, m.
maker	constructor, m.	fabricator	fabricante, m.
making	hechura, f.	construction fabrication	construcción, f. fabricación, f.
malady	dolencia, f.	infirmity	enfermedad, f.
malaise	malestar, m.	indisposition	indisposición, f.
management	régimen, m.	direction administration	dirección, f. administración, f.
manager	gerente, m.	director administrator	director, m. administrador, m.
manhood	hombría, f.	virility	virilidad, f.
mankind	genero humano, m.	humanity	humanidad, f.
manliness	hombría, f.	masculinity	masculinidad, f.
manners	maneras, f.; modales, m.	courtesy	cortesía, f.
manse		rectory	rectoría, f.
manufacturer		fabricator	fabricante, m.
marble (ball)		ball	bola, f
marriage	casamiento, m.; boda, f.	matrimony	matrimonio, m.
master	maestro, amo, dueño, m.	chief, patron	jefe, patrono, m.
match (sport)	juego, m.	encounter	encuentro, m.
match (fire)	cerilla, f; fósforo, m.		
mate	cónyugue, m.	consort	consorte, m.
mate (ship)		comrade	camarada, m.
math		mathematics	matemática, f.
matter (thing)	asunto, m.; cosa, f.	question	cuestión, f.
maze		labyrinth	laberinto, m.
meaning	sentido, m.	intention	intención, f.
meanness	bajeza, f.	vileness	vileza, f.
means	medio, recurso, m.	mode	modo, m.
meantime		interim	ínterin, m.
measurement	medida, f.	dimension	dimensión, f.
medley	mezcla, f.	miscellany	miscelánea, f.
meekness	mansedumbre, m.	humility docility	humildad, f. docilidad, f.
meet (sports)	encuentro, m.	tourney	torneo, m.
meeting	junta, f.; mitin, m.	reunion	reunión, f.
melting	fundición, f.	liquefaction	licuefacción, m.
menu	menú, m.	list	lista, f.
mercy (pity)	misericordia, f.	clemency	clemencia, f.
merger		fusion, union consolidation	fusión, unión, f. consolidación, f.
mermaid	pejemuller, f.	siren	sirena, f.
merriment	gozo, m.; alegría, f.	*jubilation	júbilo, m.

ENGLISH	SPANISH NON-CONVERSION	ENGLISH SYNONYM	SPANISH CONVERSION
merry-go-round		carrousel	carrusel, m.
mess	lío, m.	disorder	desorden, m.
		confusion	confusión, f.
messenger	mensajero, nuncio, m.	herald	heraldo, m.
middle	medio, m.	center	centro, m.
midget	enano, gorgojo, m.	miniature	miniatura, f.
mien	cara, f.; porte, m.	air	aire, m.
		appearance	apariencia, f.
might	poderío, poder, m.	force	fuerza, f.
mind	mente, f.	intelligence	inteligencia, f.
minister	sacerdote, m.	pastor, curate	pastor, cura, m
mischief	travesura, f.; daño, m.	malice	malicia, f.
miser	avaro, m.		
misfortune	desgracia, f.	affliction	aflicción, f.
		calamity	calamidad, f.
mishap	mala suerte, f.	accident	accidente, m.
mistake		error	error, m.
		equivocation	equivocación, f.
mistress	querida, f.	concubine	concubina, f.
mistrust	desconfianza, f.	doubt, suspicion	duda, sospecha, f.
mix	mescla, f.	mixture	mixtura, f.
moan (groan)	gemido, quejido, m.	lament	lamenta, f.
mob	populacho, m.	multitude	multitud, f.
moisture		humidity	humedad, f.
mongrel	mestizo, m.	hybrid	híbrido, m.
mood	humor, m.	disposition	disposición, f.
mores	usos, m.	customs	costumbres, f.
mortuary		morgue	morgue, m.
motherhood		maternity	maternidad, f.
*motion		movement	movimiento, m.
mound	montón, montículo, m.	pile, mass	pila, masa, f.
mountaineering		alpinism	alpinismo, m.
mourning	dolor, luto, m.	affliction	aflicción, f.
mouse		rat	ratón, m.
mouth organ		harmonica	armónica, f.
movie(s)		cinema	cine, m.
murder		assassination	asesinato, m.
		homicide	homicidio, m.
murderer	homicida, m.	assassin	asesino, m.
mushroom	seta, f.; hongo, m.	champignon	champiñón, m.
nakedness		nudity	desnudez, f.
name	nombre, apodo, m.	title	título, m.
		denomination	denoninación, f.
		appellation	apellido, m.
nap (sleep)	sueño, m.	siesta, f.	siesta, f.
nature	genio, m.; índole, f.	character	carácter, m.
nearness	cercanía, f.	proximity	proximidad, f.
necktie		cravat	corbata, f.
need (want)	apuro, m.	necessity	necesidad, f.
		exigency	exigencia, f.
neighbor	vecino, m.		
neighborhood	alrededores, m.	vicinity	vecindad, f.
network	red, f.	system	sistema, m.

237

ENGLISH	SPANISH NON-CONVERSION	ENGLISH SYNONYM	SPANISH CONVERSION
news (tidings)	actualidades, f.	notices	noticias, f.
newspaper	diario, m.	*periodical	periódico, m.
nicety	finura, f.	subtlety	sutileza, f.
nightclub	club m.	cabaret, cafe	cabaret, café m.
nil	nada, f.	zero	zero, m.
noise (din)	ruido, m.	clamor, tumult	clamor, tumulto, m.
nonconformist	disconforme, m.	dissident	disidente, m.
nonsense	tontería, f. desatino, disparate, m	absurdness	absurdo, m.
nostrum		panacea	panacea, f
notice (attn.)		attention	atención, f.
*notice (info)	aviso, m.	proclamation announcement	proclama, f. anuncio, m.
noun	nombre, m.	substantive	sustantivo, m.
nourishment	alimentación, f.	nutrition	nutrición, f.
nuisance	estorbo, m.	molestation	molestia, f.
nullification	anulación, f.	invalidation	invalidación, f.
number	número, m.	cipher	cifra, f.
oath (profane)	maldición, m.	blasphemy profanity	blasfemia, f. profanidad, f.
oddity	rareza, f.	singularity	singularidad, f.
odds	probabilidades, f.	disparity difference	disparidad, f. diferencia, f.
official		functionary	funcionario, m.
offset	calco, m.	compensation	compensación, f.
offspring	prole, f.	descendent progeny	descendencia, f. progenie, f.
oil	aceite, óleo, m.	petroleum	petróleo, m.
old age	vejez, f.	ancientness	ancianidad, f.
oneness	integridad, f.	unity	unidad, f.
opening (hole)		orifice aperture	orificio, m. abertura, f.
opening (start)	comienzo, m.	inauguration	inauguración, f.
openmindedness		receptivity impartiality	receptividad, f. imparcialidad, f.
*operation	operación, f.	functioning	funcionamiento, m.
opponent	contrario, m.	antagonist	antagonista, m.
order (purch.)	pedido, m.	requisition	requisición, f.
orderly	enfermero, m.	assistant	asistente, m.
ore	mena, f.	mineral	mineral, m.
outburst	arranque, m.	explosion	explosión, f.
outcast	desterrado, m.	pariah, exile	paria, exilado, m.
outcome		result, effect consequence	resultado, efecto, consecuencia, f.
outcry	alboroto, grito, m.	tumult protest	tumulto, m. protesta, f.
outfit (gear)	provisión, f.	equipment	equipamiento, m.
outing	paseo, m.	excursion	excursión, f.
outlaw	proscrito, m.	fugitive	fugitivo, m.
outline	perfil, contorno, m.	resumé silhouette	resumen, m. silueta, f.
outlook	vista, f.	perspective	perspectiva, f.
output	rendimiento, m.	production	producción, f.

ENGLISH	SPANISH NON-CONVERSION	ENGLISH SYNONYM	SPANISH CONVERSION
outrage	atropello, m.	atrocity	atrocidad, f.
		indignation	indignación, f.
outset	principio, m.	commencement	comienzo, m.
outside	parte de afuera, f.	exterior	exterior, m.
outsider	forastero, extraño, m.	intruder	intruso, m.
oversight(err)	imprevisión, m.	inadvertence	inadvertencia, f.
	olvido, descuido, m.	error, omission	error, m.; omisión, f.
oversight(care)	cuidado, m.	attention	atención, f.
		vigilance	vigilancia, f.
overture	tentativa, f.	proposition	proposición, f.
owner	amo, dueño, m.	proprietor	propietario, m.
ownership	título, m.	possesion	posesión, f.
		property	propiedad, f.
paint	pintura, f.	coloring	colorante, m.
pal	amigo, m.	companion	compañero, m.
*pan	sartén, f.	cacerol	cacerola, f.
pang (pain)	punzada, f.; dolor, m.	torment	tormento, m.
pantry		dispensary	despensa, f.
pants	calzoncillos, m.	pantaloons	pantalones, m.
paragon	ejemplar, m.	model	modelo, m.
parcel	lío, m.	package	paquete, m.
parenthood		paternity	paternidad, f.
parson	*cura, m.	pastor	pastor, m.
*part (role)	papel, m.	role	rol, m.
parting	partida, f.	separation	separación, f.
		division	división, f.
partner	compañero, m.	associate	socio, m.
partnership	sociedad, f.	asociation	asociación, f.
party (social)	fiesta, f.	reunion	reunión, f.
passage (-way)	pasillo, paso, m.	corridor	corredor, m.
past (tense)		preterite	pretérito, m.
pastime	pasatiempo, m.	distraction	distracción, f.
pat	golpecito, m.		
patch	parche, m.	remedy	remiendo, m.
pattern	dechado, m.	design, model	diseño, modelo, m.
pay	pagamento, m.; paga, f.	salary	salario, m.
	honorarios, m.	commission	comisión, f.
payee	portador, m.	beneficiary	beneficiario, m.
payment	pago, pagamento, m.	recompense	recompensa, f.
peace(-fulness)	paz, f.	calm, serenity	calma, serenidad, f.
		tranquility	tranquilidad, f.
peak (top)	cumbre, cima, f.	promontory	promontorio, m.
peer	par, m.	equal	igual, m.
peer (UK)		noble	noble, m.
pen (coop)	encerradero, m.	corral	corral, m.
penchant	afición, f.	inclination	inclinación, f.
		propensity	propensión, f.
pennant	pendón, m	insignia	insignia, f.
people (race)	pueblo, m.	race	raza, f.
people (persons)	gente, f.	population	población, f.
performance	realización, f.	execution	ejecución, f.
performance (show)	actuación, f.	representation	representación, f.
performer	ejecutante, m.	actor	actor, m.

ENGLISH	SPANISH NON-CONVERSION	ENGLISH SYNONYM	SPANISH CONVERSION
peril	peligro, m.	risk	riesgo, m.
pet	predilecto, m.	mascot	mascota, f.
petulance	malhumor, m.	impatience	impaciencia, f.
physician		medic, doctor	médico, doctor, m.
piccolo		flute	flautín, m.
picture	cuadro, m.; pintura, f.	illustration	ilustración, f.
piece (chip)	pedazo, m.; pieza, f.	fragment	fragmento, m.
pig (hog)	cochino, cerdo, m.	pork (-"er")	puerco, m.
pile (heap)	pila, f.; montón, m.	mass	masa, f.
pin	alfiler, m.	broach	broche, m.
pipe	caño, conducto, m.	tube	tubo, m.
piper		flutist	flautista, m.
pit (ditch)	fosa, zanja, f.; hoyo, m.	mine	mina, f.
pitch (tar)	brea, pez, f.	resin	resina, f.
pitcher (jug)	cántaro, m.	jar	jarro, m.
place	lugar, sitio, m.	position	posición, f.
plague	plaga, peste, f.	pestilence	pestilencia, f.
plaintiff		demander	demandante, m.
plateau	antiplano, m.	mesa, mesita	mesa, mesita, f.
plausibility	verosimilitud, f	credibility	credibilidad, f.
play (theater)		drama, piece representation	drama, pieza, f. representación, f.
playmate	compañero de juego, m.	comrade	camarada, f.
plea	empeño, ruego, m. disculpa, f.	petition promise	petición, f. promesa, f.
pleasure	placer, goce, m.	delight	deleite, m.
pledge	empeño, m.; prenda, f.	guarantee	garantía, f.
pledgee		depositary	depositario, m.
pliability	docilidad, f.	flexibility	flexibilidad, f.
plight	apuro, aprieto, m.	situation	situación, f.
plot	complot, m.	intrigue conspiracy	intriga, f. conspiración, f.
plumpness	gordura, f.	corpulence	corpulencia, f.
plunder	saqueo, m.	pillage	pillaje, m.
plunge	zambullida, f.	submersion	sumersión, f.
point of view	punto de vista, m.		
poise	serenidad, f.	aplomb equilibrium	aplomo, m. equilibro, m.
poison		venum	veneno, m.
poisoning		"envenoming" intoxication	envenenamiento, m. intoxicación, f.
pole (post)	palo, m.; estaca, f.	post	poste, m.
policeman	policía, f.	guard	guardia, f.
polish	lustre, brillo, m.	refinement	refinamiento, m.
politeness		courtesy	cortesía, f.
poll (survey)	encuesta, f.	vote	votación, f.
pollution		contamination corruption	contaminación, f. corrupción, f.
pond	estanque, charco, m.	lagoon	laguna, f.
pool (group)	mancomunidad, f.	consortium syndicate	consorcio, m. sindicato, m.
pool	piscina, f.	tank	estanque, m.
porch	porche, atrio, portal, m.	portico	pórtico, m.

ENGLISH	SPANISH NON-CONVERSION	ENGLISH SYNONYM	SPANISH CONVERSION
porpoise	marsopa, f.	dolphin	delfín, m.
portrayal	retrato, m.	representation	representación, f.
postage	porte de correos, m.	frank	franqueo, m.
postponement	aplazamiento, m.	deferment	diferimiento, m.
pot	olla, f.; puchero, m.	caldron	caldera, f.
pottery	alfarería, f.	ceramics	cerámica, f.
pouch (bag)	bolsa, f.	sack	saco, m.
poverty	pobreza, f.	misery	miseria, f.
		privation	privación, f.
		indigence	indigencia, f.
powder (dust)	pólvera, f.;polvo, m.		
power (might)	poderío, poder, m.	force	fuerza, f.
power (nation)	potencia, f.	nation	nación, f.
power (attny)	poder, m.	procuration	procuración, f.
practicability		viability	viabilidad, f.
prairie	pradera, llanura, f.	pampa	pampa, f.
praise	loa, alabanza, f.	eulogy	elogio, m.
		adulation	adulación, f.
prank	picardía,travesura, f.		
prayer	rezo, m.; oración, f.	supplication	suplicación, f.
preciseness	precisión, f.	exactness	exactitud, f.
preclusion	exclusión, f.	prevention	prevención, f.
preemption		priority	prioridad, f.
preserve	confitura, f.	conserve	conserva, f.
prevalence		frequence	frequencia, f.
prey (quarry)	presa, f.	victim	victima, f.
prick	aguijón, m.	pinch	pinchazo, m.
pride	orgullo,m.; altivez, f.	vanity	vanidad, f.
priest	sacerdote, cura, m.	cleric	clérigo, m.
primer (book)	texto elemental, m.	manual	manual, m.
primer (expl.)	carga iniciadora, f.	detonator	detonador, m.
print	impresión, f.	stamping	estampa, f.
printing	imprenta, f.	impression	impresión, f.
prize	premio, m.	recompense	recompensa, f.
prizefight	pugilato, m.	boxing	boxeo, m.
probate	legalización, f.	validation	validación, f.
probe	sonda, f.	investigation	investigación, f.
procurement	obtención, f.	acquisition	adquisición, f.
proficiency	competencia, f.	ability	habilidad, f.
profit	ganancia,f;beneficio,m.	utility	utilidad, f.
promotion(job)		ascension	ascenso, m.
pronouncement	anuncio, m.	declaration	declaración, f.
	manifiesto, m.	proclamation	proclama, f.
prosecutor	demandante, m.	accuser	acusador, m.
prospect	esperanza, f.	expectation	expectación, f.
protraction	dilatación, f.	prolongation	prolongación, f.
		extension	extensión, f.
proviso	cláusula, salvedad, f.	condition	condición, f.
		reservation	reservación, f.
		qualification	cualificación, f.
pub	bar, m.; cantina, f.	bar, tavern	bar,m.; taberna, f.
publisher	publicador, m.	editor	*editor, m.
pump	bomba, f.	inflator	inflador, m.

ENGLISH	SPANISH NON-CONVERSION	ENGLISH SYNONYM	SPANISH CONVERSION
punishment	castigo, m.; pena, f.	discipline	disciplina, f.
	punición, f.	correction	corrección, f.
purchase	compra, f.	acquisition	adquisición, f.
purpose	fin, propósito, m.	objective	objetivo, m.
push	empujón, empuje, m.	impulse	impulso, m.
puzzle	rompecabezas, m.	enigma	enigma, f.
		problem	problema, m.
puzzlement	enredo, m.	perplexity	perplejidad, f.
quaintness	rareza, f.	peculiarity	peculiaridad, f.
qualm	incertidumbre, f.	scruple	escrúpulo, m.
quandary	apuro, aprieto, m.	perplexity	perplejidad, f.
	incertidumbre, f.	dilema, doubt	dilema, duda, f.
quarry (mine)	pedrera, cantera, f.	mine	mina, f.
quart	cuartillo, m.	liter	litro, m.
quarter (town)	barrio, m.	district	distrito, m.
query	pregunta, f.	question	cuestión, f.
questioning		interrogatory	interrogatorio, m.
queue	cola, f.	file	fila, f.
quickness	presteza, f.	rapidity	rapidez, f.
quicksilver	azogue, m.	mercury	mercurio, m.
quiet(-ness)	sosiego, m.	silence	silencio, m.
	quietud, f.	calm	calma, f.
quote, -tation	comillas, f.	citation	cita, citación, f.
race track	carrera, f.	hipodrome	hipódromo, m.
rage	cólera, rabia, ira, f.	fury	furia, f.
raid	correría, f.	attack	ataque, m.
		incursion	incursión, f.
raise (in pay)		augmentation	aumento, m.
rally (meeting)		reunion	reunión, f.
rally (recovery)		recuperation	recuperación, f.
rampart	muralla, f; baluarte, m.	bastion	bastión, f.
range (prairie)	pradera, f.	pampa	pampa, f.
range (extent)	alcance, m.	dimension	dimensión, f.
	anchura, f.	extension	entensión, f.
rank	rango, m.	grade	grado, m.
		position	posición, f.
rape	ultraje, estupro, m.	violation	violación, f.
rapport	simpatía, f.	harmony	armonía, f.
		affinity	afinidad, f.
rapprochement	acercamiento, m.	reconciliation	reconciliación, f.
*rate (interest)	tipo de interés, m.	percentage	porcentaje, m.
rate (speed)	presteza, f.	velocity	velocidad, f.
		rapidity	rapidez, f.
rating	rango, m.	evaluation	evaluación, f.
ratio		relation	relación, f.
		proportion	proporción, f.
rationale	motivo principal, m.	reason	razón, f.
		justification	justificación, f.
ravage	pillaje, destrozo, m.	devastation	devastación, f.
raving	desvarío, m.	delirium	delirio, m.
reading		*lecture	lectura, f.
		recital	recital, m.
realm (field)	campo, m.	reign	reino, m.
reappraisal	retasa, f.	revaluation	revaluación, f.

241

ENGLISH	SPANISH NON-CONVERSION	ENGLISH SYNONYM	SPANISH CONVERSION
rearrangement		reordering	reordenamiento, m.
rebirth	renacimiento, m.	reincarnation	reencarnación, f.
rebuttal	impugnación, f.	refutation	refutación, f.
		contradiction	contradicción, f.
recall	llamada, f.	revocation	revocación, f.
recapture	represa, f.	recovery	recobro, m.
recess	hora de recreo, f.	intermission	intermedio, m.
recklessness	indiferencia, f.	imprudence	imprudencia, f.
		temerity	temeridad, f.
recollection	recuerdo, m.	memory	memoria, f.
		remembrance	remembranza, f.
		reminiscence	reminiscencia, f.
record	acta, anotación, f.	register	registro, m.
		inscription	inscipción, f.
		document	documento, m.
record (MUS)		disk	disco, m.
recovery	cobranza,f.;recobro, m.	recuperation	recuperación, f.
recurrence	reaparición, f.	repetition	repetición, f.
*red	rojo, m.	scarlet	escarlata, f.
reel	carrete, m.	bobbin	bobina, f.
referee	juez, m.	arbitrator	árbitro, m.
refund	reembolso, m.	restitution	restitución, f.
regard	aprecio, m.	respect	respecto, m.
		consideration	consideración, f.
regards	recuerdos, m.	salutations	saludos, m.
regret	pesadumbre,f.;pesar, m.	remorse	remordimiento, m.
rejoicing	regocijo,m.;alegría, f.	*jubilation	júbilo, m.
release	alivio, disparo, m.	liberation	liberación, f.
reliance	seguridad, f.	confidence	confianza, f.
relief	desahogo, m.	alleviation	alivio, m.
relief (aid)	socorro, m.; ayuda, f.	*assistance	asistencia, f.
		alleviation	alivio, m.
relish (like)	goce, gusto, m.	delight	deleite, m.
relish (sauce)	condimento, m.	sauce	salsa, f.
remainder	sobra, f.	rest	restante, resto, m.
remains	resto, m.	residue	residuo, m.
		remnant	remanente, m.
remark	nota, f.	observation	observación, f.
		comment	comentario, m.
remembrance	recuerdo, m.	memory	memoria, f.
remonstration		protest	protesta, f.
renewal		renovation	renovación, f.
repayment	reintegro, pago, m.	reimbursement	reembolso, m.
*report	relato, informe, m.	narration	narración, f.
reprieve	respiro, m.	alleviation	alivio, m.
request	ruego, m.; súplica, f.	demand	demanda, f.
rescue	salvamiento,rescate, m.	salvation	salvación, f.
research	averiguación, f.	investigation	investigación, f.
		experimentation	experimentación, f.
resemblance	parecido, m.	similarity	similitud, f.
	semejanza, f.		
resevoir	represa, f.	deposit	depósito, m.
resolve	propósito, m.	firmness	firmeza, f.
rest (repose)	descanso, m.	repose, quiet	reposo, quietud, f.

ENGLISH	SPANISH NON-CONVERSION	ENGLISH SYNONYM	SPANISH CONVERSION
restlessness	inquietud, f.	impatience	impaciencia, f.
restraint	refrenamiento, m.	limitation	limitación, f.
		restriction	restricción, f.
revenge	venganza, f.	vindication	vindicación, f.
revenue	ingreso, m.	rent	renta, f.
reversal	trastorno, m.	inversion	inversión, f.
review (study)	repaso, m.	reexamination	reexaminación, f.
review	revista, f.	critique	crítica, f.
revival	renacimiento, m.	restoration	restauración, f.
*revulsion	asco, m.	repugnance	repugnancia, f.
reward	premio, m.	recompense	recompensa, f.
		remuneration	remuneración, f.
riches (wealth)	riqueza, f.	opulence	opulencia, f.
riddle	acertijo, m.	enigma, mystery	enigma, f. misterio, m.
right hand	derecha, f.		
righteousness	probidad, f.	rectitude	rectitud, f.
ripeness	sazón, f.	maturity	madurez, f.
ripple	ola, f.	ondulation	ondulación, f.
rise	salida, f.	ascension	ascención, f.
road (way)	camino, m.; vía, f. carretera, f.	route	ruta, f.
robber	ratero, ladrón, m.	bandit	bandido, m.
robe	manto, abrigo, m.	tunic	túnica, f.
rod	vara, f.	cane	caña, f.
rogue (knave)	bribón, pícaro, m.	vagabond	vagabundo, m.
roll (list)	rol, m.	list, register	lista, f; registro, m.
room (space)	sitio, lugar, m.	space	espacio, m.
room (parlor)	habitación, f.	salon	sala, f.; salón, m.
roost	varal, m.	perch	percha, f.
root	raíz, f.; radical, m.	origin	origen, m.
*rope	cordón, m.	cable, cord	cable, m.; cuerda, f.
rosin		resin	resina, f.
roughness	aspereza, f.	rudeness	rudeza, f.
row (rank)	hilera, f.	file, line	fila, línea f.
rub (-bing)	roce, m.; frotación, f.	friction	fricción, f.
rule (sway)	regimen, m.	dominion	dominio, m.
		authority	autoridad, f.
rule	regla, f.	norm	norma, f.
ruler (leader)	gobernador, m.	sovereign	soberano, m.
ruling		decision	decisión, f.
ruse	astucia, f.; truco, m.	artifice	artificio, m.
rush	prisa, f.; apuro, m.	precipitation	precipitación, f.
rust	moho, orín, m.	oxidation	oxidación, f.
ruthlessness		cruelty	crueldad, f.
sadness	tristeza, f.	melancholy	melancolía, f.
safety		security	seguridad, f.
sake		reason, motive	razón, f.; motivo, m.
sale	venta, f.	liquidation	liquidación, f.
salesman		vendor	vendedor, m.
salve	ungüentino, m.	balsam	bálsamo, m.
sameness	igualdad, f.	identity	identidad, f.
saucepan	cazuela, f.	casserole	cacerola, f.
saucer		plate (small)	platillo, m.

ENGLISH	SPANISH NON-CONVERSION	ENGLISH SYNONYM	SPANISH CONVERSION
saying	dicho, decir, m.	refrain	refrán, m.
		proverb	proverbio, m.
		maxim	máxima, f.
scales	báscula, f.	balance	balanza, f.
scarcity	escasez, f	rareness	rareza, f.
		insufficiency	insuficiencia, f.
scarf	bufanda, f.	shawl	chal, m.
*scenery	paisaje, m.; vista, f.	panorama	panorama, f.
scent	olor, m.	aroma	aroma, f.
		fragrance	fragrancia, f.
scholarship	saber, m.	erudition	erudición, f.
school	escuela, f.	*college	colegio, m.
schooling	enseñanza, f.	instruction	instrucción, f.
score	tanteo, m.; cuenta, f.	result	resultado, m.
scorn	desprecio, m.	disdain	desdén, m.
scourge	azote, m.	plague	plaga, f.
scrap (paper)	trozo, pedazo, m.	fragment	fragmento, m.
script	escritura, f.	caligraphy	caligrafía, f.
scroll	nauta, f.	roll	rollo, m.
seaman		marine	marinero, m.
search (quest)	busca, búsqueda, f.	investigation	investigación, f.
seat	asiento, m.	place	plaza, f.
securities	valores, títulos, m.	obligations	obligaciones, m.
self-esteem	amor propio, m.	dignity	dignidad, f.
selfishness		egoism	egoísmo, m.
self-sacrifice	renunciamiento, m.	abnegation	abnegación, f.
seller		vendor	vendedor, m.
semblance	semejanza, f.	appearance	apariencia, f.
sending	envío, m.	transmission	transmisión, f.
		dispatch	despacho, m.
seniority	antigüedad, f.	priority	prioridad, f.
		precedence	precedencia, f.
sense (body's)	sentido, m.	faculty	facultad, f.
sentence(GRAM)		phrase	frase, f.
seriousness	seriedad, f.	severity	severidad, f.
		gravity	gravedad, f.
set	conjunto, m.	group, series	grupo, m.; serie, f.
setting(atmos)		ambience	ambiente, m.
setting(jewel)	fijación, f.	mounting	montadura, f.
settlement	arreglo, m.	accord	acuerdo, m.
settler	poblador, m.	colonist	colono, m.
severance		separation	separación, f.
		partition	partición, f.
shade	umbría, sombra, f.		
shade (hue)	matiz, f.	tint	tinte, m.
shade (window)	persiana, celosia, f.	curtain	cortina, f.
shadow	sombra, f.	penumbra	penumbra, f.
shaft	vara, f.	ray	rayo, m.
shame,-fulness	pudor, m.; vergüenza, f.	ignominy	ignominia, f.
		dishonor	deshonra, f.
shape	talle, m.	figure, form	figura, forma, f.
share	ración, f.	portion, cuota	porción, cuota, f.
		participation	participación, f.
sharpness	agudeza, f.	acrimony	acrimonia, f.

ENGLISH	SPANISH NON-CONVERSION	ENGLISH SYNONYM	SPANISH CONVERSION
shed (hut)	barraca, choza, f.	cabin	cabaña, f.
sheen	brillo, m.	luster	lustre, m.
shelter	abrigo, amparo, m.	refuge	refugio, m.
		asylum	asilo, m.
shepherd		pastor	pastor, m.
shift (work)	tanda, f.	turn	turno, m.
shift (change)		displacement	desplazamiento, m.
ship (vessel)	nave, navío, buque, m.	bark	barco, m.
shipment	embarque, despacho, m.	consignment	consignación, f.
shipping	marina, f.	navigation	navegación, f.
shirt	camisa, f.	blouse	blusa, f.
shore (coast)	ribera, playa, f.	coast	costa, f.
shortage	escasez, f.	deficit	déficit, m.
shortness	pequeñez, cortedad, f.	brevity	brevedad, f.
shout (cry)	grito, m.	acclamation	aclamación, f.
shove	empujón, m.	impulse	impulso, m.
show		exhibition	exhibición, f.
		function	función, f.
show (stage)		spectacle	espectáculo, m.
shower (bath)		douche	ducha, f.
showiness		ostentation	ostentación, f.
shrewdness		astuteness	astucia, f.
		sagacity	sagacidad, f.
shrinkage		contraction	contracción, f.
		diminution	desmunición, f.
shroud	mortaja, f.	cover	cubierta, f.
shutter (blind)	cerradura, persiana, f.	jalousie	celosía, f.
sickness	dolencia, f.; mal, m.	infirmity	enfermedad, f.
		nausea	náusea, f.
		affliction	aflicción, f.
side (flank)	lado, costado, m.	flank	flanco, m.
siege	cerco, sitio, m.	blockade	bloqueo, m.
sight (view)	vista, f.; aspecto, m.	vision	visión, f.
sight		spectacle	espectáculo, m.
sign (mark)	seña, señal, f.	mark	marca, f.
sin	pecado, m.; culpa, f.	vice	vicio, m.
		trangression	transgresión, f.
sinew		tendon, fiber	tendón, m; fibra, f.
sinfulness	maldad, f.	perversity	perversidad, f.
singer	cantante, m.	cantor	cantor, m.
site	sitio, lugar, m.	locality	localidad, f.
size (bulk)	tamaño, m.	dimension	dimensión, f.
		magnitude	magnitud, f.
size (shoes)		number	número, m.
sketch	dibujo, boceto, m.	design	diseño, m.
skill (craft)	pericia, destreza, f.	ability	habilidad, f.
	ingenio, m.	art	arte, m.
		experience	experiencia, f.
skin	piel, m.	cutis	cutis, m.
skull	casco, m.; calavera, f.	cranium	cráneo, m.
slab	rebanata, f.	plank	plancha, f.
slander	calumnia, f.	defamation	difamación, f.
slang	jerigonzo, m.; jerga, f.	vulgarism	vulgarismo, m.
slant		inclination	inclinación, f.
		obliquity	oblicuidad, f.

ENGLISH	SPANISH NON-CONVERSION	ENGLISH SYNONYM	SPANISH CONVERSION
slap	palmada, f.	buffet	bofetada, f.
slaughter	matanza, f.	carnage	carnicería, f.
sleep (nap)	sueño, m.; dormida, f.	siesta	siesta, f.
sleeplessness	desvelo, m.	insomnia	insomnia, f.
slice	rebanada, tajada, f.		
slip (paper)	papeleta, f.; trozo, m.		
slipper	zapatilla, babucha, f.	pantofle	pantufla, f.
slope	declive, m; pendiente, f.	inclination	inclinación, f.
sloth	pereza, f.	indolence	indolencia, f.
slowness	retraso, m.; lentitud, f.	tardiness	tardanza, f.
sludge	lodo, m.	sediment	sedimento, m.
slyness	disimulo, m.; astucia, f.	sagacity	sagacidad, f.
smallness	pequeñez, f.	insignificance	insignificancia, f.
smartness	ingenio, m.; agudeza, f.	intelligence	inteligencia, f.
		sagacity	sagacidad, f.
smell	olor, olfato, m.	fragrance	fragrancia, f.
		aroma	aroma, f.
smoke	fumada, f.; humo, m.		
smoothness	llanura, f.	suaveness	suavidad, f.
snake	culebra, f.	serpent	serpiente, m.
snare (trap)	trampa, f.	lasso	lazo, m.
snub	rechazo, m.	repulse	repulsa, f.
soap	sabón, m.	detergent	detergente, m.
soccer		football	fútbol, m.
softness	blandura, f.	suaveness, -vity	suavidad, f.
solicitor		procurator	procurador, m.
soot	tisne, hollín, m.		
sore	llaga, f.	ulcer	úlcera, f.
sorrow	pesar, dolor, duelo, m.	lament	lamento, m.
sort (kind)	género, tenor, m.	species, class type, variety	especie, clase, f. tipo, m.; variedad, f.
*soul	alma, ánima, f.	spirit	espíritu, m.
soundness	sanidad, f.	firmness solidity	firmeza, f. solidez, f.
source	fuente, f.	origin	origen, m.
souvenir	recuerdo, m.	memory	memoria, f.
span (space)	trecho, m.	distance	distancia, f.
speaker	conferenciante, m.	orator	orador, m.
spear (lance)	pica, f.	lance	lanza, f.
speech (talking)	palabra, habla, f.	conversation	conversación, f.
speech (lang.)	idioma, f.	language	lenguaje, f.
speech (lecture)	discurso, m.	oration conference	oración, f. conferencia, f.
speechlessness	mudez, f.	stupefaction silence	estupefacción, f. silencio, m.
speed	ligereza, f.	rapidity promptness velocity	rapidez, f. prontitud, f. velocidad, f.
spell (time)	rato, m.	interval recess	intervalo, m. receso, m.
spell (trance)	conjuro, hechizo, m.	enchantment	encanto, m.
spin	vuelta, f.; giro, m.	rotation	rotación, f.
spite	despecho, m.	rancor	rencor, m.

ENGLISH	SPANISH NON-CONVERSION	ENGLISH SYNONYM	SPANISH CONVERSION
split	grieta, hendidura, f.	division	división, f.
		fissure	fisura, f.
spoils	despojo, m.	booty	botín, m.
spool	canilla, f.	bobbin	bobina, f.
spot (place)	lugar, sitio, m.	point	punto, m.
spot (stain)	mancha, tacha, f.		
sprain (wrench)	torcedura, f.	dislocation	dislocación, f.
spray (sprinkle)	rocío, m.	douche	ducha, f.
spread	anchura, f.	diffusion	difusión, f.
		amplitude	amplitud, f.
		extension	extensión, f.
spur (impulse)	espuela, f.	impulse	impulso, m.
		stimulus	estímulo, m.
square (town)	cuadrado, m.	place, park	plaza, f.; parque, m.
square (GEOM)	cuadro, cuadrado, m.		
squeeze	abraso, apretón, m.	pressure	presión, f.
stack (heap)	montón, m.; masa, f.	pile	pila, f.
staff (people)	cuerpo, m.	personnel	personal, m.
stage (step)	etapa, f.	phase	fase, f.
stage (theater)	escenario, m.	platform	plataforma, f.
stake (wager)	apuesta, f.	interest	interés, m.
stalk (stem)	tallo, m.	cane	caña, f.
stall (booth)	barraca, f.	stable	establo, m.
stamina	aguante, m.	vigor	vigor, m.
stamp	sello, timbre, m.	stamp	estampa, f.
stance		posture, position	postura, posición, f.
standard	medida, f.	norm, criterion	norma, f; criterio, m.
standardization		uniformization	uniformización, f.
standpoint	punto de vista, m.		
start	principio, m.	commencement	comienzo, m.
statement	relato, informe, m.	declaration	declaración, f.
stay (visit)	quedada, estancia, f. permanencia, f.	visit	visita, f.
steadiness		firmness	firmeza, f.
		solidness	solidez, f.
		stability	estabilidad, f.
steak		beefsteak	bistec, biftec, m.
		fillet	filete, m.
steam	vaho, m.	vapor	vapor, m.
steeple (spire)	aguja, f; campanario, m.	tower	torre, f.
step (stride)	pisada, f.	pace	paso, m.
stern (ship)		poop	popa, f.
stick (rod)	palo, bastón, m.	cane	caña, f.
stiffness	tiesura, f.	rigidity	rigidez, f.
		inflexibility	inflexibilidad, f.
stillness		quiet, calm	qietud, calma, f.
		serenity	serenidad, f.
		silence	silencio, m.
stone	piedra, f	rock	roca, f.
stop, -page	paro, m.; parada, f.	cessation, pause	cesación, pausa, f.
storage	almacenaje, m.	deposit	depósito, m.
storm (gale)	tormenta, f.	tempest	tempestad, f.
strain (stress)	cansancio, m.	tension, fatigue	tensión, fatiga, f.

ENGLISH	SPANISH NON-CONVERSION	ENGLISH SYNONYM	SPANISH CONVERSION
strand	hilo, m.	filament	filamento, m.
strangeness	extrañeza, f.	peculiarity	peculiaridad, f.
stranger	extraño, f. desconocido, m.	intruder	instruso, m.
strap	correa, tira, f.	band	banda, f.
streak(stripe)	lista, raya, f.		
stream	arroyo, rio, m.	current	corriente, f.
strength	fortaleza, f.	force, vigor	fuerza, f; vigor, m.
stress(accent)		accent, emphasis	acento, énfasis, m.
stretch	alargamiento, m.		
strife	contienda, lucha, f.	conflict	conflicto, m.
strike (blow)	encuentro, golpe, m.	attack	ataque, m.
string (rope)	fila, hilera, f.	cord	cordel, m; cuerda, f.
strip	cinta, faja, tira, f.		
*structure		construction	construcción, f.
struggle	lucha, contienda, f.	conflict	conflicto, m.
		combat	combate, m.
stubbornness	testarudez, f.	obstinance	obstinación, f.
stuff	cosas, f.	material	materia, f.
		substance	substancia, f.
subject(citiz)	súbdito, m.		
subservience	servilisimo, m.	subordination	subordinación, f.
substantiation	comprobación, f.	justification	justificación, f.
subway	subterráneo, m.	metro	metro, m.
*success	éxito, m.	triumph	triunfo, m.
sufferance	consentimiento, m.	indulgence	indulgencia, f.
suit (LAW)	pleito, m.	process	proceso, m.
suitcase	maleta, f.	sack	saco, m.
summing up	compendio, m.	résumé	resumen, m.
summons	orden, m.	citation	citación, f.
supplier	abastecedor, m.	provider	proveedor, m.
supply	abastecimiento, m.	provision	provisión, f.
support	apoyo, m.	sustenance	susteno, m.
surface	cara, superficie, f.		
surmise		conjecture	conjetura, f.
		supposition	suposición, f.
		presumption	presunción, f.
surrender	rendición, entrega, f.	capitulation	capitulación, f.
surrogate		substitute	substituto, m.
surroundings	alrededores, m. cercancías, f.		
surveillance		vigilance	vigilancia, f.
		observation	observación, f.
survey	estudio, m.	examination	examen, m.
		inspection	inspección, f.
surveyor		topographer	topógrafo, m.
sweetheart	amante, querido, m.	enamored	enamorado, m.
sweetness	dulzura, f.		
swerve		deviation	desviación, f.
swing (motion)	balanceo, m.	oscillation	oscilación, f.
switch (ELEC)	conmutador, m.	interrupter	interruptor, m.
*sympathy		compassion	compasión, f.
taint	mancha, mácula, f.	corruption	corrupción, f.
takeover		acquisition	adquisición, f.

ENGLISH	SPANISH NON-CONVERSION	ENGLISH SYNONYM	SPANISH CONVERSION
tale (story)	relato, cuento, m.	history	historia, f.
talk (speech)	plática, f; discurso, m.	conference	conferencia, f.
talk	coloquio, m.; charla, f.	conversation	conversación, f.
tangle	enredo, m.	confusion	confusión, f.
target	blanco, m.	object, objective	objeto, objetivo, m.
task (work)	encargo, m.; tarea, f.	labor	labor, m.
taste (flavor)	gusto, m.	savor	sabor, m.
tax rate		tariff	tarifa, f.
teacher	maestro, m.	professor	profesor, m.
		pedagogue	pedagogo, m.
teaching	enseñanza, f.	instruction	instrucción, f.
teenager		adolescent	adolescente, m.
teetotaler		abstainer	abstemio, m.
temper(dispos.)		humor	humor, m.
		temperament	temperamento, m.
tenderness	terneza, f.	sensitivity	sensibilidad, f.
tenet	credo, m.	principle	principio, m.
		doctrine	doctrina, f.
term (period)	plazo, término, m.	period	período, m.
		duration	duración, f.
terms		conditions	condiciones, m.
test (exam)	prueba, f.	exam	examen, m.
thankfulness	agradecimiento, m.	gratitude	gratitud, f.
thanks	gracias, f.	gratitude	gratitud, f.
theft	hurto, m.	robbery	robo, m.
thickness	espesor, grueso, m.	density	densidad, f.
thing (matter)	cosa, f.; asunto, m.	question	cuestión, f.
thing (object)	cosa, f.	object	objeto, m.
thorn (briar)		spine	espina, f.
thought	pensamiento, m.	reflection, idea	reflexión, idea, f.
		meditation	meditación, f.
thoughtfulness	atención, f.	solicitousness	solicitud, f.
thread	hilo, m.; hebra, f.	filament	filamento, m.
threat		menace	amenaza, f.
threshold	umbral, m.	entry	entrada, f.
thrift	ahorro, m.	frugality	frugalidad, f.
		economy	economía, f.
thrill	excitación, f. estremecimiento, m.	emotion	emoción, f.
throb	latido, m.	palpitation	palpitación, f.
throng	muchedumbre, f.	multitude	multitud, f.
tie (bond)	vínculo, lazo, cordón, m.	connection	conexión, f.
		union	unión, f.
time	hora, f.; tiempo, m.	period	período, m.
		epoque	época, f.
time (s)	vez, f.	occasion	ocasión, f.
timeliness		punctuality	puntualidad, f.
		oportuneness	oportunidad, f.
tip (end)	cabo, m.; punta, f.	extremity	extremidad, f.
tip (info)	soplo, informe, m.	information	información, f.
tip (fee)	propina, f.	gratification	gratificación, f.
tirade		diatribe	diatriba, f.
togetherness		unity	unidad, f.
token	señal, m.	symbol	símbolo, m.

249

ENGLISH	SPANISH NON-CONVERSION	ENGLISH SYNONYM	SPANISH CONVERSION
tool	herramienta, f.	instrument	instrumento, m.
top (peak)	cumbre, cima, f.	crest	cresta, f.
touch	toque, tacto, m.	contact	contacto, tacto, m.
toughness	dureza, f.	tenacity	tenacidad, f.
tour	jira, f.	excursion	excursión, f.
town	pueblo, m.; ciudad, f.	village	villa, f.
township		municipality	municipalidad, f.
trace (vestige)	indicio, m.; traza, f.	vestige	vestigo, m.
trace (trail)	huella, f.; rastro, m.	indication	indicio, m.
trade	negocio, m.	commerce	comercio, m.
trade (craft)	oficio, m.	occupation	ocupación, f.
		profession	profesión, m.
trader	comerciante, m.	merchant	mercante, m.
trail (path)	senda, f.; sendero, m.	route, course	ruta, f.; curso, m.
trainee		aprentice	aprendiz, m.
		recruit	recluta, m.
training	enseñanza, f.	instruction	instrucción, f.
trait	rasgo, m.	peculiarity	peculiaridad, f.
		characteristic	característica, f.
*tramp (rover)	vago, m.	vagabond	vagabundo, m.
travel	viajar, m.	traffic	tráfico, m.
traveler	viajero, m.	tourist	turista, m.
treachery	traición, f.	perfidy	perfidia, f.
treat	obsequio, m.	delight	deleite, m.
trench (ditch)	fosa, zanja, f.	canal	canal, m.
trend	giro, m.	tendency	tendencia, f.
trespass		violation	violación, f.
		infraction	infracción, f.
trial (test)	ensayo, m.; prueba, f.	experiment	experimento, m.
trial (LAW)	juicio, m.	process	proceso, m.
trick (ruse)	engaño, truco, m.	artifice	artificio, m.
trick (knack)	maña, f.	facility	facilidad, f.
trifle	nadería, pequeñez, f.	frivolity	frivolidad, f.
		bagatelle	bagatela, f.
trim(-ming)	guarnición, f.	decoration	decoración, f.
		adornment	adorno, m.
trip (journey)	viaje, pasaje, m.	excursion	excursión, f.
trouble	pena, molestia, f.	affliction	aflicción, f.
trousers	calzónes, m.	pantaloons	pantalónes, m.
trust		confidence	confianza, f.
trust (cartel)	trust, m.	consortium	consorcio, m.
truth	veras, verdad, f.	reality	realidad, f.
		exactness	exactitud, f.
		validity	validez, f.
truthfulness		veracity	veracidad, f.
tub	cuba, tina, f.	barrel	barril, m.
	bañera, f.		
tune	tonada, f.; son, m.	melody, air	melodía, f.; aire, m.
turmoil	disturbio, m.	confusion	confusión, f.
		tumult	tumulto, m.
turn	vuelta, f.; giro, m.	revolution	revolución, f.
turncoat	tránsfuga, m.	renegade	renegado, m.
twin	gemelo, m.	double	doble, m.

ENGLISH	SPANISH	ENGLISH	SPANISH
	NON-CONVERSION	SYNONYM	CONVERSION
umbrage	ofensa. f.; pique, m.	resentment	resentimiento, m.
umpire	compromisario, m.	arbitrator	árbitro, m.
uncertainty	incertidumbre, f.	doubt	duda, f.
understanding	entendido,-dimiento, m.	comprehension	comprensión, f.
uneasiness	malestar, m.	anxiety	ansiedad, f.
unfairness	incorrección, f.	injustice	injusticia, f.
unfaithfulness	infidelidad, f.	disloyalty	deslealtad, f.
union (labor)	unión, coalición, f.	syndicate	sindicato, m.
unionist	gremialista, m.	syndicalist	sindicalista, f.
uniqueness	unicidad, f.	singularity	singularidad, f.
upstart	advenedizo, m.	presumptuous one	presuntuoso, m.
urge		impulse	impulso, m.
usefulness	provecho, m.	utility	utilidad, f.
uselessness		inutility	inutilidad, f.
utterance	dicho, m.; aserción, f.	expression	expresión, f.
		declaration	declaración, f.
vault	bóveda, f.	cave, tomb	cueva, tumba, f.
venture	empresa, f.	operation	operación, f.
vessel (cup)	vasija, f.	vase	vaso, m.
view (sight)	vista, mirada, f.	panorama	panorama, f.
view (opinion)	parecer, m.	opinion	opinión, f.
visage	rostro, m.	appearance	apariencia, f.
void (vacancy)	vacío, m.	vacuum	vacuo, m.
vow	voto, m.	promise	promesa, f.
voyage	viaje, f.	passage	pasaje, m.
voyager	viajero, m.	passenger	pasajero, m.
wage	sueldo, m.; paga, f.	salary	salario, m.
wait	demora, espera, f.	pause	pausa, f.
wakefullness	desvelo, m.	vigilance	vigilancia, f.
walk (gait)	andar, paso, m.	march	marcha, f.
walk (stroll)	vuelta, f.; paseo, m.		
want (lack)	escasez, f.	fault, privation	falta, privación, f.
want (desire)	anhelo, m.	desire	deseo, m.
ward (person)		pupil	pupilo, m.
ware(s)	mercancías, f.	articles	artículos, m.
warehouse	almacén, m.	depositary	depósitario, m.
warning	advertencia, f.	*advice	aviso, m.
waste	pérdida, f.	disipation	disipación, f.
watch	guardia, f.	vigilance	vigilancia, f.
waterfall	catarata, f.	cascade	cascada, f.
wave (ripple)	ola, f.	ondulation	onda, ondulación, f.
way (manner)		form, mode	forma, f.; modo, m.
		manner	manera, f.
way (route)	camino, m.; vía, f.	route	ruta, f.
weakness	flaqueza, f.	debility	debilidad, f.
wealth	caudal, m.	riches	riqueza, f.
		opulence	opulencia, f.
weapon(s)		arm(s)	arma, f.
wear	gasto, m.	use	uso, m.
		deterioration	deterioro, m.
weariness	cansancio, m.	fatigue	fatiga, f.
weather	tiempo, m.	climate	clima, f.
web (net)	tejido, m.; red, f.		

ENGLISH	SPANISH NON-CONVERSION	ENGLISH SYNONYM	SPANISH CONVERSION
weight	cargo, peso, m.; pesa, f.	profundity	profundidad, f.
welcome	bienvenida, f.		
welfare	salud, bienestar, f.	prosperity	prosperidad, f.
wetness		humidity	humedad, f.
wheel	rueda, f.		
while (time)	rato, m.	instant, moment	instante, momento, m.
whirl	giro, remolino, m.	rotation	rotación, f.
whisper	cuchicheo, m.	murmur	murmullo, m.
whole (total)	conjunto, todo, m.	total	total, m.
	integridad, f.	totality	totalidad, f.
whore	puta, f.	prostitute	prostituta, f.
wickedness	maldad, f.	perversity	perversidad, f.
width	anchura, f.	latitude	latitud, f.
wife		spouse	esposa, f.
wilderness	yermo, m.	dessert	desierto, m.
wildness	salvajez, f.	ferocity	ferocidad, f.
will (LAW)		testament	testamento, m.
will (free)	voluntad, f.	desire	deseo, m.
win		victory	victoria, f.
		triumph	triunfo, m.
wire (telegram)	despacho, m.	telegram	telegrama, f.
wisdom	sabiduría, f.	sagacity	sagacidad, f.
wish	anhelo, m.	desire	deseo, m.
wit (humor)	ingenio, m.; sal, f.	intelligence	inteligencia, f.
witness (person)	testigo, m.	spectator	espectador, m.
woe (sorrow)	dolor, pesar, m.	affliction	aflicción, f.
		misery	miseria, f.
wonder	milagro, pasmo, m.	marvel	maravilla, f.
word	palabra, f.	promise	promesa, f.
wordiness		verbosity	verbosidad, f.
		redundancy	redundancia, f.
work (labor)	tarea, f.; trabajo, m.	labor	labor, f.
working		explotation	explotación, f.
		elaboration	elaboración, f.
		functioning	funcionamiento, m.
world	mundo, m.	globe	globo, m.
worry	afán, m.	anxiety	ansiedad, ansia, f.
	molestia, f.	preoccupation	preocupación, f.
worship	reverencia, f.	adoration	adoración, f.
worth (value)	valor, m.	merit	mérito, m.
wrath (anger)	cólera, ira, f.	fury	furia, f.
wreckage	restos, m.	ruins	ruinas, f.
writ	mandamiento, m.	order	orden, f.
wrong (misdeed)	mal, m.	injustice	injusticia, f.
		injury	injuria, f.
yard	cercado, m.	corral, patio	corral, patio, m.
yearning	anhelo, m.	desire	deseo vivo, m.
yield	cosecha, rendición, f.	production	producción, f.
youth (time)	juventud, f.	adolescence	adolescencia, f.
zeal (ardor)	celo, m.	fervor, ardor	fervor, ardor, m.
zealot		fanatic	fanático, m.
zest	deleite, m.	enthusiasm	entusiasmo, m.
whim (fancy)	fantasia, f.	caprice	capricho, m.
whole	conjunto, m.	total, sum	total, m.; suma, f.
wound	herida, f.	lesion	lesión, f.

NOTES ON NOUN GENDER IN SPANISH

Spanish nouns are either masculine or feminine. The observations made in these notes will help determine the gender of most nouns in Spanish, but gender should be noted when adding each noun to one's vocabulary. The noun conversion category lists indicate in some cases the likely gender of the Spanish counterpart.

1. <u>FEMININE GENDER</u>: Nouns representing female beings are feminine regardless of the noun ending (*la actriz, la hermana, la madre, la mujer*). Nouns ending in *-a* (except *-ista, -grama, -pata* and *-crata*), *-dad, -ud, -ie, -umbre -ión, -sis, -itis* and *-z* are almost always feminine in gender, <u>but</u> there are some notable exceptions:

el	agua	(water)	el	diploma	(diploma)	el	oasis	(oasis)
el	análisis	(analysis)	el	día	(day)	el	monograma	(monogram)
el	angora	(angora)	el	dogma	(dogma)	el	panamá	(Panama hat)
el	aroma	(aroma)	el	drama	(drama)	el	panda	(panda)
el	astronauta	(astronaut)	el	eczema	(exzema)	el	panorama	(panorama)
el	atleta	(athlete)	el	edema	(edema)	el	papá	(papa, dad)
el	avión	(airplane)	el	emblema	(emblem)	el	paréntesis	(parenthesis)
el	ágata	(agate)	el	enfisema	(emphysema)	el	París	(Paris)
el	bastión	(bastión)	el	enigma	(enigma)	el	patriota	(patriot)
el	camarada	(mate)	el	epigrama	(epigram)	el	pie	(foot)
el	camión	(truck)	el	escorpión	(scorpion)	el	pijama	(pajama)
el	carcinoma	(carcinoma)	el	estigma	(stigma)	el	planeta	(planet)
el	carisma	(carisma)	el	extra	(extra)	el	poema	(poem)
el	centurión	(centurion)	el	génesis	(genesis)	el	problema	(problem)
el	cerviz	(cervex)	el	glaucoma	(glaucoma)	el	programa	(program)
el	chasis	(chasis)	el	gorila	(gorilla)	el	puma	(puma)
el	cinerama	(cinerama)	el	gorrión	(sparrow)	el	recluta	(recruit)
el	clima	(climate	el	guarda	(guard)	el	sintoma	(symptom)
el	cometa	(comet)	el	hematoma	(hematoma)	el	sistema	(system)
el	corneta	(bugler)	el	hosanna	(hosanna)	el	sofá	(sofa)
el	cólera	(cholera)	el	idealista	(idealist)	el	telegrama	(telegram)
el	croquis	(croquis)	el	idioma	(language)	el	tema	(theme)
el	cura	(priest)	el	iris	(iris-eye)	el	tenis	(tennis)
el	cutis	(cutis)	el	matriz	(matrix)	el	teorema	(theorem)
el	damnación	(damnation)	el	maharaja	(maharaja)	el	trauma	(trauma)
el	dentista	(dentist)	el	maná	(manna)	el	vodka	(vodka)
el	diagrama	(diagram)	el	mapa	(map, chart)	el	yoga	(Yoga)
el	dilema	(dilema)	el	melodrama	(melodrama)			

2. <u>MASCULINE GENDER</u>: Nouns representing male beings are masculine regardless of the noun ending (el actor, el dentista, el astronauta, el cura, el general). Most nouns with endings other than those listed in the preceding section as being predominantly feminine are usually masculine in gender. This includes those ending in *-e, -i, -o, -u, -ú, -al, -el, -il, -ol, -ul, -em, -lm, -um, -ium, -án, -en, -én, -in, -ín, -ón* (except *-ión), -ún, -ar, -er, -ir, -or, -ur, -es, -és, -os, -us,*

-at, -et, -ot, -ut, -ú and *-x*, but there are a few exceptions such as:

la base	(base)	la diagonal	(diagonal)	la metrópoli	(metropolis)
la catedral	(cathedral)	la dial	(dial)	la moral	(morale)
la consonante	(consonant)	la frase	(sentence)	la radio	(radio)
la constante	(constant)	la hambre	(hunger)	la señal	(signal)
la credencial	(credential)	la inicial	(initial)	la variante	(variant)
la debutante	(debutant)	la mano	(hand)	la virgen	(virgen)

Nouns ending in *-ista* are usually masculine unless the context shows that the person referred to is female.

3. <u>FEMININE NOUNS FROM MASCULINE NOUNS</u>: Masculine nouns ending in *-o* or *-e* drop the final letter and add an *-a* to form the feminine (*hijo-hija, monje-monja, chico-chica*). Masculine nouns ending in *-d, -l, -n, -r, -s* or *-z* add *-a* to form the feminine (*león-leona, profesor-profesora*)

4. <u>GENDER AND MEANING</u>: The meanings of some nouns change with gender.

MASCULINE		FEMININE	
el banco	bank, bench	la banca	banking
el capital	capital (funds)	la capital	capital (city)
el costo	cost	la costa	coast
el coma	comma	la coma	coma (Med)
el cometa	comet	la cometa	kite
el corte	cut	la corte	court, courtship
el cura	priest	la cura	cure
el duel	duel	la duela	stave
el frente	front	la frente	forehead
el fruta	fruit (on tree)	la fruta	fruit (as food)
el hermano	brother	la hermana	sister
el hijo	boy	la hija	girl
el leño	wood, log	la leña	firewood
el madero	board	la madera	wood
el libro	book	la libra	pound
el modo	manner	la moda	fashion, form
el moral	mulberry tree	la moral	morale, ethics
el naranja	orange tree	la naranja	orange
el pago	payment	la paga	pay (remuneration)
el papa	Pope	la papa	potato
el pato	duck	la pata	foot
el pez	fish	la pez	tar
el policía	policeman	la policía	police force
el político	politician	la política	politics, policy
el puerto	port	la puerta	door
el pulpo	octopus	la pulpa	pulp
el reino	kingdom, realm	la reina	queen
el velo	veil	la vela	sail, vigil, candle

The name of fruit is usually feminine and its tree masculine.

la naranja (orange) el naranjo (orange tree)
la manzana (apple) el manzano (apple tree)

C. ADJECTIVES

For the purposes of the word listings, adjectives are divided into three segments:

1. Those which are in categories that convert from English to Spanish according to a consistent pattern (Approximately 4,000 Listed);

2. Those not in a converting category but which do convert on a one-on-one basis (Approximately 350 Listed);

3. Those not in any converting category nor convertible on a one-on-one basis, but some of which can be converted indirectly through synonyms. (Approximately 1,000 Listed).

Special adjective groups such as demonstrative, possessive, indefinite, interrogative, comparative and color adjectives which require memorization are listed in APPENDIX E. Some additional frequently-used adjectives are included in the lists of APPENDIX H.

Adjectives agree with the noun they modify in gender and number. Although only the singular masculine form of the adjectives is given in the lists, most adjectives can be made feminine by changing the final -o to -a. Adjectives of nationality whose masculine singular form ends in a consonant are made feminine by adding -a, as is also the case with adjectives ending in -dor. Some adjectives have the same form for both masculine and feminine (i.e.- *interesante, realista, fácil, difícil*, etc.). The plural of adjectives is usually formed by adding -s when the adjective ends in a vowel and -es when it ends in a consonant.

1. ADJECTIVES IN CONVERTING CATEGORIES

The adjective category index lists the English adjective ending, the corresponding Spanish adjective ending, the percentage of the adjectives examined in that category which convert to Spanish according to the pattern (based on examination of a 200,000 word base), the number of adjectives (whether converting or not) included because of the high frequency of use and the category's page location. Special attention should be given to the categories with the highest conversion percentages and the largest number of adjectives listed (i.e.: -ive, -ic, -ble, -ate, -al, -an, -ar, -ant, -ent, -ary, -ory, etc.) since these afford the greatest vocabulary-building benefit. Even these high percentage conversion endings, however, won't change a non-convertible stem adjective into a convertble adjective (*talkative, foreseeable*, etc.).

ADJECTIVE CATEGORY INDEX

ENGLISH	SPANISH	CONV. %	NO. LISTED	PGE NO.	ENGLISH	SPANISH	CONV. %	NO. LISTED	PGE NO.
-istic	-ista,-ístico	95%	65	256	-i	-i	80%	7	284
-ic	-ico	95%	450	258	-ical	-ico	95%	180	284
-ed	-to,-ado,-ido	-%	190	262	-al	-al	90%	446	286
-oid	-deo,-oide	80%	8	266	-um	-o	95%	5	290
-id	-ido	95%	54	266	-an	-ano,-eo, -nse,-co,-io	85%	107	290
-nd	-ndo	80%	8	267					
-ble	Verbs -ble	95%	314	267	-an	-ano,-io,-eo	95%	65	292
-ble	-ble	70%	102	270	-o	-o	85%	6	293
-ile	-il	95%	42	271	-ar	-ar	95%	66	294
-ane	-ano	85%	10	271	-er (COMPAR)	más	-%	12	294
-ene	-eno	95%	6	271	-or	-or	90%	14	295
-ine	-ino	95%	40	271	-less		-%	16	295
-une	-uno	60%	4	272	-cious	-z	95%	26	295
-re	-re,-ro	90%	24	272	-ous	-o,-oso	85%	360	296
-ese	-és	90%	16	272	-nct	-nto	95%	8	303
-cise	-ciso	99%	3	273	-ct	-cto	95%	20	304
-nse	-nso	99%	4	273	-et	-eto	65%	10	304
-ose	-oso	99%	16	273	-it	-ito	95%	8	304
-rse	-rso	95%	8	273	-ant	-ente,-ante	70%	106	304
-use	-uso	99%	6	273	-ent	-ente	85%	196	305
-ate	-ato,-o,-ado	85%	94	274	-pt	-nto,-pto	75%	10	307
-ete	-eto	70%	8	275	-est	-este(o)	80%	9	307
-ite	-ido,-ito	70%	16	275	-ist	-ista	95%	22	308
-ute	-uto	90%	14	275	-ust	-usto	99%	4	308
-ue	-co,-uo	90%	12	275	-x	-jo,-xo	95%	6	308
-ive	-ivo	95%	317	276	-ary	-ario	85%	100	309
-ing	-nte,-or	-%	240	279	-ory	-or,-ivo,-orio	90%	94	310
-ish	-és,-co	85%	13	283					

4,000 Listed

ADJS: English *-istic* = Spanish *-ista* (70%) or *-ístico* (25%). A few drop the *-ist* and convert to Spanish *-ico*. 95%: 65 Listed

Cross-References: A *-istical* ; N *-ist, -ism*

ENGLISH	SPANISH -ico (25%)	-ista (70%)
altruistic		altruista
anachronistic	anacronístico	
anarchistic		anarquista
antagonistic	antagónico	
artistic	artístico	
atheistic	ateístico	
ballistic	balístico	
capitalistic		capitalista
characteristic	característico	

ENGLISH	SPANISH	
	-ico (25%)	-ista (70%)
chauvinistic		chauvinista
communistic		comunista
deterministic		determinista
dualistic	dualístico	
egoistic		egoista
egotistic		egotista
euphemistic	eufemístico	
evangelistic	evangélico	
expansionistic		expansionista
expressionistic		expresionista
fatalistic		fatalista
feudalistic	feudalístico	
futuristic		futurista
humanistic	humanístico	
idealistic		idealista
imperialistic		imperialista
impressionistic		impresionista
individualistic		individualista
legalistic		legalista
linguistic	lingüístico	
logistic	logístico	
masochistic	masoquístico	
materialistic		materialista
mechanistic	mecánico	mecanicista
militaristic		militarista
modernistic		modernista
monopolistic	monopolizador•	
moralistic		moralista
nationalistic		nacionalista
naturalistic		naturalista
nihilistic		nihilista
opportunistic		oportunista
optimistic		optimista
pantheistic	panteístico	
paternalistic		paternalista
pessimistic		pesimista
pluralistic	pluralístico	
populistic		populista
pragmatistic		pragmatista
pugilistic		pugilista
rationalistic		racionalista
realistic		realista
relativistic		relativista
sadistic		sadista
sensationalistic		sensacionalista
simplistic		simplista
socialistic		socialista
spiritualistic		espiritualista
statistic	estadístico	
stylistic	estilístico	
surrealistic		surrealista
synergistic	sinergético•	
theistic		teísta
totalistic		totalista
universalistic		universalista
unrealistic		no realista

ADJS: English -ic other than -istic = Spanish -ico.   95%   450 Listed

The suffix -ic is used to form adjectives meaning *of, like, having the nature of, caused by* or *consisting of*.
Cross-Reference: ADJ -ical

ENGLISH	SPANISH	ENGLISH	SPANISH
academic	académico	astigmatic	astigmático
acetic	acético	astronomic	astronómico
acoustic	acústico	athletic	atlético
acrobatic	acrobático	Atlantic	atlántico
acrylic	acrílico	atmospheric,-al	atmosférico
Adriatic	adriático	atomic	atómico
aerobic	aeróbico	authentic	auténtico
aerodynamic	aerodinámico	autobiographic	autobiográfico
aeronautic	aeronáutico	autocratic	autocrático
aesthetic	estético	automatic	automático
agnostic	agnóstico	autonomic	autonómico
alcoholic	alcohólico	axiomatic	axiomático
algebraic	algebraico	bacteriologic	bacteriológico
allegoric,-al	alegórico	Baltic	báltico
allergenic	alergénico	barbaric	barbárico
allergic	alérgico	barometric,-al	barométrico
alphabetic	alfabético	basic	básico
alphanumeric	alfanumérico	bibliographic	bibliográfico
amoebic	amíbico	bimetallic	bimetálico
analeptic	analéptico	biographic,-al	biográfico
analgesic	analgésico	biologic,-al	biológico
analytic,-al	analítico	bombastic	bombástico
anarchic	anárquico	boric	bórico
anatomic	anatómico	botanic	botánico
anemic	anémico	Britannic	británico
anesthetic	anestésico•	bubonic	bubónico
angelic	angélico	bucolic	bucólico
antibiotic	antibiótico	bureaucratic	burocrático
antisemitic	antisemítico	calligraphic	caligráfico
antiseptic	antiséptico	caloric	calórico
apathetic	apático•	calorific	calorífico
aphoristic	aforístico	carcinogenic	carcinógeno•
apocalyptic	apocalíptico	carbolic	carbólico
apologetic	apologético	carbonic	carbónico
apoplectic	apopléctico	catalytic	catalítico
apostatic	apostático	catastrophic	catastrófico
apostolic	apostólico	cathartic	catártico
aquatic	acuático	Catholic	católico
Arabic	arábico	caustic	cáustico
archaic	arcaico	Celtic	céltico
Arctic	ártico	centric	céntrico
aristocratic	aristocrático	ceramic	cerámico
arithmetic	aritmético	chaotic	caótico
aromatic	aromático	charismatic	carismático
arrhythmic	arrítmico	cherubic	querúbico
arthritic	artrítico	chloric	clórico
ascetic	ascético	choreographic	coreográfico
aseptic	aséptico	chromatic	cromático
Asiatic	asiático	chronic	crónico
asthmatic	asmático	chronologic,-al	cronológico

ENGLISH	SPANISH	ENGLISH	SPANISH
cinematic	cinemático	epileptic	epiléptico
citric	cítric	episodic	episódico
civic	cívico	epistolic	epistólico
classic	clásico	erotic	erótico
climatic	climático	erratic	errático
comic	cómico	esoteric	esotérico
concentric	concéntrico	esthetic	estético
conic	cónico	ethnic	étnico
cosmetic	cosmético	eugenic	eugenésico·
cosmic	cósmico	euphonic	eufónico
cryptic	críptico	euphoric	eufórico
cryptographic	criptográfico	evangelic	evangélico
cubic	cúbico	exoteric	exotérico
cyclic	cíclico	exotic	exótico
cystic	cístico	extrinsic	extrínseco·
dactylic	dactílico	fanatic	fanático
Delphic	délfico	fantastic	fantástico
demagogic,-al	demagógico	folkloric	folklórico
democratic	democrático	forensic	forense·
demographic	demográfico	formic	formico
despotic	despótico	frantic	frenético·
diabetic	diabético	frenetic	frenético
diabolic	diabólico	Gaelic	gaélico
diagnostic	diagnóstico	galactic	galáctico
dialectic	dialéctico	galvanic	galvánico
diametric,-al	diamétrico	gastric	gástrico
didactic	didáctico	generic	genérico
dietetic	dietético	genetic	genético
diplomatic	diplomático	geocentric	geocéntrico
dogmatic	dogmático	geographic	geográfico
domestic	doméstico	geologic,-al	geológico
Doric	dórico	geometric,-al	geométrico
dramatic	dramático	geriatric	geriátrico
drastic	drástico	Germanic	germánico
dynamic	dinámico	gigantic	gigante, gigantesco·
dynastic	dinástico	Gothic	gótico
eccentric	excéntrico	graphic	gráfico
eclectic	ecléctico	gymnastic	gimnástico
ecliptic	eclíptico	harmonic	armónico
economic	económico	Hebraic	hebraico
ecstatic	extático	hectic	hético
egocentric	egocéntrico	heretic	herético
elastic	elástico	hermetic	hermético
electric,-al	eléctrico	heroic	heroico
electromagnetic	electromagnético	Hispanic	hispánico
electronic	electrónico	historic	histórico
emblematic	emblemático	holographic	holográfico
embryonic	embriónico	honorific	honorífico
empathic	empático	hydraulic	hidráulico
emphatic	enfático	hydroelectric	hidroeléctrico
encyclopedic	enciclopédico	hydrophobic	hidrofóbico
endemic	endémico	hydroponic	hidropónico
energetic	enérgico, energético	hygienic	higiénico
enigmatic	enigmático	hyperbolic	hiperbólico
enthusiastic	entusiástico	hypnotic	hipnótico
epic	épico	hypodermic	hipodérmico
epidemic	epidémico	iambic	yámbico

ENGLISH	SPANISH	ENGLISH	SPANISH
idiotic	idióta•	oceanic	oceánico
idyllic	idílico	oceanographic	oceanográfico
impolitic	impolítico	odorific	odorífico
inorganic	inorgánico	Olympic	olímpico
interscholastic	interescolar•	optic,-al	óptico
intrinsic	intrínseco•	organic	orgánico
ionic	iónico	orgiastic	orgiástico
ironic,-al	irónico	Orphic	órfico
Islamic	islámico	orthodontic	ortodóntico
isometric,-al	isométrico	orthographic	ortográfico
isotonic	isotónico	orthopedic	ortopédico
italic	itálico	orthoscopic	ortoscópico
Judaic	judaico	osmotic	osmótico
kinetic	cinético	pacific	pacífico
laconic	lacónico	pandemic	pandémico
lactic	láctico	panic	pánico
laic	laico	panoramic	panorámico
lethargic	letárgico	pantomimic	pantomímico
lithographic	litográfico	parabolic	parabólico
lunatic	lunático	paralytic	paralítico
lymphatic	linfático	parasitic	parasítico
macroscopic	macroscópico	parenthetic	parentético
magic	mágico	pathetic	patético
magnetic	magnético	pathogenic	patogénico
majestic	majestuoso•	pathologic,-al	patológico
masonic	masónico	patriotic	patriótico
melancholic	melancólico	pectic	péctico
melodic	melódico	pedagogic,-al	pedagógico
melodramatic	melodramático	pedantic	-esco, pedante•
Messianic	mesiánico	pediatric	pediátrico
metabolic	metabólico	pelvic	pélvico
metallic	metálico	peptic	péptico
metamorphic	metamórfico	periodic	periódico
meteoric	meteórico	phallic	fálico
methodic	metódico	phantastic	fantástico
metric,-al	métrico	philanthropic	filantrópico
microscopic	microscópico	philatelic	filatélico
misanthropic	misantrópico	philharmonic	filarmónico
monarchic,-al	monárquico	philosophic	filosófico
monastic	monástico	phlegmatic	flemático
monolithic	monolítico	phonemic	fonémico
monophonic	monofónico	phonetic	fonético
monosyllabic	monosilábico	phonographic	fonográfico
moronic	morónico	photoelectric	fotoeléctrico
morphemic	morfémico	photogenic	fotogénico
mosaic	mosaico	photographic	fotográfico
myopic	miope•	photosynthetic	fotosintético
mystic	místico	photovoltaic	fotovoltaico
Napoleonic	napoleónico	plastic	plástico
narcotic	narcótico	Platonic	platónico
necrotic	necrótico	plutocratic	plutocrático
neuralgic	neurálgico	pneumatic	neumático
neurotic	neurótico	poetic	poético
nomadic	-ade, nómada•	polemic	polémico
Nordic	nórdico	polymeric	polimérico
nostalgic	nostálgico	polytechnic,-al	politécnico

ENGLISH	SPANISH	ENGLISH	SPANISH
pornographic	pornográfico	sporadic	esporádico
pragmatic	pragmático	static	estático
prehistoric,-al	prehistórico	stenographic	estenográfico
prismatic	prismático	stereophonic	estereofónico
problematic	problemático	stereoscopic	estereoscópico
prolific	prolífico	stigmatic	estigmático
prophetic	profético	stoic	estoico
prophylactic	profiláctico	strategic	estratégico
prosaic	prosaico	subsonic	subsonico
prosodic	prosódico	sulphuric	sulfúrico
psychiatric	psiquiátrico	supersonic	supersónico
psychic	psíquico	syllabic	silábico
psychoanalytic	psicoanalítico	symbolic	simbólico
psychodelic	psicodélico	symmetric	simétrico
psychopathic	psicopático	*sympathetic	simpático•
psychosomatic	psicosomático	symphonic	sinfónico
psychotic	psicótico	symptomatic	sintomático
pubic	púbico	synthetic	sintético
public	público	systematic	sistemático
puritanic	puritano•	systemic	sistémico
pyroelectric	piroeléctrico	systolic	sistólico
pyrotechnic,-al	pirotécnico	tacit	tácito
pyrrhic	pírrico	tactic,-al	táctico
quadriplegic	cuadriplégico	tannic	tánico
quadratic	cuadrático	technocratic	tecnocrático
quixotic	quijotesco•	telegraphic	telegráfico
rabbinic	rabínico	telephonic	telefónico
rheumatic	rheumático	telescopic	telescópico
rhythmic	rítmico	*terrific	terrífico
romantic	romántico	Teutonic	teutónico
rustic	rústico	thematic	temático
sarcastic	sarcástico	theoretic,-al	teorético
sardonic	sardónico	theocratic	teocrático
satanic	satánico	therapeutic	terapéutico
satiric	satírico	thermodynamic	termodinámico
scenic	escénico	thermometric	termométrico
schematic	esquemático	thermoplastic	termoplástico
schismatic	cismático	thermostatic	termostático
schizophrenic	esquizofrénico	titanic	titánico
scholastic	escolástico	tonic	tónico
sciatic	ciático	topographic,-al	topográfico
scientific	científico	toxic	tóxico
seismic	sísmico	tragic	trágico
seismographic	sismográfico	transatlantic	transatlántico
semantic	semántico	transoceanic	transoceánico
semiautomatic	semiautomático	traumatic	traumático
semitic	semítico	trigonometric	trigonométrico
septic	séptico	typographic, -al	tipográfico
serologic	serológico	tyrranic	tiránico
Slavic	eslavo•	ultrasonic	ultrasónico
Socratic	socrático	unenthusiastic	no entusiástico
sonic	sónico	unpatriotic	antipatriótico
soperific	soperífico	uremic	urémico
spasmodic	espasmódico	uric	úrico
spastic	espástico	vitriolic	vitriólico
specific	específico	volcanic	volcánico
spheric,-al	esférico	voltaic	voltaico

261

ADJS: English past participle *-ed* used as an adjective often = Spanish past participle *-ado* or *-ido* used as adjectives.

190 Listed

    This conversion occurs only if the verbs are in a conversion category. The Spanish past participle is usually formed by changing the infinitive ending *-ar* to *-ado* and the *-er* and *-ir* infinitive ending to *-ido*. A few of the many frequently used adjectives of this type derived from convertible verbs are listed here as examples.

ENGLISH PAST PART.	SPANISH INFINITIVE	SPANISH PAST PART.
abandoned	abandonar	abandonado
absorbed	absorber	absorto•
abused	abusar	abusado
accepted	aceptar	aceptado
accented	acentuar	acentuado
accredited	acreditar	acreditado
accustomed	acostumbrar	acostumbrado
acclimated	aclimatar	aclimatado
activated	activar	activado
acused	acusar	acusado
adopted	adoptar	adoptado
adulterated	adulterar	adulterado
advanced	avanzar	avanzado
affected	afectar	afectado
affiliated	afiliar	afiliado
agitated	agitar	agitado
alleged	alegar	alegado
allied	aliar	aliado
animated	animar	animado
antiquated	anticuar	anticuado
applied	aplicar	aplicado
approved	aprobar	aprobado
arched	arquear	arqueado
armed	armar	armado
arrested	arrestar	arrestado
articulated	articular	articulado
atrophied	atrofiar	atrofiado
augmented	aumentar	aumentado
authorized	autorizar	autorizado
calculated	calcular	calculado
certified	certificar	certificado
civilized	civilizar	civilizado
classified	clasificar	clasificado
coagulated	coagular	coagulado
*colored	colorar	colorado
commissioned	comisionar	comisionado
complicated	complicar	complicado
composed	componer	compuesto•
compressed	comprimir	comprimido
concentrated	concentrar	concentrado
concerted	concertar	concertado

ENGLISH PAST PART.	SPANISH INFINITIVE	SPANISH PAST PART.
concluded	concluir	concluido
condensed	condensar	condensado
conditioned	condicionar	condicionado
confirmed	confirmar	confirmado
confused	confundir	confuso•
considered	considerar	considerado
consolidated	consolidar	consolidado
continued	continuar	continuado
corrugated	corrugar	corrugado
credited	acreditar	acreditado
crucified	crucificar	crucificado
cultivated	cultivar	cultivado
decayed	decaer	decaído
decided	decidir	decidido
declared	declarar	declarado
deducted	deducir	deducido
deferred	deferir	diferido
deformed	deformar	deformado
degraded	degradar	degradado
depraved	depravar	depravado
depressed	deprimir	deprimido
derived	derivar	derivado
detailed	detallar	detallado
determined	determinar	determinado
diffused	difundir	difundido
dilapidated	dilapidar	dilapidado
dilated	dilatar	dilatado
diluted	diluir	diluído
disarmed	desarmar	desarmado
discolored	descolorar	descolorado
discovered	descubrir	descubierto•
disoriented	desorientar	desorientado
dissipated	disipar	disipado
distilled	destilar	destilado
distinguished	distinguir	disinguido
distracted	distraer	distraído
divided	dividir	dividido
divorced	divorciar	divorciado
*educated	educar	educado
elevated	elevar	elevado
*embarrassed	embarazar	embarazado
evaporated	evaporar	evaporado
exaggerated	exagerar	exagerado
exalted	exaltar	exaltado
excited	excitar	excitado
executed	ejecutar	ejecutado
exposed	exponer	expuesto•
extended	extender	extendido
fatigued	fatigar	fatigado
favored	favorecer	favorecido
figured	figurar	figurado
forced	forzar	forzado
fragmented	fragmentar	fragmentado

ENGLISH PAST PART.	SPANISH INFINITIVE	SPANISH PAST PART.
frustrated	frustrar	frustrado
generalized	generalizar	generalizado
graduated	graduar	graduado
granulated	granular	granulado
hydrated	hidratar	hidratado
impacted	impactar	impactado
imposed	imponer	impuesto•
inclined	inclinar	inclinado
included	incluir	incluso•
incorporated	incorporar	incorporado
induced	inducir	inducido
inebriated	inebriar	inebriado
infatuated	infatuar	infatuado
inflated	inflar	inflado
informed	informar	informado
inhabited	habitar	habitado
inscribed	inscribir	inscrito•
inspire	inspirar	inspirado
instructed	instruir	instruido
interested	interesar	interesado
inverted	invertir	invertido
irritated	irritar	irritado
isolated	aislar	aislado
lacerated	lacerar	lacerado
laminated	laminar	laminado
licensed	licenciar	licenciado
limited	limitar	limitado
listed	listar	listado
marked	marcar	marcado
measured	mesurar	mesurado
occupied	ocupar	ocupado
opposed	oponer	opuesto•
ordained	ordenar	ordenado•
organized	organizar	organizado
painted	pintar	pintado
paralyzed	paralizar	paralizado
perforated	perforar	perforado
perplexed	perplejar	perplejo•
perverted	pervertir	pervertido
predisposed	predisponer	predispuesto•
preferred	preferir	preferido
premeditated	premeditar	premeditado
preoccupied	preocupar	preocupado
presumed	presumir	presunto•
privileged	privilegiar	privilegiado
pronounced	pronuciar	pronunciado
proposed	proponer	propuesto•
proved	probar	probado
provided	proveer	provisto•
qualified	calificar	calificado
reactivated	reactivar	reactivado

ENGLISH PAST PART.	SPANISH INFINITIVE	SPANISH PAST PART.
reclined	reclinar	reclinado
recommended	recomendar	recomendado
reduced	reducir	reducido
referred	referir	referido
refined	refinar	refinado
reformed	reformar	reformado
registered	registrar	registrado
related	relacionar	relacionado
relaxed	relajar	relajado
repeated	repetir	repetido
repressed	reprimir	reprimido
reputed	reputar	reputado
reserved	reservar	reservado
resigned	resignar	resignado
retired	retirar	retirado
retracted	retraer	retractado•
reunited	reunir	reunido
revealed	revelar	revelado
revised	revisar	revisado
revoked	revocar	revocado
revolved	revolver	revuelto•
rounded	redondear	redondeado
ruined	arruinar	arruinado
salaried	asalariar	asalariado
sealed	sellar	sellado
secured	asegurar	asegurado
segmented	segmentar	segmentado
segregated	segregar	segregado
stamped	estampar	estampado
stipulated	estipular	estipulado
submerged	sumergir	sumergido
sugared	azucarar	azucarado
suppressed	suprimir	suprimido
surprised	sorprender	sorprendido
suspend	suspender	suspendido
toasted	tostar	tostado
titled	titular	titulado
tormented	atormentar	atormentado
truncated	truncar	truncado
ulcerated	ulcerar	ulcerado
unified	unificar	unificado
united	unir	unido
unlimited	no limitar	ilimitado
unoccupied	desocupar	desocupado
used	usar	usado
veiled	velar	velado

NOTE: Although the past participle form of verbs in both English and Spanish are often used as adjectives, it should be noted that, unlike their English counterparts, Spanish present participles cannot be used as adjectives.

    The sleeping girl.   - La muchacha que duerme.
                        (Not: La muchacha durmienda.)

    The girl is sleeping. - La muchacha esta durmiendo.
                          La muchacha duerme.

ADJS: English *-oid* = Spanish *-oide* or *-oideo*. 80%: 8 Listed

ENGLISH	SPANISH	ENGLISH	SPANISH
alkaloid	alcaloide	negroid	negroide
anthropoid	antropoide	paranoid	paranoide
fibroid	fibroideo	typhoid	tifoideo
mongoloid	mongoloide	thyroid	tiroideo

ADJS: English *-id* other than *-oid* = Spanish *-ido*. 95%: 54 Listed

ENGLISH	SPANISH	ENGLISH	SPANISH
acid	ácido	morbid	morboso, mórbido
acrid	acre•	pallid	pálido
algid	álgido	pavid	pávido
antacid	antiácido	pellucid	pelúcido
arid	árido	placid	plácido
avid	ávido	putrid	pútrido
candid	cándido	rabid	rábido
carotid	carótido	rancid	rancio•
fervid	férvido	rapid	rápido
fetid	fétido	rigid	rígido
flaccid	fláccido	semiarid	semiárido
florid	florido	solid	sólido
fluid	flúido	sordid	sórdido
frigid	frígido	splendid	espléndido
gravid	grávido	squalid	escuálido
horrid	hórrido	stolid	estólido
humid	húmedo•	stupid	estúpido
hybrid	híbrido	tepid	tibio•
insipid	insípido	timid	tímido
intrepid	intrépido	torpid	tórpido
invalid	inválido	torrid	tórrido
languid	lánguido	translucid	translúcido
limpid	límpido	tumid	túmido
liquid	líquido	turbid	túrbido
livid	lívido	turgid	túrgido
lucid	lúcido	valid	vigente, válido
lurid	sensacional•	vivid	gráfico, vívido

ADJS: English -nd = Spanish -ndo.   80%:   8 Listed

ENGLISH	SPANISH	ENGLISH	SPANISH
bland	blando	reverend	reverendo
compound	compuesto •	rotund	rotundo
fecund	fecundo	second	segundo
moribund	moribundo	vagabond	vagabundo

ADJS: English -ble from verbs in convertible categories = Spanish -ble.
                                              95%: 314 Listed

The suffix -ble denotes *able to* or *tending to*.

The Spanish adjective takes on the spelling changes which occur in their verb conversions from English to Spanish.

ENGLISH	SPANISH	ENGLISH	SPANISH
abominable	abominable	consumable	consumible
acceptable	aceptable	contestable	contestable
accessible	accesible	controvertible	controvertible
adaptable	adaptable	convertible	convertible
adjustable	ajustable	corrigible	corregible
admirable	admirable	corruptible	corruptible
admissible	admisible	countable	contable
adorable	adorable	credible	creíble
*advisable	aconsejable•	curable	curable
alienable	alienable	debatable	discutible, debatible
alterable	alterable	decipherable	descifrable
analyzable	analizable	deductible	deducible
applicable	aplicable	defensible, defendable	defendible
appreciable	apreciable	definable	definible
arbitrable	arbitrable	delectable	deleitable
assignable	asignable	demonstrable	demonstrable
attainable	realizable•	dependable	confiable•
attributable	atribuible	deplorable	deplorable
avoidable	evitable	desirable	deseable
calculable	calculable	destructible	destructible
censurable	censurable	determinable	determinable
certifiable	certificable	detestable	detestable
classifiable	clasificable	digestible	digestible
coercible	coercible	disagreeable	desagradable
combinable	combinable	discernible	discernible
combustible	combustible	disfavorable	desfavorable
comestible	comestible	dishonorable	deshonoroso•
comfortable	cómodo, confortable	dispensable	dispensable
commendable	recomendable	disposable	disponible
communicable	comunicable	disputable	disputable
comparable	comparable	distinguishable	distinguible
compatible	compatible	divisible	divisible
compensable	compensable	double	doble
computable	computable	educable	educable
conceivable	concebible	eludible	eludible
conciliable	conciliable	employable	empleable
conductible	conductible	endurable	soportable, endurable
confiscable	confiscable	enumerable	enumerable
considerable	considerable	enviable	envidiable
consolable	consolable	estimable	estimable

ENGLISH	SPANISH	ENGLISH	SPANISH
incontrovertible	incontrovertible	indecipherable	indescifrable
incorrigible	incorregible	indefatigable	infatigable
incorruptible	incorruptible	indefensible	indefensible
incurable	incurable	indefinable	indefinible
excitable	excitable	indescribable	indescriptible
excludable	excluible	indestructible	indestructible
excusable	excusable	indeterminable	indeterminable
expandible	expansible	indigestible	indigestible
explicable	explicable	indiscernible	indiscernible
exploitable	explotable	indispensable	indispensable
exportable	exportable	indisputable	indisputable
expressible	expresable	indistinguishable	indistinguible
extinguishable	extinguible	indivisible	indivisible
extractable	extraíble	ineducable	ineducable
favorable	favorable	inescapable	inevitable•
flammable	inflamable	inestimable	inestimable
flexible	flexible	inevitable	inevitable
floatable	flotable	inexcusable	inexcusable
formidable	formidable	inexhaustible	inagotable•
fungible	fungible	inexorable	inexorable
fusible	fundible, fusible	inexpiable	inexpiable
habitable	habitable	inexplicable	inexplicable
honorable	honoroso, honorable	inexpressible	inexpresable
identifiable	identificable	inextricable	inextricable
imaginable	imaginable	inflammable	inflamable
imitable	imitable	inflatable	inflable
immeasurable	inmensurable	inflexible	inflexible
immemorable	inmemorable	infusable	infusable
immovable	inmovible	inhabitable	inhabitable
immutable	inmutable	inimitable	inimitable
impalpable	impalpable	innumerable	innumerable
impassible	impasible	inoperable	inoperable
impenetrable	impenetrable	insatiable	insaciable
imperceptible	imperceptible	inscrutable	inescrutable
impermeable	impermeable	insensible	insensible
imperturbable	imperturbable	inseparable	inseparable
implacable	implacable	insociable	insociable
implausible	poco plausible	insoluble	insoluble
imponderable	imponderable	insufferable	insufrible
impracticable	impracticable	insuperable	insuperable
impregnable	impregnable	insupportable	insoportable
impressionable	impresionable	insurable	asegurable•
imputable	imputable	interminable	interminable
inaccessible	inaccesible	interpretable	interpretable
inadmissible	inadmisible	intolerable	intolerable
inalienable	inalienable	invaluable	invalorable
inalterable	inalterable	invariable	invariable
inapplicable	inaplicable	inviolable	inviolable
inappreciable	inapreciable	irreconcilable	irreconciliable
incalculable	incalculable	irredeemable	irredimible
inclinable	inclinable	irreducible	irreducible
includible	incluible	irrefutable	irrefutable
incombustible	incombustible	irremediable	irremediable
incomparable	incomparable	irreparable	irreparable
incomprehensible	incomprensible	irreplaceable	irreemplazable
inconceivable	inconcebible	irreproachable	irreprochable
inconsolable	inconsolable	irresistible	irresistible
incontestable	incontestable	irresolvable	irresoluble

ENGLISH	SPANISH	ENGLISH	SPANISH
irresponsible	irresponsable	reimbursable	reembolsable
irreversible	irreversible	remediable	remediable
irrevocable	irrevocable	removable	removible
irritable	irritable	remunerable	remunerable
justifiable	justificable	renegotiable	renegociable
lamentable	lamentable	renewable	renovable
laudable	laudable	reparable	reparable
limitable	limitable	repeatable	repetible
manageable	manejable	replaceable	reemplazable
measurable	mensurable	reprehensible	reprehensible
mentionable	mencionable	reproachable	reprochable
mitigable	mitigable	reproducible	reproducible
modifiable	modificable	rescindable	rescindible
movable (moveable)	móvil, movible	resistible	resistible
mutable	mutable	resolvable	resoluble
mystifiable	mistificable	respectable	respetable
navigable	navegable	responsible	responsable
negotiable	negociable	restrainable	restringible
noncombustible	incombustible	retractable	retractable
nonnegotiable	no negociable	reversible	reversible
nontransferable	intransferible	revisable	revisable
notable	notable	revocable	revocable
noticeable	perceptible, notable	satiable	saciable
numerable	numerable	*sensible	sensato, sensible
objectionable	objetable•	separable	separable
observable	observable	serviceable	servible
obtainable	obtenible	submergible	submergible
operable	operable	supportable	soportable
organizable	organizable	susceptible	susceptible
pardonable	perdonable	sustainable	sustenable
passable	pasable	terminable	terminable
patentable	patentable	tolerable	tolerable
payable (due)	pagadero, pagable	transferable	transferible
penetrable	penetrable	transformable	transformable
perceivable	perceptible	transmissible	transmisible
perceptible	perceptible	transmittable	transmisible
permissible	permisible	transplantable	trasplantable
placable	placable	transportable	transportable
practicable	practicable	treatable	tratable
preferable	preferible	unacceptable	inaceptable
presentable	presentable	unalienable	inalienable
presumable	presumible	unalterable	inalterable
producible	producible	uncontrollable	incontrolable
programmable	programable	undefinable	indefinible
pronounceable	pronunciable	undesirable	indeseable
punishable	penable, punible	unfavorable	desfavorable
qualifiable	calificable	unintelligible	ininteligible
quantifiable	cuantificable	unjustifiable	injustificable
questionable	cuestionable	unobjectionable	inobjetable
realizable	realizable	unpardonable	imperdonable
reasonable	razonable	unpredictable	inpredecible
recognizable	reconoscible•	unquestionable	incuestionable
reconcilable	reconciliable	unreasonable	irrazonable
recoverable	recuperable•	unusable	inusable
redeemable	redimible	usable	usable
reducible	reducible	variable	variable
referable	atribuible, referible	venerable	venerable
reformable	reformable	verifiable	verificable
refutable	refutable	violable	violable

ADJS: English -ble not formed from verbs also = -ble. 70%: 102 Listed

ENGLISH	SPANISH	ENGLISH	SPANISH
able	capaz, hábil•	intangible	intangible
affable	afable	intelligible	inteligible
amenable	receptivo•	intractable	intratable
amiable	amable	invincible	invencible
amicable	amigable	invisible	invisible
arable	arable	invulnerable	invulnerable
audible	audible	irascible	irascible
*capable	apto, hábil, capaz•	knowledgeable	bien informado•
charitable	benévolo, caritativo•	legible	legible
compatible	compatible	liable	responsable•
conscionable	razonable	malleable	maleable
contemptible	despreciable•	memorable	memorable
contractible	contractable	merchantable	vendible•
culpable	culpable	*miserable	miserable
double	doble	nimble	ágil•
dubitable	dubitable	noble	noble
durable	duradero, durable	nonviable	no viable
eligible	elegible	ostensible	ostensible
equitable	equitativo, justo•	palatable	aceptable•
exigible	exigible	palpable	palpable
exorable	exorable	partible	partible
fallible	falible	permeable	permeable
feasible	factible•	personable	agradable•
feeble	débil•	*plausible	créible•
formidable	formidable	possible	posible
frangible	frangible	potable	potable
gullible	crédulo•	practicable	practicable
horrible	horrible	probable	probable
hospitable	hospitalario•	repeatable	repetible
humble	humilde•	risible	risible
ignoble	innoble	seasonable	oportuno, estacional•
illegible	ilegible	sensible	perceptible, *sensible
immoble	inmoble	separable	separable
impalpable	impalpable	sociable	sociable
impeccable	impecable	soluble	soluble
impossible	imposible	stable	estable
improbable	improbable	susceptible	susceptible
inaudible	inaudible	tangible	tangible
incapable	incapaz•	terrible	terrible
incompatible	incompatible	treasonable	traidor•
incredible	increíble	treble	triple•
inculpable	inculpable	unsociable	insociable
indelible	indeleble	unstable	inestable
indubitable	indubitable	valuable	valioso, de valor•
ineffable	inefable	vegetable	vegetable
ineligible	inelegible	veritable	verdadero•
ineluctable	ineluctable	viable	viable
inequitable	injusto•	vincible	vencible
infallible	infalible	visible	visible
infrangible	infrangible	voluble	voluble
inhospitable	inhospitable	vulnerable	vulnerable

ADJS: English -ile other than -phile = Spanish -il.   95%: 42 Listed
The suffix *-ile* denotes *of, having to do with, that can be like* or *suitable*. The suffix *-phile* denotes *loving* or *liking*.

ENGLISH	SPANISH	ENGLISH	SPANISH
agile	ágil	mercantile	mercantil
anglophile	anglófilo	mobile	móvil
automobile	automóvil	motile	móvil
contractile	contráctil	nonvolatile	no volátil
docile	dócil	nubile	núbil
ductile	dúctil	puerile	pueril
erectile	eréctil	quintile	quintil
facile	fácil	reptile	reptil
febrile	febril	russophile	rusófilo
fertile	fértil	senile	senil
fragile	frágil	servile	servil
futile	fútil	stabile	estable•
gentile	gentil	sterile	estéril
hostile	hostil	subtile	sutil
imbecile	imbécil	tactile	táctil
immobile	inmóvil	tensile	tensor•
infantile	infantil	textile	textil
infertile	infértil	utile	útil
inutile	inútil	versatile	versátil
juvenile	juvenil	virile	viril
labile	lábil	volatile	volátil

ADJS: English -ane = Spanish -ano.   85%: 10 Listed

ENGLISH	SPANISH	ENGLISH	SPANISH
arcane	arcano	insane	loco, insano
germane	pertinente•	mundane	mundano
humane	humano	profane	profano
inane	vacío, inane•	sane	sano
inhumane	inhumano	urbane	urbano

ADJS: English -ene = Spanish -eno.   95%: 6 Listed

ENGLISH	SPANISH	ENGLISH	SPANISH
damascene	damasceno	obscene	obsceno
epicene	epiceno	serene	sereno
miocene	mioceno	slovene	esloveno

ADJS: English -ine = Spanish -ino.   95%: 40 Listed
The suffix *-ine* denotes *of, having the nature of* or *like*.

ENGLISH	SPANISH	ENGLISH	SPANISH
alkaline	alcalino	bovine	bovino
alpine	alpino	Byzantine	bizantino
antisubmarine	antisubmarino	canine	canino
aquamarine	aguamarino	clandestine	clandestino
aquiline	aquilino	crystalline	cristalino
argentine	argentino	divine	divino
asinine	asinino	elephantine	elefantino

ENGLISH	SPANISH	ENGLISH	SPANISH
endoctrine	endoctrino	routine	rutinario•
feline	felino	saccharine	sacarino
feminine	femenino	saline	salino
fine (not coarse)	fino	sanguine	sanguíno
Florentine	florentino	serpentine	serpentino
genuine	genuino	Sistine	sixtino
internecine	destructivo•	submarine	submarino•
intestine	intestino	supine	supino
libertine	libertino	tangerine	tangerino
marine	marino	ultramarine	ultramarino
masculine	masculino	ursine	ursino
Philippine	filipino	uterine	uterino
porcine	porcino	vulpine	vulpino

ADJS: English -une = Spanish -uno.   60%: 4 Listed

ENGLISH	SPANISH	ENGLISH	SPANISH
immune	inmune•	opportune	oportuno
inopportune	inoportuno	picayune	insignificante•

ADJS: English -re = Spanish -ro.   90%: 24 Listed

ENGLISH	SPANISH	ENGLISH	SPANISH
austere	austero	mediocre	mediocre•
bizarre	bizarro	miniature	en miniatura•
demure	modesto•	obscure	obscuro
entire	entero	ochre	ocre•
future	futuro	premature	prematuro
immature	inmaduro	premiere	principal•
impure	impuro	pure	puro
insecure	inseguro	rare	raro
insincere	insincero	secure	seguro
macabre	macabro	severe	severo
mature	maduro	sincere	sincero
mere	mero	sure	seguro

ADJS: English -ese = Spanish -és (m) or -esa (f).   90%: 16 Listed

The suffix -ese denotes *of a country or place* or *in the language of.*
    Cross-Reference: N -ese; Nationalities: p. 203

ENGLISH	SPANISH		ENGLISH	SPANISH	
	MASCULINE	FEMININE		MASCULINE	FEMININE
Burmese	birmanés	-esa	Maltese	maltés	-esa
Cantonese	cantonés	-esa	Milanese	milanés	-esa
Chinese	chino	-na•	Portuguese	portugués	-esa
Congolese	congolés	-esa	Sengalese	sengalés	-esa
Guianese	guayanés	-esa	Siamese	siamés	-esa
Japanese	japonés	-esa	Sudanese	sudanés	-esa
Javanese	javanés	-esa	Viennese	vienés	-esa
Lebanese	libanés	-esa	Vietnamese	vietnamés	-esa

ADJS: English *-cise* = Spanish *-ciso*. 99%: 3 Listed

ENGLISH	SPANISH	ENGLISH	SPANISH
concise	conciso	*precise	preciso
imprecise	impreciso		

ADJS: English *-nse* = Spanish *-nso*. 99%: 4 Listed

ENGLISH	SPANISH	ENGLISH	SPANISH
dense	denso	intense	intenso
immense	inmenso	tense	tenso

ADJS: English *-ose* = Spanish *-oso*. 99%: 16 Listed

The suffix *-ose* denotes *full of, containing, like.*

ENGLISH	SPANISH	ENGLISH	SPANISH
adipose	adiposo	lachrymose	lacrimoso
bellicose	belicoso	leprose	leproso
bulbose	bulboso	morbose	morboso
comatose	comatoso	*morose	moroso
globulose	globuloso	tuberose	tuberoso
grandiose	grandioso	varicose	varicoso
granulose	granuloso	verbose	verboso
jocose	jocoso	viscose	viscoso

ADJS: English *-rse* = Spanish *-rso*. 95%: 8 Listed

ENGLISH	SPANISH	ENGLISH	SPANISH
adverse	adverso	inverse	inverso
averse	averso	obverse	obverso
*converse	inverso•	perverse	perverso
diverse	variado, diverso	reverse	invertido, reverso

ADJS: English *-use* = Spanish *-uso*. 99%: 6 Listed

ENGLISH	SPANISH	ENGLISH	SPANISH
abtruse	abtruso	obtuse	obtuso
diffuse	difuso	profuse	profuso
incuse	incuso	recluse	recluso

ADJS: English -ate = Spanish -ado (70%), -ato (5%) or -o (10%).
85%: 94 Listed

The suffix -ate denotes *characteristic of* or *filled with*. It can also be the rough equivalent of the English past participle -ed.

ENGLISH	SPANISH	ENGLISH	SPANISH
accurate	exacto, preciso•	inappropriate	no apropiado
adequate	adecuado	inarticulate	inarticulado
affectionate	cariñoso, afectioso•	incarnate	encarnado
agglomerate	aglomerado	inconsiderate	inconsiderado
aggregate	agregado	indelicate	indelicado
alternate	alternado	indeterminate	indeterminado
animate	animado	indiscriminate	sin distinción•
antepenultimate	antepenúltimo	inebriate	borracho, ebrio•
appellate	apelado	innate	innato
appropriate	apropiado	inordinate	inordenado
approximate	aproximado	insubordinate	insubordinado
articulate	articulado	intemperate	intemperante•
associate	adjunto, asociado	intercollegiate	interescolar•
celebate	célibe•	intermediate	intermedio
collegiate	colegiado	interstate	interestatal•
commensurate	coextenso•	intestate	intestado
compassionate	compasivo•	intimate	íntimo
confederate	confederado	intricate	intrincado
conglomerate	conglomerado	inveterate	inveterado
considerate	considerado	inviolate	inviolado
consummate	consumado	irate	furioso•
corporate	incorporado	laureate	laureado
degenerate	degenerado	legitimate	legitimo
deliberate	deliberado	literate	literato
delicate (dainty)	fino, delicado	moderate	moderado
delicate (sickly)	débil•	oblate	oblato
designate	designado	obstinate	obstinado
desolate	desolado	ornate	ornado
desperate	desesperado	passionate	apasionado
deviate	desviado	penultimate	penúltimo
disconsolate	desconsolado	*private	particular, privado
dispassionate	desapasionado	profligate	libertino•
disproportionate	desproporcionado	proportionate	proporcionado
duplicate	duplicado	prostrate	postrado
effeminate	efeminado	proximate	próximo
*elaborate	elaborado	regenerate	regenerado
expatriate	expatriado	reprobate	vicio, réprobo
fortunate	afortunado	satiate	saciado
graduate	graduado	sedate	sosegado•
illegitimate	ilegítimo	separate	apartado, separado
illiterate	iliterato	serrate	serrado
immaculate	inmaculado	subordinate	subordinado
immediate	inmediato	temperate	temperado
immoderate	inmoderado	triplicate	triplicado
inaccurate	inexacto•	truncate	truncado
inadequate	inadecuado	ultimate	último
inanimate	inanimado	unfortunate	desafortunado

ADJS: English -ete = Spanish -eto. 70%: 8 Listed

ENGLISH	SPANISH	ENGLISH	SPANISH
complete	entero, completo	incomplete	incompleto
concrete	concreto	* indiscrete	unido•
*discrete	separado, distinto•	(indiscreet)	(indiscreto)
(discreet)	(discreto)	obsolete	obsoleto
effete	agotado, estéril•	replete	repleto

ADJS: English -ite = Spanish -ito or -ido. 70%: 16 Listed

ENGLISH	SPANISH	ENGLISH	SPANISH
composite	compuesto•	indefinite	indefinido
contrite	contrito	infinite	infinito
definite	definitivo, definido	opposite	opuesto•
erudite	erudito	petite	pequeña•
exquisite	exquisito	polite	cortés•
favorite	favorito	prerequisite	necesario•
finite	finito	recondite	recóndito
impolite	descortés•	requisite	necesario•

ADJS: English -ute = Spanish -uto or -udo. 90%: 14 Listed

ENGLISH	SPANISH	ENGLISH	SPANISH
absolute	absoluto	involute	involuto
acute	agudo	irresolute	irresoluto
astute	astuto	minute	minuto, menudo
brute	bruto	mute	mudo
destitute	indigente•	resolute	resuelto
dissolute	disoluto	substitute	substituto
hirsute	hirsuto	volute	voluto

ADJS: English -ue = Spanish -co or -uo. 90%: 12 Listed
The suffix -*esque* denotes *the manner, style* or *quality of*.

ENGLISH	SPANISH	ENGLISH	SPANISH
antique	antiguo	oblique	oblicuo
arabesque	arabesco	opaque	opaco
baroque	barroco	picturesque	pintoresco
burlesque	burlesco	statuesque	estatuario•
grotesque	grotesco	unique	único
harlequinesque	arlequinesco	vague	vago

**ADJS: English -ive = Spanish -ivo (84%), -or (5), -nte (2%),
-orio (2%) or-o (1%)   95%: 317 Listed**

The suffix -ive denotes *of the nature of*, *relating to* or *tending to*.

ENGLISH	SPANISH	ENGLISH	SPANISH
ablative	ablativo	confirmative	confirmativo
abortive	abortivo	congestive	congestivo
abrasive	abrasivo	connective	conectivo
abusive	abusivo	consecutive	consecutivo
accumulative	acumulativo	conservative	conservativo
accusative	acusativo	*conservative	conservador
acquisitive	adquisitivo	constitutive	constitutivo
active	activo	constrictive	constrictivo
adaptive	adaptivo	constructive	constructivo
additive	aditivo	consultative	consultivo
adhesive	adhesivo	consumptive	consuntivo
adjective	adjetivo	contemplative	contemplativo
administrative	administrativo	contraceptive	contraceptivo
admonitive	admonitivo	convulsive	convulsivo
affirmative	afirmativo	cooperative	cooperativo
aggressive	agresivo	corrective	correctivo
alive	vivo, viviente•	correlative	correlativo
allusive	alusivo	corroborative	corroborativo
alternative	alternativo	corrosive	corrosivo
appreciative	apreciativo	corruptive	corruptivo
apprehensive	aprensivo	creative	creativo
argumentative	argumentativo	cumulative	cumulativo
assertive	asertivo	curative	curativo
attentive	atento	dative	dativo
attractive	atractivo	deceptive	engañoso, ilusorio•
attributive	atributivo	decisive	decisivo
authoritative	autoritativo	declarative	declarativo
automotive	automóvil•	decorative	decorativo
captive	cautivo	deductive	deductivo
causative	causativo	defective	defectivo
coercive,-itive	coercitivo	defensive	defensivo
coextensive	coextensivo	definitive	definitivo
cognitive	cognitivo	degenerative	degenerativo
cohesive	cohesivo	deliberative	deliberativo
collective	colectivo	delusive	delusivo
collusive	colusorio	demonstrative	demostrativo
combative	combativo	denominative	denominativo
commemorative	conmemorativo	depressive	depresivo
communicative	comunicativo	derisive	burlón•
comparative	comparativo	derivative	derivativo
competitive	competitivo	descriptive	descriptivo
comprehensive	comprensivo	destructive	destructivo
compressive	compresivo	detective	detectivo
compulsive	compulsivo	determinative	determinativo
concessive	concesivo	digestive	digestivo
conclusive	conclusivo	digressive	digresivo
conducive	conductivo	diminutive	diminutivo
conductive	conductivo	directive	directivo

ENGLISH	SPANISH	ENGLISH	SPANISH
disjunctive	disyuntivo	inductive	inductivo
dispositive	dispositivo	ineffective	ineficaz•
disruptive	destructor•	inexpensive	barato•
dissuasive	disuasivo	infective	infectivo
distinctive	distintivo	infinitive	infinitivo
distractive	que distrae•	informative	informativo
divisive	divisivo	infusive	infusorio
donative	donativo	inhibitive,-ory	inhibitorio
* effective	efectivo	initiative	initiativo
effusive	efusivo	injunctive	inyuncto
elective	electivo	innovative	innovador•
elusive	elusivo	inoffensive	inofensivo
emulative	emulativo	inoperative	inoperante
erosive	erosivo	inquisitive	inquisitivo
eruptive	eruptivo	insensitive	insensitivo
evaporative	evaporatorio	insertive	insertivo
evasive	evasivo	instinctive	instintivo
evocative	evocador	instructive	instructivo
excessive	excesivo	intensive	intensivo
excitative	excitativo	interactive	interactivo
exclusive	exclusivo	interpretative	interpretativo
executive	ejecutivo	interpretive	interpretativo
exhaustive	exhaustivo	interrogative	interrogativo
exhortative	exhortativo	interruptive	interruptivo
expansive	expansivo	intransitive	intransitivo
expensive	costoso, caro•	introductive	introductivo
explorative,-ory	explorativo	introspective	introspectivo
explosive	explosivo	intrusive	intruso
expositive	expositivo	intuitive	intuitivo
expressive	expresivo	invasive	invasor
extensive	extensivo	inventive	inventivo
festive	festivo	investigative	investigador
fictive	fictivo	laxative	laxativo
figurative	figurativo	legislative	legislativo
formative	formativo	locomotive	locomotivo
fugitive	fugitivo	lubricative	lubricativo
furtive	furtivo	lucrative	lucrativo
generative	generativo	manipulative	manipulador
genitive	genitivo	massive	pesado, masivo
hypoactive	hipoactivo	meditative	meditativo
illusive	ilusivo	mitigative	mitigativo
illustrative	ilustrativo	mutilative	mutilativo
imaginative	imaginativo	narrative	narrativo
imitative	imitativo	native	nativo
imperative	imperativo	negative	negativo
implosive	implosivo	nominative	nominativo
impressive	impresionante•	nonconductive	no conductivo•
impulsive	impulsivo	noncorrosive	no corrosivo
inactive	inactivo	nonexclusive	no exclusivo
inattentive	desatento	nonobjective	no objetivo
incisive	incisivo	nonproductive	no productivo
inclusive	inclusivo	normative	normativo
incohesive	incohesivo	nutritive	nutritivo
indecisive	indeciso	objective	objetivo
indicative	indicativo	obsessive	obsesivo
		obstructive	obstructivo

277

ENGLISH	SPANISH	ENGLISH	SPANISH
occlusive	oclusivo	relative	relativo
offensive	ofensivo	remunerative	remunerativo
operative	operante, operativo	reparative	reparativo
oppressive	opresivo	repetitive	repetidor
palliative	paliativo	reprehensive	represor
participative	participativo	representative	representativo
partitive	partitivo	repressive	represivo
passive	pasivo	reproductive	reproductivo
pejorative	peyorativo	repulsive	repulsivo
pensive	pensativo	resistive	resistivo
perceptive	perceptivo	respective	respectivo
permissive	permisivo	responsive	responsivo
perspective	perspectivo	restive	inquieto•
persuasive	persuasivo	restorative	restaurativo
pervasive	penetrante•	restrictive	restrictivo
positive	positivo	resuscitative	resuscitador
possessive	posesivo	retentive	retentivo
preceptive	preceptivo	retributive	retributivo
predictive	predictivo	retroactive	retroactivo
preparative	preparativo	retrogressive	regresivo•
prescriptive	prescriptivo	retrospective	retrospectivo
preservative	preservativo	seclusive	solitario•
presumptive	presuntivo	*secretive	callado•
preventative	preventivo	*secretive	secretorio•
preventive	preventivo	sedative	sedativo
primitive	primitivo	seductive	seductivo
productive	productivo	*selective	selectivo
profusive	profusivo	*sensitive	sensitivo
progressive	progresivo	separative	separativo
prohibitive	prohibitivo	speculative	especulativo
projective	proyectivo	sportive	deportivo
prospective	prospectivo	stimulative	estimulador
protective	protector	subjective	subjetivo
provocative	provocativo	subjunctive	subjuntivo
punitive	punitivo	submissive	sumiso
purgative	purgativo	substantive	substantivo
putative	putativo	substitutive	substitutivo
qualitative	cualitativo	subversive	subversivo
quantitative	cuantitativo	*successive	sucesivo
radioactive	radioactivo	suggestive	sugestivo
reactive	reactivo	superactive	superactivo
receptive	receptivo	superlative	superlativo
recessive	recesivo	supportive	sustentador•
reconstructive	reconstructivo	suppositive	supositivo
recreative	recreativo	suppressive	supresivo
recuperative	recuperativo	talkative	hablador•
redemptive	redentor	*tentative	tentativo
reflective	reflector	transitive	transitivo
reflexive	reflexivo	unattractive	inatractivo
reformative	reformativo	undecisive	no decisivo
refractive	refractivo	unexpressive	inexpresivo
regenerative	regenerativo	vindictive	vindicativo
regressive	regresivo	violative	violador
regulative	regulativo	vituperative	vituperador
rehabilitative	rehabilitativo	vocative	vocativo

ADJS: English adjectives ending in *-ing* derived from the present participle of English verbs in converting categories = Spanish *-nte* or *-or* rather than the Spanish present participle *-ndo* which is used only as a verb form and not as an adjective.
240 Listed

A selected few of those often used as adjectives are listed to show the pattern.

ENGLISH	SPANISH	
	-nte	-or
absorbing	absorbente	
accepting	aceptante	
accompanying	acompañante	acompañador
accusing	acusante	acusador
acquiring	adquirente	adquiridor
adjusting		ajustador
admiring		admirador
adoring	adorante	adorador
affirming		afirmador
aggravating	agravante	agravador
agonizing	agonizante	
alarming	alarmante	alarmador
alternating	alternante	
amplifying		amplificador
appetizing		apetitoso•
ascending	ascendiente	
*aspiring	aspirante	
attacking	atacante	
*attending	asistente•	
attenuating	atenuante	
calculating		calculador
calming	calmante	
captivating	cautivante	cautivador
circulating	circulante	
classifying		clasificador
coinciding	coincidente	
comforting	confortante	confortador
compensating		compensador
competing		competidor
compomising		comprometedor
conciliating		conciliador
concluding	concluyente	
condescending	condescendiente	
confirming	confirmante	confirmador
conquering		conquistador
consenting		consentidor
conserving	conservante	conservador
consoling	consolante	consolador
conspiring	conspirante	
constraining	constringente	
contaminating		contaminador
contending	contendiente	contendedor
continuing		continuador
contracting	contrayente	

ENGLISH	SPANISH	
	-nte	-or
contradicting		contradictor
constrasting	contrastante	contrastador
contributing	contribuyente	contribuidor
convalescing	convaleciente	
converging	convergente	
convincing	convincente	
cooperating	cooperante	
coordinating		coordinador
correcting		corrector
corroborating	corroborante	
corrupting		corruptor
debilitating	debilitante	
declining	declinante	
decreasing	decreciente	
defaming	difamante	
defending		defendedor
defining		definidor
deforming		deformador
degenerating	degenerante	
degrading	degradante	
deliberating	deliberante	
delineating	delineante	delineador
demoralizing		desmoralizador
depressing	deprimente	
descending	descendente	
deteriorating		deteriorador
determining	determinante	
detonating	detonante	
detracting		detractor
devastating		devastador
differing	diferente	
diluting	diluente	
disconcerting	desconcertante	disconcertador
disgusting		disgustoso•
disquieting	inquietante	
distributing	distribuyente	distributor
diverging	divergente	
diverting		divertido•
dividing		divisor
dominating	dominante	dominador
domineering	dominante	dominador
duplicating		duplicador
edifying	edificante	edificador
electrifying	electrizante	electrizador
*embarrassing		embarazador
emerging	emergente	
enchanting		encantador
enervating	enervante	enervador
equalizing		igualador
erring	errante	
escalating		escalador
exacting	exigente	
exaggerating	exagerante	
exasperating	exasperante	
exciting	excitante	excitador

ENGLISH	SPANISH -nte	-or
excluding		excluidor
exhaling		exhalador
exhorting		exhortador
existing	existente	
expelling	expelente	
experimenting		experimentador
expiring	expirante	
exploring		explorador
exporting		exportador
extenuating	atenuante	
fascinating	fascinante	fascinador
fatiguing	fatigante	fatigoso•
flagellating		flagelador
floating	flotante	
flourishing	floreciente	
flowering	floreciente	florecedor
flowing	fluente	
fluctuating	fluctuante	
frustrating		frustratorio•
fulminating	fulminante	fulminador
galloping	galopante	
generating		generador
governing	gobernante	gobernador
gratifying		gratificador
hipnotizing		hipnotizador
humiliating	humillante	humillador
illuminating	iluminante	iluminador
imitating		imitador
impelling	impelente	
imposing	imponente	
indulging	indulgente	
initiating		iniciador
inspiring	inspirante	inspirador
instigating		instigador
insulting	insultante	insultador
interesting	interesante	
interpreting		interpretador
intervening		interventor
intriguing	intrigante	
invigorating		vigorizador
irritating	irritante	irritador
liberating		liberador
liquidating		liquidador
magnifying		magnificador
manipulating	manipulante	manipulador
meditating		meditador
menacing	amenazante	amenazador
mitigating	mitigante	mitigador
moderating	moderante	moderador
murmuring	murmurante	murmurador
nauseating	nauseante	
negotiating	negociante	negociador
objecting	objetante	
obliging	obligante	
observing	observante	observador

ENGLISH	SPANISH	
	-nte	-or
obstructing		obstructor
offending		ofendedor
officiating	oficiante	
operating	operante	operador
opposing	oponente	
oppressing		opresor
organizing		organizador
oscillating	oscilante	
palpitating	palpitante	
paralyzing		paralizador
participating	participante	
pending	pendiente	
penetrating	penetrante	penetrador
persecuting		perseguidor
perservering	perseverante	
persisting	persistente	
persuading		persuador
preceding	precedente	
preserving		preservador
prevailing	prevaleciente	
producing		producidor
projecting	proyectante	
proliferating	proliferante	
promising		prometador
propelling		propulsor
protesting	protestante	
provoking	provocante	provocador
pulsating		pulsador
purifying	purificante	purificador
pursuing		perseguidor
qualifying		calificativo·
quieting		quietador
ratifying		ratificador
recovering	recobrante	
recriminating		recriminador
recuperating		recuperador
reducing		reductor
refreshing	refrescante	refrescador
registering		registrador
regulating		regulador
regularizing		regularizador
reigning	reinante	
relaxing	relajante	
renovating		renovador
reorganizing		reorganizador
repelling	repelente	
residing	residente	
resisting	resistente	resistidor
resounding	resonante	resonador
responding	respondiente	
restraining	restringente	
resulting	resultante	
resurging	resurgente	

ENGLISH	SPANISH	
	-nte	-or
retarding		retardador
reverberating	reverberante	
rotating	rotante	
sacrificing	sacrificante	sacrificador
satisfying	satisfaciente	
saving	salvante	salvador
separating	separante	separador
serving	serviente	
stabilizing		establizador
stimulating	estimulante	estimulador
succeeding	sucediente	sucesor
suffering	sufriente	sufridor
supervening	superveniente	
supporting		soportador
surprising	sorprendente•	
surviving	sobreviviente	
sustaining	sustenante	sustentador
tempting		tentador
terrifying		aterrador
tormenting		atormentador
tranquilizing		tranquilizador
transcending	transcendente	
transgressing		transgresor
transmitting		transmisor
trembling	temblante	temblador
unceasing	incesante	
unifying		unidor
uniting		unidor
varying	variante	
venerating	venerante	venerador
vibrating	vibrante	vibrador
visiting	visitante	visitador

ADJS: English adjectives ending in *-ish* denoting nationality = Spanish *-és* or *-co*.   85%: 13 Listed

Cross-Reference: Pair Noun Conversions- Countries (p. 203)

ENGLISH		SPANISH	
	-és (40%)	-co (45%)	Misc (5%)
British		británico	
Danish	danés		
English	inglés		
Finnish	finlandés		
Flemish		flamenco•	
Irish	irlandés		
Jewish			hebreo, judío•
Moorish		morisco	moro
Polish		polaco	
Scottish	escocés•		
Spanish			español
Swedish		sueco•	
Turkish		turco	turquesco

ADJS: English adjectives ending in -i denoting nationality = -í or -i.　　　　　　　　　　　　　　　　　　　　　　　**80%: 7 Listed**

　　Cross-Reference:　　N　-Pair Conversions- Countries (p. 203)
　　　　　　　　　　　　　ADJ -an , -Nationalities (p. 290)

ENGLISH	SPANISH	ENGLISH	SPANISH
Afghani	afgano•	Osmanli	osmanlí
Bengali	bengalí	Pakistani	pakistaní, paquistaní
Hindustani	indostanés,-ano•	Tai, Thai	tai, thai
Israeli	israelí		

ADJS:　English -ical = Spanish -ico or -al.　　　　**95%: 180 Listed**
　A very large percentage of English -ical adjectives also have an -ic form with both tending to convert to -ico in Spanish.

　　　　Cross-Reference:　ADJ -ologic , -ic ;　N -ology

ENGLISH	SPANISH	ENGLISH	SPANISH
acoustical	acústico	*clerical	clerical
aeronautical	aeronáutico	clinical	clínico
allegorical	alegórico	comical	cómico
alphabetical	alfabético	conical	cónico
analogical	analógico	cosmological	cosmológico
analytical	analítico	criminological	criminológico
anarchical	anárquico	critical	crítico
anatomical	anatómico	cyclical	cíclico
angelical	angélico	cylindrical	cilíndrico
anthropological	antropológico	cynical	cínico
anticlerical	anticlerical	demoniacal	demoníaco
antithetical	antitético	diabolical	diabólico
apolitical	apolítico	dialectical	dialéctico
archeological	arqueológico	dramatical	dramático
arithmetical	aritmético	ecclesiastical	eclesiástico
arsenical	arsenical	ecological	ecológico
astrological	astrológico	economical	económico
astronautical	astronáutico	ecumenical	ecuménico
astronomical	astronómico	egotistical	egotista•
asymmetrical	asimétrico	electrical	eléctrico
atypical	atípico	elliptical	elíptico
autobiographical	autobiográfico	empirical	empírico
bacteriological	bacteriológico	epidemiological	epidemiológico
barometrical	barométrico	esoterical	esotérico
biblical	bíblico	ethical	ético
biochemical	bioquímico	ethnological	etnológico
biographical	biográfico	etymological	etimológico
biological	biológico	evangelical	evangélico
botanical	botánico	fanatical	fanático
categorical	categórico	farcical	risible, burlesco•
chemical	químico	gastronomical	gastronómico
cervical	cervical	genealogical	genealógico
chronological	cronológico	geographical	geográfico
classical	clásico	geological	geológico

ENGLISH	SPANISH	ENGLISH	SPANISH
geometrical	geométrico	pedagogical	pedagógico
geophysical	geofísico	periodical	periódico
geopolitical	geopolítico	petrochemical	petroquímico
grammatical	gramático	pharmaceutical	farmacéutico
graphical	gráfico	pharmacological	farmacológico
gynecological	ginecológico	pharmical	fármico
hemispherical	hemisférico	philanthropical	filantrópico
heretical	herético	philological	filológico
hermetical	hermético	philosophical	filosófico
hierarchical	jerárquico	physical	físico
historical	histórico	physiological	fisiológico
hypothetical	hipotético	poetical	poético
hysterical	histérico	political	político
identical	idéntico	pontifical	pontifical
ideological	ideológico	practical	práctico
illogical	ilógico	prehistorical	prehistórico
ironical	irónico	problematical	problemático
juridical	jurídico	psychological	psicológico
lethargical	letárgico	puritanical	puritano•
liturgical	litúrgico	rabbinical	rabínico
logical	lógico	radical	radical
logistical	logístico	rhetorical	retórico
lyrical	lírico	rhythmical	rítmico
magical	mágico	satanical	satánico
maniacal	maníaco	satirical	satírico
mathematical	matemático	seismological	sismológico
mechanical	mecánico	skeptical	escéptico
medical	médico	sociological	sociológico
metallurgical	metalúrgico	spherical	esférico
metaphorical	metafórico	statistical	estadístico
metaphysical	metafísico	stoical	estoico
meteorological	meteorológico	strategical	estratégico
methodical	metódico	surgical	quirúrgico•
methodological	metodológico	symbolical	simbólico
metrical	métrico	symmetrical	simétrico
mineralogical	mineralógico	tactical	táctico
monarchical	monárquico	tautological	tautológico
morphological	morfológico	technical	técnico
musical	musical, músico	technological	tecnológico
mystical	místico	theatrical	teátrico
mythical	mítico	theological	teológico
mythological	mitológico	theoretical	teórico
nautical	náutico	theosophical	teosófico
neoclassical	neoclásico	therapeutical	terapéutico
neurological	neurológico	topical	tópico
nonpolitical	no político	topographical	topográfico
numerical	numérico	*tropical	trópical
numerological	numerológico	tropical	trópico
oceanographical	oceanográfico	typical	típico
ontological	ontológico	typographical	tipográfico
optical	óptico	tyrannical	tiránico
oratorical	oratorio•	umbilical	umbilical
ornithological	ornitológico	urological	urológico
paradoxical	paradójico	vertical	vertical
parenthetical	parentético	zodiacal	zodiacal
pathological	patológico	zoological	zoológico

ADJS: English -al other than -ical = Spanish -al (85%), -rio (1%), -co (2%) or a noun phrase (2%).   90%: 446 Listed

ENGLISH	SPANISH	ENGLISH	SPANISH
abdominal	abdominal	celestial	celeste, celestial
abnormal	anormal	central	central
aboriginal	aborigen•	centrifugal	centrífugo•
abysmal	abismal	cerebral	cerebral
accidental	accidental	ceremonial	ceremonial
*actual	verdadero, actual	cervical	cervical
actuarial	actuarial	circumstantial	circunstancial
additional	adicional	*clerical	clerical
adjectival	adjetival	coastal	costero•
adverbial	adverbial	coaxial	coaxial
aerial	aério	coeducational	coeducacional
agricultural	agrícola, agrario•	coincidental	coincidente•
alluvial	aluvial	collateral	colateral
amoral	amoral	collegial	colegial
anal	anal	colloidal	coloidal
ancestral	ancestral	colloquial	coloquial
animal	animal	colonial	colonial
annual	anual	colossal	colosal
antisocial	antisocial	commercial	comercial
apocryphal	apócrifo•	communal	comunal
arbitral	arbitral	conceptual	conceptual
arboreal	arbóreo•	conditional	condicional
architectural	arquitectural	confessional	confesional
arterial	arterial	confidential	confidencial
artificial	artificial	congenial	congenial
asexual	asexual	congenital	congénito•
astral	astral	congregational	congregacional
audiovisual	audiovisual	congressional	del congreso
autumnal	autumnal	conjectural	conjetural
axial	axial	conjugal	conyugal
bacterial	bactérico	connubial	connubial
banal	banal	consentual	consensual
baptismal	bautismal, baptismal	consequential	consecuente•
beneficial	beneficial	constitutional	constitucional
bestial	bestial	continental	continental
bicameral	bicameral	continual	continuo•
biennial	bienial	contractual	contractual
bifocal	bifocal	controversial	controversial
bilateral	bilateral	conventional	convencional
bilingual	bilingüe•	conversational	conversacional
binomial	binomial	convivial	sociable, convival
biracial	biracial	cordial	cordial
bisexual	bisexual	corporal	corporal
bronchial	bronquial	correctional	correccional
brutal	brutal	criminal	criminal
cannibal	caníbal	crucial	crucial
capital	capital	crystal	cristal
cardinal	cardinal	cultural	cultural
carnal	carnal	decimal	decimal
caudal	caudal	denominational	partidista•
casual	casual	dental	dental
causal	causal	departmental	departmental

ENGLISH	SPANISH	ENGLISH	SPANISH
detrimental	perjudicial•	fundamental	fundamental
developmental	experimental•	general	general
devotional	devoto•	*genial	genial
diagonal	diagonal	genital	genital
dictatorial	dictatorial	glacial	glacial
differential	diferencial	global	global
digital	digital	governmental	gubernmental
dimensional	dimensional	gradual	gradual
directional	direccional	grammatical	gramatical
discretional	discrecional	gubernatorial	gubernativo•
disloyal	desleal	guttural	gutural
dismal	triste,depresivo•	habitual	habitual
divisional	divisional	heptagonal	heptagonal
doctoral	doctoral	heterosexual	heterosexual
doctrinal	doctrinal	hexagonal	hexagonal
dorsal	dorsal	homosexual	homosexual
dual	dual	horizontal	horizontal
editorial	editorial	ideal	ideal
educational	educacional	illegal	ilegal
electoral	electoral	immaterial	inmaterial
elemental	elemental	immemorial	inmemorial
*emotional	emocional	immoral	inmoral
environmental	ambiental•	immortal	inmortal
ephemeral	efímera•	impartial	imparcial
Episcopal	episcopal	imperial	imperial
equal	igual	impersonal	impersonal
equatorial	ecuatorial	inaugural	inaugural
equilateral	equilateral	incidental	incidental
equivocal	equívoco	inconsequential	inconsequente•
essential	esencial	incremental	incremental
eternal	eterno,eternal	individual	individual
ethereal	etéreo•	industrial	industrial
*eventual	eventual	ineffectual	sin efecto•
exceptional	excepcional	infernal	infernal
experimental	experimental	infinitesimal	infinitesimal
exponential	exponencial	inflectional	inflexional
external	externo•	influential	influyente•
extramarital	extramarital	*informal	informal
facial	facial	initial	inicial
factual	real•	inquisitorial	inquisitorial
familial	*familiar•	inspirational	inspirante•
fatal (fateful)	fatal	institutional	institucional
*fatal (deadly)	mortal•	instructional	de instrucción
federal	federal	instrumental	instrumental
feudal	feudal	integral	integral
filial	filial	intellectual	intelectual
final	final	intentional	intencional
financial	financiero•	intercontinental	intercontinental
fiscal	fiscal	intercostal	intercostal
floral	floral	intermural	intermural
*formal	formal	internal	interno•
focal	focal	international	internacional
fractional	fraccionario	interracial	interracial
fraternal	fraternal	intestinal	intestinal
frontal	frontal	intramural	intramural
frugal	frugal	irrational	irracional
functional	funcional	jovial	jovial

ENGLISH	SPANISH	ENGLISH	SPANISH
judicial	judicial	noncommittal	evasivo•
jurisdictional	jurisdiccional	nonessential	no esencial
lateral	lateral	normal	normal
latitudinal	latitudinal	notarial	notarial
legal	legal	notional	nocional
lethal	letal	nuptial	nupcial
liberal	liberal	nutritional	alimenticio•
lineal	lineal	occasional	ocasional
lingual	lingual	occidental	occidental
literal	literal	occupational	ocupacional
littoral	litoral	octagonal	octagonal
local	local	official	oficial
longitudinal	longitudinal	operational	operacional
loyal	fiel, leal	optimal	óptimo•
managerial	directivo, ejecutivo•	optional	opcional
manual	manual	oral	oral
marginal	marginal	orbital	orbital
marital	marital	orchestral	orquestral
martial	marcial	ordinal	ordinal
material	material	organizational	de organización
maternal	maternal	oriental	oriental
matriarchal	matriarcal	original	original
matrimonial	matrimonial	ornamental	ornamental
medicinal	medicinal	oval	oval
medieval	medieval	papal	papal
melancholical	melancólico	parental	parental
*memorial	conmemorativo•	parietal	parietal
menial	servil•	parochial	parroquial
menstrual	menstrual	partial	parcial
mental	mental	participial	participial
mercurial	mercurial	pastoral	pastoral
meridional	meridional	paternal	paterno, paternal
metal	metálico, de metal	patriarchal	patriarcal
mineral	mineral	pectoral	pectoral
minimal	mínimo•	penal	penal
ministerial	ministerial	periodontal	periodontal
modal	modal	peripheral,-pheric	periférico
monumental	monumental	perpetual	perpetuo•
moral	moral	personal	personal
mortal	mortal	phenomenal	fenomenal
multilateral	multilateral	pictorial	pictórico
multilingual	multilingual	plural	plural
multinational	multinacional	postal	postal
municipal	municipal	potential	potencial
mural	mural	preferential	preferencial
musical	musical	preinaugural	preinaugural
mutual	mutuo, mutual	prejudicial	perjudicial
nasal	nasal	premarital	premarital
natal	natal	prenatal	prenatal
national (native)	nacional	prepositional	preposicional
natural	natural	presidential	presidencial
naval	naval	principal	principal
navigational	navegacional	procedural	de procedimiento•
neural	neural	processional	procesional
neutral	neutral	prodigal	pródigo•
nocturnal	nocturnal	professional	profesional
nominal	nominal	professorial	profesoral

ENGLISH	SPANISH	ENGLISH	SPANISH
promotional	de promoción	tangential	tangencial
proportional	proporcional	temperamental	temperamental
proverbial	proverbial	temporal	temporal
providential	providencial	terminal	terminal
provincial	provincial	terrestrial	terrestre·
provisional	provisional	territorial	territorial
prudential	prudencial	testimonial	testimonial
punctual	puntual	textual	textual
racial	racial	thermal	termal
radial	radial	three-dimensional	tridimensional
radical	radical	tidal	de marea·
rational	racional	titular	titular
*real	real	tonal	tonal
reciprocal	recíproco	torrential	torrencial
recreational	de recreación	total	total
rectal	rectal	traditional	tradicional
regal	real·	transcendental	transcendental
regional	regional	transcontinental	transcontinental
remedial	remediador·	transitional	de transición
renal	renal	tribal	tribal
rental	de alquilar	trimestral	trimestral
residential	residencial	triumphal	triunfal
residual	residual	trivial	trivial
rival	rival	tutorial	tutelar·
rostral	rostral	two-dimensional	bidimensional
royal	real	unconditional	incondicional
rural	rural	unconstitutional	inconstitucional
sacrificial	sacrificatorio·	unequal	desigual
sacrimental	sacrimental	unequivocal	inequívoco
seasonal	estacional·	unessential	no esencial
secretarial	secretarial	ungrammatical	ingramatical
sectional	regional·	unicameral	unicameral
segmental	segmentado·	unilateral	unilateral
semifinal	semifinal	unintentional	no intencional
seminal	seminal	universal	universal
senatorial	senatorial	unnatural	no natural
sensational	sensacional	unofficial	no oficial
sensual	sensual	unreal	irreal
sentimental	sentimental	unusual	no usual, inusual
serial	de serie	usual	usual
several	varios, algunos·	venal	venal
sexual	sexual	venereal	venéreo·
signal	señalado·	venial	venial
social	social	verbal	verbal
spatial	espacial	vernal	vernal
special	especial	vertebral	vertebral
spectral	espectral	vertical	vertical
spinal	espinal	vestal	vestal
spiral	espiral	vestigial	vestigial
spiritual	espiritual	virginal	virginal
structural	estructural	virtual	virtual
subliminal	subliminal	visceral	visceral
subnormal	subnormal	visual	visual
substantial	substancial	vital	vital
superficial	superficial	vocal	vocal
supernatural	sobrenatural	vocational	vocacional
supplemental	suplemental	zonal	zonal

ADJS: English *-um* = Spanish *-o*. **95%: 5 Listed**

ENGLISH	SPANISH	ENGLISH	SPANISH
maximum	máximo	optimum	óptimo
medium	medio	vacuum	vacío, vacuo
minimum	mínimo		

ADJS: English *-an* in adjectives of nationality, region or residence = *-no, -co, -io, -eo, -nse* or *-és*. **85%: 107 Listed**

Cross-Reference: ADJ -ish, -ese ; N -an
N -Countries & People (p.203)

ENGLISH	-no 50%	-co 10%	-eo, -io 20%	-nse 5%	Misc. 15%
Abyssinian			abisinio		
Afghan	afgano				
African	africano				
Albanian					albanés
Algerian	argelino				
American	norte americano				
Andean	andino				
Anglican	anglicano				
Anglo-American	anglo-americano				
Arabian					árabe
Argentinian	argentino				
Armenian			armenio		
Asian, Asiatic		asiático			
Assyrian			asirio		
Athenian				ateniense	
Australian	australiano				
Austrian		austríaco			
Balkan		balcánico			
Belgian	bélgico				belga
Bohemian	bohemiano		bohemio		
Bolivian	boliviano				
Brazilian	brazileño				
Bulgarian					búlgaro
Canadian				canadiense	
Carribbean					caribe
Caucasian	caucasiano				
Chilean	chileno				
Colombian	colombiano				
Corinthian			corintio		
Costa Rican				costarricense	
Cretan				cretense	
Cuban	cubano				
Czechoslovakian		checoslovaco			
Danubian	danubiano				
Ecuadorian	ecuatoriano				
Egyptian			egipcio		
Estonian	estoniano		estonio		
Ethiopian		etiópico			etíope

290

ENGLISH	SPANISH				
	-no 50%	-co 10%	-eo, -io 20%	-nse 5%	Misc. 15%
European			europeo		
German		germanico			alemán
Grecian					griego
Guatemalan		guatemalteco			
Haitian	haitiano				
Hawaiian	hawaiano				
Honduran	hundureño				
Hungarian					húngaro
Indian	indiano		indio		
Indonesian			indonesio		
Iranian			iranio		
Iraquian					iraquí
Italian	italiano				
Jamaican	jamaicano				
Jordanian	jordano				
Jugoslavian					yugoeslavo
Kenyan	keniano				
Korean	coreano				
Latvian			latvio		letón
Libyan			libio		
Lithuanian	lituano				
Malayan					malayo
Malaysian			malasio		
Manchurian					manchú
Martian	marciano				
Mayan	maya				
Mediterranean			mediterráneo		
Mexican	mexicano				
Mongolian		mongólico			
Moravian					moravo
Moroccan					marroquí
Neopolitan	napolitano				
Nicaraguan	nicaragüeño				
Nigerian	nigeriano				
Norwegian					noruego
Pakistan					paquistaní
Palistinian	palestino				
Pananenian	panameño				
Paraguayan					paraguayo
Parisian				parisiense	
Persian					persa
Peruvian	peruano				
Philippian				filipense	
Polynesian	polinesio				
Prussian	prusiano				
Puerto Rican	puertorriqueño				
Roman	romano				
Rumanian	rumano				
Russian				ruso	
Salvadorian	salvadoreño				
Scandinavian					escandinavo
Siberian	siberiano				
Sicilian	siciliano				
South African	sudafricano				

ENGLISH	SPANISH				
	-no 50%	-co 10%	-eo,-io 20%	-nse 5%	Misc. 15%
South American	sudamericano				
South Korean	surcoreano				
Syrian			sirio		
Tahitian	tahitiano				
Tanzanian	tanzaniano				
Tasmanian	tasmaniano				
Texan	tejano				
Tibetan	tibetano				
Tunisian	tunecino				
Ukrainian	ucraniano				
Uruguayan					uruguayo
Vatican	vaticano				
Venetian	veneciano				
Venezuelan	venezolano				
Yugoslavian					yugoslavo

ADJS: English *-an* other than in adjectives of nationality or residence = Spanish *-ano*, *-io* or *-eo*.   95%: 65 Listed

The suffix *-an* denotes *of, belonging to, characteristic of, believing in* or *following*.

ENGLISH	SPANISH		
	-ano 55%	-io or -eo 30%	Others 15%
agrarian		agrario	
amphibian		anfibio	
antediluvian	antediluviano		
antiquarian		anticuario	
artesian	artesiano		
authoritarian		autoritario	
barbarian			bárbaro
bipartisan		bipartidario	
cesarian		cesário	
Christian	cristiano		
civilian			civil
Confucian	confuciano		
cosmopolitan			cosmopolita
diluvian	diluviano		
Draconian	draconiano		
egalitarian		igualitario	
Episcopalian			episcopalista
equalitarian		igualitario	
equestrian			ecuestre
Franciscan	franciscano		
Freudian	freudiano		
gargantuan			enorme•
Gregorian	gregoriano		
Hegelian	helegiano		
Herculean		hercúleo	

ENGLISH	SPANISH		
	-ano 55%	-io or -eo 30%	Others 15%
human	humano		
humanitarian		humanitario	
human	humano		
inhuman	inumano		
lesbian	lesbiano		
libertarian		libertario	
Lutheran	luterano		
median	mediano		
Mediterranean		mediterráneo	
metropolitan	metropolitano		
Muhammadan	mahometano		
nonpartisan			independiente•
octogenarian		octogenario	
Olympian			olímpico
orphan	huérfano		
pagan	pagano		
partisan	partisano	partidario	
patrician		patricio	
pedestrian			pedestre
plebeian		plebeyo	
postdiluvian	postdiluviano		
Presbyterian	presbiteriano		
proletarian		proletario	
puritan	puritano		
Republican	republicano		
sectarian		sectario	
superhuman	sobrehumano		
subterranean		subterráneo	
suburban	suburbano		
superhuman	sobrehumano		
Titan			titánico
totalitarian		totalitario	
Trinitarian		trinitario	
Unitarian		unitario	
urban	urbano		
utilitarian		utilitario	
utopian			utópico
vegetarian	vegetariano		
veteran	veterano		
Victorian	victoriano		

ADJS: English -o = Spanish -o.   **85%: 6 Listed**

ENGLISH	SPANISH	ENGLISH	SPANISH
albino	albino	incommunicado	incomunicado
audio	audio	negro	negro
incognito	incógnito	stereo	estereo

ADJS: English -ar = Spanish -ar. 95%: 66 Listed

The ending *-ar* denotes *pertaining to* or *like*.

ENGLISH	SPANISH	ENGLISH	SPANISH
angular	angular	ocular	ocular
avuncular	avuncular	particular (specific)	particular
bilinear	bilineal, bilinear	*particular (fussy)	escrupuloso•
bimolecular	bimolecular	*peculiar (odd)	singular•
binocular	binocular	peculiar	peculiar
bipolar	bipolar	peninsular	peninsular
cardiovascular	cardiovascular	perpendicular	perpendicular
cellular	celular	polar	polar
circular	circular	popular	popular
consular	consular	quadrangular	cuadrangular
corpuscular	corpuscular	rectangular	rectangular
dissimilar	disímil, no similar	*regular	regular
extracurricular	extracurricular	secular	secular
*familiar	familiar	semicircular	semicircular
glandular	glandular	similar	símil, similar
globular	globular	*singular	singular
granular	granular	singular (odd)	peculiar•
insular	insular	solar	solar
interlinear	interlinear	spectacular	espectacular
irregular	irregular	stellar	estelar
jocular	jocoso•	tabular	tabular
jugular	yugular	thermonuclear	termonuclear
linear	linear	titular	titular
lobar	lobar	triangular	triangular
lobular	lobular	tubular	tubular
lumbar	lumbar	unfamiliar	poco familiar
lunar	lunar	unpopular	impopular
Magyar	magiar	valvular	valvular
molecular	molecular	vascular	vascular
muscular	muscular	vehicular	vehicular
nodular	nodular	ventricular	ventricular
nuclear	nuclear	vernacular	vernáculo•
octangular	octangular	*vulgar	vulgar

ADJS: While English adjectives ending in *-er* seldom convert to Spanish in accordance with any reliable pattern, the *-er* when used to express the comparative form of the English adjective has a counterpart in Spanish expressed by the Spanish adjective preceded by *más* as shown in the listed examples.

12 Listed

ENGLISH	SPANISH	ENGLISH	SPANISH
bigger	más grande	easier	más fácil
busier	más ocupado	faster	más rápido
calmer	más calmo	harder	más difícil
cheaper	más barato	richer	más rico
cleaner	más limpio	stronger	más fuerte
clearer	más claro	taller	más alto

ADJS: English *-or* = Spanish *-or*. 90%: 14 Listed

ENGLISH	SPANISH	ENGLISH	SPANISH
anterior	anterior	multicolor	multicolor
exterior	exterior	posterior	posterior
inferior	inferior	prior	previo, anterior, prior
interior	interior	*senior	mayor•
junior	menor•	superior	superior
major	mayor	Tudor	tudor
minor	menor	ulterior	ulterior

ADJS: English *-less* usually = the Spanish noun preceded by *sin* as shown in the listed examples. Some have a separate adjective equivalent such as *guiltless* = i*nculpable* and *needless* = *innecesario*.

16 Listed

ENGLISH	SPANISH	ENGLISH	SPANISH
aimless	sin objeto	priceless	sin precio
baseless	sin base	rainless	sin lluvia
childless	sin hijos	spotless	sin mancha
endless	sin fin	styleless	sin estilo
formless	sin forma	toothless	sin dientes
friendless	sin amigos	valueless	sin valor
leaderless	sin jefe	weightless	sin peso
noiseless	sin ruido	worthless	sin valor

ADJS: English *-acious* or *-ocious* = Spanish *-az* or *-oz*. 95%:

26 Listed

The suffix *-acious* denotes *full of* or *characterized by*.

ENGLISH	SPANISH	ENGLISH	SPANISH
atrocious	atroz	perspicacious	perspicaz
audacious	audaz	pertinacious	pertinaz
capacious	capaz	precocious	precoz
contumacious	contumaz	pugnacious	pugnaz
efficacious	eficaz	rapacious	rapaz
fallacious	falaz	sagacious	sagaz
ferocious	feroz	salacious	salaz
fugacious	fugaz	sequacious	secuaz
gracious	grato, gracioso•	spacious	amplio, espacioso•
inefficacious	ineficaz	tenacious	tenaz
loquacious	locuaz	veracious	veraz
mendacious	mendaz	vivacious	vivaz
mordacious	mordaz	voracious	voraz

ADJS: English *-ous* other than *-acious* or *-ocious* = Spanish *-o* or *-oso*. 85%: 360 Listed

ENGLISH	SPANISH		
	-o 35%	-oso 45%	Misc. 20%
abstemious	abstemio		
acidulous	acídulo		
acrimonious	acrimonio		
adulterous	adúltero		
advantageous			ventajoso•
adventitious	adventicio		
adventurous	adventurero		
ambidextrous	ambidextro		
ambiguous	ambiguo		
ambitious		ambicioso	
amorous		amoroso	
amorphous	amorfo		
amphibious	anfibio		
analogous	análogo		
anomalous	anómalo		
anonymous	anónimo		
*anxious		ansioso	deseoso•
aqueous	ácueo	acuoso	
arduous	arduo		
assiduous	asiduo		
auspicious		auspicioso	
autonomous	autónomo		
avaricious		avaricioso	
barbarous	bárbaro		
bigamous	bígamo		
bilious		bilioso	
bituminous		bituminoso	
blasphemous	blasfemo		
boisterous			ruidoso•
bulbous		bulboso	
calamitous		calamitoso	
callous		calloso	
cancerous		canceroso	
capricious		caprichoso	
captious		capcioso	
carnivorous	carnívoro		
cautious	cauto	cauteloso	
cavernous		cavernoso	
censorious			censurador
ceremonious		ceremonioso	
chivalrous			caballeroso•
circuitous			tortuoso•
cirrous		cirroso	
clamorous		clamoroso	
commodious	cómodo		
compendious		compendioso	
congruous	congruo		
coniferous	conífero		
consanguineous	consanguíneo		

ENGLISH	SPANISH		
	-o 35%	-oso 45%	Misc. 20%
conscientious	concienzudo•		meticuloso•
conscious			consciente
conspicuous	conspicuo		
contagious		contagioso	
contemporaneous	contemporáneo		
contemptuous			desdeñoso•
contentious		contencioso	
contiguous	contiguo		
continuous	continuo		
copious		copioso	
coterminous	cotérmino		
courageous			valiente•
courteous			cortés
covetous			codicioso•
credulous	crédulo		
curious		curioso	
dangerous			peligroso•
deciduous	deciduo		
decorous		decoroso	
deleterious	deletéreo		
delicious		delicioso	
delirious			delirante
desirous		deseoso	
devious			desviado
dexterous	diestro•		
disadvantageous		desventajoso	
disastrous		desastroso	
discontinuous	discontinuo		
discourteous			descortés
disputatious			disputador
dubious		dudoso	
egregious	egregio		
endogenous	endógeno		
enormous			enorme
envious		envidioso	
erogenous	erógeno		
erroneous	erróneo		
euphonious			eufónico
exogamous	exógamo		
expeditious	expedito		
extemporaneous	extemporáneo		
extraneous	extraño		
fabulous		fabuloso	
facetious		jocoso•	
factious		faccioso	
factitious	facticio		
famous		famoso	
*fastidious		fastidioso	
fatuous	fatuo		
felicitous			feliz
felonious			criminal, felón
ferrous		ferroso	
fibrous		fibroso	

297

ENGLISH	SPANISH		
	-o 35%	-oso 45%	Misc. 20%
fictitious	ficticio		
flirtatious			galanteador•
fortuitous	fortuito		
frivolous	frívolo		
fungous		fungoso	
furious		furioso	
gangrenous		gangrenoso	
garrulous	gárrulo		
gaseous		gaseoso	
gelatinous		gelatinoso	
generous		generoso	
glamorous		glamoroso	
glorious		glorioso	
glutinous		glutinoso	
gluttonous			glotón
gorgeous			magnifico•
*gracious		gracioso	grato
granulous		granuloso	
gratuitous	gratuito		
gregarious	gregario		
grievous			doloroso•
harmonious		armonioso	armónico
hazardous			peligroso•
herbivorous	herbívoro		
heterogeneous	heterogéneo		
hideous			horrible•
hilarious			hilarante
homogeneous	homogéneo		
horrendous	horrendo		
humorous			chistoso, gracioso
idolatrous			idolátrico
igneous	ígneo		
ignominious		ignominioso	
illustrious			ilustre
imperious		imperioso	
impervious			impenetrable•
impetuous		impetuoso	
impious	impío		
inauspicious		no auspicioso	
incautious	incauto		descuidado•
incestuous		incestuoso	
incommodious	incómodo		
incongruous	incongruo		
inconspicuous	no conspicuo		
incredulous	incrédulo		
indecorous		indecoroso	
indigenous	indígeno		
industrious		industrioso	
infamous	infamatorio		infame
infectious		infeccioso	
ingenious		ingenioso	
ingenuous	ingenuo		

ENGLISH	SPANISH		
	-o 35%	-oso 45%	Misc. 20%
iniquitous	inicuo		
injudicious		poco juicioso	
injurious		injurioso	
innocuous	innocuo		
insectivorous	insectívoro		
insidious		insidioso	
instantaneous	instantáneo		
intravenous		intravenoso	
irreligious		irreligioso	
jealous		celoso	
joyous			alegre•
judicious		juicioso	
laborious		laborioso	
lascivious	lascivo		
lecherous			lascivo•
leguminous		leguminoso	
leprous		leproso	
libelous			difamatorio•
libidinous		libidinoso	
licentious		licensioso	
litigious		litigioso	
ludicrous			absurdo, ridículo•
lugubrious			lúgubre
luminous		luminoso	
luscious			suculento•
lustrous		lustroso	
*luxurious			lujoso•
magnanimous	magnánimo		
malicious		malicioso	
marvelous		maravilloso	
melodious		melodioso	
meritorious	meritorio		
metalliferous	metalífero		
meticulous		meticuloso	
miraculous		milagroso	
miscellaneous	misceláneo		
mischievous			malicioso•
momentaneous	momentáneo		
momentous			importante, vital•
monogamous	monógamo		
monotonous	monótono		
monstrous		monstruoso	
mountainous		montañoso	
multifarious	multifario		
multiflorous	multifloro		
multiparous	multíparo		
multitudinous	multitudiario		
murderous			asesino•
mutinous			amotinador•
mysterious		misterioso	
nauseous		nauseoso	mareado•

299

ENGLISH	SPANISH		
	-o 35%	-oso 45%	Misc. 20%
nebulous		nebuloso	
nefarious	nefario		
nervous		nervioso	
*notorious	notorio		
noxious			nocivo•
numerous		numeroso	
nutritious	nutricio		
oblivious			olvidadizo•
obnoxious			odioso•
obsequious		obsequioso	
obstreperous		estrepitoso	
obvious	obvio		
odious		odioso	
odoriferous	odorífero		
odorous		oloroso	
officious		oficioso	
ominous		ominoso	
omnifarious	omnifario		
omnivorous	omnívoro		
onerous		oneroso	
opprobrious		oprobioso	
ostentatious		ostentoso	
outrageous			atroz•
oviparous	ovíparo		
parsimonious		parsimonioso	
pecunious	pecuniario		
penurious			indigente•
perfidious	pérfido		
perilous			peligroso•
pernicious		pernicioso	
phosphorous		fosforoso	
pious	pío	piadoso	
poisonous			venenoso•
polygamous	polígamo		
pompous		pomposo	
ponderous		ponderoso	
populous		populoso	
porous, -ose		poroso	
portentous		portentoso	
posthumous	póstumo		
precancerous		precanceroso	
precarious	precario		
precious		precioso	
precipitous		precipitoso	
preposterous			absurdo,ridículo•
prestigious		prestigioso	
presumptuous		presuntuoso	
pretentious		pretencioso	
previous	previo		anterior•
prodigious		prodigioso	
promiscuous	promiscuo		
propitious	propicio		

ENGLISH	SPANISH		
	-o 35%	-oso 45%	Misc. 20%
prosperous	próspero		
punctilious		puntilloso	
querulous		quejumbroso·	
rancorous		rencoroso	
raucous			ronco·
ravenous			rapaz, voraz·
rebellious			rebelde
righteous			recto·
religious		religioso	
repetitious			repetidor
resinous		resinoso	
ridiculous	ridículo		
rigorous		rigoroso	
riotous			tumultuoso·
ruinous		ruinoso	
sacrilegious	sacrílego		
salubrious			salubre
sanctimonious			santurrón·
sanguineous	sanguíneo		
sarcomatous		sarcomatoso	
scabrous		escabroso	
scandalous		escandaloso	
scrupulous		escrupuloso	
scurrilous			procaz, grosero·
sebaceous	sebáceo		
seditious	sedicio		
self-conscious			tímido·
semi-conscious			semiconsciente
semi-precious		semiprecioso	
sensuous, -ual			sensual
serious	serio		
simultaneous	simultáneo		
sinuous		sinuoso	
slanderous			calumnioso·
solicitous	solícito		
sonorous	sonoro		
spacious		espacioso	amplio·
specious		especioso	
spirituous		espirituoso	
spontaneous	espontáneo		
spurious	espurio		
strenuous	estrenuo		
studious		estudioso	
stupendous	estupendo		
subconscious			subconsciente
subreptitious	subrepticio		
sumptuous		suntuoso	
supercilious			desdeñoso·
superfluous	superfluo		
superstitious		supersticioso	
surreptitious	subrepticio		
suspicious		sospechoso	
synchronous			sincrónico

ENGLISH	SPANISH		
	-o 35%	-oso 45%	Misc. 20%
synonymous	sinónimo		
tedious		tedioso	aburrido•
tempestuous		tempestuoso	
tenebrous		tenebroso	
tenuous			tenue
thunderous			atronador•
tortuous		tortuoso	
traitorous			traidor, infiel
treacherous			traicionero•
tremendous	tremendo		
tremulous	trémulo		
tuberous,-ose		tuberoso	
tumorous		tumoroso	
tumultuous		tumultuoso	
tyrannous	tirano		
ubiquitous	ubicuo		
ulcerous		ulceroso	
unambiguous	no ambiguo		
unanimous			unánime
unauspicious		no auspicioso	
unceremonious		inceremonioso	
unconscious			inconsciente
unctuous		untuoso	
unglamorous		poco glamoroso	
ungracious			descortés•
unharmonious		no armonioso	
uniparous	uníparo		
unscrupulous		inescrupuloso	
usurious	usurario		
vacuous	vacuo		
vainglorious		vanaglorioso	
valorous		valeroso	
vaporous		vaporoso	
various	vario		
venomous		venenoso	
venturous			aventurado
vexatious			enfadoso•
vicarious	vicario		
*vicious		vicioso	
victorious		victorioso	
vigorous		vigoroso	
villainous	villano		
virtuous		virtuoso	
viscous, -ose		viscoso	
vitreous	vítreo		
viviparous	vivíparo		
vociferous			vociferador
voluminous		voluminoso	
voluptuous		voluptuoso	
wondrous			maravilloso•
zealous		celoso	

NOTE:
    The *-ous* adjectives making up the foregoing list were chosen to exemplify the thousands of adjectives in this conversion category. Well over 90% of the English adjectives ending in the *-ous* suffixes listed below convert to Spanish adjectives with the corresponding endings indicated.

ENGLISH	SUFFIX MEANING	SPANISH
-aceous	of nature of, belonging to, characterized by, like	-áceo
-adelphous	united by filaments into parcels	-adelfo
-androus	having stamens	-andro
-cephalous	having to do with the head	-céfalo
-dactylous	having a specified number or form of fingers/toes	-dáctilo
-eous	having the nature of, like	-eo, -oso
-ferous	bearing, producing, yielding	-ífero
-florous	having many or a specified number of flowers	-floro
-gamous	referring to marriage or sexual union	-gamo
-genous	producing, generating, produced by, generated in	-geno
-gnathous	having a specified kind of jaw	-gnato
-itious	of, having the nature of, caracterized by	-icio
-merous	to have a specified number or kind of parts	-mero
-morphous	having a specified form or shape (Also -morphic)	-morfo
-parous	bringing forth, producing, bearing	-íparo
-petalous	having a specified number or kind of petals	-pétalo
-phagous	eating or destroying	-ófago
-philous	loving, having a liking for	-ófilo
-phorous	bearing, producing	-foroso
-phyllous	having a specified form or kind of leaves	-ófilo
-podous	having a specified number or kinds of feet	-podo
-pterous	having a specified number or kind of wings	-ptero
-sepalous	having a specified number or kind of sepal	-sépalo
-tropous	turning or turned in some specific way	-tropo
-ulous	tending to, full of, or characterized by	-ulo, -oso
-vorous	feeding on, eating	-ívoro

ADJS: English *-nct* = Spanish *-nto*.   **95%: 8 Listed**

ENGLISH	SPANISH	ENGLISH	SPANISH
adjunct	adjunto	extinct	extinto
defunct	difunto	indistinct	indistinto
distinct (different)	distinto	sacrosanct	sacrosanto
distinct (clear)	claro, preciso·	succinct	sucinto

ADJS: English -ct other than -nct = Spanish -cto. 95%: 20 Listed

ENGLISH	SPANISH	ENGLISH	SPANISH
abject	abyecto	imperfect	imperfecto
abstract	abstracto	incorrect	incorrecto
circumspect	circunspecto	indirect	indirecto
compact	conciso, compacto	inexact	inexacto
correct	justo, correcto	intact	intacto
derelect	derrelicto	perfect	perfecto
direct	directo	select	escogido, selecto
elect	eleito, electo	strict	estricto
erect	erecto	*subject	súbdito, subjeto•
exact	preciso, exacto	suspect	sospechoso•

ADJS: English -et = Spanish -eto. 65%: 10 Listed

ENGLISH	SPANISH	ENGLISH	SPANISH
brunet	moreno•	net	neto
coquet	coqueto	*quiet (calm)	tranquilo, quieto
discreet	discreto	quiet (silent)	silencioso•
disquiet	inquieto	secret	secreto
indiscreet	indiscreto	Soviet	soviético•

ADJS: English -it = Spanish -ito. 95%: 8 Listed

ENGLISH	SPANISH	ENGLISH	SPANISH
decrepit	decrépito	licit	lícito
explicit	explícito	preterit	pretérito
illicit	ilícito	sanskrit	sanscrito
implicit	implícito	tacit	tácito

ADJS: English -ant = Spanish -ante or -ente. 70%: 106 Listed

The suffix *-ant* often denotes *performing (the specified act)*.

ENGLISH	SPANISH	ENGLISH	SPANISH
aberrant	aberrante	concordant	concordante
abundant	abundante	consonant	consonante
adamant	obstinado•	constant	firme, constante
ambulant	ambulante	conversant	versado•
arrogant	arrogante	defiant	desafiador•
assistant	auxiliar•	determinant	determinante
attendant	acompañante•	deviant	desviante
blatant	flagrante•	discordant	discordante
brilliant	brillante	dissonant	disonante
buoyant	boyante	distant	lejano, distante
clairvoyant	clarividente•	dominant	dominante
cognizant	conocedor•	dormant	durmiente•
complaisant	complaciente	elegant	elegante
compliant	obediente•	emanant	emanante
concomitant	concomitante	emigrant	emigrante

ENGLISH	SPANISH	ENGLISH	SPANISH
errant	errante	pleasant	agradable•
exorbitant	exorbitante	pliant	flexible, dúctil•
expectant	expectante	poignant	intenso, agudo•
extant	estante	predominant	predominante
*extravagant	extravagante	pregnant	preñada, encinta•
exuberant	exuberante	preponderant	preponderante
exultant	exultante	Protestant	protestante
flagrant	flagrante	radiant	radiante
flamboyant	flamante•	rampant	agresivo, exuberante•
flippant	impertinente•	recalcitrant	recalcitrante
fragrant	fragrante	recusant	recusante
gallant	galante	redundant	redundante
giant	gigante	*relevant	pertinente•
hesitant	hesitante	reluctant	renuente, reacio•
ignorant	ignorante	remnant	remanente
important	importante	repentant	arrepentido•
incessant	incesante	repugnant	repugnante
inconstant	inconstante	resistant	resistente
indignant	indignado•	resonant	resonante
inelegant	inelegante	resultant	resultante
insignificant	insignificante	significant	significativo•
instant	instantáneo•	stagnant	estancado•
intolerant	intolerante	superabundant	superabundante
irrelevant	no pertinente•	supernatant	sobrenadante
itinerant	errante•	supplicant	suplicante
jubilant	jubilante	tolerant	tolerante
luxuriant	lujuriante	triumphant	triunfante
malignant	maligno•	truant	holgazón, tunante•
mendicant	mendicante	undulant	undulante
merchant	mercantil, mercante	unhesitant	listo, resuelto•
migrant	migratorio•	unimportant	no importante
militant	militante	unpleasant	desagradable•
nonchalant	indiferente•	vacant	desocupado, vacante
nonmalignant	no maligno•	vacillant	vacilante
observant	observador•	vagrant	vagabundo•
participant	participante	valiant	valeroso, valiente
petulant	petulante	vibrant	vibrante
piquant	picante	vigilant	vigilante

ADJS: English -ent = Spanish -ente or -ento.   85%: 196 Listed

The suffix -escent denotes *starting to be, being* or *becoming*.
The suffix -facient denotes *making* or *causing to become*.

ENGLISH	SPANISH	ENGLISH	SPANISH
abhorrent	aborrecible•	apparent	aparente
absent	ausente	ardent	ardiente
absorbent	absorbente	astringent	astringente
abstergent	abstergente	belligerent	beligerante
adherent	adherente	beneficent	benéfico•
adjacent	contiguo, adyacente	benevolent	benévolo•
adolescent	adolescente	bivalent	bivalente
affluent	afluente	clement	clemente
ambivalent	ambivalente	coalescent	coalescente
*ancient	anciano, antiguo•	coexistent	coexistente

ENGLISH	SPANISH	ENGLISH	SPANISH
cogent	persuasivo, eficaz•	fraudulent	fraudulento
coherent	coherente	frequent	frecuente
competent	competente	grandiloquent	grandilocuente
complacent	complaciente	immanent	inmanente
component	componente	imminent	inminente
concurrent	concurrente	impatient	impaciente
condescendent	condescendiente	impenitent	impenitente
*confident	confiado, seguro•	impermanent	no permanente
confluent	confluente	impertinent	impertinente
congruent	congruente	impotent	impotente
consequent	consecuente	improvident	impróvido•
consistent	consistente	imprudent	imprudente
constituent	constituyente	impudent	impudente
content	contento	inadvertent	inadvertido•
continent	continente	incandescent	incandescente
contingent	contingente	incipient	incipiente
convalescent	convaleciente	inclement	inclemente
*convenient	cómodo, conveniente	incoherent	incoherente
convergent	convergente	incompetent	incompetente
corpulent	corpulento	incongruent	incongruente
correspondent	correspondiente	inconsistent	inconsistente
crescent	creciente	incontinent	incontinente
current	corriente	inconvenient	inconveniente
decadent	decadente	indecent	indecente
decent	decente	independent	independiente
deficient	deficiente	indifferent	indiferente
delinquent	delincuente	indigent	indigento
dependent	dependiente	indolent	indolente
descendent	descendiente	indulgent	indulgente
despondent	desalentado•	inefficient	no eficiente
detergent	detergente	infrequent	infrecuente
deterrent	disuasivo•	inherent	inherente
different (various)	diferente	innocent	inocente
different (contrast)	distinto•	insipient	insipiente•
diffident	difidente	insistent	insistente
diligent	diligente	insolent	insolente
disobedient	desobediente	insolvent	insolvente
dissident	disidente	insufficient	insuficiente
divergent	divergente	insurgent	insurgente
ebullient	exuberante•	intelligent	inteligente
effervescent	efervescente	intent	atento•
efficient	eficiente	intermittent	intermitente
effluent	efluente	intransigent	intransigente
eloquent	elocuente	iridescent	iridiscente
emergent	emergente	irreverent	irreverente
eminent	eminente	latent	latente
equivalent	equivalente	lenient	indulgente•
evident	evidente	luminescent	luminiscente
excellent	excelente	magnificent	magnífico•
exigent	exigente	malcontent	malcontento
existent	existente	malevolent	malévolo•
expedient	oportuno•	multivalent	multivalente
fervent	ferviente	munificent	munificente
florescent	florescente	nascent	naciente
fluent	fluente	negligent	negligente
fluorescent	fluorescente	nonequivalent	no equivalente

ENGLISH	SPANISH	ENGLISH	SPANISH
nonexistent	inexistente	pungent	picante, punzante•
nonresident	no residente	quiescent	quiescente
nonviolent	no violento	recent	reciente
obedient	obediente	recurrent	recurrente
obsolescent	obsolescente	renascent	renaciente
omnipotent	omnipotente	resident	residente
omniscient	omnisciente	resilient	resiliente
opalescent	opalescente	resplendent	resplandeciente
opulent	opulento	resurgent	resurgente
orient	oriental•	reticent	reticente
patent	patente	reverent	reverente
patient	paciente	salient	saliente
penitent	penitente	self-sufficient	autosuficiente
permanent	permanente	silent	quieto, silencioso•
persistent	persistente	strident	estridente
pertinent	pertinente	stringent	severo, estricto•
pestilent	pestilente	subsequent	subsecuente
phosphorescent	fosforescente	subservient	subordinado•
potent	potente	succulent	suculento
preadolescent	preadolescente	sufficient	suficiente
precedent	precedente	tangent	tangente
preeminent	preeminente	transcendent	trascendente
preexistent	preexistente	transient	transitorio•
prepubescent	prepubescente	translucent	translúcido•
present	actual, presente	transparent	transparente
prevalent	usual, frecuente•	trident	tridente
proficient	proficiente	truculent	truculente
*prominent(jutting)	prominente	tumescent	tumescente
prominent(eminent)	eminente,notable•	turbulent	turbulento
provident	providente	urgent	urgente
prudent	prudente	vehement	vehemente
prurient	lascivo, sensual•	violent	violento
pubescent	pubescente	virulent	virulento

ADJS: English -pt = Spanish -pto or -nto.   75%: 10 Listed

ENGLISH	SPANISH	ENGLISH	SPANISH
abrupt	abrupto	nondescript	indescriptible•
adept	adepto	inapt	inapto
apt	apto	inept	inepto
corrupt	corrupto	prompt	pronto
exempt	exento	subscript	subscrito•

ADJS: English -est other than the superlative form = Spanish -esto or -este.   80%: 9 Listed

ENGLISH	SPANISH	ENGLISH	SPANISH
*dishonest	no honrado, deshonesto	modest	modesto
earnest	grave, serio•	northwest	del noroeste
*honest	honrado, honesto	southwest	del sudoeste
immodest	inmodesto	west	del oeste
manifest	manifiesto		

NOTE:

The English superlative adjectival form -*est* = Spanish *le* .....*más*..... or *la*........ *más* ...... as in:

The most intelligent boy	El muchacho más inteligente
The prettiest girl	La muchacha más bonita
The tallest buildings	Los edificios más altos

ADJS: English -*ist* = Spanish -*ista*.   95%: 22 Listed

Cross-Reference: N -ist ; ADJ -istic

ENGLISH	SPANISH	ENGLISH	SPANISH
alarmist	alarmista	leftist	izquierdista•
Buddhist	budista	Marxist	marxista
Calvinist	calvinista	materialist	materialista
collectivist	colectivista	Methodist	metodista
Czarist	czarista	nationalist	nacionalista
extremist	extremista	racist	racista
Fascist	fascista	rationalist	racionalista
Federalist	federalista	royalist	realista
feminist	feminista	socialist	socialista
humanist	humanista	specialist	especialista
impressionist	impresionista	surrealist	surrealista

ADJS: English -*ust* = Spanish -*usto*.   99%: 4 Listed

ENGLISH	SPANISH	ENGLISH	SPANISH
august	augusto	robust	robusto
just	justo	unjust	injusto

ADJS: English -*x* = Spanish -*xo* or -*jo*.   95%: 6 Listed

ENGLISH	SPANISH	ENGLISH	SPANISH
complex	complejo, complexo	lax	laxo
convex	convexo	orthodox	ortodoxo
duplex	dúplex•	unorthodox	no ortodoxo

NOTE: English adjectives ending in -*ow* or in -*y* other than -*ary* and -*ory* very seldom convert to Spanish according to any reliable pattern.

ADJS: English *-ary* = Spanish *-ario* or *-ar*.   85%:   100 Listed
The suffix *-ary* denotes *relating to*, *connected with* or *like*.

ENGLISH	SPANISH	ENGLISH	SPANISH
adversary	adversario	military	militar
alimentary	alimentario	missionary	misionario
ancillary	ancilario	momentary	momentáneo•
anniversary	aniversario	monetary	monetario
arbitrary	arbitrario	necessary	necesario
auxiliary	auxiliar	numerary	numerario
binary	binario	*ordinary	ordinario
capillary	capilar	papillary,-ar	papilar
cautionary	amonestador•	paramilitary	paramilitar
centenary	centenario	parliamentary	parlamentario
complementary	complementario	pecuniary	pecuniario
complimentary	elogioso•	penitentiary	penitenciario
concessionary	concesionario	pigmentary	pigmentario
contemporary	contemporáneo•	pituitary	pituitario
contrary	contrario	planetary	planetario
coronary	coronario	plenary	plenario
culinary	culinario	plenipotentiary	plenipotenciario
customary	usual, habitual•	precautionary	precautorio
dietary	dietético•	preliminary	preliminar
disciplinary	disciplinario	primary	primario
discretionary	discrecional•	proprietary	propietario
diversionary	desviador•	pulmonary	pulmonar
elementary	elemental•	reactionary	reaccionario
evolutionary	evolucionario	revolutionary	revolucionario
exclusionary	exclusionario	rotary	rotatorio
exemplary	ejemplar	rudimentary	rudimentario
expansionary	expansionista•	salivary	salival•
expeditionary	expedicionario	salutary	saludable•
*extemporary	improvisado•	sanguinary	sanguinario
extraordinary	extraordinario	*sanitary	sanitario
fiduciary	fiduciario	secondary	secundario
fragmentary	fragmentario	sedentary	sedentario
funerary	funerario	sedimentary	sedimentario
granulary	granular	solitary	solitario
hereditary	hereditario	stationary	estacionario
honorary	honorario	statuary	estatuario
illusionary	ilusorio•	subsidiary	subsidiario
imaginary	imaginario	substitutionary	substituidor•
incendiary	incendiario	summary	sumario
inflationary	inflacionario	supernumerary	supernumerario
intermediary	intermediario	supplementary	suplementario
interplanetary	interplanetario	terciary	terciario
itinerary	itinerario	temporary	temporario
involuntary	involuntario	testamentary	testamentario
judiciary	judicial•	tributary	tributario
legendary	legendario	unitary	unitario
literary	literario	unnecessary	innecesario
lunary	lunario	urinary	urinario
mammilary	mamilar	visionary	visionario
mercenary	mercenario	voluntary	voluntario

ADJS: English *-ory* = Spanish *-orio* (70%), *-or* (15%) or *-ivo* (5%).
90%: 94 Listed

The suffix *-ory* denotes *of, pertaining to, having the nature of* or *produced by*.

ENGLISH	SPANISH	ENGLISH	SPANISH
accessory	accesorio	incriminatory	incriminador
accusatory	acusatorio	inflammatory (MED)	inflamatorio
admonitory	admonitorio	inflammatory (fire)	incendiario•
advisory	avisador	inhibitory	inhibitorio
ambulatory	ambulatorio	interlocutory	interlocutorio
anticipatory	anticipador	interrogatory	interrogatorio
auditory	auditorio	introductory	introductorio
circulatory	circulatorio	investigatory	investigador
collusory	colusorio	laudatory	laudatorio
commemoratory	conmemoratorio	mandatory	obligatorio•
commendatory	comendatorio	migratory	migratorio
compensatory	compensatorio	mitigatory	mitigatorio
compulsory	compulsivo	obligatory	obligatorio
conciliatory	conciliatorio	olfactory	olfactorio
condemnatory	condenatorio	peremptory	perentorio
confirmatory	confirmatorio	perfunctory	superficial•
confiscatory	confiscatorio	persecutory	persecutorio
congratulatory	congratulatorio	possessory	posesorio
consolatory	consolatorio	precatory	suplicante•
contradictory	contradictorio	precursory	precursor
contributory	contribuidor	predatory	predatorio
corroboratory	corroborativo	prefatory	introductorio•
cursory	superficial•	premonitory	premonitorio
declamatory	declamatorio	preparatory	preparatorio
declaratory	declaratorio	preservatory	preservador
defamatory	difamatorio	probatory	probatorio
denunciatory	denunciatorio	prohibitory	prohibitorio
deprecatory	deprecatorio	promissory	promisorio
derogatory	derogatorio	provisory	provisorio
desultory	vago, inconexo•	provocatory	-ivo, provocador
dictatory	dictatorio	reconciliatory	reconciliador
dilatory	dilatorio	recriminatory	recriminatorio
discriminatory	discriminatorio	redemptory	redentor
ejaculatory	jaculatorio	reformatory	reformatorio
elusory,-ive	elusivo	regulatory	regulador
emancipatory	emancipador	respiratory	respiratorio
exclamatory	exclamatorio	responsory	responsorio
excretory	excretorio	retaliatory	vengador•
exculpatory	disculpador•	revelatory	revelado
executory	ejecutorio	revisory	revisor
exhortatory	exhortatorio	satisfactory	satisfactorio
explanatory	explicativo	savory	sabroso•
exploratory	exploratorio	sensory	sensorio
expository	expositivo	speculatory	especulador
extrasensory	extrasensorial•	statutory	estatutario
hallucinatory	alucinatorio	supervisory	supervisor
hortatory	hortatorio	transitory	transitorio
illusory	ilusorio	unsavory	desagradable•

2. ADJECTIVES CONVERTING TO SPANISH ON A ONE-ON-ONE BASIS ("PAIR CONVERSION")

There are many English adjectives not falling within any of the conversion categories but which are so similar in spelling or sound in English and Spanish that very little memorization effort is needed. Some of the most common of these adjectives are listed here.

353 Listed

ENGLISH	SPANISH	ENGLISH	SPANISH
able	hábil	carcinogenic	carcinógeno
aboriginal	aborigen	cardiac	cardíaco
above-mentioned	antes mencionado	celebate	célibe
absorbed	absorto	celebrated	célebre, famoso
abstracted	abstraído	centigrade	centígrado
absurd	absurdo	certain	cierto
acerb	acerbo	chaste	casto
addicted	adicto	chic	chic
adult	adulto	circumscript	circunscrito
affected	afectado	civil	civil
affectionate	afectuoso	clear	claro
agreeable	agradable	coastal	costero
air	aéreo	coincidental	coincidente
airy	airoso	common	común
alert	alerto	commonplace	común
alien	ajeno	compassionate	compasivo
aliquot	alícuota	composite	compuesto
amber	ambarino	compound	compuesto
ample	amplio	concave	concavo
ancient	anciano	conjoint	conjunto
another	otro	consequential	consecuento
antique	anciano, antiguo	contemporary	contemporáneo
apart	separado, aparte	content	contento
aplomb	aplomo	cooked	cocido
Arab	árabe	cossack	cosaco
assorted	surtido	costly	costoso
attentive	atento	courteous	cortés
autumn	otoñal	covered	cubierto
baritone	barítono	cowardly	cobarde
bastard	bastardo	crass	craso
benevolent	benévolo	creamy	cremoso
benign	benigno	creole	criolla
bilingual	bilingüe	crisp	crespo
*bizarre	bizarro	*crude	crudo
bland	blando	cruel	cruel
blank	en blanco	cultivated (educated)	culto
bolshevik	bolchevique	curt	corto
bourgeois	burgés	curved	curvado, curvo
*brave (courage)	bravo	delightful	deleitoso
brief (short)	corto, breve	deluxe	de lujo
brusk	brusco	demonic, demoniacal	demoniaco
*calm	tranquilo, calmado	dense	denso
*capable	capaz	devout, devoted	devoto

ENGLISH	SPANISH	ENGLISH	SPANISH
difficult	difícil	gigantic	giantesco, gigante
*dignified	digno	*grand	grandioso
*educated	instruído, educado	*graceful	gracioso
disdainful	desdeñoso	*grateful	grato
disgusting	disgustoso	gratis	gratis
disjoint,-ed	disjunto	grave	serio, grave
disloyal	desleal	greasy	grasoso
disorderly	desordenado	Greek	griego
disquite	inquieto	grippy	griposo
disrespectful	irrespetuoso	gross	grosero
divers	diversos	gummy	gomoso
doctrinaire	doctrinario	Hebrew	hebreo
doleful	triste, dolorido	hilarious	hilarante
dormant	durmiente	Hindu	hindú
double	doble	hipocritical	hipócrita
doubtful	dudoso, dudable	homicidal	homicida
east	oriental, del este	honorable	honrado
egotistical	egoista	hourly	horario
emerald	esmeraldino	humble	humilde
emeritus	emérito	idiotic	idiota
empire	imperio	illegitimate	ilegítimo
employed	empleado	illustrious	ilustre
enchanting	encantador	immune	inmune
enormous	enorme	improper	impropio
ex-cathedra	ex-cátedra	impure	impuro
excess	excesivo	indebted	endeudado
expert	experto, perito	inert	inerte
explainable	explicable	inexpert	inexperto
exposed	expuesto	infamous	infame
express	expreso	infidel	infiel
extra	extra	influential	influyente
extreme	extremo	informed	informado
extrovert	extrovertido	instant	instantáneo
false	infiel, falso	intent	atento
fierce, fiery	feroz, fiero	interim	interino
financial	financiero	intimate	íntimo
firm (fixed)	fijo, firme	introvert	introverso
flirty	coqueta, flirteo	isolated	aislado
flowery	florido	isosceles	isósceles
fossil	fósil	joined	junto
fragil, frail	frágil	just (fair)	justo
francophile	francófilo	Latin	latino
francophobe	francófobo	loyal	leal
frank (open)	cándido, franco	macabre	macabro
frantic	frenético	magnificent	magnífico
French	francés	majestic	majestuoso
fresh	fresco	malevolent	malévolo
fried	frito	maritime (sea)	marítimo
fruitful	fructuoso, fructífero	marvelous	maravilloso
frustrating	frustratorio	mediocre	mediocre
gala	gala	melancholy	triste, melancólico
genteel	gentil	mere (only)	puro, solo, mero

ENGLISH	SPANISH	ENGLISH	SPANISH
merited	merecido	profound (deep)	profundo
migrant	migratorio	prompt	puntual, pronto
minuscule	minúsculo	prone	prono
mixed	mixto	proper	correcto, propio
model	ejemplar, modelo	pulpy	pulposo
modern	moderno	*pure	puro
momentary	momentáneo	puritanical	puritano
morbid	morboso	purple	purpúreo
movable	móvil	quiet (emotion)	tranquilo, quieto
much	mucho	rank (smelly)	rancio
multiple	múltiple	rapt	rapto
mute (dumb)	silencioso, mudo	rare (scarce)	raro
myopic	miope	real	verdadero, real
Nazi	nazi	rebel	rebelde
net	neto	related	relacionado
new	moderno, nuevo	remiss	negligente, remiso
nomad	nómade	remote	remoto
nondescript	indescriptible	renegade	renegado
north	norteño, del norte	renewable	renovable
northeast	nordestal	repentant	arrepentido
northern,-erly	del norte	resentful	resentido
northwest	de noroeste	reserve	de la reserva
novel	novel	resolute	resuelto
*nude	desnudo	respectful	respetuoso
null (void)	nulo	retrograde	retrógrado
obese	obeso	revengeful	vengativo
obscene	obsceno	ribald	ribaldo
occult	oculto	rich (wealthy)	opulento, rico
ochre	ocre	risky	peligroso, arriesgado
orderly	ordenado	rocky	rocoso
other	otro	rosy	róseo, rosado
painful	penoso	routine	rutinario
pale (wane)	pálido	rubicund	rubicundo
parallel	paralelo	*rude (rough)	tosco, agreste, rudo
part	parcial	rude (impolite)	descortés, rudo
past	pasado	sacred	sacro, sagrado
pastel	pastel	saintly	santo
pasty	pastoso	salted, salty	salado, de sal
pearly	perlino	*sane	sensato, sano
perishable	perecedero	sapphire	zafirino
perplexed	perplejo	satin	satinado
phantom (-al)	fantasmal	satisfied	satisfecho
police	policial, policíaco	savage	salvaje
polished	pulido	saveable	salvable
polydactl	polidáctilo	Saxon	sajón
poor	pobre	scarce	escaso
populous	poblado	school	escolar
portable	móvil, portátil	second	segundo
post (postal)	postal	sealed	sellado
present-day	actual, presente	serene	sereno
prima facie	prima facie	short	pequeño, corto
prime	primero, primo	*simple	sencillo, mero, simple

ENGLISH	SPANISH	ENGLISH	SPANISH
sinister	siniestro	triple	triplo, triple
sober	serio, sobrio	unable	incapaz, inhábil
sole	solo	uncertain	incierto
solemn	solemne	uncivil	incivil
southeast	del sudeste	uncommon	raro, no común
southwest	del sudoeste	undecided	indeciso
sovereign	soberano	unemployed	desempleado
Soviet	soviético	unequal	desigual
sparse	esparcido	ungrateful	ingrato
spirited	espiritoso	uniform	uniforme
sport(y)	deportivo	unjust	injusto
state	del estado, estatal	unpaid	no pagado
statuesque	estatuario	unquiet	inquieto
strange	extraño	untouchable	intocable
strict	estricto	useful	útil
*suave	severo, suave	vacant	vacio
sublime	sublime	vagabond	vagabundo
subtle	sutil	vague	vago
suicidal	suicida	vain (conceit)	vanidoso
supreme	sumo, supremo	vain (futile)	fútil, vano
surplus	surplús	vast	amplio, vasto
suspect	sospechoso	vile (base)	bajo, vil
suspicious	sospechoso	vinyl	vinílico
Swiss	suizo	violet	violado
taciturn	taciturno	virgin	virgen
talented	hábil, talentoso	volunteer	voluntario
tardy	tardío, tardo	west	occidental, oeste
touchable	tocable	Yankee	yanqui
trained	entrenado	Yugoslav	yugoslavo
*tranquil	tranquilo		

3. FREQUENTLY-USED ENGLISH ADJECTIVES NOT CONVERTIBLE INTO SPANISH EXCEPT INDIRECTLY THROUGH ENGLISH SYNONYMS

The adjectives in this list are predominantly one-syllable adjectives, exceptions to converting categories and adjectives in nonconverting categories such as *-ed*, *-ing*, *-some*, *-ish*, *-le*, *-ful*, *-less* and *-y* other than *-ry*. In most cases where the English adjective has no Spanish counterpart listed in the second column, the Spanish adjective listed in the last column is given by the English-Spanish dictionary as the usual counterpart of the English adjective.

1000 Listed

ENGLISH	SPANISH NON-CONVERSION	ENGLISH SYNONYM	SPANISH CONVERSION
able	hábil	capable	capaz
above-mentioned	dicho	referred	referido
absent-minded		distracted	distraído
accomplished	acabado	realized	realizado
accountable		responsible	responsable
accurate	fiel	precise, exact	preciso, exacto
acute	agudo	severe, critical	severo, crítico
adamant	duro	obstinate	obstinado
adjoining, adjacent	vecino	contiguous	contiguo
		adjacent	adyacente
adroit	listo, diestro	able	hábil
advantageous	provechoso, ventajoso	convenient	conveniente
		beneficial	beneficioso
advisable	aconsejable	prudent	prudente
affectionate	cariñoso, afectuoso	amorous	amoroso
aforementioned	sobredicho, susodicho	referred	referido
afraid	temeroso, atemorizado	intimidated	intimidado
aged	envejecido, viejo	ancient	anciano
agreed	acordado, convenido	approved	aprobado
alien	extranjero, ajeno, extraño	different	diferente
alike	conforme, semejante, parecido	similar	similar
alive	viviente, vivo	animated, active	animado, activo
all	todo		
allowable		permissible	permisible
		admissible	admisible
		tolerable	tolerable
alluring	atrayente, tentador	attractive	atractivo
		seductive	seductor
almighty		omnipotent	omnipotente
alone	único, solo	solitary	solitario
aloof	separado	apart	apartado
amateurish	torpe	superficial	superficial
amazing	asombroso	marvelous	maravilloso
angry	enojado, enfadado	irritated	irritado
another	otro	different	diferente
		distinct	distinto
answerable		responsible	responsable

ENGLISH	SPANISH NON-CONVERSION	ENGLISH SYNONYM	SPANISH CONVERSION
anxious	inquieto, ansioso	desirous	deseoso
approachable	tratable	accessible	accesible
arguable	discutible	disputable	disputable
ascertainable	averiguable	determinable	determinable
ashamed	avergonzado		
asleep	adormecido, dormido	inactive, dormant	inactivo, durmiente
assistant	ayudante	auxiliary	auxiliar
assorted	surtido	mixed	mixto
assumed	supuesto	presumed	presunto
assured	asegurado, cierto	secure	seguro
attached	adjunto, apegado	annexed	anexo
attainable	alcanzable	realizable	realizable
attendant	*asistente	accompanying	acompañante
available	disponible	obtainable	obtenible
average(common)		ordinary	ordinario
average	mediano	medium	medio
avowed	reconocido	declared	declarado
awake	despierto	alert, conscious	alerta, consciente
aware	sensible	conscious	consciente
		informed	informado
awesome	pavoroso	imposing	imponente
awful	pésimo	terrible, atrocious	terrible, atroz
awkward	torpe	difficult	difícil
back(hind)	atrasado, de atrás	posterior, dorsal	posterior, dorsal
backward	tardo	retarded	retardado
bad(wicked, evil)	malo	infamous, vilanous	infame, villano
	malvado	vicious	vicioso
balanced	mesurado, equilibrado	symmetric	simétrico
bald	calvo		
bankrupt	quebrado	insolvent	insolvente
bare	pelado	nude	desnudo
barren	yermo	sterile	estéril
base	abyecto, bajo	vile	vil
bashful(shy)	vergonzoso	timid	tímido
beaming	brillante	radiant	radiante
bearable	soportable	sufferable	sufrible
beautiful(fair)	bello, hermoso	attractive	atractivo
believable		creditable	creíble
beloved	querido, amado	esteemed	estimado
bent	encorvado, doblado	arched, curved	arqueado, curvado
best	el(la) mejor	optimum	óptimo
betrothed		promised	prometido
better	mejor	superior	superior
bewildered	enredado	confounded	confundido
		perplexed	perlejo
biased		prejudiced	prejuiciado
		partial	parcial
big(large)	gran, grande	enormous	enorme
bigger	mayor		
bigoted	fanático	intolerant	intolerante
bitter	amargo, acre	acerb	acerbo
black	obscuro	negro	negro
blameable		culpable	culpable
		censurable	censurable

ENGLISH	SPANISH NON-CONVERSION	ENGLISH SYNONYM	SPANISH CONVERSION
blameless		innocent	inocente
blatant		flagrant	flagrante
		evident	evidente
bleak	sombrío, triste	desolate	desolado
bleeding (bloody)	sangriente		
blessed (blest)	bendito	sainted	santo
blind	ciego		
blond (fair)	rubio		
bloody	sangriento	cruel	cruel
blue		azure	azul
blunt (dull)	embotado, desafilado		
blunt (person)		rude, brusk	rudo, brusco
blurry (bleary)	borroso, nublado	indistinct	indistinto
bodily		corporal	corporal
bogus		false, spurious	falso, espurio
boisterous	ruidoso	turbulent	turbulento
bold (brazen)	atroz, atrevido	arrogant, audacious	arrogante, audaz
born	nacido	innate, natural	innato, natural
both	ambos, los dos		
bothersome	incómodo	tedious	tedioso
bound (for)		destined	destinado
boundless		unlimited, vast	ilimitado, vasto
boyish	amuchachado	puerile, juvenile	pueril, juvenil
brackish		salty, saline	salino
*brave	bravo	valiant	valiente
breakable	rompible	fragile	frágil
bright	claro	brillant	brillante
		luminous	luminoso
brisk	vivo	active	activo
brittle	quebradizo	fragile	frágil
broad (wide)	ancho	vast, general	vasto, general
brotherly		fraternal	fraternal
bulky	abultado	corpulent	corpulento
burdensome	pesado	onerous	oneroso
burning (urgent)		ardent, urgent	urgente, ardiente
busy		occupied, active	ocupado, activo
cagey		astute, evasive	astuto, evasivo
calm	calmado	tranquil	tranquilo
careful	cuidadoso	prudent	prudente
careless	descuidado	negligent	negligente
catching		contagious	contagioso
		infectious	infeccioso
ceaseless		incessant	incesante
		perpetual	perpetuo
certain	seguro, cierto	inevitable	inevitable
challenging	excitante	provocative	provocativo
changeable		variable	variable
changing		variable	variable
chargeable (suspected)		acusable	acusable
charming		enchanting	encantador
chaste	casto	continent	continente
cheap	barato	economical	económico
cheap (common)		common, vulgar	común, vulgar

317

ENGLISH	SPANISH NON-CONVERSION	ENGLISH SYNONYM	SPANISH CONVERSION
cheerful(gay,merry)	alegre	jovial	jovial
chief(head)	mayor	principal	principal
childish(-like)	aniñado	infantil,puerile	infantil,pueril
chilly	frío,fresco	frigid	frígido
choice,chosen	escogido	select	selecto
circuitous		tortuous	tortuoso
civil(polite)		gallant,courteous	galante,cortés
clean	limpio	pure	puro
clear	claro	lucid,obvious	lúcido,obvio
clever	diestro	able,ingenious	hábil,ingenioso
close(dear)	estrecho	intimate	íntimo
close(near)	cercano	proximate	próximo
closed	cerrado	concluded	concluido
cloudy	nublado	obscure	obscuro
clumsy	desmañado,torpe	crude	crudo
coarse	grosero,tosco,áspero	vulgar,rude	vulgar,rudo
cocky	presumido	arrogant	arrogante
cogent	poderoso	persuasive	persuasivo
cold	frío	frigid	frígido
colorful	pintoresco	vivid	vívido
colorless	descolorido	pale	pálido
combined	conjunto,juntos,compuesto	united	unidos
commanding	imponente	dominant	dominante
common	común	ordinary,vulgar	ordinario,vulgar
compliant		obedient,docile	obediente,dócil
concerned	ansioso	interested	interesado
*constipated	estreñido		
contemptuous	despreciativo	disdainful	desdeñoso
contrivable		imaginable	imaginable
controllable	manejable	governable	gobernable
cool		fresh	fresco
counterfeit	fingido	false,spurious	falso,espurio
countless	incontable	innumerable	innumerable
country	campestre	rustic,rural	rústico,rural
courageous	valeroso	valiant,intrepid	valiente,intépido
covert	disimulado	secret,furtive	secreto,furtivo
covetous	codicioso	ambitious	ambicioso
coy	esquivo	timid,reserved	tímido,reservado
cozy	agradable,cómodo	intimate	íntimo
cracked	agrietado	quartered	cuarteado
crafty	artificioso	able,astute	hábil,astuto
crazy	loco	absurd,demented insane	absurdo,demente insano
creditable	apreciable	estimable	estimable
crooked	torcido	curved	corvo,encorvado
crooked(bad)		dishonest fraudulent	deshonesto fraudulento
crowded	lleno,apretado		
*crude	(raw) crudo,tosco	ordinary,gross	ordinario,grosero
cunning	artero	astute,ingenious	astuto,ingenioso
curly	crespo,rizado		
cursed	maldito	abominable	abominable
cursory	sumario	superficial	superficial

ENGLISH	SPANISH NON-CONVERSION	ENGLISH SYNONYM	SPANISH CONVERSION
curt	corto	brief	breve
customary		usual,habitual	usual,habitual
cut off	retirado	isolated	aislado
daily	diario,cotidiano		
dainty		delicate,fine	delicado,fino
damned	maldito	condemned	condenado
damp(moist)	mojado	humid	húmedo
dangerous	peligroso	risky	arriesgado
dark	tenebroso	obscure	obscuro
dead	muerto	difunct	difunto
deadly	mortífero	fatal,mortal	fatal,mortal
		lethal	letal
deaf	sordo		
dear(expensive)	caro	costly	costoso
dear(loved)	querido,amado	esteemed	estimado
deceased	muerto,fallecido	difunct	difunto
deceitful	engañoso	false	falso
deep	hondo	profound	profundo
delighted	satisfecho	enchanted	encantado
delightful	encantador	precious	precioso
demure		modest,reserved	modesto,reservado
depressed	deprimido,abatido		
deserved		merited	merecido
destitute	necesitado	indigent	indigente
detached		separate	separado
devilish		diabolic	diabólico
dim(cloudy)	semioscuro,débil	indistinct	indistinto
dire		terrible	terrible
dirty (filthy)	sucio,inmundo	indecent	indecente
disappointed	desengañado	disillusioned	desilusionado
discouraged	desanimado		
diseased	morboso	infirm	enfermo
*disgraceful	vergonzoso	ignominious	ignominioso
disgruntled	malhumorado	discontent	descontento
disgusting	odioso	repugnant	repugnante
displeased	molestado	disgusted	digusto
distant(far off)	lejano		
distasteful	desagradable	repugnant	repugnante
distinct(clear)		clear,precise	claro,preciso
distraught	aturdido	perturbed	perturbado
dizzy	aturdido,mareado	vertiginous	vertiginoso
doubtful	dudoso	uncertain	incierto
doubtless	sin duda,indudable	certain	cierto
dreaded,dreadful	temido,espantoso	terrible	terrible
		horrible	horrible
dreary	triste	melancholy	melancólico
drinkable	bebible	potable	potable
drunk	borracho	inebriated	ebrio
dry(dried)	seco,paso	dehydrated	deshidratado
due (payable)	debido,pagadero		
dull(stupid)	insensato,lerdo	obtuse,stupid	obtuso,estúpido
dull(boring)	torpe	boring,insipid	abrurrido,insípido
dull(unpolished)	mate		

ENGLISH	SPANISH NON-CONVERSION	ENGLISH SYNONYM	SPANISH CONVERSION
dull(blunt)	emotado,boto,romo	w/o point	sin punta
dumb(mute)		mute,silent	mudo,silencio
dumb(stupid)	tonto	stupid	estúpido
dusty	polvoriento,polvoroso		
dying	mortecino	moribund	moribundo
eager	ansioso,deseoso	ardent,avid	ardiente,ávido
		impatient	impaciente
early	temprano	premature	prematuro
earnest	vivo	serious,grave	serio,grave
earthly	terrenal	terrestial	terrestre
		mundane	mundano
east,eastern	del este	oriental	oriental
easy		facile,simple	fácil,simple
edgy	inquieto	nervous	nervioso
edible	comestible		
educated	instruido	cultured	culto,cultivado
eerie	espectral,pavoroso	mysterious	misterioso
elated	regocijado	exalted	exaltado
else(different)	otro	different	diferente
empty	vacío	unoccupied,vacant	desocupado,vacío
endless	inacabable,sin fin	interminable	interminable
		infinite,eternal	infinito,eterno
enforceable	exigible		
engaged(marry)		promised	prometido
engaged(busy)		occupied	ocupado
enough	bastante	sufficient	suficiente
eradicable,eraseable	borrable	extirpatable	extirpable
even(level)	llano,plano	equal	igual
even(smooth)	liso,terso	uniform	uniforme
eventful		memorable	memorable
everlasting		perpetual,eternal	perpetuo,eterno
everyday	diario,corriente	common	común
evil	mal(o),nocivo,maligno	perverse	perverso
evincible		demonstrable	demostrable
exercised	intranquilo,inquieto	agitated	agitado
exhausted	cansado,agotado	prostrate	prostrado
exhaustible	agotable		
expedient	útil,conveniente	opportune	oportuno
expendable	gastable,disponible	sacrificable	sacrificable
expensive	caro	costly	costoso
experienced	hábil,experimentado	expert,versed	experto,versado
extemporary		improvised	improvisado
faint	tenue,desmayado	pale,timid	pálido,tímido
fair(just)		just,impartial	justo,imparcial
fair(weather)	despejado,bueno	clear,favorable	claro,favorable
fair(blond)	blanco,rubio		
fair (OK)		regular,adequate	regular,adecuado
faithful	fiel	loyal,constant	leal,constante
faithless	infiel,pérfido	disloyal	desleal
fancied		imaginary	imaginario
fancy	selecto	elegant,fine	elegante,fino
far(distant)	lejano	distant,remote	distante,remoto

ENGLISH	SPANISH NON-CONVERSION	ENGLISH SYNONYM	SPANISH CONVERSION
farsighted	perspicaz, previsor	prudent	prudente
fashionable	de moda	elegant	elegante
fast (quick)	veloz, pronto, vivo	rapid	rápido
fast (fixed)		fixed, firm	fijo, firme
fat (stout)	gordo, grueso	obese, corpulent	obeso, corpulento
fatherly		paternal	paternal
faultless	sin falta	perfect	perfecto
		impeccable	impecable
faulty	culpable	imperfect	imperfecto
		defective	defectuoso
fearful, afraid	temeroso, miedoso	timid, apprehensive	tímido, aprensivo
fearless	valiente	intrepid, brave	intrépido, bravo
fearsome	espantoso, temible	terrible	terrible
feeble	débil, flaco	inadequate	inadecuado
female	hembra	feminine	femenino
fickle	variable	inconstant	inconstante
fiendish	perverso, malvado	diabolic, cruel	diabólico, cruel
*fine (good)	hermoso, buen, bueno	magnificent	magnífico
first	primero	original	original
fit (able)	capaz	adequate, apt	adecuado, apto
		appropriate	apropiado
fit (sound)	sano, lozano	robust	robusto
fixed	fijo, estable	permanent	permanente
flat (level)	llano, plano		
flat (taste)	soso	insipid	insípido
flavorful		rich, savorous	rico, sabroso
flawless	sin tacha	perfect	perfecto
		impeccable	impecable
flippant	petulante	impertinent	impetinente
foggy	neblinoso, brumoso	nebulous	nebuloso
		indistinct	indistinto
following (next)	siguiente, proximo	successive	sucesivo
fond	tierno, cariñoso		
foolish	necio, tonto, bobo	imprudent, absurd	imprudente, absurdo
forbidden	vedado	prohibited	prohibido
forceful	enérgico	vigorous	vigoroso
foreign	ajeno, extranjero forastero	exotic, remote	exótico, remoto
foreseeable	previsible		
forgetful	olvidadizo	"unmemoried"	desmemoriado
forgivable		pardonable	perdonable
forgiven		pardoned	perdonado
forgotten	olvidado		
forlorn	abandonado	desolate	desolado
former	precedente, anterior	previous	previo
forward	delantero	audacious, precocious	audaz, precoz
foul (dirty)	sucio, inmundo	indecent, impure	indecente, impuro
frail	débil	fragile, delicate	frágil, delicado
free	libre	independent	independiente
free (gratis)		gratis	gratuito, gratis
fretful	inquieto	irritable	irritable
friendly	amistoso, amigable	cordial, affable	cordial, afable
frightened	asustado, espantado	terrified	aterrorizado

ENGLISH	SPANISH NON-CONVERSION	ENGLISH SYNONYM	SPANISH CONVERSION
frightening	espantoso, aterrador	alarming	alarmante
frightful	espantoso, aterrador	horrible	horrible
front	delantero	frontal	frontal
frozen	frío, helado	congealed	congelado
fruitful	fecundo	productive	productivo
		fertile	fértil
full	harto, lleno, pleno	complete	completo
full (ample)		ample, abundant	amplio, abundante
funny (comical)	divertido	comic	cómico, curioso
funny (unusual)		rare, curious	raro, curioso
furnished	amueblado		
further	nuevo	additional	adicional
gay (cheerful)	alegre, feliz	jovial, festive	jovial, festivo
*genteel	cortés	urbane, gracious	urbano, gracioso
gentle	tierno, cortés	suave, docile	suave, dócil
germane	relativo	pertinent	pertinente
		applicable	aplicable
ghastly	espantoso, horrible	pale, spectral	pálido, espectral
gifted	dotado	talented	talentoso
glad (happy)	feliz, alegre	content	contento
glass	de cristal, de vidrio		
gloomy (sad)	lúgubre, sombrío, triste	melancholy	melancólico
godly		pious, devine	pío, piadoso, divino
		devout	devoto
golden	áureo, de oro, dorado		
good (well)	buen(o)	excellent, valid	excelente, válido
gooey	pegajoso	viscous	viscoso
gorgeous	vistoso, suntuoso	magnificent	magnífico
		splendid	espléndido
grateful	agradecido		
great (famous)	gran(de)	famous	famoso
great (huge)		enormous, immense	enorme, inmenso
greedy	codicioso, avaro	voracious, avid	voráz, ávido
grievous	penoso, doloroso	lamentable	lamentable
grim (stern)	torvo	severe, somber	severo, sombrío
gross (really bad)	craso	flagrant	flagrante
gross (total)	bruto	total	total
gruesome	horrendo	horrible	horrible
gruff	áspero, ceñudo	brusk, rude	brusco, rudo
guarded	cauto	defended	defendido
		protected	protegido
guiltless		innocent	inocente
guilty	acusador	culpable	culpable
hairy	peludo, velludo	hirsute	hirsuto
hale (fit)	sano, lozano	robust	robusto
half		medium	medio
half-hearted	sin ánimo	indifferent	indiferente
handicapped	impensado	impeded	impedido
handsome	guapo, bello, hermoso		
handy	diestro, mañoso	able	hábil
haphazard	impensado	casual, fortuitous	casual, fortuito
happy	dichoso, feliz, alegre	content	contento

ENGLISH	SPANISH NON-CONVERSION	ENGLISH SYNONYM	SPANISH CONVERSION
hard(difficult)		difficult,arduous	difícil,arduo
hard(not soft)	duro	firm,solid	firme,sólido
hardy(sturdy)	resistente	robust,vigorous	robusto,vigoroso
harmless	inofensivo	innocuous,innocent	inocuo,inocente
harsh(strict)	áspero	severe,strict	severo,estricto
hasty(rash)	apresurado	precipitated	precipitado
hateful	odioso	detestable	detestable
haughty	altivo,orgulloso	arrogant,vain	arrogante,vano
hazardous	peligroso	risky	arriesgado
head(main)	mayor	principal	principal
healthy(fit)	sano,saludable	robust	robusto
heartfelt	más sentido	sincere	sincero
heartless	duro	cruel	cruel
hearty	enérgico	cordial,vigorous	cordial,vigoroso
heathen	ateo	pagan	pagano
heavenly		celestial	celeste
heavy	pesado,grueso	ponderous	ponderoso
heinous	nefando	horrible	horrible
		horrendous	horrendo
helpful	útil,provechoso	beneficial	beneficioso
helpless	inútil,desvalido débil	impotent	impotente
		incapacitated	incapacitado
high(tall)	alto	elevated	elevado
higher	más alto	superior	superior
hilly	cerril	mountainous	montañoso,montuoso
hind(behind)	atrás,trasero	posterior	posterior
hoarse	ronco		
hollow	hueco	concave	cóncavo
holy	santo	sacred	sacro,sagrado
homely(ugly)	feo,liso	repulsive	repulsivo
homesick		nostalgic	nostálgico
honest	honesto,veraz,recto	honorable	honrado
hopeful	esperanzado prometedor	optimistic confident	optimista confiado
hopeless	desesperado,sin esperanza	impossible	imposible
hot	caliente	ardent	ardiente
huge(big)	gigantesco	enormous,immense monstrous	enorme,inmenso monstruoso
humorous	chistoso,gracioso	comical	cómico
hungry	hambriento		
husky	ronco	robust	robusto
icy(frosty)	helado,frío	glacial	glacial
idle(not busy)	perezoso,ocioso	unoccupied indolent	desocupado indolente
ill(sick)	doliente	infirm	enfermo
impeachable	impugnable	censurable	censurable
impervious		impenetrable	impenetrable
impolite	grosero	discourteous	descortés
impromtu		improvised	improvisado
inacurrate		inexact incorrect	inexacto incorrecto
inadvisable	inconveniente	imprudent	imprudente

ENGLISH	SPANISH NON-CONVERSION	ENGLISH SYNONYM	SPANISH CONVERSION
inborn		innate	innato
inescapable		inevitable	inevitable
inexhaustible	inagotable	infatigable	infatigable
inexperienced	inhábil	not expert	inexperto
injurious	dañino, nocivo	prejudicial	prejudicial
inner(inside)		interior, internal	interior, interno
insured	asegurado	protected	protegido
involved	envuelto, intrincado	complicated	complicado
irate	encolerizado	furious	furioso
irksome	fastidioso, molesto	tedious	tedioso
iron	de hierro	ferrous	férreo
irrelevant	no pertinente	extraneous	extraño
		inapplicable	inaplicable
irretrievable	incobrable	unrecoverable	irrecuperable
Jewish	judio	Hewbrew	hebreo
jittery	inquieto, agitado	nervous	nervioso
joint	conjunto	united, combined	unido, combinado
jolly	alegre	jovial, festive	jovial, festivo
joyous, joyful	alegre, gozoso	jubilant	jubiloso
juicy	jugoso	succulent	suculento
jumbo(big)	gigantesco	colossal, enormous	coloso, enmorme
jumpy	aprensivo	nervous	nervioso
keen(sharp)	agudo	penetrating	penetrante
keen(eager)		anxious, avid	ansioso, ávido
key	dominante	important	importante
		principal	principal
kind	amable, bueno, bondadoso	benevolent	benévolo
known	conocido	notorious	notorio
lame	cojo, lisiado	invalid	inválido
		paralyzed	paralizado
*large(big)	gran, grande	enormous, ample	enorme, amplio
		extensive, vast	extenso, vasto
last	postero	ultimate, final	último, final
lasting		enduring, constant	duradero, constante
		permanent	permanente
late(behind time)		tardy	tarde
late(deceased)	fallecido	defunct	difunto
late(overdue)	retrasado	tardy	tardío
latest, latter	postrero	ultimate	último
laughable	risible	ridiculous	ridículo
lavish	pródigo	profuse	profuso
lawful	lícito	legal, legitimate	legal, legítimo
lawless	sin ley	illegal, illicit	ilegal, ilícito
lazy	perezoso, flojo	indolent	indolente
lean(thin)	magro, delgado, flaco		
learned	culto, sabio, letrado	erudite, lettered	erudito, letrado
least	menor	minimum	mínimo
lecherous	lujurioso	lascivious	lascivo
left	izquierdo, siniestro		
lengthy	dilatado	large, prolonged	largo, prolongado
lenient	clemente	indulgent	indulgente
less	menos		
level(flat)	plano, llano	horizontal	horizontal
liable	obligado	responsable	responsable

ENGLISH	SPANISH NON-CONVERSION	ENGLISH SYNONYM	SPANISH CONVERSION
libelous		defamatory	difamatorio
light(color)		clear	claro
light(weight)	leve,ligero,liviano		
likable	agradable,*simpático	amiable	amable
like(alike)	parecido,semejante	similar	similar
		equivalent	equivalente
likely		probable	probable
limp	laxo,flojo	flacid,relaxed	flácido,relajado
little,small	chico,pequeño,poco	short,brief	corto,breve
livable	sufrible,soportable	tolerable	tolerable
live,lively	vivo,enérgico	vivacious	vivaz
living	viviente,vivo	active	activo
loaded		charged	cargado
lone	solo,único	solitary	solitario
lonesome(lonely)	señero,solo	solitary	solitario
*long		large	largo
loose	suelto,flojo		
lost	perdido	disoriented	desorientado
loud	ruidoso,alto,fuerte	strident	estridente
lovable	amable	adorable	adorable
love(be in ..)		enamored	enamorado
lovely	bello,precioso,hermoso	enchanting	encantador
loving	amante,afectuoso,cariñoso	amorous	amoroso
low	bajo	inferior	inferior
low(vile)	bajo,abyecto	vile	vil
lowly(mean)	bajo,mezquino,humilde	modest,inferior	modesto,inferior
lucky	venturoso,dichoso	fortunate	afortunado
ludicrous		absurd	absurdo
		ridiculous	ridículo
luscious	sabroso	succulent	suculento
		delicious	delicioso
mad(crazy)	insensato,loco	insane,demented	insano,demente
mad(rabies)		rabid	rabioso
mad(angry)	enfadado	furious	furioso
main(head)	mayor	principal	principal
male	varón,macho	masculine	masculino
mandatory	forzoso	obligatory	obligatorio
maneuverable	maniobrable	manageable	manejable
manifold		multiple	múltiple
		diverse,various	diverso,vario
manly	varonil,macho	viril,noble	viril,noble
marketable	comerciable	vendible	vendible
married	casado	conjugal	conyugal
matchless	sin igual,sin par	incomparable	incomparable
mature	maduro	seasoned	sazonado
maudlin	lloroso	sentimental	sentimental
mean(low)	bajo,mezquino	miserable	miserable
mean(cruel)	maléfico,malo	cruel	cruel
meaningful		significant	significativo,-cante
meek(humble)	manso,humilde	docile	dócil
mellow	maduro,tierno	suave	suave
merciful	misericordioso	compassionate	compasivo
		clement	clemente
merciless	despiadado	cruel	cruel

325

ENGLISH	SPANISH NON-CONVERSION	ENGLISH SYNONYM	SPANISH CONVERSION
merry(cheerful)	alegre,feliz	content	contento
middle	medio	intermediate	intermedio
mighty(powerful)	poderoso,fuerte	potent,vigorous	potente,vigoroso
mild(gentle)	apacible,manso	suave,bland	suave,blando
		benign	benigno
milky	lechoso	lacteous	lácteo
mischievous	dañoso, malévolo	malicious	malicioso
missing	desaparecido,perdido	absent	ausente
mistaken	errado,equivocado	incorrect	incorrecto
		erroneous	erróneo
mixed	mezclado,mixto	varied	variado
mock	fingido	false,simulated	falso,simulado
model	de modelo	exemplary	ejemplar
moist(damp)	mojado	humid	húmedo
moldy	mohoso		
momentous	de momento	important,vital	importante,vital
monthly	mensual		
moot	discutible	debatable	debatible
more	más	additional	adicional
morning	de la mañana	matinal	matinal
most	lo más,casi todo		
motherly	materno	maternal	maternal
motionless	inmóvil,fijo	static	estático
motley	moteado	varied,diverse	variado,diverso
mournful	triste,dolorido	lamentable	lamentable
muddy	fangoso,lodoso,barroso		
muggy		humid	húmedo
murderous	asesino,devastador	violent	violento
mute	callado,mudo	silent	silencioso
naive	ingenuo	credulous,natural	crédulo,natural
naked(bare)	sin vestido	nude	desnudo
narrow	apretado,estrecho	limited	limitado
nasty	sucio,desagradable	detestable	detestable
naughty	travieso,malvado	disobedient	desobediente
near(close)	vecino,cercano	contiguous,intimate	contiguo,íntimo
nearsighted		myopic	miope
neat	arreglado,limpio	orderly	ordenado
needless	inútil	unnecessary	innecesario
needy	necesitado,menesteroso	indigent,poor	indigente,pobre
neighboring	vecino		
neighborly	amistoso	sociable	sociable
new	nuevo	recent,modern	reciente,moderno
next	siguiente,próximo	contiguous	contiguo
next to last		penultimate	penúltimo
nice	amable,agradable	decent,attractive	decente,atractivo
night	de noche	nocturne	nocturno
nimble	ligero	agile,active	ágil,activo
noiseless	sin ruido	silent	silencioso
noisy	ruidoso	clamorous	clamoroso
nonchalant	imperturbable	indifferent	indiferente
noncommittal		evasive,reserved	evasivo,reservado
north(northern)	norteño,del norte		
noteworthy		notable	notable
		conspicuous	conspicuo

ENGLISH	SPANISH NON-CONVERSION	ENGLISH SYNONYM	SPANISH CONVERSION
noticeable	sensible	perceptible	perceptible
numb	aterido,entumecido		
obnoxious	molesto,odioso	detestable	destestable
odd(strange)	singular	curious,rare	curioso,raro
odd(not even)	impar	irregular	irregular
old(elderly)	de edad,viejo	mature,ancient	maduro,anciano
old(longstanding)		antique	antiguo
old-fashioned	pasado de moda	antiquated	anticuado
only	único	sole,mere,unique	solo,mero,único
open	libre,abierto		
opposite	opuesto	contary	contrario
orderly	ordenado	methodical	metódico
		obedient	obediente
ordinary(trite)	ordinario	vulgar,common	vulgar,común
ordinary(usual)	corriente	usual,habitual	usual,habitual
		regular,normal	regular,normal
outer,outside	al aire libre	exterior,external	exterior,externo
outrageous		atrocious	atroz
outside		exterior	exterior
outspoken(open)	abierto,ingenuo	frank,candid	franco,cándido
outstanding	destacado	distinguished	distinguido
		notable	notable
over(past)		past	pasado
over	sobrante,más alto	superior	superior
		excessive	excesivo
overall		total,complete	total,completo
		general	general
overcome	vencido	subjugated	subyugado
overseas	ultramar		
overt	abierto	evident,public	evidente,público
own	propio		
painful	penoso	dolorous	doloroso
painless	indoloro		
paramount	sumo	superior,maximum	superior,máximo
part		partial	parcial
		incomplete	incompleto
passing	pasajero	transitory	transitorio
peaceful	apacible	pacific	pacífico
		serene,tranquil	sereno,tranquilo
peak	de cresta	maximum	máximo
peculiar(odd)	extraño	singular,special	singular,especial
perilous	peligroso	risky	arriesgado
petty	despreciable,mezquino	trivial	trivial
		insignificant	insignificante
phoney		false,falsified	falso,falsificado
picayune	mezquino	insignificant	insignificante
pink		rosy	rosado
pious	pío,piadoso	devout	devoto
pitiable	sensible	lamentable	lamentable
		deplorable	deplorable
pitiful	triste,lastimoso	miserable	miserable
plain(clear)		clear,reasonable	claro,razonable
plain(simple)	fácil,sencillo	simple	simple

ENGLISH	SPANISH NON-CONVERSION	ENGLISH SYNONYM	SPANISH CONVERSION
plausible	creíble	possible	posible
		reasonable	razonable
playful	travieso, juguetón	festive	festivo
pleasant	grato, agradable, gustoso	affable	afable
pleasing	grato, agradable	affable	amable
plentiful		ample, copious	amplio, copioso
		abundant	abundante
pliable (pliant)	plegable	ductile, flexible	dúctil, flexible
plump (fat)	rechoncho, gordo		
pointed	agudo, puntiagudo	obvious, evident	obvio, evidente
poisonous		venomous	venenoso
polite	culto, atento	courteous, fine	cortés, fino
poor	necesitado, pobre	indigent	indigente
powerful	poderoso, fuerte	robust, potent	robusto, potente
powerless	ineficaz	impotent, inept	impotente, inepto
praiseworthy	loable	laudable	laudable
pregnant	preñado, encinta	*embarassed	embarazada
preposterous	disparatado	absurd	absurdo
		ridiculous	ridículo
*present-day	actual	current, present	corriente, presente
		modern	moderno
pressing	apremiante	urgent	urgente
pretty	guapo, bonito, lindo, hermoso	attractive	atractivo
prevalant	generalizado	usual, frequent	usual, frecuente
preventable		avoidable	evitable
prior	precedente	previous, anterior	previo, anterior
prize	premiado	excellent	excelente
profitable	provechoso	advantageous	ventajoso
		beneficial	beneficioso
		lucrative	lucrativo
prominent		eminent, notable	eminente, notable
prompt	listo, pronto	rapid, punctual	rápido, puntual
prone	prono	prostrate	postrado
proper	apropiado	correct, exact	correcto, exacto
protracted	largo	extensive	extenso
proud	orgulloso	arrogant	arrogante
quaint	extraño	exotic, rare	exótico, raro
quarterly		trimestral	trimestral
queer (strange)	extraño	singular, rare	singular, raro
		*peculiar	peculiar
quick (fast)	veloz, pronto, vivo	rapid	rápido
quiet (silent)	quieto	silent	silencioso
		tranquil	tranquilo
quotable		citable	citable
ragged	roto, rasgado, raído	irregular	irregular
rainy	lluvioso, pluvioso	inclement	inclemente
rampant	imperioso	exuberant	exuberante
		agressive	agresivo
random	fortuito	casual, accidental	casual, accidental
rank	rancio	gross, vulgar	grosero, vulgar
rash (reckless)	temerario, atrevido	imprudent	imprudente
raw	sin cocer, *crudo		
readable		legible	legible

ENGLISH	SPANISH NON-CONVERSION	ENGLISH SYNONYM	SPANISH CONVERSION
ready-made	confeccionado, hecho		
ready	listo, dispuesto	prepared	preparado
real	*real, verdadero	authentic, genuine	auténtico, genuino
rear	trasero	posterior	posterior
reckless	precipitado, temerario	imprudent	imprudente
red	rojo	scarlet	escarlata
refined	fino	cultivated	culto
regrettable	sensible, deplorable	lamentable	lamentable
relentless		inexorable	inexorable
		implacable	implacable
relevant	a propósito	pertinent	pertinente
reliable	confiable, seguro	creditable	acreditado
reluctant	reacio, renuente	contrary	contrario
remarkable	no común	notable	notable
		extraordinary	extraordinario
remiss	descuidado	negligent	negligente
		deficient	deficiente
reputable	estimable	respectable	respetable
		honorable	honorable
required, requisite	forzoso	obligatory	obligatorio
		necessary	necesario
restful	descansado, quieto	tranquil, calm	tranquilo, calmado
restless	inquieto	not tranquil	intranquilo
resulting		emergent	emergente
		consequent	consiguiente
retrievable	recuperable	recoverable	recobrable
right (correct)	cierto, justo	correct	correcto
right (not left)	derecho, diestra		
right (angle)	recto		
ripe (mature)	en sazón	mature	maduro
rotten	podrido, putrefacto	decomposed	descompuesto
rough (uncouth)	grosero	crude	*crudo
rough (sea)		agitated	agitado
rough (to touch)	áspero		
round	redondo, rotundo	circular	circular
roundabout		tortuous	tortuoso
		indirect	indirecto
rude	rudo	discourteous	descortés
rusty	rojizo, mohoso	oxidized	oxidado
ruthless	insensible	cruel, inhuman	cruel, inhumano
sad (gloomy)	triste, sombrío	melancholy	melancólico
safe (secure)	salvo	secure, intact	seguro, intacto
sage (wise)	sabio, juicioso	prudent	prudente
said	antedicho	cited	citado
saleable	realizable	vendible	vendible
same	mismo, propio	identical, equal	idéntico, igual
same (time)		simultaneous	simultáneo
sandy	arenoso		
saucy	atrevido	impertinent	impertinente
		insolent	insolente
scant (scanty)	escaso, magro	insufficient	insuficiente
scarce	escaso	rare, limited	raro, limitado
scented		perfumed	perfumado

329

ENGLISH	SPANISH NON-CONVERSION	ENGLISH SYNONYM	SPANISH CONVERSION
scholarly	letrado	erudite	erudito
school	escolar	scholastic	escolástico
scornful	despreciativo	disdainful	desdeñoso
sea	del mar	maritime, marine	marítimo, marino
secluded	apartado, aislado	solitary	solitario
self-conscious	cohibido	timid	tímido
self-evident		manifest, patent	manifiesto, patente
set		fixed, established	fijo, establecido
selfish	interesado	egoistic	egoísta
several		various, diverse	varios, diversos
shady	umbroso, sombreado, sombroso		
shallow	poco profundo	superficial	superficial
		trivial	trivial
sham	fingido, supuesto	false	falso
shameful	vergonzoso	scandalous	escandaloso
sharp (shrewd)	agudo, sagaz	astute	astuto
sharp (tart)	picante	pungent	pungente
sharp (pointed)	afilado, agudo	pointed	puntiagudo
sheepish	manso, avergonzado	timid	tímido
sheer	puro, ligero	fine, transparent	fino, transparente
short (brief)	corto	brief	breve
shrewd	sagaz, listo	astute	astuto
shrill	agudo, chillón	penetrating	penetrante
shut	cerrado	secured	asegurado
shy (bashful)	temeroso, vergonzoso	timid	tímido
sick (ill)	doliente	infirm	enfermo
side (lateral)		lateral	lateral
silk (en)	de seda, sedoso	suave	suave
silly	tonto, bobo, necio	absurd	absurdo
		ridiculous	ridículo
silvery	plateado	argentine	argentino
sinful	pecador, pecaminoso	malevolent	malévolo
single (bachelor)	soltero	celebate	célibe
single	sencillo, único	sole, singular	solo, singular
		individual	individual
sinkable	hundible	submergible	sumergible
sizable	grande	considerable	considerable
skilled, skillful	diestro	expert, able	experto, hábil
skinny	delgado, flaco, magro		
slack	flojo	lax	laxo
slanderous	calumnioso	defamatory	difamatorio
slanting	en declive	oblique, inclined	oblicuo, inclinado
		diagonal	diagonal
sleepy	soporoso, soñoliento	lethargic	letárgico
slight (small)	chico, pequeño, menudo	diminutive	diminuto
slim (slight, slender)	flaco, delgado	svelte	esbelto
slippery	resbaloso	evasive	evasivo
slow	lento, despacio		
sluggish	ocioso, perezoso	indolent	indolente
		inactive	inactivo
sly	hábil, mañoso, diestro	astute	astuto
sly (furtive)	malicioso	furtive	furtivo

ENGLISH	SPANISH NON-CONVERSION	ENGLISH SYNONYM	SPANISH CONVERSION
small(little)	chico,pequeño,menudo	diminutive,short	diminuto,corto
smart(chic)	apuesto	elegant	elegante
smart(able)	listo,sagaz	intelligent	inteligente
		astute	astuto
smooth	liso,pulido	suave,tranquil	suave,tranquilo
snowy	nevado,nevoso		
snug(tight)	cómodo,apretado	comfortable	confortable
soft(quiet)	tierno,dulce	suave	suave
soft(texture)	suave,muelle	bland	blando
sole(only)	solo,único	exclusive	exclusivo
sore	adolorido	sensitive	sensitivo
		inflamed	inflamado
sorrowful	triste,doloroso	disconsolate	desconsolado
sorry	doloroso,triste	miserable	miserable
sound(fit)	saludable,sano	robust	robusto
sour	picado,agrio	acid,fermented	ácido,fermentado
		rancid	rancio
south(southern)	del sur,austral	meridional	meridional
spare	de reserva,de sobra	additional	adicional
		supplementary	suplementario
speechless	callado	mute,stupefied	mudo,estupefacto
speedy(fast)	veloz,pronto,vivo	rapid	rápido
spent	gastado,agotado	exhausted	exhausto
		consumed	consumido
split	cuarteado,hendido	parted,divided	partido,dividido
spoiled	pasado	putrid	podrido,pútrido
spotless	sin mancha	immaculate,pure	inmaculado,puro
spring(season)	primaveral		
square(d)	cuadrado	rectangular	rectangular
		exact	exacto
stale	pasado,duro,añejo,viejo	rancid	rancio
standard		normal,regular	normal,regular
state	del estado,estatal	public	público
stately	imponente	majestic,solemn	majestuoso,solemne
steadfast	resuelto	constant,fixed	constante,fijo
		immutable	inmutable
steady(regular)	regular	stable,constant	estable,constante
steady(firm)		firm,fixed	firme,fijo
steep	pendiente,pino	precipitous	precipitoso
stern(harsh)	duro,austero	strict,severe	estricto,severo
		rigorous	rigoroso
sticky	pegajoso	viscose	viscoso
stiff	duro,tieso	rigid,inflexible	rígido,inflexible
still(calm)	inmóvil,plácido	tranquil,quiet	tranquilo,quieto
		serene,silent	sereno,silencioso
still(motion)		immobile,fixed	inmóvil,fijo
stingy	avaro,mezquino,avariento	miserly	mísero
stolen	hurtado	robbed	robado
stone	pétreo,de piedra		
stony	lapidoso,pedregoso		
stormy	ventoso	tempestuous	tempestuoso
		turbulent	turbulento

331

ENGLISH	SPANISH NON-CONVERSION	ENGLISH SYNONYM	SPANISH CONVERSION
stout(fat)	gordo	corpulent	corpulento
stout(robust)	fuerte	robust,brave	robusto,*bravo
straight	derecho	direct	directo
straight(erect)	derecho	erect	recto,erecto
straight(forward)		direct,frank	directo,franco
		consecutive	consecutivo
		sincere,honest	sincero,honesto
strange(odd)	ajeno,extraño	curious,rare	curioso,raro
	desconocido	singular,peculiar	singular,peculiar
		excentric	excéntrico
strict	estricto	severe,rigorous	severo,rigoroso
striking	impresionante	surprising	sorprendente
stringent		severe,strict	severo,estricto
		rigorous	rigoroso
strong	fuerte, poderoso	robust,potent	robusto,potente
stubborn	terco	obstinate	obstinado
stuffy(no air)	mal ventilado	suffocating	sofocante
stuffy(proud)		pompous	pomposo
sturdy	resuelto	robust,firm	robusto,firme
stylish	de moda	elegant	elegante
successful	*exitoso,afortunado	prosperous	próspero
sudden	imprevisto,súbito,repentino	precipitous	precipitado,-toso
suitable	conveniente	appropriate	apropiado
		adequate	adecuado
		satisfactory	satisfactorio
sullen	hosco	bad humored	malhumorado
		unsociable	insociable
		taciturn	taciturno
sundry		various,diverse	varios,diversos
		miscellaneous	misceláneo
sunny	soleado		
supple	manejable	flexible	flexible
		adaptable	adaptable
sure(certain)	seguro	certain,firm	cierto,firme
surly	áspero	rude	rudo
surplus	sobrante	excess	excedente
sweet	dulce,lindo	delicious	delicioso
swift(fast)	súbito,veloz,vivo	rapid	rápido
swollen	hinchado	expanded	expandido
tactful	político,cauto	discreet,prudent	discreto,prudente
tactless	falto de tacto	indiscreet	indiscreto
tall(high,lofty)	alto	elevated	elevado
tame	manso	domesticated	domesticado
tan		toasted,bronzed	tostado,bronceado
tantamount		equivalent	equivalente
tardy	tardo,tardío,lento	dilatory	dilatorio
tasty	gustoso	savorous	sabroso
		appetizing	apetitoso
taut	tirante,tieso	tense	tenso
teachable	instruible,enseñable	educable,docile	educable,dócil
tender	tierno	bland,suave	blando,suave
terse	breve	concise,succinct	conciso,sucinto
tested	ensayado	proved	probado

ENGLISH	SPANISH NON-CONVERSION	ENGLISH SYNONYM	SPANISH CONVERSION
thankful	reconocido, agradecido	appreciative	apreciador
thick	espeso, grueso	dense	denso
thin (slender)	flaco, delgado, magro	fine	fino
thirsty	seco, sediento	arid	árido
thorough	minucioso, cabal, acabado	complete, perfect	completo, perfecto
		detailed	detallado
thoughtful (thinking)	meditabundo	pensive	pensativo
thoughtful (kind)	atento	considerate	considerado
		meditative	meditativo
thoughtless	incauto, desatento	inconsiderate	desconsiderado
		imprudent	imprudente
		negligent	negligente
thrifty	ahorrativo	frugal	frugal
		economical	económico
ticklish	cosquilloso	delicate	delicado
tidy	limpio	orderly	ordenado
tight	estrecho, apretado, ajustado	compact, dense	compacto, denso
timely		punctual, oportune	puntual, oportuno
tin	de hojalata		
tiny (little)	pequeño, chico	diminutive	diminuto
		minuscule	minúsculo
tired	rendido, cansado	fatigued	fatigado
		exhausted	exhausto
tireless	incansable	indefatigable	infatigable
tiresome	pesado, aburrido	tedious	tedioso
top	más alto	ultimate, eminent	último, eminente
tough	duro, fuerte	robust, firm	robusto, firme
touchy	quisquilloso	irritable	irritable
		delicate	delicado
traceable		attributable	atribuible
trade	de comercio	commercial	comercial
		mercantile	mercantil
trainable		educable	educable
tremendous		enormous, immense	enorme, inmenso
trim	pulcro, bonito	compact	compacto
trite	gastado	trivial	trivial
troubled	agitado	disturbed	disturbado
		preoccupied	preocupado
troublesome	pesado, penoso, gravoso	importune	importuno
true (genuine)	verdadero, fiel	authentic	auténtico
true	verdadero	certain, real	cieto, real
truthful	verídico	veracious	veraz
ugly (homely)	feo	repulsive	repulsivo
		repugnant	repugnante
unable	inhábil	incapable	incapaz
unavoidable	ineludible	inevitable	inevitable
unaware	inconsciente, imprevisto	*ignorant	ignorante de
unbearable	insoportable	intolerable	intolerable
unbelievable		incredible	increíble
unbreakable	irrompible	indestructible	indestructible
uncanny		strange	extraño
		mysterious	misterioso
unclean	inmundo, sucio	impure	impuro

333

ENGLISH	SPANISH NON-CONVERSION	ENGLISH SYNONYM	SPANISH CONVERSION
undercover	escondido	clandestine	clandestino
		secret	secreto
underdeveloped	desarrollado	primitive	primitivo
underground		subterranean	subterráneo
underground(secret)		clandestine	clandestino
		secret	secreto
understandable		comprehensible	comprensible
undressed(bare)	desnudo		
undue	indebido	inappropriate	impropio,inapropiado
		excessive	excesivo
uneasy	inquieto	not tranquil	intranquilo
unemployed	disempleado	unoccupied	desocupado
uneven	impar	unequal	desigual
		different	diferente
unfair	inicuo	unjust	injusto
unfaithful	infiel	disloyal	desleal
unfinished	inconcluso	incomplete	incompleto
unfit	incapaz,inservible	improper,inept	impropio,inepto
		incompetent	incompetente
		inadequate	inadecuado
unforgettable	inolvidable	memorable	memorable
unforgivable	indisculpable	unpardonable	imperdonable
		inexcusable	inexcusable
unfriendly	no amigable	hostile,enemy	hostil,enemigo
ungodly	malvado,impío	irreligious	irreligioso
		profane,vile	profano,vil
unhappy	infeliz,desgraciado	discontented	descontento
unhealthy	insalubre,malsano	indisposed	indispuesto
	nocivo	infirm	enfermo
unkind	poco amable,duro	cruel,rude	cruel,rudo
unknown	desconocido	incognito	incógnito
unlawful		illegal,ilicit	ilegal,ilícito
		illegitimte	ilegítimo
unlike	desemejante	dissimilar	disímil
		different,diverse	diferente,diverso
unlucky	desgraciado	unfortunate	desafortunado
unmistakable	inequívoco	obvious,evident	obvio,evidente
unpleasant	molesto	disagreeable	desagradable
unreadable		illegible	ilegible
unruly	ingobernable,indócil	turbulent	turbulento
		undisciplined	indisciplinado
unsafe	peligroso	insecure	inseguro
unseen	inadvertido	invisible	invisible
unselfish	desprendido	generous	generoso
		altruistic	altruista
unspeakable	indecible	abominable	abominable
		atrocious	atroz
unsteady	inseguro	unstable	instable
		fluctuating	fluctuante
unsuitable	inservible	improper	impropio
		inadequate	inadecuado
untiring	incansable	indefatigable	infatigable

ENGLISH	SPANISH NON-CONVERSION	ENGLISH SYNONYM	SPANISH CONVERSION
untrue		false,inexact	falso,inexacto
untrue(not loyal)	engañoso,infiel	disloyal	desleal
unwise	tonto,necio	imprudent	imprudente
unworthy	indigno	w/o merit	sin mérito
upper	más elevado	superior	superior
upright	derecho,recto	vertical	vertical
upright(good)	justo,probo	honorable	honrado
upset	enfadado,trastornado	perturbed	perturbado
useful	útil,provechoso	beneficial	beneficioso
useless	inútil,inservible	inept,in vain	inepto,vano
utmost	sumo	extreme,maximum	extremo,máximo
utter	cabal	complete,total	completo,total
		entire,absolute	entero,absoluto
vain(conceit)	vanidoso	ostentatious	ostentoso
vain (in..)	vano		
valid(in force)	vigente	valid	válido
void(null)		invalid,null	inválido,nul
void(empty)	hueco	vacant	vacio,vacante
wandering		errant,vagabond	errante,vagabundo
		nomad	nómada
wanton	insensible	perverse,cruel	perverso,cruel
warlike(martial)	guerrero	martial,bellicose	belicoso,marcial
warm	caliente	tepid	tibio
warm(emotion)		cordial,ardent	cordial,ardiente
wary	cauteloso,cuidadoso	prudent	prudente
washable	lavable		
wasteful	malgastador	prodigal	pródigo
watchful		vigilant,alert	vigilante,alerto
		attentive	atento
water	acuoso	aquatic	acuático
		hydraulic	hidráulico
waterproof		impermeable	impermeable
watery	aguado	aqueous,liquid	acuoso,líquido
wavy	ondeado	undulated	ondulado
weak(feeble)	flaco,flojo,débil	fragile,infirm	frágil,enfermizo
wealthy	adinerado	rich,opulent	rico,opulento
weary(tired)	tedioso,cansado	fatigued	fatigado
weird	sobrenatural	mysterious,rare	misterioso,raro
welcome	bienvenido	agreeable	agradable
well	bueno	adequate	adecuado
well(health)	sano	cured	curado
west(westerly)	del oeste	occidental	occidental
wet	mojado,empapado	humid	húmedo
wet(paint)		fresh	fresco
whole	todo	entire,total	entero,total
wicked	pícaro,malo,malvado	vile,perverse	vil,perverso
		iniquitous	inicuo
wide(broad)	ancho	comprehensive	comprensivo
		extensive,vast	extenso,vasto
widespread		extended	extendido
		disseminated	diseminado
wild(fierce)	fiero	ferocious	feroz

335

ENGLISH	SPANISH NON-CONVERSION	ENGLISH SYNONYM	SPANISH CONVERSION
wild(uncultured)	silvestre, agreste	savage	salvaje
willing	deseoso, listo	disposed to	dispuesto
		voluntary	voluntario
windy	ventoso	tempestuous	tempestuoso
wintry	invernizo	hibernal	invernal, hibernal
wise(sage)	sabio, sagaz	prudent	prudente
wishful	anhelante	desiring, anxious	deseoso, ansioso
witty	chistoso, agudo, gracioso	ingenious	ingenioso
wonderful		admirable	admirable
		marvelous	maravilloso
wont	habituado	accustomed	acostumbrado
wooden	de madera		
woolen	de lana		
worldly	terreno	mundane, secular	mundano, secular
		terrestial	terrestre
worldwide	mundial	global	global
worn	raído, agotado, gastado	used	usado
worried	inquieto	preoccupied	preocupado
worst	(el) peor		
worthless(useless)	sin valor	inutile	inútil
worthwhile	útil	meritorious	meritorio
worthy	apreciable, digno, merecedor	meritorious	meritorio
		estimable	estimable
wounded	herido	afflicted	afligido
woven	tejido		
wretched	infeliz, doloroso	deplorable	deplorable
		miserable	miserable
written	impreso, escrito		
wrong(mistaken)	errado	incorrect, false	incorrecto, falso
		erroneous	erróneo
wrong(unjust)	malo	unjust	injusto
yearly		annual	anual
young(youthful)	joven	juvenile	juvenil

D. ADVERBS

Just as most English adjectives can be transformed into adverbs by adding -ly, most Spanish adjectives can be transformed into adverbs by adding the ending -mente to the feminine form of the adjective.

ENGLISH ADJECTIVE	ENGLISH ADVERB	SPANISH ADJECTIVE	SPANISH ADVERB
divine	divinely	divino (-a)	divinamente
generous	generously	generoso (-a)	generosamente
possible	possibly	possible	posiblemente

Since the exceptions and spelling changes encountered in converting English adjectives to Spanish adjectives usually carry over into the corresponding Spanish adverb, it seems best to use the Spanish rather than the English adjective or adverb as the base. English adverbs formed from adjectives in categories that don't convert to Spanish adjectives usually don't convert to Spanish adverbs (i.e. childishly = puerilmente). To avoid repetition of the long lists of adjectives, just enough of the most commonly used adverbs derived from each of the converting adjective categories are listed here to demonstrate the pattern. Although most Spanish adjectives are convertible into the -mente adverbial form, the dictionary should be checked to be sure that other such adverbs not listed have been accepted. The base adjective's usual stress or written accent is retained in the adverb as if the -mente had not been added. When two or more more Spanish adverbs ending in -mente occur in a series, the -mente is omitted in all but the last adverb.

> El jefe habló lenta y claramente.

In addition to the 1,200 adverbs converting from adjective categories, the Pair Conversion list (p.353) provides another 200 adverbs converting to Spanish on a one-on-one basis, and the Synonym Conversion list (p.355) provides approximately 500 more. Almost 500 of the most used Spanish adverbs not derived from adjectives are listed separately in Appendix F (page 404), bringing the total adverbs listed to about 2,400. Some Spanish adjectives are transformed to adverbial use by means of an adverbial phrase rather than the -mente ending (i.e. immorally = de modo inmoral; indescribably = de manera indescriptible).

1. ADVERBS DERIVED FROM ADJECTIVES IN CONVERTING CATEGORIES

ADVERBS: Most adverbs ending in *-bly* from Adjectives ending in *-ble* = Spanish *-blemente*. 92 Listed

ENGLISH	SPANISH	ENGLISH	SPANISH
admirably	admirablemente	irrevocably	irrevocablemente
amiably	amablemente	irritably	de modo irritable•
appreciably	apreciablemente	justifiably	justificadamente•
audibly	audiblemente	lamentably	lamentablemente
comfortably	confortablemente	laudably	loablemente•
demonstrably	demostrablemente	measurably	mensurablemente
deplorably	deplorablemente	miserably	miserablemente
desirably	deseablemente	nobly	noblemente
doubly	doblemente	notably	notablemente
equitably	equitativamente•	noticeably	notablemente•
favorably	favorablemente	ostensibly	ostensiblemente
flexibly	flexiblemente	palpably	palpablemente
forcibly	forzamente•	passably	pasablemente
formidably	formidablemente	peaceably	pacíficamente•
honorably	honorablemente	perceptibly	perceptiblmente
horribly	horriblemente	possibly	posiblemente
impeccably	impecablemente	preferably	preferiblemente
imperceptibly	imperceptiblemente	presumably	presumiblemente
impossibly	imposiblemente	probably	probablemente
improbably	improbablemente	profitably	provechosamente•
inalterably	inalterablemente	reasonably	razonablemente
incalculably	incalculablemente	regrettably	lamentablemente•
incomparably	incomparablemente	remarkably	notablemente•
inconceivably	inconcebiblemente	reparably	reparablemente
incredibly	increíblemente	respectably	respetablemente
incurably	incurablemente	responsibly	responsablemente
indefinably	indefiniblemente	revocably	revocablemente
indelibly	indeleblemente	sensibly	sensiblemente
indispensably	indispensablemente	separably	separablemente
indisputably	indisputablemente	sociably	sociablemente
indubitably	indubitablemente	stably	establemente
inevitably	inevitablemente	susceptibly	susceptiblemente
inexcusably	inexcusablemente	tangibly	tangiblemente
inexorably	inexorablemente	terminably	terminablemente
inexplicably	inexplicablemente	terribly	terriblemente
inextricably	de modo inextricable•	tolerably	tolerablemente
inflexibly	inflexiblemente	unalterably	inalterablemente
inseparably	inseparablemente	unavoidably	inevitablemente
intolerably	intolerablemente	understandably	comprensiblemente•
invaluably	invalorablemente	unfavorably	desfavorablemente
invariably	invariablemente	unforgettably	inolvidablemente•
invincibly	invenciblemente	unjustifiably	injustificadamente•
invisibly	invisiblemente	unquestionably	incuestionablemente
irreconcilably	irreconciliablemente	unreasonably	desrazonablemente
irreparably	irreparablemente	visibly	visiblemente
irresistibly	irresistiblemente	vulnerably	vulnerablemente

ADVERBS: Most adverbs ending in -ically from adjectives ending in -ic or -ical = Spanish -icamente or sometimes -almente.

162 Listed

Cross-Reference: ADJ -ic, -ical

ENGLISH	SPANISH	ENGLISH	SPANISH
academically	académicamente	erotically	eróticamente
aesthetically	estéticamente	erratically	erráticamente
alphabetically	alfabéticamente	ethically	éticamente
analytically	analíticamente	evangelically	evangélicamente
anatomically	anatómicamente	exotically	exóticamente
angelically	angelicamente	fanatically	fanáticamente
apologetically	apologéticamente	fantastically	fantásticamente
artistically	artísticamente	genetically	genéticamente
authentically	auténticamente	geographically	geográficamente
autocratically	autocráticamente	geologically	geológicamente
automatically	automáticamente	geometrically	geométricamente
basically	básicamente	grammatically	gramaticalmente
biographically	biográficamente	graphically	gráficamente
biologically	biológicamente	hermetically	herméticamente
catastrophically	catastróficamente	heroically	heroicamente
categorically	categóricamente	hipnotically	hipnóticamente
chemically	químicamente	historically	históricamente
chronically	crónicamente	hypothetically	hipotéticamente
chronologically	cronológicamente	hysterically	de modo histérico•
classically	clásicamente	identically	idénticamente
clinically	clínicamente	ideologically	ideológicamente
comically	cómicamente	intrinsically	intrínsecamente
critically	críticamente	ironically	irónicamente
cynically	cínicamente	juridically	jurídicamente
democratically	democráticamente	lackadaisically	lánguidamente•
despotically	despóticamente	lethargically	letárgicamente
diabolically	diabólicamente	logically	lógicamente
diametrically	diametralmente	lyrically	líricamente
diplomatically	diplomáticamente	magically	mágicamente
dogmatically	dogmáticamente	majestically	majestuosamente•
domestically	domésticamente	mathematically	matemáticamente
dramatically	dramáticamente	mechanically	mecánicamente
drastically	drásticamente	melodically	melódicamente
dynamically	dinámicamente	metaphysically	metafísicamente
ecclesiastically	eclesiásticamente	methodically	metódicamente
economically	económicamente	microscopically	microscópicamente
ecstatically	extáticament	musically	musicalmente
ecumenically	ecuménicamente	mystically	místicamente
egoistically	egoístamente•	mythically	míticamente
elastically	elásticamente	nautically	náuticamente
electrically	eléctricamente	nostalgically	nostálgicamente
electronically	electrónicamente	numerically	numéricamente
elliptically	elípticamente	optically	ópticamente
emphatically	enfáticamente	optimistically	de manera optimista•
empirically	empíricamente	organically	orgánicamente
energetically	enérgicamente	pacifically	pacíficamente
enigmatically	enigmáticamente	paradoxically	paradójicamente
enthusiastically	entusiásticamente	parenthetically	de modo parentético•
equivocally	equívocamente	pathetically	patéticamente

ENGLISH	SPANISH	ENGLISH	SPANISH
patriotically	patrióticamente	scientifically	científicamente
pathologically	patológicamente	semantically	semánticamente
pedagogically	pedagógicamente	skeptically	escépticamente
periodically	periódicamente	sociologically	sociológicamente
pessimistically	con pesimismo•	socratically	socráticamente
philanthropically	filantrópicamente	spasmodically	espasmódicamente
philosophically	filosóficamente	specifically	especificamente
phonetically	fonéticamente	sporadically	esporádicamente
photographically	fotográficamente	stoically	estoicamente
physically	físicamente	strategically	estratégicamente
physiologically	fisiológicamente	surgically	quirúrgicamente•
poetically	poéticamente	symbolically	simbólicamente
politically	políticamente	symmetrically	simétricamente
practically	prácticamente	*sympathetically	simpáticamente•
pragmatically	pragmáticamente	symptomatically	sintomáticamente
prophetically	proféticamente	synthetically	sintéticamente
prosaically	prosaicamente	systematically	sistemáticamente
psychologically	psicológicamente	tactically	tácticamente
publicly	públicamente	technically	técnicamente
radically	radicalmente	technologically	tecnológicamente
realistically	de manera realista•	telegraphically	telegráficamente
reciprocally	recíprocamente	telephonically	telefónicamente
rhetorically	retóricamente	theatrically	teatralmente
rhythmically	rítmicamente	theologically	teológicamente
romantically	románticamente	theoretically	teóricamente
rustically	rústicamente	therapeutically	terapéuticamente
sadistically	sadísticamente	tragically	trágicamente
sarcastically	sarcásticamente	tropically	tropicalmente
satanically	satánicamente	typically	típicamente
satirically	satíricamente	tyrannically	tiránicamente
schematically	esquemáticamente	uneconomically	no económicamente
scholastically	escolásticamente	vertically	verticalmente

ADVERBS: Some English adverbs ending in *-edly* = Spanish *-damente* or *-tamente*.   32 Listed
Cross-Reference: Adj *-ed*

ENGLISH	SPANISH	ENGLISH	SPANISH
advisedly	avisadamente	perplexedly	perplejamente•
affectedly	afectadamente	perturbedly	perturbadamente
complicatedly	complicadamente	premeditatedly	premeditadamente
confessedly	por confesión•	presumedly	presuntamente
confusedly	confusamente•	repeatedly	repetidamente
contentedly	contentamente	reservedly	reservadamente
decidedly	decididamente	resignedly	resignadamente
depravedly	depravadamente	sacredly	sagradamente
devotedly	devotamente	unaffectedly	sin afectación•
disconcertedly	desconcertadamente	undoubtedly	indudablemente•
exaggeratedly	exageradamente	unitedly	unidamente
exaltedly	exaltadamente	unjustifiedly	injustificadamente
interestedly	interesadamente	unlimitedly	ilimitadamente
limitedly	limitadamente	unpremeditatedly	impremeditadamente
malcontentedly	malcontentamente	unreservedly	sin reserva•
markedly	marcadamente	variedly	variadamente

ADVERBS: Most English adverbs ending in *-idly* = Spanish *-idamente*.
20 Listed

Cross-Reference: ADJ - *id*

ENGLISH	SPANISH	ENGLISH	SPANISH
acidly	ácidamente	rigidly	rígidamente
avidly	ávidamente	solidly	sólidamente
candidly	cándidamente	sordidly	sórdidamente
fervidly	férvidamente	splendidly	espléndidamente
invalidly	inválidamente	squalidly	escuálidamente
languidly	lánguidamente	stupidly	estúpidamente
lucidly	lúcidamente	timidly	tímidamente
morbidly	mórbidamente	torridly	tórridamente
placidly	plácidamente	validly	válidamente
rapidly	rápidamente	vividly	vívidamente

ADVERBS: English adverbs ending in *-ilely* = Spanish *-ilmente*.
10 Listed

Cross-Reference: ADJ *-ile*

ENGLISH	SPANISH	ENGLISH	SPANISH
agilely	ágilmente	hostilely	hostilmente
docilely	dócilmente	puerilely	puerilmente
facilely	fácilmente	servilely	servilmente
fertilely	fértilmente	subtilely(subtly)	sutilmente
futilely	fútilmente	vilely	vilmente

ADVERBS: English adverbs ending in *-emely* = Spanish *-emamente*.
2 Listed

Cross-Reference ADJ *-eme*

ENGLISH	SPANISH	ENGLISH	SPANISH
extremely	extremamente	supremely	supremamente

ADVERBS: English adverbs ending in *-nely* = Spanish *-namente*.
24 Listed

Cross-Reference: ADJ: *-ane, -ene, -ine, -une*

ENGLISH	SPANISH	ENGLISH	SPANISH
arcanely	arcanamente	mundanely	mundanamente
asininely	asininamente	obscenely	obscenamente
clandestinely	clandestinamente	opportunely	oportunamente
divinely	divinamente	pristinely	prístinamente
felinely	felinamente	profanely	profanamente
finely	finamente	routinely	rutinariamente·
genuinely	genuinamente	sanely	sensatamente, sanamente
humanely	humanamente	sanguinely	sanguínament
inanely	inanemente	serenely	serenamente
inhumanely	inhumanamente	serpentinely	serpentinamente
inopportunely	inoportunamente	supinely	supinamente
insanely	locamente, insanamente	urbanely	urbanamente

ADVERBS: Some English adverbs ending in *-rely* = Spanish *-ramente*.

15 Listed

Cross-Reference: ADJ *-ere, -ure*

ENGLISH	SPANISH	ENGLISH	SPANISH
austerely	austeramente	prematurely	prematuramente
demurely	modestamente•	purely	puramente
entirely	enteramente	rarely	raramente
impurely	impuramente	securely	seguramente
insecurely	inseguramente	severely	severamente
leisurely	pausadamente•	sincerely	sinceramente
merely	meramente	surely	seguramente
obscurely	obscuramente		

ADVERBS: English adverbs ending in *-sely* = Spanish *-samente*.

Cross-Reference: ADJ *-cise, -nse, -ose, -rse*   **20 Listed**

ENGLISH	SPANISH	ENGLISH	SPANISH
abstrusely	abstrusamente	intensely	intensamente
adversely	adversamente	inversely	inversamente
concisely	concisamente	obtusely	obtusamente
conversely	recíprocamente•	obversely	obversamente
densely	densamente	perversely	perversamente
diffusely	difusamente	precisely	precisamente
diversely	diversamente	profusely	profusamente
falsely	falsamente	purposely	de prepósito•
grandiosely	grandiosamente	sparsely	escasamente•
immensely	inmensamente	tensely	tensamente

ADVERBS: English adverbs ending in *-ately* = Spanish *-adamente, -atamente* or *-iamente*.

48 Listed

Cross-Reference: ADJ *-ate*

ENGLISH	SPANISH	ENGLISH	SPANISH
accurately	exactamente•	fortunately	afortunadamente
adequately	adecuadamente	illegitimately	ilegítimamente
affectionately	afectuosamente•	immaculately	inmaculadamente
alternately	alternadamente	immediately	inmediatamente
appropriately	apropiadamente	immoderately	inmoderadamente
approximately	aproximadamente	inaccurately	inexactamente•
articulately	articuladamente	inadequately	inadecuadamente
compassionately	compasivamente•	inappropriately	impropiamente
consummately	consumadamente	inarticulately	inarticuladamente
degenerately	degeneradamente	inconsiderately	inconsideradamente
deliberately	deliberadamente	indiscriminately	indistintamente•
delicately	delicadamente	innately	de manera innata•
desolately	desoladamente	inordinately	inordenadamente
desperately	desesperadamente	intimately	íntimamente
disconsolately	desconsoladamente	intricately	intrincadamente
dispassionately	desapasionadamente	legitimately	legítimamente
effeminately	afeminadamente	moderately	moderadamente
*elaborately	detalladamente•	obstinately	obstinadamente

ENGLISH	SPANISH	ENGLISH	SPANISH
ornately	ornadamente	separately	separadamente
passionately	apasionadamente	subordinately	subordinadamente
privately	privativamente•	temperately	temperadamente
proportionately	proporcionadamente	*ultimately	últimamente
proximately	próximamente	undeliberately	indeliberadamente
sedately	sosegadamente•	unfortunately	infortunadamente

ADVERBS: English adverbs ending in *-etely* = Spanish *-etamente.*

4 Listed

Cross-Reference: ADJ *-ete*

ENGLISH	SPANISH	ENGLISH	SPANISH
completely	completamente	discretely	discretamente
concretely	concretamente	incompletely	incompletamente

ADVERBS: English adverbs ending in *-itely* = Spanish *-idament* or *-itamente.*

10 Listed

Cross-Reference: ADJ *-ite*

ENGLISH	SPANISH	ENGLISH	SPANISH
contritely	contritamente	impolitely	descortésmente•
*definitely	definativamente•	indefinitely	indefinidamente
eruditely	eruditamente	infinitely	infinitamente
exquisitely	exquisitamente	oppositely	opuestamente
finitely	finitamente	politely	cortésamente•

ADVERBS: English adverbs ending in *-otely* and *-utely* = Spanish *-otamente, -udamente* or *-utamente.*

8 Listed

Cross-Reference: ADJ *-ote, -ute*

ENGLISH	SPANISH	ENGLISH	SPANISH
remotely	remotamente	irresolutely	irresolutamente
absolutely	absolutamente	minutely	menudamente
acutely	agudamente	mutely	mudamente
astutely	astutamente	resolutely	resueltamente

ADVERBS: English adverbs ending in *-quely* = Spanish *-camente.*

6 Listed

Cross-Reference: ADJ *-que*

ENGLISH	SPANISH	ENGLISH	SPANISH
brusquely	bruscamente	opaquely	de modo opaco•
grotesquely	grotescamente	picturesquely	pintorescamente•
obliquely	oblicamente	uniquely	únicamente

ADVERBS: English adverbs ending in *-ively* = Spanish *-ivamente*.

Cross-Reference: ADJ *-ive*

136 Listed

ENGLISH	SPANISH	ENGLISH	SPANISH
abusively	abusivamente	excessively	excesivamente
actively	activamente	exclusively	exclusivamente
administratively	administrativamente	exhaustively	completamente•
affirmatively	afirmativamente	expansively	expansivamente
aggressively	agresivamente	expensively	costosamente•
allusively	alusivamente	explosively	explosivamente
alternatively	alternativamente	expressively	expresivamente
appreciatively	apreciadamente•	extensively	extensivamente
apprehensively	aprensivamente	festively	festivamente
argumentatively	argumentativamente	figuratively	figurativamente
assertively	asertivamente	furtively	furtivamente
attentively	atentamente•	imaginatively	con imaginación•
attractively	atrayentemente•	imperatively	imperativamente
attributively	atributivamente	impulsively	impulsivamente
augmentatively	aumentativamente	imputatively	imputativamente
authoritatively	autorizadamente•	inactively	inactivamente
coextensively	coextensivamente	inclusively	inclusivamente
cohesively	cohesivamente	incomprehensibly	incomprensivamente
collectively	colectivamente	inconclusively	inconclusamente•
collusively	colusoriamente•	indecisively	indecisamente•
comparatively	comparativamente	indicatively	indicativamente
comprehensively	comprensivamente	inductively	inductivamente
compulsively	compulsivamente	ineffectively	ineficazmente•
conclusively	concluyentemente•	inexpensively	baratamente•
consecutively	consecutivamente	inexpressively	inexpresivamente
conservatively	conservativamente	inoffesively	inofensivamente
constructively	constructivamente	inquisitively	inquisitivamente
convulsively	convulsivamente	insensitively	insensiblemente•
correlatively	correlativamente	instinctively	instintivamente
corroboratively	corroborativamente	intensively	intensivamente
corrosively	corrosivamente	introspectively	introspectivamente
creatively	creadoramente•	intuitively	intuitivamente
cumulatively	acumulativamente	lucratively	lucrativamente
deceptively	engañosamente•	meditatively	meditativamente
decisively	decisivamente	negatively	negativamente
defensively	defensivamente	nutritively	nutritivamente
definitively	definitivamente	objectively	objetivamente
deliberatively	deliberativamente	obstructively	obstructivamente
demonstratively	demostrativamente	offensively	ofensivamente
derisively	irrisoriamente•	operatively	operativamente
descriptively	descriptivamente	oppressively	opresivamente
destructively	destructivamente	passively	pasivamente
determinatively	determinantemente•	pensively	pensativamente
diffusively	difusamente•	perceptively	perceptivamente
digressively	digresivamente	permissively	permisivamente
disjunctively	disyuntivamente	persuasively	persuasivamente
distinctively	distintamente•	positively	positivamente
divisively	divisivamente	possessively	posesivamente
effectively	efectivamente	preceptively	preceptivamente
effusively	efusivamente	presumptively	presuntivamente
evasively	evasivamente	preventively	preventivamente

ENGLISH	SPANISH	ENGLISH	SPANISH
primitively	primitivamente	restrictively	restrictivamente
productively	productivamente	retroactively	retroactivamente
progressively	progresivamente	retrospectively	retrospectivamente
provocatively	provocativamente	selectively	selectivamente
qualitatively	cualitativamente	sensitively	sensiblemente•
quantitatively	cuantitativamente	speculatively	especulativamente
reactively	reactivamente	subjectively	subjetivamente
receptively	receptivamente	substantively	substantivamente
recreatively	recreativamente	successively	sucesivamente
reflexively	reflexivamente	suggestively	sugestivamente
regressively	regresivamente	superlatively	superlativamente
relatively	relativamente	suppositively	supositivamente
remuneratively	remunerativamente	tentatively	tentativamente
repressively	represivamente	transitively	transitivamente
repulsively	repulsivamente	unobtrusively	discretamente•
respectively	respectivamente	unproductively	improductivamente
responsively	responsivamente	vindictively	vindicativamente

ADVERBS: English adverbs ending in *-rily* (from *-ary* and *-ory* adjectives = Spanish *-riamente*. 52 Listed

Cross-Reference: ADJ *-ary, -ory*

ENGLISH	SPANISH	ENGLISH	SPANISH
adversarily	adversariamente	perfunctorily	perfunctoriamente
arbitrarily	arbitrariamente	precautionarily	precautoriamente•
complementarily	complementariamente	preliminarily	preliminariamente
contradictorily	contradictoriamente	preparatorily	preparatoriamente
contrarily	contrariamente	primarily	primariamente
customarily	habitualmente•	promissorily	promisoriamente
dilatorily	dilatoriamente	proprietarily	propietariamente
disciplinarily	disciplinariamente	reactionarily	reaccionariamente
elementarily	elementalmente•	rudimentarily	rudimentariamente
exclamatorily	exclamatoriamente	sanguinarily	sanguinariamente
extraordinarily	extraordinariamente	sanitarily	sanitariamente
fragmentarily	fragmentariamente	satisfactorily	satisfactoriamente
honorarily	honoríficamente•	secondarily	secundariamente
imaginarily	imaginariamente	sedentarily	sedentariamente
involuntarily	involuntariamente	solidarily	solidariamente
legendary	legendariamente	solitarily	solitariamente
literarily	literariamente	stationarily	estacionariamente
mercenarily	mercenariamente	statutorily	estatutariamente
militarily	militarmente•	subsidiarily	subsidiariamente
momentarily	monentáneamente•	summarily	sumariamente
necessarily	necesariamente	supplementarily	suplementariamente
obligatorily	obligatoriamente	temporarily	temporalamente•
ordinarily	ordinariamente	transitorily	tansitoriamente
parlamentarily	parlamentariamente	unitarily	unitariamente
pecuniarily	pecuniariamente	unnecessarily	innecesariamente
peremptorily	perentoriamente	voluntarily	voluntariamente

ADVERBS: English adverbs ending in *-ally* from *--al* adjectives = Spanish *-a(l)mente*.   200 Listed

Cross-References: ADJ *-al*

ENGLISH	SPANISH	ENGLISH	SPANISH
abnormally	anormalmente	especially	especialmente
abysmally	abismalmente	essentially	esencialmente
accidentally	accidentalmente	eternally	eternamente
*actually	en efecto, actualmente	*eventually	eventualmente
additionally	adicionalmente	exceptionally	excepcionalmente
adverbially	adverbialmente	experimentally	experimentalmente
amorally	amoralmente	exponentially	exponencialmente
annually	anualmente	externally	externamente
artificially	artificialmente	facially	facialmente
asexually	asexualmente	fatally	fatalmente
biennially	bienalmente	federally	federalmente
bilaterally	bilateralmente	finally	finalmente
brutally	brutalmente	financially	financieramente•
capitally	capitalmente	formally	formalmente
carnally	carnalmente	fraternally	fraternalmente
casually	casualmente	frugally	frugalmente
celestially	celestialmente	functionally	funcionalmente
centrally	centralmente	fundamentally	fundamentalmente
ceremonially	ceremonialmente	generally	generalmente
circumstantially	circunstancialmente	genially	genialmente
coincidentally	coincidentalmente	governmentally	gubernativamente•
collaterally	colateralmente	gradually	gradualmente
commercially	comercialmente	gutturally	guturalmente
conceptually	conceptualmente	habitually	habitualmente
conditionally	condicionalmente	horizontally	horizontalmente
confidentially	confidencialmente	ideally	idealmente
conjecturally	conjeturalmente	illegally	ilegalmente
constitutionally	constitucionalmente	immaterially	inmaterialmente
continually	continuamente	immorally	inmoralmente
contractually	contractualmente	immortally	inmortalmente
conventionally	convencionalmente	impartially	imparcialmente
cordially	cordialmente	imperially	imperialmente
correctionally	correccionalmente	impersonally	impersonalmente
criminally	criminalmente	incidentally	incidentalmente
crucially	críticamente•	individually	individualmente
cruelly	cruelmente	industrially	industrialmente
culturally	culturalmente	infinitesimally	infinitesimalmente
denominationally	sectariamente•	informally	informalmente
diagonally	diagonalmente	initially	originalmente•
dictatorially	dictatorialmente	institutionally	institucionalmente
differentially	diferencialmente	instrumentally	instrumentalmente
discretionally	discrecionalmente	integrally	integralmente
disloyally	deslealmente	intellectually	intelectualmente
doctrinally	doctrinalmente	intentionally	intencionalmente
editorially	editorialmente	internally	internamente
effectually	efectivamente•	internationally	internacionalmente
emotionally	emocionalmente	irrationally	irracionalmente
equally	igualmente	jovially	jovialmente

ENGLISH	SPANISH	ENGLISH	SPANISH
judicially	judicialmente	provisionally	provisionalmente
laterally	lateralmente	prudentially	prudencialmente
latitudinally	latitudinalmente	punctually	puntualmente
legally	legalmente	racially	racialmente
liberally	liberalmente	radially	radialmente
literally	literalmente	rationally	racionalmente
longitudinally	longitudinalmente	really	realmente
loyally	lealmente	regally	regiamente•
manually	manualmente	regionally	regionalmente
marginally	marginalmente	ritually	ritualmente
materially	materialmente	royally	regiamente•
maternally	maternalmente	rurally	ruralmente
matrimonially	matrimonialmente	seasonally	en cada estación•
menially	servilmente•	sensationally	sensacionalmente
mentally	mentalmente	sensually	sensualmente
ministerially	ministerialmente	sentimentally	sentimentalmente
monumentally	monumentalmente	severally	separadamente•
morally	moralmente	sexually	sexualmente
mortally	mortalmente	socially	socialmente
municipally	municipalmente	specially	especialmente
mutually	mutualmente	spiritually	espiritualmente
nationally	nacionalmente	structurally	estructuralmente
naturally	naturalmente	substantially	substancialmente
neutrally	neutralmente	superficially	superficialmente
nocturnally	nocturnamente	supernaturally	sobrenaturalmente
nominally	nominalmente	tangentially	tangencialmente
normally	normalmente	temporally	temporalmente
notionally	nocionalmente	terminally	terminalmente
occasionally	ocasionalmente	territorially	territorialmente
octagonally	octagonalmente	textually	textualmente
officially	oficialmente	totally	totalmente
optimally	óptimamente	traditionally	tradicionalmente
orally	oralmente	trivially	trivialmente
originally	originalmente	unconditionally	incondicionalmente
ornamentally	ornamentalmente	unequally	desigualmente
partially	parcialmente	unequivocally	claramente•
paternally	paternalmente	unilaterally	unilateralmente
penally	penalmente	unintentionally	sin intención•
perennially	perennemente•	universally	universalmente
peripherally	periféricamente•	unmorally	amoralmente
perpetually	perpetuamente	unnaturally	anormalmente
personally	personalmente	unofficially	extraoficialmente
phenomenally	fenomenalmente	unusually	excepcionalmente•
plurally	pluralmente	usually	usualmente
potentially	potencialmente	venally	venalmente
preferentially	preferentemente	verbally	verbalmente
prejudicially	perjudicialmente	virtually	virtualmente
principally	principalmente	viscerally	visceralmente
professionally	profesionalmente	visually	visualmente
proportionally	proporcionalmente	vitally	vitalmente
proverbially	proverbialmente	vocally	vocalmente
providentially	providencialmente	vocationally	vocacionalmente

ADVERBS: English adverbs ending in *-arly* from *-ar* adjectives
 = Spanish *-armente*. **16 Listed**

Cross-Reference: ADJ *-ar*

ENGLISH	SPANISH	ENGLISH	SPANISH
angularly	angularmente	peculiarly	peculiarmente
circularly	circularmente	perpendicularly	perpendicularmente
clearly	claramente•	popularly	popularmente
familiarly	familiarmente	regularly	regularmente
insularly	insularmente	similarly	similarmente
irregularly	irregularmente	singularly	singularmente
molecularly	molecularmente	spectacularly	espectacularmente
particularly	particularmente	vulgarly	vulgarmente

ADVERBS: English adverbs ending in *-orly* from *-or* adjectives =
 Spanish *-ormente*. **4 Listed**

Cross-Reference: ADJ *-ory*

ENGLISH	SPANISH	ENGLISH	SPANISH
anteriorly	anteriormente	superiorly	superiormente
exteriorly	exteriormente	ulteriorly	ulteriormente

ADVERBS: English adverbs ending in *-aciously* and *-ociously* = Spanish
 -azmente and *-ozmente* respectively. **18 Listed**

Cross-Reference: ADJ *-acious, -ocious*

ENGLISH	SPANISH	ENGLISH	SPANISH
atrociously	atrozmente	pertinaciously	pertinazmente
audaciously	audazmente	precociously	precozmente
capaciously	capazmente	pugnaciously	pugnazmente
contumaciously	contumazmente	rapaciously	rapazmente
efficaciously	eficazmente	sagaciously	sagazmente
fallaciously	falazmente	spaciously	espaciosamente•
ferociously	ferozmente	tenaciously	tenazmente
graciously	amablemente•	vivaciously	vivazmente
loquaciously	locuazmente	voraciously	vorazmente

ADVERBS: Most English adverbs ending in *-ously* other than *-aciously* and *-ociously* = Spanish *-(os)amente* or *-emente*. 202 Listed

Cross-Reference: ADJ *-ous*

ENGLISH	SPANISH	ENGLISH	SPANISH
abstemiously	abstemiamente	extemporaneously	extemporáneamente
advantageously	ventajosamente•	extraneously	extrañamente
ambiguously	ambiguamente	fabulously	fabulosamente
ambitiously	ambiciosamente	facetiously	chistosamente•
amorously	amorosamente	famously	famosamente
anomalously	anómalamente	fastidiously	fastidiosamente
anonymously	anónimamente	felicitously	felizamente
anxiously	ansiosamente	fictitiously	ficticiamente
arduously	arduamente	fortuitously	fortuitamente
assiduously	asiduamente	frivolously	frívolamente
auspiciously	auspiciosamente	furiously	furiosamente
autonomously	autónomamente	generously	generosamente
avariciously	avariciosamente	gloriously	gloriosamente
barbarously	bárbaramente	gorgeously	magníficamente•
calamitously	calamitosamente	gratuitously	gratuitamente
callously	insensiblemente•	gregariously	gregariamente
calumniously	calumniosamente	harmoniously	armoniosamente
capriciously	caprichosamente	hideously	horriblemente•
captiously	capciosamente	hilariously	chistosamente•
cautiously	cautamente	homogeneously	homogéneamente
ceremoniously	ceremoniosamente	horrendously	horrendamente
congruously	congruamente	humorously	humorísticamente•
conscientiously	conscienzudamente•	ignominiously	ignominiosamente
consciously	conscientemente•	imperiously	imperiosamente
conspicuously	conspicuamente	imperviously	inpenetrablemente•
contagiously	contagiosamente	impetuously	impetuosamente
contemptuously	desdeñosamente•	incestuously	incestuosamente
contentiously	contenciosamente	incongruously	incongruamente
contiguously	contiguamente	inconspicuously	discretamente•
continuously	continuamente	incredulously	incrédulamente
copiously	copiosamente	indecorously	indecorosamente
courageously	valerosamente•	industriously	industriosamente
courteously	cortésmente	infamously	infamemente
covetously	codiciosamente•	ingeniously	ingeniosamente
curiously	curiosamente	ingenuously	ingenuamente
dangerously	peligrosamente•	injuriously	injuriosamente
decorously	decorosamente	innocuously	inocuamente
deliciously	deliciosamente	insidiously	insidiosamente
deliriously	delirantemente•	instantaneously	instantáneamente
dexterously	diestramente•	irreligiously	irreligiosamente
disastrously	desastrosamente	jealously	celosamente
discourteously	descortésmente•	judiciously	juiciosamente
dubiously	dudosamente	laboriously	laboriosamente
egregiously	egregiamente	lasciviously	lascivamente
enormously	enormement	licentiously	licenciosamente
enviously	envidiosamente	ludicrously	ridículamente•
erroneously	erróneamente	luxuriously	lujosamente•
expeditiously	expeditamente	magnanimously	magnánimamente

ENGLISH	SPANISH	ENGLISH	SPANISH
maliciously	maliciosamente	sensuously	sensualmente•
marvelously	maravillosamente	seriously	seriamente
mellifluously	melifluamente	simultaneously	simultáneamente
melodiously	melodiosamente	sinuously	sinuosamente
meritoriously	meritoriamente	solicitously	solícitamente
meticulously	meticulosamente	sonorously	sonoramente
miraculously	miraculosamente	speciously	especiosamente
mischievously	maliciosamente•	spontaneously	espontáneamente
monotonously	monótonamente	strenuously	vigorosamente•
monstrously	monstruosamente	studiously	estudiosamente
mysteriously	misteriosamente	stupendously	estupendemente
nebulously	nebulosamente	subconsciously	subconscientemente
nefariously	nefariamente	sumptuously	suntuosamente
nervously	nerviosamente	superfluously	superfluamente
notoriously	notoriamente	superstitiously	supersticiosamente
obsequiously	obsequiosamente	surreptitiously	subrepticiamente
obviously	obviamente	suspiciously	sospechosamente
odiously	odiosamente	synonymously	sinónimamente
officiously	oficiosamente	tediously	tediosamente
ominously	ominosamente	temerariously	temerariamente
onerously	onerosamente	tempestuously	tempestuosamente
ostentatiously	ostentosamente•	tenuously	tenuemente
parsimoniously	parsimoniosamente	tortuously	tortuosamente
perilously	peligrosamente•	traitorously	traidoramente
perniciously	perniciosamente	treacherously	traidoramente•
picturesquely	pintorescamente	tremendously	tremendamente
piously	piadosamente	tremulously	trémulamente
pompously	pomposamente	tumultuously	tumultuosamente
ponderously	ponderosamente	tyrannously	tiranizadamente•
portentously	portentosamente	ubiquitously	ubicuamente
precariously	precariamente	unambigiously	no ambiguamente
preciously	preciosamente	unanimously	unánimemente
precipitously	precipitosamente	unceremoniously	inceremoniosamente
presumptuously	presuntuosamente	unconsciously	inconscientemente•
pretentiously	pretenciosamente	unctuously	untuosamente
previously	previamente	unscrupulously	inescrupulosamente
prodigiously	prodigiosamente	uproariously	ruidosamente•
promiscuously	promiscuamente	usuriously	usurariamente
propitiously	propiciamente	vangloriously	vanagloriosamente
prosperously	prósperamente	variously	variamente
querulously	quejumbrosamente•	venomously	venenosamente
rancorously	rencorosamente	vicariously	de vicario•
raucously	roncamente*	viciously	viciosamente
rebelliously	rebeldemente*	victoriously	victoriosamente
religiously	religiosamente	vigorously	vigorosamente
ridiculously	ridiculamente	villainously	villanamente
righteously	rectamente•	virtuously	virtuosamente
rigorously	rigurosamente	vituperously	vituperosamente
ruinously	ruinosamente	vociferously	con clamor•
sacrilegiously	sacrílegamente	voluminously	voluminosamente
scandalously	escandalosamente	voluptuously	voluptuosamente
scrupulously	escrupulosamente	wondrously	maravillosamente•
seditiously	sediciosamente	zealously	celosamente

ADVERBS: English adverbs ending in *-ctly* = Spanish *-ctamente*.
(The *-c* of the *-nctly* ending is usually dropped.)
                                                                 16 Listed
             Cross-Reference: ADJS *-ct*

ENGLISH	SPANISH	ENGLISH	SPANISH
abjectly	abyectamente	imperfectly	imperfectamente
abstractly	abstractivamente•	incorrectly	incorrectamente
circumspectly	circunspectamente	indirectly	indirectamente
correctly	correctamente	indistinctly	indistintamente
directly	directamente	inexactly	inexactamente
distinctly	distintamente	perfectly	perfectamente
erectly	rectamente•	strictly	estrictamente
exactly	exactamente	succinctly	sucintamente

ADVERBS: English adverbs ending in *-etly* = Spanish *-etamente*.
                                                                 5 Listed
             Cross-Reference: ADJS *-et*

ENGLISH	SPANISH	ENGLISH	SPANISH
discreetly	discretamente	secretly	secretamente
indiscreetly	indiscretamente	unquietly	inquietamente
quietly	tranquilamente, quietamente		

ADVERBS: English adverbs ending in *-itly* = Spanish *-itamente*.
                                                                 6 Listed
             Cross-Reference: ADJS *-it*

ENGLISH	SPANISH	ENGLISH	SPANISH
decrepitly	decrépitamente	illicitly	ilícitamente
explicitly	explícitamente	implicitly	implícitamente
exquisitly	exquisitamente	tacitly	tácitamente

ADVERBS: English adverbs ending in *-ntly* = Spanish *-ntemente*.
                                                                 112 Listed
             Cross-Reference: ADJS *-ant* , *-ent*

ENGLISH	SPANISH	ENGLISH	SPANISH
abundantly	abundantemente	competently	competentemente
adamantly	firmemente•	complacently	complacientemente
affluently	afluentemente	concurrently	concurrentemente
apparently	aparentemente	confidently	confidentemente
ardently	ardientemente	consequently	consecuentemente
arrogantly	arrogantemente	consistently	consistentemente
belligerently	beligerantemente	constantly	constantemente
brilliantly	brillantemente	contingently	contingentemente
cogently	persuasivamente•	conveniently	convenientemente
coherently	coherentemente	currently	corrientemente
coincidently	coincidentalmente•	decently	decentemente

ENGLISH	SPANISH	ENGLISH	SPANISH
deficiently	deficientemente	insistently	insistentemente
dependently	dependientemente	insolently	insolentemente
differently	diferentemente	instantly	instantáneamente•
diligently	diligentemente	insufficiently	insuficientemente
disobediently	desobedientemente	intelligently	inteligentemente
distantly	distantemente	intermittently	intermitentemente
divergently	divergentemente	intolerantly	intolerantemente
dominantly	dominantemente	irreverently	irreverentemente
efficiently	eficientemente	leniently	indulgentemente•
elegantly	elegantemente	magnificently	magníficamente•
eloquently	elocuentemente	malignantly	malignamente•
eminently	eminentemente	negligently	negligentemente
evidently	evidentemente	obediently	obedientemente
excellently	excelentemente	patently	patentemente
exorbitantly	exorbitantemente	patiently	pacientemente
extravagantly	extravagantemente	permanently	permanentemente
fervently	fervientemente	persistently	peristentemente
fluently	corrientemente•	pertinently	pertinentemente
fraudulently	fraudulentemente	petulantly	petulantemente
frequently	frecuentemente	pleasantly	agradablemente•
gallantly	galantemente	predominantly	predominantemente
hesitantly	vacilantemente•	preeminently	preeminentemente
ignorantly	ignorantemente	presently	presentemente
impatiently	impacientemente	prominently	prominentemente
impertinently	impertinentemente	providently	próvidamente•
importantly	importantemente	prudently	prudentemente
impotently	impotentemente	radiantly	radiantemente
imprudently	imprudentemente	recently	recientemente
impudently	impudentemente	redundantly	redundantemente
inadvertently	inadvertidamente•	relevantly	pertinentemente•
incessantly	incesantemente	reverently	reverentemente
incidently	incidentemente	significantly	significativamente•
incoherently	incoherentemente	silently	silenciosamente•
incompetently	incompetentemente	subsequently	subsiguientemente
incongruently	incongruentemente	subserviently	servilmente•
inconveniently	inconvenientemente	sufficiently	suficientemente
indecently	indecentemente	transparently	transparentemente
independently	independentemente	triumphantly	triunfantemente
indifferently	indiferentemente	turbulently	turbulentamente
indulgently	indulgentemente	unpleasantly	desagradablemente•
inefficiently	ineficazmente•	urgently	urgentemente
infrequently	infrecuentemente	valiantly	valientemente
inherently	inherentemente	vehemently	vehementemente
innocently	inocentemente	violently	violentemente
insignificantly	insignificantemente	virulently	virulentemente

ADVERBS: **English adverbs ending in *-ptly* = Spanish *-ptamente*.**

6 Listed

Cross-Reference: ADJS *-pt*

ENGLISH	SPANISH	ENGLISH	SPANISH
abruptly	abruptamente	corruptly	corruptamente
adeptly	adeptament	ineptly	ineptamente
aptly	aptamente	promptly	prontamente

2. ADVERBS CONVERTING NOT BY ADJECTIVAL CATEGORY BUT ON A ONE-ON-ONE BASIS ("PAIR CONVERSIONS")

186 Listed

ENGLISH	SPANISH	ENGLISH	SPANISH
ably	hábilmente	depressingly	depresivamente
absurdly	absurdamente	despairingly	desesperadamente
accusingly	acusativamente	devotedly	devotamente
admiringly	admirativamente	devouringly	devoradamente
adoringly	con adoración	devoutly	devotamente
affectedly	afectadamente	difficultly	difícilmente
affectionately	afectuosamente	disapprovingly	con desaprobación
aggravatingly	agravantemente	disconcertedly	desconcertadamente
agonizingly	agonizadamente	disdainfully	desdeñosamente
agreeably	agradablemente	disrespectfully	irrespetuosamente
airily	airosamente	divertingly	divertidamente
alarmingly	alarmantamente	doubtfully	dudosamente
alertly	alertamente	doubtingly	dudosamente
amply	ampliamente	embarassingly	embarazosamente
approvingly	con aprobación	enchantingly	encantadoramente
aptly	aptamente	entirely	enteramente
augustly	agustamente	equitably	equitativamente
benignly	benignamente	exceedingly	excesivamente
bravely	bravamente	expertly	expertamente
briefly	brevemente	expressly	expresamente
bruskly	bruscamente	falsely	falsamente
calmly	calmadamente	fiery	fieramente
capably	capazmente	finely	finamente
certainly	por cierto, ciertamente	firmly	firmemente
charitably	caritativamente	flowery	floridamente
chastely	castamente	fragilely	frágilmente
circumspectly	circunspectamente	frankly	francamente
civily	civilmente	freshly	frescamente
clearly	claramente	fruitfully	fructuosamente
commonly	comúnmente	genteelly	gentilmente
complexly	complexamente	gracefully	graciosamente
condescendingly	condescendientemente	grandly	grandiosamente
confusingly	confusamente	gratefully	agradecidamente
continuingly	continuamente	gravely	gravemente
convexly	convexamente	greasily	grasosamente
convincingly	convincentemente	grossly	groseramente
correspondingly	correspondientemente	humanly	humanamente
courteously	cortézmente	humbly	humildemente
courtly	cortésmente	immodestly	inmodestamente
cowardly	cobardemente	imploringly	implorantemente
crassly	crasamente	improperly	impropiamente
crisply	crispamente	indulgingly	indulgemente
crudely	crudamente	inertly	inertamente
cruelly	cruelmente	inexpertly	inexpertamente
curtly	cortamente	inhumanly	inhumanamente
daily	diariamente	inquiringly	inquisitivamente
decidedly	decidamente	interestingly	interesantemente
delightfully	deleitosamente	inopportunely	inoportunamente
densly	densamente	justly	justamente

353

ENGLISH	SPANISH	ENGLISH	SPANISH
manifestly	manifiestamente	sacredly	sagradamente
menacingly	amenazadamente	satisfyingly	satisfactoriamente
merely	meramente	savagely	salvajemente
minimally	como mínimo	secondly	segundamente
minisculely	miniscúlamente	serenely	serenamente
modernly	modernamente	shortly	cortamente
modestly	modestamente	simply	simplemente
morbidly	mórbidamente	singly	singularmente
mundanely	mundanamente	sinisterly	siniestramente
mutely	mudamente	soberly	sobriamente
newly	nuevamente	solely	solamente
noteworthily	notablemente	solemnly	solemnemente
obscenely	obscenamente	sovereignly	soberanamente
obtusely	obtusamente	spiritedly	espiritosamente
opportunely	oportunamente	sportingly	deportivamente
orderly	ordenadamente	strangely	extrañamente
painfully	penosamente	strictly	estrictamente
partly	parcialmente	suavely	suavemente
perplexedly	perplejamente	sublimely	sublimemente
perseveringly	perseverantemente	subtly	sutilmente
poorly	pobremente	superhumanly	sobrehumanamente
precisely	precisamente	supplicatingly	suplicantemente
presumedly	presuntamente	surprisingly	sorprendentemente
profanely	profanamente	tardily	tardíamente
profoundly	profundamente	temptingly	tentadoramente
profusely	profusamente	timely	a tiempo
promptly	prontamente	tranquilly	tranquilamente
properly	propiamente	triply	triplemente
protectingly	protectoramente	unceasingly	incesantemente
provokingly	provocativamente	uncertainly	inciertamente
purely	puramente	unfruitfully	infructuosamente
rarely	raramente	ungracefully	sin gracia
*really	realmente	ungratefully	ingratamente
refreshingly	refrescantemente	uniformly	uniformemente
remotely	remotamente	uniquely	únicamente
reproachfully	con reproche	unjustly	injustamente
resentfully	resentidamente	urbanely	urbanamente
respectfully	respetuosamente	vacillatingly	vacilantemente
revengefully	vengativamente	vaguely	vagamente
richly	ricamente	vainly	inútilmente, vanamente
robustly	robustamente	varyingly	variamente
royally	*realmente	vastly	vastamente
rudely	rudamente	vilely	vilmente

3. FREQUENTLY-USED ENGLISH ADVERBS FORMED FROM ADJECTIVES NOT CONVERTIBLE INTO SPANISH EXCEPT THROUGH ENGLISH SYNONYMS

500 Listed

Cross-Reference: ADJS -Synonym Conversions

ENGLISH	SPANISH NON-CONVERSION	ENGLISH SYNONYM	SPANISH CONVERSION
accordingly	por consiguiente	in conformity	en conformidad
accurately	con precisión	exactly	exactamente
		precisely	precisamente
actually	verdaderamente	*really	realmente
adamantly		obstinately	obstinadamente
adroitly	diestramente	ably	hábilmente
aimlessly		w/o objective	sin objeto
amazingly	asombrosamente		
amusingly	divertidamente	graciously	graciosamente
angrily	con ira, con cólera	furiously	furiosamente
annoyingly	incómodamente	molestingly	molestamente
approvingly		with approval	con aprobación
artfully	con artificio	ingeniously	ingeniosamente
		astutely	astutamente
astonishingly	asombrosamente		
awfully(very)	muy	terribly	terriblemente
barely	apenas, escasamente	merely	meramente
bashfully		timidly	tímidamente
beautifully	bellamente	splendidly	espléndidamente
becomingly	apropiadamente	decorously	decorosamente
bimonthly	bimestralmente		
bitterly	amargamente	rancorously	rencorosamente
blatantly		flagrantly	flagrantemente
blissfully	dichosamente		
bluntly		bruskly	bruscamente
		frankly	francamente
boastfully	jactanciosamente		
bodily		corporally	corporalmente
bountifully		generously	generosamente
breathlessly		expectantly	expectantemente
brightly		brillantly	brillantemente
briskly	vivamente	energetically	enérgicamente
busily	atareadamente	diligently	diligentemente
calmly	sosegadamente	tranquilly	tranquilmente
carefully	cuidadosamente	prudently	prudentamente
carelessly	descuidadosamente	negligently	negligentemente
ceaselessly		incessantly	incesantemente
charmingly		enchantingly	encantadoramente
cheaply	barato		
cheerfully	alegremente	jovially	jovialmente
chiefly	sobre todo	principally	principalmente
childishly		puerilely	puerilmente
cleanly	nitidamente, limpiamente		

ENGLISH	SPANISH NON-CONVERSION	ENGLISH SYNONYM	SPANISH CONVERSION
cleverly		ably	hábilmente
		ingeniously	ingeniosamente
closely	cerca, estrechamente	contiguously	contiguamente
cloudily		nebulously	nebulosamente
clumsily	torpemente		
coarsely	toscamente	grossly	groseramente
consequently	por consiguiente	in consequence	en consecuencia
	por lo tanto, por ende		
cooly	fríamente	tranquilly	tranquilamente
courageously		valiently	valientemente
covertly	furtivamente	secretly	secretamente
cozily	cómodamente		
craftily	mañosamente	astutely	astutamente
crazily	alocadamente	senselessly	insensatamente
cunningly	graciosamente, diestramente	astutely	astutamente
curtly	fríamente	briefly	brevemente
customarily	comúnmente	usually	usualmente
		habitually	habitualmente
daily	diariamente	all the days	todos los días
daintily	finamente	delicately	delicadamente
daringly	atrevidamente	audaciously	audazmente
darkly		obscurely	obscuramente
dearly (costly)	caramente	costly	costosamente
dearly (intensely)		profoundly	profundamente
dearly (lovingly)	cariñosamente		
deathly		mortally	mortalmente
		gravely	gravemente
deceitfully	engañosamente	fraudulently	fraudulentamente
deeply	hondamente	profoundly	profundamente
deftly	diestramente	ably	hábilmente
designingly		insidiously	insidiosamente
devilishly		diabolically	diabólicamente
dimly	débilmente	obscurely	obscuramente
		indistinctly	indistintamente
discerningly	juiciosamente	sagaciously	sagazmente
disgracefully	vergonzosamente	ignominiously	ignominiosamente
disgustingly		repugnently	repugnantemente
dishonestly	deshonestamente	fraudulently	fraudulentamente
disparagingly	despectivamente	disdainfully	desdeñosamente
distastefully	desagradablemente	repugnantly	repugnantemente
distressfully	penosamente		
distrustfully	desconfiadamente	suspiciously	sospechosamente
disturbingly	perturbadoramente		
dolefully	tristemente	lamentably	lamentablemente
doubtfully	dudosamente	uncertainly	inciertamente
doubtlessly		indubitably	indubitablemente
dreadfully		terribly	terriblemente
		extremely	extremamente
drunkenly		enebriatedly	ebriamente
dryly	fríamente, secamente		
duly	debidamente	appropriately	apropiadamente
dutifully	debidamente	obediently	obedientemente
eagerly	afanosamente	anxiously	ansiosamente
early	pronto, temprano	prematurely	prematuramente

ENGLISH	SPANISH NON-CONVERSION	ENGLISH SYNONYM	SPANISH CONVERSION
earnestly	de veras	seriously	seriamente
		intensely	intensamente
easily	sin dificultad	facilely	fácilmente
easterly	desde el éste		
eerily	espectralmente	mysteriously	misteriosamente
effortlessly		facilely	fácilmente
encouragingly	alentadoramente		
endearingly	cariñosamente		
endlessly(enduringly)	sin fin	perpetually	perpetuamente
		infinitely	infinitamente
engagingly	simpáticamente	graciously	graciosamente
enticingly	tentadoramente	seductorily	seductoramente
entreatingly		supplicantly	suplicantemente
equitably	equitativamente	justly	justamente
evenly(equally)		equally	igualmente
		impartially	imparcialmente
evenly(on level)	llanamente	tranquilly	tranquilamente
eventfully	de modo memorable	extraordinary	extraordinariamente
everlastingly		eternally	eternamente
		perpetually	perpetuamente
evilly	malvadamente	perversely	perversamente
exactingly		exigently	exigentemente
expensively		costly	costosamente
fairly		justly	justamente
		impartially	imparcialmente
		objectively	objetivamente
fairly (quite)	bastante	moderately	moderadamente
faithfully	fielmente	loyally	lealmente
faithlessly	incrédulamente	disloyally	deslealmente
falteringly	con titubeo	vacilatingly	vacilantemente
fancifully		capriciously	caprichosamente
fatefully	fatídicamente	ominously	ominosamente
faultily	erradamente	defectively	defectuosamente
		imperfectly	imperfectamente
fearfully	temerosamente	timidly	tímidamente
fearlessly		intrepidly	intrépidamente
		valiently	valientemente
fearsomely	temerosamente	terribly	terriblemente
feelingly	con sentimiento	expressively	expresivamente
feverishly	febrilmente	passionately	apasionadamente
		ardently	ardientemente
firstly	en primer lugar	primarily	primeramente
fitfully	por intervalos	capriciously	caprichosamente
		irregularly	irregularmente
fittingly		properly	propiamente
flashily	brillantemente	ostentatiously	con ostentación
flatly(level)	de plano	horizontally	horizontalmente
flatly(entirely)		categorically	categóricamente
flatteringly	lisonjeramente		
flauntingly		ostentaciously	ostentosamente
flawlessly	sin tacha	perfectly	perfectamente
		impeccably	impecablemente
fleetingly	fugazmente, velozmente		
foolhardily	temerariamente	audaciously	audazmente

ENGLISH	SPANISH NON-CONVERSION	ENGLISH SYNONYM	SPANISH CONVERSION
foolishly	tontamente	simply	simplemente
forbiddingly	en forma amenazante	ominously	ominosamente
forcefully		energetically	enérgicamente
		vigorously	vigorosamente
forgivingly	con clemencia o perdón	indulgently	indulgentemente
formerly	antés, antiguamente		
fretfully	con mal humor		
friendly	amistosamente	amicably	amigablemente
frighteningly	espantosamente	alarmingly	alarmantemente
fruitfully	fructuosamente	productively	productivamente
fruitlessly	infructuosamente	inefficaciously	ineficazmente
fully	plenamente	completely	completamente
		entirely	enteramente
gaily	alegremente	jovially	jovialmente
gainfully	ventajosamente	lucratively	lucrativamente
gently	dulcemente	suavely	suavemente
gingerly	cuidadosamente	delicately	delicadamente
glaringly	penetrantemente	evidently	evidentemente
	notoriamente	furiously	furiosamente
gleefully	alegremente	jubilantly	jubilosament
gloomily	obscuramente	melancholically	melancólicamente
gratefully	agradecidamente	with gratitude	con gratitud
greatly	muy, grandemente	enormously	enormamente
greedily	codiciosamente	voraciously	vorazmente
		avariciously	avaramente
grievously	penosamente	dolorously	dolorosamente
		deplorably	deplorablemente
grimly	sombríamente	severely	severamente
grudgingly	de mala gana	with hesitation	con hesitación
gruffly	ásperamente	rudely	rudamente
guiltily		culpably	culpablemente
haltingly	inseguramente	vacilatingly	vacilantemente
handily	diestramente	ably	hábilmente
handsomely	hermosamente	generously	generosamente
happily	por fortuna, felizmente	fortunately	afortunadamente
hardily	osadamente	robustly	robustamente
harmfully	dañosamente	prejudicially	perjudicialmente
harmlessly		innocuously	inocuamente
harshly	ásperamente, agriamente	severely	severamente
		cruelly	cruelmente
hastily	apresuradamente	rapidly	rápidamente
		precipitously	precipitadamente
hatefully	odíosamente	detestably	detestablemente
haughtily	altivamente	arrogantly	arrogantemente
		disdainfully	desdeñosamente
hazily	nebulosamente	vaguely	vagamente
healthfully	saludablemente		
heartily	con entusiasmo	cordially	cordialmente
		sincerely	sinceramente
		completely	completamente
heartlessly	desalmadamente	cruelly	cruelmente
heavily	lentamente, pesadamente	laboriously	laboriosamente
heedfully	cuidadosamente	attentively	atentamente
heedlessly	descuidamente	disattentively	desatentamente

ENGLISH	SPANISH NON-CONVERSION	ENGLISH SYNONYM	SPANISH CONVERSION
hellishly		infernally	infernalmente
helpfully	servicialmente	beneficially	beneficiosamente
helplessly	débilemente	irremediably	irremediablemente
		impotently	impotentemente
hesitating	con indecisión o titubeo	vacillatingly	vacilantemente
hideously		horribly	horriblemente
highly	muy, sumamente, altamente	extremely	extremadamente
hoarsely	roncamente		
honestly	rectamente, honradamente	correctly	correctamente
		sincerely	sinceramente
hopefully	esperanzadamente	optimistically	con optimismo
hopelessy	sin esperanza	despairingly	desesperadamente
hotly	ardientemente	vehemently	vehementamente
		violently	violentamente
hourly	a cada hora	frequently	frecuentamente
hungrily	hambrientamente	voraciously	vorazmente
impolitely	groseramente	discourteously	descortésamente
increasingly	crecientemente		
intriguingly	de manera intrigante		
irrately	airadamente	furiously	furiosamente
jointly	conjunctamente	collectively	colectivamente
jokingly	en broma		
joyfully	alegremente	jubilantly	jubilosamente
keenly	agudamente	profoundly	profundamente
kindly	bondadosamente	benevolently	benévolamente
		cordially	cordialmente
knowingly	con conocimiento	intentionally	intencionalmente
		astutely	astutamente
lastingly	duraderamente	permanently	permanentemente
lastly	al fin, finalmente	ultimately	últimamente
lately	ultimamente	recently	recientemente
laughingly	con risa, riendo		
lavishly	pródigamente	generously	generosamente
		copiously	copiosamente
		profusely	profusamente
lawfully	lícitamente	legally	legalmente
		legitimately	legítimamente
lawlessly		illegally	ilegalmente
lazily	perezosamente	indolently	indolentemente
leniently	misericordiosamente	indulgently	indulgentemente
lightly	ligeramente	gently	gentilmente
likely		probably	probablemente
limply		flaccidly	fláccidamente
listlessly	desganadamente	apathetically	apáticamente
		indifferently	indiferentemente
lively	vivamente	energetically	enérgicamente
		vivaciously	vivazmente
longingly	anhelosamente	desirously	deseablemente
loosely	sueltamente, libremente	approximately	aproximadamente
lovingly	cariñosamente	amorously	amorosamente
luckily		fortunately	afortunadamente
lustily	poderosamente	vigorously	vigorosamente
		sensually	sensualmente
masterfully	diestramente	ably	hábilmente

ENGLISH	SPANISH NON-CONVERSION	ENGLISH SYNONYM	SPANISH CONVERSION
mainly	mayormente	principally	principalmente
meagerly	escasamente, pobremente		
meaningfully		significantly	significativamente
meekly	sumisamente, mansamente	humbly	humildmente
		docilely	dócilmente
mercifully	misericordiosamente	compassionately	compasivamente
mercilessly	despiadadamente	cruelly	cruelmente
merrily	alegremente	festively	festivamente
mightily	poderosamente	extremely	extremadamente
mildly	apaciblemente	suavely	suavemente
mindfully	cuidadosamente	attentatively	atentamente
mistakenly	equivocadamente	erroneously	erróneamente
mistrustfully	desconfiadamente		
mockingly	burlonamente		
modernly	*actualmente	recently	recientemente
monthly	mensualmente		
mostly	en su mayor parte	principally	principalmente
		generally	generalmente
mournfully	tristemente		
movingly	conmovedoramente	pathetically	patéticamente
naively	cándidamente	ingenuously	ingenuamente
namelessly		anonymously	anónimamente
namely	es decir, a saber	specifically	específicamente
narrowly	estrechamente	precisely	precisamente
nearly	casi	approximately	proximadamente
neatly	con cuidado, diestramente	ably	hábilmente
needlessly	inútilmente	unnecessarily	innecesariamente
newly	de nuevo, nuevamente	recently	recientemente
nightly	por las noches		
noiselessly		silently	silenciosamente
noisily	ruidosamente		
northeasterly	hacia el nordeste		
northerly	hacia el norte		
northwesterly	hacia el noroeste		
noteworthily	digno de atención	notably	notablemente
noticeably	notablemente	perceptibly	perceptiblamente
oddly	extrañamente	curiously	curiosamente
		singularly	singularmente
often	a menudo	frequently	frecuentamente
only	solo	solely	solamente
		uniquely	únicamente
openly	abiertamente	publicly	públicamente
outrageously	afrentosamente	atrociously	atrozmente
outstandingly	destacadamente	notably	notablamente
overly		excessively	excesivamente
overtly	abiertamente	publicly	públicamente
overwhelmingly	abrumadoramente	irresistibly	irresistiblemente
painfully	penosamente	dolorously	dolorosamente
painlessly	sin causar dolor		
painstakingly	cuidadosamente		
partly	en parte	partially	parcialmente
peacefully	apaciblemente	pacifically	pacíficamente
		serenely	serenamente
pettily	mezquinamente		

ENGLISH	SPANISH NON-CONVERSION	ENGLISH SYNONYM	SPANISH CONVERSION
pitifully	lastimosamente	lamentably	lamentablemente
pityingly	misericordiosamente	compassionately	compasivamente
plainly		clearly	claramente
		visibly	visiblemente
		evidently	evidentemente
playfully	de modo juguetón	festively	festivamente
pleasingly	agradablemente		
plentifully		abundantly	abundantemente
		copiously	copiosamente
pointlessly	inútilmente		
powerfully	poderosamente	potently	potentemente
prayerfully	piadosamente		
prettily	lindamente, hermosamente	attractively	atractivamente
pridefully	orgullosamente	arrogantly	arrogantemente
properly	propiamente	correctly	correctamente
purposefully	de propósito	resolutely	resueltamente
quarterly	trimestralmente		
queerly	estrafalariamente	strangely	extrañamente
quickly (speedily)	prontamente	rapidly	rápidamente
quietly	calladamente	silently	silenciosamente
		calmly	calmadamente
randomly	fortuitamente	casually	casualmente
rashly	temerariamente	imprudently	imprudentamente
readily (easily)	prontamente	facilely	facilmente
really (truly)	verdaderamente	really	*realmente
recklessly	temerariamente	imprudently	imprudentemente
regretfully, -ably	sentidamente	lamentably	lamentablemente
relentlessly	implacablemente	inexorably	inexorablemente
restfully	descansadamente	tranquilly	tranquilamente
restlessly	inquietamente	nervously	nerviosamente
revengefully	vengativamente	vindicatively	vindicativamente
revoltingly	escandalosamente	repugnantly	repugnantemente
		offensively	ofensivamente
richly (wealthily)	ricamente	opulently	opulentamente
rightfully		legitimately	legítimamente
		properly	propiamente
rightly	rectamente	justly	justamente
		correctly	correctamente
roughly	toscamente, ásperamente	brutally	brutalmente
		rudely	rudamente
ruthlessly	despiadadamente	cruelly	cruelmente
scathingly	acerbamente	severely	severamente
scornfully	despectivamente	disdainfully	desdeñosamente
searchingly		penetratingly	penetrantemente
seemingly		apparently	aparentemente
selfishly	con egoísmo	egoistically	egoístamente
selflessly	abnegadamente	disinterestedly	desinteresadamente
semimonthly	quincentalmente		
senselessly	insensatamente		
shabbily	andrajosamente	miserably	miserablemente
shallowly		superficially	superficialmente
		trivially	trivialmente
shamefully	vergonzosamente	scandalously	escandalosamente

ENGLISH	SPANISH NON-CONVERSION	ENGLISH SYNONYM	SPANISH CONVERSION
shamelessly	desvergonzosadamente	insolently	insolentemente
sharply	agudamente	precisely	precisamente
sheepishly	con vergüenza	timidly	tímidamente
shiftily	mañosamente	evasively	evasivamente
		furtively	furtivamente
shockingly	espantosamente	horribly	horriblemente
shortly	al instante, cortamente	briefly	brevemente
shrewdly(slyly)	sagazmente	astutely	astutamente
shyly	temerosamente	timidly	tímidamente
sickeningly		repugnantly	repugnantemente
simply	sencillamente	purely	puramente
		merely	meramente
sinfully	pecaminosamente		
skillfully	diestramente	ably	hábilmente
		expertly	expertamente
slantingly	con inclinación	obliquely	oblicuamente
		diagonally	diagonalmente
slavishly		servilely	servilmente
slightly	ligeramente		
sloppily, slovenly	descuidadamente	disorderly	desordenadamente
slowly	despacio, lentamente	gradually	gradualmente
sluggishly	perezosamente	indolently	indolentemente
slyly		astutely	astutamente
		furtively	furtivamente
smartly	briosamente	sagaciously	sagazmente
smoothly	llanamente, lisamente	suavely	suavemente
sneakingly, -ily	solapadamente	furtively	furtivamente
snootily	altivamente	disdainfully	desdeñosamente
softly	blandamente	suavely	suavemente
solely	únicamente, solamente	exclusively	exclusivamente
somberly	lúgubremente	melancholically	melancólicamente
soothingly	de modo calmante	consolingly	consoladoramente
sorely	penosamente, dolorosamente	urgently	urgentemente
		severely	severamente
sorrowfully	con pena, tristemente		
soulfully		sentimentally	sentimentalmente
southeasterly	hacia el sudeste		
southerly	hacia el sur		
southwesterly	hacia el sudoeste		
sparingly	escasamente	frugally	frugalmente
		economically	económicamente
sparsely	escasamente		
speedily	velozmente	rapidly	rápidamente
spitefully	con rencor		
spryly	vivazmente	agilely	ágilmente
squarely	en cuadro	honorably	honradamente
starkly	rigurosamente	severely	severamente
		aridly	áridamente
stately		magestically	majestuosamente
staunchly		firmly	firmemente
steadfastly	constantemente	resolutely	resueltamente
steadily	fijamente, seguramente	firmly	firmemente

ENGLISH	SPANISH NON-CONVERSION	ENGLISH SYNONYM	SPANISH CONVERSION
stealthily		furtively	furtivamente
		clandestinely	clandestinamente
steeply	de modo escarpado		
sternly		severely	severamente
		firmly	firmemente
stiffly	tiesamente	rigidly	rígidamente
stormily		tempestuously	tempestuosamente
		violently	violentamente
stoutly		valiently	valientemente
		resolutely	resueltamente
strangely	extrañamente	curiously	curiosamente
		rarely	raramente
		peculiarly	peculiarmente
		singularly	singularmente
strikingly		impressively	impresionantemente
strongly	fuertamente	vigorously	vigorosamente
		emphatically	enfáticamente
stubbornly	tercamente	obstinately	obstinadamente
stylishly	a la moda	elegantly	elegantemente
successfully	con éxito		
suddenly	de repente, súbitamente	precipitately	precipitadamente
sullenly	con malhumor		
surely	sin duda	certainly	ciertamente
		indubitably	indudablemente
sweetly	dulcemente	suavely	suavemente
swiftly(speedily)	velozmente	rapidly	rápidamente
tactfully	políticamente	discreetly	discretamente
		politically	políticamente
tactlessly	sin tacto	indiscreetly	indescretamente
tamely	debilmente	docilely	dócilmente
tastefully	con gusto	elegantly	elegantemente
tastelessly	sin gusto	insipidly	insípidamente
tastily	sabrosamente	appetizingly	apetitosamente
tearfully	llorosamente		
temptingly	tentadoramente		
tenderly	tiernamente		
tersely		concisely	concisamente
		succinctly	sucintamente
thankfully	agradecidamente		
thanklessly	desagradecidamente		
thickly	espesamente	densely	densamente
		abundantly	abundantemente
thinly	delgadamente	finely	finamente
thoroughly	detalladamente	completely	completamente
thoughtfully		pensively	pensativamente
thoughtlessly	incautamente	imprudently	imprudentemente
tightly	apretadamente, estrechamente		
timely	a tiempo	opportunely	oportunamente
tirelessly	incansablemente		
tiresomely	cansadamente	tediously	tediosamente
truly	verdaderamente	certainly	ciertamente
trustingly	confiadamente		

ENGLISH	SPANISH NON-CONVERSION	ENGLISH SYNONYM	SPANISH CONVERSION
trustworthily	confiablemente		
truthfully	verazmente		
unassumingly	sin pretensiones	modestly	modestamente
		discreetly	discretamente
unbearably	insoportablemente	intolerably	intolerablemente
unbelievably		incredibly	increíblemente
unbelievingly		incredulously	incrédulamente
		skeptically	escépticamente
uncommonly		extraordinarily	extraordinariamente
		notably	notablemente
understandingly	compasivamente	tolerantly	tolerantemente
undoubtedly	sin duda	indubitably	indudablemente
unduly	indebidamente	unappropriately	impropiamente
		excessively	excesivamente
uneasily	inquietamente	anxiously	ansiosamente
unerringly	certeramente	infallibly	infaliblemente
unevenly		irregularly	irregularmente
		unequally	desigualmente
unfairly		unjustly	injustamente
unfaithfully	infielmente	disloyally	deslealmente
unhappily	infelizmente	disconsolately	desconsoladamente
unknowingly	sin saber	inadvertently	inadvertidamente
unlawfully		illegally	ilegalmente
		illegitimately	ilegítimamente
		illicitly	ilícitamente
unluckily	desgraciadamente	unfortunately	desafortunadamente
unmercifully	despiadadamente	cruelly	cruelmente
unrelentingly	sin truega	inexorably	inexorablemente
		inflexibly	infexiblemente
unseemly	impropiamente	indecently	indecentemente
		indecorously	indecorosamente
unselfishly		generously	generosamente
unsparingly	despiadamente	prodigally	pródigamente
unsteadily		unstably	inestablemente
		inconstantly	inconstantemente
unsuccessfully	sin éxito	unfruitfully	infructuosamente
unthankfully	desagradecidamente	ungratefully	ingratamente
untimely	intempestivamente	inopportunely	inoportunamente
		prematurely	prematuramente
untruly, untruthfully	engañosamente	falsely	falsamente
unwaveringly	sin vacilar	firmly	firmemente
unwillingly	de mala gana		
unwisely	neciamente	imprudently	imprudentemente
unwittingly	inconscientemente	inadvertently	inadvertidamente
uprightly	rectamente	vertically	verticalmente
usefully	útilmente	advantageously	ventajosamente
uselessly	inútilmente		
utterly (wholly)		entirely	enteramente
		totally	totalmente
		absolutely	abolutamente
		completely	completamente
wantonly	insensiblemente	cruelly	cruelmente

ENGLISH	SPANISH NON-CONVERSION	ENGLISH SYNONYM	SPANISH CONVERSION
warmly	calorosamente, cariñosamente		
wastefully		prodigally	pródigamente
watchfully		attentively	atentamente
waveringly	de modo vacilante	tremulously	trémulamente
weakly	débilmente		
wealthily		opulently	opulentamente
		richly	ricamente
wearily	cansadamente	fatiguingly	fatigosamente
weekly	semanalmente		
westerly	hacia el oeste		
wholly		totally	totalmente
		absolutely	absolutamente
		entirely	enteramente
		completely	completamente
willfully, willingly	de buena gana	voluntarily	voluntariamente
		intentionally	intencionalmente
wisely	sabiamente	prudently	prudentemente
wishfully	anhelosamente		
woefully	tristemente	lamentably	lamentablemente
wonderfully		marvelously	maravillosamente
		stupendously	estupendamente
worthily	dignamente, merecidamente		
wrongfully	sin razón	unjustly	injustamente
		illicitly	ilícitamente
		illegally	ilegalmente
wrongly	sin razón	erroneously	erróneamente
		incorrectly	incorrectamente
yearly	cada año	annually	anualmente
youthfully	de modo juvenil		

SPELLING CHANGES FROM ENGLISH TO SPANISH

Familiarity with this list of the most common spelling changes between English and Spanish will not only enhance proper spelling in Spanish, but will also help in the recognition of conversions which might be somewhat obscured by the spelling changes.

1. <u>Elimination of One Consonant in English Double Consonants except *rr*</u>

bb = b	abbreviate=abreviar, abbatial=abacial
cc = c	acceleration=aceleración, successor=sucesor, flaccid=flácido

        <u>BUT</u>: The double *c* is used in Spanish when the first *c* has a *k* sound and the second an *s* sound.

        action=acción, correction=corrección, accident=accidente

dd = d	addition=adición, addict=adicto
ff = f	affirmative=afirmativo, official=oficial, offend=ofender different=diferente
gg = g	aggregate=agregar, suggestion=sugestión, aggression=agresión
ll = l	allege=alegar, collective=colectivo, ballad=balada, alleviate=aliviar, collusion=colusión, nullity=nulidad.

        <u>BUT</u>: Spanish has the *ll* as a separate letter of the alphabet.

        street=calle, arrival=llegada, quarrel=querella, brilliant=brillante, roller=rodillo, rain=lluvia.

mm = m	commence=comenzar, mummy=momia, summary=sumario, commission=comisión
nn = n	annex=anexar; flannel=franela, innocent=inocente, annul=anular, manner=manera, anniversary=aniversario, tennis=tenis

        <u>BUT</u>: The double *n* remains when the first is part of a prefix.

        connivance=connivencia, ennoble=ennoblecer, innate=innato, connotation=connotación

pp = p	apparent=aparente, appetite=apetito, applicable=aplicable, opportunity=oportunidad, supplememntary=suplementario
rr = rr	aberration=aberración, arrogant=arrogante, correct=correcto, error=error, irrational=irracional, irritate=irritar
ss = s	assault=asalto, expressive=expresivo, assume=asumir, assistance=asistencia, necessity=necesidad, possible=posible, professor=profesor, progressive=progresivo
tt = t	attack=atacar, attention=atención, attribute=atributo, attractive=atractivo, battery=batería, battle=batalla

2. Other Frequent Spelling Changes (Not always applicable)

a to e	rancor=rencor, pardon=perdón
ab to a, au	abnormal=anormal, absent=ausente
apt to aut	captive=cautivo, baptize=bautizar
au to o	pauper=pobre, paucity=poco
b to pt	subscriber=subscriptor
b to v	automobile=automóvil, mobility=movilidad
bm to m	submersion=sumersión, submission=sumisión
bt to t	subtle=sutil
bt to st	subtractive=sustractivo
c to z	force=fuerza, race=raza, place=plaza
c to g	cabinete=gabinete, carafe=garrafa, sacred=sagrado, secure=seguro
ch to c	technology=tecnología, synchronize=sincronizar, saccharine=sacarina
ch to c	character=carácter, charge=cargar, chastise=castigar

ch to qu	architect=arquitecto, trachea=tráquea, orchestra=orquesta
ck to qu	attack=ataque, sack=saquear, picket=piquete
ct to t	distinct=distinto, extinct=extinto, object=objeto, punctual=puntual, respect=respetar, subjective=subjetivo

BUT: Many remain *ct* : Octubre, activo, efectivo, productivo.

ct to x	reflective=reflexivo
dv to d	advance=avanzar, advise=avisar, adventure=aventura

BUT: Some remain *dv* : adverbio, adverso, adversidad.

e to ie	serpent=serpiente, cent=ciento, ardent=ardiente, recent=reciente, dependent=dependiente
e to i	penguin=pingüino
ea to e	reveal=revelador, pearl=perla
eau to o	bureaucratic=burocrático
ei to i	seismograph=sismógrafo
ei to e	seignior= señor
ent to iant	student=estudiante
fl to ll	flame=llama
g to j	paraplegia=paraplejia, percentage=porcentaje, garage=garaje
gm to m	augment=aumentar, phlegmatic=flemático
gn to n	reign=reinar, prognosticate=pronosticar
gn to ñ	signal=señal, seignior=señor

gua to ga	guarantee=garantizar
i to e	incarnate=encarnado, superintend=superentender, minor=menor, reimbursable=reemolsable
i to ie	sinister=siniestro
ia to a	parliament=parlamento
i to y	Pompeian=pompeyano (i.e.- an *i* between two vowels)
j to y	abject=abyecto, project=proyecto, pejorative=peyorativo, adjacent=adyacente, trajectory=trayectoria
k to c	alkaline=alcalino, obelisk=obelisco, plankton=plancton
k to qu	park=parque, pekingese=pequinés, skeleton=esqueleto (before *e* or *i*)
m to n	symphonic=sinfónico, triumphant=triunfante
mm to nm	commemorative=conmemorativo, immense=inmenso, immobile=inmóvil, immoral=inmoral, immunity=inmunidad
mon to mos	demonstrative=demostrativo
mp to n	assumption=asunción, assumption=asunción, presumptive=presuntivo, peremptorily=perentoriamente, temptation=tentación, redemption=redención
nct to nt	adjunct=adjunto
o to au	restoration=restauración
o to ue	resolved=resuelto, sole=suelo
o to u	secondary=secundario
ou to o	tournament=torneo, troubador=trovador
ou to u	pronounce=pronunciar, recourse=recurso, tourist=turista
p to ap	placate=aplacar (Verb forms)

p to b	April=abril, superb=soberbio, saporous=sabroso
ph to f	philospher=filósofo, elephant=elefante, telephone=teléfono, pamphlet=panfleto, sapphire=zafiro
pn to n	pneumonia=neumonía, pneumatic=numático
ps to s	psychoanalyst=(p)sicoanalista, psychology=(p)sicología pseudonym=seudónimo, psalm=salmo
pt to c	absorption=absorción, resumption=reasunción
pt to t	prompt=pronto
qu to cu	eloquent=elocuente, frequency=frecuencia, oblique=oblicuo, quartz=cuarzo, question=cuestión, squadron=escuadrón, sequel=secuela

BUT: The *qu* is often retained before *i*:
adquirir, liquidación, obsequioso, quieto, quintuple

r to l	recruitment=reclutamiento
r to arr	ruin=arruinar
rh to r	rhapsody=rapsodia, rhizome=rizoma, rheostat=reóstato rhythm=ritmo, rhumba=rumba, rhombic=rómbico
s to z	sapphire=zafiro, vicecount=vizconde, sarsaparilla=sarzaparrilla
s to as	salaried=asalariado, secure=asegurar (Verb forms)
s to c	sentinel=centinela, sendal=cendal

s to es — English words beginning with *s* followed by a consonant sound add an *e* before the *s*:
Spain=España, station=estación, scholar=escolar, spirit=espíritu, skeleton=esqueleto, stupid=estúpido, scrupulous=escrúpulo, special=especial, scheme=esquema, space=espacio, specify=especificar, sterile=estéril

sc to c	conscience=conciencia, resuscitate=resucitar, science=ciencia.

t to d	state=estado, regulator=regulador, mater=madre, mature=maduro, accelerator=acelerador, creator=creador, dictator=dictador, generator=generador, orator=orador,
th to t	authentic=auténtico, cathedral=catedral, catholic=católico, sympathize = simpatizar, author=autor
ti to ci	action=acción, condition=condición, nation=nación, patient=paciente, partial=parcial, satiable=saciable

BUT: The ti is retained in words ending in
-gestion : congestión, digestión, sugestión

tor to tro	spector=espectro
trans to tras	transcend=trascender
u to o	current=corriente, suffocate=sofocar, trumpet=trompeta
un to in	unjustified=injustificado, unconditional=incondicional
v to b	approve=aprobar, govern=gobernar, receive=recibir, savour=sabor, overture=obertura
w to v	swastika=svástica, waltz=vals, watt=vatio
x to j	example=ejemplo, executor=ejecutor, fix=fijar relaxation= relajación
y to i	agency=agencia, analysis=análisis, decency=decencia, hymn=himno, hygiene=higiene, hysteria=histeria, system=sistema, gymnasium=gimnasio
z to c	benzene=benceno, zero=cero, zinc=cinc (zinc)
z to s	Brazil=Brasil

ACCENT MARKS & ACCENT PLACEMENT

The location of the pronounciation stress in Spanish words is determined by the application of the following rules:

1. For Spanish words ending in *n* , *s* or a vowel, the stress is normally placed on the next to the last (penultimate) syllable, and no written accent mark is needed.

    dentista, posible, hablan, estamos, caballo, crisis

2. For Spanish words endings in a consonant other than *n* or *s*, the stress is normally placed on the last syllable, and no written accent mark is needed.

    tractor, postal, edad, solicitud, azul

3. For Spanish words having the stress placed on a syllable other than that indicated by the first two rules, the stressed syllable is marked by a written accent.

    adiós, aquí, árbol, azúcar, café, carbón, decisión, dramático, francés, inglés, lápiz, público, hindú

4. Some Spanish words bear the written accent over the normally accented syllable when they are used as interrogatory words.

    ¿cómo?, ¿qué?, ¿dónde?, ¿cuándo?, ¿cuál?, ¿por qué?

5. Some Spanish words bear the written accent over the normally accented syllable to distinguish them from identical words with different meanings.

aquel	(that-ADJ)		áquel	(that-PRON)
de	(of)		dé	(give!)
el	(the)		él	(he)
ese	(that-ADJ)		ése	(that-PRON)
este	(this-ADJ)		éste	(this-PRON)
mas	(but)		más	(more)
mi	(my)		mí	(me)
si	(if)		sí	(yes)
solo	(only,sole)		sólo	(only-ADV)
te	(you)		té	(tea)

<u>NOTE</u>: Unlike in French, Spanish accents (except ñ and ü) aren't used to change the pronunciation of a letter but only to indicate the location of the stress. The accents placed on the ñ *and* ü do change the pronounciation.

boy	niño		antiquity	antigüedad
canyon	cañón		drain	desagüe
loving	cariñoso		ointment	ungüento
owner	dueño		penguin	pingüino
Spanish	español		shame	vergüenza
small	pequeño		stork	cigüeña

PREFIXES

Most English prefixes of Latin or Greek origin convert to similar prefixes in Spanish, but affixing such a prefix to an English word that doesn't convert to a Spanish word won't make that word convertible. Since such prefixes often help identify an English-Spanish conversion, some of those most frequently used are listed here to show the similarities. More precise definitions of these prefixes may be found in any good English or Spanish dictionary.

PREFIX	PREFIX MEANING	ENGLISH	SPANISH
a-	lack of (Also often used to convert a word into a verb)	amoral, apolitical bring near accomodate embrace	amoral, apolítico acercar (cerca) acomodar (cómodo) abrazar (brazo)
ab-	from, away, down from	abduct, absorb	abducir, absorber
ad-	toward, to, addition to, nearness to	admit, adrenal	admitir, adredal
ac-	Before c and q	acclaim	aclamar
af-	Before f	affirm, afflict	afirmar, afligir
ag-	Before g	aggregate, aggressive	agregar, agresivo
al-	Before l	allude, allegation	aludir, alegación
an-	Before n	annotate, annihilate	anotar, aniquilar
ap-	Before p	approve, appreciate	aprobar, apreciar
ar-	Before r	arrest, arrogant	arrestar, arrogante
as-	Before s	ascend, assign	ascender, asignar
at-	Before t	attend, attack	atender, atacar
aero-	air, flying, gas	aerodynamic	aerodinámico
agro-	field, earth, soil	agrology	agrología
al-	the	alchemy, almanac	alquimia, almanaque
ambi-	both	ambidextrous	ambidextro
amphi-	on both sides	amphibious	anfibio
an-	not, without	anandrous, anemia	anandriario, anemia
ante-	before in time	antecedent, ancestor	antecedente, antecesor
anthropo-	man	anthropology	antropología
anti-	against, opposite	antipathy, antibiotic	antipatía, antibiótico
apo-	separation, off	apostasy, apogee	apostasía, apogeo
arch-	superior	archangel	arcángel
audio-	hearing	audiometer	audiómetro

PREFIX	PREFIX MEANING	ENGLISH	SPANISH
auto-	self	autograph, autocracy	autógrafo, autocracia
biblio-	book	bibliography	bibliografía
bi(n)-	two, double, twice	bilingual, binary	bilingüe, binario
bio-	life	biography, biology	biografía, biología
cata-	down, downward	catastrophe	catástrofe
centi-	hundred	centigram, centipede	centigramo, centípedo
chromo-	color, pigment	chromosome	cromosoma
chron(o)-	time	chronometer	cronómetro
circum-	around, surrounding	circumference	circunferencia
com-	together, with, joint	combine, compact	combinar, compacto
co-	Before h, w & vowel	cooperate, coexistence	cooperar, coexistir
col-	Before l	collateral, collusion	colateral, colusión
con-	Before c, d, g, j, n, q, s, t, v	connote, congeal, conquest, constant, context, convert	connotar, congelar, conquista, constante, contexto, convertir
cum-	Before m	cummulative	(a)cumulativo
cor-	Before r	corrupt, correlation	corromper, correlación
contra-	against, contrary	contradiction	contradicción
cosmo-	world	cosmopolitan	cosmopolita
counter-	against, contrary	counterespionage	contraespionaje
dactylo-	finger	dactylic, dactyl	dactílico, dáctilo
de-	away, from, down	degenerate, defunct	degenerar, difunto
dia-	through, across	diagonal, diagnose	diagonal, diagnosticar
dis-	separation, negation	disarm, dishonest discover, discount	desarmar, deshonesto descubrir, descontar
di-	Before b, d, g, v, m, n, l, t	digression, divert dissent, dilatory	digresión, divertir disidir, dilatorio
dif-	Before f	differ, diffusion	diferir, difusión
dyna-	power	dynamics, dynamo	dinámica, dínamo
dys-	hard, bad, difficult	dysentery, dyspepsia	disentería, dispepsia
electro-	electric	electrocute, electron	electrocutar, electrón
en-	in, into	enthrone, endemic	entronar, endémico
em-	Before p, b, m	embark, emplacement	embarcar, emplazamiento

PREFIX	PREFIX MEANING	ENGLISH	SPANISH
equi-	equal	equivalent	equivalente
ex-	out of, from	expel, excoriate export, expose	expeler, excoriar exportar, exponer
ec-	Before c or s	eccentric, ecstasy	excéntrico, éxtasis
ef-	Before f	effusive, effigy	efusivo, efigio
e-	Before b, d, g, h, l, m, n, r and v	educe, elect, emit, emigrate, erosive	educir, elegir, emitir, emigrar, erosivo
ex-	former, previous	ex-president	ex-presidente
extra-	outside, beyond	extraordinary	extraordinario
gastro-	stomach	gastrology	gastrología
graph-	writing	graphology, graphic	grafología, gráfica
geo-	earth	geocentric, geology	geocéntrico, geología
hemi-	half	hemisphere	hemisferio
hydro-	water	hydrostatic, hydrogen	hidrostático, hidrógeno
hyper-	excessive, over, above	hyperactive	hiperactivo
hypo-	under, beneath, below	hypodermic, hypocrasy	hipodérmico, hipocresía
ideo-	idea	ideology, ideogram	ideología, ideograma
in-	no, not, without	inactive, inapt	inactivo, inepto
il-	Before l	illiterate	iliterato
im-	Before b, m and p	impossible, imbecile	imposible, imbécil
ir-	Before r	irresponsible	irresponsable
in-	in, into, within	infer, indulgent	inferir, indulgente
il-	Before l	illuminate	iluminar
im-	Before b, m and p	immigrate, impale	inmigrar, empalar
ir-	Before r	irritate, irrigate	irritar, irrigar
infra-	below, beneath	infrared, infrasonic	infrarrojo, infrasónico
inter-	between, among	intercept, internal	interceptar, interno
intra-	within, inside of	intravenous	intravenoso
intro-	inward, into, within	introvert, introduce	introverso, introducir
juxta-	near, beside	juxtaposition	yuxtaposición
kilo-	1000	kilogram, kilocycle	kilogramo, kilociclo
loco-	place	locomotion	locomoción

PREFIX	PREFIX MEANING	ENGLISH	SPANISH
magni-	great,big,large	magnitude	magnitud
mal-	badly,wrong,ill	malign,malediction	maligno,maldición
mega-	large,great,powerful	megaphone,megalith	megáfono,megalito
meta-	after,transposed	metaphore,metaphrase	metáfora,metáfrasis
metro-	measure	metrology,metronome	metrología,metrónomo
micro-	little,small,minute	microscope,microgram	microscopio,micrograma
milli-	1000th part	millimeter,milligram	milímitro,miligramo
mini-	small	minibus	minibús
mono-	one,along,single	monotheism,monotone	monoteísmo,monotonía
morph-	form	morpholgy,morpheme	morfología,morfema
multi-	many	multilateral	multilateral
necro-	death	necrology	necrología
neo-	new,recent,latest	neoclassic,neophyte	neoclásico,neófito
neuro-	nerve	neuropath,neurology	neurópata,neurología
non-	no,not,negative	nonbelligerent nonproductive	no beligerante improductivo
ob- o- oc- of- op-	to,toward,against Before m Before c Before f Before p	oblige,objective omit occur,occupy offer,offense oppress,opponent	obligir,objetivo omitir ocurrir,ocupar ofrecer,ofensa oprimir,oponente
octa-	eight	octagon,October	octágono,octubre
oleo-	oil	oleomargarine	oleomargarina
omni-	all,everwhere	omniscient,omnivore	omnisciente,omnívoro
ortho-	straight,regular	orthodontic	ortodóntico
osteo-	bones	osteopath,osteotomy	osteópata,osteotomía
ovi-	egg	oviduct,oviform	oviducto,oviforme
paleo-	ancient	paleographer	paleógrafo
pan-	all,common to all	Pan-American	panamericano
para-	beside,beyond,for	parallel,paradox	paralelo,paradoja
patho-	suffering,disease	pathology,pathogenic	patología,patogénico

PREFIX	PREFIX MEANING	ENGLISH	SPANISH
pedi-	foot or feet	pedicure	pedicuro
ped(o)-	children	pediatrics	pediatría
pen-	almost	peninsula,penultimate	península,penúltimo
pent(a)-	five	pentagon,pentamerous	pentágono,pentámero
per-	through,complete	persuade,perforate	persuadir,perforar
peri-	around,encircling	periscope,peritoneum	periscopio,peritoneo
phago-	eating	phagocyte	fagocito
philo-	loving,liking	philology	filología
phleb-	veins	phlebotomy,plebitis	flebotomía,flebitis
phono-	sound	phonology,phonograph	fonología,fonógrafo
photo-	light	photographic	fotográfico
physio-	nature,natural	physiology	fisiolgía
poly-	much,many	polygamy,polyphagia	poligamia,polifagia
post-	after,behind	posterior,posthumous	posterior,póstumo
pre-	before,earlier	precede,preeminent	preceder,preeminente
pro-	in front of,before	prophet,project	profeta,proyectar
pro-	moving forward	progress,proceed	progreso,proceder
proto-	original,first	protocol,protagonist	protocolo,protagonista
pseudo-	pretended,sham	pseudonym,pseudocarp	seudónimo,seudocarpo
psycho-	mind	psychology	psicología
pulmo-	lung	pulmonary	pulmonar
pyro-	fire,heat	pyromania,pyrometer	piromanía,pirómetro
quadri-	four times	quadriplegic	cuadriplégico
quasi-	almost	quasi-public	cuasipúblico
radio-	ray,raylike	radiogram,radiology	radiograma,radiología
re-	back,again	restore,reappear	restaurar,reaparecer
retro-	backward,back,behind	retrospection	retrospección
rhino-	nose	rhinitis,rhinoceros	rinitis,rinoceront

PREFIX	PREFIX MEANING	ENGLISH	SPANISH
semi-	half	semiconductor	semiconductor
Sino-	Chinese	Sino-Japanese	sinojaponés
socio-	society	society, sociologist	sociedad, sociólogo
stereo-	2-dimensional	stereoscope	estereoscopio
stylo-	pointed, sharp	stylograph	estilógrafo
sub-	under, beneath, below	submerge, subdivision	sumergir, subdivisión
suc-	Before c	succession, succinct	sucesión, sucinto
suf-	Before f	suffer, sufficient	sufrir, suficiente
sug-	Before g	suggestive	sugestivo
sum-	Before m	submission	submisión
sur-	Before r	surrogate	subrogar
sus-	Before p and t	sustain, suspend	sostener, suspender
sulf-	sulpher	sulfonic, sulfuric	sulfónico, sulfúrico
super-	over, above, on top	superior, superintend	superior, superentender
sur-	over	surrealist	surrealista
syn-	with, together	synergetic, synthesis	sinergético, síntesis
syl-	Before l	syllogism, syllable	silogismo, sílaba
sym-	Before m, p and b	symbole, symetry	símbolo, simetría
sys-	Before s	system, systole	sistema, sístole
tauto-	the same	tautology	tautología
techno-	science, skill	technology, technical	tecnología, técnico
tele-	at a distance	telegraph, television	telégrafo, televisión
theo-	God	theology, theocentric	teología, teocéntrico
thermo-	heat	thermodynamics	termodinámica
trans-	over, across	transatlantic, transmission, transfuse	transatlántico, transmisión, transfundir
tri-	three	triangle, tricycle	triángulo, triciclo
typo-	type	typical, typography	típico, tipografía
ultra-	beyond, extreme	ultraviolet, ultraism	ultravioleta, ultraísmo
un-	not, opposite of	unable, unarm, unconscious	inhábil, desarmar, inconsciente

PREFIX	PREFIX MEANING	ENGLISH	SPANISH
uni-	having only one	unicellular	unicelular
vermi-	worm	vermicide	vermicida
vice-	subordinate, deputy	vice-president	vicepresidente
zoo-	animal	zoology	zoología

NOTE: English prefixes not having Latin or Greek origins such as those listed below very seldom follow any reliable pattern of conversion from English to Spanish.

be-	beset, bemoan, befriend, beloved
by-	bystander, by-product
cross-	crossbow, crossbreed
for-	forbid, forget, forgo
fore-	forecast, foreman, forearm, forehead
grand-	grandfather, grandmother
mis-	misjudge, misobey, mistake, misfortune
out-	outlying, outboard, outrun
over-	overcharge, overalls, overview
self-	self-centered, self-conscious, self-control
under-	undernourish, underpass, underscore, undershirt
up-	uproot, upstage, uphill, upset, upgrade
with-	withdraw, withhold, withstand, within

AUGMENTATIVES

While English usually uses an adjective to indicate that something is large, Spanish often adds an augmentative ending to the word (after dropping the final unstressed vowel). The resulting augmentatives often also impart the meaning of derogativeness as well as largeness so they are to be used with care. The following are some of the most common augmentative endings

-ón (-ona)

caja (box)	cajón	= drawer	mujer	mujerona	= stout lady
calle	callejón	= lane	piedra	pedrejón	= big stone
casa	casón	= big house	señora	señorona	= great lady
cuchara	cucharón	= big spoon	silla	sillón	= armchair
gigante	gigantón	= big giant	soltero	solterón	= old bachelor
hombre	hombrón	= big fellow	vientre	ventrón	= big belly
jarra	jarrón	= large jar	zapato	zapatón	= big shoe
lanza	lanzón	= large lance			

-acho(a)

hombre	hombracho	= big man	vulgo	vulgacho	= mob, rabble
populación	populacho	= mob			

-azo(a)

animal	animalazo	= big animal	boca	bocaza	= large mouth
árbol	arbolazo	= big tree	hombre	hombrazo	= big man
barba	barbaza	= thick beard	libro	librazo	= big book
bobo	bobazo	= blockhead	mujer	mujeraza	= big woman

-ote

camisa	camisote	= long coat	pájaro	pajarote	= big bird

DIMINUTIVES

While English usually uses an adjective to indicate that something is small Spanish often adds a diminutive ending to the word (after dropping the final unstressed vowel). The resulting diminutives often impart a sense of affection as well as smallness. Sometimes the resulting word has a new meaning such as is seen in the change from *paño* (cloth) to *pañuelo* (handkerchief). The following are among the most common diminutive endings:

-*ito(a)*; -*cito(a)* ; -*ecito (a)*   (Often indicate endearment)

abuelo	abuelito	= grandpa	Juan	Juanito	= Johnnie
ahora	ahorita	= right away	jovenes	jovencitos	= youngsters
amigo	amiguito	= pal	mano	manecita	= little hand
Carlos	Carlitos	= Chuck	perro	perrito	= puppy
casa	casita	= cottage	poco	poquito	= little bit
flor	florecita	= little flower	probre	pobrecito	= poor little guy
gato	gatito	= kitten	pronto	prontito	= quite soon
hermana	hermanita	= little sister	rato	ratito	= little while
hombre	hombrecito	= little man	señora	señorita	= young lady
jardín	jardincito	= small garden	vieja	viejecita	= little old lady
joven	jovencito	= kid			

-*illo(a)*; -*cillo(a)*   (Often indicate insignificance or vulgarity)

campana	campanilla	= hand bell	dolor	dolorcillo	= minor pain
chica	chiquilla	= little girl	guerra	guerrilla	= small war
cigar	cigarrillo	= cigarette	ladrón	ladroncillo	= petty thief
cuchara	cucharilla	= small spoon	pájaro	pajarillo	= small bird

-*uelo(a)*; -*zuelo(a)*   (Often indicate scorn or vulgarity)

arroyo	arroyuelo	= small stream	piedra	piedrezuela	= pebble
autor	autorzuelo	= petty writer	rey	reyezuelo	= petty king
huevo	ovezuelo	= small egg	rueda	ruedezuela	= small wheel
paña	pañuelo	= handkerchief	puerta	portezuela	= small door
pequeño	pequeñuelo	= youngster	viejo	vejezuelo	= little old man

NOTE: The following suffixes are also used to form diminutives: **-ico, -in, -ino, -ete, -ajo, -ejo , -ato, -enzo, -icho, -icula** and **-ijo.**

DECEPTIVE COGNATES

One of the main obstacles standing in the way of broader reliance on the similarity between English and Spanish words has been the fear of errors caused by a limited number of words that look or sound alike in the two languages but have quite different meanings. Since no more than 1% of the 30,000 commonly used words listed in this book face any serious problems of this kind, the tremendous benefits of vocabulary conversion seem to justify the time spent in becoming familiar with the 500 or so misleading cognates listed here. Some are real cognates which have evolved into different meanings and some are words which look alike in English and in Spanish simply by chance. Although most of the seriously misleading cognates are included in the list, no effort has been made to collect all the cases where either the English or Spanish words have alternative meanings not following through to the other language nor where the divergence is just a shade of meaning. The deceptive cognates are flagged by an asterix* when they appear in the other lists in this book. It should be noted too that many Spanish words have different meanings in different countries just as certain English words may also have different meanings in England and in the United States. Spanish cognates often have several meaning other than the listed English equivalent.

ENGLISH	SPANISH EQUIVALENT	SPANISH COGNATE	ENGLISH EQUIVALENT
abductor	raptor	abductor	aducent muscle
accord	ortogar, conceder	acordar	resolve, conciliate
accost	abordar	acostarse	go to bed
acre (land)	acre	acre (ADJ)	acrid, harse
actual (real)	verdadero, efectivo, real	actual	present-day, current
actuality	realidad	actualidad	present time
actually	en realidad, en efecto	actualmente	at present, currently
adagio (MUS)	adagio	adagio	adage, proverb
addition	adición, suma	adición	addition, bill, check
admit (concede)	conceder	admitir	let enter
advertisement	anuncio	advertencia	advice
advertize	anunciar	advertir	warn, advise, observe
advice	consejo	aviso	warning
advise	aconsejar	avisar	inform, advise, warn
affect	afectar, influir	afecto	affection, fondness
agony	angustia, agonía	agonía	death throes
ailment	dolencia, indisposición	alimento	food, fuel, alimony
aim	aspirar a, apuntar	amar	love
alms	limosna	alma	soul, spirit
alto	contralto	alto	tall, high
alumnus (-a)	ex-alumno (-a)	alumno	student, pupil
American (US)	norteamericano, yanqui, estadounidense	americano	any Western Hemisphere person
amount to	subir a, sumar	montar	mount, ride, get on
ancient	antiguo	anciano	old
anxious (eager)	deseoso	ansiosos	anxious (worried)

ENGLISH	SPANISH EQUIVALENT	SPANISH COGNATE	ENGLISH EQUIVALENT
apology	excusa,disculpa	apología	defense,praise
appeal	apelación	apellido	surname
appearance(act)	aparición	apariencia	looks,appearance
application(job)	solicitud	aplicación	zeal,application
appreciate(add)	aumentar	apreciar	esteem
arena	estadio,campo,coliseo	arena	sand
argument	disputa,discusión	argumento	proof,summary
arial(radio)	antena	aério(ADJ)	air,aerial
arm	brazo	arma (el)	weapon
arrest(stop)	detener	arrestar	arrest,jail
as	como	as	ace(card)
aspire	ambicionar	aspirar	inhale
assist	ayudar,apoyar	asistir	attend,be present
assistance	ayuda,asistencia	asistencia	attendance
assumption	suposición,hipótesis	asunción	taking on authority
attend	asistir	atender	attend to,care for
attendant	sirviente,acompañante	atendedor	proofreader's aid
audience	auditorio,oyentes,	audiencia	hearing,audition
auditorium	salón de actos	auditorio	audience
auto	auto,automóvil	auto	judicialdecree,file
axe	hacha	axis	axis(neck vertebra)
axis	eje	axis	axis(neck vertebra)
bachelor	soltero	bachiller	high school grad
baggage	equipaje	bagaje	military,equipment
ball	pelota	bala	bullet,shot
barracks	cuartel	barraca	cabin,hut
bastard	bastardo	bastardilla	italics
bizarre	raro,excéntrico	bizarro	brave,gallant
blank	blanco	blanco	blank,white
bozo	tipo,sujeto	bozo	mouth,muzzle
brave	valiente,bravo	bravo	fierce,wild,brave
bride	novia	brida	rein,bridle
cabinet	armario,cómoda	gabinete	government body
cafe	restaurante,café	café	bar,coffeehouse
calm	calmado,sereno,quieto	calmo	barren,uncultivated
camera(photo)	cámera	cámera	camera,chamber,room
camp	campamento	campo	field,country
cannon(gun)	cañon	canon	canon,precept
canyon	cañón	cañón	canyon,gun
cap(hat)	gorro	capa	cloak,cape
capable	capaz	capable	castratable
car	coche(auto),vagón RR	carro	wagon,cart
		caro (ADJ)	expensive
carbon	carbono	carbón	charcoal,coal
card	tarjeta	carta	letter
care	cuidado,atención	cara	face,countenance
cargo(load)	carga,cargamento	cargo	duty,responsibility
carpet	alfombra	carpeta	folder,briefcase
cart	carro	carta	letter,card,map,menu
cartel	monopolio,documento	cartel	poster,chart
cartoon	dibujo,caricatura	cartón	cardboard
casualty(injury)	baja(MIL),accidente	casualidad	chance,coincidence
cement	cemento	cimiento	foundation,origin

ENGLISH	SPANISH EQUIVALENT	SPANISH COGNATE	ENGLISH EQUIVALENT
chagrin	mortificación	chagrín	tooled leather
chance	fortuna, casualidad oportunidad, ocasión	chanza	joke, jest
chance (to take.)	aventurar	chancear	joke, fool
chaparon	chapparrona	chaparrón	downpour, shower
		chaperón	hood, cowl
character (play)	personaje	carácter	nature, personality
charge (.a price)	precio	carga	load, burden
cholera	cólera	cólera	anger, cholera
cigar	puro, tabaco, habano	cigarro	cigarette
coast	costa	costo	cost
collapse (fall)	derrumbe	colapso	collapse (MED)
collar	cuello	collar	necklace, flange
college	universidad	colegio	school
colon (GRAM)	dos puntos	colon	colon (ANAT)
			colón (El Salv. coin)
color (to..)	pintar, colorear	encolerizar	anger, enrage
colored (dyed)	teñido	colorado	red, ruddy
comma	coma	coma	comma, coma
commercial (TV)	anuncio	comercial	re commerce
commode	cómoda, retrete	comodidad	comfort, convenience
commodity	mercancía, géneros	comodidad	comfort, convenience
compact (agrmt)	pact, convenio	compacto	dense, tight
compensation (pay)	remuneración	compensación	recompense, redress
competence	capacidad	competencia	competition
competition	competencia, concurso	competición	sporting event
complacency	afabilidad, deferencia	complacencia	pleasure, satisfaction
complexion	tez	complexión	character, temperament
compromise	arreglo, concessión acuerdo, convenio	compromiso	appointment, promise, obligation, pledge
compromise (VERB)	arreglar, componer	comprometer	bind, obligate
conception (idea)	concepto	concepción	conception (beginning)
concrete	hormigón, concreto	concreto	specific, concrete
concurrence	coincidencia, acuerdo	concurrencia	crowd, competition
condition	estado, circunstancia	condición	nature, disposition
conductor (MUS)	director	conductor	driver, motorman
conductor (tram)	cobrador (street-car)	conductor	driver, motorman
conductor (driver)	conductor, guía	conductor	driver, motorman
confection	dulce, pastel	confección	workmanship, handiwork
conference	consulta, junta	conferencia	lecture, talk
confidence (faith)	confianza	confidencia	secret, confidence
confident	confiado	confidente	true, faithful, trusty
congratulate	felicitar	congratular	be glad, congratulate
conservative	conservador	conservativo	preservative
constipate	estreñirse	constiparse	catch cold
constipated	estreñido	constipado	having a cold
constipation	estreñimiento	constipación	common cold
consumption (use)	consumo, destrucción	consunción	wasting away, tuberc.
contest (to..)	disputar, contender	contestar	answer, reply, confirm
convene	reunirse, juntarse	convenir	agree, fit, suit
convenience	comodidad	conveniencia	suitability, usuage
convenient	cómodo	conveniente	suitable, fit, proper
converse	inverso	converso	converted
conviction (crime)	condena	convicción	strong belief
copy (book)	ejemplar	copia	duplicate, reprod, copy

ENGLISH	SPANISH EQUIVALENT	SPANISH COGNATE	ENGLISH EQUIVALENT
corporal (MIL)	caporal, cabo	corporal	corporal (relig. cloth)
correspond	comunicarse	corresponder	correspond, belong to
correspondent	corresponsal	correspond-	corresponding
cost	costo, precio	costa /iente	coast
count	contar	contar	relate, tell, count
courage	valor, valentía	coraje	anger, bravery
course (ACAD)	asignatura	curso	school year
court (LAW)	tribunal, corte	corte	yard, entourage, court
		corto	short
crude	tosco, rudo, vulgar	crudo	raw
cry	llorar, grit	criar	bring up
crystal	cristal	cristal	glass, pane, cristal
cup	taza	copa	goblet, trophy
cure (healing)	cura, f.	cura, m.	priest
curious (strange)	curioso, rara	curioso	inquisitive, odd
date (apptmt)	cita	data	information, facts
date (fruit)	dátil	data	information, facts
date (time)	fecha	data	information, facts
deception	engaño, impostura	decepción	disappointment
decline (refuse)	rehusar	declinar	decline, worsen
deduct (subtract)	subtraer, rebajar	deducir	deduce, conclude
defile	contaminar	desfilar	defile (MIL)
definitely	definitivamente	definidamente	in defined manner
delicious	sabroso, delicioso	delicioso	delightful
delight	deleite, encanto	delito	crime, offense
demand	reclamar, exigir	demandar	request, ask for
depletion (COM)	disminución	depleción	depletion (MED)
deportation	deportación	deporte	sport, recreation
depreciation	depreciación	desprecio	contempt, scorn
dessert	dulce, postre	desertar	desert, abandon
destination	destino	destinación	assignment
devise (to..)	inventar	divisar	see, perceive
dignified	serio, grave, decoroso	digno	worthy
dinner	cena, comida	dinero	money
direction	dirección, orientación	dirección	management, address
disgrace	vergüenza, deshonra	desgracia	misfortune, grief
disgraceful	vergonzoso, lamentable	desgraciado	unfortunate, clumsy
disgust (to..)	repugnar, indignar	disgustar	displease
disgust	repugnancia, aversión	disgusto	displeasure, annoyance
dishonest	no honrado, fraudulento	deshonesto	indecent, lewd
dismay	consternación	desmayo	faint, swoon
dispatch	mensaje, despacho	despacho	office, dispatch
distress	angustia, pena	destreza	skill, dexterity
divert	desviar, distraer	divertir	amuse, entertain
divide	dividir	divisar	see, perceive
doctor (MD)	médico, doctor	doctor	academician, M.D.
dormitory	residencia	dormitorio	bedroom
drugstore	farmacia, botica	droguería	drug & misc. store
druggist	farmacéutico	droguero	drug dealer, chemist
duel	duelo	duela	barrel stave
Dutch	holandés	ducha	shower, douche
edit	redactar, repasar	editar	publish
editor	redactor, director	editor	publisher
educate	instruir	educar	raise, bring up
educated	instruido, culto	educado	urbane, polite

ENGLISH	SPANISH EQUIVALENT	SPANISH COGNATE	ENGLISH EQUIVALENT
education	instrucción	educación	breeding, manners
effective	eficaz	efectivo	real, true, actual
elaborate	perfeccionar	elaborar	prepare, make
elaborate	detallado, suntuoso	elaborado	manufactured
elevator	ascensor	elevador	silo, elevating (ADJ)
embargo	embargo	sin embargo	however
embarkation (goods)	embarque	embarco	embark (people)
embarrassed	confundido, confuso	embarazada	pregnant
emersion	salida	emersión	reappearance
emotional	emocional	emocionante	thrilling
engineer (RR)	maquinista	ingeniero	engineer (profession)
entertain (amuse)	divertir	entretener	entertain, delay
enter	entrar	enterar	inform, make known
envy	envidiar	enviar	send
equipment	equipamiento	equipo	team
escalate	intensificar	escalar	climb
estate	finca, herencia, bienes	estado	state
estimate	calcular, avaluar	estimar	esteem, respect
estimate	cálculo	estima	esteem, respect
estimation (value)	valoración	estimación	esteem, valuation
eventual	final	eventual	accidental, unexpected
eventually	finalmente	eventualmente	by chance
evidence	prueba, testimonio	evidencia	certainty, evidence
example	ejemplo	ejemplar	copy
exit	salida, éxit	éxito	success, outcome
expectation (hope)	esperanza	expectación	expectancy, suspense
explode	detonar, estallar	explotar	exploit, plunder
extemporary	improvisado	extemporáneo	untimely, inopportune
extravagant	excesivo, gastador	extravagante	odd, strange, eccentric
fabric	tejido, tela	fábrica	factory
faculty (academic)	profesorado	facultad	physic. faculty, skill
factory	fabrica	factoría	agency, commission
familiar	conocido	familiar	domestic, re family
fastidious	melindroso, pulcro	fastidioso	annoying, boring
fault	culpa, defecto	falta	lack, want
feast	festín, banquete	fiesta	holiday, party
felon	criminal, felón	felón	villain, scoundrel
figure (number)	cifra	figura	figure, form, shape
file (record)	archivo	fila	line, row, tier, file
file (tool)	lima	fila	line, row, tier, file
fine (good)	excelente, bueno	fino	small, delicate, pure
finesse	finura, delicadeza	fineza	fineness
firm (COM)	casa, empresa	firma	firm, signature
float	flotador	flota	fleet
formal	metódico, ceremonioso	formal	serious, reliable
friction (strife)	discordia	fricción	rubbing, friction
gain	ganancia, beneficio	gana	desire, hunger, wish
gala	fiesta, celebración	gala	formal dress
Geneva	Ginebra	ginebra	gin (liquor)
genial	cordial, afable	genial	brilliant, inspired
gentle	dócil, suave, manso	gentil	refined, courteous
genteel (polite)	gentil, fino, cortes	gentil	gentile, pagan
graceful	elegante, garboso	gracioso	amusing, charming
gracious	amable, cortés, afable	gracioso	amusing, charming
grade (mark)	nota	grado	degree (ACAD), measure

ENGLISH	SPANISH EQUIVALENT	SPANISH COGNATE	ENGLISH EQUIVALENT
grand	grandioso, majestuoso	grande	large, tall, great
grateful	agradecido	grato	kind, pleasant
gratification	gusto, placer	gratificación	tip, reward, gratuity
gratify	satisfacer, agradar	gratificar	tip, reward
gratuity	donación, propina	gratuidad	freeness
grocer	abacero	grocero	crude, vulgar
grocery	bodega	grosería	vulgarity, coarseness
guardian	custodio, guardián	guardián	tutor, warden
gulf	golfo	golf	golf
habit	costumbre	hábito	dress, attire, habit
hall	vestibulo, salón	halo	halo
honest	honrado	honesto	decent, virtuous
honesty	honradez, integridad	honestidad	decency, modesty
idiom	modismo, giro	idioma	language
ignore	no hacer caso de	ignorar	be ignorant of
import	importancia, sentido	importe	amount, cost, value
import (VERB)	importar	importar	import, be important
indignant (angry)	indignado	indigno	unworthy, contemptible
individual	individuo	individual (ADJ)	individual
induct	admitir, reclutar	inducir	induce, lead, persuade
infant	criatura	infante	king's son
informal	íntimo, sencillo	informal	unconventional
information	información	informe	report, acct, inquiry
		información	accusation, info.
ingenuity	ingeniosidad, destreza	ingenuidad	naivete, simplicity
injure	herir, lesionar	injuriar	abuse, insult, offend
injury	daño, herida	injuria	injustice, harm
instance	ejemplo	instancia	insistence, petition
intend	querer hace	entender	understand
		intentar	try
intimation	insinuación, indicio	intimación	warning, announcement
intoxicate	embriagar, emborrachar	intoxicar	poison
intoxication	embriaguez (drunk)	intoxicación	poisoning
introduce (person)	presentar	introducir	usher in
introduction	presentación	introducción	insertion, preface
inversion	inversión	inversión	inversion, investment
invest (finance)	invertir	investir	install
investment (COM)	inversión	investidura	installation
Japan	Japón	jabón	soap
journal	diario	jornal	day's work
journalist	periodista, cronista	jornalero	day laborer
jubilation (glee)	júbilo	jubilación	pension, retirement
label	etiqueta, rótulo	etiqueta	etiquette, label
laborer	trabajador, obrero	labrador	farmer
large	grande, extenso	largo	long, generous
lecture	disertar, instruir	lectura	reading
lecture	disertación, sermón conferencia, curso	lectura	reading
lecturer	conferenciante	lector	reader
librarian	bibliotecario	librero	bookseller
library	biblioteca	librería	bookstore
lily	lirio	lila	lilac
liquidate (kill)	asesinar	liquidar	liquefy, settle, sell
location	colocación, posición	locación	lease, rental
luxurious	lujoso	luxurioso	lecherous

ENGLISH	SPANISH EQUIVALENT	SPANISH COGNATE	ENGLISH EQUIVALENT
luxury	lujo	lujuria	lechery,lust,excess
manners(social)	modales	maneras	ways,means
mantle(cloak)	manto	mantel	tablecloth
		manto	mantel(fireplace)
mark	señal,mancha	marca	brand,trademark
		marco	frame,window case
mascara	cosmético para las pestañas	máscara	mask,masquerade
mason(trade)	albañil	masón	freemason
matrimony	casamiento	matrimonio	married couple
mayor(official)	alcalde	mayor(ADJ)	older,greater
		mayor(NOUN)	major(MIL)
measure	medida	mesura	moderation
media	medios publicitarios	media	stocking,average
memo	nota,memorandum	memo	fool,simpleton
memorial	recuerdo,monumento	memorial	notebook,brief
meter	metro,medidor	meter(VERB)	insert,put into
miserable	desgraciado,vil	miserable	poor,wretched,stingy
misery	miseria,calamidad	miseria	misery,stinginess
mold(BOT)	moho	molde	pattern,form
moral	moral(ADJ)	moral, f.	morals,ethics
		moral, m.	black mulberry tree
morose	áspero,malhumorado	moroso	slow,in default
motto	lema,devisa	moto	motorcycle
mount	monte	monte	mount,woodland
native(NOUN)	natural	nativo	native(ADJ)
note	comentario,billete	nota	grade,musical note
notice	aviso	noticia(s)	news
notice(to..)	notar	noticiar	give notice
notorious	de mala reputación	notorio	famous,well-known
nude(naked)	desnudo	nudo	knot
obliteration	borradura,extinción	obliteración	extirpation(MED)
occasion(event)	acontecimiento,suceso	ocasión	opportunity
occurrence	suceso	ocurrencia	witticism
office	oficina despacho	oficio	trade,occupation
official	funcionario	oficial	officer,official(ADJ)
once	una vez	once	eleven
operate(handle)	manejar	operar	operate(surgery)
operation(event)	funcionamiento	operación	operation(surgery)
or(CONJ)	o	oro	gold
oration	discurso,oración	oración	prayer,oration,speech
ordinary	común,corriente,usual	ordinario	vulgar,common
page(book)	página	paje	messenger page
pan	sartén,cacerola	pan	bread
parable	parábola	parábola	parabola,parable
parade	procesión,desfile	parada	stop,pause
parents	padres	parientes	relatives
part (role)	papel	parte	part(..of whole)
particular(ADJ)	singular,determinado	particular	private,unofficial
particular(NOUN)	detalle	particular(ADJ)	private,unofficial
party(social)	fiesta	partido	political party
pastel(colors)	pastel	pastel	pastry,pie,cake
pastor	pastor,cura	pastor	pastor,shepherd
patron(of event)	patrocinador	patrón	owner,boss
patron(saint)	patrono	patrón	owner,boss

ENGLISH	SPANISH EQUIVALENT	SPANISH COGNATE	ENGLISH EQUIVALENT
pear	pera	perro,pero	dog,but
peculiar(odd)	singular,extraño	peculiar	innate,characteristic
pension(pay)	pensión,jubilación	pensión	pension,boarding house
perfusion	afusión,aspersión	perfusión	bath,perfusion(MED)
persecution	persecución	persecución	pursuit,persecution
peso (CURR)	peso	peso	weight
petulence	malhumor	petulancia	insolence,flippancy
phrase	frase	frase	phrase,sentence
pillar	pilar,columna	pillar(VERB)	plunder,pillage
place	poner,colocar	placer	pleasure,joy
plant(BOT)	planta	planta	foot sole,floor(bldg)
plant(factory)	fábrica	planta	plant(BOT)
plausible	creible,razonable	plausible	laudable,commendable
plume	pluma	pluma	plume,pen,handwriting
policy(GOVT)	política,táctica	policía	police
policy(INS))	póliza	policía	police
precise	preciso,exacto	preciso	precise,necessary
precision	precisión,exactitud	precisión	obligación,necessity
preparations	preparativos	preparaciones	medicine
prescription	receta	prescripción	property acquisition
present(gift)	regalo,presente	presente	gift,present time
preserve(VERB)	conservar	preservar	protect against
pretend	fingir,simular	pretender	try to get,seek
primer	manual,detonador	primero(ADJ)	first
private(ADJ)	particular	privado	personal
procure(VERB)	adquirir,obtener, try,transact,produce, conseguir,comprar	procurar	try,produce,manage endeavor
prominent	eminente,notable	prominante	projecting,elevated
promote(rank)	ascender	promover	promote,push
propose(to wed)	declararse	proponer	propose,suggest
pulchritude	belleza, encanto	pulcritud	neatness
pulp	pulpa	pulpo	octopus
punch(blow)	puñada	ponche	punch(drink)
pupil(student)	alumno, discípulo	pupilo	roomer,ward
pure	puro	puro	cigar
purple	morado, púrpura	púrpura	crimson,purple
question	pregunta	cuestión	problem,dispute,matter
quit	dejar, salir de	quitar	remove,take away
quotation(words)	citación	cotización	price quotation
radio	radio	radio	radio,radius,zone
rat(big mouse)	rata	rato	short space of time
real	verdadero,real,genuino	real	real,actual;royal
realist	realista	realista	realist,royalist
realize(VERB)	darse cuenta de,comprender	realizar	achieve a goal,effect, carry out
rebate	rebaja, descuento	rebate	dispute,fight
receipt	recibo	receta	prescription
recollection	memoria, recuerdo	recolección	collection,harvest summary,compilation
record(VERB)	registrar, inscribir	recordar	remember,remind
recur	repetir,reiterar	recurrir	appeal,resort to
red	rojo	red	net
reflection(idea)	reflexión	reflejo	image
register(ACAD)	matricular,inscribir	registrar	inspect,examine

ENGLISH	SPANISH EQUIVALENT	SPANISH COGNATE	ENGLISH EQUIVALENT
regular	regular	regular	common, average
reign	reinado, imperio	reno	reindeer
		reino	kingdom, realm
		reina	queen
relate	relacionar	relatar	tell, relate
relative (family)	pariente	relativo (ADJ)	related, relative
relevant	pertinente	relevante	excellent, eminent
relief	desahogo, ayuda	relieve	relief art work
remark (VERB)	observar	remarcar	mark again
rent (VERB)	alquilar, arrendar	rentar	produce income
rent	alquilar	renta	income
report (VERB)	informar, dar cuenta	reportar	check, curb, control
report	informe, noticia	reporte	printing transfer
resort	balneario	resorte	spring (MECH)
rest (VERB)	descansar	restar	deduct, reduce, remain
retire	jubilar	retirar	remove, withdraw
retreat	refugio, retirada	retrete	toilet, bathroom
revolver (gun)	revólver	revolver (VERB)	mix, consider, return
revulsion	repugnancia, aversion	revulsión	revulsion (MED)
rodeo	rodeo	rodeo	twist, encircling
roll (bread)	bollo, panecillo	rollo	roll of paper
		rol	list, part
romance	amorío, encanto	romance	ballad, romance
rope	cuerda	ropa	clothing
rude	grosero, descortés	rudo	rustic, rough, crude
sable (ZOOL)	cebellina	sable	saber, cutlass
saga (legend)	saga	saga	witch, sorceress
salad	ensalada	salado	salty
salary	sueldo	salario	wages (laborers')
salt	sal	salto	jump, leap
salve	ungüento, bálsamo	salva	salvo, greeting
sane	cuerdo, sensato	sano	healthy, wholesome
sanity	juicio, sensatez	sanidad	sanitation, health
scenery (stage)	decorado, decoraciones	escenario	stage, setting
scenery (view)	paisaje, panorama	escenario	stage, setting
scholar	erudito, docto	escolar	pupil
season (year)	estación	sazón	spice, seasoning
secrete (hide)	esconder	secretar	ooze, secrete
secure (obtain)	obtener	asegurar	secure (safeguard)
security (docum.)	valores	seguridad	security (safety)
senior (ADJ)	padre, superior	señor	master, mister
sensible	razonable, sensato	sensitivo	sensitive, lamentable
sentence (GRAM)	frase	sentencia	judgment, verdict
serious	serio, grave	serio	reliable, worthwhile
sierra	cordillera, sierra	sierra	saw, jagged mountains
signature	firma	signatura	filing number or mark
		asignatura	school course
smoking	acción de fumar	smoking	dinner jacket, tuxedo
soap	jabón	sopa	soup
soul	ala, espíritu	sol	sun
		solo	alone, only
spade (shovel)	pala, azada	espada	sword, spade (cards)
spice	especia	especie	species
stationery	papelería	estacionario	fixed, stable
stretch (VERB)	estirar, alargar	estrechar	tighten, narrow, reduce

ENGLISH	SPANISH EQUIVALENT	SPANISH COGNATE	ENGLISH EQUIVALENT
suave (urbane)	fino, culto	suave	gentle, soft
subject	asunto, materia, tema	sujeto	person, subject (GRAM)
substantiate	justificar	substanciar	abstract, abridge
succeed	lograr, tener éxito	suceder	happen, follow
success	éxito	suceso	event, happening
successful	de éxito	sucesivo	followimg, consecutive
suggestion	sugerencia	sugestión	personal influence
support (VERB)	apoyar, soportar, sostener	sorportar	endure, bear, put up with
sympathetic	compasivo	simpático	likeable, agreeable, pleasant, nice
sympathize (VERB)	congeniar, condolerse	simpatizar	to be congenial with
sympathy (pity)	compasión	simpatía	liking, affection
talent	talento, capacidad	talante	countenance, mien
talon (claw)	talón	talón	claw, heel, stub
tariff	arancel	tarifa	rate, price list
tea	té	tío	uncle
temple	sien	templo	temple (bldg)
tentative	provisorio, indeciso	tentativa	attempt, endeavor
terrific	magnifico, excelente	terrífico	terrifying
terrify	aterrorizar, alarmar	aterrizar	land a plane
timber	madera	timbre	stamp, seal, doorbell
torment	tormento, angustia	tormenta	storm, tempest
tramp	vagabundo	trampa	trap, snare
tranquil	tranquilo, quieto	tranquil (NOUN)	plumb line
transpire (happen)	acontecer, suceder	transpirar	perspire, sweat
tuition	derechos de matrícula	tuición	legal defense
tuna	atún (fish)	tuna	prickly pear (BOT)
tutor	instructor, profesor	tutor	guardian
ultimately	finalmente	ultimamente	recently
urge (VERB)	instar, impulsar, roger	urgir	be urgent
vegetables	legumbres (edibles)	vegetales	plants
versatility	universalidad	versatilidad	changeableness, instability
vase	jarrón	vaso	glass (drinking)
veil	velo	vela	candle
veil (hide)	velar	velar	watch, keep vigil
vicious	maligno, vicioso	vicioso	depraved
villain	bribón	villano	rustic, peasant, boor
vulgar	indecente, deshonesto	vulgar	common, ordinary
wagon	carro, carreta	vagón	railway car
wine	vino	viña	vineyard
zero	cero	cerro	hill

APPENDICES

AREAS OF NON-CONVERSION

Although the purpose of the CONVOCAB approach is to facilitate the building of an extensive Spanish vocabulary through the conversion of an existing vocabulary of English verbs, nouns and adverbs derived from adjectives, there are many essential words which must be learned without the benefit of conversion patterns. Since virtually all of the pronouns, articles, prepositions, conjunctions, short adverbs and numbers require memorization, they are arranged in separate lists in the Appendices to facilitate the learning process. The 40 subject matter lists contained in Appendix H provide easy access to key words in subject matter groups that might be of special interest.

APPENDIX	PAGE
A. PRONOUNS	396
B. ARTICLES	398
C. PREPOSITIONS	398
D. CONJUNCTIONS	400
E. SPECIAL NONCONVERTING ADJECTIVES	401
F. SPECIAL NONCONVERTING ADVERBS	403
G. NUMBERS	408
H. SUBJECT MATTER GROUPS	410

A. PRONOUNS

Although pronouns are primarily a subject for grammar study, this appendix sets forth the most commonly used pronouns in the various pronoun categories.

1. Personal Pronouns

These pronouns vary in form according to the five different roles indicated in the chart's column titles: i.e.-as the subject of a clause or sentence; the indirect object of a verb; the direct object of a verb; a reflexive pronoun referring back to the subject and as the object of a preposition.

SUBJECT	INDIRECT OBJECT	DIRECT OBJECT	REFLEXIVE	AFTER PREPOSITION
I = yo	me = me	me = me	myself = me	me = mí
you = +tú	you = +te	you = +te	yourself = +te	you = +ti
you = usted	you = le	you = lo, la, le	yourself = se	you = usted
he = él	him = le	him = lo, le	himself = se	him = él
she = ella	her = le	her = la	herself = se	her = ella
it = ello	it = le	it = lo	itself = se	it = ello
we = nosotros / nosotras	us = nos	us = nos	ourselves = nos	us = nosotros / nosotras
you = +vosotros / +vosotras	you = +os	you = +os	yourselves = +os	you = +vosotros / +vosotras
you = ustedes	you = les	you = los, las	yourselves = se	you = ustedes
they = ellos / ellas	them = les	them = los / them = las	themselves = se	them = ellos / ellas

NOTE:
The second person forms identified by a + sign are the familiar forms used for close personal relationships and do not appear as often in written Spanish as the formal form of the second person pronouns. When the object of the Spanish preposition *con* is *mí* or *ti*, the special combined form *conmigo* and *contigo* are used.

2. Possessive Pronouns

These pronouns agree in gender and number with the object possessed.
Cross-Reference: ADJ -Possessive Adjectives

ENGLISH	SPANISH			
	Masc.Singular	Masc.Plural	Fem.Singular	Fem.Plural
mine	el mío	los míos	la mía	las mías
yours	el tuyo	los tuyos	la tuya	las tuyas
his	el suyo	los suyos	la suya	las suyas
hers	el suyo	los suyos	la suya	las suyas
its	el suyo	los suyos	la suya	las suyas
ours	el nuestro	los nuestros	la nuestra	las nuestras
yours	el vuestro	los vuestros	la vuestra	las vuestras
theirs	el suyo	los suyos	la suya	las suyas
yours	el suyo	los suyos	la suya	las suyas

3. **Demonstrative Pronouns**
These pronouns indicate a particular person or object. They agree in gender and number with the nouns they replace.

ENGLISH	SPANISH		ENGLISH	SPANISH	
	Masculine	Feminine		Masculine	Feminine
this	éste	ésta	that (close)	ése	ésa
			that (far)	aquél	aquélla
these	éstos	éstas	those (close)	ésos	ésas
			those (far)	aquéllos	aquéllas

4. **Relative Pronouns**
Unlike in English, the relative pronoun may not be omitted in Spanish.

ENGLISH	SPANISH	ENGLISH	SPANISH
that	que	who	quien, quienes, que
what	(lo) que	whom	a quien, que
which	que	whose	cuyo, cuya
		of which	

5. **Interrogatory Pronouns**

ENGLISH	SPANISH		ENGLISH	SPANISH	
how many?	¿cuántos?	¿cuántas?	who?	¿quién?	¿quiénes?
how much?	¿cuánto?	¿cuánta?	whom?	¿a quién?	¿a quiénes?
what?		¿qué?	whose?	¿de quién?	¿de quiénes?
which?	¿qué? ¿cuál	¿cuáles?			

6. **Miscellaneous Pronouns**
These pronouns usually refer to a nonspecific class or thing.

ENGLISH	SPANISH	ENGLISH	SPANISH
all	todo	nobody, no one	nadie
another	otro	none	ninguno
any	alguno, cualquiera	nothing	nada
anybody	alguien, alguno	one	uno
(anyone)	cualquiera, quienquiera	other	otro
anything	algo, alguna cosa	same	mismo
both	los dos; ambos	self	mismo
each (one)	cada uno	several	varios
either	uno u otro	some	algunos
everybody	todo el mundo	somebody	alguien
everyone	cada uno, todo el mundo	someone	alguien
everything	todo	something	alguna cosa, algo
few	algunos, pocos	such	tal
former	aquél	whatever	cualquier cosa que
latter	último, éste	when	cuándo
much	mucho	whoever	quienquiera que
neither	ninguno	whomever	a quienquiera

B. ARTICLES

Spanish definite and indefinite articles agree in gender and number with the noun they accompany.

ENGLISH	SPANISH			
	Masc.Singular	Masc.Plural	Fem.Singular	Fem.Plural
Definite Article				
the	el	los	la	las
Indefinie Article				
Singular a, an	un		una	
Plural a few, some		unos		unas

C. PREPOSITIONS

Prepositions are words or phrases that indicate a (spatial, temporal, causal, effective, directional or some other) relationship between a noun or pronoun and another portion of the sentence.

Very few Spanish prepositions resemble their English counterparts. It is often difficult to determine whether the word or phrase is used as an adverb or as a preposition. Although not all prepositions and prepositional phrases have been included, the list contains most of those which are most frequently used.

ENGLISH	SPANISH	ENGLISH	SPANISH
aboard	a bordo de	at(time)	a, en
about	alrededor de, de, sobre, cerca de	at(place)	a, en
	respecto a, tocante a, acerca de	at home of	en casa de, a casa de
above	arriba de, encima de, sobre	at the end of	al cabo de
according to	según	at the side of	al lado de
across	al otro lado de	because of	por, a causa de
	por, a través de	before(time)	antes de
after(place)	detrás de	before(place)	frente a, delante de
after(following)	tras	behind(place)	tras, detrás de
after(time)	después de	behind(time)	después de
against	enfrente de, contra	below	debajo de
ahead(place)	de frente a, delante de	beneath	por debajo de, debajo de
ahead(time)	antes de	beside(place)	cerca de, al lado de
along	entre, por, al lado de	besides(other than)	además de
	a lo largo de	between	entre
among(amid)	en medio de, entre	beyond(place)	fuera de, más allá de
around	cerca de, alrededor de	beyond(time)	después de
as(like)	como	but	salvo, excepto
as against	por, comparado con	by(accdg to)	según, conforme a
as far as	hasta	by(beside)	al lado de, cerca de
as for	en cuanto a	by(multiply)	por
at(by)	con, a	by(near)	junto a
at (in, on)	en	by(prior to)	antes de
at (toward)	a	by(via)	por

ENGLISH	SPANISH	ENGLISH	SPANISH
by (agency)	por	next to	junto a, al lado de
by means of	a fuerza de, mediante por medio de	notwithstanding	a pesar de
		of	desde, de
concerning	sobre, concerniente a de, acerca de, respecto a	off	de, desde
		on (place)	encima de, a, en, sobre
considering	en vista de	on account of	en favor de, a causa de
depending on	según	on behalf of	por, a favor de
despite	a pesar de, a despecho de no obstante	on the part of	de parte de
		on the point of	a punto de
down	a lo largo de, abajo, por	on top of	además de, encima de
during (in)	mientras, durante	onto	encima de, sobre, en, a
except	menos, salvo, excepto aparte de, sino	opposite	frente a, en frente de contra, al otro lado de
facing	frente a	out of	fuera de, por, de
far from	lejos de	outside of	fuera de
following	después de	over (above)	sobre, encima de
for (on behalf of)	por, para	over (across)	a través de
for (..period of time)	durante	over (more)	más de
for the sake of	por motivo de, por	past (beyond)	más de, más allá de
for want of	a falta de	per (for each)	según, por
from (place)	de	plus	más
from (time)	desde	regarding	sobre, con respecto a en cuanto a, tocante a
from (result)	por, a causa de		
in	a, dentro, en	save	sino, menos, excepto, salvo
in accordance with	de acuerdo con	since (after)	después de, desde
in addition to	además de, a más de	thanks to	gracias a
in back of	detrás de	through	a través de, por
in behalf of	por, por parte de	through (by means of)	por medio de
in compliance with	de acuerdo con	throughout (time)	durante todo
in comparison with	comparado con	throughout (in every part)	por todo
in consequence of	como resultado de	to	a, para, hasta
in consid. of	en consideración a	to (destination)	hacia, a
in behalf of	por, en nombre de	to (in order to)	para
in case of	en caso de	to (time)	hasta
in favor of	en favor de	to the left of	a la izquierda de
in front of	frente a, delante de en frente de	to the right of	a la derecha de
		toward(s)	hacia, para
in lieu of	en lugar de, en vez de	under (underneath)	bajo, debajo de
in the midst of	en medio de	unless	excepto, salvo
in the name of	en nombre, de parte de	until (up to, till)	a, hasta
in order to	a fin de, para	until (before)	antes de
in place of	en lugar de	unto	hacia, hasta
in the presence of	delante de, ante	up	a lo alto de, hacia arriba de
in regard to	con respecto a en cuanto a	up to	hacia, hasta
		upon, on	en, a, sobre
in return for	por	versus	contra
in spite of	no obstante, a pesar de a despecho de	vis-á-vis	comparado con, frente a
		whenever	toda vez que
in view of	en vista de	with	a, con
inside of (within)	dentro de	with reference to	con respecto a
instead of	en vez de, en lugar de	with respect to	con respecto a
into	dentro, adentro, a, en	within	adentro de, dentro de
less (minus)	menos	within sight of	a la vista de
like	como, a manera de	without (lacking)	sin
minus	menos, sin	without (outside)	fuera de
near (nearby)	junto a, cerca de	worth	digno de

D. CONJUNCTIONS

Conjunctions are words used to link or connect sentences or parts of sentences. The same word or phrase can often also be used as an adverb or preposition.

ENGLISH	SPANISH	ENGLISH	SPANISH
according to(depending on)	según	now that	puesto que,ya que,ahora que
after	después (de) que	now then	conque
although,albeit	no obstante,bien que	on the other hand	por otra parte
	aunque,aun cuando		por otra lado,en cambio
and	y(e)	once	cuando,tan pronto como
and so	así que,pues,conque	only	pero,sólo que
as(since)	pues,puesto que	*or	o(u)
as(manner)	según,como	provided that	como,con tal que
as..as	tan..como		provisto que,siempre que
as it seems	según parece	rather than	antes
as if	como si	save	con excepción de
as it were	por decirlo así	scarcely..when	apenas..cuando
as long as	tanto como,ya que	seeing(..that)	visto que,puesto que
as regards	en cuanto a	since (because)	pues,puesto que
as soon as	tan pronto como		desde que,ya que
as though	como si	since(time)	desde que,después que
as well as	tan bien como,así como	so long as	mientras que,hasta que
because of	debido a,a causa de	so(in order that)	de modo que,pues
because(for)	pues,ya que,porque		así que,para que,conque
before(time)	antes que,antes de que		de modo(manera) que
both..and	tanto..como	still	sin embargo,no obstante
but(if not)	a menos que	than	que
but(yet)	pero,mas,sino	then	conque
either	o	that	para que,que,de modo que
either..or	o...o	though	a pesar de que,aunque
else	de otro modo	unless	a no ser que,a menos que
even if	aunque,aun cuando	until(till)	hasta que
even though	aunque,aun cuando	when	aun cuando,cuando
every time that	siempre que	whence	de dónde
except	pero,sino,fuera de que	whenever	siempre que,cada vez que
for(because)	puesto que,pues,porque	where	por donde,adonde,donde
	puesto que	whereas	por cuanto,puesto que
how	como,que		mientras que,en visto de que
however,yet	mas,pero,sin embargo	whereby	por medio del cual
if	en caso de,si	wherefrom	de lo cual,desde donde
	siempre que,supuesto que	wherein	en que,donde
immediately	tan pronto como	whereof	de que,de lo que
in as much as	visto que,puesto que	whereon	en que,sobre
in case	en caso de que	whereto	adonde,a lo que
in order that	para que,a fin de que	whereupon	sobre que,después de lo cual
in that	ya que,porque	wherever	dondequiera que
lest	por miedo de,para que no	wherewith	con que,con lo cual
like	como,del mismo modo	whether(if)	si
neither..nor	ni..ni	while(during)	mientras que
nor	ni	while(whereas)	en tanto que
no sooner than	apenas	whither	adonde
not,only,but	no sólo..sino también	why	porque,por lo cual
notwithstanding	aunque,a pesar de que	without	sin que,a menos que

E. SPECIAL GROUPS OF NON-CONVERTING ADJECTIVES

1. Demonstrative Adjectives (Agree with noun in number and gender)

ENGLISH		SPANISH			
Singular	Plural	Singular		Plural	
		Masculine	Feminine	Masculine	Feminine
this	these	este	esta	estos	estas
that	those	ese (nearby)	esa	esos	esas
		aquel (distant)	aquella	aquellos	aquellas

2. Possessive Adjectives (Agree with noun in number and gender)

ENGLISH	SPANISH			
	Before the Noun		After the Noun	
	Singular	Plural	Singular	Plural
my	mi	mis	mío, -a	míos, -as
your(sing)	tu (familiar)	tus	tuyo, -a	tuyos, -as
	su (formal)	sus	suyo, -a	suyos, -as
his	su	sus	suyo, -a	suyos, -as
her	su	sus	suyo, -a	sujos, -as
its	su	sus	suyo, -a	suyos, -as
our	nuestro, -a	nuestros, -as	nuestro, -a	nuestros, -as
your(plur)	vuestro, -a (fam)	vuestros, -as	vuestro, -a	vuestros, -as
	su (formal)	sus	suyo, -a	suyos, -as
their	su	sus	suyo, -a	suyos, -as

3. Indefinite Adjectives (Agree with noun in number and gender)

ENGLISH	SPANISH	ENGLISH	SPANISH
all	todo	most	lo más, casi todo
another	otro	neither	ningún
any (some)	alguno	no	ningun(o)
any (whatever)	cualquier	only	único
both	ambos	other	otro
each	cada	several	algunos, varios
either	uno u otro	some	alguno
every	cada, todo	such	tal
few	algunos, pocos	what	que, cualquier
many	muchos	which	cualquiera
more	más	whichever	cualquiera

4. Interrogative Adjectives (Agree with the noun in number and gender)

ENGLISH	SPANISH	ENGLISH	SPANISH
how many?	¿cuántos? (-as)	which?	¿qué?
how much?	¿cuánto? (-a)		¿cuál(-es)?
what?	¿qué?		

5. Irregular Comparative and Superlative Adjectives

ENGLISH			SPANISH		
Positive	Comparative	Superlative	Positive	Comparative	Superlative
bad	worse	worst	malo	peor	el peor
big	bigger	biggest	gran(de)	mayor	el mayor
good	better	best	buen(o)	mejor	el mejor
small	smaller	smallest	pequeño	menor	el menor

F. SPECIAL GROUPS OF FREQUENTLY-USED ADVERBS WHICH ARE NOT DERIVED FROM ADJECTIVES AND DON'T CONVERT FROM ENGLISH TO SPANISH

The adverbs listed here are arranged in groups according to the meaning or function they contribute to the sentence. The groupings are rather arbitrary since many could reasonable be placed in more than one group.

1. Interrogatory Adverbs

ENGLISH	SPANISH	ENGLISH	SPANISH
how?	¿cómo?	how soon?	¿cuándo?
how else?	¿de qué otra manera?	how often	¿cuántas veces?
how far?	¿a qué distancia?	when?	¿cuándo?
how fast?	¿con qué rapidez?	where?	¿dónde?
how long?	¿cuánto tiempo?	where from, whence?	¿de dónde?
	¿hasta cuándo?	where to, whither?	¿adónde?
how many?	¿cuántos?	why?	¿por qué?, ¿para qué?
how much?	¿cuánto?		

2. Adverbs of Place, Arrangement, Direction & Motion

ENGLISH	SPANISH	ENGLISH	SPANISH
aboard	a bordo	east	al este, hacia el este
above(upstairs)	encima, arriba	elsewhere	en otra parte
abroad	en el extranjero	everywhere	en todas partes
across(beyond)	a través	facing	enfrente
across(other side)	al otro lado	far(far away)	a gran distancia, lejos
ahead(forward)	más allá, adelante	farther	más adelante, más lejos
ahead(in front)	delante	forth	afuera, adelante
along(lengthwise)	a lo largo	forward	hacia adelante
anywhere(not..)	en cualquier parte	from a distance	desde lejos
anywhere	dondequiera	further(extent)	más, además
apart	separadamente, aparte		más allá, más adelante
around	cerca, alrededor	hence(henceforth)	de aquí, en adelante
around here	por acá	here	en este lugar, acá, aquí
aside	a lado, aparte, a un lado	hereabouts	por aquí, en la vecindad
at a distance	a lo lejos	here and there	acá y allá
at home	en casa, a casa	herein	aquí dentro, en esto
away(place)	a distancia, lejos	hereinabove	antes, más arriba
back (rearward)	detrás, atrás	hereinbelow	más abajo
backward	hacia atrás	hereof	de esto
before(in front)	al frente, delante	hereto	a esto, a este fin
behind(in back)	hacia atrás, detrás	hither	acá, hacia acá
below(downstairs)	debajo, abajo	home(at..)	en casa
beneath	debajo, abajo	home(homeward)	hacia casa, a casa
between	de por medio, entre los dos	in here	aquí dentro
beyond	allende, más allá	in the first place	en primer lugar
by(near)	cerca, al lado	in front of	en frente, delante
close(near)	próximo a, cerca	in the distance	a lo lejos
down(downwards)	hacia abajo, abajo	indoors	adentro, bajo techo
downstairs	abajo	inside(within)	dentro, adentro
downwind	con el viento	inward	interiormente, hacia dentro

403

ENGLISH	SPANISH	ENGLISH	SPANISH
just beyond	un poco más allá	thereat	allí,allá,ahí
near(not far)	próximadamente,cerca	therefrom,thence	de allí,desde ahí
nearby	cercano,a la mano,cerca	therein	adentro
next to	a lado de,junto a	thereinafter	en adelante
north	hacia el norte,al norte	thereof	de eso,de esto
nowhere	en ninguna parte	thereon	sobre,encima
off	a distancia,lejos	thereto	a eso,a ello
on the left	a la izquierda	thereunder	por debajo,debajo
on the right	a la derecha	thereupon	por lo tanto,encima de eso
on top	encima	this way	por acá,por aquí
onward	hacia adelante	thither	allá
opposite	enfrente	through(across)	a través
out(forth)	hacia afuera,fuera	throughout	en todas partes
out(not in)	afuera	to one side	al lado,aparte
outdoors	fuera de casa,al aire libre	together	uno con otro,juntamente
outside	afuera	underneath (under)	debajo
over(across)	al otro lado	up(upstairs)	arriba
over(above)	encima	up and down	de arriba a abajo
over here	acá	upward(s)	hacia arriba
over there	allí,allá	west	hacia el oeste
overhead	arriba	whence(from where)	de dónde
past	más allá	where(in which)	en dónde,dónde
seaward(s)	hacia el mar	where(through which)	por dónde
side by side	codo a codo	where to(whither)	adónde
sideways(-ward)	de lado,lateralmente	wherein	en qué,en dónde
somewhere(..place)	en alguna parte	whereto	para qué,adónde
south	hacia el sur	wherever	dónde
there	allí,allá,ahí	within (on inside)	dentro,adentro
thereabouts	por ahí,alrededor		

3. Adverbs of Time

ENGLISH	SPANISH	ENGLISH	SPANISH
after	tras,después	at night	de noche,por la noche
afterward	después,luego,más tarde	at once	en seguida,al instante
again	otra vez,de nuevo		ahora mismo,al momento,al punto
ahead	antes		inmediatamente,desde luego
all of a sudden	de súbito,de pronto	at present	al presente,ahora
all the time	todo el tiempo	at the end	a fines de
already	desde entonces,ya	at the latest	a más tardar
always(all along)	para siempre,siempre	at the same time	en mismo tiempo
any more	nunca más,no más		a la vez
as long as	ya que	at the time	por entonces
as soon as	luego que,cuanto antes	at times	algunas veces,a veces
	así que,tan pronto como		de vez en cuando
as soon as possible	lo mas pronto	awhile	por un rato
	tan pronto posible	before(earlier)	anteriormente,antes
at a time	a la vez	beforehand	antes, de antemano
at first	al pronto,al principio	before long	dentro de poco
at first sight	a primera vista	behind(late)	con retraso,atrasado
at last	al cabo,por fin,al fin	by and by	poco a poco,pronto
at least	por lo menos,al menos	daily	todos los días,diariamente
	a lo menos,cuando menos	day after tomorrow	pasado mañana
at most	a todo,por lo más	day before yesterday	anteayer
	a lo más,cuando más	early	temprano

ENGLISH	SPANISH	ENGLISH	SPANISH
ever(all times)	siempre	no longer	ya no, no...más
ever(at any time)	alguna vez, jamás	not yet	aún no, todavía no
every day	todos los días	now	actualmente, ya, ahora
every time	cada vez	nowadays	en estos días, hoy día
finally	en fin, por último, por fin finalmente, al fin, al cabo	now and then	de vez en cuando
		often	muchas veces, a menudo
first(-ly)	primeramente	on time	a tiempo
first of all	en primer lugar ante todo	*once and for all	de una vez
		*once (one time)	una vez
for the present	por ahora	once (formerly)	en otro tiempo
for the time being	por de pronto	per day	al día
forever, for good	para siempre	presently	luego, ya, a poco
formerly	antiguamente, antes	previously	anteriormente
forthwith	ahora mismo, al instante en seguida	right away(now)	desde luego, ahora mismo
		seldom	raramente, raras veces pocas veces
from now on(henceforth)	en adelante		
from that time on	desde entonces	several times	varias veces
from then on	desde entonces	since then	desde entonces
from time to time	de vez en cuando de cuando en cuando	so often	tantas veces
		someday	de algún día
hardly ever	casi nunca	sometime	algún día, alguna vez
henceforth	en adelante	sometimes	a veces, algunas veces
hereafter	de aquí, en adelante	soon(early)	temprano
hereinafter	después, más adelante	soon(shortly)	en breve, luego, pronto
hitherto(thus far)	hasta ahora	soon after	poco después
immediately	desde luego, al punto	sooner	antes
in the evening	por la tarde	still(yet)	aún, todavía
in the morning	por la mañana	the other day	el otro día
in time	a tiempo	then(after that)	pues, luego
just as(then)	al momento que	then(that time)	entonces, después
just in time	justo a tiempo	thereafter	después de
just now	ahora mismo	thereinafter	en adelante
last night	anoche	theretofore	hasta entonces
last week	la semana pasada	this evening	esta tarde
lastly	al fin, finalmente	this morning	esta mañana
late(after all)	al final	thus far	hasta ahora
late(tardily)	tardíamente	today	hoy
late(time)	tarde	tomorrow(day after)	pasado mañana
lately	recientemente, últimamente	tomorrow evening	mañana por la tarde
later	luego, más tarde	tomorrow	mañana
long ago	hace much tiempo	tomorrow morning	mañana por la mañana
many times(often)	muchas veces	tonight	esta noche
meantime(-while)	mientras tanto entretanto	two weeks ago	hace dos semanas
		week from today	de hoy en ocho días
monthly	mensualmente	when	cuando
never	jamás, nunca	whenever	cada vez que, siempre que
next	después, luego	yesterday(day before-)	anteayer
next week	la semana próxima	yesterday	ayer
nightly	cada noche, por las noches	yet(until now)	ya, todavía

4. Adverbs of Manner

ENGLISH	SPANISH	ENGLISH	SPANISH
accordingly	en conformidad	how	cómo
actually	en efecto, en realidad	in a whisper (quietly)	en voz baja

ENGLISH	SPANISH	ENGLISH	SPANISH
alike(similarly)	de la misma manera	in addition	además
all right	bien,bueno	in any case	en todo caso
alone	sólo,solamente	in earnest	de veras
aloud	en voz alta	in fact	de hecho,en realidad
anyhow(in any case)	de cualquier modo	in like manner	igualmente,simismo
anyhow(in any case)	de todos modos	in no way	nada más,de ningún modo
anyway	en todo caso,de todos modos	in passing	de pasada,al paso
as(like)	como	in short	en breve,en fin
as a last resort	en último caso	in such a case	en tal caso
as follows	así	in that way	de esta manera,así
as it were	por decirlo así	in this way	de este modo
as well	también	in truth	de veras
as well as	así como	in turn	a su vez
at every step	a cada paso	in vain	inútilmente,en vano
badly(poorly)	sin éxito,mal	indeed	de veras,verdaderamente
besides	también,además	instance(for..)	por ejemplo
better	mejor	instead	en lugar,en vez,más bien
better and better	cada vez mejor	just(exactly)	exactamente
by all means	sin falta,de todos modos	just as	así
by and large	de manera general	just so	a su gusto
by chance	acaso,por casualidad por suerte	like	así como,semejante a,como
by far	con mucho	likewise(also)	también
by heart	de memoria	maybe	acaso,tal véz,quizá(s)
by means of	mediante	no way(nowise)	de ningún modo
by no means	de ningún modo	on foot	a pie
by the way	de paso,a propósito	on other occasions	otras veces
carefully	con cuidado	on purpose	de propósito
certainly	como no,de seguro ciertamente,por supuesto claro,por cierto,seguramente	on the contrary	al contrario
		on the other hand	por otra parte
		otherwise	por lo contrario de otra manera, de otro modo
contrary to	en contra a	out loud	en voz alta
doubtless(-ly)	sin duda	piecemeal	poco a poco,en pedazos
downright	muy,claramente	really	de veras
either(negative)	tampoco	right	bien,correctamente,justamente
else(instead)	además,de otro modo	scarcely	apenas
even	hasta,aun	slow(slowly)	lentamente,despacio
fast(quickly)	rápidamente,de prisa	so(how)	así,de esta manera
first place(in the.)	en primer lugar	somehow(someway)	de algún modo
frequently	a menudo	sooner the better	cuanto antes mejor
from afar	de lejos	step by step	paso a paso
further(extent)	más,además más allá,más adelante	such as	tal como
		suddenly	de pronto,de repente súbitamente
general(in.)	en general,generalmente	surely	seguramente,sin duda
gladly	con placer,de buena gana con mucho gusto	thereby	de tal modo,con eso
		thereof	de allí,de eso,de esto
hardly	casi no,escasamente,apenas por lo tanto,así,luego	therewith	con eso,con esto
		this way	de esta manera
hereby	por este acto,por la presente	thus(how)	así,de este modo
hereof	de esto,de eso	too(also)	asimismo,además,también
hereto	a esto,a este fin	truly	en verdad,de veras verdaderamente
hereupon	luego,con esto,sobre esto		
herewith	con esto,incluso,ajunto	w.pleasure	con placer,con mucho gusto
high	altamente,sumamente	worse,worst	peor
well	bien	wrong(amiss)	sin razón,mal
wherewith	con qué		

5. Adverbs of Degree, Amount & Number

ENGLISH	SPANISH	ENGLISH	SPANISH
at least	por lo menos, a lo menos	little	algo, poco
a little	un poco	little by little	poco a poco
about (approx)	cerca, alrededor, casi	merely (only)	meramente, solamente
above all	especialmente, sobre todo	more	más
all (entirely)	todo, enteramente	more and more	más y más
almost	casi	more or less	más o menos
altogether	en totalidad, enteramente	most	sumamente, más
around (about)	cerca, aproximadamente	mostly	en su mayor parte
as (equally)	tan	much	muy, mucho
as...as	tan...como	nearly (almost)	proximadamente, casi
as much	tanto	only	sólo, solamente
as much as	tanto como, cuanto	over	más
at most	por lo más	partly	parcialmente, en parte
at any rate	en todo caso	quite	muy, enteramente, bastante
at all	en modo alguno, de ningún modo	rather (somewhat)	bastante, algo
enough	bastante	scarcely (hardly)	apenas
entirely	del todo	so (degree)	tan, tanto
especially	especialmente, sobre todo	so much	tanto
ever so much	muchísimo	some	poco más
halfway	en el medio, a medias	somewhat	algo
hardly	apenas	too much (-many)	demasiado
just (merely)	casi, apenas, solamente	too	demasiado
least (at .)	a lo menos, al menos	twice	dos veces
less and less	de menos en menos	very (greatly)	mucho, bien, muy
less	menos	wholly	totalmente, por completo

6. Adverbs of Negation & Affirmation

ENGLISH	SPANISH	ENGLISH	SPANISH
no	no	not even	ni aun
not	no	noway	de ningún modo
not at all	nada, de ningún modo	nowise	de ningún modo
not either	tampoco	yes	sí

7. Adverbs of Inference & Result

ENGLISH	SPANISH	ENGLISH	SPANISH
because of	por causa de, a causa de	now then	ahora bien, no obstante
consequently	por consiguiente	of course	sin duda, por supuesto
for instance	por ejemplo		claro, cómo no, desde luego
furthermore	a más de esto, además	perhaps	acaso, quizás, tal vez
however (yet)	sin embargo, no obstante	rather (preferably)	más bien
in so much as	puesto que, ya que	regardless	a pesar de todo
indeed	de veras, verdaderamente	therefore (so, hence, thus)	por lo tanto, así, por eso, luego
moreover	por otra parte, además		
namely	es decir, a saber	though	sin embargo, no obstante
nevertheless (yet, notwithstanding)	empero, con todo, sin embargo, no obstante	whereby	cómo, por qué medio
		wherefore	por qué, por lo cual
		why	por lo cual, para qué, por qué

G. NUMBERS

1. Cardinal Numbers

ENGLISH	SPANISH
zero (naught)	cero
one	uno, un, una
two	dos
three	tres
four	cuatro
five	cinco
six	seis
seven	siete
eight	ocho
nine	nueve
ten	diez
eleven	once
twelve	doce
thirteen	trece
fourteen	catorce
fifteen	quince
sixteen	dieciséis
seventeen	diecisiete
eighteen	dieciocho
nineteen	diecinueve
twenty	veinte
twenty-one	veintiuno
twenty-two	veintidós
twenty-three	veintitrés
twenty-four	veinticuatro
twenty-five	veinticinco
twenty-six	veintiséis
twenty-seven	veintisiete
twenty-eight	veintiocho
twenty-nine	veintinueve
thirty	treinta
thirty-one	treinta y uno
forty	cuarenta
fifty	cincuenta
sixty	sesenta
seventy	setenta
eighty	ochenta
ninety	noventa
one hundred	ciento, cien
one hundred one	ciento uno
two hundred	doscientos
three hundred	trescientos
four hundred	cuatrocientos
five hundred	quinientos
six hundred	seiscientos
seven hundred	setecientos
eight hundred	ochocientos
nine hundred	novecientos
one thousand	mil

2. Ordinal Numbers

ENGLISH	SPANISH
-------	-------
first	primero
second	segundo
third	tercero
fourth	cuarto
fifth	quinto
sixth	sexto
seventh	séptimo
eighth	octavo
ninth	noveno
tenth	décimo
eleventh	undécimo
twelfth	duodécimo
thirteenth	decimotercio
fourteenth	decimocuarto
fifteenth	decimoquinto
sixteenth	decimosexto
seventeenth	decimoséptimo
eighteenth	décimoctavo
nineteenth	decimonoveno
twentieth	vigésimo
twenty-first	vigésimoprimo
twenty-second	vigésimosegundo
twenty-third	vigésimotercero
twenty-fourth	vigésimocuarto
twenty-fifth	vigésimoquinto
twenty-sixth	vigésimosexto
twenty-seventh	vigésimoséptimo
twenty-eighth	vigésimoctavo
twenty-ninth	vigésimonono
thirtieth	trigésimo
thirty-first	trigésimoprimo
fortieth	cuadragésimo
fiftieth	quincuagésimo
sixtieth	sexagésimo
seventieth	septuagésimo
eightieth	octogésimo
ninetieth	nonagésimo
hundredth	centésimo
last	último
two hundredth	ducentésimo
three hundredth	tricentésimo
four hundredth	cuadringentésimo
five hundredth	quingentésimo
six hundredth	sexcentésimo
seven hundredth	septingentésimo
eight hundredth	octingentésimo
nine hundredth	noningentésimo
thousandth	milésimo

ENGLISH	SPANISH	ENGLISH	SPANISH
fifteen hundred	mil quinientos		
two thousand	dos mil	2/1000	dosmilésimo
two thousand five	dos mil cinco		
hundred thousand	cien mil	1/100,000	cienmilésimo
million	un millón	millionth	millonésimo
billion	mil milliones, billón	billionth	billonésimo

3. Dates

	SPANISH
1492	mil cuatrocientos noventa y dos
1945	mil novecientos cuarenta y cinco
1989	mil novecientos ochenta y nueve

4. Fractions

ENGLISH	SPANISH	ENGLISH	SPANISH
one half	una mitad	one sixth	un sexto
one third	un tercio	one seventh	un séptimo
two thirds	dos tercios	one eight	un octavo
one fourth (quarter)	un cuarto	one ninth	un noveno
three fourths	tres cuartos	one tenth	un décimo
one fifth	un quinto	eight tenths	ocho décimos
three fifths	tres quintos	one hundredth	un centavo

5. Quantities

ENGLISH	SPANISH	ENGLISH	SPANISH
dozen	docena, f.	pair	par, m.
half a dozen	media docena, f.	portion (part)	parte, f.
gross	gruesa, f.	score (20)	veintena, f.

6. Multiples

ENGLISH	SPANISH	ENGLISH	SPANISH
double	doble	threefold (thrice)	tres veces
fivefold	quíntuplo	triple	triple, triplo
hundredfold	céntuplo	twentyfold	veinte veces
tenfold	diez veces	twofold (twice)	dos veces

7. Other Numerical Terms

ENGLISH	SPANISH	ENGLISH	SPANISH
by halves	por mitades	once	una vez
first time	primera vez	second time	segunda vez
last time	última vez	twice	dos veces

H. FREQUENTLY-USED WORDS IN SUBJECT MATTER GROUPS

Appendix H provides lists of key frequently used words pertaining to forty important subject matter groups. This grouping will facilitate concentration on particular areas of interest. Some converting words have been included in these lists, but the majority require memorization or gradual assimilation through exposure to the Spanish language.

About 7,000 Listed

SUBJECT MATTER LIST INDEX

	Page		Page
1. FOODS & FOOD RELATED WORDS	412	21. VEGETABLES & GRAINS	447
2. BEVERAGES	416	22. PLANTS & FLOWERS	448
3. COOKING, EATING & DRINKING	417	23. TREES & FOREST	450
4. HOUSEHOLD & YARD	418	24. PHENOMENA OF NATURE	451
5. NEIGHBORHOOD & COMMUNITY	421	25. MINERALS & MATERIALS	454
6. BODY PARTS, AILMENTS & CARE	423	26. MEASUREMENTS	455
7. BODY SENSES, FUNCTIONS & CHARACTERISTICS	427	27. TIME, SEASONS & HOLIDAYS	456
8. FAMILY	430	28. SPORTS & GAMES	458
9. DEATH & FUNERALS	431	29. RECREATION & AMUSEMENT	463
10. APPAREL & ACCESSORIES	432	30. MUSIC & THEATER	463
11. PERSONAL GROOMING	433	31. ART & ARCHITECTURE	465
12. TEXTILES, SEWING & TAILORING	434	32. COLORS	465
13. OCCUPATIONS & ROLES	435	33. EDUCATION & LITURATURE	466
14. SHOPS & WORK PLACES	439	34. COMMUNICATIONS	469
15. TOOLS & DEVICES	440	35. BUSINESS & COMMERCE	470
16. ANIMALS	442	36. LAW & LEGAL AFFAIRS	474
17. FISH AND CRUSTACEA	444	37. RELIGION	477
18. REPTILES	445	38. TRAVEL & ACCOMODATIONS	478
19. INSECTS	445	39. GOVERNMENT	483
20. BIRDS	446	40. ARMED FORCES & DEFENSE	484

SUBJECT LIST CROSS-REFERENCES:

	Page		Page
NATIONS & NATIONALITIES	203	MOUNTAINS	208
CITIES & REGIONS	206	FIRST NAMES	208
ISLANDS	207	MONTHS	210
LAKES, OCEANS & RIVERS	208	PLANETS	210

1. FOOD AND FOOD-RELATED WORDS

a) MEAT

ENGLISH	SPANISH	ENGLISH	SPANISH
bacon	tocineta, f.; tocino, m.	mutton	carne de carnero, f.
baked meat	cocida en el horno, f.	overdone meat	carne requemada, f.
baloney	salchicha, f.	pork	cerdo, m.; carne de puerco, f.
beef	carne de vaca, f.	porkchop	chuleta de cerdo, f.
beefsteak	biftec, bistec, m.	rabbit	conejo, m.
biscuit	bollo, bizcocho, m.	rare meat	carne jugosa, f.
boiled meat	carne hervida, f.		carne poco (hecha) asada, f.
bologna	mortadela, f.	raw meat	carne cruda, f.
brains	sesos, m.	rib	costilla, f.
broiled meat	carne a la parrilla, f.	roast (meat)	(carne) asado, m.
calf	becerro, ternera, f.	roastbeef	rosbif, m.
chop (cutlet)	chuleta, f.	salami	salchichón, m.
cold cuts	fiambres, m.	sausage	salchicha, f.; chorizo, m.
cold meat	carne fiambre, f.	serloin	lomo, m.
game	caza, f.	steak	bistec, biftec, m.
ham	jamón, m.	stew	guisado, puchero, m.
hamburger	hamburguesa, f.	stew (to..)	guisar
hash	picadillo, m.	stewed meat	carne guisada, f.
kidneys	riñones, m.	tripe	callos, m.
lamb	carne de cordero, f.	tender meat	carne tierna, f.
lambchop	chuleta de carnero, f.	tenderloin	filete, m.
liver	hígado, m.	tough meat	carne dura, f.
meat	carne, f.	veal	carne de ternera, f.
meatball	albóndiga, f.	veal cutlet	chuleta de ternera, f.
meatloaf	carne mechada, f.	venison	caza, f.; venado, m.
medium meat	carne poco asada, f.	well done	carne bien cocida, f.
	carne medio cruda, f.		carne bien asada, f.
medium cooked	a punto	wurst	salchicha, f.

b) FOWL

ENGLISH	SPANISH	ENGLISH	SPANISH
chicken	pollo, m.	fowl	ave, m.
-breast	pechuga de pollo, f.	goose	ganso, m.
-croquettes	croquetas de pollo, f.	partridge	perdiz, f.
-a la king	pollo a la reina, f.	pheasant	faisán, m.
-broiled	pollo a la parrilla, m.	squab	pichón, m.
-fricassee	fricasé de pollo, f.	turkey	pavo, m.
-roast	pollo asado, m.	-roast	pavo asado, m.
duck	pato, m.	-stuffed	pavo relleno, m.

c) FISH

ENGLISH	SPANISH	ENGLISH	SPANISH
anchovy	anchoa, f.	pickled fish	escabeche, m.
caviar	caviar, m.	plaice	platija, acedía, f.
cod	abadejo, m.	salmon	salmón, m.
cod (dried)	bacalao, m.	sardine	sardina, f.
fish (food)	pescado, m.	seafood	pescado, m.
flounder	rodaballo, m.	smelt	eperlano, m.
haddock	robalo, m.	snapper	cubera, f.
hake	merluza, f.	sole	lenguado, m.
halibut	hipogloso, m.	squid	calamar, m.
herring	arenque, m.	swordfish	espada, f.
mackerel	caballa, f.	trout	trucha, f.
octopus	óctopo, pulpo, m.	tunafish	atún, bonito, m.
perch	perca, f.	turbot	turbo, m.

d) SHELLFISH

ENGLISH	SPANISH	ENGLISH	SPANISH
clam	almeja, f.	oyster	ostra, f.
crab	cangrejo, m.	scallop	valva de concha, pechina, f.
craw(y)fish	langostino, m.	shellfish	molusco, mariscos, m.
lobster	langosta, f.	shrimp	gamba, f.; camarón, m.
mussel	mejillone, m.	snail	caracol, m.

e) EGGS

ENGLISH	SPANISH	ENGLISH	SPANISH
egg	huevo, m.	poached eggs	huevos escalfados, m.
fried	huevos fritos, m.	shirred eggs	huevos al plato, m.
hardboiled	huevos duros, m.	scrambled eggs	huevos revueltos, m.
medium	huevos no muy cocidos, m.	softboiled eggs	huevos pasados, m.
omelet	tortilla de huevos, f.		por agua, m.
-with ham	tortilla con jamón, f.	yolk (egg)	yema, f.
-mushrooms	tortilla de setas, f.	white (egg)	clara de huevo, f.
-with herbs	de finas hierbas, f.		

f) BREAD

ENGLISH	SPANISH	ENGLISH	SPANISH
biscuit	bizchocho, m.; galleta, f.	knead (to..)	amasar
bread	*pan, m.	loaf	bollo, m; hogaza, f.
bread-butter	-con mantequilla, m.	muffin	panecillo, mollete, m.
bread (piece of..)	pedazo de pan, m.	pastry	pastel, m
brown bread	pan moreno, m.	roll	bollito, panecillo, m.
bun	bollo, m.	roll (sweet)	pan dulce, bollo, m.
corn bread	pan de maíz, m.	rye bread	pan de centeno, m.
cracker (biscuit)	bizcocho, m.	sandwich	emparedado, sandwich, m.
crumb	migaja, miga, f.	slice of bread	rebanada de pan, f.
crust	corteza, f.	stale	duro
dough	pasta, masa, f.	toast	tostada, f.
doughnut	buñuelo, m.	white bread	pan blanco, m.
flour	harina, f.	whole-wheat bread	pan integral, m.
French bread	pan francés, m.	yeast	levadura, f.

g) VEGETABLES

ENGLISH	SPANISH	ENGLISH	SPANISH
artichoke	alcachofa, f.	onion	cebolla, f.
asparagus	espárrago, m.	parsley	perejil, m.
bean (string)	habichuela, f.	parsnip	pastinaca, chiviría, f.
bean (broad)	haba, f.	pea	arveja,f.; guisante, m.
bean (kidney)	judía, f.; frijol, m.	pea (chick..)	garbanzo, m.
beet (root)	remolacha, f.	pepper	pimienta, f.
broccoli	bróculi, m.	pickle	encurtido, m.
cabbage	berza, col, f.	plantain	plátano, m.
carrot	zanahoria, f.	popcorn	rosetas de maiz, f.
cauliflower	coliflor, m.	potato	papa, patata, f.
celery	apio, m.	boiled..	papas hervidas, f.
chick pea	garbanzo, m.	fried...	papas fritas, f.
chips (potato)	papas fritas, f.	mashed..	majado, puré de papas, m.
chive	cebolleta,f.;cebollino, m.	pumpkin	calabaza, f.
coleslaw	ensalada de col picada, f.	radish	rábano, m.
corn (maize)	maíz, m.	rhubarb	ruibarbo, m.
cucumber	pepino, m.	rice	arroz, m.
eggplant	berenjena, f.	sauerkraut	chucrut, m.
endive	escarola, f.	spinach	espinaca, f.
garlic	ajo, m.	sprout	brote, m.
gherkin	pepinillo, m.	squash	calabaza, f.
gourd	güira, calabaza, f.	sweet potato	boniato,m.; batata, f.
greens	verduras, f.	swiss chard	acelega, f.
kale	col, m.	tomato	tomate, m.
leek	puerro, m.	turnip	nabo, m.
lentil	lenteja, f.	*vegetable	verdura, legumbre, f.
lettuce	lechuga, f.	watercress	berro, m.
mushroom	seta, f.; hongo, m.	zucchini	calabacín, m.
okra	quimbombo, m.	yam	ñame, m.

h) FRUITS & BERRIES

ENGLISH	SPANISH	ENGLISH	SPANISH
apple	manzana, f.	guava	guayaba, f.
apricot	albaricoque, m.	huckleberry	arándano, m.
avocado	aguacate, m	lemon	limón, m.
banana	plátano, banano, m.	lime	limón verde, lima agria, f.
barberry	bérbero, m.	mandarin	mandarina, f.
bayberry	baya del laurel, f.	mango	mango, m.
berry	baya, mora, f.	melon	melón, m.
blackberry	mora, f.	mulberry	mora, f.
blueberry	arándano, m.	olive	aceituna, f.
cantaloupe	melón, m.	orange	naranja, f.
cherry	cereza, f.	papaya	papaya, f.
cranberry	agrio, arándano, m.	peach	melocotón, m., pérsico, m.
currant	grosella, f.	pear	pera, f.
date	dátil, m.	pineapple	piña, ananá, f.
dewberry	zarzamora, f.	plum	ciruela, f.
dried fruit	frutas secas, f.	pomegranate	granada, f.
elderberry	baya de saúco, f.	prune	ciruela pasa, pruna, f.
fig	higo, m.	raisin	pasa, f.
fruit	fruta, f.	raspberry	frambuesa, f.
gooseberry	uva espina, f.	strawberry	fresa, f.
grape	uva, f.	tangerine	mandarina, f.
grapefruit	toronja,f.; pomelo, m.	watermelon	sandía, f.

i) NUTS

ENGLISH	SPANISH	ENGLISH	SPANISH
almond	almendra, f.	hazelnut (filbert)	avellana, f.
Brazil nut	nuez del Brasil, f.	nut	nuez, f.
butternut	nogal ceniciento, m.	peanut	maní, cacahuete, m.
cashew	acajú, m.	pecan	pacana, f.
chestnut	castaña, f.	pistacho	pistacho, m.
coconut	coco, m.	walnut	nuez, f.

j) DESSERT

ENGLISH	SPANISH	ENGLISH	SPANISH
bonbon	bombón, m.	ice cream	helado, m.
cake	torta, f., pastel, m. bizcocho, m.	lollipop	chupete, m.; paleta, f.
		macaroon	macarrón, m.
candy	bombón, dulce, m.	meringue	merengue, m.
chocolate	chocolate, m.	mousse	crema, espuma, f.
compote	compota, f.	pastry	pasta, f.; pastel, m.
cookie	bizcochito, m.; galletita, f.	pie	pastel, m.; tarta, f.
cream	crema, f.	pudding	flan, budín, pudín, m.
custard	flan, m.	sherbet	sorbete, m.
dessert	postre, m.	spongecake	bizcochuelo, m.
doughnut	rosquilla, f.; buñuelo, m.	sweet	dulce, m.
fritter	fritura, f.	tapioca	tapioca, f.
fruit (preserves)	compota, f.	tart	torta, f.
ginger bread	pan de jenibre, m.	yogurt	yogurt, m.

k) SEASONING & CONDIMENTS

ENGLISH	SPANISH	ENGLISH	SPANISH
bitter	amargo	molasses	miel de caña, melaza, f.
caper	alcaparra, f.	mustard	mostaza, f.
catsup	salsa de tomate, f.	nutmeg	nuez moscada, f.
chili (chile)	ají, m.; chile, m.	oil	aceite, m.
chive	cebollino, m.	oil (olive)	aceite de oliva, m.
cinnamon	canela, f.	paprika	paprika, pimentón, m.
clove	clavo, clavero, m.	pepper (blk or white)	pimienta, f.
conserve	conserva, f.	preserve	confitura, f.
dressing (sauce)	aliño, m; salsa, f. aderezo, m.	relish	salsa, f.
		saffron	azafrán, m.
dressing (stuffing)	relleno, m.	sage	salvia, f.
flour	harina, f.	salt	sal, f.
garlic	ajo, m.	salty	salado
ginger	jengibre, m.	sauce (gravy)	salsa, f.
gravy	salsa, f.; caldo, m.	seasoned	sazonada
herb	yerba, hierba, f.	sour	agrio
honey	miel, f.	spice	especia, f.
horseradish	rábano picante, m.	spicy	picante
hot pepper	ají, chile, m.	sponge cake	bizcocho, m.
jam	confitura, compota, f.	sugar	azúcar, m.
jelly	jalea, f.	sweet	dulce
lard, shortening	manteca, f.	syrup	almíbar, jarabe, m.
lemon	limón, m.	tasty (flavorful)	sabroso
marmalade	mermelada, f.	thyme	tomillo, m.
mayonnese	mayonesa, f.	vanilla	vainilla, f.
mint	menta, f.	vinegar	vinagre, m.

1) MISCELLANEOUS EDIBLES

ENGLISH	SPANISH	ENGLISH	SPANISH
appetiser	tapa, f.	meal (grain)	grano molido, m.
batter	batido, m.	milk	leche, f.
broth	caldo, m.	noodle	tallarine, f.; fideo, m.
butter	mantequilla, f.	oatmeal	harina de avena, f.
cheese	queso, m.	pancake	tortilla, hojuela, f.
consommé	consomé, m.		panqueque, m.
cottage cheese	requesón, m.	pasta	pasta, f.
cream	crema, nata, f.	pickle	encurtido, m.
cream cheese	queso crema, f.	pizza	piza, f.
dish (food)	manjar, plato, m.	popcorn	rosetas de maíz, f.
fat (lard)	grasa, manteca, f.	porridge	gachas, f.
flour	harina, f.	salad	ensalada, f.
food	alimento, m.	sandwich	emparedado, sandwich, m.
gazpacho	gazpacho, m.	snack	bocado, tentempié, m.
grease	grasa, f.	snails	caracoles, m.
hors d'oeuvres	entremeses, m.	*soup	sopa, f.
leftovers	sobras, f.; restos, m.	spaghetti	espagueti, m.
licorice	regaliz, orozuz, m.		macarrón delgado, m.
macaroni	macarrones, m.	sweetbreads	lechecillas, mollejas, f.
margarine	margarina, f.	stew	puchero, guisado, m.

2. BEVERAGES (DRINKS)

ENGLISH	SPANISH	ENGLISH	SPANISH
absinthe	ajenjo, m.	milk	leche, f.
alcohol	alcohol, m.	milk (condensed)	leche condensada, f.
ale (beer)	cerveza, f.	milk (malted)	leche malteada, f.
anise	anís, m.	milk (past'd)	leche pasteurizada, f.
aperitif	aperitivo, m.	mineral water	agua mineral, m.
beer	cerveza, f.	orange juice	jugo de naranja, m.
brandy	coñac, aguardiente, m.	orangeade	naranjada, f.
champagne	champaña, f.	pop (soda)	refresco, m.; gaseosa, f.
chocolate	chocolate, m.	port	oporto, m.
cider	sidra, f.	punch	ponche, m.
cocoa	cacao, f.	rum	ron, m.
cocktail	coctel, m.	rye	whiski de centeno, m.
coffee	café, m.	scotch	escocés, m.
coffee/black	café solo, m.	sherry	jerez, m.
coffee/milk	café con leche, m.	soda water	agua de Seltz, m.
cognac	coñac, m.	soft drink	refresco, m.
cold drink	refresco, m.	spirits	alcohol, m.
drink	bebida, f.; trago, m.	tea	té, m.
drinkable	potable	tequila	tequila, f.
drop	gota, f.	vermouth	vermut, m.
gin	ginebra, f.	vodka	vodka, f.
half bottle	media botella, f.	water	agua, f.
ice water	agua helada, f.	whiskey	whiski, m.
liqueur	licor, m.	wine	vino, m.
juice	zumo, jugo, m.	wine (red..)	vino tinto, m.
lemonade	limonada, f.	wine sparkling..)	vino espumoso, m.
liquor	bebida alcohólica, f.	wine (table..)	vino de mesa, m.
Manhattan	manhattan, m.	wine (white..)	vino blanco, m.
martini	martini, m.	wine list	lista de vinos, f.

3. COOKING, EATING & DRINKING

ENGLISH	SPANISH	ENGLISH	SPANISH
bake	hornear, cocer al horno	drink (beverage)	bebida, f.
banquet	banquete, m.	drinking	beber, m.
bar	bar, m.	drunk (to get..)	emborrachar(se)
bill (of fare)	lista de platos, f.	eat (VERB)	comer
bill (check)	cuenta, f.	eating	comer, m.
bite	bocado, m.	fast (not eating)	ayuno, m.
bitter	amargo	fast (VERB)	ayunar
blender	mezcladura; licuadora, f.	faucet	llave, f.; grifo, m.
board (food)	pensión, f.	feast	festín, m.; fiesta, f.
bottle	botella, f.	flavor (VERB)	saborear
bowl (dish)	escudilla, f.	food	alimento, m.; comida, f.
	cuenco, tazón, bol, m.	fork (table)	tenedor, m.
breadbasket	panera, f.	freezer	congelador, m.
breakfast	desayuno, m.	fry (VERB)	freír
breakfast (VERB)	desayunar(se)	frying pan	sartén, f.
broil (VERB)	asar a la parrilla	gas	gas, m.
broiler	parrilla, f.	glass (goblet)	vaso, m.
broom	escoba, f.	goblet	copa, f.
cacerol	cacerola, f.	hunger	hambre, f.
can (tin)	lata, f.	hungry (to be..)	tener hambre
can opener	abrelatas, m.	ice	hielo, m.
carve (meat)	trinchar	icebox	nevera, f.
chew (VERB)	masticar	invite (VERB)	convidar, invitar
clean	limpiar	jar	tarro, m.; jarra, f.
clear the table	quitar la mesa	jug (pitcher)	porrón, jarro, m.
coffee pot	cafetera, f.	kettle	tetera, olla, marmita, f.
colander	colador, m.		
cook (chef)	cocinero, m.	kitchen	cocina, f.
cook (VERB)	guisar, cocer	kitchen closet	aparador, m.
cork (stopper)	corcho, tapón, m.	knife	cuchillo, m.
corkscrew	sacacorchos, m.	ladle	cucharón, m.
counter(table)	mostrador, m.	larder	despensa, f.
cover (lid)	tapa, cubierta, f.	lid (cover)	cubierta, tapa, f.
crockery	loza, f.	lunch (-eon)	almuerzo, m.
cruet	vinagrera, f.	lunch (VERB)	almorzar
cup (mug)	taza, f.	main course (entree)	entrada, f.
cupboard	armario, aparador, m.	match	cerilla, f.;fósforo, m.
cut (slice)	rebanar,cortar,tajar	meal	comida, f.
cutlery	cuchillería, f.	menu	carta, lista, f.; menú, m.
decanter (carafe)	garrafa, f.	microwave	microonda, f.
demitasse	tacita, f.	mixer	batidora, f.
diet	régimen, m.; dieta, f.	morsel	manjar, pedazo, bocado, m.
dine (VERB)	comer	mug (cup)	taza, jarra, f.
dining room	comedor, m.	napkin	servilleta, f.
*dinner	comida, cena, f.	nourish (feed)	alimentar
dipper	cucharón, m.	nut-cracker	cascanueces, m.
dish	plato, m.; fuente, f.	oven	horno, m.
dish (side..)	entremés, m.	*pan (frying)	sartén, f.
dishcloth	repasador, fregador, m.	*pan	cacerola, cazuela, f.
dishes (tableware)	vajilla, f.	pantry	despensa, f.
dishtowel	secador, m.	pension (Rm & Bd)	pensiøn, f.
dishwasher	lavaplatos, m.	picnic	jira, f.; picnic, m.
draft (draught)	trago, m.	piece	pedazo, m.
drain	desagüe, desaguadero m.	pitcher (jug)	jarro, cántaro, m.
drink (VERB)	tragar, beber	place (at table)	cubierto, m.

417

ENGLISH	SPANISH	ENGLISH	SPANISH
plate	plato, m.	stove	estufa, f.; hornillo, fogón, m.
platter	fuente, f.	stuff (VERB)	rellenar
pot	olla, caldera, f.; puchero, m.	sugar bowl	azucarera, f.
pot holder	almohadilla, f.	supper	cena, f.
pressure cooker	olla a presión, f.	supper (sup, to have..)	cenar
provisions	provisiones, víveres, m.	swallow (VERB)	tragar
recipe	receta, f.	sweet	dulce
refreshments	colación, f.	table	mesa, f.
refrigerator	refrigerador, m.	tablecloth	mantel, m.
	nevera, f.	table linen	mantelería, f.
restaurant	restaurante, f.	tap (sink)	grifo, m.
rolling pin	rodillo, m.	taste (flavor)	gusto, sabor, m.
roast (VERB)	asar	taste (VERB)	probar, saborear, gustar
salt (VERB)	salar		
salt shaker	salero, m.	tea (afternoon)	merienda, f.
saucepan	cacerola, f.	teacup	taza de té, f.
saucer	platillo, m.	teapot	tetera, f.
set the table	poner la mesa	teaspoon	cucharita, cucharilla, f.
sideboard	aparador, m.	teaspoonful	cucharadita, f.
side dish	entremés, m.	thirst	sed, f.
sink	fregadero, vertedero, m.	thirsty (VERB)	tener sed
slice	rebanada, f.	tip	propina, f.
skillet	sartén, caldereta, f.	toast (salute)	brindis, m.
slice (piece)	tajada, f.	toast (to give a ..)	brindar
snack	bocado, tentempié, m.	toaster	tostadora, f.
spatula	espátula, f.	tray	bandeja, f.; platillo, m.
spice (VERB)	condimentar	tumbler	vaso, m.
spill (pour)	verter	utensils	utensilios, m.
spoon (soup)	cuchara, f.	waiter	mozo, camarero, m.
spoon (tea)	cucharita, f.	waitress	camarera, f.
stew (VERB)	guisar, estofar	wine-glass	copa, f.

4. HOUSEHOLD & YARD

Words relating to cooking and eating are listed on page 417.
Cross-Reference: Travel, & Accomodations p. 478

ENGLISH	SPANISH	ENGLISH	SPANISH
air-cond'ng	aire acondicionado, m.	bathtub	bañera, f.
aisle	pasillo, m.	beam (rafter)	madero, m.; viga, f.
alarm clock	despertador, m.	bed (couch, cot)	cama, f.; lecho, m.
alcove (niche)	nicho, m.	bed table	mesa de noche, f.
apartment	cuarto, m.	bedding	ropa de cama, f.
armchair	butaca, f.; sillón, m.	bedroom	dormitorio, m. alcoba, f.
ash	ceniza, f.	bedspread	colcha, cubrecama, f.
ashtray	cenicero, m.	bell	campana, f.; timbre, m.
attic	ático, m.		campanilla, f.
balcony	balcón, m.	bench	banco, m.
banister	barandilla, f.; balaustre, m.	blanket	manta, f.
basement	sótano, m.	blind (shutter)	celosía, persiana, f.
basin	lavabo, tazón, m.	bolt	cerrojo, pasador, m.
basket	cesta, canasta, f.	board	tabla, f.
bassinet	cuna de mimbre, f.	book	libro, m.
bath	baño, m.	dust pan	pala para la basura, f.
bathmat	alfombrilla de baño, f.	bookcase	estante de libros, m.
bathroom	(cuarto de) baño, m.	bottle	botella, f.
bath towel	toalla de baño, f.	box	caja, f.

ENGLISH	SPANISH	ENGLISH	SPANISH
broom	escoba, f.	dust	polvo, m.
brush (paint)	pincel, m.	duster	plumero, m.
brush	cepillo, m.; brocha, f.	dust cloth	trapo, m.
bucket(pail)	cubeta,f.;balde,cubo, m.	dwelling	morada, vivienda, f.
buffet (dresser)	aparador, m.		habitación, residencia, f.
bulb (light)	bombilla, f.	eaves	alero, m.
bunk	litera, f.	elevator	ascensor, m.
bureau (chest)	cómoda, f.	face cloth	paño, m.; toallita, f.
buzzer	timbre, zumbador, m.	fan	abanico, ventilador, m.
cabinet	armario, m.	farmyard	corral, m.
candle	candela, vela, f.	faucet	llave de agua, f.;grifo, m.
candelabra	candelabro, m.	fence	valla, cerca, f.
candlestick	candelero, m.	fire	fuego, m.
card table	mesa de juego, f.	fire escape	escalera de incendios, f.
carpet (rug)	alfombra, f.;tapete, m.	fire ext.	extintor de incendios, m.
ceiling	techo, cielo raso, m.	fireplace	chimenea, f.; hogar, m.
cellar (basement)	sótano, m.	firewood	leña, f.
cellar (wine..)	bodega, f.	flap (table)	hoja, f.
cent.heating	calefacción central, f.	flashlight	rayo, destello, m.
chair	silla, f.		linterna eléctrica, f.
chamber(room)	cuarto, m.;sala, f.	flat(furnished..)	piso amueblado, m.
chandelier	araña, candelabro, m.	flat	piso, apartamento, m.
chest of drawers	cómoda, f.	floor (story)	piso, m.
chest (box)	arca, f;cofre;cajón, m.	floor	suelo, m.
chimney	chimenea, f.	footstool	taborete, escabel, m.
clock	reloj, m.	foundation	cimiento, m.
closet	armario, gabinete, m.	frame	cuadro, marco, m.
coal	carbón, m.	furnace	horno, m.
cork (stopper)	corcho, tapón, m.	furnished	amueblado
corner	rincón, m.	furniture	muebles, m.
corridor	pasillo, m.	garbage (rubbish,trash)	basura, f.
cot (bed)	cama, camilla, f.	garbage can	tacho de la basura, m.
	lecho, catre, m.	garden	jardín, m.
cottage	casita, choza, f.	glassware	cristalería, f.
couch (bed)	cama, f.; lecho, m.	glue	cola, f.
couch (sofa)	sofá, f.;diván, m.	grate (grill)	parrilla, f.
counter (table)	mostrador, m.	ground floor	piso bajo, m.
courtyard (patio)	patio, m.		planta baja, f.
cradle (crib)	cuna, f.	guest	invitado, m.
cupboard	aparador, armario, m.	gutter	canal, canalón, m.
curtain	cortina, f.	hall (room)	salón, m.;sala, f.
cushion (pad)	cojinete, cojín, m.	hall (entry)	vestíbulo, m.
desk	escritorio, m.	hamper	cesto, m.
dining room	comedor, m.	hatrack	sombrerera, percha, f.
doll	muñeca, f.	headboard	cabecera, f.
door (entrance)	entrada, f.	hearth	hogar, fogón, m.
door	puerta, f.	heater	calentador, m.
doorbell	campanilla, f.;timbre, m.	heating	calefacción, f.
doorknob	perilla, f.	hinge	bizagra, f.; gozne, m.
downstairs	piso bajo, m.	hook	gancho, m.
drain	desagüe, m.	house (home)	casa, f.; hogar, m.
drape (curtain)	cortina, f.		residencia, f.;domicilio, m.
drawer	cajón, m.; gaveta, f.	house (country..)	casa de campo, f.
drawers	cajón, m.; *cómoda, f.	household	casa, f.
drawing room	salón, m.; sala, f.	hut (shed)	barraca, choza, f.
dresser	aparador, tocador, m.	inside	interior, m.
driveway	camino de entrada, m.	iron (clothes)	plancha, f.

419

ENGLISH	SPANISH	ENGLISH	SPANISH
ironing board	tabla de planchar, f.	playroom	cuarto de juegos, m.
key	llave, f.	plug (stopper)	tapón, m.
keyhole	bocallave, m.	plug (ELEC)	enchufe, m.
knife	cuchillo, m.	poker (tool)	atizador, m.
knob	botón, tirador, m.	polish (VERB))	dar brillo
knock(on door)	llamar a la puerta, m.	porch	pórtico, atrio, porche, m.
knocker	aldaba, f.	porch (front door)	portal, m.
ladder	escalera, f.	passage	pasilla, f.
lamp	lámpara, f.	portrait	retrato, m.
lampshade	pantalla, f.	pottery	cerámica, f.
landing (stairs)	descanso, m.	premises	local, m.
landlord(owner)	propietario,dueño, m.	prop (strut)	apoyo, sustén, m.
latch	aldabilla, f.; picaporte, m.	property	propiedad, m.
laundry	lavado, m.;ropa lavada, f.	pump	bomba, f.;inflador, m.
laundry (room)	lavandería, f.	quilt(comforter)	edredón,m;colcha, f.
*library	biblioteca, f.	radiator	radiador, m.
lid (cover)	cubierta, tapa, f.	record (MUS)	disco, m.
light	luz eléctrica, f.	recorder	grabadora, f.
lighting	iluminación, f.	refrigerator	nevera, f.
lint	pelusa, f.		refrigerador, m.
lobby	pasillo, vestíbulo, m.	rent (let)	alquilar, f.
	foyer, m.;sala de espera, f.	restroom	baño, retrete, tocador, m.
lock	cerradura, f.;cerrojo, m.	rocker	mecedora, f.
lock (VERB)	cerrar con llave	roof	tejado,techo, m.;cubierta, f.
lounge	salón, m.	room (parlor)	sala, f.; salón, m.
mailbox	buzón, m.	room	cuarto, m.; sala, f.
mantelpiece	reprisa de chimenea, f.		habitación, f.
masonry	albañilería, f.	room (space)	lugar, espacio, m.
mat (straw)	estera, f.	rug	alfombra, f.;tapete, m.
match	cerilla, f.;fósforo, m.	running water	agua corriente, m.
mattress	colchón, m.	scissors	tijeras, f.
medicine chest	botiquín, m.	screen (partition)	mampara, f.
mirror	espejo, m.	scrub	fregar, frotar
mop	aljofifa, f.	seat	asiento, m.;plaza, f.
needle	aguja, f.	sewer	albañal, m.
nook (corner)	rincón, m.	sewing machine	máquina de coser, f.
ornament	adorno, m;decoración, f.	shade (window)	estor, m.;cortina, f.
outlet (ELEC)	toma, f.	sheet (bed..)	sábana, f.
outside	exterior, m.	shelf	estante, anaquel, m.
paint	pintura, f.;colorante, m.	shovel	pala, f.
painting	pintura, f.; cuadro, m.	shower (bath)	ducha, f.
pane (window)	cuadro de vidrio, m.	shutter (blind)	celosía, f.
paper	papel, m.	shutter (outside)	contraventana, f.
parlor (living room)	sala, f.	sideboard	aparador, m.
partition	tabique, m.	sink (basin)	lavabo, fregadero, m.
passage	pasillo, m.	sitting room	sala de estar, sala, f.
path(-way)	senda, f.;sendero, m.	slipcover	funda, f.
peg	percha,clavija, f.;gancho, m.	soap	jabón, m.
piano	piano, m.	socket (ELEC)	portalámpara, f.
picture	pintura, f.; cuadro, m.	sofa	sofá, m.
pigeonhole	casilla, f.	soot	tizne, hollín, m.
pillow	almohada, f.; cojín, m.	spark	chispa, f.
pillowcase	funda de almohada, f.	sponge	esponja, f.
pin	alfiler, broche, m.	stairs (stairway)	escalera, f.
pipe	cañería,caño,conducto,tubo, m.	step	grada, f.;peldaño,escalón, m.
pipe (smoking)	pipa, f.	stool	banqueta, f.;taburete, m.
plaster	yeso, emplasto, m.	story (floor)	piso, m.

ENGLISH	SPANISH	ENGLISH	SPANISH
stove	estufa, f.	upholstery	tapicería, f.
sweep	barrer	vacuum cleaner	aspiradora, f.
switch	conmutador, interruptor, m.	vase	jarrón, m.
table	mesa, f.	venetian blinds	persianas, f.
tap (faucet)	grifo, m.; canilla, f.	veranda	terraza, f.
tape (ribbon)	cinta, f.	wall (room)	pared, f.
tape recorder	grabador de cinta, m.	wall (outside)	muro, m.
	grabadora magnetofónica, f.	wall paper	empapelado, m.
tapestry	tapiz, m.; tapicería, f.		papel pintado, m.
telephone	teléfono, m.	wardrobe	vestuario, ropero, m.
television	televisión, f.		guardarropa, f.; armario, m.
tenant	inquilino, m.	wash basin	lavabo, m.
terrace	terraza, f.	washing machine	lavadora, f.
thimble	dedal, m.	wastebasket	canasta, f.
thread	hilo, m.	well	pozo, m.
threshold	umbral, m.; entrada, f.	window	ventana, f.
tile	losa, f.	window blind	persiana, f.
toilet	retrete, inodoro, m.	windowpane	cristal, m.
towel	toalla, f.	wine cellar	bodega, f.
toy	juguete, m.	wire	alambre, m.
tray	bandeja, f.; platillo, m.	woodwork	entablado, enmaderado, m.
tub	cuba, tina, bañera, f.	writing desk	bufete, escritorio, m.

5. NEIGHBORHOOD, CITY & COMMUNITY

Cross-References: Shops (p.439) and Objects of Nature List (p.451)

ENGLISH	SPANISH	ENGLISH	SPANISH
airport	aeropuerto, m.	cemetery	cementerio, m.
alley	calleja, f.; pasillo, m.	chateau	castillo, m.
aquarium	acuario, m.	checkroom	guardarropa, m; consigna, f.
arch	arco, m.	church	iglesia, f.
auditorium	anfiteatro, m.	cinema	cine, m.
avenue	avenida, f.	city	ciudad, f.
bank	banco, m.	City Hall	alcaldía, ayuntamiento, m.
bar	taberna, f.	consulate	consulado, m.
bar (cafe)	cantina, f.	convent	convento, m.
barn	granero, establo, m.	coop (hen)	gallinero, m.
barnyard	corral, m.	corner (street)	esquina, f.
barracks	cuartel, m.	cottage	casa de campo, f.; chalet, m.
belfry	campanario, m.	court (sport)	campo, m.; pista, f.
block	manzana, cuadra, f.	courthouse	palacio de justicia, f.
boarding house	pensión, f.	court (yard)	patio, corral, m.
booth(stall)	barraca, f; quiosco, m.	crossroads	cruce, m.; encrucijada, f.
bridge	puente, m.	crosswalk	paso para peatones, m.
building	edificio, m.	crowd	muchedumbre, m.
bus	ómnibus, m.	curb (street)	bordillo, m.
business section	centro, m.	dam	presa, represa, f.
by-pass	desvío, m.	depot	estación, f.
cabin	cabaña, f.	deptmt store	almacén, m.; tienda, f.
canal	presa, f.; canal, m.	detour	desvío, m.
castle	castillo, m.	district (ward)	barrio, m.
cathedral	catedral, f.	ditch (trench)	zanja, f.; foso, m.
cellar	bodega, f.	dock (wharf)	dique, muelle, m.

ENGLISH	SPANISH	ENGLISH	SPANISH
dome	cúpula, f.	neighbor	vecino, m.
downtown	centro, m.	neighborhood	barrio, alrededores, m.
drain	sumidero, m.		vecindario, m.; vecindad, f.
driveway	camino de entrada, m.	newsstand	puesto de periódicos, m.
drugstore	farmacia, f.	nightclub	cabaret, m.
embassy	embajada, f.	outskirts	alrededores, m.
factory	fábrica, f.	palace	palacio, m.
farm	granja, f.	park	parque, m.
farmhouse	granja, alquería, f.	pavilion	pabellón, m.
field	campo, m.	people	pueblo, m.; gente, f.
fire engine	coche de bomberos, m.	pier (dock)	muelle, m.
flagpole	mástil de bandera, m.	placard (poster)	cartel, m.
flat (aptmt)	piso, aposento, m.	place	lugar, sitio, m.
fort	fortaleza, f.	platform (RR)	andén, m.
foundation	cimientos, m.	parish	parroquia, f.
fountain	fuente, f.	path	senda, f.; sendero, m.
gallery	galería, f.	pavement	pavimiento, m.; acera, f.
gallows	horca, f.	police station	comisaría, f.
garage	garaje, m.; cochera, f.		estación de policía, f.
gateway	portal; portón, m.; entrada, f.	populous	poblado
graveyard	cementerio, m.	port	puerto, m.
greenhouse	invernadero, m.	post	poste, m.
grocery	tienda de comestibles, f.	post office	correo, m.
gutter	cuneta, f.	prison	prisión, f.
hall (city..)	ayuntamiento, m.	pub	bar, m.; cantina, taberna, f.
hamlet	aldea, f.; poblado, m.	quarry (mine)	pedrera, cantera, f.
hedge	seto, m.; cerca, f.	quarter	barrio, distrito, m.
highway	autopista, carretera, f.	railway station	estación de
hospital	hospital, m.		ferrocarril, f.
hotel	hotel, m.	resevoir	represa, f.
house	casa, f.	restaurant	restaurante, m.
hut	choza, cabaña, f.	road	camino, m.; vía, ruta, f.
hydrant	boca de agua, f.	route (way)	ruta, carretera, f.
incinerator	incinerador, m.	rural (rustic)	rural, campestre
inn	posada, f.	school	escuela, f.; colegio, m.
jail	cárcel, m.; prisión, f.	sewer	albañal, m.
kingdom	reino, m.	shed (hut)	cabaña, barraca, choza, f.
kiosk (newsstand)	kiosco, quiosco, m.	shop	tienda, f.; taller, almacén, m.
lamppost	poste de alumbrado, m.	sidewalk	acera, f.
land (real estate)	bienes raíces, m.	sign (shop)	rótulo, m.
lane	senda; calleja, f.; sendero, m.	signpost	poste, hito, m.; guía, f.
lavatory	lavabo, retrete, m.	skyscraper	rascacielos, m.
letterbox	buzón, m.	slum	barrio bajo, m.
*library	biblioteca, f.	spire	aguja, f.
lighthouse	faro, m.	square (town)	plaza, f.; parque, m.
lodge	casa de campo, f.	stable	establo, m.; cuadra, f.
main entrance	entrada principal, f.	statue	estatua, f.
manse (rectory)	rectoría, f.	steeple (spire)	aguja, torre, f.
market	mercado, m.	store	tienda, f.; almacén, m.
mill	molino, m.	street	calle, f.
mine	mina, f.	streetcar	tranvía, f.
ministry	ministerio, m.	streetlight	farol, m.
moat (pit)	foso, m.	streetlighting	alumbrado público, m.
monument	monumento, m.	subway	subterráneo, metro, m.
mosque	mezquita, f.	synagogue	sinagoga, f.
movie	cine, m.	taxi	parada de taxis, f.
museum	museo, m.	telegraph	telégrafo, m.

ENGLISH	SPANISH	ENGLISH	SPANISH
telephone	teléfono, m.	university	universidad, f.
*temple	templo, m.	vane	veleta, f.
theater	teatro, m.	zoo	jardín zoológico, zoo, m.
town hall	ayuntamiento, m.	village	aldea,f.;poblado,pueblo, m.
townsman (citizen)	ciudadano, m.	walk (drive)	paseo, m.
traffic	circulación,f.; tráfico, m.	wall (city)	muro, m.; tapia, f.
traffic light	luz de tráfico, f.	warehouse	almacén, depósito, m.
trench (ditch)	fosa, zanja, f.	well	pozo, m.
trolley	tranvía, m.	Wet Paint	recién pintado,
trough	pila, f.		pintura fresca, f.
tunnel	túnel, m.	windmill	molino, m.
turnpike	autopista, carretera, f.	yard	corral, patio, m.

6. BODY PARTS, AILMENTS & CARE

a) HUMAN BODY PARTS

ENGLISH	SPANISH	ENGLISH	SPANISH
abdomen	abdómen, m.	ear	oreja, f.
ankle	tobillo, m.	eardrum	tímpano, m.
appendics	apéndice, m.	elbow	codo, m.
arm	brazo, m.	enamel	esmalte, m.
armpit	axila, f.	esophagus	esófago, m.
artery	arteria, f.	eye	ojo, m.
back	espalda, f.	eyeball	globo de ojo, m.
backbone	espina dorsal, f.	eyebrow	ceja, f.
espinazo, m.;columna vertebral, f.		eyelash	pestaña, f.
beard	barba, f.	eyelid	párpado, m.
belly	vientre, m.;barriga, f.	face	rostro, m.;*cara, frente, f.
bile	bilis, f.	finger	dedo, m.
bladder	vejiga, f.	fingernail	uña, f.
blood	sangre, f.	finger (ring..)	anular, m.
body (live)	cuerpo, m.	fist	puño, m.
body (corpse)	cadáver, m.	flesh	carne, f.
bone	hueso, m.	foot	pie, m.
bosom	seno, pecho, m.	forefinger	dedo índice, m.
bowel(s)	intestinos, m.	forehead	frente, f.
braid (hair)	trenza, f.	gallbladder	vesícula biliar, f.
brain	cerebro, m.	gland	glándula, f.
breast	pecho, m.; seno, m.	groin	ingle, f.
brow	frente, f.;ceja, f.	gullet	gola, f.
buttock(s)	nalga(s), f.	gum (teeth)	encía, f.
cadaver	cadáver, m.	hair	pelo, cabello, m.
calf	pantorrilla, f.	hand	mano, f.
cheek	mejilla, f.	head	cabeza, f.
cheekbone	pómulo, m.	heart	corazón, m.
chest	pecho, m.; seno, m.	heel	talón, m.
chin	barba,barbilla, f.;mentón, m.	hip	cadera, f.
clavicle	clavícula, f.	index finger	(dedo) índice, m.
collarbone	clavícula, f.	instep	empeine del pie, m.
colon	colon, m.	intestine	intestino, m.
complexion	tez, f.	jaw (jowl)	mandíbula, quijada, f.
cornea	córnea, f.	joint	coyuntura, f.
cranium	cráneo, m.	jowl	carrillo, m.
diaphragm	diafragma, f.	kidney	riñón, m.

423

ENGLISH	SPANISH	ENGLISH	SPANISH
knee	rodilla, f.	shin	tibia, espinilla, canilla, f.
kneecap	rótula, f.	shoulder	hombro, m.; espalda, f.
knuckle	nudillo, m.	shoulder blade	escápula, f.
lap	regazo, m.	side	lado, flanco, costado, m.
lash (eye)	pestaña, f.	sinew	tendón, m.; fibra, f.
leg	pierna, f.	skeleton	esqueleto, m.
limb	miembro, m.	skin	piel, f.; cutis, m.
lip	labio, m.	skull	calavera, f.; cráneo, m.
little finger	meñique, m.	socket (eye)	órbita, f.
liver	hígado, m.	sole (foot)	planta del pie, f.
lung	pulmón, m.	spine	espina dorsal, f.
marrow	médula, f.	spleen	bazo, m.
mouth	boca, f.	stomach	estómago, m.
muscle	músculo, m.	*temple	sien, f.
mustache	bigote, mostacho, m.	tendon	tendón, m.
nail (finger)	uña, f.	thigh	muslo, m.
nape	nuca, f.	throat (gorge)	garganta, gola, f.
navel	ombligo, m.	thumb	pulgar, m.
neck	cuello, m.	toe	dedo del pie, m.
nerve	nervio, m.	tongue	lengua, f.
nose	nariz, f.	tonsil	amigdala, tonsila, f.
nostril	ventana de la nariz, f.	tooth	diente, m.
organ	órgano, m.	trunk	tronco, m.
palate	paladar, m.	uterus	útero, m.
palm (hand)	palma, f.	vein	vena, f.
pancreas	páncreas, m.	vertebra	vértebra, f.
pelvis	pelvis, f.	viscera	vísceras, f.
pupil (eye)	pupila, f.	waist	talle, m.; cintura, f.
rear	espalda, f.	wart	verruga, f.
rib	costilla, f.	womb	útero, matriz, m.
scalp	cuero cabelludo, m.	wrist	muñeca, f.

b) DISEASES & AILMENTS

In addition to those listed, there are hundreds of nouns in this subject area falling within such converting categories as -a, -ion, -ectomy, -otomy, -ism, -ergy, -pathy, -ity, -sis and -itis.

ENGLISH	SPANISH	ENGLISH	SPANISH
abortion	aborto, m.	blister	ampolla, f.
abscess	absceso, m.	boil	grano, furúnculo, m.
accident	accidente, m.	bruise	cardenal, m.; magulladura, f.
ache	dolor, m.	bump	chichón, m.
acne	acné, m.	bunion	juanete, m.
afraid (to be..)	tener miedo	burn	quemadura, f.
*ailment	dolencia, indisposición, f.	cancer	cáncer, m.
appendicitis	apendicitis, f.	canker	úlcera, f.; cancro, m.
appetite	apetito, m.	cataract	catarata, f.
asphyxia	asfixia, f.	cavity	cavidad, f.
asthma	asma, f.	chickenpox	varicela, f.
backache	dolor de espalda, m.	childbirth	parto, m.
baldness	calvicie, f.	chill (shiver)	escalofrío, m.
bite	mordedura, f.	cholera	cólera, f.
blind	ciego	clot	coágulo, m.
blindness	ceguera, f.	cold	catarro, resfriado, m.

ENGLISH	SPANISH	ENGLISH	SPANISH
cold (to catch..)	resfriar(se)	influenza	gripe, f.
contagious	contagioso	insanity (madness)	locura, f.
contusion	contusión, f	insomnia	insomnio, m.
corn (toe)	callo, m	itch	picazón, f.
corpse (body)	cadáver, m	jaundice	ictericia, f.
cough	tos, f	lame	cojo
cough (VERB)	toser	lameness	cojera, f.
cramp	calambre, m	leper	leproso, m..
cripple	lisiado, cojo, m	leprosy	lepra, f..
cut	incisión, f.; corte, m	limp	cojera, f..
dead man	muerto, m	lisp	balbuceo, ceceo, m..
dead	muerto	lockjaw	trismo, tétano, m.
deaf	sordo	mad (insane)	demente, loco
deafness	sordera, f	madness	demencia, locura, f.
death	muerte, f	malaria	malaria, f.; paludismo, m..
diarrhea	diarrea, f	measles	sarampión, f..
diabetes	diabetes, f	microbe	microbio, m..
die (VERB)	morir(se)	migraine	migraña, f.
disease	mal, m.; enfermedad, f.	miscarriage	aborto, m.
disentery	disentería, f.	mumps	parotitis, parotiditis, f.
dizziness	mareo, vértigo, m.	nausea	náusea, f.
dizzy	aturdido, mareado	nightmare	pesadilla, f.
drunk	ebrio, embriagado, borracho	numbness	entumecimiento, m.
drunkenness	embriaguez, f.	old	anciano, viejo
earache	dolor de oído, m.	old age	vejez, m.
emergency	urgencia, emergencia, f.	pain (ache)	dolencia, f.; dolor, m.
epidemic	epidemia, f.	pain (grieve)	doler
faint (-ing,-ness)	desmayo, m.	painful	penoso, doloroso
fear	miedo, m.	pale	pálido
fever	fiebre, f.	pestilence	pestilencia, f.
flue	gripe, f.	pimple	grano, f.
fracture (break)	fractura, f.	plague	plaga, peste, f.
germ	microbio, m.	pneumonia	pulmonía, neumonía, f.
gout	gota, f.	poison	veneno, m.
grippe	influenza, gripe, f.	poisoning	envenenamiento, m.
grow old	envejecer	poisoning (food)	intoxicación, f.
handless (armless)	manco	ptomaine	(p)tomaína, f.
hangover	resaca, f.	restless	inquieto
hay fever	fiebre para forraje, f.	rheumatism	reumatismo, m.
headache	dolor de cabeza, m.	scar	cicatriz, f.
health	salud, sanidad, f.	scarlet fever	escarlatina, f.
healthy	saludable, sano	scratch	arañazo, m.; rascadura, f.
heartache	angustia, f.	scurvy	escorbuto, m.
heart attack	ataque cardiaco, m.	seasickness	mareo, m.
hemorrhage	hemorragia, f.	shiver (tremble)	temblar
hemorrhoids	hemorroides, m.	shock	choque, m.
hernia	hernia, f.	sick (ailing)	enfermo
hiccup	hipo, m.	sick(to be.)	estar malo (enfermo)
hives	urticaria, f.	sick(to become.)	ponerse enfermo
hoarse	ronco	sickness	mal, m.; enfermedad, f.
hoarseness	ronquera, f.	smallpox	viruela, f.
hunger	hambre, f.	sore	llaga, f.
hurt (to..one's self)	herir(se)	sore throat	dolor de garganta, m.
ill	enfermo	soreness	dolor, m.; armagura, f.
ill (to become..)	enfermar	sorrow	pesar, m.; tristeza, f.
illness	mal, m.; enfermedad, f.	splinter	astilla, f.
indigestion	indigestión, f.	sprain (wrench)	torcedura, f.

425

ENGLISH	SPANISH	ENGLISH	SPANISH
stammer	tartamudeo, m.	temperature	temperatura, f.
stiffness	tiesura, f.	tetanus	tétano, m.
stigmatism	estigmatismo, m.	thirst	sed, f.
stomach ache	dolor de estómago, m.	tired	cansado
strain (exertion)	esfuerzo, m.	toothache	dolor de diente, m.
stroke	ataque fulminante, golpe, m.	tumor	tumor, m.
	conmoción cerebral, f.	twist	torcedura, f.
sty	orzuelo, m.	typhoid	fiebre tifoidea, f.
stupid (foolish)	tonto	typhus	tifus, m.
suffer (to..)	padecer	ulcer	úlcera, f
suffering (ailing)	sufrimiento, m.	weakness	debilidad, f.
sunburn	quemadura de sol, f.	whooping cough	tos ferina, f.
sweat (perspiration)	sudor, f.	wound	herida, f.
sweat (to..)	sudar	wounded	herido
swollen	inflamado, hinchado	wrench (sprain)	torcedura, f.
sympathize (to pity)	compadecer	yellow fever	fiebre amarilla, f.

c) TREATMENT AND CARE

Cross-Reference: N -ine, -ectomy; -tomy; -in;
Personal Grooming List p.433

ENGLISH	SPANISH	ENGLISH	SPANISH
adhesive tape	esparadrapo, m.	extract (tooth)	extraer, sacar
alcohol	alcohol, m.	fill (tooth)	empastar
ambulance	ambulancia, f.	filling (tooth)	empaste, m.
ammonia	amoníaco, m.	first aid	primeros auxilios, m.
ampoule	ampolla, f.	first-aid kit	botiquín, m.
anaesthetc	anestésico, m.	forceps	pinzas, f.; forceps, m.
antidote	antídoto, m.	gauze	gasa, f.
antiseptic	antiséptico, m.	glasses	anteojos, m.; gafas, f.
aspirin	aspirina, f.	healing (cure)	cura, f.
asylum	asilo, m.	hospital	hospital, m.
balm	bálsamo, m.	hygiene	higiene, f.
bandage	venda, f.	incurable	incurable
better (get..)	mejorar	infirmary	enfermería, f.
bicarbonate	bicarbonato de soda, m.	injection	inyección, f.
boric acid	ácido bórico, m.	insulin	insulina, f.
*care (attention)	cuidado, m.	iodine	yodo, m.
care for (nurse)	cuidar de	laboratory (lab)	laboratorio, m.
castor oil	aceite de ricino, m.	laxative	laxante, m.;purgante, f.
catheter	catéter, m.	lens (glasses)	cristal, m.
certif.	certificado de sanidad, m.	massage	masaje, m.
comfort	consolar, confortar	medical	médico
comforting	consolador	medicine (medication)	medicina, f.
cotton	algodón hidrófilo, m.	medicine chest	botiquín, m.
cough syrup	jarabe para la tos, m.	medicine dropper	cuentagotas, m.
*cure (healing)	cura, f.	needle	aguja, f.
cure (VERB)	curar	nourishment	alimento, nutrimiento, m.
cured	curado		nutrición, f.
dentist	dentista, f.	novocaine	novocaína, f.
diet	dieta, f.; régimen, m.	nurse	enfermera, f.
dispensary	dispensario, m.	nursery	cuarto de los niños, m.
doctor (physician)	médico, m.	oculist	oculista, m.
druggist	boticario, m.	ointment	pomada, f.; ungüento, m.

ENGLISH	SPANISH	ENGLISH	SPANISH
operate	operar	splint	tablilla, astilla, f.
operation	operación, f.	spray (VERB)	rociar
optician	óptico, m.	stretcher	camilla, f.
patient	paciente, m.	surgeon	cirujano, m.
pharmacy	farmacia, f.	syringe	jeringa, f.
pill	píldora, f.	tablet	tableta, pastilla, f.
plaster	emplasto, m.	thermometer	termómetro, m.
prescription	*receta, f.	tweezers	pinzas, f.
quinine	quinina, f.	transfusion	transfusión de sangre, f.
recover	curar(se), restablecer(se)	treatment	trato, tratamiento, m.
remedy	remedio, m.	vaccinate	vacunar
salve	bálsamo, m.; pomada, f.	vitamins	vitaminas, f.
sanitation	*sanidad, f.	ward	sala de hospital, f.
scissors	tijeras, f.	well (to be..)	estar (bueno) sano
sedative	calmante, m.	worsen (get worse)	empeorar
smelling salts	sales aromáticas, f.	x-ray	rayos X, m.; radiografía, f.

7. BODY SENSES, FUNCTIONS & CHARACTERISTICS

ENGLISH	SPANISH	ENGLISH	SPANISH
affection	afecto, cariño, m.	coagulation	coagulación, f.
alive	vivo	comfort	bienestar, m.
anger	*cólera, ira, f.; enojo, m.	complain	quejar(se)
angry	enfadado	complaint	queja, f.
anxious	ansioso	complexion	tez, f.
appearance	apariencia, f.	conceive	concebir
appetite	apetito, m.	confidence	confianza, f.
asleep	dormido	corpulent (stout)	corpulento
awake (to be..)	estar despierto	courage	ánimo, coraje, valor, m.
awaken	despertar(se)	coward	cobarde, m.
bad temper	mal genio, m.	cowardice	cobardía, f.
bathe	bañar(se)	crazy	loco
bed (go to..)	acostar(se)	cry (VERB)	llorar
behavior	comportamiento, conducta, f.	curl	rizo, m.
bite (to..)	morder	curly (hair)	crespo, rizado
blind	ciego	dark-haired	trigueño, moreno
blindness	ceguera, f.	depressed	abatido
blink	pestañeo, m.	desire	deseo, m.
blond	rubio, m.	determination	determinación, f.
blow (VERB)	soplar	digestion	digestión, f.
blush	rubor, m.	dimple	hoyuelo, m.
brave	valiente	disappointment	disgusto, m.
breathe	respirar	disillusion	desilusión, f.
breath	aliento, hálito, m.	disloyalty	deslealtad, f.
breathing	respiración, f.	displeased	descontento
brunet	moreno, m.	disposition	disposición, f.; genio, m.
bun (hair knot)	moño, m.	doubt	duda, f.
careful	cuidadoso	dream (VERB)	soñar
careless	descuidado	dream	sueño, m.
caress	caricia, f.	dry (to..one's self)	secar(se)
character	carácter, m.	dumb (mute)	mudo
charm	encanto, m.	dumb (stupid)	tonto, estúpido
cheerfulness	alegría, f.	dumbell (stupid)	tonto, bobo, m.
cherish	apreciar, acariciar, *estimar	dwarf	enano, m.
		eager	deseoso
circulation	circulación, f.	eagerness (anxiety)	afán, m.

ENGLISH	SPANISH	ENGLISH	SPANISH
eat	comer	kind	amistoso, cariñoso, bueno, bondadoso
effort	esfuerzo, m.		
embrace (VERB)	abrazar	kindness	bondad, f.
emotion	emoción, f.	kiss (VERB)	besar
endurance	aguante, m.; resistencia, f.	kiss	beso, m.
enjoyment	placer, disfrute, goce, m.	knot (hair)	moño, m.
envy	envidia, f.	know (be acquainted)	conocer
expression (face)	semblante, gesto, m. ademán, m.	know	saber
		knowledge	conocimiento, m.
face (grimace)	mohín, m.; mueca, f.	lap	falda, f.; regazo, m.
fair	rubio	laugh (VERB)	reir
fat	grueso, gordo	laugh (-ter)	risa, f.
fatigue	fatigo, m.	lay down	acostar(se)
fear (fright)	miedo, m.	lazy	perezoso
fear (VERB)	temer	lie	mentira, f.
feel	sentir	life	vida, f.
feeling	sentido, m.; sensación, f.	like	gustar
foolish	bobo, tonto	likeness	semejanza, f.; parecido, m.
forget	olvidar	listen to	escuchar
forgive	perdonar	live	vivir
friendship	amistad, f.	lock (hair)	mechón, bucle, m.
gall	hiel, bilis, f.	look	mirada, f.
generosity	generosidad, f.	look at	mirar
genius	genio, m.	longing	ansia, f.
gesture	ademán, m.	love (VERB)	amar
get up	levantar(se)	love	amor, m.
glad	alegre	loyal	leal
greet	saludar	loyalty	lealtad, f.
grief (sorrow)	tristeza, f.	luck	fortuna, suerte, f.
grow	crecer	manners	modales, f.
grow fat	engordar	memory	memoria, f.
grow old	envejecer	mien	semblante, m.
guess (VERB)	adivinar	mind	ánimo, m.; mente, f.
hallucination	alucinación, f.	miserable	deplorable, desdichado
happiness	dicha, alegría, f.	misfortune	desgracia, f.
happy	feliz	moan (groan)	gemido, quejido, m.
hate (VERB)	odiar	mole (skin)	lunar, m.
hatred	odio, m.	morality	moralidad, f.
hear	oir	murmur (VERB)	murmurar
hearing	oído, m.	negligent	negligente
heartbeat	latido, m.	old	viejo
height	talla, estatura, f.	pain	dolor, m.
hesitation	vacilación, f.	passion	pasión, f.
hope	esperanza, f.	perceive	percibir
hope (VERB)	esperar	perspire	transpirar
hormone	hormona, f.	pleased	contento
hunger	hambre, f.	pleasure	placer, m.
hungry (to be..)	tener hambre	polite	*educado, cortés
idea	idea, f.	praise (VERB)	alabar
illusion	ilusión, f.	pride	orgullo, m.
imagination	imaginación, f.	proud	orgulloso
imagine	imaginar	pulse	pulso, m.
impolite	*mal educado, descortés	rage (fury)	rabia, f.
insult	insultar	reason (VERB)	razonar
intelligence	inteligencia, f.	redhead	pelirrojo, m.
intuition	intuición, f.	remember	acordar(se)
joy	alegría, f.; gozo, m.	resemble	parecer(se)

ENGLISH	SPANISH	ENGLISH	SPANISH
respiration	respiración, f.	surprise	sorpresa, f.
rest (VERB)	descansar(se)	swallow	trago, bocado, m.
sad	triste	swallow (VERB)	tragar
sadness	tristeza, f.	sweat (perspiration)	sudor, m.
saliva (spit)	saliva, f.	sweat (VERB)	sudar
sanity	juicio, m.	talk	hablar, conversar
say	decir	talent (gift)	talento, m.
scab	costra, f.	tall	alto
see	ver	taste (VERB)	gustar
selfishness	egoismo, m.	taste	gusto, m.
sensation	sensación, f.	tear (eyes)	lágrima, f.
sense	sentido, m.	tell	contar
shame	vergüenza, f.	temper	*cólera, f.; humor, m.
shape (figure)	talle, m.	thank	agradecer
short (in height)	pequeño, bajo	thankful	agradecido
shout (cry)	grito, m.	think	pensar
shout (VERB)	gritar	thin (reduce)	adelgazar
shrewd	sagaz, astuto	thin	delgado
shy	timido	thirst	sed, f.
sigh	suspiro, m.	thirsty (to be..)	tener sed
sigh (VERB)	supirar	thought	pensamiento, m.
sight	vista, f.	threaten	amenazar
silly	tonto, bobo	thrill (shudder)	estremecimiento, m.
sincere	sincero	throb	latido, m.;palpitación, f.
sit	sentar(se)	touch (feel)	tacto, m.
sleep (VERB)	dormir	touch (VERB)	tocar
sleep (nap)	sueño,m.; siesta, f.	trembling	temblor, m.
sleepy	tener sueño	trustworthy	de confianza
slim	delgado	truth	verdad, f.
small	pequeño	ugly	feo
smell	oler	understand	comprender, entender
smelling (smell)	olfato, m.	unhappy	infeliz, *desgraciado
smile	sonrisa, f.	vanity	vanidad, f.
smile (VERB)	sonreír	vice	vicio, m.
smoke	fumar	virtue	virtud, f.
smug	presumido	voice	voz, f.
sneer	mofa, f.	wake up	despertar(se)
sneeze (VERB)	estornudar	want	querer
snore	roncar	wash (VERB)	lavar(se)
sob	sollozo, m.	weak	débil
sober	sobrio, moderado	weep	llorar
sorrow	tristeza, f.	weeping	llanto, lloro, m.
sorry (be..)	sentir	well-being	bienestar, m.
soul	espíritu, m.; alma, f.	whim	capricho, m.
speak	hablar	whisper	cuchicheo, m.
speech (talking)	habla, f.	whistle (VERB)	silbar
spirit	ánimo, espíritu, m.	wickedness	maldad, f.
spit	escupir, espectorar	will	voluntad, f.
stand (endure)	tolerar,soportar	wink	parpadeo, m.
stand up	ponerse en pie	wisdom	sabaduría, f.
step	paso, m.	wise	sabio
stern	severo,firme,estricto	wish	desear
stout (courageous)	valiente	wit (humor)	ingenio, m.
stout (fat)	corpulento	worry	preocupar(se)
straight (hair)	lacio, liso	wrinkle	arruga, f.
strong	robusto, fuerte	yawn	bostezo, m.
stubborn	tenaz, obstinado	young	joven

8. THE FAMILY

ENGLISH	SPANISH
adoption	adopción, f.
adult	adulto
adult	persona mejor, f.
affection	afecto, cariño, m.
affectionate (fond)	cariñoso
age (old...)	vejez, f.
age (years)	edad, f.
alias	alias, m.
ancester	antepasado, m.
aquaintance	conocido, m.
aunt	tía, f.
baby	criatura, f.; bebé, m.
bachelor	soltero, m.
bachelorhood	soltería, f.
*best man	padrino, m.
birth	nacimiento, m.
birthday	cumpleaños, m.
born	nacido
born (to be..)	nacer
boy	muchacho, m.
boyfriend	novio, amigo, m.
boyhood	niñez, f.
*bride (fiancée)	prometida, novia, f.
bridegroom (fiancé)	novio, m.
bridesmaid	dama de honor, f.
brother	hermano, m.
brother-in-law	cuñado, m.
brotherhood	fraternidad, f.
call (by name)	llamar
camaraderie	camaradería, f.
child	hijo, niño, m.
childhood	niñez, f.
christen	bautizar
Christian name	nombre de pila, m.
citizen	ciudadano, m.
compatriot	compatriota, m.
comrade	camarada, compañero, m.
countryman	paisano, m.
couple	matrimonio, m.; pareja, f.
cousin, f.	prima, f.
cousin, m.	primo, f.
dad	papá, m.
darling	querida, f.
daughter	hija, f.
daughter-in-law	nuera, f.
dear (beloved)	querido
dearest	queridísimo, m.
descendant	descendiente, m.
divorce	divorcio, m.
divorcee	divorciada, f.
dowry	dote, m.; dotación, f.
engaged	prometida, prometido
engaged (to get..)	prometer(se)
engagement	compromiso, m.
engmnt ring	anillo de compromiso, f.
family	familia, f.
family name	apellido, m.
father (dad, pop, pa)	papá, padre, m.
father-in-law	suegro, m.
fatherhood	paternidad, f.
fellowship	confraternidad, f.
female	hembra, f.
fiancé(e)	novia, f.; novio, m.
first name	nombre de pila, m.
forefather	antepasado, m.
fosterchild	hijo adoptivo, m.
fosterfather	padre adoptivo, m.
fraternity	fraternidad, f.
friend	amigo, m.
friendship	amistad, f.
gentleman	caballero, señor, m.
girl (lass)	niña, muchacha, chica, f.
girlfriend	amiga, novia, f.
girlhood	niñez, f.
godchild	ahijado, m.
goddaughter	ahijada, f.
godfather	padrino, m.
godmother	madrina, f.
godson	ahijado, m.
grandchild	nieto, m.
granddaughter	nieta, f.
grandfather	abuelo, m.
grandmother	abuela, f.
grandson	nieto, m.
great granddaughter	biznieta, f.
great grandfather	bisabuelo, m.
great grandmother	bisabuela, f.
great grandson	biznieto, m.
gr. great grandson	tataranieto, m.
groom	novio, m.
grow up	crecer
guardian	tutor, guardián, m.
guardianship	tutela, f.
guest	invitado, huésped, m.
half-brother	medio hermano, m.
half-sister	media hermana, f.
heir	heredero, m.
heiress	heredera, f.
heritage	herencia, f.
honeymoon	luna de miel, f.
husband	esposo, marido, m.
infancy	infancia, f.
issue	progenie, f.
kinship	parentesco, m.
lady	dama, señorita, señora, f.
lineage	linaje, m.
love	amor, m.
love (in..with)	enamorado de

ENGLISH	SPANISH	ENGLISH	SPANISH
love (VERB)	amar, querer	*relative,-tion	pariente, m.
lover	amante, amador, m.	sibling(s)	hermano(s), m.
loving	afectuoso	single	soltero
maiden	joven soltera, f.	sister	hermana, f.
maiden name	apellido de soltera, m.	sister-in-law	cuñada, f.
male	varón, m.	son	hijo, m.
man	hombre, m.	son-in-law	yerno, m.
manhood	hombría, f.	spinster	solterona, f.
mankind	humanidad, m.	spinsterhood	soltería, f.
marriage	casamiento, m.; boda, f.	spouse	esposo, m.
	matrimonio, m.	stepbrother	hermanastro, m.
married man	casado, m.	stepchild	hijastro, m.
marry	casar(se)	stepdaughter	hijastra, f.
maternity	maternidad, f.	stepfather	padrastro, m.
*matrimony	matrimonio, m.	stepmother	madrastra, f.
matron of honor	madrina, f.	stepsister	hermanastra, f.
minor	menor, m.	stepson	hijastro, m.
mother (mom)	mamá, madre, f.	surname	apellido, m.
mother-in-law	suegra, f.	sweatheart	novio, m.
motherhood	maternidad, f.	trousseau	ajuar, m.
name	nombre, apellido, m.	twins	gemelos, m.
name (family..)	apellido, m.	uncle	tío, m.
neighbor	vecino, m.	virgin	doncella, virgen, f.
nephew	sobrino, m.	ward	pupilo, m.
nickname	mote, apodo, m.	wedding	boda, nupcias, f.
niece	sobrina, f.	wedding ring	anillo de boda, m.
	nombre de familia, m.	widow	viuda, f.
old age	ancianidad, vejez, f.	widower	viudo, m.
old man	viejo, anciano, m.	widowhood	viudez, f.
old woman	vieja, anciana, f.	wife	esposa, mujer, f.
orphan	huérfano, m.	woman	mujer, f.
pal (buddy)	camarada, compañero, m.	young	joven
parentage	ascendencia, f.	young lady	joven, señorita, f.
parenthood	paternidad, f.		muchacha, chica, f.
*parent(s)	padre(s), m.	youngster	chico, mozo, jovencito, m.
paternity	paternidad, f.	youth (period)	juventud, f.
playmate	compañero de juego, m.	youth (boy)	muchacho, mozo, joven, m.

9. DEATH & FUNERALS

ENGLISH	SPANISH	ENGLISH	SPANISH
burial	entierro, m.	inheritance	patrimonio, m.
bury	sepultar, enterrar		herencia, f.
cemetery	cementerio, m.	mourner	doliente, m.
coffin	ataúd, m.	mourning (be in..)	estar de luto
corpse (body)	cadáver, m.	mourning clothes	luto, m.
cremation	cremación, f.	mourning	duelo, m.
dead man	muerto, m.	shroud	sudario, m.; mortaja, f.
death	fallecimiento, m.; muerte, f.	tombstone	lápida, f.
deathbed	lecho mortuorio, m.	undertaker	dueño de funeraria, m.
die	fallecer, morir	wake (vigil)	velorio, m.
funeral	funeral, entierro, m.	widow	viuda, f.
grave (tomb)	tumba, f.	widow (to become a..)	enviudar
hearse	coche fúnebre, m.	widower	viudo, m.
inherit	heredar	wreath	corona, f.

10. APPAREL & ACCESSORIES

ENGLISH	SPANISH	ENGLISH	SPANISH
apron	delantal, m.	gabardine	gabardina, f.
attire (adorn)	adornar	galosh	chanclo, m.
bag (purse)	bolsa, f.	garment	vestido, m.
bathingsuit	trusa, traje de baño, m.	garter(s)	liga(s), f.
bathrobe	bata de baño, f.	girdle (corset)	cinturón, m; faja, f.
beads (of necklace)	cuentas, f.	glasses	lentes, m.; gafas, f.
beads (religious)	rosario, m.		anteojos, m.
belt	cintura, f.; cinturón, cinto, m.	glove (mitten)	guante, m.
bib	babero, babador, m.	gown	traje, vestido, m.
blouse	blusa, f.	handbag	cartera, f.; bolso, m.
bonnet	sombrero, m.	handkerchief	pañuelo, m.
boot	bota, f.	hat (bonnet)	sombrero, m.
bow tie	corbatín, m.	heel (shoe)	tacón, m.
bracelet	pulsera, f.; brazalete, m.	hood (hat)	gorro, capucho, m.
braces	tirantes, m.	hose (stocking)	media, calceta, f.
brassiere (bra)	sostén, m.	in fashion	de moda
breeches	calzones, m.	jacket	saco, m.; chaqueta, f.
brim (hat)	ala, f.		americana, f.
broach (clasp)	broche, m.	jeans	jeans, pantalones, m.
buckle	hebilla, f.	jewel (gem)	joya, alhaja, pedrería, f.
button	botón, m.	jewelry	joyería, joyas, f.
buttonhole	ojal, m.	jumper	jersey, m.
cane	bastón, m.	knickers	bragas, f.
*cap	gorra, f.; gorro, m.	lace (cord)	cordón, m.
*cape (cloak)	capa, f.	lace (fancy)	encaje, m.
case (glasses)	estuche, m.	lapel	solapa, f.
chemise	camisa, f.	linen	ropa blanca, f.
cigar	cigarro, *puro, m.	lining	forro, m.
cigarette	cigarillo, m.	locket	relicario, medallón, m.
cloak	capa, f.; manto, m.	*mantle	manto, m.
clothes (-ing)	vestido, m.; *ropa, f.	mitten	mitón, m.
coat	abrigo, m.	mounting	montadura, f.
coat (suit)	chaqueta, f.; saco, m.	muff	manguito, m.
coattail	faldón, f.	muffler	bufanda, f.
*collar	cuello, m.	neckerchief	pañuelo de cuello, m.
compact	polvera, f.	necklace	collar, m.
contact lens	lente de contacto, f.	necktie	corbata, f.
corset	corsé, m.	negligee	negligé, m.
costume (clothes)	atuendo, traje, m.	nightgown	camisa de dormir, f.
costume (disg.)	disfraz, m; máscara, f.	nightshirt	camisa de dormir, f.
crown	corona, f.	out of fashion	pasado de moda
cuff (sleeve)	puño, m.	overcoat	abrigo, gabán, m.
cuff (trousers)	vuelta, f.		sobretodo, m.
cufflinks	gemelos, m.	overalls	pantalones de trabajo, m.
diaper	pañal, m.; servilleta, f.	overshoe	chanclo, m.
drawers (shorts)	calzoncillos, m.	pajamas	pijama, m.
dress (gown)	traje, vestido, m.	pants	calzoncillos, pantalones, m.
dress (VERB)	vestir(se)	parasol	quitasol, m.; sombrilla, f.
dress (clothes)	*ropa, f.	pearls	perlas, f.
dressmaker	modista, f.	petticoat	enagua, f.; fustán, m.
earring	arete, m.; pendiente, m.	pin (broach)	broche, m.
fashion	moda, f.	pipe	pipa, f.
footwear	calzado, m.	pocket	bosillo, m.
frock	vestido, hábito, m.	pocketbook	cartera, f.; bolso, m.
fur	piel, f.	pullover	jersey, suéter, pulóver, m.

ENGLISH	SPANISH	ENGLISH	SPANISH
purse	bolsa, f.; bolsillo, m.	sun glasses	gafas contra el sol, f.
	cartera, f.; monedero, m.	suspenders	tirantes, m.
put on	poner(se)	sweater	jersey, suéter, m.
raincoat	impermeable, m.	swimsuit	traje de baño, m.
ready-made	hecho	tailor	sastre, m.
ribbon	cinta, f.	take off	quitar(se)
ring (finger)	sortija, f.; anillo, m.	tie (necktie)	corbata, f.
robe	manto, m.; bata, f.	trinket	dije, m.; chuchería, f.
rubbers	chanclos, m.	trousers	calzón, m.; pantalones, m.
sandal	sandalia, f.	tunic	túnica, f.
scarf	bufanda, f.; chalina, f.	tuxedo	esmoquin, smoking, m.
seam	costura, f.	umbrella	sombrilla, f.; paraguas, m.
shawl	mantón, m. chal, m.	underdrawers	calzoncillos, m.
shirt	camisa, f.	underpants	bragas, f.
shoe	zapato, m.	undershirt	camiseta, f.
shoelace	cordón de zapato, m.	underskirt	enaguas, combinación, f.
shorts	calzoncillos, m.	underwear	ropa interior, f.
size (clothes)	talla, f.; tamaño, m.	undress	desnudar(se)
size (hats)	medida, f.	valet	camarero, m.
size (shoes)	número, m.	veil	redecilla, f.; velo, m.
skirt	falda, f.	vest	chaleco, m.
sleeve	manga, f.	waist	talle, m.; cintura, f.
slip(dress)	enaguas, combinación, f.	waistcoat	chaleco, m.
slipper	zapatilla, pantufla, f.	wallet	cartera, billetera, f.
smock	bata corta, f.	wardrobe (apparel)	vestuario, m.
sock	media corta, f.; calcetín, m.	watch	reloj de bosillo, m.
sole (shoe)	suela, f.	wear (to..)(carry, use)	llevar
spectacles	gafas, f.; anteojos, m.	wig	peluca, f.
step-ins	bragas, f.	worn out	usado
stockings	*medias, calcetas, f.	wristwatch	reloj de pulsera, m.
stud	botón, m.	zipper	cierre relámpago, m.
suit (clothes)	saco, traje, m.		cremallera, f.

11. **PERSONAL GROOMING**

ENGLISH	SPANISH	ENGLISH	SPANISH
bath	baño, m.	curling iron	tenacillas, f.
bathe	bañar(se)	cuticle	cutícula, f.
bathing cap	gorro de baño, m.	dental floss	seda dental, f.
beauty salon	salón de belleza, m.	deodorant	desodorante, m.
bobby pin	horquilla de presión, f.	diapers	pañales, m.
brush (VERB)	cepillar	dress (VERB)	vestir(se)
brush	cepillo, m.	eye-shadow	sombra de ojos, f.
cake(soap)	(pastilla)pan de jabón, m.	eyebrow pencil	lápiz de cejas, m.
chain	cadena, f.	face cloth	toallita, f.; paño, m.
change clothes	mudar(se) de ropa	facial	facial, masaje de cara, m.
chewing gum	chicle, m.	fan (hand..)	abanico, m.
cigar	tobaco, puro, cigarro, m.	flints (lighter)	pedernales, f.
cigarette case	pitillera, f.	hairbrush	cepillo para el pelo, m.
cigarette	cigarrillo, m.		cepillo de cabeza, m.
cologne	agua de colonia, m.	haircut	corte de pelo, m.
comb (hair)	peine, m.	hairnet	redecilla, f.
comb (VERB)	peinar(se)	hairpin	horquilla, f.
compact	polvera, f.	hairstyle	peinado, m.
cosmetics	cosmético, m.	lather	espuma, f.
cream (cold..)	crema, f.	lighter (cigarette..)	encendedor, m.

433

ENGLISH	SPANISH	ENGLISH	SPANISH
lighter fluid	bencina, f.	shampoo	champú, m.
lipstick	lápiz de labios, m.	shave	afeitar(se)
lotion	loción, f.	shaver (elec)	máquina de afeitar, f.
make-up (put on..)	maquillar(se)	shaver	afeitadora, f.
make-up	maquillaje, m.	shaving brush	brocha de afeitar, f.
manicure	manicura, f.	shaving cream	crema de afeitar, f.
manicurist	manicura, f.	shaving soap	jabón de afeitar, m.
mascara	rimel, m.	shine (to..shoes)	lustrar
matches	cerillas, f.; fósforos, m.	shoehorn	calzador, m.
mirror (looking glass)	espejo, m.	shoelace	cordón, m.
mouthwash	enjuague, f.	shoes(to take.off)	descalzar(se)
nail polish	esmalte de uñas, m.	shower	ducha, f.
nailbrush	limpiauñas, m.	smoke (VERB)	fumar
nail clippers	cortaclavos, m.	soap (cake of)	pastilla de jabón, f.
nailfile	lija, lima de uñas, f.	soap	jabón, m.
ointment	ungüento, m.; pomada, f.	sponge	esponja, f.
perfume	perfume, m.	spot remover	sacamanchas, m.
perm.wave	permanente, m.	talcum powder	talco, m.
pin	afiler, m.	tobacco pouch	petaca, f.
pipe	pipa, f.	tobacco	tabaco, m.
polish remover	disolvente, m.	toilet paper	papel higiénico, m.
powder (cosmetic..)	polvos, m.	toilette	tocado, arreglo, m.
powder puff	mota, borla, f.	toothbrush	cepillo de dientes, m.
powder room	tocador, m.	toothpaste	pasta dentífrica, f.
pumice	piedra pómez, f.	towel	toalla, f.
razor	navaja de afeitar, f.	tweezers	pinzas, f.
razor(ELEC)	maquinilla de afeitar, f.	undress	desnudar(se)
razorblade	hoja de afeitar, f.	valet	camarero, m.
rouge	colorete, m.	Vaseline	Vaselina, f.
safety pin	imperdible, m.	wash	lavar(se)
salve	emplasto, ungüento, m.	washroom	lavabo, m.
scissors	tijeras, f.	wig	peluca, f.

12. TEXTILES, SEWING & TAILORING

ENGLISH	SPANISH	ENGLISH	SPANISH
braid	tenza, f.	fringe	fleco, m.
button	botón, m.	fur	piel, f.
canvas	lona, f.	hem	dobladillo, m.; bastilla, f.
cloth	paño, m.; tela, f.	hook & eye	broche, m.
corduroy	pana, f.	iron (VERB)	planchar
cotton	algodón, m.	knitting	tejido de punto, m.
crease	pliegue, m.	knot	*nudo, m.
crepe	crepé, crespón, m.	label	etiqueta, f.
crochet	crochet, m.	lace	encaje, m.
cut (VERB)	cortar	leather	cuero, m.
darn	zurcir	linen	lino, m.
dressmaker	modista, f.	material	tela, f.; paño, material, m.
dry cleaning	limpieza en seco, f.	measure	tomar medida
dyeing	tintorería, f.	measurement	medida, f.
embroider	bordar	measuring tape	cinta métrica, f.
fabric	tela, f.; material, paño, m.	mend	remendar
fashion (style)	moda, f.	milliner	sombrerero, m.
felt	fieltro, m.	muslin	gasa, musalina, f.
fold	pliegue, doblez, m.	needle	aguja, f.

ENGLISH	SPANISH	ENGLISH	SPANISH
nylon	nilón, m.	stitch	puntada, f.
organdy	organdí, m.	suede	gamuza, f.
percale	percal, m.	style	moda, f.
petit point	petit point, m.	taffeta	tafetán, m.
pin	afiler, m.	tailor	sastre, m.
plaid	plaid, m.	tartan	tartán, m.
rayon	rayón, m.	tassel	borla, f.
ribbon (tape)	cinta, f.	terry cloth	tela de esponja, f.
safety pin	imperdible, m.	thimble	dedal, m.
satin	raso, satén, m.	thread (strand)	hilo, m.
scissors	tijeras, f.	try on	probar
seam	costura, f.	tuft	borla, f.; mechón, m.
seamstress	costurera, f.	velvet	terciopelo, velludo, m.
serge	sarga, f.	velour	veludillo, m.
sew	coser	velveteen	pana, f.
sewing basket	costurero, m.	wool (cloth)	paño, m.
sewing machine	máquina de coser, f.	wool (fleece)	lana, f.
silk	seda, f.	worsted	estambre, m.
size	bulto, tamaño, m.	wrinkle	arruga, f.
starch (VERB)	almidonar	yarn	hilado, m.; hilaza, f.
starch	almidón, m.	zipper	cremallera, f.

13. OCCUPATIONS & ROLES

Cross-Reference: N -er, -or and -ist (Doers)

ENGLISH	SPANISH	ENGLISH	SPANISH
acrobat	acróbata, m.	boxer	boxeador, m.
actress	actriz, f.	boyscout	niño explorador, m.
administrator	administrador, m.	brewer	cervecero, m.
admiral	almirante, m.	bricklayer	albañil, ladrillero, m.
apprentice	aprendiz, m.	builder	constructor, m.
arbitrator	árbitro, m.	bull fighter	torero, m.
architect	arquitecto, m.	businessman	hombre de negocios, m.
artist	artista, m.		comerciante, negociante, m.
atronaut	astronauta, m.	butcher	carnicero, m.
attorney	abogado, m.	buyer	comprador, m.
author	autor, m.	cab driver	cochero, taxista, m.
aviator	aviador, m.	cabinet maker	ebanista, m.
babysitter	niñera, f.	canvasser	solicitador, m.
baker	panadero, m.	captain	capitán, m.
banker	banquero, m.	caretaker	guardián, cuidador, m.
barber	peluquero, barbero, m.	carpenter	carpintero, m.
bartender	barman, tabernero, m.	career	carrera, f.
bellboy	botones, m.	cashier	cajero, m.
bidder	licitador, postor, m.	caterer	abastecedor, proveedor, m.
blacksmith	herrero, m.	chairman	presidente, m.
boarder	pensionista, f.	chambermaid	camarera, f.
bodyguard	guardaespaldas, f.	chauffeur	conductor, chófer, m.
bookkeeper	contable, m.	chef	cocinero, m.
bookseller	librero, m.	chemist	químico, m.
bootblack	limpiabotas, f.	chemist (druggist)	farmacéutico, m.
borrower	prestatario, m.	chiropodist	pedicuro, m.

435

ENGLISH	SPANISH	ENGLISH	SPANISH
cleaner	tintorero, lavandero, m.	fruit vendor	frutero, m.
cleric	clérigo, m.	furrier	peletero, m.
clerk (sales)	vendedor, dependiente, m.	gambler	jugador, m.
clerk (off.)	empleado de oficina, m.	gangster	pandillero, bandido, m.
clerk (writer)	escribano, m.	garbageman	basurero, m.
clothier	ropero, m.	gardener	jardinero, m.
clown	payaso, m.	general	general, m.
coach (trainer)	entrenador, m.	girlscout	niña exploradora, f.
*correspndent	corresponsal, m.	glazier	vidriero, m.
cobbler	zapatero, m.	goldsmith	orfebre, m.
coiffeur	peinador, peluquero, m.	governess	aya, institutriz, f.
colonel	coronel, m.	greengrocer	verdulero, m.
comic	cómico, m.	*grocer	especiero, tendero, m.
commander	comandante, m.	groom (horse)	mozo, m.
commissioner	comisario, m.	guarantor	fiador, m.
composer	compositor, m.	guard	guardia, f.
constable	alguacil, guardia rural, f.	guest (visitor)	huésped, m.
contractor	contratista, f.	gypsy	gitano, m.
cook	cocinero, m.	haberdasher	mercero, camisero, m.
count	conde, m.	hairdresser	peluquero, m.
cowboy	vaquero, gaucho, m.	harlot	puta, zorra, f.
critic	crítico, m.	helper	ayudante, m.
custom officer	aduanero, m.	historian	historiador, m.
cutlery shop	cuchillería, f.	horseman	caballero, jinete, m.
dancer	bailarina, f.	host	anfitrión, m.
dealer	comerciante, negociante, m.	hostess	anfitriona, f.
debtor	deudor, m.	housekeeper	ama, casera, f.
decorator	decorador, m.	housewife	ama de casa, f.
dentist	dentista, m.	hunter	cazador, m.
doctor (ACAD)	doctor, m.	innkeeper	posadero, hostelero, m.
doctor (phys.)	doctor, médico, m.	jailer	carcelero, m.
doorman	portero, m.	janitor	portero, m.
dressmaker	modista, f.	jeweler	joyero, m.
driver	cochero, chofer, conductor, m.	jobber	corredor, m.
		joiner (carpenter)	ebanista, m.
*druggist (chemist)	boticario, m.	jouneyman	jornalero, m.
dyer	tintorero, m.	journalist	periodista, m.
*editor	redactor, editor, m.	judge	juez, m.
electrician	electricista, m.	juggler	malabarista, m.
employee	empleado, m.	king	rey, m.
engine operator	maquinista, m.	knight	paladín, caballero, m.
engineer	ingeniero, m.	*laborer	trabajador, obrero, m.
expert	experto, perito, m.		jornalero, m.
farmer	granjero, labrador, agricultor, m.	lady	dama, señora, f.
		landlady	casera, propietaria, f.
fellow worker	compañero, colega, m.	landlord	dueño, arrendador, m.
fiddler	violinista, m.		casero, propietario, m.
fighter	guerrero, boxeador, m.	laundryman	lavandero, m.
financier	financiero, m.	lawyer	letrado, abogado, m.
fireman	bombero, m.		licenciado, jurista, m.
fisherman	pescador, m.	leader (MIL)	jefe, m.
fishmonger	pescadero, m.	leader (MUS)	director, m.
florist	florista, m.	*lecturer	conferenciante, m.
foreman	capataz, m.	liar	mentiroso, embustero, m.
founder	fundidor, m.	librarian	bibliotecario, m.
friar (monk)	fraile, monje, m.	lieutenant	teniente, m.

ENGLISH	SPANISH	ENGLISH	SPANISH
lifeguard	salvavidas, m.	obstetrician	obstétrico, m.
	guarda de playa, m.	oculist	oculista, m.
lighthouse keeper	guardafaro, m.	office (role)	cargo, m.
linesman	guardalínea, m.	office boy	mensajero, mandadero, m.
linguist	lingüista, m.	office holder	titular, m.
lithographer	litógrafo, m.	office manager	jefe de oficina, m.
locksmith	cerrajero, m.	office worker	oficinista, m.
logger	maderero, m.	official, officer	funcionario, m.
longshoreman	cargador, estibador, m.	oilman	petrolero, m.
Lord	Señor, m.	optician	óptico, m.
machinist	mecánico, maquinista, m.	optometrist	optometrista, f.
magician	mago, m.	orator	orador, m.
magistrate	magistrado, m.	organist	organista, m.
maid	camarera, criada, moza, f.	osteopath	osteópata, m.
mailman (letter carrier)	cartero, m.	outlaw	fugitivo, m.
manager	gerente, director, m.	owner	dueño, m.
manicurist	manicura, f.	page	botones, paje, m.
manufacturer	fabricante, m.	painter	pintor, m.
mapmaker	cartógrafo, m.	palmist	palmista, m.
mariner	marinero, m.	paperboy	diarero, m.
mason	albañil, m.	paperhanger	empapelador, m.
master	jefe, amo, dueño, m.	parishioner	parroquiano, m.
matador	matador, m.	parlormaid	camarera, f.
mathematician	matemático, m.	passerby	transeunte, m.
*mayor	alcalde, m.	*pastor (parson)	clérigo, pastor, m.
mechanic	mecánico, m.	pastry-cook	pastelero, m.
merchant	vendedor, comerciante, m.	patrolman	patrullero, policía, m.
messenger	mensajero, nuncio, m.	patternmaker	modelista, m.
metalworker	metalario, m.	pawnbroker	prestamista, m.
midwife	partera, f.	peasant	campesino, aldeano, m.
milkmaid	lechera, f.	pedagogue	pedagogo, m.
milkman	lechero, m.	peddler	buhonero, m.
miller	molinero, m.	pharmacist	farmacéutico, m.
milliner	modista, sombrerero, m.	philosopher	filósofo, m.
mime	pantomimo, mimo, m.	photographer	fotógrafo, m.
miner	minero, m.	physician	médico, m.
minister	pastor, cura, sacerdote, m.	pianist	pianista, f.
miser	avaro, m.	pickpocket	carterista, ratero, m.
mistress (lover)	concubina, f.	pilgrim	peregrino, m.
mistress	ama, dueña, señora, f.	pilot	piloto, m.
monarch	monarca, m.	pioneer	pionero, m.
monk (friar)	fraile, monje, m.	pipefitter	cañero, m.
mortician	funerario, m.	piper	flautista, f.
motorman	conductor, m.	pirate	pirata, m.
murderer	asesino, m.	pitcher (ball)	lanzador, m.
musician	músico, m.	planner	proyectista, m.
newsboy	diariero, m.	planter	sembrador, m.
newscaster	comentarista, m.	plasterer	yesero, m.
newspaperman	periodista, m.	playwright	dramaturgo, m.
nightwatchman	sereno, m.	plumber	cañero, plomero, m.
notary public	notario público, m.	poacher	cazador furtivo, m.
	escribano, m.	poet	poeta, m.
nun	monja, f.	poetess	poeta, f.
nurse	enfermera, f.	policeman	policía, f.
nursemaid	niñera, f.	politician	político, m.
nurseryman	vivero, m.	Pope	papa, m.
pediatrician	pediatra, m.	porter (bearer)	cargador, portero, m.

437

ENGLISH	SPANISH	ENGLISH	SPANISH
position	puesto, m.	singer	cantante, cantor, m.
postman	cartero, m.	sinner	pecador, m.
poultryman	gallinero, pollero, m.	skill	pericia, f.
practitioner	practicante, m.	smith	herrero, m.
preacher	predicador, m.	soldier	militar, soldado, m.
president	presidente, m.	speaker	orador, m.
priest	padre, sacerdote, cura, m.	specialist	especialista, f.
prince	príncipe, m.	spokesman	portavoz, vocero, m.
princess	princesa, m.	squire	escudero, m.
printer	impresor, m.	statesman	estadista, m.
prizefighter	boxeador, m.	stationer	papelista, papelero, m.
profession	profesión, f.	steam fitter	tubero, m.
professor	profesor, m.	stenographer	taquígrafo, m.
programmer	programador, m.		estenógrafa, f.
prophet	profeta, m.	stevedore	estibador, m.
prostitute	puta, prostituta, f.	steward	camarero, m.
*publisher	editor, m.	stewardess	asistenta, azafata, f.
queen	*reina, f.	stockbroker	agente de bolsa, m.
rabbi	rabí, rabino, m.		bolista, m.
racer	corredor, m.	stone-cutter	picapedrero, m.
ragman	trapero, m.	storekeeper	tendero, almacenero, m.
rancher (cow man)	ranchero, m.	striker	huelguista, m.
rector	rector, m.	student	estudiante, m.
referee	árbitro, juez, m.	surgeon	cirujano, m.
reporter	reportero, informador, m.	surveyor	topógrafo, agrimensor, m.
representative	representativo, m.	tailor	sastre, m.
retailer	detallista, m.	tanner	curtidor, m.
rider	jinete, caballero, m.	teacher	maestro, m.
robber	ladrón, bandido, m.	technician	técnico, m.
role (part)	papel, m.	telephone operator	telefonista, f.
ruler	soberano, m.	teller (bank..)	cajero, m.
sailmaker	velero, m.	tentmaker	tendero, m.
sailor	marinero, m.	thief	ladrón, ratero, m.
saint	santo, m.	tobacconist	tabaquero, estanquero, m.
salesman	vendedor, m.	trade (role)	oficio, m.
saloonkeeper	tabernero, m.	trainer	entrenador, m.
savior	salvador, m.	trainee	aprendiz, m.
scholar	sabio, erudito, m.	treasurer	tesorero, m.
scientist	hombre de ciencia, m.	trucker	camionero, m.
scout (exploror)	explorador, m.	trustee	fiduciario, m.
scout (runner)	corredor, m.	typist	mecanógrafo, m.
scribe	escritor, m.	undertaker	funerario, m.
sculpter	escultor, m.	underwriter	asegurador, m.
seaman	marino, marinero, m.	upholsterer	tapicero, m.
seamstress	costurera, f.	valet	paje, camarero, m.
secretary	secretaria, f.	vendor	vendedor, m.
senator	senador, m.	veterinarian	veterinario, m.
servant	criado, sirviente, m.	viceroy	virrey, m.
settler (colonist)	colono, m.	victor	vencedor, m.
shepherd	pastor, m.	villager	aldeano, m.
sheriff	alguacil, m.	vine-grower	viñador, m.
shoeblack	limpiabotas, m.	vintner	vinatero, m.
shoemaker	zapatero, m.	voyager	viajero, m.
shopkeeper	tendero, m.	waiter	camarero, mozo, m.
silversmith	platero, m.	watchmaker	relojero, m.

ENGLISH	SPANISH	ENGLISH	SPANISH
watchman	vigilante, guardián, m.	witch	bruja, hechicera, f.
	sereno, m.	witness	testigo, m.
weaver	tejedor, m.	wizard	hechicero, brujo, mago, m.
welder	soldador, m.	woodcarver	tallista, m.
well digger	pocero, m.	worker	obrero, trabajador, m.
wholesaler	mayorista, m.	workman	obrero, operario, m.
whore	prostituta, puta, f.		jornalero, trabajador, m.
wine dealer	vinatero, m.	wrestler	luchador, m.
		writer	autor, escritor, m.

14. SHOP OR WORK PLACE

Cross-Reference: Neighborhood, City & Community (p.421)

ENGLISH	SPANISH	ENGLISH	SPANISH
antique shop	tienda de.. antigüedades, f.	hairdresser shop	peluquería, f.
bakery	panadería, f.	hardware store	quincallería, f.
			ferretería, f.
bank	banco, m.	hatchery	criadero, m.
bar (cafe)	cantina, f.	hospital	hospital, m.
barber shop	peluquería, barbería, f.	hostelry	hospedería, f.
boarding house	*pensión, f.	hotel	hotel, m.
*bookshop	librería, f.	inn	posada, fonda, hostería, f.
booth (stall)	barraca, f.	jewelry store	joyería, f.
boutique	tienda de modas, f.	laundry	lavandería, f.
brewery	cervecería, f.	liquor store	licorería, f.
butcher shop	carnicería, f.	mach. shop	taller de maquinaria, m.
candy shop	confitería, f.	market	marcado, m.
	bombonería, f.	mill	molino, m.
cannery	fábrica de conservas, f.	millinery	sombrerería, f.
cattle ranch	ganadería, f.	nunnery	convento de monjas, m.
chemist's	botica, droguería, f.	nursery	guardería infantil, f.
church	iglesia, f.	pastry shop	dulcería, pastelería, f.
classroom	clase, m.; aula, f.	pawnshop	casa de empeños, f.
cleaners	tintorería, f.	perfume shop	perfumería, f.
coffee house	cafetería, f.	pharmacy	farmacia, f.
creamery	lechería, f.	power station	generadora, f.
customs	aduana, f.	printing office	imprenta, f.
dairy	lechería, f.	restaurant	restaurante, m.
deptmnt store	almacén, m; tienda, f.	sawmill	aserradero, m.
distillery	distilería, f.	shipyard	astillero, m.
*drugstore (chemist)	farmacia, f.	shoe store	zapatería, f.
drugstore (U.S.type)	botica, f.	shop	tienda, f.
dye-works	tintorería, f.	spinning mill	hilandería, f.
*factory	fabrica, f.	stationery store	papelería, f.
farm	finca, hacienda, granja, f.	store	tienda, f.
fishery	pesquería, f.	supermarket	supermarcado, m.
florist shop	florería, f.	tailor's shop	sastrería, f.
forge	fragua, f.	tannery	tenería, f.
gas station	gasolinera, f.	textile mill	fábrica de paño, f.
gas works	fábrica de gas, f.	tobacco shop	tabaquería, estanco, m.
glass works	fábrica de vidrio, f.	toy shop	jugetería, f.
grocery	bodega, especería, f.	warehouse	almacén, m.
	tienda de comestibles, f.	windmill	molino de viento, m.
haberdashery	mercería, camisería, f.	workshop	taller, m.

15. TOOLS, INSTRUMENTS & DEVICES

<u>Cross-Reference</u>: Specialized tools, instruments and devices can be found under Cooking-Eating p.417 & Household p.418

ENGLISH	SPANISH	ENGLISH	SPANISH
anchor	ancla, f.	dial	disco graduado, m; esfera, f.
anvil	yunque, m.	die	matriz, molde, m.
apparatus	aparato, m.	drill	taladro, m.; broca, f.
arrow	flecha, f.; dardo, m.	elevator	ascensor, m.
axe (hachet)	hacha, f.	eyelet	ojete, ojillo, m.
baler	empacadora, f.	*file	lima, f.
bar (pole)	palanca, f.	flashlight	destello, rayo, m.
bar (grating)	reja, verja, f.	forge	fragua, f.
barril	barril, m.	fork (garden)	horca, laya, f.
basket	cesta, canasta, f.	frame	cuadro, m.
battery (cell)	pila seca, f.	gauge	indicador, m.
battery (storage)	acumulador, m.	gear	engranaje, m.
bin	cajón, m.	gimlet	barrena, f.
blade (knife)	hoja, f.	grommet	anillo, m.
blower	soplador, m.	hammer	martillo, m.
boiler	caldera, f.	handle	puño, mango, m.
bolt	tornillo, perno, m.	handlebar	manillar, m.
box	caja, f.; cajón, m.	harness	harnés, m. guarniciones, f.
broom	escoba, f.	harrow	rastra, grada, f.
brush (paint)	pincel, m.	harvester	cosechadora, segadora, f.
brush (tool)	cepillo, m.; brocha, f.	hatchet	hacha, f.
bucket (pail)	cubo, balde, m.	hinge	gozne, m.
buffer	pulidor, m.	hoe	azadón, m.; azada, f.
bulldozer	rasador, m.	hook (fishing)	anzuelo, m.
cable	cable, m.	hook	garabato, gancho, m.
can opener	abrelatas, m.	hose (tube)	manga, manguera, f.
candle	*vela, f.	incubator	incubadero, m.
cane (stick)	bastón, m.	instrument	instrumento, m.
cash register	caja registradora, f.	iron (flat)	plancha, f.
cask	cuba, f.; tonel, barril, m.	jack	cric, gato, m.
cast	molde, m.	jigsaw	sierra caladora, f.
chain (fetter)	cadena, f.	key	llave, f.
chisel	cincel, m.	knife	cuchillo, m.
churn	mantequera, f.	ladder	escalera, escala, f.
club (stick)	palo, m.	lathe	torno, m.
coil	carrete, m.; espiral, f.	lawn mower	cortadora de césped, f.
compass (magn.)	brújula, f.	lens	lente, cristal, m.
compass (drawing)	compás, m.	level	nivel, m.
container	vasija, f.; envase, m.	lever	palanca, f.
cord	cuerda, f.	line (rope)	cuerda, f.; cordel, m.
corkscrew	sacacorchos, m.	link (chain)	eslabón, m.
crane (mech.)	grúa, f.	lock	cerradura, f.
crowbar	palanca, f.	loom	telar, m.
crutch	muleta, f.	machete	machete, m.
cultivator	cultivadora, f.	magnet	imán, m.
cutlass	machete, m.	match (fire)	fósforo, m.
dagger	puñal, m.; daga, f.	meter	medidor, metro, m.
derrick	grúa, f.	mill	molino, m.
device	aparato, m.	milling machine	fresadura, f.

ENGLISH	SPANISH	ENGLISH	SPANISH
mixer	mezcladors, f.	snare (trap)	trampa, f.
mold	matriz, f.;molde, m.	socket	hueco, enchufe, m.
	plantilla, f.	*spade (shovel)	pala, azada, f.
mop	estropajo, m.	spanner	llave de tuercas, f.
nail (tack)	clavo, m.	spare	pieza de recambio, f.
nail (VERB)	clavar	spear (lance)	pica, lanza, f.
nail puller (claw)	sacaclavos, m.	spigot	grifo, m.
needle	aguja, f.	spike	púa, f.
net	*red, malla, f.	spindle	huso, carretel, m.
noose	dogal, m.	spinning wheel	rueca, f.
nut (fastener)	tuerca, f.	spoke	rayo, m.
oil can	aceitera, f.	spool	canilla, bobina, f.
outlet (Elec.)	toma, f.	spring	*resorte, muelle, m.
padlock	candado, m.	sprinkler	regadera, f.
pail (bucket)	cubo, balde, m.	spur (on boot)	espuela, f.
paintbrush	pincel, m.;brocha, f.	square	escuadra, f.
penknife	cortaplumas, m.	staff (stick)	palo, bastón, m.
pick	zapapico, pico, m.	stapler	grapador, m.
pin	afiler, m.	stave (barrel)	duela, f.
pincers	alicates, m.;tenazas, f.	stirrup	estribo, m.
pitchfork	horca, f.	storage battery	acumulador, m.
plane	cepillo, m.	string	cuerda, f.;cordón, m.
pliers	pinzas, alicates, f.	support (prop)	apoyo, sustento, m.
plow (plough)	arado, m.	switch (ELEC)	interruptor, m.
plow (VERB)	arar	sword	espada, f.
plug (ELEC)	enchufe, m.	syphon	sifón, m.
plug (stopper)	tapón, m.	syringe	jeringa, f.
poker	atizador, m.	tack	tachuela, f.; clavete, m.
post(pole)	palo,poste, m.;estaca, f.	tank	tanque, m.
pump	bomba, f.	tap (faucet)	grifo, m.
radio	radio, m.	tape measure	cinta métrica, f.
rake	rastrillo, m.	tape recorder	magnetófono, m.
rasp	lima, f.; raspador, m.	thimble	dedal, m.
reel	carrete, m.;bobina, f.	thrasher	trilladora, f.
rod (bar, shaft)	vara, f.	tongs	tenazas, f.
rod (fishing)	caña, f.	tool	herramienta, f.
*rope	soga, cuerda, f.;cordón, m.	tractor	tractor, m.
ruler (inst)	regla, f.	trowel (garden)	desplantador, m.
safety pin	imperdible, m.	trowel (mason)	llana,f; badilejo, m.
sandpaper	papel abrasivo, m.	tub	cuba, tina, bañera, f.
saw	sierra, f.	tweezers	pinzas, f.
scaffold	andamio, m.	unscrew	destornillar
scales	balanza, f.	utensil	utensilio, m.
scissors	tijeras, f.	vacuum cleaner	aspiradora, f.
screen (partition)	mampara, f.	ventilator	ventilador, m.
screw	tornillo, m.; rosca, f.	vise	prensa de tornillo, f.
screwdriver	destornillador, m.	wedge	cuña, f.
scythe	guadaña, f.	weld	soldadura, f.
seeder	sembradora, f.	wheel	rueda, f.
sewer	albañal, m.	wheelbarrow	carretilla, f.
sewing machine	máquina de coser, f.	whip (lash)	azote, látigo, m.
shears	cizallas, tijeras, f.	wire	alambre, m.
shovel	pala, f.	wire (barbed..)	alambre de púas, m.
sickle	hoz, f.	wrench (socket)	llave de tubo, f.
sieve	tamiz, cedazo, m.; criba, f.	wrench	llave, f.
sled (sleigh)	trineo, m.	zipper	cierre relámpago, m.
sledgehammer	almádena, f.		cremallera, f.

441

16. ANIMALS
a) Kinds of Animals

ENGLISH	SPANISH	ENGLISH	SPANISH
animal	animal, m.	kangaroo	canguro, m.
ape	mono, m.	koala	koala, f.
ass	burro, asno, m.	kid (goat)	cabra, f.; cabrito, m.
badger	tejón, m.	kitten	gatito, m.
bat	murciélago, m.	lamb	cordero, m.
bear	oso, m.	leopard	leopardo, m.
beast	bestia, f.	lion, lioness	león, m.; leona, f.
beaver	castor, m.	llama	llama, f.
beef	vaca, f.	lynx	lince, m.
bloodhound	sabueso, m.	mammal	mamífero, m.
boar	jabalí, verraco, m.	mare	burra, yegua, f.
buck	macho del ciervo, m.	marsupial	marsupial, m.
buffalo	búfalo, m.	mastiff	mastín, m.
bull	toro, m.	mink	visón, m.
burro	burro, m.	mole (animal)	topo, m.
calf (animal)	becerro, ternero, m.	mongoose	mangosta, m.
camel	camello, m.	monkey	mono, m.
cat	gato, m.	moose	anta, f.
cattle	ganado, m.	mountain lion	puma, m.
cheetah	leopardo, m.	mouse	ratón, m.
chipmunk	ardilla listada, f.	mule	mulo, m.
colt	potro, m.	muskrat	rata almizclera, f.
cow	vaca, f.	mustang	mustango, m.
deer (stag)	ciervo, m.	ocelot	ocelote, m.
doe	gama, f.	opossum	oposum, m.
dog	perro, m.	orangutang	orangután, m.
dolphin	delfín, m.	otter	nutria, f.
dom. animals	animales domésticos, m.	ox	buey, m.
donkey	asno, burro, m.	panda	panda, f.
dragon	dragón, m.	panther	puma, pantera, f.
elephant	elefante, m.	pig (hog)	puerco, cerdo, m.
elk	alce, m.	polar bear	oso polar, m.
ewe	oveja, f.	polecat	mofeta, veso, turón, m.
filly	potranca, f.	pony	jaca, caballito, m.
fox	zorro, m.	poodle	perro de lanas, m.
foxhound	perro zorro, m.	porcupine	puerco espín, m.
giraffe	jurafa, f.	pork	cerdo, m.
goat (kid)	cabra, f.	porpoise	marsopa, f.
gopher	tuza, f.	puppy	perrito, m.
gorilla	gorila, f.	pussy (-cat)	gatito, m.
greyhound	galgo, m.	rabbit	conejo, m.
hamster	hámster, m.	racoon	mapache, m.
hare	liebre, f.	ram	carnero, morueco, m.
hedgehog	erizo, m.	rat	rata, f.
heifer	becerro, m.	reindeer	reno, m.
hippopotamus	hipopótamo, m.	rhinoceros	rinoceronte, m.
hog	puerco, cerdo, m.	sable	marta cebellina, f.
horse (steed)	caballo, m.	seal	foca, f.
hound	perro de caza, m.	sheep (ewe)	carnero, m.; oveja, f.
jackal	chacal, m.	skunk	zorrino, mofeta, tejón, m.
jackass	asno, burro, m.	sow	cerda, f.
jaguar	jaguar, m.	spaniel	perro de aguas, m.

ENGLISH	SPANISH	ENGLISH	SPANISH
squirrel	ardilla, f.	weasel	comadreja, f.
stag	ciervo, venado, m.	whale	ballena, f.
stallion	semental, m.	wildcat (lynx)	gato montés, lince, m.
steed (horse)	caballo, m.	wildebeast	ñu, m.
steer	res, novillo, m.	wolf	lobo, m.
swine (boar)	marrano, m.	wolfhound	barsoí, galgo ruso, m.
terrier	terrier, m.	wolverine	glotón, m.
tiger	tigre, m.	woodchuck	marmota, f.
vampire	vampiro, m.	yak	yak, m.
walrus	morsa, f.	zebra	cebra, f.

b) Words Relating to Animals

ENGLISH	SPANISH	ENGLISH	SPANISH
back (of animal)	lomo, m.	livestock	ganado, m.
bark (VERB)	ladrar	male	varón, macho, m.
bark	ladrido, m.	manger	comedero, pesebre, m.
barn	granero, m.	mane	melena, f.; crin, m.
barnyard (corral)	corral, m.	mate	pareja, f.
bite	mordedura, f.	mew (VERB)	maullar
bite (VERB)	morder	muzzle (snout)	hocico, morro, m.
breed (stock)	raza, f.	pack (hounds)	jauría, f.
breed (to..)	criar	paddock	potrero, m.
brood	cría, f.	pasture	pastura, f.
burrow	madriguera, f.	paw (foot)	pata, garra, f.
cage	jaula, f.	pet	animal mimado, m.
carcass	res muerta, f.	pigpen	chiquero, m.; zahúrda, f.
cattle raising	ganadería, f.	ranch	ganadería, f.
claw	garra, uña, f.	rein (bridle)	rienda, f.; freno, m.
cow shed	establo, m.; cuadra, f.	roar	rugido, bramido, m.
den (lair)	cubil, m.; guarida, f.	roar (VERB)	rugir, bramar
feed	comida, f.	saddle	silla de montar, f.
feed (VERB)	cebar	shepherd	pastor, m.
female	hembra, f.	skin (hide)	piel, f.; pellejo, m.
fleece	vellocino, vellón, m.	snout	trompa, f.
flesh (meat)	carne, f.	squeal	berrido, grito, chillido, m.
flesh eating	carnicero	stable	establo, m.
flock	manada, bandada, f. rebaño, m.	stirrup	estribo, m.
foal	potro, m.	stock	ganado, m.
fodder (forage)	foraje, m.	straw	paja, f.
fur	piel, f.	tail	rabo, m.; cola, f.
gallop	galope, m.	tame	manso
game (prey)	presa, caza, f.	tame (VERB)	domar
harness	guarniciones, f; arnés, m.	team (horses)	yunta, f.; tronco, m.
hay	heno, m.	train (VERB)	amaestrar
herd (cattle)	rebaño, m.	trap (snare)	trampa, f.; lazo, m.
herd (pigs)	piara, f.	trough	abrevadero, m.
hide (skin)	cuero, piel, m.	tusk	colmillo, m.
hoof	casco, m.; pezuña, f.	udder	ubre, f.
horn	asta, f.; cuerno, m.	water (VERB)	dar de beber
horseshoe	herradura, f.	whip	látigo, m.
howl (bellow)	grito, maullido, m.	wild (savage)	salvaje
hunting	caza, f.	wildlife	fauna silvestre, f.
leather	cuero, m.	yoke (oxen)	junta, f.; jugo, m.

17. FISH AND CRUSTACEA

a) Kinds of Fish & Crustacea

Cross-Reference: List of Fish as Food (p.413)

ENGLISH	SPANISH	ENGLISH	SPANISH
anchovy	anchoa, f.	pike	lucio, sollo, m.
barracuda	barracuda, f.	piranha	piraña, f.
bass	róbalo, m.	plaice	platija, f.
catfish	siluro, m.	pollack	gado, m.
clam	almeja, f.	porpoise	marsopa, f.
cod	abadejo, bacalao, m.	prawn	camarón, m.; gamba, f.
crab	cangrejo, m.	sailfish	pez vela, f.
crawfish (cray-)	cangrejo de rio, m.	salmon	salmón, m.
dolphin	delfín, m.	sardine	sardina, f.
eel	anguila, f.	scallop	venera, pechina, f.
fish (alive)	pez, m.	sea horse	hipocampo, m.
flounder	lenguado, m.	sea urchin	erizo marino, m.
goldfish	carpa dorada, f; dorado, m.	shark	tiburón, m.
guppy	olomina, f.	shellfish	crustáceos, molusco, m.
haddock	abadejo, m.		marisco, m.; conchas, f.
hake	merluza, f.	shrimp	gamba, f.; camarón, m.
halibut	hipogloso, m.	skate	raya, f.
herring	arenque, m.	smelt	eperlano, m.
jellyfish	aguamar, medusa, f.	sole	lenguado, m.
lobster	langosta, f.	squid	calamar, m.
mackerel	caballa, f.; escombro, m.	starfish	estrella de mar, f.
manta	manta, f.	stingray	pastinaca, f.
marlin	pez vela, m.	sturgeon	esturión, f.
minnow	pez pequeño, m.	sunfish	pez luna, m; rueda, f.
moray eel	morena, f.	swordfish	pez espada, m.
mussel	mítulo, mejillón, m.	tarpon	tarpón, m.
octopus	óctopo, pulpo, m.	trout	trucha, f.
oyster	ostra, f.	tuna	atún, m.
perch	perca, f.	turbot	rodaballo, m.
pickerel	lucio pequeño, m.	whale (animal)	ballena, f.

b) Words Relating to Fish & Crustacea

ENGLISH	SPANISH	ENGLISH	SPANISH
bait	cebo, m.	fishhook	anzuelo, m.
bobber	flotador, m.	fishing	pesca, f.
cast (throw)	lance, m.	fishing line	sedal, m.
catch	pesca, f.	gill	agalla, branquia, f.
fin	aleta, f.	net	*red, f.
fish (to)	pescar	scale (flake)	escama, f.
fish (caught)	pescado, m.	shell	concha, f.
fish pole (rod)	caña de pescar, f.	strike	mordedura, f.
fisherman	pescador, m.	worm	lombriz, f.; gusano, m.

18. REPTILES

ENGLISH	SPANISH	ENGLISH	SPANISH
alligator	caimán, m.	rattlesnake	cascabel, m.
asp	áspid, m.	reptile	reptil, m.
boa	boa, f.	salamander	salamandra, f.
cobra	cobra, f.	serpent	serpiente, m.
creep (to crawl)	arrastrar	snake	culebra, serpiente, f.
crocodile	crocodilo, m.	tadpole	renacuajo, m.
frog	rana, f.	toad	sapo, m.
lizard	lagarto, m.	tortoise (turtle)	tortuga, f.
poison	veneno, m.	viper	víbora, f.

19. INSECTS

a) Kinds of Insects

ENGLISH	SPANISH	ENGLISH	SPANISH
ant	hormiga, f.	ladybug	mariquita, f.
aphid	áfido, pulgón, afidio, m.	locust	langosta, cigarra, f.
bedbug	chinche, f.	louse	piojo, m.
bee	abeja, f.	mantis	mantis, f.
beetle	escarabajo, m.	mosquito	mosquito, m.
bug	bicho, m.	moth	polilla, f.
bumblebee	abejorro, m.	scorpion	escorpión, m.
butterfly	mariposa, f.	silkworm	gusano de seda, m.
caterpillar	oruga, f.	spider	araña, f.
cockroach	cucaracha, f.	sting (VERB)	picar
cricket	grillo, m.	tarantula	tarántula, f.
flea	pulga, f.	termite	termita, f.; comején, m.
fly	mosca, f.	tick	ácaro, pito, rezno, m.
gnat (midge)	jején, mosquito, m.		garrapata, f.
grasshopper	saltamontes, m.	wasp	avispa, f.
	langosta, cigarra, f.	weevil	calapatillo, gorgojo, m.
hornet	avispón, m.	worm (grub)	gusano, m.
insect	insecto, m.	yellow jacket	avispa, f.

b) Words Relating to Insects

ENGLISH	SPANISH	ENGLISH	SPANISH
beehive	colmena, f.	honeycomb	panal, m.
buzz	zumbido, m.	honey	miel, f.
cobweb	telaraña, f.	larva	larva, f.
cocoon	capullo, m.	sting	picar
grub	gusano, m.	wax	cera, f.
hive (bee)	colmena, f.	web	telaraña, f.

c) Miscellaneous Creepers

ENGLISH	SPANISH	ENGLISH	SPANISH
earthworm	lombriz, f.	snail	caracol, m.; babosa, f.
slug	babosa, f.	worm	gusano, m.

20. BIRDS
a) Kinds of Birds

ENGLISH	SPANISH	ENGLISH	SPANISH
albatross	albatros, m.	nightingale	ruiseñor, m.
bird	ave, f.; pájaro, m.	oriole	oriol, m.
blackbird	mirlo, m.	osprey	halieto, m.
canary	canario, m.	ostrich	avestruz, m.
catbird	tordo, m.	owl	buho, m.; lechuza, f.
chick	polluelo, m.	parakeet	periquito, perico, m.
chicken	pollo, m.	parrot	loro, papagayo, m.
cock (rooster)	gallo, m.	partridge	perdiz, f.
condor	cóndor, m.	peacock	pavo real, m.
cuckoo	cuclillo, m.	pelican	alcastraz, pelícano, m.
crane	grulla, f.	penguin	pingüino, m.
crow	cuervo, m.	pheasant	faisán, m.
dove	paloma, f.	pigeon	paloma, f.; pichón, m.
duck	pato, m.	puffin	pufino, m.
duckling	patito, m.	quail	codorniz, f.
eagle	águila, f.	raven	cuervo, m.
falcon	halcón, m.	robin	pechirrojo, petirrojo, m.
finch	pinzón, m.	rooster	gallo, m.
fowl	aves de corral, pollo, m.	seagull	gaviota, f.
goose	ganso, m.	skylark	alondra, calandria, f.
gosling	gansarón, m.	sparrow	gorrión, m.
grouse	ortega, f.	squab	pichón, m.
gull	gaviota, f.	starling	estornino, m.
hawk	halcón, m.	stork	cigüeña, f.
hen	gallina, f.	swallow	golondrina, f.
hummingbird	colibrí, picaflor, m.	swan	cisne, m.
kingfisher	martín pescador, m.	tanager	tanagra, f.
jay	arrendajo, grajo, m.	tern	gaviotín, m.
lark	alondra, f.	thrush	malvía, zorzal, tordo, m.
macaw	guacamayo, m.	turtledove	tórtola, f.
magpie	urraca, f.	turkey	pavo, m.
mallard	pato silvestre, m.	vulture	buitre, m.
martin	vencejo, m.	warbler	sílvido, m.
meadowlark	sabanero, m.	woodpecker	carpintero, picaposte, m.
mockingbird	sinsonte, m.	wren	abadejo, reyezuelo, m.

b) Words Relating to Birds

ENGLISH	SPANISH	ENGLISH	SPANISH
beak	pico, m.	feather	pluma, f.
bill (beak)	pico, m.	fly (VERB)	volar
brood	cría, nidada f.	hen house	gallinero, m.
brood (to hatch)	empollar	nest	nido, m.
cage	jaula, f.	nest (VERB)	anidar
claw	garra, f.	perch	percha, f.
comb	cresta, f.	pluck (VERB)	desplumar
coop	gallinero, m.	plume	penacho, m.
coxcomb	cresta, f.	poultry	aves de corral, m.
crest	cresta, f.	roost	percha, f.
egg	huevo, m.	wing	ala, aleta, f.
egg (to lay eggs)	poner huevos	yard	corral, m.

21. VEGETABLES & GRAINS

Cross-Reference: List of Vegetables as Food (p.414)

a) Kinds of Vegetables & Grains

ENGLISH	SPANISH	ENGLISH	SPANISH
artichoke	alcachofa, f.	mushroom	seta, f.; hongo, m.
asparagus	espárrago, m.	oat(s)	avena, f.
banana	plátano, banano, m.	okra	quimbombó, m.
barley	cebada, f.	onion	cebolla, f.
bean (broad)	haba, f.	parsley	perejil, m.
bean (kidney)	frijol, m.; judía, f.	parsnip	chiviría, f.
bean (lima)	frijol de media luna, m.	pea	guisante, m.
bean (string)	judía verde, f.	pea (chick)	garbanzo, m.
beet (root)	remolacha, f.	pepper	pimiento, m.
broccoli	bróculi, m.	potato	papa, patata, f.
Brussel sprouts	col de Bruselas, f.	pumpkin	calabaza, f.
cabbage	berza, col, f.	radish	rábano, m.
cabbage (red)	col morada, f.	rice	arroz, m.
carrot	zanahoria, f.	rhubarb	ruibarbo, m.
cauliflower	coliflor, f.	rye	centeno, m.
celery	apio, m.	scallion	escalonia, f.
cereal	cereal, m.	shallot	chalote, m.
chick pea	garbanzo, m.	soy bean	semilla de soja, f.
chives	cebolleta, f.; cebollino, m.	spinach	espinaca, f.
corn (maize)	maíz, m.	sprout	brote, m.
cucumber	pepino, m.	squash	calabaza, f.
eggplant	berenjena, f.	sugarbeet	remolacha, f.
endive	escarola, f.	sweet potato	patata dulce, f.
garlic	ajo, m.	Swiss chard	acelga, f.
gherkin	pepinillo, m.	tomato	tomate, m.
gourd	calabaza, f.	turnip	nabo, m.
grain	grano, m.	vegetable	legumbre, verdura, f.
kale	col, m.		vegetal, m.
kohlrabi	colirrábano, m.	watercress	berro, m.
leek	puerro, m.	wheat	trigo, m.
lentil	lenteja, f.	yam	ñame, m.
lettuce	lechuga, f.	zucchini	calabacín, m.

b) Words Related to Vegetables and Grains

ENGLISH	SPANISH	ENGLISH	SPANISH
acre	hectária, f.	cultivator	cultivadora, f.
agriculture	agricultura, f.	dirt (soil)	tierra, f.; suelo, m.
alfalfa	alfalfa, f.	dry (barren)	árido
baler	empacadora, f.	ear (corn)	espiga, f.
bushel	fanega, f.	fallow(leave.)	dejar en barbecho
coffee plantation	cafetal, m.	farm	granja, f.
corncob	mazorca de maíz, f.	farmer	labrador, agricultor, m.
corncrib	granero, m.	fertilizer	fertilizante, abono, m.
crop	cosecha, f.	field	prado, campo, m.
cultivate(work)	labrar, cultivar	furrow	surco, m.; zanja, f.
cultivation	cultivo, m.	garden (veg.)	huerta, f.

ENGLISH	SPANISH	ENGLISH	SPANISH
grain	grano, m.	root	raíz, f.
harrow	grada, f.	scatter	esparcir
harvest	siega, cosecha, f.	seed (grain)	grano, m.; semilla, f.
harvest (VERB)	cosechar	seeder	sembradora, f.
harvester	cosechadora, segadora, f.	sheaf	gavilla, f.; haz, m.
hoe	azadón, m.	shell (VERB)	desvainar
husbandry	manejo, m.	shovel	pala, f.
husk (shell)	vaina, cáscara, f.	sickle	hoz, f.
irrigate (to water)	regar	sow (VERB)	sembrar
irrigation	riego, m.; regadura, f.	sowing	siembra, f.
manure	estiércol, m.	spade	azada, f.
mill	molino, m.	sprout (shoot)	brote, m.
plantation	hacienda, f.	team (horses)	tiro de caballos, m.
planting	plantación, f.	thrasher	trilladora, f.
plow	arado, m.	tractor	tractor, m.
pod (shell)	vaina, f.	truck garden	huerta, f.
rake	rastrillo, m.	untilled land	campo inculto, m.
reap (to mow)	segar	wheat field	trigal, m.
reaping machines	segadora, f.	yield (production)	rendimiento, m.

22. PLANTS, BUSHES & FLOWERS
Other than Vegetables & Grains

a) Kinds of Flowers and Plants

ENGLISH	SPANISH	ENGLISH	SPANISH
banana	banano, plátano, m.	herb	hierba, yerba, f.
bittersweet	dulcamara, f.	holly	acebo, m.
bluebell	campánula, f.	hollyhock	malva real, f.
bush (shrub)	arbusto, m.	hyacinth	jacinto, m.
buttercup	botón de oro, m.	ivy	hiedra, f.
cane	caña, f.	jasmine	jazmín, m.
carnation	clavel, m.	larkspur	consuelda, f.
chrysanthemum	crisantemo, m.	laurel	laurel, m.
clover	trébol, m.	lavender	lavándula, f.
coriander	cilantro, coriandro, m.	lilac	lilac, lila, f.
cornflower	aciano, m.	lily	azucena, f.; lirio, m.
cotton	algodón, m.	lily of valley	muguete, m.
currant bush	grosellero, m.	lotus	loto, m.
daffodil	narciso trompón, m.	marigold	caléndula, f.
daisy	maya,, margarita, f.	milkweed	asclepiadea, f.
dandelion	diente de león, m.	mint	menta, f.
fern	helecho, m.	mistletoe	liga, f.; muérdago, m.
flax	lino, m.	morning glory	dompedro, m.
flower	flor, f.	moss	musgo, m.
forget-me-not	nomeolvides, f.	mountain laurel	calmia, f.
gardenia	gardenia, f.	mulberry	morera, f.
nasturtium	nastuerzo, m.	myrtle	mirto, m.
geranium	geranio, m.	narcissus	narciso, m.
goldenrod	vara de oro, f.	nettle	ortiga, f.
grape vine	vid, f.	orchid	orquídea, f.
grass (lawn)	césped, hierba, yerba, f.	pansy	pensamiento, m.
hay	heno, m.	passion flower	pasionaria, f.
heather (heath)	brezo, m.	peony	peonía, f.
hedge (shrub)	arbusto, seto, m.	petunia	petunia, f.

ENGLISH	SPANISH	ENGLISH	SPANISH
philodendron	filodendro, m.	shrub (bush)	arbusto, m.
phlox	flox, m.	snap dragon	dragón, m.
pineapple	piña, ananá, f.	snow drop	amarilis, f.
*plant	planta, f.	Spanish moss	barbón, m.
plantain	plátano, m.	strawberry plant	fresal, m.
poinsettia	flor de Pascua, f.	sugar cane	caña de azúcar, f.
poison ivy	zumaque venenoso, m.	sunflower	girasol, m.
portulaca	verdolaga, f.	sweetpea	guisante de olor, m.
poppy	amapola, f.	syringa	jeringuilla, f.
primrose	primavera, f.	thistle	cardo, m.
Queen Anne's lace	dauco, m.	thyme	tomillo, m.
ragweed	ambrosia, f.	tiger lily	trigidia, f.
rasberry bush	frambueso, m.	tulip	tulipán, m.
rose	rosa, f.	violet	violeta, f.
rosebush	rosal, m.	watercress	berro, m
sage	salvia, f.	water lily	nifea, f.; nenúfar, m.
seaweed	alga marina, f.	weed	maleza, mala hierba, f.
shamrock	trebol, m.	wistaria	glicina, vistaria, f.
		zinnia	cinnia, f.

b) Words Relating to Flowers and Plants

ENGLISH	SPANISH	ENGLISH	SPANISH
aroma	aroma, f.	garland	guirnalda, f.
blade (grass)	hoja, brizna, f.	haystack	almiar, m.
blooming	florido	lawn (grass)	césped, m.
blossom (bloom)	flor, f.	lawnmower	cortacésped, m.
bouquet	ramo de flores, m.	landscape	paisaje, m.; vista, f.
bud	botón, m.; yema, f.	leaf	hoja, f.
	capullo, brote, m.	leaves (full of..)	frondoso
bud (VERB)	brotar	meadow	prado, m.; pradera, f.
bulb	bulbo, m.; cebolla, f.	mower	dallador, m.
bunch	racimo, ramillete, m.	peel (husk)	cáscara, f.
bush	mata, f.; arbusto, m.	petal	pétalo, m.
corsage	corpiño, ramillete, m.	plant	plantar
creeper	enredadera, f.	pod	vaina, f.
creeping (climbing)	trepador	pollen	polen, m.
dirt	tierra, f.	pot	tiesto, m.; maceta, f.
enclosure	cerrado, m.	reed (grass)	junco, m.
fade (to wither)	marchitar(se)	root	raíz, f.
fence	cerca, f.	scent	fragancia, f.
fertilizer	fertilizante, abono, m.	seed	semilla, f.
field (meadow)	pradera, f; prado, m.	sod (turf)	césped, m.
florist	florero, m.	sowing	siembra, f.
flower	flor, f.	spade (fork)	laya, f.
flower (to blossom)	florecer	sprout	brote, m.
flowerbed	cuadro de flores, m.	stalk (stem)	tallo, m.
	arriate, m.	straw	paja, f.
flowerpot	florero, m.	thicket	maleza, f.
folliage	follaje, m.	thorn (briar)	espina, f.
furrow	surco, m.; zanja, f.	vine	parra, vid, f.
garden	jardín, m.	vineyard	viñedo, m.; viña, f.
gardener	jardinero, m.	water	regar
gate	entrada, barrera, f.	watering can	regadera, f.
greenhouse	invernadero, m.	weed (VERB)	escardar, desherbar
ground (soil)	tierra, f.; suelo, m.	wheelbarrow	carretilla, f.

449

23. TREES

a) Kinds of Trees

Tree names are often the name of the fruit with the ending changed to the masculine ending -o or -ero.

ENGLISH	SPANISH	ENGLISH	SPANISH
almond	almendro, m.	mahogany tree	caobo, m.
apple tree	manzano, m.	mandarin tree	mandarino, m.
apricot tree	albaricoquero, m.	mango	mango, m.
ash	fresno, m.	maple	arce, m.
bamboo	bambú, m.	oak	roble, m.
beech	haya, f.	olive tree	olivo, m.
birch	abedul, m.	orange tree	naranjo, m.
cedar	cedro, m.	palm	palmera, palma, f.
cherry tree	cerezo, m.	papaya tree	papayo, m.
chestnut tree	castaño, m.	peach tree	melocotonero, m.
coconut tree	cocotero, m.	pear tree	peral, m.
conifer	conífero, m.	pecan tree	pacana, f.
cork tree	alcornoque, m.	pine	pino, m.
cypress	ciprés, m.	plane tree	plátano, m.
date tree	datilero, m.	plum tree	ciruelo, m.
ebony	ébano, m.	pomegranate tree	granado, m.
elm	olmo, m.	poplar	álamo, m.
fig tree	higuera, f.	quince tree	membrillero, m.
fir	abeto, m.	rosewood	palisandro, m.
fruit tree	árbol frutal, m.	rubber tree	caucho, m.
grapefruit tree	toronjo, m.	sequoia	secoya, f.
guava tree	guayabo, m.	sycamore	sicomoro, m.
hazelnut tree	avellano, m.	teak	teca, f.
horse chestnut	castaña de Indias, f.	tree	árbol, m.
juniper	junípero, m.	tulip tree	tulipero, m.
lemon tree	limonero, m.	walnut tree	nogal, m.
lime tree	tilo, limero agrio, m.	willow	mimbre, sauce, m.
linden	tilo, m.	yew	tejo, m.

b) Nouns Relating to Trees & Tree Products

ENGLISH	SPANISH	ENGLISH	SPANISH
acorn	bellota, f.	limb	rama, f.
bark	corteza, cáscara, f.	log	leño, m.
board (plank)	tabla, f.; madero, m.	lumber	madera, tablas, f.
branch (bough)	rama, f.	maple syrup	jarabe de arce, m.
brier	brezo, m.	nut	nuez, f.
bud	brote, m.	pitch	brea, pez, resina, f.
climb (VERB)	trepar	plywood	madera terciada, f.
clump	acizo, m.	prune (VERB)	podar
cone	cono, m.; piña, f.	*pulp	pulpa, f.
cork	corcho, m.	rosewood	palo de rosa, m.
foliage	follaje, m.	orchard	huerto, m.
forest (woods)	bosque, m.; selva, f.	root	raíz, f.
fruit	fruta, f.	rosin	resina, f.
grove	bosque, m.; arboleda, f.	rubber (foam)	caucho esponjoso, m.
lath	listón, m.	rubber	caucho, m.; goma, f.
leaf	hoja, f.	sap	savia, f.

ENGLISH	SPANISH	ENGLISH	SPANISH
sawdust	aserrín, m.	*timber	árboles de monte, m.
shed leaves	deshojar(se)	trunk	tronco, m.
shell (husk)	cáscara, f.	twig	rama, ramita, f.
stump	tocón, m.; toza, f.	wood (lumber)	madera, leña, f.
*timber	maderaje, m.	woody	silvoso

24. OBJECTS & PHENOMENA OF NATURE

a) Geographic Directions

ENGLISH	SPANISH	ENGLISH	SPANISH
east	oriente, este, m	northwest	norueste, noroeste, m.
latitud	latitud, m.	south	sud, sur, m.
longitud	longitud, m.	southeast	sudeste, m.
north	norte, m.	southwest	suroeste, sudoeste, m.
northeast	noreste, nordeste, m.	South Pole	Polo Sur, m.
North Pole	Polo Norte, m.	west	occidente, oeste, m.

b) General

ENGLISH	SPANISH	ENGLISH	SPANISH
air	aire, m.	comet	cometa, m.
archipelago	archipiélago, m.	constellation	constelación, f.
atmosphere	atmósfera, f.	continent	continente, m.
atlas	atlas, m.	cool	fresco
avalanche	avalancha, f.; alud, m.	coolness	frescura, f.
bank(river)	margen, orilla, ribera, f.	cosmos	cosmos, m.
basin (river)	cuenca, f.; cauce, m.	country (-side)	campo, m.
bay	bahía, f.	crater	cráter, m.
bayou	canalizo, m.	creek	arroyo, riachuelo, m.
beach (strand)	playa, f.	crevice	grieta, hendedura, f.
blizzard	ventisca, f.	current	corriente, f.
bluff	barranca, f.	dale	valle, m.
bog	pantano, m.	dampness	humedad, f.
boulder	pedrón, m.	darkness	tinieblas, obscuridad, f.
breeze	brisa, f.	dark (to get..)	anochecer
brook	arroyo, m.	dawn	aurora, alba, madrugada, f.
canal	canal, m.	dawn (to..)	almanecer
cape	cabo, m.	daylight	luz del día, f.
cave	cueva, f.	death	muerte, f.
cavern	caverna, f.	desert	desierto, m.
chain (mountains)	cordillera, f.	dew	rocío, m.
chill	frío, m.; frialdad, f.	dirt (soil)	tierra, f.; suelo, m.
cliff	risco, precipicio, m.	downpour	*chaparrón, aguacero, m.
clear (cloudless)	despejado	draft	corriente de aire, f.
clear up	aclarar, despejar(se)	drop	gota, f.
climate	clima, m.	drought	sequía, f.
cloud	nube, f.	dryness	aridez, sequedad, f.
cloudy	nublado	dust	polvo, m.
coast	litoral, m.; costa, f.	earth	suelo, m.; tierra, f.
cold	frío, m.	earth (planet)	globo, m.
coldness	frialdad, f.	earthquake	terremoto, m.

ENGLISH	SPANISH	ENGLISH	SPANISH
ebb (low tide)	reflujo, m; bajamar, f.	hurricane	huracán, m.
eclipse	eclipse, m.	ice	hielo, m.
element	elemento, m.	island	isla, f.
energy	energía, f.	isthmus	istmo, m.
equator	ecuador, m.	jungle	selva, f.
erupt	entrar en erupción	knoll	otero, m.; loma, f.
explore (VERB)	explorar	lake	lago, m.
explorer	explorador, m.	land	tierra, f.
falls	cascada, f.	landscape	paisaje, m.
field	campo, m.	lava	lava, f.
fire	fuego, m.	ledge (rock)	reborde, m.; berma, f.
firmament	firmamento, m.	life	vida, f.
flame	llama, f.; fuego, m.	light	luz, iluminación, f.
flash (lightning)	relámpago, m.	lightning	relámpago, rayo, m.
flood (VERB)	inundar	lightning conductor	pararrayos, m.
flood	diluvio, m.; inundación, f.	lowland	tierra baja, f.
flood tide	marea creciente, f.	mainland	tierra firme, f.
foam	espuma, f.	map	mapa, f.
fog (mist)	niebla, bruma, f.	marsh	pantano, m.
foggy (misty)	nebuloso, brumoso	*matter	materia, f.
ford	vado, m.	meadow	pradera, f.; prado, m.
forest (woods)	selva, f. bosque, m.	meteor	meteoro, m.
freeze	helar	milky way	vía láctea, f.
fresh (cool)	fresco	mist (fog)	neblina, niebla, bruma, f.
frost	helada, escarcha, f.	moon	luna, f.
frozen	helado	moon (full)	luna llena, f.
gale (storm)	tempestad, f.	moonbeam	rayo de luna, m.
	tormenta, f.; ventarrón, m.	moonlight	luz de la luna, f.
geography	geografía, f.	moor	páramo, m.
glacier	glaciar, m.	mountain	monte, m.; montaña, f.
glen (dale)	hoya, f.; valle, m.	mountain range	cordillera, sierra, f.
globe	globo, m.	mountainous	montañoso
gloom (darkness)	obscuridad, f.	mountainside	ladera, f.
God	Dios, m.	mountain top	cumbre, cima, f.
gorge	cañón, paso, m.	mouth (river)	desembocadura, f.
grove (woods)	bosque, m.; selva, f.	mud	lodo, barro, m.
grow dark	anochecer	nature	natura, naturaleza, f.
gulf (big bay)	golfo, m.	night	noche, f.
gully	arroyo, m.	noise	ruido, m
gust	ráfaga, ventolera, f.	northeaster	tempestad nordestal, f.
hail	granizo, m.	North Pole	Polo Norte, m.
hail (VERB)	granizar	North Star	estrella polar, f.
heat (warmth)	calor, m; temperatura, f.	oasis	oasis, m.
heaven	cielo, paraíso, m.	ocean	océano, m.
hell	infierno, m.	open air	aire libre, m.
hemisphere	hemisferio, m.	outdoors	exterior, aire libre, m.
highland	tierra de altura, f.	peak	cumbre, cima, f.; pico, m.
hill (ridge)	colina, f.; cerro, m.	pebble	piedrecilla, f.
	loma, f.; collado, otero, m.	peninsula	península, f.
hillside	ladera, f.	pile (heap)	pila, f.
hilltop	cima, cumbre, f.	pit (ditch)	fosa, f.; hoyo, m.
hilly	montañoso	plain	pampa, llanura, f.; llano, m.
horizon	horizonte, m.	planet	planeta, m.
humidity	humedad, f.	plateau	meseta, mesa, f.

ENGLISH	SPANISH	ENGLISH	SPANISH
pond	estanque, m.; laguna, f.	steam	vapor, m.
pool	estanque, pozo, m.	steep	empinado
prairie	pradera, pampa, llanura, f.	stone	piedra, f.
prism	prisma, m.	storm	tormenta, tempestad, f.
quagmire	lodazal, m.; ciénaga, f.	stormy	borrascoso
quake	terremoto, temblor, m.	strait	estrecho, m.
rain (rainfall)	lluvia, f.	stream	arroyo, río, m.
rain (VERB)	llover	subsoil	subsuelo, m.
rainbow	arco iris, m.	summit (top)	cumbre, cima, f.
rainy	lluvioso	sun	sol, m.
range (mountains)	cordillera, f.	sunbeam	rayo de sol, m.
ray (beam of light)	rayo, m.	sunlight	luz solar, f.
reef	escollo, arrecife, m.	sunshine	sol, m.; luz del sol, f.
ridge (mountains)	sierra, arruga, f.	sunny	soleado
	cordillera, loma, f.	sunrise	salida del sol, f.
rim	borde, m.; orilla, f.	sunset	puesta del sol, f.
river	río, m.	sunshine	luz del sol, f.
riverside	ribera, f.	surface	superficie, f.
rock	piedra, roca, f.	swamp (bog, marsh)	pantano, m.
sand	arena, f.	tempest (storm)	tempestad, f.
satellite	satélite, m.	thaw	deshielo, m.
*scenery	paisaje, m.; vista, f.	thaw (VERB)	deshelar(se)
sea	mar, m.	thunder	trueno, m.
seacoast	litoral, m.; costa, orilla, f.	thunder (VERB)	tronar
sea level	nivel del mar, m.	thunderbolt	rayo, m.
seashore	costa, playa, f.	thunderclap	tronido, m.
seaside	costa, f.; litoral, m.	thundercloud	nubarrón, m.
set (sun)	poner(se)	thunderstorm	tronada, f.
shade, in the..	a la sombra	tide (H)	pleamar, marea (alta), f.
shadow (shade)	sombra, f.	tide (L)	bajamar, marea (baja), f.
shine (sun)	brillar	to be clear.	hcer buen tiempo
shore (river)	orilla, ribera, f.	to be stormy.	hacer mal tiempo
shower (downpour)	aguacero, m.	tornado	tornado, m.
	chaparrón, m.; lluvia, f.	twilight	crepúsculo, anochecer, m.
sky (heaven)	cielo, m.	typhoon	tifón, m.
sleet	aguanieve, f.	universe	universo, m.
slope	cuesta, ladera, f.	valley	valle, m.
	pendiente, m.	view	vista, f.
slush	cieno, fango, m.	volcano	volcán, m.
smoke	humo, m.	warmth (heat)	calor, m.
snow	nieve, f.	water	agua, f.
snow (VERB)	nevar	waterfall	catarata, cascada, f.
snowflake	copo, m.	wave	onda, ola, f.
snowstorm	ventisca, nevasca, f.	weather	tiempo, m.; clima, f.
snowy	nevoso	well (water)	pozo, m.
soil	suelo, m.	whirlpool	vórtice, m.
solar system	sistema solar, m.	whirlwind	torbellino, m.
sound	sonido, m.	wind	viento, m.
South Pole	Polo Sur, m.	windstorm	ventarrón, m.
space	espacio, m.	windy	ventoso
spark	chispa, f.	woods (forest)	bosque, m.
spring (source)	fuente, f.	world	mundo, m.
star	estrella, f.; astro, m.	zodiac	zodíaco, m.

25. MINERALS, GEMS, METALS & EARTHEN MATERIALS

Cross-Reference: N -um, -ite

ENGLISH	SPANISH	ENGLISH	SPANISH
agate	ágata, f.	mineral	mineral, m.
alloy	aleación, mezcla, f.	mold	molde, m.
aluminum	aluminio, m.	mold (VERB)	moldar
amethyst	amatista, f.	mortar	argamasa, f.
asphalt	asfalto, m.	mud	lodo, barro, m.
brass	latón, m.	nickel	níquel, m.
brick	ladrillo, m.	oil	aceite, óleo, m.
bronze	bronce, m.	onyx	ónix, f.
cast iron	hierro fundido, m.	opal	ópalo, m.
cement	cemento, m.	ore	mineral, m.
chalk	tiza, creta, greda, f.	paraffin	parafina, f.
chromium	cromo, m.	petroleum	petróleo, m.
chromium plated	cromado	pewter	peltre, m.
cinder	cenizas, cernada, f.	plaster	emplasto, yeso, m.
clay	barro, m.; arcilla, f.	plastic	plástico, m.
coal	carbón, m.	platinum	platino, m.
concrete	hormigón, m.	porcelain	porcelana, f.
copper	cobre, m.	quarry	cantera, f.
crystal	cristal, m.	rock	roca, f.
diamond	diamante, m.	ruby	rubí, m.
emerald	esmeralda, f.	rust	herrumbre, orín, m.
extract (dig out)	extraer	rusty	oxidado, herumbrado, mohoso
flint	pedernal, m.	sand	*arena, f.
forge (smithy)	fragua, f.	sandstone	arenisca, f.
forge (VERB)	forjar, fraguar	sapphire	zafiro, m.
gem	piedra preciosa, f.	sheet (metal)	hoja, f.; pliego, m.
glass	vidrio, m.	silver	plata, f.
gold	oro, m.	silver plated	argentado
granite	granito, m.	slate	pizarra, f.
gravel	arenillas, grava, f.	soil (earth)	tierra, f.; suelo, m.
iron (scrap)	hierro viejo, m.	solder (VERB)	soldar
iron	hierro, m.	stainless steel	acero inoxidable, m.
iron (ADJ)	ferreo	steel	acero, m.
lava	lava, f.	stone	piedra, f.
lead	plomo, m.	stone-cutter	picapedrero, m.
lime	cal, f.; ajonje, m.	stony	pedregoso
limestone	piedra caliza, f.	stucco	estuco, m.
macadam	macadán, macadam, m.	sulphur	azufre, m.
marble	mármol, m.	tar	brea, f.; alquitrán, m.
matter	materia, f.	tile	losa, teja, f.
melt (to smelt)	fundir	tin	lata, f.; estaño, m.
mercury	mercurio, m.	tin-plate	hojalata, f.
metal	metal, m.	topaz	topacio, m.
mine	mina, f.	turquoise	turquesa, f.
mine (VERB)	explotar	wax	cera, f.
miner	minero, m.	zinc	cinc, zinc, m.

26. MEASUREMENTS

Terms of weight and measurement often differ from country to country both as to name and equivalency.

Cross-Reference: Time (p.456)

ENGLISH	SPANISH	ENGLISH	SPANISH
acre	acre, m.; hectárea, f.	milligram	miligramo, m.
area	área, f.	millimicron	milimicrón, m.
barrel	barril, tonel, m.; cuba, f.	millimeter	milímetro, m.
bushel	fanega, f.	millivolt	milivoltio, m.
centimeter	centímetro, m.	milliwatt	milvatio, m.
contents	contenido, m.	minute	minuto, m.
degree	grado, m.	narrow	estrecho
depth	profundidad, f.	none (no)	ninguno
dozen	docena, f.	ohm	ohm, ohmo, m.
foot	pie, m.	ounce	onza, f.
gallon	galón, m.	peck	9 litros
gram	gramo, m.	percent	por ciento, m.
gross (144)	gruesa, doce docenas, f.	piece	pedazo, m.
half	mitad, f.	pint	pinta, f.
half dozen	media docena, f.	pound	libra, f.
handful	puñado, manojo, m.	quart (quarter)	cuarto, m.
heavy	pesado	quintal (100 lbs)	quintal, m.
hectare	hectárea, f.	quite	bastante
hectoliter	hectolitro, m.	ream	resma, f.
height	altura, f.	rod	5029 metros
inch	pulgada, f.	scoop	cucharada, f.
kilogram	kilogramo, m.	score (20)	veintena, f.
kilometer	kilómetro, m.	several	varios, algunos
large	grande	short	corto
league	legua, f.	size	tamaño, m.
length	longitud, f.; largo, m.	small (little)	pequeño
light	ligero	some	algunos
liter	litro, m.	square meter	metro cuadrado, m.
long	largo	tablespoon	cucharada, f.
lots	mucho	tall	alto
maxwell	máxwel, maxwelio, m.	teaspoon	cucharadita, f.
many	muchos	thick	grueso, denso, espeso
measure (measurement)	medida, f.	thickness	grosor, espesor, m.
measure (to..)	medir	ton	tonelada, f.
megacycle	megaciclo, m.	volt	voltio, m.
meridian	meridiano, m.	volume	volumen, m.
meter	metro, m.	watt	wat, vatio, m.
meter (square..)	metro cuadrado, m.	weigh	pesar
metric system	sistema métrico, m.	weight	peso, m.
microgram	microgramo, m.	whole	entero, m.
micrometer	micrómetro, m.	wide	ancho
middle (center)	medio, centro, m.	width (breadth)	anchura, f.
mile	milla, f.	yard	yarda, f.

27. TIME

Hours, Days, Weeks, Months, Seasons and Holidays

a) Hours & Parts of an Hour

ENGLISH	SPANISH	ENGLISH	SPANISH
clock	reloj, m.	minute	minuto, m.
day (24 hours)	día, m.	moment	momento, m.
early	temprano	quarter hour	cuarto de hora, m.
fast (clock)	adelantado	slow (clock)	atrasado
half an hour	media hora, f.	time	hora, f.; tiempo, m.
hour and a half	hora y media, f.	second	segundo, m.
hour	hora, f.	watch	reloj de pulsera, m.
late	tarde	wall clock	reloj de pared, m.

b) Days

ENGLISH	SPANISH	ENGLISH	SPANISH
afternoon	tarde, f.	night	noche, f.
all day	todo el día	night before last	anteanoche
daily	diario	noon (midday)	mediodía, m.
day	día, m.	sunrise	salida del sol, f.
day before (eve)	víspera, f.	sunset	puesta del sol, f.
day after tomorrow	pasado mañana	this morning	esta mañana
day before yesterday	anteayer	today	hoy
daybreak (dawn)	alba, f; amanecer, m.	tomorrow	mañana
dusk (nightfall)	anochecer, m.	-afternoon	mañana por la tarde
evening	anochecer, m.; tarde, f.	-morning	mañana por la mañana
every day	todos los días	tonight	esta noche
last night	anoche	twilight	anochecer, crepúsculo, m.
midnight	medianoche, f.	yesterday	ayer
morning (early..)	madrugada, f.	yesterday afternoon	ayer tarde
morning (forenoon)	mañana, f.		

c) Weeks

ENGLISH	SPANISH	ENGLISH	SPANISH
Sunday	domingo, m.	Thursday	jueves, m.
Monday	lunes, m.	Friday	viernes, m.
Tuesday	martes, m.	Saturday	sábado, m.
Wednesday	miércoles, m.		

every week	todas las semanas	next week	semana entrante, f.
fortnight	quincena, quince días, m.		semana próxima, f.
fortnightly	quincenal, bimensual	week	semana, f.
last week	semana pasada, f.	weekend	fin de semana, m.
		weekly	semanal

d) Months
The names of the months also appear in the "Noun Pair" list

ENGLISH	SPANISH	ENGLISH	SPANISH
January	enero, m.	July	julio, m.
February	febrero, m.	August	agosto, m.
March	marzo, m.	September	septiembre, m.
April	abril, m.	October	octubre, m.
May	mayo, m.	November	noviembre, m.
June	junio, m.	December	diciembre, m.
calendar	calendario, m.	monthly	mensual
every month	todos los meses	quarterly	trimestral
every two months	bimestral	next month	mes próximo, m.
last month	mes pasado, m.	six months (1/2 Year)	semestre, m.
month	mes, m.	this month	este mes

e) Seasons

ENGLISH	SPANISH	ENGLISH	SPANISH
autumn (fall)	otoño, m.	summer	estío, verano, m.
season	temporada, estación, f.	summer (to spend.)	veranear
spring	primavera, f.	winter	invierno, m.

f) Years

ENGLISH	SPANISH	ENGLISH	SPANISH
anniversary	aniversario, m.	last year	año pasado, m.
centenary	centenario, m.	leap year	año bisiesto, m.
century	siglo, m.	New Year	año nuevo, m.
date	fecha, f.	next year	año prómixo, m.
decade	década, f.	semiannual	semianual
half year (6 Months)	semestre, m.	year bef. last	año antepasado, m.

g) Holidays

ENGLISH	SPANISH	ENGLISH	SPANISH
Ash Wednes.	miércoles de ceniza, m.	holiday	día feriado, m.
birthday	día natal, cumpleaños, m.	Lent	cuaresma, f.
Christmas	Navidad, f.	New Year's Day	día de Año Nuevo, m.
Christmas Eve	víspera de Navidad, f.	New Year's Eve	Nochevieja, f.
Easter	Pascua de Resurreción, f.	Palm Sunday	Domingo de Ramos, m.
festival (feast)	fiesta, f.	Passover	Pascua de los hebreos, f.
Good Friday	Viernes Santo, m.	vacation	vacaciones, f.

h) Relative Time

ENGLISH	SPANISH	ENGLISH	SPANISH
always	siempre	future	futuro, porvenir, m.
begin (to)	comenzar, empezar	late	tarde
beginning	principio, m.	next	que viene, proximo
early	temprano	pass (to..by)	pasar
end	fin, m.	past (last)	pasado
epoch (period)	época, f.	present (Adj.)	presente
finish (to end)	acabar, terminar	present	presente, m.

28. SPORTS & GAMES
a) General

ENGLISH	SPANISH	ENGLISH	SPANISH
amusement	diversión, f.	Olympic Games	juegos olímpicos, m.
athlete	atleta, m.	Olympics	olimpiadas, f.
athletics	atletismo, m.	opponent	adversario, m.
auditorium (theater)	anfiteatro, m.	play (game)	juego, m.
auditorium (hall)	auditorium, m.	play (VERB)	jugar
beat (to defeat)	vencer	player	jugador, tocador, m.
bet	apuesta, postura, f.	practice	práctica, f.
bounce	salto, brinco, m.	prize	premio, m.
broadcast	radiofusión, f.	record	marca, f.; récord, m.
championship	campeonato, m.	referee	árbitro, m.
champion	campeón, m.	rules (of game)	reglas del juego, f.
cheat	engañar	run	corrida, carrera, f.
cheer	aclamar	rule	regla, f.
club (assoc.)	círculo, club, m.	runner-up	subcampeón, m.
competition	competencia, f.	run off	carrera final, f.
contest	lucha, f.	score	tanteo, resultado, m.
court	pista, f.; campo, m.	scorecard	anotador, m.
cup (trophy)	copa, f.	scorekeeper	marcador, tanteador, m.
defeat	derrota, f.	scrimmage	escaramuza, f.
dressing-room	vestuario, m.	season	temporada, f.
dirty play	juego sucio, m.	seat	asiento, m.; localidad, f.
fair play	juego limpio, m.	semifinal	semifinal, f.
fan (enthusiast)	aficionado, m.	semifinalist	semifinalista, m.
final	final, f.	skill	habilidad, f.
gallery	galería, f.	sports	deportes, m.
game (match)	juego, partido, m.	sportsman	deportista, m.
gymnasium	gimnasio, m.	team	equipo, m.
half-time	descanso, m.	stadium	estadio, m.
helmet	yelmo, casco, m.	stands	graderias, tribuna, f.
jump (leap, spring)	salto, brinco, m.	throw	tiro, lanzamiento, m.
jump (to leap)	saltar	ticket	billete, m.
kick	patada, f.; puntapié, m.	tie (draw)	empate, m.
lineman	delantero, m.	time (VERB)	cronometrar
liner	pelota rasa, f.	time-out	interrupción, intervalo, m.
linesman	juez de línea, m.	toss a coin	lanzar al aire
lineup	formación, alineación, f.	tournament	torneo, m.
lose	perder	training	entrenamiento, m.
loss (forfeit)	pérdida, f.	trainer	entrenador, m.
mallet	mallete, m.	whistle	silbato, m.
major league	liga mayor, f.	win (VERB)	ganar
match	juego, partido, m.	winner	ganador, m.
offside	en posición adelantada	world record	récord mundial, m.

b) Bull Fighting

ENGLISH	SPANISH	ENGLISH	SPANISH
bull fighter	torero, m.	dartsman	banderillero, m.
bullfight	corrida de toros, f.	picador	picador, m.
bullring	redondel, m.	spear	pica, f.
dart	banderilla, f.	sword	espada, f.

c) Baseball & Cricket

ENGLISH	SPANISH	ENGLISH	SPANISH
ball	bola, pelota, f.	left fielder	jardinero izquierdo, m.
ballplayer	pelotero, m.	mask	máscara, f.
base (bag)	base, m.	mound	montículo, m.; lomita, f.
baseball	béisbol, m.	out	"aut", m
baserunner	corredor, m.	outfield	jardín, m.
bat (baseball)	bate, m.	outfielder	jardinero, m.
bat (cricket)	paleta, f.	overhand	por lo alto
bat (VERB)	golpear con la paleta	pitch (ball)	lanzamiento, m.
batter	bateador, m.	pitcher	lanzador, m.
catch (ball)	cogida, f.	rubber	goma, f.
catcher	cogedor, m.	run	carrera, f.
cricket	cricket, criquet, m.	second base	segunda base, f.
diamond	diamante, m.	southpaw (lefty)	zurdo, m.
double	doble, m.	strike	bola buena, pasada, f.
field	campo, m.	strikeout	"ponchado aut", m.
fielder	jardinero, m.	switch-hitter	bateador ambidextro, m.
first base	primera base, f.	third base	tercera base, f.
glove (mit)	guante, m.	triple	triple, m.
hit	batazo, hit, golpe, m.	throw	lanzamiento, m.
home plate (wicket)	base meta, f.	throw (pitch))	lanzar
home run	jonrón, m.	walk (4 balls)	quatro bolas malas, f.
inning	turno, m.; entrada, f.	walk (4 balls)	base por bola, m.
left field	jardín izquierdo, m.		

d) Football & Soccer

ENGLISH	SPANISH	ENGLISH	SPANISH
block	bloqueo, m.	kick	patada, f.; puntapié, m.
center-forward	delantero centro, m.	left half	medio izquierdo, m.
defenders	defensas, m.	outside-	
*football (game)	fútbol, m.	left (wing)	extremo izquierdo, m.
	fútbal americano, m.	right (wing)	extremo derecho, m.
football (ball)	balón, m.	penalty-kick	penalty, m.
football field	campo (de fútbol), m.	rugby	rugby, m.
forwards	delanteros, m.	rugby-player	jugador de rugby, m.
fullback	back, m.; defensa, f.	soccer	*fútbol, m.
goal	meta, f.; gol, m.	soccer player	futbolista, m.
goalkeeper	guardameta, portero, m.	tackle (VERB)	agarrar, atajar
half-backs	medios, m.	tackle	atajo, atajador, m.

e) Racquet Sports

ENGLISH	SPANISH	ENGLISH	SPANISH
backhand	golpe revés, m.	ping-pong	ping pong, m.
badminton	badminton, m.	racquet	raqueta, f.
baseline	línea de fondo, f.	service	saque, m.
deuce	a dos	shuttlecock	volante, m.
forehand	golpe directo, m.	table tennis	tenis de mesa, m.
let	let, m	tennis	tenis, m..
love	cero, m	tennis ball	pelota, f..
net	*red, f	tennis court	cancha de tenis, f..

f) Boating

Cross-Reference: Travel (p.480)

ENGLISH	SPANISH	ENGLISH	SPANISH
boom	botavara, f.	row boat	bote de remos, m.
canoe	canoa, f.	rower	remero, m.
cruise	viaje por mar, f.	row (VERB)	remar
dinghy	dinga, lancha, f.	rudder	timón, m.
hull	casco, m.	sail	vela, f.
launch (shallop)	lancha, chalupa, f.	sailboat	velero, m.
lifebelt	cinturón salvavidas, m.	sailing	náutica, vela, f.
mainsail	vela mayor, f.	schooner	goleta, f.
marina	marina, f.	sheet (rope)	escota, f.
motorboat	bote a motor, m.	sloop	balandra, f.
oar	remo, m.	speedboat	lancha de carreras, f.
oarsman	remero, m.	stern	popa, f.
paddle (canoe)	canalete, m.	topsail	gavia, f.
rope	maroma, f.	yacht	yate, m.

g) Boxing & Wrestling

ENGLISH	SPANISH	ENGLISH	SPANISH
bout	turno, m.	nelson (hold)	llave nelson, f.
boxing	boxeo, m.	prizefight	pelea profesional, f.
boxing glove	guante de boxeo, m.	punch	puñetazo, m.
boxer	púgil, boxeador, m.	referee	árbitro, m.
judo	judo, m.	ring (boxing)	cuadrilátero, m.
light heavyweight	semipesado, m.	round	ronda, vuelta, f.; partido, m.
light weight	peso ligero, m.	welterweight	peso medio, m.
mat	colchoneta, f.	wrestler	luchador, m.
middleweight	peso medio, m.	wrestling	lucha, f.

h) Hockey, Skating, Sledding & Skiing

ENGLISH	SPANISH	ENGLISH	SPANISH
hockey	hockey, m.	ski (VERB)	esquiar
hockey stick	palo de hockey, m.	ski	esquí, m.
puck	disco de goma, m.	ski lift	telesquí, m.
roller skate	patín de ruedas, m.	skier	esquiador, m.
skate	patín de hielo, m.	skiing	esquiar, esquí, m.
skate (VERB)	patinar	ski jump	salto con esquí, m.
skater	patinador, m.	ski pole	bastón de esquiar, m.
skating	patinaje, patinar, m.	sled (sledge, sleigh)	trineo, m.
skating rink	pista de patinaje, f.	snowshoe	raqueta, f.

i) Archery, Target Shooting & Hunting

ENGLISH	SPANISH	ENGLISH	SPANISH
archery	ballestería; tiro de arco, m.	marksmanship	puntería, f.
		miss (target)	errar
arrow	dardo, m.; flecha, f.	quiver	aljaba, f.
bow	arco, m.	shoot (VERB)	tirar
catch (prey)	presa, f.	shooting	tiro, m.
game (prey)	caza, f.	shot	tiro, m.
		shot (Ammunition)	bala, f.
hunt (hunting)	caza, f.	shotgun	escopeta, f.
hunt (VERB)	cazar	skeet	tiro de platillo, m.
hunter	cazador, m.	target (hit the..)	hacer blanco
hunting (for game)	caza, f.	target	blanco, m.
hunting (horse & hounds)	montería, f.	trap (snare)	trampa, f.

j) Fishing

ENGLISH	SPANISH	ENGLISH	SPANISH
angler	pescador de caña, m.	fisherman	pescador, m.
bait	cebo, m.	fishhook	anzuelo, m.
fish (alive)	pez, m.	fishing	pesca, f.
fish (caught)	pescado, m.	fishing rod	caña de pescar, f.
fish (VERB)	pescar	fishing tackle	avíos de pescar
fish net	*red, f.	harpoon	arpón, m.

k) Golf

ENGLISH	SPANISH	ENGLISH	SPANISH
bunker (trap)	hoyo de arena, m.	golf club (stick)	palo, m.
caddie	caddie, m.	golfer	golfista, m.
drive	golpe de salida, m.	green	césped, m.
flag	bandera, f.	hole (cup)	hoyo, m.
golf	golf, m.	putt (VERB)	tirar al hoyo
golf bag	bolsa, f.	sandtrap	hoyo de arena, m.
golf course	campo de golf, m.	tee	salida, f.; tee, m.

l) Hiking, Climbing & Camping

ENGLISH	SPANISH	ENGLISH	SPANISH
ascent	escalada, f.	path	senda, f.
camping	camping, m.	picnic	jira campestre, f.
camp (VERB)	acampar	rucksack	mochilla, f.
campfire	hoguera de campamento, m.	sleeping-bag	saco de dormir, m.
hike	caminata, f.; paseo, m.	step	paso, m.
mountaineering	alpinismo, m.	tent	tienda de campaña, f.
mountaineer	alpinista, m.	walk (stroll)	paseo, m.
outing	jira, excursión, f.	walk (gait)	andar, paso, m.; marcha, f.

m) Riding

ENGLISH	SPANISH	ENGLISH	SPANISH
bet (wager)	apuesta, f.	race	carrera, corrida, f.
bet (to..)	apostar	race course	pista, carrera, f.
bit	bocado, m.	racetrack	hipódromo, m.
bookmaker	corredor de apuestas, m.	*reins	riendas, f.
bridle	freno, m.	rider (horseman)	jinete, m.
dismount	desmontar del caballo	run (to..)	correr
gallop	galopar	saddle	silla de montar, f.
horse race	carrera de caballos, f.	spurs	espuelas, f.
horsemanship	equitación, f.	starting post	puesto de salida, m.
jockey	jockey, m.	stirrups	estribos, m.
mount (to..)	montar a caballo	whip	látigo, m.

n) Swimming

ENGLISH	SPANISH	ENGLISH	SPANISH
backstroke	brazada de espalda, f.	goggles	gafas de inmersión, f.
bathingsuit	traje de baño, m.	pool	estanque, m.; piscina, f.
beach	playa, f.	sidestroke	brazada de costado, f.
breaststroke	brazada de pecho, f.	sun bathe	tomar el sol
butterfly stroke	mariposa, f.	sun tan (to get..)	broncear(se)
crawl stroke	crawl, m.	surfing	patinaje sobre las olas, m.
dive (to..)	bucear	swim (to..)	nadar
dive	salto, m.	swimmer	nadador, m.
diving board	trampolín, m.	swimming	natación, f.
diving	buceo, m.	water polo	polo acuático, m.
flippers	aletas para nadar, f.	water-skiing	esquí acuático, m.

o) Track

ENGLISH	SPANISH	ENGLISH	SPANISH
broad jump	salto largo, m.	miler	corredor de la milla, m.
discus	disco, m.	pole vault	salto con garrocha, m.
hammer	martillo, m.	put the shot	lanzar el peso
high jump	salto alto, m.	record	récord, m.; marca, f.
hurdle	valla, f.	relay	carrera de relevos. f.
javelin	jabalina, f.	runner	corredor, m.
jump	salto, m.	shot-put	lanzamiento de peso, m.
long jump	salto largo, m.	throw the discus	lanzar el disco, m.
marathon	maratón, m.	track	pista, f.

p) Miscellaneous Sports

ENGLISH	SPANISH	ENGLISH	SPANISH
basketball	baloncesto, m.	gymnastics	gimnasia, f.
bicycle (bike)	bicicleta, f.	polo	polo, m.
falconer	halconero, m.	pushup	plancha, f.
fencing	esgrima, f.	volleyball	voleibol, balonvolea, m.
gymnasium	gimnasio, m.	weight lifting	levantamiento de pesas, m.
gymnast	gimnasta, m.		

29. RECREATION & AMUSEMENTS

ENGLISH	SPANISH	ENGLISH	SPANISH
amuse	recrear, divertir	gambler	jugador, m.
amusements	diversión, f; recreos, m.	games	juegos, m.
amusing	ameno, divertido	joke	burla, broma, f.
billiards	billar, m.	nightclub	club nocturno, café, m.
bowling	bolos, m.		cabaret, m.
bowling alley	bolera, f.	paint (VERB)	pintar
bridge (cards)	bridge, m.	pastime	pasatiempo, m.
card(playing..)	carta, f.; naipe, m.	playground	patio de recreo, m.
checkers	juego de damas, m.	playing cards	cartas, f.
chess	ajedrez, m.	poker	póker, m.
dance (VERB)	bailar	pool	billar, m.
deck (cards)	baraja, f.; monte, m.	popular	concurrido, frecuentado
dice	dados, m.	puzzle	rompecabezas, m.
entertaining	divertido	shuffle (VERB)	barajar
fair	feria, f.	shuffleboard	juego de tejo, m.
fun	diversión, f.	tenpins	juego de bolos, m.
gamble (VERB)	jugar, apostar	zoo	jardín zoológico, m.

30. MUSIC & THEATER

Cross-Reference: Musical terms listed in N -*o* and N -*a*

ENGLISH	SPANISH	ENGLISH	SPANISH
accompaniment	acompañamiento, m.	chime	repique, campaneo, m.
accordion	acordeón, m.	choir	coro, m.
act	acto, m.	chorus	coro, m.
actor (player)	actor, m.	cinema (movie)	cine, m.
actress	actriz, f.	circus	circo, m.
applaud (clap)	aplaudir	clarinet	clarinete, m.
applause	aplausos, m.	comedy	comedia, f.
audience	público, auditorio, m.	company	compañía, f.
auditorium	auditorium, anfiteatro, m.	composer	compositor, m.
bagpipe	gaita, f.	concert	concierto, m.
balcony	balcón, m.	contralto	contralto, m.
ball (dance)	baile, f.	cornet	corneta, f.
ballet	ballet, baile, m.	curtain (theater)	telón, m.
ballroom	salón de baile, m.	dance (ball)	baile, m.
band	banda de música, f.	dance (step)	danza, f.
band leader	director, conductor, m.	dance (VERB)	danzar, bailar
baritone	barítono, m.	dancer	bailarina, f.
bass	bajo, m.	dancing	danza, f., baile, m.
booking office	taquilla, f.	debut	estreno, m.
bow (violin)	arco, m.	din	estrépito, m.
box (theater)	palco, m.	drum	tambor, m.
box office	boletería, taquilla, f.	drummer	tambor, m.
bugle	trompeta, corneta, f.	ear (hearing)	oído, m.
buy tickets	comprar localidades	entrance	entrada, f.
camera	cámara, f.	exit	salida, f.
cast (theater)	reparto, m.	fail (be a dud)	fracasar
castanets	castañuelas, m.	fiddle	violín, m.
character (play)	personaje, m.	fiddler	violinista, m.

ENGLISH	SPANISH	ENGLISH	SPANISH
fife	pífano, m.	pit	platea, f.; patio, m.
film	filme, m.; película, f.	play	representación, función, f.
flute	flauta, f.	play (piece)	pieza, f.
gallery	galería, f.	play (to..on)	tocar
gleeclub	coro, m.	bells	sonar
guitar	guitarra, f.	guitar	tañer la guitarra
harmonica	armónica, f.	drum	tocar el tambor
harmony	harmonía, f.	player	ejecutante, tocador, m.
harp	arpa, f.	player piano	pianola, f.
horn	trompeta, corneta, f.	puppet	muñeca, f.
hymn	himno, m.	recording	grabación, f.
instrument:	instrumento, m.	refrain (chorus)	estribillo, m.
-percussion	.de percusión, m.	rehearsal	ensayo, m.
-string	..de cuerda, m.	rhythm	ritmo, m.
-wind	..de viento, m.	saxaphone	saxófono, m.
intermission	entreacto, m.	scene	cuadro, m.; escena, f.
jazz	jazz, m.	scenery	decoraciones, f.
jew's harp	birimbao, m.	screen (theater)	pantalla, f.
jig	jiga, f.	script	guión, m.
kettle drum	timbal, m.	seat(place)	asiento, m.; localidad, f.
lute	laúd, m.	sextet	sexteto, m.
lyre	lira, f.	show	espectáculo, m.
make-up	caracterización, f.	sing	cantar
mandolin	mandolina, f.	singer	cantor, cantante, m.
maraca	maraca, f.	slide trombone	trombón de varas, m.
mariachi band	maríachi, m.	solo	solo, m.
marimba	marimba, f.	soloist	solista, m.
mask	máscara, f.	song	canto, m.; canción, f.
melodeon	melodión, m.	soprano	soprano, m.
melody	melodía, f.	sound	sonido, m.
merengue	merengue, m.	spectator	espectador, m.
meter	metro, m.	stage	escenario, m.
minuet	minuete, m.	stanza	estrofa, f.
mouth organ	armónica, f.	star	estrella, f.
mouthpiece	boquilla, f.	symphony	sinfonía, f.
movie	cine, m.; película, f.	tambour	tambor, m.
movie-camera	cámara de cine, f.	tambourine	pandereta, f.
music (play..)	hacer música	taps	toque de silencio, m.
music	música, f.	tenor	tenor, m.
musical	músico, m.	theater	teatro, m.
musician	músico, m.	theatrical	teatral
mute	sordina, f.	ticket	billete, m.
oboe	oboe, m.	ticket window	ventanilla, f.
octet	octeto, m.	tone	tono, m.
opera	ópera, f.	triangle	triángulo, m.
operetta	opereta, f.	trombone	trombón, m.
orchestra	orquesta, f.	trumpeter	trompetero, m.
orchestra(seats)	patio de butacas, m.	tuba	tuba, f.
organ	órgano, m.	usher	acomodador, m.
organ-grinder	organillero, m.	vaudville	variedades, f.
organist	organista, m.	viola	viola, f.
overture	obertura, f.	violin	violín, m.
part (role)	papel, m.	violinist	violinista, m.
performance	representación, función, f.	waltz	vals, m.
		woodwinds	maderas, f.
piano	piano, m.	xylophone	xilófono, m.
pianist	pianista, m.	zither	cítara, f.

31. ART & ARCHITECTURE

ENGLISH	SPANISH	ENGLISH	SPANISH
aesthetic	estético	masterpiece	obra maestra, f.
arch	arco, m.	model (to shape)	modelar
architect	arquitecto, m.	model	modelo, m.
architecture	arquitectura, f.	museum	museo, m.
artist	artista, f.	paint (VERB)	pintar
background	fondo, m.	painter	pintor, m.
brush	pincel, m.	painting	pintura, f.
bust	busto, m.	palette	paleta, f.
carve (chisel)	tallar	portrait	retrato, m.
chisel	cincel, m.	potter's clay= barro de alfarero, m.	
column	columna, f.	potter's wheel=torno de alfarero, m.	
contrast	contraste, m.	pottery	alfarería, f.
cupola (dome)	cúpula, f.	print (picture)	estampa, f.
draftsman	dibujante, m.	sculptor	escultor, m.
draw (design)	dibujar	sculpture	escultura, f.
drawing	dibujo, m.	statue	estatua, f.
easel	caballete, m.	tower (steeple)	torre, f.
engrave	grabar	vault (arched roof)	bóveda, f.
engraving	grabado, m.	work of art	obra, f.
exhibition	exhibición, exposición, f.	workshop	taller, m.

32. COLORS

ENGLISH	SPANISH	ENGLISH	SPANISH
beige	color de lana, beige	ochre	ocre
black	negro	orange	anaranjado
blond	rubio	orchid	purpurino
blue	azul	oxblood	rojo oscuro
bright	claro	peach	melocotón
brightness	claridad	pink	rosado, roso
brown	pardo, marrón	purple	morado, purpúreo
brunette	moreno	red	encarnado, rojo
chestnut	castaño	rose	roso, rosado
clear	claro	ruby	rubí
color	color	ruddy	rosado, rojizo
colored (ruddy)	colorado	russet	bermejo
crimson	carmesí	rust	rojizo
dark	obscuro	salmon	salmón
darkness	obscuridad	scarlet	escarlata
dull	sombrío, mate	silver	de plata, argentino
gild	dorar	sky blue	azul celeste
gold (golden)	de oro, dorado	slate blue	azul pizarra
green	verde	sorrel	alazano
grey	pardo, gris	steel blue	azul acero
lavender	color de lavándula	straw colored	pajizo
light	claro	tan	tostado, bronceado
lillac	lila	turquoise blue	azul turquesa
magenta	magenta	ultramarine blue= azul ultramarino	
many-colored	multicolor	violet	violeta, violado
maroon	rojo obscuro	white	blanco
mauve	malva	yellow	amarillo

33. EDUCATION, LITERATURE & CORRESPONDENCE

a) Objects Found in Schools

ENGLISH	SPANISH	ENGLISH	SPANISH
ballpoint pen	bolígrafo, m.	fountain pen	pluma de fuente, f.
blackboard	encerado, m.; pizarra, f.	ink	tinta, f.
blot	mancha, tacha, f.	inkwell	tintero, m.
blotting paper	papel secante, m.	map	mapa, f.
book	libro, volumen, m.	notebook	cuaderno, m.
bookcase	armario, m.	page (book)	página, f.
booklet	folleto, m.	paper	papel, m.
chair (university)	cátedra, f.	pen	pluma, f.
chalk	tiza, f.	pencil	lápiz, m.
chart	cuadro, m.; tabla, f.	picture	cuadro, m.
	gráfica, mapa, f.	*primer	manual, m.
class	clase, f.	pupil	discípulo, alumno, m.
classroom	aula, sala de clase, f.	sheet (paper)	pliego, m.; hoja, f.
copy (book)	ejemplar, m.	student	alumno, estudiante, m.
crayon	creyón, m.	teacher	maestro, m.
desk	escritorio, m.	text	texto, m.
drawing (sketch)	dibujo, m.	textbook	libro de texto, m.
eraser	borrador, m.; goma, f.	theme (paper)	ensayo, m.; tema, f.

b) Grammar & Language

ENGLISH	SPANISH	ENGLISH	SPANISH
accent	acento, m.	phrase	frase, f.
adjective	adjetivo, m.	preposition	preposición, f.
adverb	adverbio, m.	present	presente, m.
alphabet	alfabeto, m.	present	presente, m.
antecedent	antecedente, m.	pronoun	pronombre, m.
article	artículo, m.	pronounce	pronunciar
clause	cláusula, f.	punctuation	puntuación, f.
colon	dos puntos, m.	question	pregunta, f.
comma	coma, f.	question	interrogar, preguntar
conjunction	conjunción, f.	question mk	punto interrogante, m.
consonant	consonante, f.	quotation marks	comillas, f.
dictionary	diccionario, m.	semi-colon	punto y coma, m.
exclamation	exclamación, f.	sentence (GRAM)	frase, f.
English	inglés, m.	slang (jargon)	jerga, f.
future	futuro, m.	Spanish	castellano, español, m.
gender	género, m.	speech (talking, word)	habla, m.
grammar	gramática, f.	speech (lang.)	idioma, lenguaje, f.
hyphen	guión, m.	spell (to..)	deletrear
*idiom	modismo, dialecto, m.	spelling	ortografía, f.
interjection	interjección, f.	syllable	sílaba, f.
italics	bastardilla, cursiva, f.	talk	coloquio, m.; charla, f.
language	idioma, m.; lengua, f.		conversación, f.
letter (abc)	letra, f.	tense (GRAM)	tiempo, m.
narrate (to relate)	relatar	tongue (lang)	lengua, idioma, f.
noun	substantivo, nombre, m.	translate	traducir
paragraph	párrafo, m.	translator	traductor, m.
participle	participio, m.	translation	traducción, f.
past (tense)	pretérito, m.	verb	verbo, m.
period (GRAM)	punto, m.	word	palabra, f.

c) Literature

ENGLISH	SPANISH	ENGLISH	SPANISH
author	autor, m.	play (theater)	representación, f.
autobiography	autobiografía, f.		drama, pieza, f.
biography	biografía, f.	poem	poema, m.
chapter	capítulo, m.	poet	poeta, m.
comedy	comedia, f.	poetry	poesía, f.
drama	drama, m.	preface	prefacio, m.
essay	ensayo, m.	prose	prosa, f.
fable	fábula, f.	quotation	citación, cita, f.
fairytale	cuento de hadas, m.	rhyme	rima, f.
fiction	novelística, ficción f.	story	cuento, m.; narración, f.
literature	literatura, f.	short story	narración, f.; cuento, m.
magazine (review)	revista, f.	table-contents	índice de materias, f.
masterpiece	obra maestra, f.	tale	historia, f; relato, cuento, m.
memoirs	memorias, f.	tragedy	tragedia, f.
narration	narración, f; relato, m.	title	título, m.
novel	novela, f.	verse	verso, m.
novelist	novelista, m.	writer	escritor, m.
*periodical	revista, f.; periódico, m.	writing	escritura, f.

d) Mathematics & Science

ENGLISH	SPANISH	ENGLISH	SPANISH
acute angle	ángulo recto, m.	geometry	geometría, f.
add	añadir	lab	laboratorio, m.
add (to..up)	sumar, adicionar	magnet	imán, m.
algebra	álgebra, f.	math (mathematics)	matemática, f.
angle	ángulo, m.	mechanics	mecánica, f.
arithmetic	aritmética, f.	multiply	multiplicar
calculus	cálculo, m.	number	número, m.
chemical	químico	parallel	paralelo, m.
chemistry	química, f.	physics	física, f.
circle	círculo, m.	product	producto, m.
circumference	circunferencia, f.	rectangle	rectángulo, m.
compound	compuesto	ruler (inst.)	regla, f.
computer	computadora, f.	science	ciencia, f.
diameter	diámetro, m.	square	cuadrado, m.
divide	partir, dividir	straight	recto
division	división, f.	subtract	sustraer, restar
equal	igual	subtraction	sustracción, f.
figure (number)	cifra, f.	sum (addition)	adición, suma, f.
formula	fórmula, f.	triangle	triángulo, m.
fraction	fracción, f.	trigonometry	trigonometría, f.

e) Education in General

ENGLISH	SPANISH	ENGLISH	SPANISH
annotation	anotación, f.	attention	atención, f.
answer	contestación, repuesta, f.	attentive	atento
answer	responder, contestar	behavior (conduct)	conducta, f.
ask	preguntar	briefcase	cartera, f; portafolio, m.
assignment (school)	tarea escolar, f.	busy (phone)	ocupado
attention (to pay..)	atender	cheat	engañar, defraudar

ENGLISH	SPANISH	ENGLISH	SPANISH
college	universidad, f.	naughty	desobediente, revoltoso
college student	estudiante universitario, m.	note (VERB)	notar
		note	nota, f.
correct (VERB)	corregir	notes (to take..)	tomar notas
correct	correcto	notice	aviso, anuncio, m.
count (VERB)	contar	outline	bosquejo, resumen, m.
course	curso, m.	pamphlet	panfleto, folleto, m.
date (calendar)	fecha, f.	pencil	lápiz, m.
debate	debate, m.	placard	letrero, cartel, m.
degree	grado, m.; licenciatura, f.	playground	campo de recreo, m.
diligent	aplicado	practice (VERB)	practicar
diploma	diploma, f.	prize	premio, m.
doctorate	doctorado, m.	professor	profesor, m.
draft	bosquejo, borrador, m.	punish	castigar
draft (document)	proyecto, m.	punishment	castigo, m.
*education	educación, instrucción, f.	read	leer
enroll	matricular(se)	reader	lector, m.
erase	borrar	reading	lectura, f.
examination (to pass..)	aprobar	register (letter)	certificar
examination	examen, m.	rejoinder	respuesta, f.
examination (to take.)	examinar(se)	remainder (MATH)	residuo, m; resta, f.
example	ejemplo, m.	remark	comentario, m.
exercise	ejercicio, m.		observación, f.
explain	explicar	*report	relato, informe, m.
explanation	explicación, f.	reprimand	reprender
false (wrong)	falso	review	revista, crítica, f.
forget	olvidar	review (study)	repaso, m.
grade (acad.mark)	grado, m; nota, f.	reward	recompensa, f.
grant (scholarship)	beca, f.	reward (VERB)	recompensar, premiar
handwriting	letra, f.	saying	refrán, m.
high school	escuela secundaria, f.	*scholar	letrado, erudito, docto, m.
history	historia, f.	scholarship (grant)	beca, f.
homework	tareas, f.; deberes, m.	scholarship	saber, m.; erudición, f.
illustration	ilustración, f.	school	colegio, m.; esquela, f.
improve	mejorar, progresar	schooling	instrucción, f.
inattentive	desatento	script	escritura, caligrafía, f.
index	índice, m.	scroll	rollo, m.
ink	tinta, f.	semester	semestre, m.
intellect	entendimiento, m.	sheet of paper	hoja, f.
kindergarten	kindergarten, m.	signature	firma, f.
	escuela de infantes, f.	sketch	dibujo, m.; boceta, f.
knowledge (acqaint.)	conocimiento, m.	speaker (orator)	orador, m.
knowledge	saber, entendimiento, m.	speech	discurso, m.; oración, f.
	información, f.		conferencia, f.
lazy	perezoso	speech	habla, conversación, f.
learn	aprender	statement	estado de cuenta, m.
learning	sabiduría, f.; saber, m.	study	estudio, m.
	erudición, f.	study (VERB)	estudiar
lecture	discurso, m; conferencia, f.	style	estilo, m.
lesson	lección, f.	talk	plática, f.; discurso, m.
marks	clasificación, nota, f.	teach	enseñar
matter (subj)	materia, f.; asunto, m.	teaching	instrucción, enseñanza, f.
mean (VERB)	querer decir	term (semester)	curso, m.
meaning	sentido, significado, m.		período académico, m.
memorandum	nota, f.; memorándum, m.	test (exam)	prueba, f.; examen, m.
memorize	aprender de memoria	thesis	tesis, f.

ENGLISH	SPANISH	ENGLISH	SPANISH
think	pensar	university	universidad, f.
treatise	tratado, m.	*upbringing	crianza, educación, f.
tuition	matricula, f.	wisdom	sabiduria, f.
tutor	tutor, m.	write	escribir
understand	comprender	writing (hand.)	caligrafía, letra, f.
understanding	entendimiento, m.	yearbook	anuario, m.

34. COMMUNICATIONS
Newspaper, Mail, Telephone, Radio & TV

ENGLISH	SPANISH	ENGLISH	SPANISH
account (report)	relación, f.	parcel post	paquete postal, m.
aerial	antena, f.	phone book	guía telefónica, f.
airmail	correo aéreo, m.	phone booth	cabina telefonica, f.
address	señas, dirección, f.	phone number	número del teléfono, m.
broadcasting	radiodifusión, f.	postal order	giro postal, m.
cable	cable, m.	postcard	tarjeta postal, f.
call (telephone..)	llamada, f.	poster (bill)	cartel, m.
call (VERB)	llamar	postage	franqueo, m.
card	tarjeta, f.	postman	cartero, m.
collect	cobrar, recoger	post office	oficina de correos, f.
collection (mail)	recogida, f.	post office box	apartado postal, m.
communication	comunicación, f.	press (news)	prensa, f.
critic	crítico, m.	print	impresión, estampa, f.
deliver (VERB)	entregar	print (VERB)	imprimir
delivery	entrega, f; reparto, m.	printed matter	impresos, m.
dial (VERB)	marcar	printing	impresión, imprenta, f.
directory	guía de teléfono, f.	program	programa, m.
editorial	artículo de fondo, m.	publish	imprimir, editar
enchange (telephone.)	central, f.	radio	radio, m.
envelope	sobre, m.	reader	lector, m.
film	película, f.	record (disk)	disco, m.
forward (VERB)	expedir	record (VERB)	grabar
free (phone not in use)	libre	record library	discoteca, f.
hang up (..telephone)	colgar	record player	tocadiscos, m.
heading	encabezamiento, m.	recording	grabación, f.
headline	titular, m.	registered	certificado
information	información, f.	seal (VERB)	sellar
inquiry(ques)	cuestión, pregunta, f.	send	enviar
interview	entrevista, f.	shortwave	onda corta, f.
leaflet	panfleto, folleto, m.	special delivery	correo urgente, m.; entrega inmediata, f.
letter(mail)	carta, epístola, f.	stamp	timbre, sello, m.
listener	oyente, m.	stamp (VERB)	timbrar, franquear
loudspeaker	megáfono, altavoz, m.	tape (recording)	cinta magnética, f.
magazine	revista, f.	tape recorder	grabadora, f.
mail (post)	correo, m.	telegram	telegrama, f.
mailbox (letter box)	buzón, m.	telegraph	telélgrafo, m.
mail a letter	echar al buzón	telegraph (VERB)	telegrafiar
message	mensaje, m.	telephone	teléfono, m.
microfilm	microfilm, m.	television	televisión, f.
news	noticias, f.	transistor	transistor, m.
newsreel	noticiario, m.	TV channel	canal, m.
newsstand	quiosco, m.	TV set	televisor, m.
number (telephone)	número, m.	volume	volumen, m.
newspaper	periódico, diario, m.	writing paper	papel de escribir, m.
parcel	paquete, m.		

35. BUSINESS AND COMMERCE

ENGLISH	SPANISH
account	factura, cuenta, f.
accounting	contabilidad, f.
acquire	adquirir
adding machine	máquina de sumar, f.
address (speech)	discurso, m.
address	señas, dirección, f.
addressee	destinatario, m.
*advertisement	anuncio, m.
advertising	publicidad, f.
	propaganda, f.
advice (warning)	aviso, m.
agent	agente, m.
agreement	acuerdo, contrato, m.
airmail	correo aéreo, m.
amount	cantidad, f.
annual report	anuario, m.
answer	contestación, respuesta, f.
appointment	cita, f.; compromiso, m.
appraisal (valuation)	evaluación, f.
apprenticeship	aprendizaje, m.
articles	artículos, m.
asset	activo, bienes, m.
assets (fixed)	activo fijo, m.
assignee	cesionario, m.
assignment	asignación, cesión, f.
associate (VERB)	asociar
associate	socio, m.
audit	intervención, f.
balance	saldo, m.
balance sheet	balance, m.
ballpoint pen	bolígrafo, m.
bank	banco, m.
bank account	cuenta de banco, f.
banker	banquero, m.
banking	banca, f.
banknote	billete de banco, m.
bankruptcy (failure)	quiebra, f.
	bancarrota, insolvencia, f.
bargain (windfall)	ganga, f.
bargain (deal)	trato, convenio, m.
Bd. of Directors	junta directiva, f.
bearer	portador, m.
benefit	beneficio, m.
bid	postura, f.
bidder	licitador, postor, m.
bill (poster)	cartel, m.
bill	factura, cuenta, f.
bill of exch.	letra de cambio, f.
bill of lading	carta de porte, f.
billboard	cartelera, f.
blueprint	copia azul, f.
board (council)	junta, f.
bond (certif.)	bono, m.
bonus	sobresueldo, m.; prima, f.
book-keeping	contabilidad, f.
	teneduria de libros, f.
boom (economic)	prosperidad, f.
borrower	prestatario, m.
boss	patrón, jefe, m.
branch	sucursal, f.
brand (mark)	marca, f.
breach	infracción, contravención, f.
briefcase	cartera, f; portafolio, m.
broker	cambista, corredor, agente, m.
brokerage	correduría, f; corretaje, m.
budget	presupuesto, m.
bundle	bulto, m.
bureau	oficina, f.
business (occup)	ocupación, f.
business	asunto, negocio, m.
businessman	negociante, m.
	comerciante, m.
buy	comprar
buyer	comprador, m.
by-law	estatuto, m.
cancel an order	anular un orden
capital	capital, m.
carbon (copy)	copia, f.
card (business)	tarjeta, f.
care (custody)	custodia, f.
cartage	porte, acarreo, m.
case (criminal)	proceso, m.
cash	efectivo, m.
cash (for..)	al contado
cent	centavo, m.
chairman	presidente, m.
change	cambio, vuelto, f.
change (small..)	suelto, m.
charge (price)	precio, m.
charge (VERB)	cobrar
charge acct	cuenta de crédito, f.
charter	escritura, patente, f.
cheap (inexpensive)	barato
check	cheque, m.
check (to verify)	comprobar
check-book	talonario, m.
	libreta de cheques, f.
chief (head)	jefe, m.
claim	reclamación, demanda, f.
clearance sale	liquidación, f.
clerk	vendedor, dependiente, m.
client	cliente, m.
coin	moneda, f.
collateral	guarantía, f; colateral, m.

ENGLISH	SPANISH	ENGLISH	SPANISH
commerce	comercio, m.	employee	empleado, m.
committee	junta, f.; comité, m.	employment	empleo, m.
company	sociedad, compañía, f.	enclosure	adjunto, anexo, m.
competition	competencia, f.	endorse (VERB)	endosar
complaint	lamento, m.; queja, f.	engagement	cita, f.; compromiso, m.
consignment	remesa, consignación, f.	enterprise	empresa, f.
contents	contenido, m.	errand	mandato, recado, m.
contract	contrato, m.	estate	bienes, m.
conveyance	conducción, f.	estimate	presupuesto, m.
	transmisión, f.	exchange (barter)	trueque, m.
copy	copia, f.	exchange (stock)	bolsa, f.
corporation	corporación, sociedad, f.	exchange rate	tipo de cambio, m.
correspondence	correspondencia, f.	exchange (VERB)	cambiar
cost	costo, precio, m.	expenses	gastos, m.
council	junta, f.	expert	perito, m.
counter	mostrador, m.	export	exportación, f.
counterclaim	contrademanda, f.	export (VERB)	exportar
credit	crédito, m.	face value	valor nominal, m.
craft (trade)	oficio, arte, m.	fall due	vencer
creditor	acreedor, m.	fee	honorario, m.; remuneración, f.
currency	moneda corriente, f.	file (folders)	archivo, m.
current acct	cuenta corriente, f.	finance	finanzas, f.
customer	parroquiano, cliente, m.	*firm (company)	casa, firma, f.
customs	aduana, f.		sociedad, compañía, f.
damage	avería, f.; daño, m.	folder	hoja, f.; folleto, m.
date (calendar)	fecha, f.	foreign currency	divisas, f.
date (VERB)	fechar	form	planilla, f.
date (aptmt)	cita, compromiso, m.	foundation	fundamento, m.
dealer	negociante, m.	franc	franco, m.
debate	debate, m.	freight	carga, flete, f.
debit	débito, m.	goods (wares)	efectos, m; mercancía, f.
debt	deuda, f.	grantee	cesionario, donatario, m.
debt (to be in..)	endeudar(se)	grow rich	enriquecer(se)
delay	retraso, plazo, m.	guarantor	fiador, m.
delivery	entrega, f.	handshake	apretón de manos, m.
demand	demanda, f.	hardware	ferretería, f.
depot	almacén, depósito, m.	headquarters	sede, oficina central, f.
deposit	depósito, m.	import (importation)	importación, f.
desk	despacho, escritorio, m.	import (significance)	importancia, f.
disbursement	desembolso, gasto, m.	import (VERB)	importar
discount	descuento, m.	income	ingresos, m.; renta, f.
discount (VERB)	descontar	inc. tax	impuesto sobre la renta, m.
dollar	dólar, m.	inform	avisar
down payment	primer pago, m.	injury	perjuicio, m.
draft (sket.)	bosquejo, m; borrador, f.	inquiry	cuestión, pregunta, f.
draft (document)	proyecto, m.	installment	plazo, m.; cuota, f.
draft (on bank)	giro, cheque, m.	insurance	seguro, m.
	letra, libranza, f.	insurer	asegurador, m.
draw on account	girar	intercourse (COM)	intercambio, m.
due	vencido		comunicación, f.
due course (in..)	en su tiempo	interst rate	tipo de interés, m.
duty (customs)	derechos de aduana, m.	interest	interés, m.
	arancel, m.	*investment	inversión, f.
duty (oblig.)	obligación, f.; deber, m.	invoice	factura, f.
earn a living	ganar(se) la vida	issue	punto en cuestión, f.
earning(s)	ingresos, f.	job	empleo, trabajo, m.; obra, f.

471

ENGLISH	SPANISH	ENGLISH	SPANISH
lab	laboratorio, m.	note	nota, f.
laborer	obrero, operario, m.	note (payable)	pagaré, m.
lease	alquiler, arrendamiento, m.	note (bank)	billete, m.
ledger	libro mayor, m.	notice	aviso, anuncio, m.
legal tender	moneda legal, f.	occupation	ocupación, f.
lessee	arrendatario, inquilino, m.	offer (VERB)	ofrecer
lessor	arrendador, locador, m.	offer	oferta, f.
letter (mail)	carta, epístola, f.	office	oficina, f.; despacho, m.
letter of attorney	poder, m.	open an account	abrir cuenta
letter of cred.	carta de crédito, f.	operating expense	gastos de explotación, f.
letter of exchange (draft)	letra, f.	order	encargo, pedido, m.
letterhead	membrete, m.	outlet	salida, f.
liabilities	obligaciones, f; pasivo m.	output	producción total, f.
liability	responsibilidad, f.	overhead	gastos generales, m.
licensee	licenciado, m.	overpayment	pago excesivo, m.
load (burden)	cargo, m.	overtime	horas adicionales, f.
loan	préstamo, m.	owner	propietario, dueño, m.
loss	pérdida, f.	package (parcel)	bulto, m.
lot	lote, m.	packing	embalaje, m.
lump sum	suma total, f.	paper	papel, m.
mail (post)	correo, m.	paperclip	presilla, f.
mailbox	buzón, m.	papercutter	cortas papeles, m.
mail order	pedido postal, m.	paperweight	pisa papeles, f.
management	gerencia, dirección, régimen, m.; administración, f.	parcel post	paquete postal, m.
		part payment	pago a cuenta, m.
manager	administrador, gerente, m.	partner	socio, m.
margen	margen, m.	partnership	asociación, f.; sociedad, f.; consorcio, m.
mark (sign)	señal, m.		
markdown	rebaja, reducción, f.	party (participant)	cómplice, m.
market	mercado, m.	patent	patente, m.
market (stock..)	bolsa, f.	pay	sueldo, pagamento, salario, m. honorarios, m; comisión, paga, f.
marketing	mercadero, m.		
marketplace	mundo mercantil, m.	pay (VERB)	pagar
market value	valor comercial, m.	payable to bearer	pagadero al portador
markup	margen de ganancia bruta, m.		
matter (substance)	materia, f.	payload	carga útil, f.
maturity (expiration)	vencimiento, m.	payee	portador, beneficiario, m.
measure	medida, f.	payment	pago, pagamento, m.
measure (VERB)	medir	payment (part..)	pago a cuenta, m.
meeting	junta, f.; mitin, m.	payroll	planilla de pagos, f.
member	miembro, m.	pencil sharpener	afilalápiz, m.
memorandum	nota, f.; memorándum, m.	penholder	portaplumas, m.
merchandise	mercadería, f.	percent	por ciento, m.
merchant	comerciante, vendedor, m.	percentage	porcentaje, m.
merger	fusión, consolidación, f.	peseta	peseta, f.
millionaire	millonario, m.	peso	peso, m.
minutes (record)	actas, f.	*plant (factory)	fábrica, f.
minute book	libro de actas, m.	plat	plano, diseño, m.; mapa, f.
money	moneda, plata, f.; *dinero, m.	pledge	abono, empeño, m. promesa, garantía, prenda, f.
money order	giro postal, m.		
mortage	hipoteca, f.	pledgee	depositario, m.
mortage (VERB)	hipotecar	*policy	póliza, f.
mortgagee	hipotecario, m.	policyholder	asegurado, m.
motto (tradename)	mote, m.; lema, f.	postage	franqueo, m.
net weight	peso neto, m.	pound (currency)	libra esterlina, f.
newsletter	boletín de noticias, m.		

ENGLISH	SPANISH	ENGLISH	SPANISH
poverty	pobreza, f.	sample	muestra, f.
power of attorney	mandato, m.	save (to accumulate)	ahorrar
prepayment	pago adelantado, m.	savings	ahorros, m.
president	presidente, m.	savings acct	cuenta de ahorros, f.
price (cost)	tarifa, f.; precio, m.	savings bank	banco de ahorros, m.
price list	lista de precios, f.; tarifa, f.	savings bond	bono de ahorros.
		secretary	secretario, m.
price rise	subida de precios, f.	securities	valores, títulos, m. obligaciones, m.
price tag	etiqueta de precio, f.		
procedure	procedimiento, m.	sell	vender
proceeds	ganancias, f.; ingresos, m.	seller	vendedor, m.
profit	beneficio, provecho, m. utilidad, ganancia, f.	send to	mandar, enviar
		sender	remitente, m.
P & L	ganancias y perdidas, f.	settle account	ajustar la cuenta
pro forma	pro forma	settlement	arreglo, m.
promissory note	pagaré, m.	share (stock)	acción, f.
proposal	propuesta, oferta, f.	shareholder	accionista, m.
proxy (by..)	por poder	shift workers)	turno, m.
proxy	delegado, apoderado, m.	ship (VERB)	enviar
purchase	compra, f.	shipment	despacho, embarque, m.
quality	calidad, f.	shipping agent	expedidor, m.
quantity	cantidad, f.	shop	tienda, f.
rating	evaluación, f.	shorthand	taquigrafía, f. estenografía, f.
raw material	materia prima, f.		
real estate	bienes raíces, m.	showcase	escaparate, m; vitrina, f.
*rebate	rebaja, f.; descuento, m.	sight draft	letra a la vista, f.
receipt	recibo, m.	sign (shop)	rótulo, letrero, m.
*receipts (income))	ingresos, m.	sign (VERB)	firmar
receivables	activo, corriente, m.	signature	firma, f.
receiver	recipiente, m.	special delivery	correo urgente, m. entrega especial, f.
record	registro, m.; inscripción, f.		
reduction	rebaja, f.	spend (waste)	gastar
refund	reembolso, m.	staff	cuerpo, personal, m.
refund(VERB)	reembolsar, devolver	staff (editorial)	redacción, f.
registration	matrícula, f.	stamp	sello, timbre, m.
release	renuncia, cesión, f.	standard	medida, f.
remittance	giro, m.; remesa, f.	statement	estado de cuenta, m.
*rent	alquiler, m.; renta, f. arrendamiento, m.	stationery (store)	papelería, f.
		stenographer	estenógrafo, f.
reply	respuesta, f.	sterling	libra esterlina, f.
*report	relato, informe, m.	stock (supply)	existencias, f.
resale	reventa, f.	stock (share)	acción, f.
retail	venta al por menor, f. venta al detalle, f.	stock exchange	bolsa, f.
		stockbroker	bolsista, m.
retailer	detallista, minorista, m.	stockholder	accionista, m.
return (give back)	devolver	stockmarket	bolsa, f.
revenue	ingreso, m.; rentas, f.	stop payments	suspender pagos
right	derecho, m.	storage	almacenaje, m.
risk	riesgo, m.	strike (labor)	huelga, f.
royalty (fee)	derechos, m.	strike(VERB)	declararse en huelga
safe (strong box)	caja fuerte, f.	style	tipo, estilo, m.
*salary	sueldo, salario, m.	subject (business)	asunto, m.
sale	venta, f.	sublease	subarriendo, m.
sale (bargain)	barato, m.; ganga, f.	supplier	abastecedor, proveedor, m.
salesman	vendedor, m.	supply (..& demand)	oferta, f.
salesman (traveling)	viajante, m.	supply (VERB)	abastecer

ENGLISH	SPANISH	ENGLISH	SPANISH
surety bond	fianza, f.	typing	mecanografía, f.
surplus	sobrante, m.	typist	mecanógrafa, f.
surtax (surcharge)	recargo, m.	undertaking	empresa, f.
tag (label)	rótulo, m.; etiqueta, f.	underwriter	asegurador, m.
takeover	adquisición, f.	unemployed	desempleado
tariff	arancel, m.	unemployment	desempleo, m.
task (job,work)	labor, m.;tarea, f.	union (labor)	sindicato, m.
tax exempt	libre de impuestos	vault	bóveda, f.
tax rate	tarifa, f.	vendor	vendedor, m.
tax	impuesto, m.;contribución, f.	vote	voto, m.
taxpayer	contribuyente, m.	wage	sueldo, m.; paga, f.
tenant	inquilino,arrendatario, m.		salario, jornal, m.
terms (on..)	a plazos	ware(s)	mercancías, f.
tender	oferta, f.	warehouse	almacén, m.
trade	negocio, comercio, m.	wealth	riqueza, f.
trade(craft)	ocupación,profesión, f.	weigh	pesar
	oficio, m.	windfall	ganga, f.
trade (VERB)	comerciar, negociar	wholesale	venta (al) por mayor, f.
trademark	marca de fábrica, f.	wholesaler	mayorista, m.
trader	comerciante, mercante, m.	wire	despacho, m.;telegrama, f.
tradesman	tendero, m.	witness (person)	testigo, m.
tragedy	tragedia, f.	witness (info)	testimonio, m.
transfer	traspaso,transferencia, f.	work (labor)	labor, trabajo, m.
transferee	cesionario, m.		obra, tarea, f.
transportation	transportación, f.	workman	jornalero, trabajador, m.
traveling salesman	viajante, m.	wrong	injuria, f.; perjuicio, m.
turnover	movimiento total, m.		injusticia, f.
typewriter	máquina de escribir, f.	yield	rédito, rendimiento, m.

36. LAW AND LEGAL MATTERS

ENGLISH	SPANISH	ENGLISH	SPANISH
accuse (VERB)	culpar, acusar	auction	remate judicial, m.
accused	acusado, m.	audit	intervención, f.
acquit (to absolve)	absolver	award	fallo, m.
acquital	absolución, f.	bail	fianza, caución, f.
adopt	adoptar	bailee	depositario, m.
advise	aconsejar	bailment	depósito, m.
advocate	abogado, m.	bandit	bandido, m.
affidavit	declaración escrita, f.	bankruptcy (failure)	quiebra, f.
agent	agente, m.		bancarrota, insolvencia, f.
agreement	acuerdo, contrato, m.	bill (legislation)	proyecto, m.
appeal	apelación, f.	blackmail	chantaje, m.
arraignment	emplazamiento, m.	bondsman	fiador, m.
arrest	arresto, m.	breach	contravención, f.
arrest (VERB)	arrestar, detener	bribery	soborno, m.
assessment	avaluación, tasación, f.	capital punishment	pena de muerte, f.
assignee	cesionario, m.	charge (indictment)	acusación, f.
assignment	asignación, cesión, f.	charter	escritura, patente, f.
attachment (LAW)	embargo, m.	chief of police	jefe de policía, m.
attorney (lawyer)	abogado, m.	cite	citar
(proxy)	apoderado, m.	citation	citación, f.

ENGLISH	SPANISH	ENGLISH	SPANISH
citizenship	ciudadanía, f.	handcuffs	esposas, f.
civil rights	derechos civiles, m.	hearing (appearance)	audiencia, f.
claim	demanda, f.	heir	heredero, m.
claimant	demandante, m.	illegal	ilegal
clerk (scrivener)	escribano, m.	impeachment	impugnación, f.
client	cliente, m.	imprison	encarcelar
code	codigo, m.	imprisonment	encarcelamiento, m.
complaint (LAW)	demanda, f.	indictment	acusación, f.
condemn (VERB)	condenar	infraction	infracción, f.
copyright	propiedad intelectual, f.	infringement	infracción, f.
court (LAW)	foro, tribunal, m.	inherit (VERB)	heredar
courtroom	sala de tribunal, f.	inheritance	herencia, f.
	juzgado, m.; sala de justicia, f.	injure (to..)	perjudicar, dañar
creditor	acreedor, m.	injury	perjuicio, m.
crime	delito, crimen, m.	injustice	injusticia, f.
criminal	criminal, reo, m.	innocent	inocente
	delincuente, m.	insolvency	quiebra, insolvencia, f.
criminal (ADJ)	criminal	insult (VERB)	insultar
damage	daño, m.	jail	prisión, cárcel, f.
debt	deuda, f.	judge	juez, m.
debtor	deudor, m.	judge (VERB)	juzgar
deceit (fraud)	engaño, m.	judgment	juicio, dictamen, m.
decree	decreto, m.		decisión, f.
decree (VERB)	decretar	jurisprudence	jurisprudencia, f.
deed (document)	escritura, f.	jury	jurado, m.
	instrumento, m.	just	justo
defendant (criminal)	acusado, m.	justice	justicia, f.
(civil)	demandado, m.	juvenile crt	tribunal de menores, m.
defense	defensa, f.	kill (murder)	asesinar, matar
defend (protect)	defender	law	jurisprudencia, f.; derecho, m.
delinquent	culpable, delincuente, m.	lawsuit	pleito, proceso, m.
detective	detective, m.	law (statute)	código, estatuto, m.
dispute	disputa, riña, f.		ley, legislación, f.
docket	agenda, f; orden del día, m.	lawyer	abogado, m.
draft (document)	proyecto, m.	lease	alquiler, arrendamiento, m.
easement	servidumbre, f.	legal	legal
embezzlement	desfalco, m.	levy	recaudación, f.
escrow	depósito, m.	liability	responsabilidad, f.
evidence	evidencia, f.; testimonio, m.	libel	libelo, escrito difamatorio, m.
execute	ejecutar	litigate	pleitar, litigar
executioner	verdugo, m.	litigation	litigio, m.
fact	hecho, m.	memorandum	nota, f.; memorándum, m.
fault	culpa, f.	mercy	clemencia, misericordia, f.
fee	honorario, m.; remuneración, f.	minutes (record)	actas, f.
fine	multa, f.	misdemeanor (crime)	delito, m.
forbidden	prohibido	murder (VERB)	matar, asesinar
force (be in force)	regir	murderer	asesino, m.
forgery	falsificación, f.	negligence	negligencia, f.
form	planilla, f.	nonpayment	falta de pago, f.
garnishment	embargo, m.	notary	notario, m.
grantee	cesionario, donatario, m.	notice	aviso, anuncio, m.
guarantor	fiador, m.	oath (swearing)	juramento, m.
guilt	culpa, f.; delito, m.	offender	ofensor, reo, m.
guilty	culpable	offense	ofensa, f.

ENGLISH	SPANISH	ENGLISH	SPANISH
office (law..)	estudio, bufete, m.	sentence (penalty)	sentencia, f.
order (command)	ordenar	sentence (VERB)	sentenciar
order	orden, m.	settlement	arreglo, m.
pardon (VERB)	indultar	sign (VERB)	firmar
pardon	perdón, indulto, m.	signature	firma, f.
parole	liberación condicional, f.	slander	calumnía, difamación, f.
patent	patente, m.	solicitor	procurador, m.
patrol car	carro patrullero, m.	statute	estatuto, m.
perjure (commit..)	perjurar	subornation	suborno, m.
perjury	perjurio, m.	subpoena	citación, f.
permit	permiso, m.	suit (process)	pleito, proceso, m.
plaintiff	demandante, m.	summons	citación, f.
plead guilty	declarar culpable	supreme court	tribunal supremo, m.
plead not glty	declarar inocente	suspicion	sospecha, f.
police	policía, f.	swear (VERB)	jurar
policeman	agente de policía, m.	testament	testamento, m.
power of attorney	poder, m.	testimony	testimonio, f.
prejudice	prejuicio, m.	theft	robo, hurto, m.
prison	cárcel, prisión, f.	thief	ladrón, m.
prisoner	prisionero, preso, m.	tort	agravio, daño, m.
procedure	procedimiento, m.	trademark	marca de fábrica, f.
proceedings	actuación, f.	transcript	trasunto, m.; copia, f.
proof	prueba, f.	transgress	transgredir
prosecution	proceso, m.	trespass	infracción, violación, f.
protect	proteger	trial	juicio, proceso, m.
punish	castigar	tribunal	juzgado, tribunal, m.
punishment	castigo, m.	trust	confianza, f.
quarrel (dispute)	riña, f.	truth	verdad, f.
ransom	rescate, m.	unjust	injusto
record	registro, m.; inscripción, f.	vice	vicio, m.
register	registro, m.	victim	víctima, f.
register (VERB)	registrar	violation	violación, f.
reprehend	reprender	violate	violar, contravenir
reward (VERB)	premiar	warrant	autoridad, f.
right	derecho, m.	warranty	guarantía, f.
rob (steal)	robar	whistle (police)	pito, m.
robber (thief)	ladrón, m.	will	testamento, m.
robbery	robo, m.	witness (person)	testigo, m.
rule	regla, f.	witness (to bear..)	atestiguar
ruling	decisión, f.	writ	mandamiento, m.
sentence (decision)	dictamen, m.	wrong	injuria, f.; perjuicio, m.

37. RELIGION

ENGLISH	SPANISH	ENGLISH	SPANISH
abbey	abadía, f.	holy (saintly)	sagrado, santo
altar	altar, m.	hymn	himno, m.
angel	ángel, m.	hymnal	libro de himnos, m.
apostle	apóstol, m.	Jesus Christ	Jesucristo
archbishop	arzobispo, m.	Jesus	Jesús
baptism	bautismo, m.	Jew	judío, m.
belfry	campanario, m.	Jewish	judío
belief (creed, faith)	creencia, f.	Koran	Corán, m.
believe	creer	Lent	cuaresma, f.
believer	creyente, m.	Lord	Señor
bell (church..)	campana, f.	martyr	mártir, m.
benediction (blessing)	bendición, f.	mass	misa, f.
Bible (Scriptures)	biblia, f.	mercy	merced, f.
bishop	obispo, m.	minister	pastor, m.
bless	bendecir	miracle	milagro, m.
cardinal	cardenal, m.	missionary	misionero, m.
cathedral	catedral, f.	Mohammedan	musulmán, mahometano, m.
Catholic	católico, m.	monastery	monasterio, m.
chapel	capilla, f.	monk	monje, m.
chaplain	capellán, m.	nun	monja, f.
charity	caridad, f.	omnipotent (almighty)	omnipotente
Christian	cristiano, m.	pagan (heathen)	pagano
Christianity	cristianismo, m.	pardon (to forgive)	perdonar
Christmas Eve	Nochebuena, f.	pardon	perdón, m.
Christmas	Navidad, f.	parish priest	párroco, m.
church	iglesia, f.	piety	piedad, f.
clergy	clero, m.	pilgrim	peregrino, m.
clergyman	clérigo, m.	pity	compasión, piedad, f.
commandment	mandamiento, m.	Pope	Papa, m.
communion	comunión, f.	pray	rezar
convent	convento, m.	preach	predicar
convert (VERB)	convertir	preacher	predicador, m.
creation	creación, f.	priest (parson)	cura, sacerdote, m.
creator	Creador	Protestant	protestante, m.
cross	cruz, f.	psalm	salmo, m.
cult	culto, m.	rabbi	rabino, m.
curse (VERB)	maldecir	redeem (VERB)	redimir, rescatar
damnation	condenación, f.	religion	religión, f.
damned	condenado	religious	religioso
demon	demonio, m.	repentant	arrepentido
devil	satán, demonio, diablo, m.	sacred	sagrado
disciple	discípulo, m.	saint	santo, m.
divine	divino	salvation	salvación, f.
Easter	Pascua de Resurrección, f.	sanctuary	santuario, m.
faith	fe, f.	save (obtain salvation)	salvar
faithful (congregation)	fieles, m.	Savior	Salvador, m.
God	Dios, m.	sermon	sermón, m.
Good Friday	Viernes santo, m.	shrine	santuario, m.
gospel	evangelio, m.	sin (VERB)	pecar
Grace	gracia, f.	sin	pecado, m.
heaven	cielo, m.	spirit	espíritu, m.
hell	infierno, m.	synagogue	sinagoga, f.
heresy	herejía, f.	temple	templo, m.
heretic	hereje, m.	worship (VERB)	adorar

38. TRAVEL AND TRIP ACCOMODATIONS

a) Travel in General

ENGLISH	SPANISH
accident	accidente, m; desgracia, f.
accomodation	acomodación, f.
arrival	arribo, m.; llegada, f.
bag (suitcase)	maleta, f.
bag	maletín, m.
baggage chk	talón, m; contraseña, f.
baggage	equipaje, m.
baggage room	sala de equipajes, f.
bellboy	botones, mensajero, m.
bill	factura, cuenta, f.
blanket	frazada, manta, f.
boarding house	pensión, f.
	casa de huéspedes, f.
book (VERB)	reservar, encargar
border	frontera, f.
bridge	puente, m.
brush (VERB)	cepillar
cabaret	cabaret, m.
carrier (bags)	cargador, portador, m.
chambermaid	camarera, f.
change (small..)	cambio, m.
change (to..currency)	cambiar
charter	alquilar, fletar
claim	reclamación, f.
cloakroom	guardarropa, f.
coins	moneda, f.
collide	chocar
collision	choque, m.
compartment	compartimiento, m.
connection	connexión, f; empalme, m.
corridor	pasillo, m.
crew	tripulación, f.
cushion	cojín, m.
customs	aduana, f.
customs officer	aduanero, m.
dangerous	peligroso
declare	declarar
delay	retraso, m.
departure	partida, salida, f.
deposit (VERB)	depositar
doorman	portero, m.
double room	habitación doble, f.
dry cleaning	limpieza en seco, f.
duty (tax)	derechos, m.
emergency cord	señal de alarma, f.
entrance	entrada, f.
exchange off.	oficina de cambio, f.
excursion	excursión, f.
exit	salida, f.
fare (rate)	tarifa, f.; pasaje, m.

ENGLISH	SPANISH
fill out form	rellenar una ficha
first class	primera clase, f.
free (not occupied)	libre
freight	flete, m.
frontier	frontera, f.
Gentlemen (restroom)	Caballeros
guard	guarda, m.
guest	huésped, m.
guidebook	guía, f.
hanger (clothes)	colgador, m.
host	huesped, anfitrión, m.
hotel	hotel, m.
ice	hielo, m.
inland	interior, m.
inn	fonda, hospedería, posada, f.
inquire	informar(se)
interpreter	intérprete, m.
itinerary	itinerario, m.
label	rótulo, m.
Ladies (restroom)	Damas, Señoras
laundry	lavandería, f.
lavatory	lavabo, retrete, m.
leave (to depart)	salir
level crossing	paso a nivel, m.
luggage	equipaje, m.
maid	camarera, f.
map	plano, m; mapa, m.; carta, f.
money exchange	cambio, m.
No Smoking	Prohibido Fumar
noisy	ruidoso
passenger	viajero, pasajero, m.
passport	pasaporte, m.
popular	popular, frecuentado
postcard	tarjeta postal, f.
press (clothing)	planchar
pub (inn)	taberna, f.
rate of exchange	cambio, m.
refreshment room	cantina, f.
resort (spa)	lugar de temporada, m.
	balneario, m.
respectable (decent)	respetable
restaurant	restaurante, m.
restroom	baño, retrete, lavabo, m.
room	habitación, f.; cuarto, m.
round trip	ida y vuelta, f.
running water	agua corriente, m.
schedule (timetable)	horario, m.
seat	asiento, m.
service incl.	servicio incluído
service	servicio, m.

ENGLISH	SPANISH	ENGLISH	SPANISH
sheets	sábanas, f.	tourism	turismo, m.
sight-seeing	excursión, turismo, m.	tourist	turista, f.
signal	señal, f.	towels	toallas, f.
sojourn (stay)	estancia, f.	travel (VERB)	viajar
souvenir	recuerdo, m.	travel agency	agencia de viajes, f.
spend money	gastar dinero	traveler	viajero, turista, m.
spend holidays	pasar vacacion	traveler's chk	cheque de viajero, m.
starch (VERB)	almidonar	trip (journey)	viaje, pasaje, m.
stay overnight	pasar la noche	trip (take a..)	hacer un viaje
stop (VERB)	parar	trunk	cofre, baúl, m.
stop	parada, f.	tunnel	túnel, m.
strap	correa, f.	twin beds	camas gemelas, f.
suitcase	maleta, f.; saco, m.	vacation	vacaciones, f.
taxi	taxi, m.	valise	valija, maleta, f.
ticket	pasaje, billete, m.	waiting room	sala de espera, f.
tip (VERB)	dar una propina, f.	wash (VERB)	lavar
tip	propina, f.	weekend	fin de semana, m.
tour	jira, excursión, f.	whistle	silbato, m.
tour (to travel)	viajar, recurrir	window	ventanilla, f.

b) Train Travel

ENGLISH	SPANISH	ENGLISH	SPANISH
baggage car	furgón, m.	platform	andén, m.
berth	litera, f.	porter	mozo, m.
boxcar	furgón, m.	rack (baggage)	rejilla, f.
brake	freno, m.	rail	rail, carril, riel, m.
brake (VERB)	frenar	railroad(-way)	ferrocarril, m.
car (RR)	coche, vagón, m.	round trip	ida y vuelta, f.
carriage	coche, m.	seat	asiento, m.
check baggage	facturar	signal	señal, f.
coach	coche, vagón, m.	sleeping car	coche cama, m.
coachman	cochero, m.	smoking (allowed)	Permitido Fumar
compartment	compartimento, m.	smoking car	salón de fumar, m.
conductor	revisor, cobrador, m.	station (depot)	estación, f.
corridor	pasillo, m.	station master	jefe de estación, m.
crossing (RR)	cruce ferroviario, m.	stop (train)	parada, f.
derailment	descarrilamiento, m.	stop (VERB)	parar
diner	coche comedor, m.	streetcar	tranvía, f.
engine	locomotora, f.	subway	subterráneo, metro, m.
express train	tren expreso, m.	ticket	billete, m.
first class	vagón de primera, m.	ticket collector	revisor, m.
freight train	tren de carga, m.	ticket office	taquilla, f.
get on (to board)	subir al	ticket window	ventanilla, f.
get off	bajar del	time table	horario, m.
guard	guarda, m.	track (RR)	vía, f.; carril, m.
late (behind sched.)	de retraso	train	tren, m.
locomotive	locomotora, f.	train (fast)	rápido, expreso, m.
lower berth	litera baja, f.	train (mail)	tren correo, m.
luggage car	furgón de equipajes, m.	train (through)	tren directo, m.
luggage rack	portaequipajes, m.	trolley	tranvía, f.
monorail	monocarril, m.	tunnel	túnel, m.
one way ticket	viaje de ida, m.	upper berth	litera de arriba, f.
parlor car	coche salón, m.	waiting room	sala de espera, f.

c) Air Travel

ENGLISH	SPANISH	ENGLISH	SPANISH
air current	corriente de aire, f.	jet	avión de reacción, m.
airfield	aeródromo, m.	jet engine	reactor, m.
airplane	aeroplano, m. avión, m.	land (VERB)	aterrizar
air pocket	bache, m.	landing	aterrizaje, m.
airport	aeropuerto, m.	landing gear	tren de aterrizaje, m.
air terminal	terminal aérea, f.	landing strip	pista de aterrizaje, f.
altimeter	altímetro, m.	orbit	órbita, f.
altitude	altura, f.	pilot	aviador, piloto, m.
aviation	aviación, f.	propeller	hélice, f.
cabin	cabina, f.	rocket	cohete, m.
cockpit	cabina, f.	rudder	timón, m.
control stick	palanca de mando, f.	runway	pista, f.
control tower	torre de mando, m.	safetybelt	cinturón de seguridad, f.
descend	descender	seaplane	hidroavión, m.
fasten (belt)	abrochar	seat	asiento, m.
flight	vuelo, m.	stabilizer	estabilizador, m.
fly (VERB)	volar	stewardess	azafata, camarera, f.
fuselage (body)	cuerpo, fuselaje, m.	tail	cola, f.
gate	barrera, f.	take off	despegar
glider	planeador, m.	window seat	asiento interior, m.
helicopter	helicóptero, m.	wing	ala, f.

d) Ship Travel

ENGLISH	SPANISH	ENGLISH	SPANISH
anchor	ancla, f.	embarcation	embarcación, f.
anchor (VERB)	fondear, anclar	embark	embarcar
anchorage	anclaje, m.	engine room	sala de máquinas, f.
barge	lanchón, m.; barcaza, f.	engineer	ingeniero, m.
bell	campanilla, f.	excursion	excursión, f.
board (VERB)	abordar	ferry	transbordador, m.
board (on..)	a bordo	flag	pabellón, m.; bandera, f.
boat	barco, bote, m.	freight	carga, f.; flete, m.
	barca, lancha, f.	freighter	buque de carga, fletero, m.
boiler	caldera, f.	funnel	chimenea, f.
boom	botavara, f.	gang-plank	plancha de desembarco, f.
bow (ship)	proa, f.	gang-way	pasaje, m.; pasarela, f.
bridge	puente, m.	gong	gong, m.
buoy	boya, f.	harbour	puerto, m.
cabin (berth)	camarote, m.	headwind	viento de proa, m.
canoe	canoa, piragua, f.	helm	timón, m.
captain	capitán, m.	helmsman	timonel, m.
cargo	carga, f.	high sea	alta mar, f.
compass	brújula, f.	hold	bodega, cala, f.
course (route)	rumbo, m.	hose	manguera, f.
craft	embarcación, f.	hull	casco, m.
crane	grúa, f.	keel	quilla, f.
crew (ship company)	tripulación, f.	knot	nudo, m.
crossing (trip)	travesía, f.	land (to disembark)	desembarcar
cruise	viaje por mar, m.	landing	desembarco, m.
disembark (to land)	desembarcar	latitude	latitud, f.
deck	cubierta, f.	launch	chalupa, lancha, f.
desk chair	silla de cubierta, f.	lifebelt	cinturón salvavidas, m.
dock (pier)	muelle, dique, m.	lifeboat	bote salvavidas, m.

ENGLISH	SPANISH	ENGLISH	SPANISH
lighthouse	faro, m.	sailor	marinero, m.
lightship	buque faro, m.	sea	mar, m.
liner	transatlántico, m.	seaman	marinero, marino, m.
lock (sluice)	esclusa, f.	seaport	puerto marítimo, m.
lounge	salón, m.	seasickness	mareo, m.
lower deck	cubierta inferior, f.	seasick (get..)	marear(se)
main deck	cubierta principal, f.	seawater	agua de mar, m.
manifest	manifiesto, m.	ship (vessel)	barco, buque, m.
mariner	marinero, m.		embarcación, f. nave, navío, m.
mast	mástil, m.	shipping	embarque, m.; navegación, f.
mate	piloto, m.	shipwreck	naufragio, m.
merchantman	barco mercante, m.	shore (coast)	litoral, m.
mooring	amarradero, m.	sink (VERB)	hundir
oar	remo, m.	starboard (right side)	estribor, m.
paddle (canoe)	canalete, m.	stateroom	cabina, f.; camarote, m.
pier(dock)desembarcadero, muelle, m.		steamship,-mer	buque de vapor, m.
pilot (ports)	práctico, m.	stearage	tercera clase, f.
port (left side)	babor, m.	stern (poop deck)	popa, f.
port (harbor)	puerto, m.	steward	camarero, m.
porthole	portilla, f.	sun deck	cubierta superior, f.
power boat	autobote, m.	tanker	buque tanque, m.
promenade dk	cubierta de paseo, f.	tide	marea, f.
propeller	hélice, f.	tonnage	tonelaje, m.
prow	proa, f.	tug (towboat)	remolcador, m.
pump	bomba, f.	unload	descargar
purser	contable, contador, m.	vessel	buque, barco, m.
quarterdeck	alcázar, m.	voyage	viaje, f.
rope	soga, cuerda, f.	wharf (pier)	muelle, m.
rowboat	bote de remo, m.	wharfage	muellaje, m.
rudder	timón, m.	wheel	timón, m.
sail	vela, f.	wreck (ship)	naufragio, m.
sail (VERB)	zarpar, salir	yacht	yate, m.

e) Road Travel

ENGLISH	SPANISH	ENGLISH	SPANISH
accelerate	acelerar	bus	autobús, m.
accelerator	acelerador, m.	bus stop	parada de autobús, f.
air pressure	presión de aire, f.	cab (hack)	coche, taxi, m.
automobile	automóvil, m.	car	carro, coche, automóvil, m.
avenue	avenida, f.	caravan	caravana, f.
axle	eje, m.	carburetor	carburador, m.
battery	acumulador, m.	carriage	coche, m.
bearing	cojinete, m.	cart	carro, m.; carreta, f
bend (curve)	curva, f.	Caution!	¡Cuidado!
bicycle	bicicleta, f.	chain	cadena, f.
blinker	faro intermitente, m.	charge battery	cargar la batería
blowout (flat)	pinchazo, m.	chassis	chassis, m.
body (of car)	carroceria, f.	chauffer	chófer, conductor, m.
bolt	perno, m.	circle (roundabout)	redondel, m.
brake (VERB)	frenar	clutch	embrague, m.
brake(s)	freno(s), m.	coach (wagon)	vagón, carruaje, m.
breakdown	avería, f.	collide	chocar
bridge	puente, m.	collision	choque, m.
buggy	coche ligero, m.	conductor	conductor, cobrador, m.
bulb	bombilla, f.	convertible	convertible, m.
bumper	defensa, f.; parachoqes, m.	corner	esquina, f.

ENGLISH	SPANISH	ENGLISH	SPANISH
crossroads	encrucijada, f.	motor bike	bicicleta a motor, f.
crosswalk	cruce, paso de peatones, m.	motor bus	autobús, m.
curve	curva, f.	motor car	automóvil, m.
cycling	ciclismo, m.	skid	patinazo, m.
cylinder	cilindro, m.	sleigh	trineo, m.
Danger!	¡Peligro!	slippery	resbaladizo
detour	desviación, f.; desvío, m.	motor	motor, m.
door (car)	puerta, portezuela, f.	motorcycle	moto, m.; motocicleta, f.
drive (take a ..)	pasear	motoring	automovilismo, m.
drive (VERB)	conducir	mudguard	guardafango, guardabarros, m.
drive	paseo, m.	muffler	silenciador, m.; sordina, f.
drive shaft	eje de transmisión, m.	No Entry	se prohibe entrar
driver	chofer, conductor, m.	noise	ruido, m.
driv.lic.	licencia para conducir, m.	nut	tuerca, f.
emerg.brake	freno de emergencia, m.	oil	aceite, m.
engine	máquina, f.; motor, m.	oil filter	filtro petrolero, m.
exhaust	escape, m.	oil gauge	oleómetro, m.
exhaust pipe	tubo de escape, m.	oil pump	bomba de aceite, f.
fan belt	correa del ventilador, f.	omnibus	omnibus, m.
fare	pasaje, precio de billete, m.	one way	dirección única, f.
fender	guardafango, guardabarro, m.	overdrive	sobremarcha, f.
fine	multa, f.	overpass	paso superior, m.
flat tire	pinchazo, m.	park (VERB)	aparcar, estacionar
fuse	fusible, m.	parking	estacionamiento, m.
garage	garaje, m.	pkg light	luz de estacionamiento, f.
gas (petrol)	gasolina, f.	parking lot	parque, m.
gas station	gasolinera, f.	pkg meter	reloj de estacionamiento, m.
gas tank	tanque de gasolina, f.	part (MECH)	pieza, f.
gauge	calibrador, m.	pedal	pedal, m.
gear	engranaje, m.	pedestrian	peatón, m.
get off (bus)	bajar	piston	pistón, m.
Go!	¡Marcha!	plug (stopper)	tapón, m.
grade crossing	paso a nivel, m.	power brakes	servofrenos, m.
grease (VERB)	engrasar	pump	bomba, f.
greasing	engrase, m.	puncture	pinchazo, m.
headlight	farol delantero, m.	radiator	radiador, m.
highway	carretera, autopista, f.	rear mirror	espejo de retrovisión, m.
hood (car)	capó, m.	rear window	ventanilla trasera, f.
horn (car)	bocina, f.	repair	reparación, f.
horsepower	caballos de fuerza, m.	reverse	revés, m.
hub	cubo, m.	ride (car)	paseo en auto, m.
ignition	encendido, m.	right	derecha, f.
inflate	inflar	rim	llanta, f.
jack	gato, cric, m.	road	vía, carretera, f.; camino, m.
Keep left	Conserve la izquierda	route	ruta, f.
Keep right	Conserve la derecha	RR crossing	cruce, paso a nivel, m.
left	izquierda, f.	running board	estribo, m.
lever	palanca, f.	rut	carril, m.; carrilada, f.
low gear	primera velocidad, f.	scooter	motoneta, f.; escúter, m.
lubrication	engrase, m.	screw	tornillo, m.
manifold	colector, m.	screwdriver	destornillador, m.
map	mapa de carreteras, m.	seat	asiento, m.
mechanic	mecánico, m.	sedan	sedán, , m.
meter (guage)	contador, m.	shift (gear.)	palanca de cambio, f.
milage	distancia en millas, f.	shock absorber	amortiguador, m.
mirror(rear..)	espejo retrovisor, m.	signpost	poste indicador, m.

ENGLISH	SPANISH	ENGLISH	SPANISH
Slow!	¡Despacio!	tire	llanta, f.; neumático, m.
spare parts	piezas de recambio, f.	tire chains	cadenas de rueda, f.
	repuestos, m.	tire iron	desmontador, m.
spare tire	neumático de repuesto, m.	tire pump	inflador, m.; bomba, f.
spare wheel	rueda de recambio, f.	tire tread	rodadura, f.
spark	chispa, f.	token (coin)	ficha, f.
spark plug	bujía, f.	tow	remolque, atoaje, m.
speed (limited)	velocidad limite, f.	tow truck	camión remolcador, m.
speed limit	velocidad máxima, f.	traffic	tráfico, tránsito, m.
speed	velocidad, f.		circulación, f.
speedometer	velocímetro, m.	traffic jam	embotellamiento, m.
spring	muelle, m.	traffic signals	semáforo, m.
stall (VERB)	calar, parar		señales de tráfico, f.
start a car	poner en marcha	trailer	remolque, m.
starter	arranque, m.	transfer	tranferencia, transbordo, m.
steering	dirección, f.	tread (tire)	cara, llanta, f.
steering wheel	volante, m.	truck	camión, carro, m.
Stop!	¡Pare!, ¡Parada!	trunk (car)	portaequipaje, m.
stoplight	luz de parada, f.	tube	cámara de aire, f.
stopping place	parada, f.	valve	válvula, f.
storage battery	acumulador, m.	van	camión, m.
straight ahead	para adelante	vehicle	vehículo, m.
street (road)	calle, f.	wagon	camionete, f.; vagón, carro, m.
street car	tranvía, f.	wheel	rueda, f.
street lamp (light)	farola, f.	window	ventanilla, f.
stuck (get..)	atascar	windshield	parabrisas, m.
switch	interruptor, m.	wiper	limpiaparabrisas, m.
tail light	luz de cola, f.	wire	alambre, m.
taxi	taxi, m.	wrench	llave (de tuercas), f.

39. GOVERNMENT

Cross-References: Armed Forces & Weapons
Law & Legal Maters

ENGLISH	SPANISH	ENGLISH	SPANISH
ambassador	embajador, m.	country	patria, tierra, f.; país, m.
army	ejército, m.	countryman	compatriota, paisano, m.
Attorney General	Fiscal General, m.	court (royal)	corte, m.
bill (legis.)	proyecto de ley, m.	courtier	cortesano, m.
cabinet	Consejo de Ministros, m.	crown (VERB)	coronar
campaign	campaña, f.	crown	corona, f.
castle	castillo, m.	defense	defensa, f.
chamber	cámara, f.	democracy	democracia, f.
citizen	ciudadano, m.	Department of....	Ministerio de..
city hall	ayuntamiento, m.	Agriculture	..Agricultura, m.
Communist	comunista, m.	Commerce	..Comercio, m.
Congress	Congreso, m.	Defense(War)	..(Guerra)Defensa, m.
Conservative	conservador, m.	Interior	..Interior, m.
consul	cónsul, m.	Labor	..Trabajo, m.
consulate	consulado, m.	Navy	..Marina, f.
council	consejo, m.	State	..Estado, m.
councillor	consejero, m.	Treasury	..Hacienda, m.

ENGLISH	SPANISH	ENGLISH	SPANISH
dictator	dictador, m.	police	policía, f.
dictatorship	dictadura, f.	politician	político, m.
diplomat	diplomático, m.	politics	política, f.
elect	elegir	President	presidente, m.
election	elección, f.	Prime Minister	Primer Ministro, m.
embassy	embajada, f.	prince	príncipe, m.
emperor	emperador, m.	princess	princesa, f.
empire	imperio, m.	queen	*reina, f.
empress	emperatriz, f.	referendum	referéndum, m.
Foreign Office	Ministerio de Asuntos Exteriores, m.	regime	régimen, m.
		rein (VERB)	*reinar
govern	gobernar	republic	república, f.
government	gobierno, m.	republican	republicano, m.
governor	gobernador, m.	royal	*real
inhabitant	inhabitante, m.	Secretary	ministro, m.
king	rey, m.	Senate	Senado, m.
law	legislación, ley, f.	socialist	socialista, m.
legislature	legislatura, f.	sovereign	soberano, m.
liberty	libertad, f.	Speaker	Presidente de la Cámara, m.
magesty	majestad, f.	state	estado, m.
majority	mayoría, f.	subject (citizen)	súbdito, m.
*mayor	alcalde, m.	Supreme Court	Tribunal Supremo, m.
minister	ministro, m.	taxation (tax)	impuesto, m.
ministry	ministerio, m.	throne	trono, m.
monarch	monarquía, f.	title	título, m.
native land	tierra natal, patria, f.	traitor	traidor, m.
native of..	natural de.., m.	treaty	tratado, m.
official	oficial, funcionario, m.	tyrant	tirano, m.
ordinance	ordenanza, f.; estatuto, m.	United Nations	Naciones Unidas, f.
pacifism	pacifismo, m.	veto (VERB)	negar, vetar
pacifist	pacifista, m.	Vice-President	Vicepresidente, m.
palace	palacio, m.	viceroy	virrey, m.
party (political)	partido, m.	vote	votar
platform (agenda)	programa, f.	White House	Casa Blanca, f.

40. ARMED FORCES & WEAPONS

ENGLISH	SPANISH	ENGLISH	SPANISH
admiral	almirante, m.	atomic bomb	bomba atómica, f.
aide	ayudante, m.	attack (to..)	atacar
air base	base aérea, f.	attack	ataque, m.
air shelter	refugio antiaéreo, m.	aviation	aviación, f.
aircraft carrier	portaaviones, m.	band	banda, f.
airfield	campo de aviación, m.	banner	estandarte, m.; bandera, f.
airforce	fuerzas aéreas, f.	barracks	barracas, f.; cuartel, m.
airraid	bombardeo aéreo, m.	base	base, m.
ambush	emboscada, f.	battalion	batallón, m.
ammunition	municiones, f.	battery	batería, f.
arm (VERB)	armar	battle	batalla, f.
armada	armada, f.	battlefield	campo de batalla, m.
armistice	armisticio, m.	battleship	acorazado, m.
army	ejército, m.	bayonet	bayoneta, f.
arrow	dardo, m.; flecha, f.	belt	cinturón, m.
artillery	artillería, f.	boatswain	contramaestre, m.
assault (to storm)	asaltar	bomb (to shell)	bombardear

ENGLISH	SPANISH
bomb	bomba, f.
bombardier	bombardero, m.
bombardment	bombardeo, m.
bomber	bombardero, m.
brigade	brigada, f.
brigadier	general de brigada, m.
bugler	corneta, m.
bullet	bala, f.
bunker	casamata, f.
cadre	cuadro, m.
call the roll	pasar lista
camouflage (VERB)	camuflar
camouflage	camuflaje, m.
campaign	campaña, f.
cannon	cañón, m.
captain	capitán, m.
cargo	carga, cargamento, m.
carrier (planes)	portaaviones, m.
cartridge	cartucho, m.
cavalry	caballería, f.
chaplain	capellán, m.
chief/staff	jefe de estado mayor, m.
colonel	coronel, m.
column	columna, f.
combat	combate, m.
combatant	combatiente, m.
comdr-in-chief	general en jefe, m.
command (auth)	mando, m.
command (order)	orden, f.
commandant	jefe, comandante, m.
company	compañía, f.
conquest	conquista, f.
conscript	quinto, recluta, m.
*corporal	cabo, m.
counterespionage	contraespionaje, m.
court-martial	tribunal militar, m.
crew	tripulación, f.
cruiser	crucero, m.
cutlass	machete, m.
dagger	puñal, m.
defeat (rout)	derrota, f.
defense	defensa, f.
deserter	desertor, m.
desertion	deserción, f.
destroyer	destructor, m.
detachment	destacamento, m.
disarm	desarmar
discharge (gun)	disparo, m.
discharge (to fire)	descargar disparar
discipline	disciplina, f.
division	división, f.
doctor	doctor, médico, m.
draft	cuota, leva, f. conscripción, f.

ENGLISH	SPANISH
draftee	conscripto, recluta, m.
drill (VERB)	ejercitar
drown	ahogar
drummer	tambor, m.
enemy	enemigo, m.
engagement	encuentro, m.
engineers	ingenieros, m.
enlistment	alistamiento, m.
ensign	alférez, subteniente, m.
equip	equipar
*equipment	equipo, m.
escape	huída, f.
escort	escolta, f.
exercise (drill)	ejercicio, m.
expedition	expedición, f.
explode	estallar
feat (deed, exploit)	hazaña, f.
field glasses	gemelos de campaña, f.
field hosp.	hospital de campaña, m.
fight	combate, m.; lucha, f.
fighter plane	avión de caza, m.
file (row, rank)	fila, f.
firearm	arma de fuego, f.
flag (ensign)	bandera, f.
flamethrower	lanzallamas, m.
flank (side)	lado, flanco, m.
flee	huir
fleet (navy)	flota, armada, f. escuadra, f.
flight (escape)	huída, f.
float (VERB)	flotar
flyer (pilot)	aviador, m.
foot soldier	infante, m.
fortification	fortificación, f.
foxhole	trinchera individual, f.
frontier	frontera, f.
fuel	combustible, m.
furlough	licencia, f.; permiso, m.
garrison	guarnición, f.
gas mask	máscara antigás, f.
gear (kit)	equipo, m.
general	general, m.
glider	planeador, m.
grade (rank)	grado, m.
grenade (shell)	granada, f.
guard (watch)	guardia, f.
guerrilla	guerrillero, m.
gun (rifle)	fusil, m.; escopeta, f.
gun (canon)	cañón, m.
gun fire	fuego, disparo, m.
gun shot	tiro, m.
gun powder	pólvora, f.
gunner	artillero, m.
harbour	puerto, m.
headquarters	cuartel general, m.

485

ENGLISH	SPANISH	ENGLISH	SPANISH
helm	timón, gobernalle, m.	permission	permiso, m.
helmet	yelmo, casco, m.	pilot (helmsman)	piloto, m.
hero	héroe, m.	pilot (aviator)	aviador, piloto, m.
heroine	heroína, f.	pilot (port)	práctico del puerto, m.
infantry	infantería, f.	pistol	pistola, f.
intelligence	inteligencia, f.	plane	aeroplano, avión, m.
invasion	invasión, f.	platoon	pelotón, m.
kit	equipo, m.	plunder	saqueo, pillaje, m.
latrine (sump)	letrina, f.	port (harbor)	puerto, m.
leave	licencia, f.;permiso, m.	post(position)	guarnición,puesto, m.
left flank	flanco izquierdo, m.	prisoner	prisionero, m.
lieutenant	teniente, m.	private	soldado raso, m.
lt.colonel	teniente coronel, m.	quartermaster	intendencia, f.
lt.general	teniente general, m.	quay	muelle, m.
lighthouse	faro, m.	radar	radar, m.
line of battle	frente de batalla, f.	rampart	baluarte, m.
load	carga, f.	rank	rango, grado, m.
machine gun	ametralladora, f.	rapier	espadín, m.
maneuvers	maniobras, f.	ration	ración, f.
major	mayor, m.	rear admiral	contraalmirante, m.
maj.general	general de división, m.	rear-guard	retaguardia, f.
march	marcha, f.	recruit	recluta, m.
marine	marino, m.	recruitment	reclutamiento, m.
martial	marcial	refugee	refugiado, m.
master sergeant	sargento mayor, m.	regiment	regimiento, m.
mate	piloto,camarada,maestre, m.	reinforcement	refuerzo, m.
mauser	máuser, m.	repulse	rechazar
medal	medalla, f.	retreat	retiro, m. retirada, f.
Medical Corp	servicio de sanidad, m.	*revolver	revólver, m.
medics	cuerpo de enfermeros, m.	rifle	rifle, fusil, m.
mess (dining)	plato, m.; ración, f.	right flank	flanco derecho, m.
mess (hall)	rancho, m.	riot	motín, m.
military	militar	rocket	cohete, m.
military serv.	servicio militar, m.	roll	registro, rol,m.; lista, f.
mine	mina, f.	roster	lista, f.; rol, m.
mortar	mortero, m.	rout	derrota, f.
mount guard	montar la guardia	row (line)	fila, f.
muster	asamblea, reunión, f.	rudder(helm)	gobernalle, timón, m.
navigator	navegante, m.	saber	sable, m.
navigate (to sail)	navegar	sailor	marinero, m.
navy	armada, marina, m.	searchlight	faro, m.
oath	juramento, m.	section	sección, f.
occupation	ocupación, f.	seige	bloqueo, sitio, m.
officer	oficial, m.	sentry	centinela, m.
order	orden, m.	sergeant (1st)	sargento primero, m.
order (give an..)	ordenar	sergeant	sargento, m.
orderly	ordenanza, asistente, m.	shell (expl)	casquillo, m.;bomba, f.
outfit (kit)	equipo, m.	shelter	refugio, m.
parachute	paracaídas, m.	shield	escudo, m.
parachutist	paracaidista, m.	ship	navío, buque, m.
parade	desfile, m.;parada, f.	shipwreck	naufragio, m.
paratroops	tropas paracaidistas, f.	shoot (to kill)	fusilar
patrol	patrulla, f.	shot	tiro, disparo, m.
paymaster	pagador, m.	siege (to lay..)	sitiar
peace	paz, f.	siege	sitio, bloqueo, m.
periscope	periscopio, m.	Signal Corps	cuerpo de señales, m.

ENGLISH	SPANISH	ENGLISH	SPANISH
signal (VERB)	señalar	torpedo	torpedo, m.
signal	señal, f.	tow (VERB)	remolcar
sink (VERB)	hundir	trainee	soldado bisoño, recluta, m.
soldier	soldado, m.	training	entrenamiento, m.
sortie	salida, f.		enseñanza, f.
spear	lanza, f.	traitor	traidor, m.
spy (VERB)	espiar	trench	fosa, trinchera, f.
spy	espía, m.	triumph	triunfo, m.
squad	cuadrilla, f.; grupo, m.; patrulla, f.	troops	tropas, f.
		tugboat	remolcador, m.
squadron (military)	escuadrón, m.	turret	torreta, torre blindada, f.
squadron (naval)	escuadra, f.	uniform	uniforme, m.
squadron (planes)	escuadrilla, f.	vessel	navio, nave, m.
staff	estado mayor, m.	victor	triunfador, vencedor, m.
standard-bearer	abanderado, m.	victorious	victorioso, vencedor
strategy	estrategia, f.	victory	victoria, f.
struggle	lucha, f.	volunteer	voluntario, m.
submarine	submarino, m.	wage war	hacer la guerra
surrender	rendición, entrega, f.	war	guerra, f.
surround	rodear	warlike	belicoso, guerrero
sword	espada, f.	warship	buque de guerra, m.
tactics	táctica, f.	watch	vigilancia, guardia, f.
target	blanco, objetivo, m.	wharf (quay)	muelle, m.
tent	tienda de campaña, f.	wounded (ADJ)	herido
torpedo boat	torpedero, m.	wounded	herido, m.